Encyclopedia of Furniture Making

By ERNEST JOYCE

Revised and Expanded by
Alan Peters

Technical Consultant
Patrick Spielman

Sterling Publishing Co., Inc.   New York

Published in 1987 by
Sterling Publishing Co., Inc.
387 Park Avenue South
New York, N.Y. 10016

First published in the United States in 1973 by Drake
Publishers, Inc., and in 1979 by Sterling Publishing
Co., Inc.
Published by arrangement with B.T. Batsford Ltd.,
London
This editon available in the United States, Canada
and the Philippine Islands only

Library of Congress Cataloging-in-Publication Data

Joyce, Ernest
   Encyclopedia of furniture making.

   Includes index.
    1. Furniture making.   I. Peters, Alan, 1933-
II. Title.
TT194.J69   1987   684.1   86-30181
ISBN0-8069-6440-5

ISBN 0-8069-6441-3 pbk.

Manufactured in the United States of America

Contents

Preface
Introduction

Part I Basic materials

1 Woods (hardwoods and softwoods) 1
2 Veneers 46
3 Manufactured boards 50
4 Plastics and leathers 58
5 Metals 68
6 Adhesives 73
7 Abrasives 81

Part II Tools and Equipment

8 Cabinet maker's bench and accessories 87
9 Hand tools 90
10 Portable power tools and accessories 118
11 Woodworking and allied machinery 129
12 Workshop layout and furnishings 141

Part III Basic techniques and joint construction

13 Wood preparation 146
14 Jointing techniques and methods 150
15 Edge jointing 152
16 Housing/dado, halving and bridle joints 156
17 Mortise and tenon joints 160
18 Dowelled joints 167
19 Dovetailing 170
20 Mitre, scribed and scarf joints 182

Part IV Advanced areas of furniture construction

21 Carcass construction 187

22 Leg and frame construction 208
23 Door construction 227
24 Drawer and tray construction 244
25 Fall flaps, secretaires, cylinder falls and tambours 256

Part V Metal fittings/fasteners and their application

26 Screws, nails and pins 265
27 Hinges and hinging 267
28 Locks and locking actions 275
29 Stays, bookcase fittings and castors 282
30 Catches, bolts and handles 286
31 Knock-up (KU) and knock-down (KD) fittings 291

Part VI Advanced techniques

32 Veneering, marquetry and inlay 294
33 Table lining 323
34 Mouldings and lippings/edgings 325
35 Curved work 332

Part VII Running a professional workshop

36 Setting out and cutting lists 348

Part VIII Draughtsmanship and workshop geometry

37 The drawing office 352
38 Projections commonly used 355
39 Perspective drawing 359
40 Workshop geometry 363

Part IX Furniture designs and constructional details

41 Tables and desks (domestic and office) 380
42 Chests, cabinets and sideboards 422
43 Bedroom furniture 440
44 Seating and upholstery 458
45 Church furniture 481
46 Miscellaneous furniture 492

Part X Restoration, repairs and wood finishing

47 Structural repairs 500
48 Surface damage 503
49 Wood finishing 505

Appendix: *Costing and estimating* 512
Index 515

Preface to the revised edition

It was with some trepidation that I accepted the task of revising Ernest Joyce's work, for in the eyes of so many it had become the woodworker's bible, helping countless people in their search for woodworking knowledge and their own personal search for excellence. This reluctance to tamper with the bible, which was strong, and shared by many other people, was tempered by the knowledge that much had changed in the world of craft furniture since 1970 when this work was first published—changes that Ernest Joyce himself would well have approved. Writing as he did in the late sixties, he could never have envisaged the tremendous boom that was to take place in the crafts, nor how this was to spread so rapidly around the world. In particular, the craft of furniture making as practised in small workshops is now more healthy, relevant and exciting than at any time since the turn of the century.

We no longer have to apologize for working in wood, for using hand skills and traditional joints, nor for stressing quality and individuality or any of the other qualities of the individual craftsman. These are now so widely recognized that I have purposely shifted the emphasis in this book even further towards the self-employed craftsman and away from industry, not from any feeling of antipathy to the latter, but simply because, just as the craftsman has moved on these past fifteen years, so too has the furniture industry. Streamlined and increasingly international, so much of its technology and marketing techniques is far removed from the message this book has to give and Joyce himself was so anxious to impart.

If much has changed in regard to the status of the craftsman and the role of industry, many other things have not. Many of the skills and techniques practised in workshops today vary little from those of centuries ago. The hand tools we use daily differ little from those of 15 or even 150 years ago. What has changed,

however, is the choice available. From the humblest hand tool to the most powerful woodworking machine, we are now no longer restricted to what is made in our own country but have a wide choice from all over the world. Also, because power tools were relatively new fifteen years ago, it is natural that the biggest advance in choice and technical development should have been in this area, and consequently this section of the book has been expanded.

It would be impossible to revise this book without getting involved in the question of furniture design, for here, too, thinking has changed. It was inevitable that fashions would change since 1970, and no craftsman can afford to ignore fashion, whether he wishes to follow its dictates or not. But more important than the changes in fashion has been the emergence of such strong influences as the American school of craft furniture making, led by such international figures as Wendell Castle and James Krenov, and magazines, such as *Fine Woodworking* in the United States; the rise, too, of the Crafts Council in Britain, and the influence of such household names as John Makepeace, Habitat and MFI; and lately in Europe, as a climax to a decade of Italian domination of the industrial and contract furniture scene, the impact of Memphis design.

All these influences have combined to throw wider open than ever before that thorny question—what is good design? In 1970 it was somewhat easier to answer that in Britain. People tended to look to the Council of Industrial Design and its London Design Centre to give us the answer. But the public was becoming bored with acres of clinical, flush veneered doors and surfaces, and craftsmen too began to question the relevance of industrial design to their own work, where they were using low scale technology and designing not for a mass market with all the restrictions imposed by the production line, but for individuals and for themselves.

know about, and he should be prepared to undertake any work within the general context of 'Furniture', with the possible exception of deep upholstery and hand and spray polishing, both of which require other aptitudes and training. The tendency, therefore, is to replace the term 'cabinet-maker' with the more comprehensive 'furniture-maker', but custom dies hard and both terms must be regarded as synonymous.

It remains to define what precisely is meant by furniture as distinct from joiners' work. The traditional sharp division between the two types of craftsmen has to some extent disappeared and is now more a matter of approach than anything, for each follows the same principles of construction and both have the same basic skills. Joiners' work which is normally considered to be part of the fabric of a building is usually strong, sturdy and not so intimately concerned with appearance, whereas the cabinet-maker's approach is towards compactness, lightness and delicacy of treatment. In self-contained, free-standing furniture there is no doubt as to the more suitable type of craftsman, but a good deal of fixed church-work, panelled work and particularly built-in fitments could be done equally well by either and it is difficult to draw sharp demarcations. In substance, however, the book is concerned with furniture only, which includes chair-work and those types of built-in fitments which are designed to replace free-standing furniture. It excludes such things as shop fitting, museum- and ship-work, etc., as specialist trades outside its province.

Ernest Joyce
1970

Introduction to the first edition

Any textbook concerned with the techniques of furniture-making must deal primarily with the basic handcrafts for it is upon this groundwork that machine production is built, and in fact all the machine can ever do is to translate the essential hand operations into rotary movements of the cutting tool. In effect, therefore, mechanised production is no more than a speeding up of hand production, simplifying wherever possible but not radically interfering with methods which have taken over 4000 years to perfect, for wood is a natural material and imposes its own strict limitations. Where other forms of material are concerned techniques can of course differ, and not doubt in the future both plastics and metal will usurp much of the importance of wood, but it is hardly likely that it will be altogether supplanted, at least in the foreseeable future, for quite apart from aesthetic values it is still the cheapest medium; it can be worked with the simplest hand tools and is always easily repairable. To those pundits, therefore, who may claim that the teaching of hand skills is no longer relevant in this day and age it can be pointed out that anyone who has only been shown how to force a piece of wood against a mechanised saw will have learnt very little, but if he has had to saw that piece of wood by hand he will be more likely to know that much more about it, he will have greater respect for it and will understand in greater depth the problems that will have to be faced in its manipulation.

Additional to this need for all machine operators to know their material and how best it can be shaped are questions of quality, not only in the artefact, but also of the artificer himself. Actuating a lever all day long is soul destroying, and modern civilisation must eventually deal with the inherent problems the machine imposes. Handwork allows a man to express his own individuality; it is creative, it is definitely therapeutic. The ideal of more handwork, more individual fulfilment, less automation of both man and machine may be economically impracticable, but it should not be dismissed out of hand for sooner or later we shall be forced to come to terms with the leisure automation will increasingly thrust upon us. Handwork, whether it be sawing a piece of wood or shaping a lump of clay, is one answer, and no apologia is needed.

Scope of the work

Terms in daily use often stretch their meanings and the expression 'handmade' can no longer be accepted as signifying only that work which is produced exclusively by hand-methods without recourse to the machine. Instead, it must now be taken as more descriptive of the approach than the means adopted, and a fair interpretation would include pure hand methods and those other methods which enlist the help of the machine without allowing it to dictate in any way. The inherent danger of mass production is that costly and complex machinery is always greedy for output in order to justify its existence, and it will tend to impose limitations on the designer and actively influence his work. In the so-called 'handwork' no such limitation is permissible and man continues to be the master, using the machine as an extension of his hands only and not as an independent entity liable at any time to question his decisions. It is with this 'handwork' and with this 'machine-assisted work' that the book is chiefly concerned and not with the mechanics of quantity production which belong more properly to the theory of wood machining, a subject which calls for a high degree of engineering skill. Having made the point, the term 'handmade' is retained failing a more comprehensive description.

The general term 'cabinet-maker' is also outdated, for so-called 'cabinet-work' is no longer confined to straight carcase furniture, with chair-making and other special activities as separate trades. Moreover, the Furniture Industry increasingly uses plastics, plastic laminates, metal sections, and many other new materials, all of which the cabinet-maker should

Thus there has been a reaction against the anonymity of much of the industrial furniture of the early 1970s, and a greater emphasis on individual creative work amongst craftsmen, and, more generally, a wider use of colour and decoration in the furniture in our shops.

The result in 1987 is that furniture design is very much in the melting pot. Some worthless gimmickry is thrown up side by side with much that excites and stimulates, and there is a sense of expectancy in the craft field that makes furniture making no longer one of our weaker surviving crafts, but one of the strongest and most vibrant.

Alan Peters
1987

Part I Basic materials
1 Woods (hardwoods and softwoods)

WOOD SPECIES

In all, some 43,000 different species of wood-forming plants have been identified, of which some 30,000 could be regarded as timber producers in some form or other and about 10,000 commercially exploitable. Many of these are of local interest only owing to unsuitability, high cost of logging, non-availability in commercial quantities, etc., but many hundreds remain which are of sufficient importance to merit serious consideration. Certain timber species continually recur, i.e. oak types, walnut types, mahogany types, beech types, etc. whose names are familiar, but in any tropical forest there may be only about 18 timber trees to the acre (0.40 ha) and of these only two or three will be varieties with known names, and the logger must therefore strive to find markets for the remainder in order to make logging a commercial proposition. For this reason new species are constantly being introduced into world markets, but large-scale furniture manufacturers cannot afford to experiment, relying chiefly upon oak, ash, beech, etc., which are always in uninterrupted and plentiful supply, so the newcomers tend to be much cheaper in comparison, although not necessarily inferior in any way.

WOOD CLASSIFICATION

In the classification of plants, including wood, the biological classifications determined by microscopic inspection of the structure are written in Latin, which is the international language adopted, with the genus first (the class or kind of things contained in the particular plant family), then the species (the subordinate kinds within the genus), and lastly the family. Thus European oak will be *Quercus* (genus), *robur* (species), family Fagaceae. Within the same family grouping will also be beech, hornbeam, sweet chestnut, etc., but true oaks will always be *Quercus* although the species will differ, i.e. *alba* for American white, *borealis* for American red and *mongolica* for Japanese. However, as timber species are usually discovered and put to use long before the botanist arrives to identify them, they will have been given common names arrived at either by adoption of the local or native nickname, the district of source, the port of shipment or some peculiarity of the wood itself.

The precise botanical classification is not of pressing importance to the cabinet-maker (and half an ounce of practical experience with the wood in question is worth a pound of academic knowledge), but it will at least warn him of what to expect. Thus Australian silky oak belongs to the family Proteaceae, and has nothing in common with true oaks (Fagaceae) except a fancied resemblance in the medullary ray structure; while on the other hand both Honduras mahogany (*Swietenia macrophylla* Meliaceae) and Cuban (Spanish) mahogany (*Swietenia mahogani* Meliaceae) will have more in common than African mahogany (*Khaya grandifolia* Meliaceae), sapelewood (*Entandrophragma septentrionale* Meliaceae) and guarea (*Guarea thompsonii* Meliaceae) because in the latter group the genus differs. If, however, the designer or craftsman wishes to pursue his scientific enquiries further, he will usually find that there are classes of instruction in wood technology widely available, and increased knowledge of his material will never be wasted, since for all practical purposes the study of wood does begin at the bench and under the impact of the cutting-tool.

All trees are exogens, increasing their woody fibre by the annual addition of a new layer (annual ring) under the bark, and forming a typical cone-like structure of yearly increments. As producers of structural material they are conveniently grouped within two main classifications:

Softwoods – Coniferous or cone bearing, needle-leafed, usually evergreen, trees that provide the typical commercially-used softwoods.

Hardwoods – Deciduous or broad-leafed trees that comprise the so-called commercially-used hardwoods.

In botanical terms the words 'softwood' or 'hardwood' do not indicate their actual physical hardness or softness. A third classification includes palms and bamboos which are, strictly speaking, giant grasses. There are the inevitable exceptions, of course, for the very soft poplars and willows are broad-leafed and therefore classed as hardwoods, while the harder, needle-leafed larch remains a softwood even though it is deciduous, and yews and hollies are true hardwoods though they are evergreen. However, the classifications are near enough for all practical purposes.

GROWTH AND STRUCTURE

Every tree has a complete circulatory system in which water and dissolved mineral salts, collected by the roots and commonly known as 'sap', are drawn upwards in the growing season through innumerable pipes or hollow vessels by the rapid evaporation from the surfaces of the leaves. In turn, the action of sunlight on the chlorophyll or green colouring matter in the leaves converts the rising sap, through a complex process of photosynthesis, into the essential food sugars and starches which then travel down the bast or inner skin underlying the bark, and are conveyed into the heart of the tree at every point by an elaborate system of radial medullary rays, clearly visible in the so-called 'flash' or flower of quartered oak. There is also a respiratory system whereby the leaves inspire oxygen and carbon dioxide during the day, which is again diffused throughout the living structure of the tree, while the waste products of combustion, chiefly carbon dioxide, are transpired at night. All this constant passage of essential water, food and oxygen throughout every part of the tree necessitates a complex honeycomb structure of pipes or vessels, soft pithy cells and structural wood fibre, which, even when fully dried, retains sufficient elasticity to behave as a typical sponge, capable of absorbing or giving up moisture in a ceaseless effort to maintain itself in a constant state of equilibrium with its surroundings.

The actual structure of the tree is illustrated in Figure 2 and the sectional drawings show the details. The function of the bark is to protect the tree from injury and shield the precious bast layer, which is the sole conveyor of food. Immediately under the bast is the cambium or growth layer, one cell thick and therefore only visible as a coat of slime. This layer creates new bast on one side and sapwood on the other, while the sapwood in turn ages and creates fresh heartwood. The function of the sapwood is to convey the water to the leaves, while the heartwood acts as a stiffening rib to the tree. At the exact centre of the annual rings, but not necessarily at the centre of the tree, lies the pith which is merely the decayed remnants of the original twig.

The growth in the cambium layer is very rapid during the spring when the constant evaporation from the leaf surfaces and the continual unfolding of fresh leaves exercise the strongest pull on the rising sap, therefore ensuring an abundant supply of food. It is not so rapid in summer, when the first impetus has been lost, and ceases altogether in winter when the tree remains dormant. Both rapid spring and slower summer growth combine together to create one annual ring whose number determines the exact age of the tree, while the heartwood itself is sapwood which, deprived of essential food and oxygen, has been literally choked to death by the ever-encircling rings of sapwood. Once the tree has started to make heartwood the amount of sapwood remains constant throughout the life of the tree, and for each new growth ring added, one matures and dies. Before it dies, however, all food is withdrawn from its cells, the fibres harden forming stiffer, denser heartwood, while the typical darker coloration evident in most—but not all—woods is the result of subtle chemical changes in the nature of the wood. The point to be stressed is that these chemical changes must take place within the living tree; no amount of after-treatment will darken sapwood, harden its fibres or drive out the sugars and starches locked in its cells which form the essential food-stuffs of all destructive wood-boring pests. This is the only reason why sapwood might not be recommended for use in furniture, although apart from that there is little, if any, difference in the structural strength. Sapwood will,

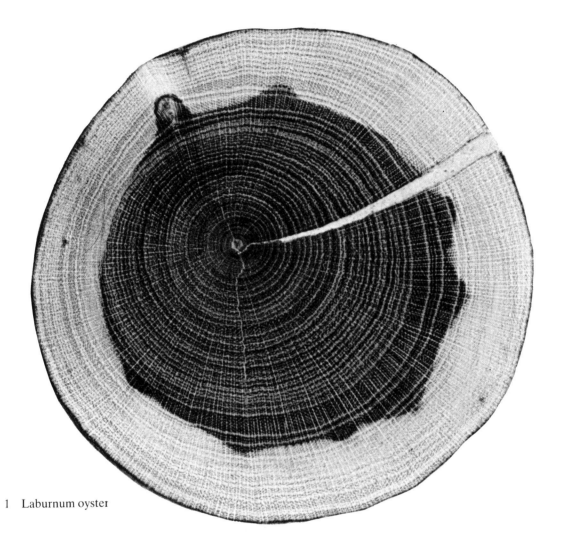

1 Laburnum oyster

however, always be wetter, for the pores of heartwood are blocked with gum-like bladders (*tyiosis*) which prevent the free movement of water, and therefore they contain more air and froth.

Figure 1 shows a slice cut from a laburnum tree (laburnum oyster) illustrating very clearly the sharp division between heartwood and sapwood which need not necessarily follow the annual rings. The spacing of the rings, the alternation between rapid and slow growth in succeeding years, the greater freedom of growth on one side due possibly to climatic conditions, prevalent winds, etc., or overshadowing or poor soil on the narrow side, is clearly visible, as are the medullary rays radiating inward from every point on the bast to the centre pith. These rays are always the weakest link as the split plainly shows, for they deflect the longitudinal fibres and thus form the natural cleavage-lines along which most timbers will readily split.

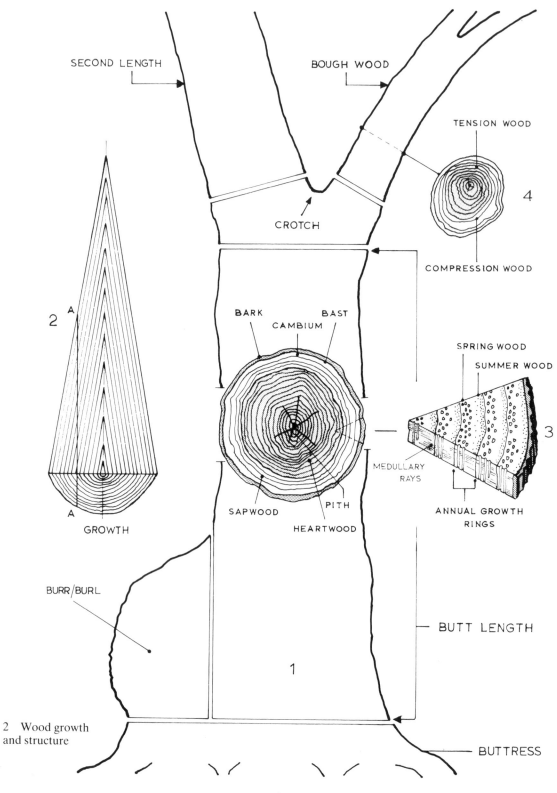

SECOND LENGTH

BOUGH WOOD

TENSION WOOD

CROTCH

4

COMPRESSION WOOD

2   A

BARK   BAST
CAMBIUM

SPRING WOOD
SUMMER WOOD

MEDULLARY
RAYS

3

A
GROWTH

SAPWOOD   PITH
HEARTWOOD

ANNUAL GROWTH
RINGS

BURR/BURL

BUTT LENGTH

1

2 Wood growth
and structure

BUTTRESS

FELLING AND SAW-MILLING

Exceptionally valuable timbers standing alone or in isolated groups are usually bargained for separately; each tree is measured and the price per foot cube of usable timber in each butt negotiated.

It is customary to fell standing timber in autumn and winter, although there is no real objection to summer felling, for a growing tree can transpire up to 50 gal (227 l) of water a day through its leaves in hot weather, thus depleting the moisture content of the trunk. However, summer felling does increase the risk of too rapid drying and consequent severe checking and splitting of the logs, and therefore winter schedules are usually adopted. Tropical timbers are felled at any time dependent on the prevailing conditions, for they have no fixed period of growth (and therefore no pronounced annual rings), while certain heavy timbers, notably teak, greenheart, etc., are *girdled* or *ring-barked* at the base of the trunk about two years before felling, thus cutting off the supply of food and sap. As the tree continues to transpire through its leaves the overall weight is drastically reduced, enabling it to be hauled or floated.

If a tree is a large one and the timber above the first main break is usable, then the whole trunk is felled and taken to the saw-mill; alternatively the second length above the break (branch or fork) is split for cordwood, and only the butt or main trunk is used. Except in tropical rain forest trees, where lack of light and over-crowded conditions encourage very straight, clear cylindrical poles often up to 180 ft (55 m) high in emergent trees, second length timber is usually inferior in quality, with large knots, twisted grain and a much smaller percentage of heartwood. Such timber is, therefore, only suitable for building construction work, although an occasional second length will yield good-quality narrow planks. Branches are not used, for not only is the proportion of heartwood very small but the pith is off centre, with the annual rings in tension at the top and in compression underneath, therefore causing considerable shrinkage. Occasional prime walnut, mahogany and ash trees, etc. yield at the convergence of the two sets of annual rings the exceptionally beautiful crotch, curl and feather figuring, while good burrs or burls, when they occur, are cut off and sold to the veneer-merchants. The stumps or root bases of some walnuts, notably the American black walnut, can also yield the very bold stump figuring, and these trees are uprooted bodily and not felled. It is a little sad for the craftsman that all the best of timber—prime oaks of 40 in (1 m) quarter girth and up, fine walnuts, clean sycamores, and in fact all exceptional trees—are immediately bought for veneer cutting at prices far higher than they would reach for conversion into solid board and plank.

Home-grown hardwood logs are not debarked at the saw-mill, for, although the bark does encourage insect pests, it helps to protect the trunk from over-rapid drying. Imported timbers are, however, always debarked, and sometimes also desapped which helps to cut down the weight, for the logs are sold with the customary allowance for bark and wane, and there is little point in incurring heavy transport costs for useless tonnage. Where logging costs are high, with long distances to be covered, and where there are ample forest reserves to cover the capital costs, local saw-mills are usually erected to convert the logs into square edge timber or lumber. Teak and other valuable hardwoods are invariably exported square edge, while most of the common woods can be obtained in round logs trimmed of sap or in square edge timber, the latter usually only 'shipping dry', with a moisture content below the danger level for fungus attack (25 per cent), but otherwise unseasoned.

Methods of saw-milling

Plain sawn or flat sawn
Produces full width waney/wane edge and squared up boards (Figure 3.5) with the annual rings in a series of contour markings. Boards cut this way are known as tangential cut.

Quarter sawn
Figure 3.4 shows a true quarter sawn or radial cut log. However, due to cost, this is rarely done, and the majority of quarter sawn timber is produced as in 3.3. Here, many boards do not

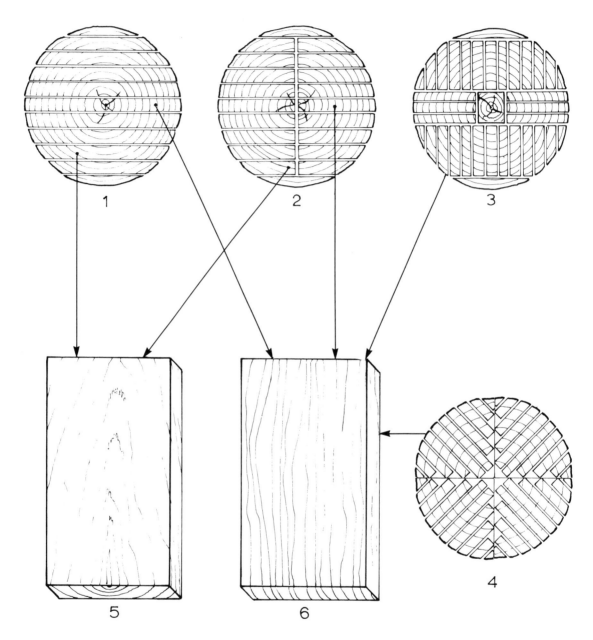

3   Wood conversion or milling

have the annual rings running at 90 degrees to the surface as on the true radial cut board.

Billet sawn (Figure 3.2)
This is frequently done to produce more stable timber than results from the plain sawn method,

and it is often passed off as quarter sawn timber, whereas in fact only a few centre boards (3.6) are produced on the true quarter. The differences in behaviour between plain sawn and quarter sawn timber are described later under *Movement and shrinkage* (p. 15).

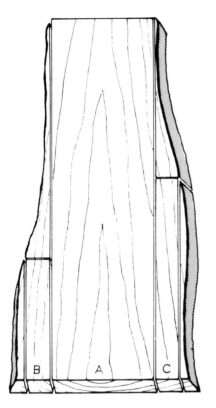

4　Waney/wane-edge board showing square edge wood (**A**) and short and long narrow boards (**B** and **C**)

Saw-milling

Prior to the conversion of the logs into timber or lumber they are cross-cut to length, odd kinks adzed or sawn off, and debarked if the bark is loose or gritty or if hidden nails are suspected (a constant hazard in hedgerow timber).

Treatment of the butt, the side or angle from which it is to be cut, whether it is to be plain sawn to provide waney/wane edge boards, or cut 'billet' fashion for quartered, is at the discretion of the head sawyer, for inexperienced saw-milling can destroy much of the value of a prime butt. The actual 'breaking down' of the log is done either by large circular saws, or more usually by vertical band mills in which only $3/32$ in (2.4 mm) is lost in sawdust for each cut, as against $1/4$ in (6.3 mm) for the heavy circular rip-saws. Logs are also cut with the horizontal band mill, which is slower but gives a more even cut,

as the weight of the plank is downwards and not against the side of the saw.

The primitive method of pit-sawing by hand, in which the log is placed over an open pit with one man on top of the trunk and another underneath to pull the long pit-saw downwards, it still used in native districts where labour is cheap and power facilities not available. The expression 'top-sawyer' originated from this method of sawing, for the man on top guided the saw, while his helper below did most of the hard work in cramped and difficult conditions.

Where the cut includes the natural shape of the log without preliminary squaring or trimming then the plank or board is known as *waney* (or *wane*) *edge*, and square edged is obtained by trimming off on either side. If the plank is wide enough the offcuts/cut offs are used to provide narrow boards (*short narrows* and *long narrows*), both of which are sound, but correspondingly cheaper. It is obvious that square edge timber/lumber will be more expensive than waney edge, owing to the extra sawing, waste, etc., but the economy in the latter is largely illusory. Imported sawn hardwoods are usually square edge to save shipping space, but some producers export in the form of 'boules' or complete logs totally flat cut, while a fair proportion of African timbers are exported in the round. Very valuable timbers—ebonies, kingwood, blackwood, lignum vitae, etc.— which are of small dimension are exported in log form and sold by weight.

Portable chain mills

These are, in essence, large chainsaws that operate horizontally on a felled log to produce sawn planks to any thickness required. Their great advantage is that they can be taken into the woodlands and the log can be converted on the site, which enables the individual boards to be easily transported by normal van or trailer.

This machine does, therefore, enable the furniture-maker to recover logs that might otherwise simply rot away due to their not being economically viable in terms of normal commercial considerations. Furthermore, in some parts of the world it is the only way to obtain complete logs of sawn timber as opposed to the squared up and graded boards.

5 Sperber portable chain mill

6 First cut with ladder support

7 Subsequent cuts do not require the ladder support. (By courtesy of Philip Cole)

SEASONING AND MOISTURE CONTENT

The growing tree which is full of sap can contain anything from 50 per cent free water up to 200 per cent in certain swamp-grown softwoods. A single cubic foot (0.02832 m³) of green oak, for instance, can contain up to 28 pt (16 l) of water which must be reduced to at least 4 pt (2.27 l) before the timber is fit for use. The object of seasoning is, therefore, to accelerate the evaporation of this surplus moisture, rendering the wood lighter, harder, stronger, less susceptible to discoloration and mould attack, and much less liable to shrinkage and distortion.

The water in the tree is contained in the actual fibres which are saturated (bound moisture), and in the open pores or vessels which are filled with a mixture of water and water vapour. Immediately the tree is felled the vessels will start to dry. This process is very slow in whole logs, but can be speeded up by converting the log into plank form, when the water-level will fall steadily until a fibre saturation point is reached (usually 30 per cent moisture content) in which the vessels are empty but the fibres remain saturated. From then on the water loss will be at a slower rate until the board has reached an equilibrium with the surrounding atmosphere. The amount of moisture thus left in the wood is termed the 'equilibrium moisture content' according to the 'relative humidity' of the prevailing atmosphere, and before describing methods of seasoning it is necessary to define these terms.

Relative humidity

Even in the driest of weather the atmosphere will always contain a certain amount of invisible water vapour which can vary considerably from hour to hour. The actual degree of moisture vapour present at any one time (relative humidity) is measured with a wet and dry hygrometer, and is expressed as the percentage of moisture in the air at a given temperature, compared with the maximum amount (saturation point) the air would hold at the same temperature without actual precipitation. The humidity rate can fluctuate rapidly, but fortunately wood is a slow conductor, and therefore rapid fluctuations either side of the seasonal average can usually be ignored.

Equilibrium moisture content

As wood is an organic and hydroscopic material susceptible to moisture changes it will always endeavour to reach a state of equilibrium with the surrounding atmosphere, giving up or taking in water like a sponge until the balance is achieved. The term 'equilibrium moisture content' is therefore an evaluation of the prevailing atmospheric humidity in terms of the corresponding actual water content the wood has achieved in that humidity; it is expressed as a percentage of the dry weight of wood substance (see *Measurement of moisture*, p. 13). *The important point to remember is that no matter how old the timber happens to be it will always respond in precisely the same way*, and that as its environment changes so will its moisture content.

Methods of seasoning

The whole object of seasoning is to bring the moisture content of the wood down to acceptable levels, according to the use to which it will be put, as speedily but as gently as possible. The drying out of the actual fibres after the pores are emptied is accomplished by surface evaporation and consequent capillary attraction from the moist interior of the wood. If the evaporation rate is too fast then partial vacuums will be created in the wood substance and the cell walls will collapse, causing widespread splitting and distortion. If, however, the drying-rate is controlled, then the water loss will be replaced by air and the natural strength and elasticity of the wood will always strive to accommodate the strains imposed. In the literal sense, therefore, 'seasoning' means controlled drying, and any wood which has been satisfactorily dried down to an acceptable level is usually regarded as seasoned timber/lumber. There is no doubt, however, that additional storage time over the prescribed minimum does bring certain advantages not measurable in any scientific way. In effect it will have matured like wine—it will be no drier but the moisture will be more evenly distributed, and it will be kinder, more mellow, and more mature, and therefore not so liable to distort. These advantages may be fractional but they do exist and the old craftsmen who matured their oak for 14 years under the shade of apple trees, and surrounded by chest-high nettles, did so not through any mystique but for definite practical reasons.

Two methods of seasoning currently practised are *air drying* and *kiln drying*. Generally speaking air drying is slower and cheaper, kiln drying is simpler but more expensive. However, as air drying can never reduce the moisture content to much below 15 per cent, kiln drying is always necessary for lower levels; but as certain timbers do not respond satisfactorily to kiln drying in the green state, preliminary air drying is advisable. Any lingering prejudice against kiln drying—and it still exists—has no basis in actual fact, for both methods are complementary.

8 Brushing sawdust from log prior to next cut

Air drying

Ideally, hardwoods should be sawn and piled for drying when humidity values are high and initial drying relatively slow; but in practice most merchants or dealers cut and pile timber throughout the year, stacking the boards fairly close so that the drying-rate is not too rapid. *On no account should green wood be close piled without air spaces between each plank*, as this will inevitably invite mould and fungi attack (the same applies to seasoned wood unless it can be adequately protected from the rain). The normal procedure, therefore, is to sweep the sawdust from each plank as it is cut and stack as soon as possible on firm, level foundations in such a way that an uninterruped flow of air is maintained over every surface. The stack itself should be built up on brick or concrete piers or creosoted timber/lumber sleepers, with wood bearers across the piers not less than 9 in (23 cm) above ground level, and the planks or boards piled exactly over each other and separated by stickers of neutral wood—fir, poplar, horse-chestnut, etc. — placed from 18 in (45 cm) to 24 in (60 cm) apart according to the thickness (Figure 9). These stickers can be 1 in square section (25 mm) for thick planks and ¾ in (19 mm) by ½ in (12.5 mm) for thinner boards, the ¾ in (19 mm) dimension laid flat so that the stickers do not roll over as the boards are positioned. The line of the stickers must correspond with the position of the lower bearers, and they must be exactly over each other throughout the height of the stack, *with the ends of the planks or boards well supported and not overhanging each other in random lengths*, for the function of the sticker is not only to permit the free passage of air throughout the stack but also to restrain as much as possible any tendency to warping.

When completed the top of the stack should be weighted down with odd wood slabbing, and well protected from heavy rain and hot sun by a suitable lean-to roof with a generous overhang all round. Rain driving into the sides of the stack is not harmful, always provided the timber has a chance to dry out, and therefore the stack should be kept as narrow as possible and never over 6 ft (1.82 m) wide. Shielding from very hot sun, however, particularly at the ends, is advisable in the early stages. Some form of

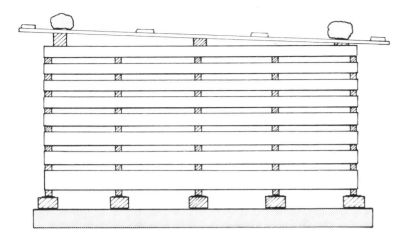

9   Stacking wood for air drying

10   Wood in stick at Sheffield Park Sawmills, Sussex, England

degrade (splitting, checking, etc.) must be expected on the ends where the moisture is drawn from the cut pores fairly rapidly, but this can be kept within reasonable limits by covering the ends with special paint. Unfortunately, merchants or dealers usually cannot afford these extra precautions for the common run of wood, but some square edge woods imported from tropical countries are end coated in this manner.

11

As a general rule most hardwoods are air dried out of doors and can remain there indefinitely, although at a later stage the better logs are usually moved into open-sided storage-sheds where they can be fully protected from the rain.

Drying times The usual time allowed for the air drying of timber to the normal equilibrium moisture content of from 15 to 22 per cent, according to the season, is one year for every inch in thickness; but given favourable conditions 1 in (25 mm) hardwoods piled in autumn will in all probability be down to 20 per cent by the following summer, and 2 in (50 mm) planks to the same moisture content a few months later. (Softwoods will dry to about 20 per cent moisture content in three months.) Further drying to 15 per cent is only possible in very dry weather, and in exceptional heatwaves 12 per cent might be reached, but under normal conditions the moisture content will swing backwards and forwards within the higher range, and any further drying time will make no difference beyond distributing the remaining moisture more evenly, and helping to equalize the built-in stains. For lower moisture contents other methods must, therefore, be adopted.

Kiln drying

The use of hot air in drying wood requires specialized knowledge, and therefore the process is described in broad outline only.

The principles are simple enough, but expert handling is required at every stage. In essence, wood is stacked as for air drying in enclosed compartments or buildings through which hot air is passed, either by natural draught or by power-driven fans. As the heated air would induce very rapid moisture evaporation from the wood surfaces, with consequent severe shrinkage and distortion, live steam is injected into the compartment, so that the rate of evaporation is always maintained at a safe level. Constant control is necessary, as the degree of heat and level of humidification must be adjusted so that there is a progressive fall in the relative humidity, until the wood has reached the required moisture content. As woods differ widely in their reactions, specific schedules have been laid down for practically all those in common use; but other factors, i.e. wood quality, intended use, thickness, whether quartered or plain sawn, etc., permissible degrade (defects), must also be taken into account, so that much depends on the skill and judgement of the operator.

The advantages of kiln drying are obvious, for green wood can be satisfactorily dried down to any given moisture content in a matter of weeks only, moreover much lower values are possible than with air drying. While it is true that any tendency to warp or buckle is increased in kiln drying, this can be mitigated by keeping the initial temperature low and thus extending the drying time, or by air drying the wood down to 20 per cent and then kiln drying, and this latter method is probably ideal. As a rough guide, green hardwoods can be kiln dried to a moisture content of 10 per cent in from three to 12 weeks, according to the species and the schedules adopted, and air-dried hardwoods with 20 per cent moisture content down to the same value in one to four weeks. It must not be forgotten, however, that as soon as the timber leaves the kiln it will begin to take up moisture again (moisture pick-up), and will gradually revert to the normal equilibrium content of 15 to 22 per cent. It should, therefore, be placed in a warm store, or otherwise close piled and covered with tarpaulins until used.

Permissible moisture contents

Wood which has been stored in the open, even under the most favourable conditions, is hardly dry enough for use in heated interiors. While little shrinkage takes place in wood seasoned from green to fibre saturation point (30 per cent), from then on the shrinkage is appreciable with maximum movement within the range 20 per cent down to 10 per cent. The maximum moisture content of timber in use should, therefore, not exceed the amounts shown below if excessive shrinkage is to be avoided.

22 to 15 per cent Usual limits of moisture content in thoroughly air dried wood.

20 per cent	Dry rot safety line.
16 per cent	Outdoor furniture.
15 per cent	Joiners' work in new buildings. Normal church-work in intermittently heated interiors.
12 to 14 per cent	Bedroom furniture with only occasional heating.
11 to 13 per cent	Living-room furniture with normal heating, including reasonable central heating.
9 to 11 per cent	Furniture in flats, offices and public buildings, etc. with continuous high degree of central heating.
8 per cent	Radiator shelves and casings, etc.

The upper values in each case are usually safe enough, dependent on the wood species, as there is always some air movement from open doors, windows, etc.

It should not be assumed that because a workshop happens to be continuously heated throughout the winter months wood stored in it will automatically dry down to the lower levels. It might conceivably fall to 6 per cent in exceptional circumstances, but owing to the continual movement, opening of doors, etc. it is more likely to be within the range 10 to 12 per cent and even 14 per cent and it is the average value which counts, for wood moves slowly and is virtually unaffected by day to day changes. Some method of conditioning the wood before use may have to be adopted, therefore; but while the old adage that it should be stored for at least six weeks in the room in which the completed furniture is to stand is very sensible, it is hardly practicable. However, it is possible to create a small warm store, or even a very simple kiln, built of insulating materials and with a gentle source of heat, for even electric light bulbs in a closed compartment will give sufficient for small sections, though care must be taken not to overdry and at too rapid a rate. On occasions the writer has even pressed a heated linen-cupboard into service, but a close watch should be kept for splitting and distortion, with the wood sections cut slightly oversize so they can be squared later.

Additionally, it is always wise to protect the completed furniture at the first possible opportunity, for oil-paint (three coats) will give 50 per cent protection, French polish and cellulose (two coats) 30 per cent, and wax-polish 3 per cent against moisture absorption over a period of one month, with much higher values over seven days.

Dehumidifiers

In recent years, the dehumidifier as a wood seasoner has completely revolutionized the kiln drying process. Many small furniture making concerns can now undertake drying economically both for their own use and for resale.

Until this breakthrough, hot air steam kilns were in normal use demanding both specialist expertise and expensive equipment. The dehumidifier, first developed to reduce humidity in store rooms and basement conditions, works on the refrigeration principle, and is actually kinder to the wood in the process as no real heat is involved.

Timber/lumber seasoners using this method come in a variety of sizes and are easy to install and to operate. The small portable dehumidifying unit is also invaluable to the furniture maker for controlling the humidity within the workshops, or, quite frequently, within a small part of the premises as previously described, in the form of an insulated room or chamber with the dehumidifier replacing the light bulbs.

Small kilns or drying areas with these smaller portable units are ideal for the craftsman who does not wish to undertake serious kiln drying, but wishes simply to condition and finish off air dried stock, particularly when humidity is high.

Measurement of moisture

The most accurate method of measuring the moisture content is the oven method, in which thin slices of the wood to be tested are accurately weighed, heated in an oven or drying-chamber, repeatedly reweighed until it has been established beyond question that all the moisture has been driven off, and the

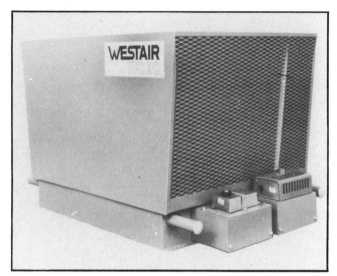

moisture loss then calculated in accordance with the formula—net weight minus dry weight over dry weight and multiplied by 100, to yield the percentage moisture content. Thus, if the timber sample weighed initially 5 gm, and after reweighing only 4 gm, then the calculation would be:

$$\frac{5\ gm - 4\ gm}{4\ gm} \times 100 = 25\ percent\ moisture\ content$$

Care must be taken not to scorch the wood, and the weighing must be done on an accurate chemical balance, while knots and other defects should not be included in the sample.

A simple oven using one or more 40 watt electric light bulbs is illustrated in Figure 12.

While the results obtained by the oven

11   Dehumidifiers
HPD30: A compact 3 kW model for use where space is at a premium

PD15: An easily portable model with similar performance to the HPD30

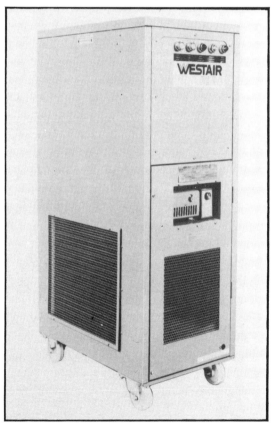

PD75: Can be placed inside or outside the drying chamber with ducting. This 9 kW model is for more serious wood drying.

method are extremely reliable, they are more applicable to scientific research, and for field-work the electric moisture-meter will give instantaneous readings accurate enough for most practical purposes. These meters work on the principle that, as wood itself is a bad conductor of electricity, any moisture present will facilitate the passage of an electrical current passing between two electrodes spaced apart and inserted into the wood, and the measure of resistance to the passage of the current can be expressed in terms of moisture present as a percentage of the total bulk. One such meter uses a transistorized sensing-plate to record the effect of the material being tested in a high-frequency electrostatic field; but most common forms of meter employ contact, clamp or drive-in pin electrodes attached to cable leads, with the meter actuated either direct from the mains, or with standard dry-cell high- and low-tension batteries.

The range of measurement varies according to the type of meter, with a normal coverage of from 6 to 30 per cent, and a margin of error of from 1 to 2 per cent. It should be borne in mind, however, that the presence of mineral salts in the wood may affect the readings, while some woods give large errors, especially in the upper moisture range; but most manufacturers give a table of adjustments covering many of the commonly used woods.

In taking any measurement, whether by oven method or moisture-meter, the readings should not be taken from the end of the plank, but from the thickness of a cut section at least 9 in (228 mm) in from the end and immediately the cut has been made, otherwise surface evaporation may falsify the test. If an approximate moisture content only is required, then the electrodes should be pushed into the surface at several points throughout the length of the plank not less than 3/16 in (4.5 mm) deep, and then the average of the reading used.

MOVEMENT AND SHRINKAGE

Sound jointing techniques upon which the stiff-ness, appearance and general usefulness of furniture depend must take into account the natural movement of wood, and its propensity to shrink, swell and warp under fluctuating

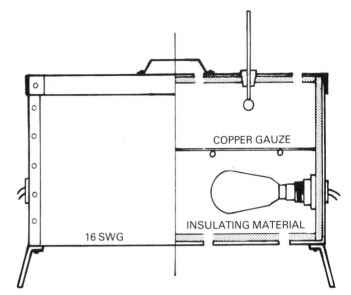

12   Drying-oven for testing moisture content

COPPER GAUZE

INSULATING MATERIAL

16 SWG

13   Measuring moisture content

atmospheric conditions. *It is, therefore, vitally important that the woodworker should understand exactly what kind of structural material it is which ceaselessly moves in sympathy with its surroundings*, and what precautions he can usefully adopt to minimize that movement. Surface protection with paint, polish or even metal coatings may conceivably delay the natural process but can never entirely arrest it; and it is not generally realized that while age itself may exercise a certain restraining influence, no matter how old the wood may be, the innate tendencies will continue to persist throughout its effective life.

14 Effect of strong sunlight on freshly sawn wood

Shrinkage

A full understanding of the reasons for the shrinkage of wood, the probable extent of the movement and the direction it is likely to take (wood is not a homogeneous solid and the movement is not equal in all directions) is essential if furniture is to be soundly constructed, *for it is impossible to lock wood fibre permanently against its natural inclinations*, and its strength is such that it will eventually overcome every effort to confine it. Furthermore, the increasing use of artificial heating means drier atmospheres and greatly increased shrinkage values, and this equally applies no matter how old the wood is, for even antique furniture will rapidly disintegrate in over-heated surroundings. It should be pointed out, however, that heat alone is not inimical to wood: it is the degree of dryness occasioned by the heat which is the deciding factor.

The probable extent and direction of the shrinkage is best understood by visualizing the tree as a compact cylinder composed of innumerable smaller cylinders or annual growth rings fitted tightly within each other (Figure 15).

As the tree dries out so the shrinkage will take place in every direction except in the length, the circumference of the outer cylinder will grow shorter and the cylinders within will each grow progressively smaller and more tightly packed (1, 2). This circumferential shrinkage along the length of the annual rings is always greater than the shrinkage between the rings, and while a precise ratio is not possible (for the figures depend upon the density of the wood species and the oil and resin content of the fibres), it is generally assumed that the amount of shrinkage between the rings will only be a little over half that along the length of the rings.

The effect of these shrinkage values is illustrated in 3 and 4. In 3 the greater amount of shrinkage in a tangentially cut plank will be across the width, as shown by the heavy arrows, with about half that amount between the rings as indicated by the smaller arrows; whereas in radial or quarter cut wood the main shrinkage will be in the thickness, which is relatively unimportant (the amount shown in the drawings is exaggerated for illustration purposes). *Thus, the radial or quarter cut plank (4, 5A) is always*

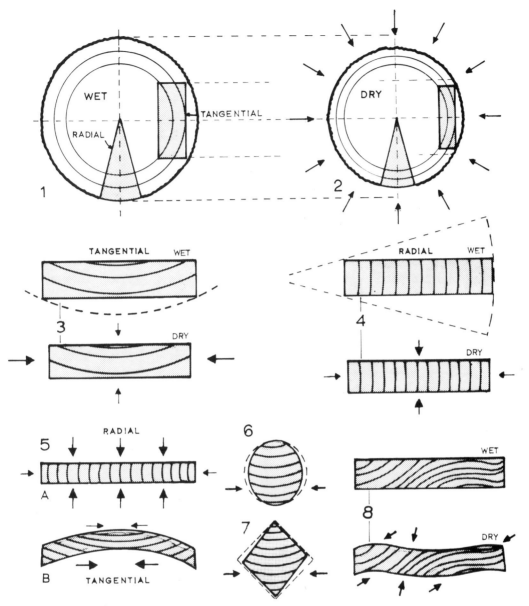

15 Shrinkage of wood

more stable, for not only is there less shrinkage across the width, but the pull is fairly equal from one annual ring to another, and therefore there is no tendency towards distortion. In 5B the annual rings in the tangentially cut plank are of different lengths, and the pull on the underside away from the heart will be much greater than on the side nearer the heart. A tangentially cut plank will, therefore, pull in, rounding as it dries, as shown by the arrows, while circular sections (6) will go oval, and square sections (7) diamond shaped. Where the grain direction is irregular as in 8, then the plank may twist in several directions across the width, while a further complication in tangential timber is that when it is cut from the log the saw cut is parallel to the long axis of the tree and, therefore, diagonal to the growth rings. It must be accepted, therefore, that wood is always somewhat unpredictable in its behaviour, and only very generalized rules are possible.

17

Shrinkage factors

Shrinkage factors along the length can usually be ignored for they are only fractional, but both tangential and radial shrinkages can be considerable, according to the particular species. Unfortunately, the greatest degree of shrinkage takes place between the critical moisture contents of air dried wood (20 per cent) and fully conditioned wood (9 to 10 per cent). For example, English oak, which is usually classed as a medium stable timber, will shrink approximately 5/16 in (8 mm) for every 12 in (304 mm) of width across the face of a tangentially cut board, and 3/16 in (4.5 mm) for a radially cut board, if dried down from 20 to 12 per cent moisture content; while beech, which has a large shrinkage value, will shrink 3/8 in (9.5 mm) and 7/32 in (5.5 mm) respectively. There is, however, no conformity between species, and other woods will exhibit less tangential and more radial shrinkage.

Dimensional changes for some of the more commonly used types are given below. As the moisture content of wood at any given humidity rate varies with the species, the values are based on conditioning from an outdoor humidity rate of 90 per cent down to an environmental humidity of 60 per cent.

Approximate comparative movement

Timber	Moisture content range 90%-60% humidity %	Tangential shrinkage		Radial shrinkage		Class
		in per ft	mm per m	in per ft	mm per m	
Afzelia	14-9.5	1/8	10.4	1/16	5.2	Very small
Abura	18-12.5	13/64	16.9	1/8	10.4	Small
Afrormosia	15-11	5/32	13.0	5/64	6.5	Small
Agba	17-12	7/32	18.2	3/32	7.8	Small
Beech	20-12	3/8	31.2	13/64	16.9	Large
Chestnut	17.5-12.5	5/32	13.0	5/64	6.5	Small
Elm	20.5-12	9/32	23.4	3/16	15.6	Medium
Idigbo	15-11	1/8	10.4	1/16	5.2	Very small
African mahogany	20-13.5	5/32	13.0	7/64	9.1	Small
C. Amer. mahogany	19-12.5	5/32	13.0	1/8	10.4	Small
Muninga	13-10	5/64	6.5	1/16	5.2	Very small
English oak	20-12	5/16	26.0	3/16	15.6	Medium
Yellow pine	17-11	3/16	15.6	7/64	9.1	Small
Ramin	20-12	3/8	31.2	3/16	15.6	Large
Sitka spruce	19-12.5	5/32	13.0	7/64	9.1	Small
Teak	15-10	5/32	13.0	3/32	7.8	Small
Utile	22-14	3/16	15.6	11/64	14.3	Small

Distortion, i.e. warping, twisting, etc., is not dependent on shrinkage values, but generally speaking timbers whose tangential and radial shrinkages are near to each other distort very little.

CHARACTERISTICS AND DEFECTS

Grain, texture and figure

While the general term *grain* is normally used to cover many different characteristics of wood, e.g. straight grain, coarse grain, curly grain, raised grain, etc., strictly speaking it should only denote the direction or arrangement of the wood fibres in relation to the longitudinal axis of the tree or of the converted plank, with the term *texture* as descriptive of the relative size and arrangement of the constituent cells, and *figure* denoting the ornamental markings brought about by structural characteristics.

Grain

Where the wood fibres follow or are parallel to the long axis of the tree or plank then the term *straight grain* is used. Any slight deviation from the parallel is known as *oblique* or *diagonal* grain, and pronounced deviation *cross grain*. If the arrangement of the fibres twists about the long axis then the twist is known as *spiral*; while regular waves or ripples create *wavy* grain, and irregular curves *curly* grain. The term *interlocked grain* refers to a condition in which, for some unknown reason, the direction of the fibres regularly changes or reverses in successive growth layers, and is often known as *ribbon* or *stripy* grain (sapele, etc.). All these grain arrangements occur naturally in the tree, although diagonal grain can be caused by poor saw-milling, and spiral grain cut through and through in the normal way will show as simple diagonal grain on the face. Additionally, the term 'grain' is used in connection with methods of milling, etc.; thus a straight cut across the face of the plank will show *end grain*, while cuts parallel to the long axis (ripping cuts) produce *long-grain*, and oblique cuts *short-grain*. Quarter sawn timber/lumber is sometimes known as *edge-grain* timber, and plain or flat sawn as *flat sawn* timber. The terms *rough grain*, *raised grain*, *smooth grain*, etc. are not descriptive of the innate characteristics of the wood, but only of the finished surface.

Texture

Texture is concerned with the relative size and arrangement of the cells. Thus a wood with large open pores usually referred to as *coarse grain* is more correctly *coarse textured*; with small pores set close together which can be brought to a good finish as *fine* or *close textured*; with uniform pores showing little difference between springwood and summerwood *even textured*, with the reverse for *uneven textured*. Oak, ash and elm are coarse textured (coarse grained) woods, because there is an alternation of large open pores of the springwood with the densely packed fibres of the summerwood.

Figure

Structural characteristics, medullary rays, pronounced or irregular growth rings, variations in colour or texture, knots and abnormalities all produce the ornamental markings or 'figure' on the surface of the wood, and are of great importance to the furniture-maker. All these are innate, i.e. natural characteristics, and can be further developed or exaggerated by the methods of sawing adopted. For example, radial cuts in true quartered oak and chestnut follow the path of the medullary rays, and show the typical 'flash' or 'silver grain' to best advantage. These rays are also visible in quarter-cut beech, while sycamore will sometimes produce a magnificent flame figure, and plane a rich lacy pattern (lacewood). Again, quarter sawing of some timbers produces very straight regular grain patterns, instead of the usual contour markings of flat sawn timber where the saw cuts through the annual growth rings. If there are concentric bands of colour encircling the tree, as in Rio rosewood, Macassar ebony and other exotics, then quartering will produce boldly marked vertical stripings, and plain sawn wood large irregular blazes of predominant colour. Woods with a marked contrast between springwood and summerwood often show the annual growth rings very conspicuously if plain cut, and even more so if rotary cut into veneers, of which typical examples are the resinous softwoods, Douglas fir (Columbian pine), yellow pine, pitch-pine, etc., and the ring-porous hardwoods, ash, oak, elm, etc. Bold demarcations between sap and heartwood yield the prized laburnum oysters, the strong pattern of royal walnut, and the delicate feathering of some walnut crotches.

Some of the most beautiful figurations are obtained from irregular grain structure. Wavy and curly grain can yield quilted and swirl figure, and the very beautiful dapple and mottle in which alternate light and dark bands cross the grain direction instead of running with it. This transverse movement can occur in many woods, and has always been highly prized in sycamore for the backs of violins. A variation of the stripy figure is 'roe', in which local irregularities break up the stripe, while similar irregularities or dimples in the cambium layer produce the blister grain of Douglas fir, and smaller inward-growing dimples one type of burr or burl as in burr maple. Sometimes the crotch or fork of the

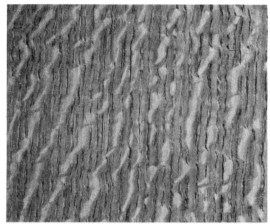

English oak

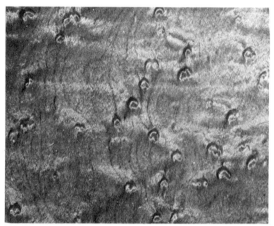

Bird's eye maple

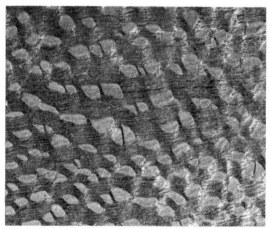

Australian silky oak

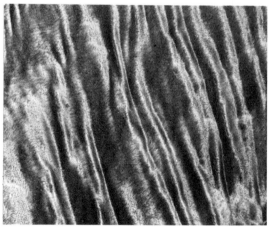

Quilted maple

Satinwood

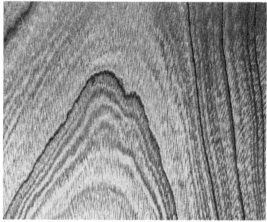

African mahogany

tree produces the self-descriptive and highly prized fan, feather, swirl and curl figuring; while the buttress or root base of some trees, notably walnuts, the very bold-patterned stump figure.

Some abnormalities produce striking figure, notably burr formations caused either by fungal irritation of the cambium layer, severe pollarding or lopping, or in the case of elm, natural growth irregularities. Burrs or burls can also be caused by large numbers of small twigs which fail to develop, and yield the familiar bird's eye in maple, etc. Examples of some of these figure markings are shown in 16, but it would be impossible to include all the known varieties, for practically every species of tree is capable of yielding outstanding effects in grain, texture and colour, and there are many recorded instances of exceptional logs suitable for veneering bringing very large sums of money.

Coloration

The natural colouring agents in wood are water soluble, and will tend to leach out if repeatedly soaked or exposed to weathering for long periods. Typical colour examples are logwood, which yields a commercial water soluble fierce red dye, and fustic a khaki yellow. Generally speaking, wood is lighter in colour when freshly sawn and gradually darkens as the wood surfaces oxidize, but as the colours are not permanent they may ultimately fade. The sapwood is usually lighter than the heartwood, and this serves as the usual method of identification; but some species exhibit little if any difference, notably ash, sycamore, beech, holly, silver fir, etc.

The precise description of colour in any specimen is virtually impossible, as so many factors apply. No two trees are ever alike, and at best a wood can only be described as having general characteristics modified or accentuated by growth conditions, exposure to air, heat, sunlight, etc. In general, most woods, with the exception of jet-black ebonies and blackwood, and pure white holly, have a yellowish cast which can never be bleached out completely. It is this predominant yellow in conjunction with reds and blacks which give the innumerable

shades of brown. Greens do exist, but are usually the result of abnormalities, while clear greys are the result of weathering or treatment by chemical means.

Woods which change colour under normal indoor conditions, with only occasional exposure to direct sunlight, include the following:

Those which fade – rosewood, walnut, mansonia, teak, agba, gaboon, etc.

Those which yellow – African mahogany, sapele, walnut (most species), agba, gaboon, maple, plane, sycamore, oak, etc.

Those which redden – cherry, yew, beech, kingwood, purpleheart, padouk, etc.

The lists are by no means complete, and individual specimens may not necessarily behave in the manner indicated, while all polishes tend to darken wood in time, and oil and wax pronouncedly so.

Odour

Most timbers have trace odours, some very pronounced, due to the presence of essential oils which often decide the use of the wood. Notable examples are cedar, camphorwood, etc. Some timbers are also known by their particular scent or odour, such as sandalwood, rosewood, jamwood, sneezewood, stinkwood, etc. Teak, Australian walnut and certain African woods have a highly objectionable smell when freshly worked; but most scents and odours, with the notable exception of camphor and cedar which are used as moth deterrents, rapidly fade on exposure to the air, due to the surface evaporation or drying out of the essential oils.

Durability

Hardness is no criterion of durability even though most, but not all, durable woods are essentially hard and dark in colour, due to the higher content of wood substance and the presence of antiseptic tannins and resins. A notable exception is western red cedar, which is not a true cedar but a very light softwood so impregnated with phenolic-type resins that it is almost impervious to decay.

The question of durability hardly arises in indoor domestic furniture, for all woods are sufficiently durable under controlled conditions. Where, however, continuous moist conditions occur in the presence of free oxygen then the wood is immediately subject to decay in various forms. Beech or elm, for instance, will last for centuries, either as furniture or totally immersed in water or deeply buried in the earth; but if either is laid on wet soil, or only shallowly buried in the upper layers which contain free oxygen, it will speedily rot.

Wood for all work exposed to weathering must, therefore, be chosen carefully for natural durability and resistance to decay. Unfortunately, it cannot be assumed that because a wood is highly resinous it is therefore extremely durable, although it will be more durable than wood with a low resin content. Woods of proven durability include oak, chestnut, yew, teak and greenheart; while if the work is to be painted or otherwise protected then obviously woods of only average durability can be used. Some woods are, however, inclined to repel paint, while others will not absorb sufficient preservative except under pressure, therefore reference should be made to the standard textbooks on wood preservation (see Bibliography).

Fire resistance of wood

Although wood might appear to be one of the most inflammable of materials, some species, notably crabwood, jarrah, iroko, padouk and teak, are very resistant, and all woods of large dimension char outwardly, cutting off the supply of oxygen necessary to support combustion. However, built-in fixtures in exhibition-work, public buildings, etc. are sometimes required to be fireproofed, or composed of fire-retardant materials. Plywoods and chipboards in fire-retardant quality can be obtained to special order; or the completed product can be coated with special paints or clear varnishes, or treated with various chemical preparations, the most widely used of which is ammonium phosphate. Alternatively, plywood panels or partitions can be interleaved with plasterboard or soft asbestos to give a 'one hour' standard resistance.

It is, or should be, the responsibility of the buyer or his agent to specify precisely the degree of resistance required, and the materials or treatment to be used; but the terms 'fireproof' or 'fire-resistant' should not be accepted without qualification, otherwise they may be liable to serious misconstruction. It is usually more correct to claim that a combustible material suitably treated is 'fire-retardant' only.

Defects

Every tree is a prey to defects from the moment it emerges as a seedling to the last stages of seasoning, and these defects can be innate (inherent vice), such as the characteristic natural shrinkage of wood; acquired defects occasioned by seasonal checks, insect and fungal attack, etc.; and artificial defects caused by incorrect sawing and seasoning. As, however, any one defect may arise from several causes it is more convenient to classify them as *natural* or *artificial*.

Natural defects

Knots These are in effect the basal stumps of incipient or cast-off branches in the living tree. Where the tree itself naturally prunes its branches owing to lack of light caused by overcrowding, or where such branches are artificially pruned in controlled forestry and cleanly sawn, then the cambium layers will heal over the wound and the knot is then live or embedded (17:1A). Where, however, a mature branch is broken off, leaving a long ragged stump, then the cambium layer cannot heal the wound and the stump dies, forming a deal or loose knot, often rot affected (17:2A).

All knots whether live or dead affect the mechanical strength of the timber, owing to the abrupt change in the direction of the fibres, and constitute blemishes which detract from the value. They are, therefore, graded as follows:

Pin knots Small knots ½ in (12.5 mm) or under, often caused by the shedding of early branches. Usually allowable in prime timber.

Spike or splay knots (17:3) Knots sliced through their length during sawing, and commonly known as 'slash' knots. They are difficult to plane up, especially in softwood, while large specimens are not permissible in hardwood unless allowed for in the measurement.

Encased knots Dead knots which are still sound and difficult to dislodge, and often ringed with resin in softwood.

Branched knots Two or three knots springing from a common centre.

Knots are classified as small, medium and large, the latter usually 1½ in (38 mm) in diameter and over; but gradings are not precise and vary according to the country of origin.

Shakes Both the medullary ray and springwood cells of ring-porous hardwoods are weaker than the remainder, and built-in tensions are created which tend to level out, either in the growing tree under certain adverse conditions or in the felled log during seasoning. Thus extensive splitting may occur in the weakest links, i.e. radially along the medullary rays, and tangentially at the junction of springwood and summerwood. Various forms of shake are common, as follows:

Radial shakes The log splits from the pith or heart radially along the medullary rays, usually indicating that the tree has passed its prime. Sawing losses can be minimized by placing the cuts either side of the shake, always provided the growth of the tree does not twist upon its axis, in which case the shakes become spiral, rendering the log useless for long lengths. Where only one shake is present it is known as a 'simple heart shake', while two shakes in line compose a 'double heart shake' (17:4), and several a 'star shake' (17:5).

Frost shakes (17:7) project inwardly from a definite frost rib on the cambium and are, as their name implies, the result of severe weather.

Tangential shakes The soft springwood of the log splits away from the harder summerwood, either during seasoning or through shearing stresses in the growing tree caused by old age, excessive bending under strong winds, intense heat, etc. A frequent cause in oak is the depradations of the tortrix viridána moth, whose caterpillars strip the young leaves in early summer, with the result that growth is checked

and the wood rings fail to cohere. Where such shakes run along part of the annual ring only, then they are known as 'cup shakes' (17:6A); but where the log is completely encircled then they become 'ring shakes' (17:6B). Usually such shakes seriously detract from the value of the timber. English walnuts are particularly prone to cup and ring shakes, as the trees are rarely felled until they are long past maturity.

Cross shakes (*thunder shakes*) These failures are caused by compression and not by splitting or shearing, while the actual rupture is across the grain and not with it as with all other shakes. The probable cause is not thunder, as the name suggests, but either felling shatter (the sudden impact as the felled log hits either hard ground or another fallen log), or mechanical strain in the living tree. Chiefly confined to the softer varieties of tropical hardwoods, and appearing either as a definite fracture or an overriding of the fibres, showing only as a faint raised line across the width of the wood, which will snap like a carrot under strain. This particular type of shake often occurs with a soft condition in the heartwood, known as 'brittle heart', 'carrot heart', etc., and agba is particularly liable to this defect. End splitting and sun checking (see below) are usually regarded as artificial defects due to errors, in seasoning, but a marked propensity to split and check may be inherent in some species and such defects may be part natural and part artificial.

Pitch veins, pitch pockets, etc. Sometimes known as resin pockets, they can appear either as thin veins or shallow cavities filled with resin. Usually caused by damage to the cambium layer in resinous woods, they may remain hidden and thus constitute a serious danger if the wood is used structurally.

Pith flecks Repeated damage to the cambium layer by small insects is often healed over with bark, and may show as small dots or patches of brown cork deeply buried in some woods, notably birch, alder and sycamore. They have no effect other than that of unsightliness.

Rind galls, etc. Patches of ingrowing bark, probably caused by exterior damage to the

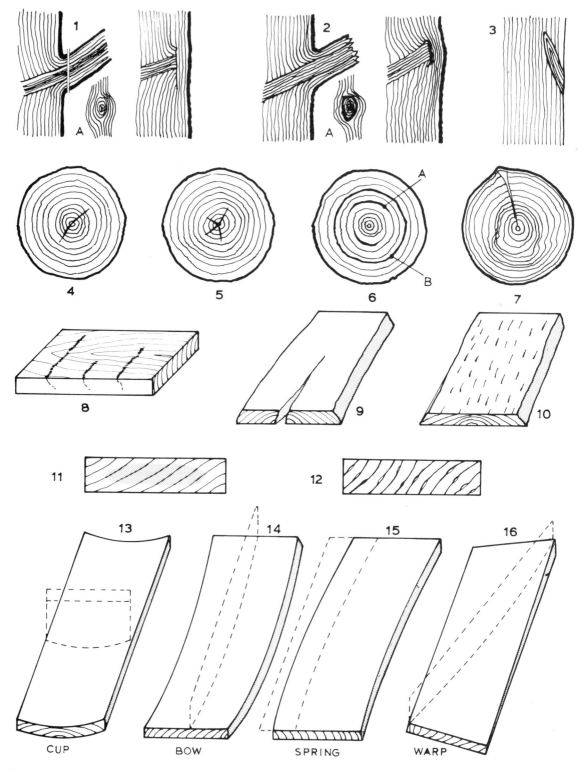

17   Defects in wood

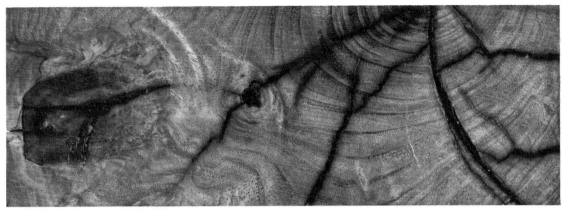

18 Shakes and knots in English walnut

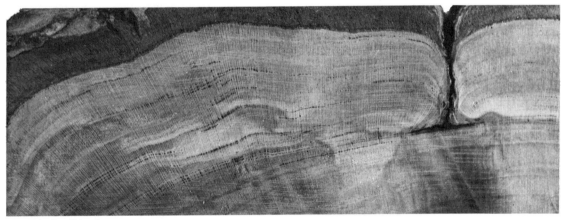

19 Rind gall in cherry

growing tree. Other natural defects include 'callus', or tissue formed over a wound in a tree resulting in unnatural growth incorporated in the normal wood growth; 'canker', caused by fungoid disease; and 'cat face', a partially healed fire scar.

Internal sapwood Normally, the sapwood dies ring by ring, forming heartwood, but on occasions patches of sapwood survive within the heartwood, and show as lighter patches as sometimes seen in Rio rosewood. It is not known how the condition arises. Sapwood also can be prematurely killed by frost or other agents, while the cambium is repaired and continues to grow, forming new sapwood over the dead patches which appear in later years as a dark ring. The wood usually separates and breaks away along the ring during conversion.

Burrs/Burls These are not usually classed as defects as they may enhance the value of the timber considerably; they are, however, true defects. They can be caused either by fungal or insect attack irritating the cambium layers, and resulting in large rapid growths, usually at the base of the tree, or by numbers of small twigs which fail to develop owing to insufficient nourishment, forming a dense mass. The knobs in severely lopped or pollarded trees, and the witch's broom in birch trees, are typical examples.

Artificial defects

All woods shrink on drying, some pronouncedly so, thus creating internal strains and stresses. Normally, the natural elasticity of a healthy

25

wood structure will distribute these stresses evenly, but if the structure is unequal or lacking in elasticity (innate defect), and if incorrect seasoning imposes too great a strain, then various forms of distortion, splitting, etc. will occur. Weighting down during seasoning helps to reduce distortion.

Cupping or rounding (17:13) The plank hollows across the width, forming a rounding on the underface, often due to incorrect piling.

Bowing (17:14) The plank is curved like a bow throughout its length. A succession of short bows is usually caused by sagging between too widely spaced stickers or by stickers which are not placed exactly over each other.

Springing (17:15) Sometimes known as 'edge bend', the wood remains flat but bends edgewise on its own plane.

Twisting (17:16) The plank twists on its longitudinal axis with the result that the long edges are straight, but the diagonals are curved. Usually known as 'in winding'.

Warping, casting Synonymous terms for distortion in one or more directions (see Twisting, above).

End splitting (17:9) The butt end of the plank splits open, usually caused by too rapid drying, but some species will always split.

Sun checking (17:10) The wood surface is covered with small splits along the grain caused by too rapid drying in hot sun. Not serious unless the splits penetrate deeply.

Flaking The surface of the wood lifts in innumerable small flakes or layers which spring under the cutting action, preventing a smooth surface. Sometimes due to structural weakness, but can also be caused by incorrect seasoning.

Diagonal grain The grain runs obliquely to the longitudinal axis, usually due to incorrect sawing, but some timbers exhibit marked deviations in grain direction which cannot be avoided. Although the condition may make surfacing more difficult it is not important, except in structural members where the impact strength loss is high, and in bending where a grain slope of 1 in 25 may mean a bending strength loss of 4 per cent, and a 1 in 5 slope a loss of 45 per cent.

Case hardening (17:11) If the wood is kiln dried too quickly then the surfaces dry out at a rate quicker than the rate of movement of moisture by capillary attraction from the centre of the plank, with the result that the dry outer layers are in tension, and the moist interior in compression. Cuts which close ahead of the saw are often due to case hardening. Provided the actual wood fibres are not ruptured the condition can be cured by steaming and redrying.

Honeycombing (17:12) If the kiln drying of case-hardened timber is continued to dryness then the natural shrinkage movement of the moist interior as it dries will be locked in by the rigid outer skin, resulting in severe internal stresses and subsequent checking or disruption of the wood fibres, not visible from the outside. There is no cure for the condition, which severely depreciates the value of the timber.

Collapse The too rapid kiln drying of green timber can result in a flattening of the wood cells, caused by vacuums created by the withdrawal of water to below fibre saturation point at a rate faster than it can be replaced by either air or live steam. This condition is known as 'collapse' and is characterized by extensive shrinking and warping, particularly in the springwood, giving a washboard effect. It can also be caused by too slow drying at too high a temperature, or too high a humidity rate, and can sometimes be remedied by steaming and reworking in the dry kiln.

DISEASES AND PESTS

Wood which is deeply buried in the ground or completely submerged in water does not decay, as witness the highly prized black bog oak which has been buried for centuries under layers of wet peat, and the use of timber baulks for underwater piles and breakwaters. However, where there is free oxygen, living fungi will attack the wood, provided there is moisture present; and although most of these fungi are relatively harmless, causing little more than local staining, two main types of rot actively feed upon the wood substance and eventually destroy it.

White rots

These are usually outdoor types, commonly known as 'wet rots' (rotting logs, fence posts, etc.). They consume both the cellulose and lignin content of the wood, leaving only a white pithy or slimy residue.

Brown rots

These are mainly of the indoor type, but can also occur out of doors. They attack the cellulose content only, leaving the lignin content intact, and are commonly known as 'dry rots', with the wood residue usually brown, spongy, dry and deeply cracked with and across the grain, giving a characteristic charred appearance.

Dote

This is an outdoor type of brown rot known commercially as 'dote' or 'punk'. Living trees are affected, also felled logs full of sap and awaiting sawing, the infection spreading through the heartwood and finally emerging as a bracket-shaped fruit-body on the bark. Incipient dote is easily recognizable, as the wood is peppered with round or oval greyish-white spots which do not appear to affect the mechanical strength to any great extent, but in later stages the wood becomes brown, dry, with spongy white streaks. The fungus cannot exist in the dry state, therefore sound unaffected wood need not be treated. As some harmless fungi cause similar brown staining, doteiness can be tested for by lifting a small splinter of the wood surface with a knife; if dote is present the splinter will break easily with a brash fracture. Fruit woods such as pear, apple, cherry, plum, etc. are particularly susceptible to this form of rot.

It is dote that causes the now much sought after spalted timber. Favoured by wood turners and some furniture-makers, maple, beech and walnut produce the most highly prized markings.

True dry rot (Lacrymans merulius)

This is an indoor type, and of all the wood-destroying fungi the most serious as it will attack dry seasoned timber if the conditions are suitable. Initially, the infection needs damp,

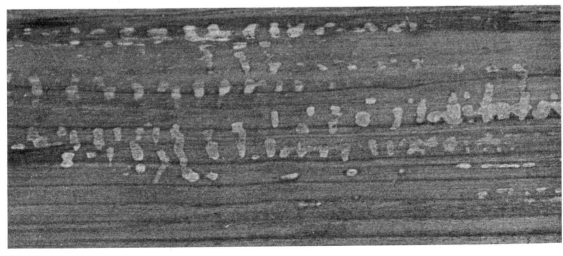

20   Dote in cherry

badly ventilated surroundings, but once the fungus has taken hold it will carry its own water in wide thread-like hyphae which can penetrate thick brickwork in search of fresh material which it rapidly consumes, leaving the characteristic deeply cleft, cube-like charring, often hardly noticeable under painted surfaces except as local sinkages. In dark conditions the fungus may appear as a white woolly growth, or a smooth fan-shaped grey skin with ragged edges exuding moisture droplets, but if light is present then the typical fruit-bodies will appear. Those who have seen a fully formed fruit-body, sometimes many feet across, with its leprous-grey skin suffused with livid patches of white, yellow and lilac-blue, and peppered with rust-red spores are hardly likely to forget the experience.

Treatment for dry rot must be drastic: all infected woodwork cut away and burnt, infected brickwork and non-wood materials scorched with a blow torch, and treated with an efficient antiseptic. Sound wood in the vicinity should be thoroughly brushed over with either a water soluble preservative such as commercial sodium fluoride (4 per cent), zinc chlorate (5 per cent), applied hot if possible; or one of the commercial solvent-type preservatives recommended for the purpose. Care should be taken with all these chemicals in confined spaces, for although they are not intrinsically dangerous to handle they must necessarily be highly toxic if they are to be effective.

Several other dry rots, notably the cellar fungus (*Coniophora cerebella*), attack house woodwork, but they require continuous moisture and therefore present no hazard to dry timber.

Insect pests

Most important of these are the lyctus, death-watch and furniture beetles; and of secondary importance, in that they attack only unseasoned, sickly or softwood timber, the pinhole borers, longhorn beetles and giant wood-wasp. All these pests are winged and capable of flight in search of suitable breeding-places and in every case it is the larva or worm which actually attacks the wood.

Pinhole borers (ambrosia beetles)

These are confined to tropical countries and attack the sapwood and heartwood of freshly felled logs waiting for milling. Wood attacked by pinhole borers can be recognized immediately by the very small neat exit holes, usually stained with fungus, and the straight tunnels empty of dust running both with and across the grain. Structural damage is usually slight, and wood which has been attacked can safely be used in this country, although obviously there must be prejudice against it owing to the apparent similarity with the ravages of the true furniture beetle.

Lyctus (powder-post) beetle (21:B)

Several species exist and are common to timber-yards where they attack the sapwood of hardwoods with large pores, notably oak, ash, elm and coarse-grained walnuts. Close-grained woods and softwoods are usually immune, as the large eggs are not laid in cracks or crevices but in the actual pores of the wood which must be wide enough to receive them. The attack usually dies out as the wood becomes seasoned and the available starch is exhausted, but in the meantime the entire sapwood can be reduced to a flour-like dust. The mature beetle is dun coloured, with a narrow body about 3/16 in (4.7 mm) long, slightly larger than the furniture beetle, and with a more pronounced head.

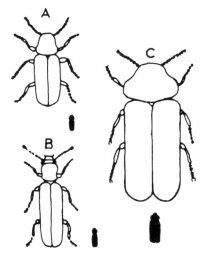

21   Wood-boring beetles

Common furniture beetle
(Anobium punctatum) (21:A)

Commonly known as *woodworm*, this is the most serious pest, and commonly occurs in roof rafters, floors or general woodwork, including furniture. A few flight holes on the surface of polished timber may not appear serious, but the wood below may be so tunnelled as to reach the point of total collapse, therefore a constant watch should be kept on every item of woodwork.

The mature beetle is oblong shaped, from $1/10$ to $1/5$ in long (2.5 to 5 mm) and dusty dark brown in colour, with wing-cases covered with lines of small punctures (hence the specific name). It commonly breeds in the dead branches of living trees, fencing-posts, etc., to enter the house by any open window during the dry summer season. After the female beetle has mated about 20 eggs are laid in any suitable crack or crevice, and in particular the exit or flight holes of previous larvae, and the curved white grub, which is equipped with strong biting jaws, hatches in about six weeks to commence its tunnelling by consuming the wood and excreting small pellets of granular dust. When it has reached maturity, which can be anything from one to two years according to the starch content of the wood, the grub, which is now about $1/4$ in (6.3 mm) long, moves to close under the surface, where it pupates and tunnels its way upwards to emerge finally as an adult beetle at any time from late May to August. It can then fly off to mate and renew the cycle.

While the sapwood of any wood is particularly liable to infestation (and it is for this reason that in some countries sapwood should never be used in furniture), the heartwoods of certain sweet woods, notably birch, beech, alder and some soft walnuts, are also attacked, while any wood affected by dampness or incipient decay is also prone. Alder, in particular, speedily becomes riddled with furniture beetle, hence the wiseacre's claim that it is better to have a plank or two of alder lying about the timber- or lumber-yard to attract any migrant beetles—a highly invidious contention, for the alder then becomes a first-class breeding-ground. Polished and painted surfaces do, of course, accord protection against the egg-laying female beetle, but invariably there is some hidden crack or crevice or an old flight hole which invites attack, therefore carcass backs and the underframing of furniture should be periodically examined for freshly expelled fine dust. Birch or alder plywoods glued with animal or vegetable glues are particularly susceptible, but resin-glued ply is normally resistant.

Death-watch beetle (Xestobium rufovillosum) (21:C)

This is a larger cousin of the furniture beetle, about $1/4$ in (6.3 mm) to $1/3$ in (8.5 mm) long and without the characteristic punctures on the wing-cases. The mature beetle raps the wood with its head during the mating season in early summer, producing the familiar ticking sound which is magnified by the wood and can travel considerable distances—hence the specific name of 'death-watch' beetle.

The life-cycle closely resembles that of the furniture beetle, but can extend over anything from one and a half to several years, dependent on the condition of the wood; while after pupation the mature beetle does not emerge immediately, but usually waits until the following spring. The seasoned heartwood of most timbers can be attacked, but infestation is usually confined to old oak in which some subtle change, probably induced by damp conditions, has rendered the wood more digestible, hence its incidence in old buildings, church roofing, etc. where the stoutest structural timbers can be reduced to mere shells. Infestation is rare in furniture, and is immediately recognizable by the large exit holes and characteristic bun-shaped pellets of wood-dust.

House longhorn beetle
(Hylotrupes)

The pest is extremely destructive on the continent of Europe, though in England virtually confined to certain pine-forest regions of Surrey. Softwood only is attacked, and infestation is usually limited to roof or attic. The mature beetle is from $1/4$ in (6.3 mm) to $3/4$ in (19 mm) in length, varying in colour from brown to iridescent green, with characteristic long curved feelers, while the oval exit holes can be very large and up to $3/8$ in (9.5 mm) in size.

Certain other types of longhorn beetle infest the sapwood of both hardwoods and softwoods. They do not as a rule attack seasoned timber/lumber, and are, therefore, confined to forest and timber-yard.

Giant wood-wasps

These only attack the living tree, and are, therefore, the foresters' concern. An occasional mature wasp of somewhat terrifying aspect, much bigger than a hornet and with a long egg-laying probe which could be mistaken for a sting, can sometimes be seen haunting the wood-pile in late summer, but can safely be disregarded.

Methods of treatment for insect pests

No treatment is required for pinhole borer as the tunnels are always empty, but infestation by furniture and death-watch beetle should be taken in hand immediately. The entire surface should be cleaned with a powerful vacuum-cleaner to clear the flight holes of dust, and a proprietary woodworm killer of the solvent type, usually a metallic or chlorinated naphthalene, liberally brushed or swabbed over the surface. Each flight hole should also be injected with the fluid, using the cheap polystyrene squeeze bottles with nozzle stoppers available, so that the hidden tunnelling can carry the fluid into the body of the wood. The entire treatment should be repeated in the following spring just before the beetles emerge (for the insecticide will not necessarily reach all the hidden grubs which will continue to pupate), after which a yearly check should be made for any signs of fresh dust, and measures taken accordingly. Most proprietary wood-worm destroyers do not stain the wood permanently or interfere with the existing polish, and should be applied as liberally as possible, for they are quite safe to handle. However, spraying in confined spaces should not be done unless efficient face masks are worn; and in any case liberal brushing is always preferable to spraying, as the oily fluid tends to bridge over existing flight holes; thus failing to penetrate.

STAINS IN WOOD

Stains can be caused by harmless fungi as distinct from wood-rotting fungi, soil conditions, frost factors, etc., chemical contamination, and natural oxidization or weathering.

Stain identification

Positive identification of any particular type of stain can be difficult, but as a rule fungal and mineral stains are of variable intensity, fading slightly at the edges and following the grain. Stains with a hard edge which do not follow the grain are usually chemical in origin, while overall discoloration is probably due to weathering or incorrect seasoning.

Mould- and sap-staining fungi, etc.

Certain harmless moulds feed on the carbo-hydrates in the wood cells and can produce grey, grey-blue, pink, white and black stains. Usually this type of staining is confined to the surfaces of the wood, and can, therefore, be eradicated by brushing or sanding down; but several types, of which the best known is *Ceratostomella pini*, attack the sapwood, producing the characteristic bluing of badly seasoned softwoods. This discoloration cannot be satisfactorily bleached out, and is due almost entirely to an optical effect, similar to the apparent blueness of watered milk. All these fungi have little if any mechanical effect on the wood, as the hyphae or mould threads constrict considerably where they pierce the cell walls, whereas wood-destroying fungi bore large apertures, and consume the cellulose.

Some fungi actually increase the value of the wood, as in the case of the beef-steak fungus (*Fistulina hepatica*) which can sometimes be seen growing on old, standing oak trees, the early stages of which produce a rich golden brown; and the much rarer *Chlorosplenium* sp. which stains oak a vivid green. Both have some mechanical effect on the timber, but not enough to impair its usefulness in decorative-work. All species of fungi require a certain minimum moisture content, usually well over 20 per cent, and therefore dry, seasoned timber is not affected.

Mineral stains

Certain soil conditions can cause pronounced staining, usually in brown or greyish streaks, as, for example, black-hearted ash, brown-hearted beech, and the reddish-brown mineral streak in the heartwood of Parana pine. As these are natural pigment-stains they do not affect the mechanical properties of the wood. They cannot be satisfactorily bleached out. Some timbers show actual deposits of white and grey crystalline mineral salts in the grain, and at times actual calcium stones which penetrate some distance into the wood. The difficult working properties of some exotic woods is often due to the dulling action of these mineral salts on cutting edges.

Chemical stains

Practically all woods contain sufficient colour-forming compounds to produce staining when brought into contact with acidic or alkaline chemicals, and in this respect behave much like litmus paper, producing reds, pinks and browns with acid reactions (french polish, urea glues, etc.), and blues and greens with alkaline reactions (soap, detergents, etc.). Additionally, most woods contain appreciable amounts of tannic acid which, if wetted, will react in greater or lesser degree with iron in any form, producing the characteristic blue-black staining of iron nails in exterior oak-work. Other woods besides oak showing strong reactions are afromosia, camphorwood, Douglas fir and sweet chestnut; while African mahogany, coigue, idigbo, gedunohor, sapele and utile react slightly to produce minor staining. Wood for scrubbed table-tops, draining-boards, etc. should be as neutral as possible. Teak, maple, sycamore, oak and deal are usually unaffected by soap and water, but agba, ayan, idigbo and afzelia are known to be unsuitable. Where there is any doubt a thorough test should be made beforehand.

Natural oxidization, weathering, etc.

Freshly converted green timber will oxidize rapidly if the wood surfaces remain wet for any length of time, due to the formation of chemical compounds which act on the colour-forming properties of the wood, producing brown or grey staining. This chemical effect is most marked in light-coloured woods, such as sycamore, which must be surface dried immediately it is converted if the overall whiteness is to be preserved. Moreover, sticker marks can penetrate quite deeply, particularly where there is chemical action between the actual sticker and the wood surface, and for this reason stickers should always be neutral woods—deal, horse-chestnut or poplar—which have been thoroughly dried.

Additional to seasoning discolorations is the effect of weather and sunlight on wood which can either bleach or darken surfaces very appreciably. Cherry, for instance, will darken considerably if exposed to strong sunlight for a few hours, so also will mahogany, while freshly sawn dry teak will rapidly oxidize from light green to dark brown. On the other hand, direct sunlight will bleach dark rosewood to a medium walnut colour, and walnut itself will lighten considerably, while kingwood will rapidly fade from deep purple to dark red-brown. The general rule would appear to be that dark woods lighten and light woods darken, but it is hardly safe to assume that the rule applies automatically, and tests should always be made. Some synthetic lacquers contain ultra-violet light barriers which to some extent inhibit the bleaching action of strong sunlight, but only certain woods are protected and the results are never altogether permanent.

Bleaching stains

Iron stains can be satisfactorily bleached out with either a saturated solution of oxalic acid in water or methylated spirit, hydrogen peroxide, some household bleaches, ink-eradicators, etc., and light chemical staining from other sources may also respond to several applications. The bleaching out of fungal stains, mineral discolorations and natural oxidization is never really feasible, although proprietary two-solution bleaches can assist in masking the discoloration by rendering the surfaces of the wood more opaque. Bleaching of entire surfaces, often—and to the writer's way of thinking, horribly—perpetrated on oak and pine, owes much to the lavish use of white grain fillers which choke the wood surface. The action of most bleaches is, of course, the release of free oxygen as the active bleaching agent.

PROPERTIES OF COMMON WOODS

The following list gives descriptions of some of the more widely known woods suitable for furniture-making. In each case, colour, texture, figure, working properties and behaviour can only be an approximation or general average, *for individual trees within each species may differ very considerably*. There will be marked differences between trees of the same species and accorded the same commercial gradings grown some 2000 miles apart, but there can also be an appreciable difference between trees grown only a few hundred miles apart. Movement or dimensional change is arrived at by adding together the tangential and radial movement values occasioned by a change in environmental humidity of 90 per cent (equivalent to a moisture content in timber of

approximately 20 per cent according to the species), down to a humidity of 60 per cent (12 per cent moisture content), with a total movement of 3 per cent denoting a stable wood; 3 to 4.5 per cent a medium, and over 4.5 per cent a relatively unstable wood. Thus idigbo will shrink approximately $3/32$ in (2.4 mm) tangentially and $1/16$ in (1.5 mm) radially for every 12 in (305 mm) in width within the range 18 per cent moisture content (90 per cent air humidity) down to 12 per cent (60 per cent humidity), and can be classed as a small movement or stable wood, whereas beech will shrink $3/8$ in (9.5 mm) tangentially and about $3/16$ in (5mm) radially under the same conditions, and must, therefore, be regarded as a large movement or relatively unstable wood. In practice, actual stability under normal working conditions will depend on the sum of the dimensional changes as given above, and also on the difference between the tangential and radial shrinkage value, with large differences giving greater tendency to warp and twist.

Home-grown wood

Origin	Colour, texture, figure	Working properties, behaviour, etc.
Ash	White to pinky cream or brown. Coarse textured. Plain figure sometimes with large flash or ripple.	Tough, strong but easy working, ideal bending wood. Stable.
Acacia	Lime green to golden brown in colour. Straight grained with a coarse texture but smooth to finish.	Requires careful seasoning. Hard, strong and very durable; ideal for cabinet work.
Apple	Light brown in colour with varying zones of light and dark browns. Fine grain and texture.	Hard and rather brittle. Easy to work but care must be taken in seasoning. Used mainly in turnery, small cabinet work and carving and in the past for many saw handles.
Beech	Whitish yellow. Fine even texture. Plain speckled grain. Quality variable.	Medium hard, strong, clean and easy working. A universal wood. Fairly stable.

Origin	Colour, texture, figure	Working properties, behaviour, etc.
Boxwood	Distinctive yellow colour, and one of the finest textured commercial woods available.	Dense and heavy and must be dried carefully to avoid splitting. Once dry is an excellent wood for fine turnery or carving. Also used for engraving, chessmen and bandings.
Cedar of Lebanon	Light brown, strongly aromatic, with clearly marked annual rings. Prone to large dead knots.	The wood is soft and light but durable. Fine grain but brittle, works easily. Ideal for cabinet work and panelling. Used in the past in blanket chest bottoms as a deterrent to moths.
Cherry	Pale yellow to light reddish brown. Fine even texture with silky sheen resembling pale yew.	Medium hard, tough, clean working. Fine finish. Excellent cabinet wood. Stable.
Chestnut, sweet (Spanish)	Resembling oak in appearance but not so dense.	Softer than oak. Clean working. Very stable.
Elm, (English or common)	Pale dull brown to medium brown. Coarse texture. Bold attractive figure.	Hard, tough, clean working. Warps badly if not bone-dry. Bends extremely well.
Elm, Dutch	Straighter grain than common elm.	As English elm but not so liable to warp.
Elm, Wych	Very pale brown. Straight grain.	Very clean working. Fairly stable.
Holly	Greenish white to grey. No distinct heartwood. Dense texture. Some holly can be pure white if correctly seasoned.	Medium hard, very clean working, very fine finish. Suitable for inlays, and for staining as blackwood. Fairly stable.
Larch	Reddish brown. Straight grained with a distinctive spring and summer wood. Reasonably free from knots, but when these occur they are hard and tend to loosen in seasoning.	Moderately hard and heavy. Strong, durable and tough.
Lime	Even white to pale brown. Fine uniform texture. Little figure.	Softish, close grained and very clean working. Ideal for carving. Fairly stable.
Macrocarpa	A softwood resembling yew.	Very durable and stable. Strong scent. Ideal for bookshelves, etc.
Maple	Not so white as sycamore. Fine texture with natural lustre. Plain figure.	Medium hard to very hard. Fine finish. Reasonably stable.

Origin	Colour, texture, figure	Working properties, behaviour, etc.
Oak	Cream to light yellow-brown. Coarse even texture. Attractive figure with quartered wood showing bold flash.	Medium hard to hard, tough, clean working, good finish. Bends well. Fairly stable.
Oak, brown	Very rich brown colour.	Much sought after for fine furniture.
Oak, tiger	Streaked brown on a white ground.	Properties as normal oak.
Pear	Pinkish brown with fine even texture and no apparent figure.	Medium hard, clean working, fine lustrous finish. Stable.
Plane	Resembling beech in appearance but with broader rays. When quartered is known as 'lace wood'.	Medium hard, fine finish. Stable.
Sycamore	White to yellow-white. Fine texture, natural silky lustre, sometimes with outstanding 'fiddle' figure when quartered. Known as 'Harewood' when stained silver-grey with iron salt.	Medium hard to hard, fine finish. Stable.
Walnut	Greyish yellow to brown with brown-black markings, often finely figured. Fine grain, but some open texture in coarser varieties. One of the most beautiful of all woods.	Medium hard, very clean and easy working. Bends well if straight grained. Stable.
Yew	A very dense softwood. Orange to rich brown in colour with purplish tints, stripes and darker spots. Very smooth and lustrous. Handsome close even grain with fine texture and figure which finishes well. Distinctive white sapwood.	Tough, strong, durable, heavy, hard and elastic. Knots, heart shake, ingrown bark and other growth characteristics are an attractive feature, accounting for its use in woodware and fine cabinet work. Bends extremely well.

Imported hardwoods

Origin	Colour, texture, figure	Working properties, behaviour, etc.
Abura West Africa	Light brown with pinkish tinge. Fine even texture. No figure.	Medium hard, clean working with some interlocked grain. Fairly stable.
Afrormosia West Africa	Resembling teak but paler and finer textured.	Moderately hard, easy working. Non-greasy substitute for Burmah teak. Very stable.
Agba West Africa	Light cream. Close even texture. No figure.	Medium hard, clean, easy working. Excellent for construction work. Stable.

Origin	Colour, texture, figure	Working properties, behaviour, etc.
Beech 　　Europe	White to brownish red when steamed. Fine even texture. Plain figure.	Medium hard, clean working. Good bending wood. Not very stable.
Bubinga 　　West Africa	Purplish brown ground colour, bordering in some specimens on deep crimson. Deeper tints run across either as irregular bands or as mottled or marbled variegations.	Dries slowly but well, and once dry is stable in use. Strong, hard and machines to a fine finish. Similar to rosewood in weight and grain, and often used as a cheaper alternative. Used for cabinet work and fine wood-ware items.
Guarea 　　(Nigerian 　　pearwood) 　　West Africa	Pinkish brown. Fine texture. Straight grain occasionally curled.	Medium hard, easy working with some interlocked grain. Reasonably stable.
Hydeua/ 　　Amazakoue/ 　　Ovangkol. 　　West Africa	Dark golden brown in colour with attractive dark brown to black markings. Close grain and fine texture.	Hard, heavy, clean working. Stable
Idigbo 　　West Africa	Pale yellow. Even texture. No figure. Good oak substitute.	Medium hard, easy working. Very stable.
Mahogany, 　　African 　　(Dry land)	Deep red brown. Coarse texture. Stripy figure.	Fairly hard, dense, easy working but grain interlocked. Not stable.
Mahogany, 　　African (Lagos, 　　Nigerian, Grand 　　Bassam, etc.)	Light pink brown to red brown. Fairly coarse texture. Stripy figure.	Medium hard, easy working but with interlocked grain. Fairly stable to stable.
Mahogany, 　　Brazilian	Darker and richer than Honduras. Some resembles Cuban.	Superior to all African species. Second only to Honduras.
Mahogany, 　　Cuban		It is regrettable that Cuban (Spanish) mahogany, the most universally known of all timbers, is no longer available owing to over-exploitation.
Mahogany, 　　Honduran	Yellowish brown. Close even texture. Plain lustrous figure.	Medium hard, excellent working properties. Very stable.
Makoré 　　(Cherry 　　mahogany) 　　West Africa	Reddish brown. Fine even texture. Lustrous, stripy figure. Peppery scent.	Medium hard, clean working. Stable.

Origin	Colour, texture, figure	Working properties, behaviour, etc.
Mansonia West Africa	Dark greyish brown, resembling walnut. Fine even texture. No figure.	Medium hard, clean working. Very stable.
Muninga Africa	Handsome gold to red-brown with darker markings.	Moderately hard, clean working. Stable.
Oak Europe	Pale cream to light brown. Coarse texture. Good figure. Large flash.	Hard, clean working. Fairly stable.
Oak Japan	Pale cream to light brown. Coarse even texture. Little figure. Small flash.	Medium hard, milder working than other oaks. Very stable.
Oak USA	White or red according to species. Coarse even texture closer than European oak. Very little figure.	Hard, heavy, clean working. Moderately stable.
Obeche West Africa	White to pale straw. Soft, open but firm texture. No figure.	Softish, easy working and suitable for core work only. Stable.
Olivewood Europe	Yellowish brown with variegated darker streaks.	Hard, heavy and gives a fine lustrous finish. Used for decorative work, inlays and turnery.
Padauk West Africa, Burma, Andaman Islands	Rich deep red/brown in colour. Coarse texture with an interlocked grain.	A heavy timber. Dries slowly but exceptionally stable in use. Used in furniture, fine joinery and for tool handles.
Pao Rosa West Africa	Dense, attractive, straight grained, rose coloured wood, which gives a pleasing lustre when finished.	Hard and heavy, used mainly in turnery and fine cabinet work.
Ramin Malaya	White to pale straw. Medium texture. Little figure.	Medium hard, clean working. Fairly stable.
Redwood, Scandinavian. Northern Europe, Scandinavia, Britain and Western Siberia	A white sapwood with light brown heartwood. Some small sound knots may be found.	Soft, stable and fairly durable. Good furniture quality boards available.
Rosewood, Amazon South America	Dark rust brown with some lighter markings.	Very dense, hard and heavy. An ideal rosewood for turnery as it is one of the few available in thick sections.

Origin	Colour, texture, figure	Working properties, behaviour, etc.

Rosewood, Brazilian, Rio – *see* Exotic hardwoods

Rosewood, Honduran Honduras	Distinct mauve/red colour with lighter and darker markings.	Heavy, dense and machines to an excellent finish. Available in reasonable sized boards; used extensively in musical instruments and furniture.

Rosewood, Indian, Bombay – *see* Exotic hardwoods

Rosewood, Mexican Mexico	Brown with black lines, extremely decorative.	Very popular as a fine turnery timber.
Rosewood, Santos Brazil	Light brown/red with purple streaks.	A dense heavy timber which finishes with a fine silky lustre.
Sapelewood West Africa	Reddish brown. Coarse even grain. Lustrous stripe.	Fairly hard, easy working but with interlocked grain. Fairly stable when quarter sawn.
Teak Burmah Africa	Golden brown with occasional black streaks. Lustrous plain figure sometimes rippled.	Medium hard, very easy working but severe on cutting edges. A greasy wood but remarkably stable. The best all-round wood.
Utile West Africa	Greyish pink to red, resembling sapelewood but coarser texture and without pronounced stripe.	Moderately hard, clean working. Stable.
Walnut USA	Purplish black-brown, fine even texture, often boldly marked.	Strong, elastic, hard, clean working. Stable.
Walnut, African. West Africa	Bronze yellow and lustrous with dark streaks. Coarse even texture with ribbon stripes.	Moderately hard, clean working but grain interlocked. Not a true walnut. Reasonably stable.

The dust of both makoré and mansonia is non-poisonous but highly irritant to mucous membranes and occasionally to the skin in susceptible cases, and for this reason they are little used in production runs where large quantities of dust are raised. Hand-creams, light face-masks or respirators will give protection to those not unduly allergic to the dust.

Exotic hardwoods

Black bean Australia	Chocolate-brown with grey-brown streaks somewhat resembling a coarse walnut. Straight-grained even texture.	Hard, strong, somewhat difficult to work but capable of fine finish. Fairly stable.

Origin	Colour, texture, figure	Working properties, behaviour, etc.
Laurel India	Light brown to brown-black. Superficially resembling walnut but with coarse though even texture.	Hard, heavy, tough working and very strong. Capable of fine finish. Fairly stable.
Rosewood, Indian, Bombay	Dark brown to purple-black. Straight grain without violent colour fluctuations of Rio rosewood. Medium, coarse, oily texture.	Rather harder than Rio rosewood, but fairly easy to work and capable of fine finish. Stable.
Rosewood, Brazilian, Rio. South America	Tan to violet-brown or purple-black with ink-black streaks and patches. Medium coarse texture. Oily with characteristic scent when freshly worked.	Hard, fairly easy to work, but hard on tools. Capable of fine finish. Stable.
Satinwood, East Indian. India	Light straw to golden yellow, sometimes exceptionally figured. Fine even texture with remarkable lustre. An outstanding wood.	Hard, very dense and difficult to work, but capable of fine finish. Stable.
Silky oak Australia East Africa	Pinky red-brown with characteristic dark eye or ray. Straight even grain, coarse texture. Not a true oak.	Fairly soft but remarkably strong and tough. Easy working but difficult to finish. Fairly stable.

Other exotic woods occasionally available

Blackwood (African)
Exceptionally hard, heavy, brown-black, giving the appearance of almost total blackness as it has no visible grain. An oily, extremely stable and valuable wood reserved for musical instruments, chessmen, knife handles, brush backs, etc.

Cocobolo (Nicaraguan rosewood)
Similar to Rio rosewood but with a pronounced reddish tinge and coarse, visible grain. Not so common as other rosewoods and principally used for brush backs, knife handles, door knobs, etc.

Ebony (Macassar ebony, Andaman marble wood, coromandel, calamander wood, etc.)

All are extremely hard and heavy, very finely textured and somewhat cold to the touch with a marble-like quality. The colours are showy, ranging from dark grey streaked with saffron-green, brown, red and purple to pure black. The trees do not grow much beyond 8 in (203 mm) to 10 in (254 mm) in girth and uses are, therefore, confined to small articles.

Kingwood (Violetta—Brazil)
The veritable king of all woods, violet-brown with black or violet-black streaks. Very hard, heavy and most finely textured. Diameters are never more than about 8 in (203 mm) and uses are confined to inlays and small articles owing to scarcity and high cost. A near cousin is Pernambuco wood, the most expensive of woods and used exclusively in the best violin bows.

Purplewood (Aramanth, violetwood)
Colour intense purple or violet. Very hard, heavy, medium coarse to fine texture. Chief uses for ornamental wood are turning, inlays and billiard-cue butts.

Snakewood (Leopardwood, letterwood)
Brown or reddish brown striped with black. Very hard and heavy, fine uniform texture. Small heartwood and only suitable for inlays, door handles, walking-sticks, etc.

Tulipwood (Brazil)
Pink to crimson stripes with a straw-coloured ground. Fine texture with a straight to interlocked grain. Heavy, dense and machines to a fine finish. An ideal timber for small woodware but its main use is for furniture bandings.

BUYING WOOD, AND TRADE TERMS
Notes on buying wood

Buyers of waney/wane edge timber in small quantities direct from the saw-mill or timber-merchant or dealer must expect to pay considerably more per foot than buyers of complete logs of any one variety. Moreover, they cannot assume the right to pick and choose invidividual planks, but must be prepared to accept them 'as they rise' from the pile. However, most co-operative merchants will allow selection, particularly to known customers, although they must necessarily charge higher prices. Imported square edge timber is stacked according to thickness; the planks may be from different logs but the quality is usually fairly consistent throughout the pile, and therefore it is reasonably safe to buy 'as they rise' and only pay extra for small quantities. Wide, flat sawn boards are usually obtainable in home-grown and some African woods, but as they are cut from the centre of the tree, pith defects and pronounced cupping must be expected. Quartered wood can sometimes be obtained in fairly wide boards, particularly in English oak, but are obviously more expensive. Wide boards in teak, Honduras mahogany and other valuable woods are unfortunately now almost unobtainable owing to past over-exploitation; any such extra wide or long boards and planks command considerably higher prices. A fair average specification for teak and Honduras mahogany is now about 8 in (200 mm) wide and 8 ft (2.4 m) long, but African woods have not yet been over-exploited, and greater widths and lengths are commonly available. In ordering teak it is more economical to give the timber-merchant exact descriptions of the minimum widths, thicknesses and lengths required so that he can pick the nearest. Assuming that planks 8 in (200 mm) wide and 7 ft (2.1 m) long will suffice, then he may be able to supply widths of 8¼ in (210 mm) and lengths of 7 ft 3 in (2.2 m), thus saving valuable timber. Thicknesses are usually very full indeed, but only charged for at the nominal grading.

Seasoned wood

The terms *dry, bone dry, well seasoned* are relatively meaningless without supporting evidence, for any wood which has been sticked one year for every inch (25 mm) of thickness may be counted as air dry or seasoned, as distinct from green. The moisture content will, of course, depend on the season of the year, and not on the number of years in stick; it should not exceed 20 or 22 per cent in exceptional circumstances in Britain, unless it is water wet with drifting rain or snow. *While further drying over the prescribed minimum will not make any difference to the moisture content, nevertheless additional years in stick help to equalize out the built-in strains and stresses*; and while a 1 in (25 mm) board of English oak which has been seasoned for five years might show little intrinsic difference from one which has been dried for one year only, nevertheless it will be more mature and tend to be milder mannered and more stable.

Timber-merchants or lumber-dealers converting their own logs keep exact records, and will always give the number of years in stick, while if they have bought the logs from other merchants the pedigree is usually available. Retail merchants who do not convert their own can rarely give the seasoning time, marketing the wood as 'seasoned' only. This also applies to all square edge imported wood, which may only be 'shipping dry' (approximately 25 per cent moisture content) when received from the importer. However, reputable merchants can be trusted to advise the buyer to the best of their ability.

Choosing wood

There is no consistency of quality in wood and every merchant or dealer can only offer the best of what is available in the particular species at any given time. First-hand inspection of the stock is always essential, therefore. Again, only active experience can give the knowledge of what constitutes good quality in any particular species. As an example, the writer would probably accept large rotten cores in rosewood logs, large knots in prime quality English walnut, very small pin knots in prime English oak, but no defects whatsoever in Honduras and African (grand bassam) mahoganies, sapelewood or Burmah teak.

In choosing wood the planks or boards should be turned over and abnormal defects rejected or allowed for in the measurement. Top boards which are badly cast or showing considerable sap should not be included. Thicknesses up to 1 in (25 mm) should be reasonably free from splits except at the extreme ends, and if there are knots or shaky patches they should be ringed with chalk and allowed for in the final measurement. A certain degree of splitting in thicker planks must be expected, but is only permissible if usable wood is left on either side. Some degree of warp in wide boards is inevitable (but not in quartered stuff), but here again a centre-cut should yield reasonably flat surfaces on either side. Again, slight bowing in the length is allowable, but pronounced kinking, casting or cupping is not, although much depends on the nature of the wood, and a richly figured log might exhibit very considerable distortion. Heart and star shakes in the pith or crown plank are almost inevitable in logs from mature trees, but pronounced cup

Examples of well-grown wood showing evenly spaced rings

22 English oak

23 Yellow pine

40

Douglas fir

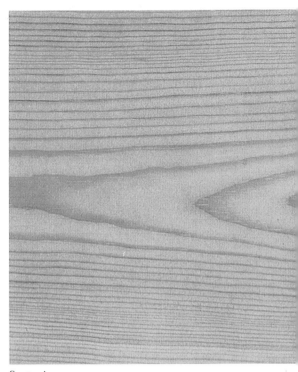

Scots pine

Brazilian rosewood

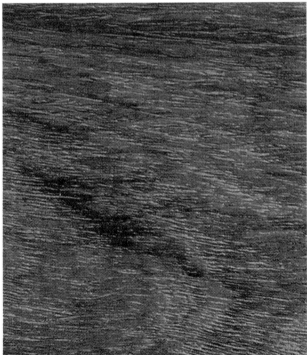

Indian rosewood

Muninga

Padauk

Walnut

Mahogany

Ash

Elm

Plane

Robinia

Oak

Beech

Cherry

Sycamore

or ring shakes should be rejected out of hand as they have a habit of following up the tree for considerable distances, and may thus render the planks useless for all normal purposes. Seasoning defects should be looked for, *particularly deep sticker-marks*, extensive discoloration, sun checking, etc., although dry English oak may show large tarry patches which do not penetrate below the surface. If a mild working wood is required then the annual rings should be examined; they should be evenly spaced and as regular as possible and from eight to 16 rings per in (25 mm). Generally speaking, the wider the rings in hardwoods the stronger the wood, but the reverse applies to softwoods. Figures 22 & 23 show an example of beautifully grown yellow pine with tight, evenly spaced rings beside a comparable example of mild English oak. As the true colour of the wood and the extent of the sap is usually masked by dirt or weathering, most merchants will allow scoring the butt end with a knife, although they would object to its use across the face; it is therefore better to carry a small block-plane for testing. Thicknesses should be more but never less than the nominal size quoted, *and a sharp eye should be kept for badly sawn or taper-cut planks* which occasionally pass unnoticed. Imported square edge wood does not, as a rule, exhibit the same defects as waney/wane edge timber, as these have been rejected during conversion; moreover the plank and boards are usually graded before shipment. Points to look for are bowing in the length and inferior gradings slipped into the pile, otherwise the board can be accepted as it rises, choosing the most suitable widths and lengths. As the length of seasoning time is unknown the moisture content should be tested before use, and it is always better to buy square edge wood well in advance of requirement. Kiln-dried wood will be more expensive than air-dried, unless the latter has been in stick for several years. *It is not wise to assume that kiln-dried wood will contain any less moisture as this depends entirely on how long it has been in storage since drying.* On the whole, however, good kiln-dried wood, no matter where it has been stored, will tend to be less liable to subsequent distortion as the initial drying will have been carefully controlled.

Terms

The following terms are used in the timber trade, but although some are more applicable to softwood gradings they are also used in American hardwood gradings and are therefore included.

Terms denoting quality

Butt Butt length	Main trunk. Specifically lowest part of trunk next to stump.
Boule	French term for superior timber or wood, but specifically imported logs sawn through and through and reassembled in order of cutting.
Prime	The best available in the particular species at any particular time. First quality.
Selects	Selected wood.
Clean	Free from knots.
Clear	Free from visible defects.
C and S	Common and Selects.
Mercantable	Free from defects impairing strength, i.e. sound construction timber.
FAS	Firsts and Seconds.
FAQ	Fair Average Quality.
U/S	Unsorted.
Av spec	Average specification, i.e. dimensions according to the species.

Broken spec	Denoting withdrawal of certain dimensions from original specification.
Rising in the pile	As stacked without grading or selection.
Crown plank } Pith plank }	Centre plank containing pith and heart shakes.
Boxed heart	Wood converted so that the whole of the heart including pith and centre shakes is contained in one piece.
Crook } Knee }	Short length of naturally curved wood.
Slabbing	Outside slices of the log containing bark and sap.
Brashy	Short-grained or old, dead or carroty wood.
Brittleheart	Brashy heart caused by compression failures in fibres during growth.
Blackheart	Abnormal black or dark brown discoloration in heartwood not necessarily decayed as in blackhearted ash, etc.
Shipping dry	Sufficiently dry to prevent deterioration (fungoid growths, mould, etc.) during shipment only. (Average moisture content 25 per cent.)
Bone-dry	Meaningless term suggesting thoroughly dry wood.

Terms denoting treatment

Converted timber	Timber/lumber sawn from log.
t and t	Sawn through and through/plain sawed. Waney/wane edge timber.
W/E	Waney edge timber following the shape of the log.
S/E	Square edge timber, i.e. waney edge timber trimmed up with edges parallel.
U/E	Unedged boards.
1 W/E, 1 S/E	One waney edge, one square edge from logs squared one side before sawing.
Quartered } Quarter sawn }	Radial cut timber following path of medullary rays.
Rift sawn } Plain cut } Slash cut } Flat cut }	Tangentially cut flat sawed through the log (the middle planks will be quarter cut).
Cleft	Split or riven along the natural cleavage-lines following the medullary rays.
Surfaced	Planed on faces but not to final thickness.
Thicknessed	Planed to exact thickness.
Prepared	Planed to final width and thickness.
par	Planed all round, i.e. prepared.
pe	Planed edge, or plain edge not tongued as in floor-boards.
t & g	Tongued and grooved.
t g & b	Tongued, grooved and beaded.
t g & v	Tongued, grooved and vee-jointed.
Deeping	Resawing through the thickness, i.e. parallel to the wide faces.
Flat Cutting	Resawing through the width, i.e. parallel to the edges.
ad	Air-dried
kd	Kiln-dried.

For other terms refer to appropriate chapters.

Terms denoting dimension

Quarter girth	Quarter of the girth taken as one side of the equivalent square in measuring wood in the round.
Hoppus measure	System used in timber measurement of round logs which allows about 27 per cent for waste in milling (bark and wane, etc.).
afb	Allowance for bark.
Billet	Short round log. Short timber split or hewn. Log centre cut and squared or dressed.
Blank	Timber cut to specified dimension and left full to allow for subsequent treatment.
Lumber	Square-edged boards of random widths.
Plank	Sawn timber over 2 in (50 mm) thick and of varying widths (British Standard 565:1963).
Board	Sawn timber up to 2 in (50 mm) thick. (Many home-grown timber-merchants or lumber dealers prefer to regard Boards as up to 1¼ in (32 mm) thick and Planks as over 1¼ in (32 mm) thick).
Batten	Wood of small cross-section. Specifically square sawn softwood 1⅞ in (48 mm) to 4 in (102 mm) thick and 4 in (102 mm) to 8 in (204 mm) wide.
Lath	Strip wood of small section. Specifically ³⁄₁₆ in (5 mm) to ⅜ in (9.5 mm) thick and 1 in (25 mm) to 1¼ in (32 mm) wide.
Strip	Square sawn timber 2 in (50 mm) and under thick and 2 in (50 mm) to 5½ in (140 mm) wide.
Squares	Square sawn timber 2 ft (0.60 m) and 2 ft 6 in (0.76 m) long by 1½ in (38 mm) by 1½ in (38 mm) and up.
Scantlings	Square edged dimensions not conforming to other standard terms.
Dimension stock	Timber sawn to specified sizes.
Shorts	Short lengths 3 ft (0.91 m) to 5 ft 9 in (1.75 m) long and widths 6 in (152 mm) and up.
SN	Short narrows less than 6 in (152 mm) wide.
Cube foot / cf	Cubic foot 12 in (304.8 mm) by 12 in (304.8 mm) by 12 in (304.8 mm), i.e. 0.02832 m³.
Foot super / fs	Square foot (0.09290 m²) superficial or face measure.
bd ft, fbm / bm	Board foot, board measure, denoting 1 sq. ft (0.09290 m²) (25 mm) thick.
Foot run / ft, run	Running foot (25 mm) length measurement in the particular width.
Av L	Average lengths.
A W	All widths.
Nom	Nominal or sawn size before machining.
Scant	Converted timber/milled wood of less than specified dimension.
Sawn size	Sawn size before machining, i.e. planing.
Finish / Finished	Net measurement after machining.
Dead / Dead length	Exact length/finished length.
Tolerance	The maximum permissible variation for a specified dimension in the sawn size.

Marking and measuring timber (metric measure)

Continental exporters cut to inch dimensions for the British and American markets and are content to do so for so long as the demand exists. However, the general adoption of metric weights and measures will necessitate a complete overhaul of existing practices, and it has yet to be decided what conventional units will be adopted. At present bulk quantities of timber in continental countries are often measured in cubic metres (stères) but as a cubic metre contains 35.3150 cu. ft some smaller unit may eventually be adopted. In the meantime the procedures already mentioned are the same. The average of three widths over the face usually favours the buyer, and a measuring device incorporating sensitive fingers has been developed which will give extremely accurate readings. A similar device has been used for many years in the leather trade for measuring hides.

Metrication

Some confusion still exists within the Timber Trade in the implementation of the metric system of weights and measures, and attempts to introduce intermediate units of measurement (centimetres, decimetres, etc.) have so far failed. Timber continues to be sold by the cubic foot (foot cube) as the cubic metre is too large an amount for most individual requirements, although metres and millimetres are increasingly being used for linear, cross section and surface measurements. Wood-working tools, brasswork, etc. are still made to imperial measure with metric equivalents, and this is likely to continue for the foreseeable future.

Metric conversions: imperial to metric units

Length
1 inch = 25.4 mm (millimetres)
1 foot = 0.3048 m (metres)

Area
1 square inch (1 in^2) = 6.4516 cm^2 (square centimetres)
1 square foot (1 ft^2) = 0.092 903 04 m^2 (square metres)

Volume
1 cubic inch (1 in^3) = 16.387 064 cm^3 (cubic centimetres)
1 cubic foot (1 ft^3) = 0.028 32 m^3 (cubic metres)
1 UK fluid ounce = 28.41 ml (millilitres)
1 UK fluid gallon = 4.545 96 l (litres) (160 fl oz)

Mass
1 ounce (avoirdupois) = 28.350 g (grams)
1 pound (avoirdupois) = 0.45359237 kg (kilograms)

Density
lbs per cu ft to kilograms per cu metre:
1 lb/cf = 16.018 kg/m^3

Pressure
lbs force per sq in to kilograms per sq cm:
1 lbf/in^2 = 0.070 31 kgf/cm^2

Metric conversions: inches to millimetres

in	mm	in	mm
1/32	0.793	13/16	20.637
1/16	1.587	7/8	22.225
3/32	2.381	15/16	23.812
1/8	3.175		
5/32	3.969		cm
3/16	4.762	1	2.54
7/32	5.556	2	5.08
1/4	6.350	3	7.62
9/32	7.144	4	10.16
5/16	7.937	5	12.70
11/32	8.731	6	15.24
3/8	9.525	7	17.78
13/32	10.319	8	20.32
7/16	11.112	9	22.86
15/32	11.906	10	25.4
1/2	12.700	20	50.8
9/16	14.288	30	76.2
5/8	15.875	40	101.6
11/16	17.462	40	127.0
3/4	19.050	100	254.0

Temperature

Degrees Fahrenheit to degrees Celsius (Centigrade):

$$\frac{5 \ (\text{degrees F}-32)}{9} = \text{degrees Celsius}$$

Degrees Celsius to degrees Fahrenheit:

$$\frac{9 \ (\text{degrees C})}{5} + 32 = \text{degrees Fahrenheit}$$

Conversion factors

To convert	multiply by
inches into	
millimetres	25.4
millimetres into	
inches	0.039 37
square inches into square	
centimetres	6.4516
square centimetres into	
square inches	0.155

Wood-scribe

This is a folding knife with hooked blade giving a gouge-like cut, and sometimes called a 'raze-knife'. It is used for marking the superficial footage on the ends of planks, and for scoring the weathered face of the wood to determine grain and colour.

24 Wood-scribe

2 Veneers

The term 'veneer' is unfortunate as it can mean to 'gloss over' or 'to cover up', but the practice of veneering dates from before the time of the Pharaohs, and is not, as some people still mistakenly imagine, a cheap method of glossing over poor workmanship and materials. Cogent reasons for the practice are fourfold:

(a) a more balanced construction is achieved, free from the inevitable splitting, checking, warping and distortion of solid wood;

(b) the availability of rare and highly decorative timbers is vastly extended by using them in sheet form;

(c) decorative effects, duplication of identical grain configurations to form matched panels and patterns are possible which would be extremely difficult with timber in solid form;

(d) certain rare and costly burrs, burls, curls and abnormal grain effects have very little structural strength, and would split, buckle or distort if used in any appreciable thickness.

The only disadvantages of veneered work, i.e. chipping and lifting of edges, fragility of top surfaces, etc., and lack of sparkle in the wood itself due to excessive glue penetration, have now been largely eliminated with the use of resin glues which form permanent bonds that do not—or should not—penetrate to the wood surface; and synthetic lacquers which provide extremely hard protective coverings which are proof against most risks in normal use.

MANUFACTURE OF WOOD VENEERS

Before the introduction of power-driven circular saws all veneers were sawn by hand, usually $1/8$ in (3 mm) and over in thickness, with deep saw kerfing which had to be planed off before laying or the ribbing would ultimately show through the polish. At the turn of the century specially large circular saws up to 18 feet (5.48 m) in diameter with very fine saw teeth and little set were introduced which could cut veneers from $1/32$ in (0.8 mm) to $1/16$ in (1.5 mm) in thickness, or about 12 sheets to the inch (25 mm). In all cases about half the wood substance was lost in sawdust, and with the exception of certain difficult woods, notably the kingwoods, ebonies and some satinwood, which must still be cut with the saw, all veneers are now sliced with the knife and waste is eliminated. It should be pointed out, however, that saw-cut veneers are always better quality, for the slicing action of the knife across the grain does to some extent tear or distress the wood fibres.

Two methods of knife slicing are currently practised: *rotary cutting or peeling*, and *flat slicing*. A third method of semi-rotary slicing is now only used in special cases.

Rotary peeling

Most woods can be cut by this method, but apart from certain special effects (bird's-eye maple, etc.) its use is confined to the production of core veneers for plywood and laminated work, etc., using the more common hardwoods of large dimension, clean cylindrical boles and free cutting grain structure which allow easy peeling. Suitable logs are first cross cut to length, debarked, adzed to shape and, after prolonged immersion in boiling water, mounted on a giant lathe while still hot and peeled with a fixed knife which is fed forward with each revolution. The lathe is run slowly at first until the bole or bolt is a true cylinder and there is little if any torque, then the speed is greatly increased and the bole unwinds as a continuous ribbon of veneer the full length of the log, after which it is cut into sheets by pre-set guillotines and force dried in mechanical driers. Veneers can be cleanly cut by this method from $1/80$ in (0.3 mm) to $3/8$ in (9.5 mm) in thickness, but the grain effect follows round the annual rings, giving an exaggerated onion-slice effect; moreover in some species the fibres tend to crack under the knife (all veneers are sliced across the grain), and microscopic examination will disclose innumerable slight tears or cracks. *For this reason all veneers should be laid at right angles to the grain direction* of the groundwork, otherwise the fibres are not locked in position and unseen cracks will tend to open. The true advantages of rotary slicing are cheapness of production, and the extremely large dimensions possible, but despite these factors flat slicing is always the better method.

Flat cutting or slicing

Originally carefully selected flitches of wood suitable for veneers were dogged down to a horizontal bed within the machine, and a heavy knife mounted on a rigid carriage slid backwards and forwards over the table to give a shearing cut. In more modern machines, however, the bed is vertical, moving upwards and downwards, again with a diagonal shearing action, against a fixed knife usually ½ in (12.5 mm) thick, 7 in (178 mm) wide and capable of cutting a 17 ft (5.18 m) length with every stroke. The knife is fed forwards by the thickness of the veneer being cut for each downward stroke of the bed, and is capable of very fine adjustment and accurate cutting of veneers from $\frac{1}{250}$ in (0.1 mm) to ¼ in (6 mm) or more in thickness.

Flat slicing of veneers gives a smoother, finer cut than rotary peeling, but even so there is always a tendency for the fibres to be plucked or torn, as in hand-planing across the grain. The best and most decorative results are obtained from true quartered flitches, where the direction of the cut is at right angles to the annual rings; whereas if the cut transverses the full width of the log it will go with the rings for half the width and against them for the other half. The effect can often be seen in sliced gaboon construction veneers, where one half of the width of the sheet is cleanly cut and the other half woolly and uneven.

The cutting of all veneers is highly specialized, for the logs must be steamed correctly, at exactly the right temperature for cutting (wet heat softens wood), and dogged down at the right angle, with the thickness and speed of cut determined by long experience only, and an instinctive appreciation of how the wood is likely to behave. Face veneers, as distinct from construction veneers, are usually cut either 0.88 mm, 0.83 mm or 0.71 mm thick (28, 30 or 35 to the inch), the last familiarly known as 'seven mil' (0.71 mm), with the thicker veneers a better compromise against excessive glue penetration and torn grain. Continental veneer-cutters often cut 40, 50 or even 60 sheets to the inch (25 mm) with little regard for plucked grain and tissue-thin patches. Such veneers are much cheaper, but should not be used in good work.

Reference has already been made to 'Semi-rotary' cutting, in which suitably shaped flitches are mounted off centre in the lathe so that the cut is half-slice, half-rotary peeling action. This cutting method is sometimes employed for special grain effects, notably in Rio rosewood, etc., but has been largely abandoned owing to the enormous torque created by the off-centre flitch, and consequent heavy wear on the lathe.

Veneer thicknesses

Veneer gauge no.	thickness (in)	Approx. no. to inch (25 mm)	thickness (mm)
8	0.160	6¼	4.064
11	0.116	8½	2.946
12	0.104	9¾	2.642
14	0.080	12½	2.032
17	0.056	18	1.422
19	0.040	25	1.016
20	0.036	28	0.914
21	0.032	31¼	0.813
22	0.028	35¾	0.711
25	0.020	50	0.508
27	0.016	62½	0.406
35	0.008	125	0.203

TYPES OF VENEER Page 47

While rotary peeling is usually reserved for plywood manufacture, constructional veneers for laminated work are normally sliced in 1, 1.5, 2.5, 3 and 4 mm thicknesses from beech, obeche, gaboon, limba and similar woods. Backing quality veneers used as balancers on the underside of groundworks (see Veneering, marquetry and inlay, Chapter 32) are usually peeled or sliced to $\frac{1}{32}$ in (0.7 mm) or thinner out of sapele, straight-grain mahogany, makore (cherry mahogany), etc. Both constructional and backing veneers are normally sold in bulk quantities, but can be obtained in small amounts from retail dealers if specially ordered. They are considerably cheaper than the usual run of face veneers, and one suspects that backing veneers are often used for face-work in cheap furniture. There can be no objection to this for the veneers are cleanly cut from prime logs and are usually lacking only in decorative effect, although occasional bundles will be the equivalent of a good African mahogany or sapelewood face veneer. Saw-cut veneers are now virtually unobtainable except as odd lots, but kingwood is still saw-cut. Face or decorative veneers are usually sold by the cutters in part or complete logs, composed of several bundles according to the number of flitches the log has yielded. This 'buying as they rise' and taking the good with the bad—for practically all trees have some defect or other—is obviously much cheaper than choosing selected bundles from any one stock, and most veneer-cutters in a large way of business will not permit 'breaking the log'. For the small user there are many retail dealers who buy in bulk and sell a few leaves at a time, although the price asked must necessarily be several times that of a bulk purchase.

In choosing veneers it is always a wise precaution to examine each bundle very thoroughly, for beautiful veneers are international currency. They may pass through several hands and are easily damaged. Reputable firms do not hide defective or damaged leaves in the middle of the bundle as a matter of policy, but transposition can occur. Curls, burrs/burls and feathers, etc. are numbered and should be in strict order as cut, for although there may be no apparent difference between adjacent sheets, the small variations build up, and the difference between the first and last sheet of, say, a 30-leaf bundle can be very considerable. Such bundles are rarely, if ever, split, and must be bought as a whole. Highly decorative veneers should never be ordered from one sample leaf only; inspection of the whole stock is essential. To cite just one example—a single Rio rosewood log may yield bundles ranging from a very plain light tan to rich inky black figuring.

Veneer varieties

It would be impossible to list all the varieties available at any one time, for every wood species is capable of yielding veneers, and every tree in the species is an individual with different grain structure, coloration and abnormalities. Add to this different methods of cutting, rotary peeling, semi-rotary peeling, quartered slicing, crown cut (tangential cut), etc., and the permutations are endless. There are, for example, over 300 different species of oak commercially available; the mahoganies form a vast family, while walnuts include English, French, Italian, Ancona (Italian), Circassian, Caucasian (Persian), Australian and American. Names also change according to the locality or at the whim of the dealer, with common agba elevated to tola branca, white tola, etc., to give only one example. Add to this abnormal grain effects— roe, bird's eye, blister, dapple, mottle, quilted, stripy, swirled, burr/burl, crotch, stump, pollard, fiddleback, curl, fan, feather and flame—and the endless variety ensures that wood as a means of decoration is irreplaceable so long as people remain individuals and hanker after individual things. A full description of the matching, jointing, preparation and laying of all types of veneer is given in Chapter 32.

MAN-MADE VENEERS

Reference should be made to a comparatively recent development which for lack of a better term can only be described as 'man-made veneers'. The process, first developed by John Wright (Veneers) Ltd and known as *Fineline* veneers, and later also by Aaronson Ltd under the trade-name *Arofleur*, is prefabricated in the sense that stacks of different-coloured veneers are glued up into a solid block, and then sliced across the artificial grain thus created by the separate layers to yield a regular and repeatable pattern. A crown-cut pattern is also introduced by Aaronson Ltd into the middle of the sheet. Some of the veneers so produced, which are, of course, free from all defects and therefore much more economical in use, are rather too brash and regular, but the best have a quiet dignity and a subtle colour modulation which lends itself to simple contemporary designs of good shape and proportionment. In normal veneers the waste factor is high, and a minimum of 50 per cent is generally allowed, but with these fabricated veneers dimensions are fairly constant, and do not vary throughout the stock. Prices compare very favourably with normal straight-cut veneers, taking into account the low waste factor.

Coloured Veneers

An even more recent development has been the process of dyeing veneers with fast dyes. Usually made from white sycamore, they are available in a wide range of colours from the smaller veneer merchants.

3 Manufactured boards

These can be grouped within three broad classifications:

Plywoods
These are composed of layers or strips of solid wood glued together in simulation of solid wood, viz. plywood, laminboard, blockboard, battenboard, each layer being at right angles in grain direction to the one above or below.

Particle boards
Commonly known as chipboard, they are composed of wood chips bonded together with synthetic resin glue and pressed or extruded into rigid sheets.

Fibre boards
These are composed of wood fibre macerated in water and pressed at high temperatures, often with a little resin, into sheets and boards of varying densities, according to the degree of heat and pressure applied, viz. hardboards, softboards, and medium density fibreboard. The later, MDF, is rapidly superseding both particle board and plywood in industrialized production of furniture.

PLYWOOD (THREE-PLY, MULTIPLY, ETC.)

The technique of gluing together thin sheets of wood in a balanced construction with each layer crossed at right angles so that the wood grains are locked in position, effectively preventing all shrinkages across the width, dates from the seventeenth century, but it was only in 1896 that plywood was commercially produced for cheap tea-chests. Since then ceaseless development has produced a bonded sheet which is completely free from lamination, and which is generally available in thicknesses from $1/32$ in (0.8 mm) to 1 in (25 mm), in a range of qualities for every purpose.

The original tea-chest ply was composed of three layers—a central core and two balancing veneers—thence the familiar term 'three-ply'

which is still used for three-layer construction. Plywoods with more than three layers are usually classed as multiply, although the term 'five-ply' is sometimes used for five-layer construction. Obviously, the layers or veneers of which the ply is composed must be relatively thin or the strength of the timber and its tendency to shrink and distort will be greater than the strength of the bonding adhesive; therefore for strong plywood additional layers must be used, one on either side for each increase in thickness, so that the total number will always be odd for a balanced construction, as distinct from an unbalanced assembly of an even number of veneers which will have a greater tendency to pull or distort. In practice, the central core can be relatively thick ($1/8$ in [3 mm] or $1/6$ in [4 mm]), and of lower density wood to reduce the overall weight; but wherever possible the combination of veneer thickness and wood species should be chosen to give the finished sheet equal stiffness both parallel and perpendicular to the grain of the face veneers. For this reason each pair of balancing veneers, including the face and backing veneers, is usually of the same thickness and of the same or comparable species. The number of glue-lines also affects the overall stiffness, and the thinner the veneers, with the consequent increase in the number of glue-lines, *the greater the rigidity of the finished sheet will be.*

Grading and classification of plywood

Clear distinction must be drawn between the grading of ply, which is concerned only with the quality of the face veneers, and the classification into groups or types, which is concerned with the nature of the bonding adhesive and the durability of the actual wood used. Hitherto plywoods were loosely grouped into *interior* and *exterior* qualities, but these terms are fairly meaningless. Admittedly,

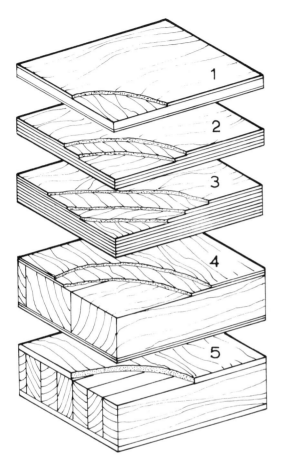

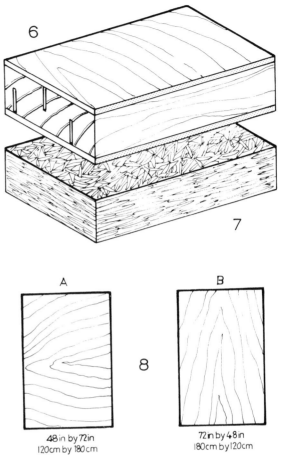

25 Manufactured boards
1 3 ply construction   **2** 5 ply construction
3 Multi-ply construction   **4** Blockboard
5 Laminboard   **6** Battenboard (unsuitable for
quality furniture-making)   **7** Particle board
(chipboard)   **8** Grain direction when ordering
plywoods or veneered chipboards (A = cross
grained; B = long grained). Medium Density
Fibre Board (not shown) (MDF) resembles an
inexpensive, light-coloured hardboard but sanded
on both surfaces.

furniture-makers do not require weather-
resistant plywoods, but they must be confident
that the plies are well bonded and will not
laminate, and that they will withstand bacterial
and fungoid attack; therefore the type of
bonding medium used is of importance. It is, for
instance, hardly sufficient to describe a plywood
as *well-glued* or *resin-bonded*, for the former
term may include weak vegetable glues, while
the latter may be so extended with fillers
compounded of cereal flours, etc. that the
implicit moisture-resistant properties are lost.

Plywood grades

Grading rules differ according to the country of
origin, and the following list is therefore a
general indication only.

A   Face and back veneers practically free
      from all defects.
A/B   Face veneers practically free from all
      defects. Reverse veneers with only a few
      small knots or discolorations.
A/BB Face as A but reverse side permitting
      jointed veneers, large knots, plugs, etc.

B   Both sides as reverse of A/B.

B/BB   Face as reverse of A/B. Reverse side as reverse of A/BB.

BB   Both sides as reverse of B/BB.

WG   Guaranteed well glued only. All broken knots plugged.

X   Knots, knot-holes, cracks and all other defects permitted.

Marine Quality High-quality product usually of fir, makoré, mahogany or similar highly durable wood throughout, bonded with phenolic resin glue to WBP specification. (Must withstand 72 hours boiling in water without failure of the glue-lines.)

Additionally the United Africa Company grade their Cresta plywoods under Gold, Silver and Blue labels. Construction is the same throughout, and the grading refers to the face appearance only. The bonding is phenolic resin to WBP specification, and every sheet is impregnated against insect attack (lyctus, furniture beetle, termites, etc.), which does not affect the gluing or polishing properties.

In practice it is not wise to go below B/BB, BB or grade 2 for veneering, while Douglas fir ply is altogether unsuitable owing to the upraised grain, and therefore grading rules for this particular kind of ply have not been included. It can be assumed that, unless specifically stated, all plywoods are dry glued, i.e. the veneers dried before gluing, and that except for the very lowest grades not suitable for furniture both the face and reverse are sanded flat for immediate use.

Plywood dimensions

In all usual sizes the length of the face grains is given first, irrespective of the length of the sheet. Thus a plywood sheet quoted as 48 in (122 cm) by 72 in (183 cm) will be 72 in (183 cm) in actual length and 48 in (122 cm) wide across the sheet and parallel to the direction of the face grain. Such a sheet is cross grained as distinct from long grained, as the face grain of the former runs counter to the length of the sheet, and it is important to remember this when choosing sheet sizes, for subsequent face-veneering which must be at right angles to the face grain of the sheet. Thus two wardrobe ends each 6 ft (183 cm) by 18 in (46 cm) which are to

be face-veneered must be cut from a sheet 36 in (92 cm) by 72 in (183 cm), and not from one quoted as 72 in (183 cm) by 36 in (92 cm) in which the face grain runs the length of the sheet. Thicknesses in plywood commonly available with their nearest inch equivalents are as follows:

mm	in	mm	in
0.8	$1/32$	8	$5/16$
1.2		9	$3/8$
1.5	$1/16$	12	
2	$3/32$	12.5	$1/2$
3	$1/8$	15	$5/8$
4	$5/32$	18	$3/4$
5	$3/16$	22	$7/8$
6	$1/4$	25	1

Plywoods can normally be obtained in any of the following wood species: agba (tola branca), alder, basswood (Japanese lime), European and Japanese beech, European birch, Chilean pine, Douglas fir (Columbian or Oregon pine), elm, gaboon (okoumé), lauan, limba (afara), African mahogany, makoré, red meranti, obeche, Parana pine, European pine, poplar, sapele, sen, red and white seraya, red and white sterculia, tamo (Japanese ash), utile and yang. Most suppliers will, however, only stock the most popular, i.e. gaboon, lauan, birch, alder, Douglas fir, and limba, etc. Of these gaboon, birch and limba are excellent for veneering, but gaboon is inclined to woolliness in face-work, and birch is difficult to stain evenly. On the other hand, limba is medium textured, moderately hard and stiff, and its natural light gold-brown colour can be stained in simulation of oak, walnut and mahogany, therefore making it a good all-round choice. In all cases the wood species quoted refer to the face veneers only, and not to the cores, which may be of low-density woods.

Bending properties

Although plywood is normally used as a flat material, its natural resilience enables it to be bent to reasonably small radii of curvature without fracturing. The safe minimum of curvature will depend on the overall thickness, the individual thickness of the veneers, the species of timber employed and, to a lesser extent, the nature of the adhesive, while three-layer plywoods composed of equal veneers will bend more easily than plywoods composed of thick cores and thin outer veneers. It is always better, therefore, to make up thick curved panels out of several thin plies rather than one thick ply, as the following table shows:

Radius of curvature

Thickness	Along grain	Across grain
¼ in (6.3 mm)	2 ft 0 in (0.609 m)	1 ft 3 in (0.381 m)
⅜ in (9.5 mm)	4 ft 6 in (1.371 m)	3 ft 0 in (0.914 m)
½ in (12.7 mm)	8 ft 0 in (2.438 m)	6 ft 0 in (1.828 m)
⅝ in (15.8 mm)	10 ft 0 in (3.048 m)	8 ft 0 in (2.438 m)
¾ in (19.0 mm)	12 ft 0 in (3.657 m)	10 ft 0 in (3.048 m)

The above figures were prepared by the Forest Products Research Laboratory in connection with the use of Douglas fir plywood, but also offer a reliable guide as to the bending movements of most other hardwoods bent dry at ordinary room temperatures. Synthetic resin bonded plywoods can also be soaked or steamed, and will then bend to smaller radii dependent upon the wood species. As will be seen from the table above the bending movement is greater across the grain than along the grain, therefore cross-grained panels should be chosen (see below). Plywood can also be scarf jointed provided the same type of adhesive be used, and the inclination of the joint is not less than 1 in 10 for boards under ½ in (12.5 mm) thick and 1 in 8 for over ½ in (12.5 mm).

Stability

As wood is a hygroscopic material, shrinking and swelling under varying temperature/humidity conditions, plywood, which is composed entirely of wood, must also shrink and swell, but the total movement is very small owing to the strength of the glue-lines which lock the fibres in all directions. For instance, the Forest Products Research Laboratory has established in tests on 22 different species of 3/16 in (5 mm) thick three-ply that the mean swelling is only 0.18 per cent along the grain, and 0.27 per cent across the grain when subjected to a humidity range of 30 to 90 per cent, equivalent to raising the moisture content from 7 to 20 per cent. For all practical purposes in furniture the movement can be disregarded, although it will show on the edges of untreated

ply as a fractional creep of long-grain veneers. The thicker the ply the less the movement is and the greater the measure of stability, while synthetic resin glues give greater measures of stability over the other glues. An additional advantage is that plywood has no line of cleavage and therefore will not split under adverse atmospheric conditions. This absence of lines of cleavage also affects the impact strength of plywood which is greater than that of solid wood subjected to a similar loading; and in all practical applications thicknesses over solid timber can be reduced, with a ¾ in (19 mm) thickness of ply roughly equivalent to a 1 in (25 mm) thickness of solid wood.

Blockboards, laminboards, etc.

In these the principle of construction is a series of wood core strips glued together side by side to form a slab, which is sandwiched between outer layers of veneer or thin plywood whose grains are crossed at right angles to the length of the core strips. In blockboard the core strips should not exceed 1 in (25 mm) in width, although they can be of any thickness dependent on the thickness of the completed board, and in theory at least the grain direction of the strips should run counter to each other, although in practice a random selection is adopted. The outer or face veneers can be a single thickness of from 3/32 in (2 mm) to 9/64 in (3.5 mm); or two veneers glued together with grains parallel to make up a 3/32 in (2 mm) thickness; or, where the length of the sheet exceeds the width, a five-ply construction of core strips, 3/32 in (2 mm) veneer either side at right angles to the core, and outer veneers of about 1/16 in (1.5 mm) parallel to the core.

Laminboard adopts the same construction, but the core strips must not exceed 9/32 in (7 mm) wide, and some varieties, notably Finnish birch, utilize core strips made up from plywood trimmings. Laminboard is heavier and stiffer than blockboard owing to the greater number of glue-lines, and the use of gaboon or spruce for core strips rather than low-density softwoods; the cost, therefore, is greater, and use is limited to high-class work for which it is eminently suited as it does not exhibit the bumpiness or ripple, i.e. core-strip sinkage, sometimes found in cheaper grades of blockboard.

Battenboard is a variation in which the core strips can be up to 3 in (76 mm) wide, unglued and saw kerfed either side to allow for shrinkage, but it has little if any application in furniture. Both blockboard and laminboard can be obtained in sizes up to 60 in (152 cm) by 120 in (305 cm) and occasionally 144 in (366 cm) in Finnish birch, and up to 60 in (152 cm) by 201 in (510 cm) in gaboon, beech, etc., both measured in the same way as plywood, with the length of the face grain first quoted. Sheet thicknesses range from $1/2$ in (12.5 mm) to $1 3/4$ in (44 mm) and $1 7/8$ in (47 mm) in flush door sizes only.

Blockboards and laminboards are usually obtainable in beech, birch, limba, gaboon and agba glued to MR and BP specifications. They are not normally marketed in 'exterior' quality, although WBP specification can be obtained. Their chief merits lie in the larger sizes available, their increased rigidity (they cannot be bent to any appreciable radii unless deeply saw kerfed) and the ease with which they can be jointed by the usual methods. They are thus eminently suitable for general carcass-work, table-tops, flush doors, etc.

PARTICLE BOARDS (CHIPBOARDS)

These are composed of wood chips carefully graded, mixed with synthetic resin glue and either pressed or extruded into rigid, self-supporting sheets of uniform thickness which are sanded down to close tolerances. Flax-sheaves are sometimes used instead of wood chips (flax boards) and have virtually the same properties, although they tend to be lighter in weight and not so strong for any given density. Considerable research has gone into the development of both types of board, and wood-chip boards are marketed in several forms: flooring grade for general purpose in the building industry, low-density boards for door cores, partitioning, etc., standard all-purpose boards for built-in fitments, panelling, etc., and special furniture-boards (Weyroc 38) for carcass components. The last-mentioned boards are of graded density construction, with the finest chips near to the face, giving a high-density, smooth, close-textured surface eminently suitable for veneering, as there is little tendency for the individual wood chips to show through under high polishes. They are invariably pressed, as distinct from extruded, boards in which the wood chips lie at right angles to the board surfaces, resulting in poor bending strength and lower stability.

Particle boards are heavier than most other wood materials (33 to 40 lb per cu. ft or 528.609 to 640.739 kg per cu. m according to the density) as the glue content is relatively high; moreover they have no long fibres and thus have little bending strength and tend to crumble at the edges if roughly treated. Always provided that these boards are not treated merely as substitutes for solid timber and forced to conform to long-established constructional methods, but regarded as valid materials in their own right, well worthy of new methods and applications, there is no doubt whatever that their use will continue to expand, and indeed they will become the standard material for furniture-making. With their obvious advantages this is almost inevitable, for not only do they make use of what is virtually waste material (forest thinnings, bough wood, etc.) but the very fact that they are man-made materials means that there is always scope for research and development in the production of lighter, stronger, stiffer and cheaper boards.

Working properties

Particle boards are very stable with little dimensional change (shrinking, warping, etc.), and even the absence of long fibres can be turned to advantage, for, as there is no end grain, boards can be glued and butt joined together at any angle without supporting constructional joints. Working properties are as for other prefabricated woods and present no problems; they can be cut, planed, shaped, routed and bored with all normal tools, provided the cutting edges are kept sharp and feed speeds a little slower than for solid timber. For quantity production, tungsten-carbide cutting edges are recommended, as the high glue content dulls normal steels. Planing to thickness is not advised, as cross planing is inevitable and bound to create rough patches, but the boards are obtainable in a variety of thicknesses to close tolerances, and where surfaces have to be reduced it is better to sand them down. They are not intended for exterior use as the edges are susceptible to moisture penetration, although some manufacturers now incorporate a proportion of wax emulsion in the glue which gives a certain measure of protection. Screw- and nail-holding properties are not as good as long-grain materials, but sufficient for all but the heaviest loadings.

Uses for particle boards are the same as for blockboards and laminboards, viz. carcasses, flush doors, shelving, panelling, partition-work, etc. A point in their favour is that they have no hidden defects (see *Defects in plywoods, etc.,* below) and are thus eminently suitable for large veneered table-tops polished to a high gloss, and as a substrate for plastic laminates. They can be satisfactorily veneered and the best-quality boards no longer require counter-veneering to hold back any tendency for the wood chips to show through the face veneers. Thicknesses of standard boards range from ³⁄₈ in (9 mm) to 1³⁄₈ in (36 mm), and furniture-boards from ¹⁄₂ in (12.5 mm) to ⁷⁄₈ in (21 mm), and boards can be obtained already veneered with a wide range of woods.

FIBRE BOARDS

Fibre boards have been used extensively in the building industry for many years in various densities, but until recently the only application for furniture-making was the dense hardboard used for back panels and drawer bottoms. More recently, a medium density fibreboard (MDF) has been manufactured for the furniture industry, and it is available in thicknesses from ¹⁄₄ in (6 mm) up to 1 in (25 mm), which gives it a versatility in use that previously only plywood enjoyed.

On average it is about half the price of plywood, and although it is more expensive than particle board it is superior in that the edges do not have to be lipped. Industry can simply mould, colour and polish the edges as if they were solid wood. Its application for the craftsman would be similar to that of good quality plywood or chipboard, but it has a great disadvantage in that it will swell up like a sponge

if the untreated edges are ever exposed to water. It is extremely stable and ideal for veneering, but its weight can be another disadvantage.

PURCHASING THE APPROPRIATE QUALITY

Like many other products, manufactured boards are available in a wide range of quality. An expensive oil-tempered sheet of hardboard, for example, is quite a different product from a cheap sheet produced with next to no resin, which is virtually only compressed cardboard. It may, however, be quite adequate for laying out surfaces or storage jobs around the workshop.

The same is equally true of particle board and plywood, and the higher the quality the lower the likelihood of the defects referred to below.

DEFECTS IN PLYWOODS, ETC.

Certain defects regularly occur during or after manufacture, and should be diligently searched for otherwise they may give endless trouble. Figure 26 gives the most common defects. Ripples or bumpiness (26:1) caused by swelling of the core strips in laminated construction can be detected with a knife-edge straight edge, or passing the palm of the hand over the surface (closing the eyes increases the sensibility). Planing off the bumps is not always satisfactory, as the cores may shrink back in drier conditions, forming undulating hollows; therefore it is better to reject bumpy boards for face-work and use them only for unseen interiors. Figure 26:2 shows hidden blisters which can only be detected by tapping the surface with the finger-nail for any hollow sound; they must be glued back or subsequent veneering is bound to lift them. Overlapping veneers are shown in 26:3, and will eventually show as a long spine under a high polish. Long splits in the face (26:4) are easily rectified, but hidden gaps in the core (26:5) are often difficult to detect and may only declare themselves at later stages. Here again laboriously tapping with the finger-nail is the only answer, while all freshly cut ends should be critically examined. Figure 26:6 shows a method adopted in some constructions, in which the core strips are grooved across to take a string

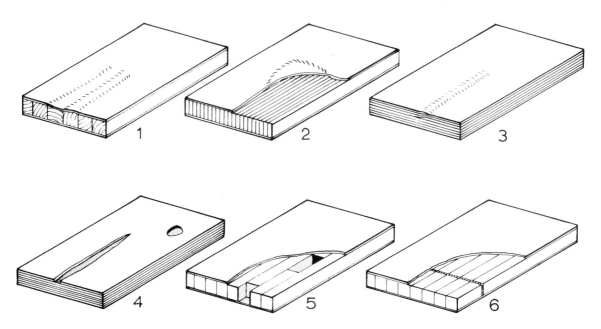

26 Defects in plywoods, etc.

binder during assembly, and such boards should not be used in face-work. All these defects may not necessarily detract from the structural strength, but will certainly mar the surface quality if not rectified. Badly warped boards, particularly in the thicker grades, should be rejected out of hand, for it is never wise to assume that holding frameworks will pull them straight or subsequent veneering correct them. More often than not the whole carcass will be pulled in wind.

All prefabricated woods are dried to a moisture content of around 9 per cent during manufacture. They pick up moisture slowly but also give it up as slowly, therefore they should be stored flat on level foundations and in dry conditions.

COMPARATIVE PROPERTIES OF SOLID WOODS AND MANUFACTURED BOARDS

Advantages of manufactured boards

1 Plywood and laminboards, etc. have no natural line of cleavage and cannot be split across the length or width, as the grain direction of each alternate layer is opposed to the direction of the force. General stiffness and rigidity is also much greater, and a strip of plywood is stiffer than a strip of steel of equal weight, and therefore thicknesses as opposed to solid wood can be reduced by as much as 25 per cent. Particle boards do not have the same high strength weight ratio and are relatively weak in all directions, nevertheless they have much the same dimensional stability, and sufficient strength and stiffness for most purposes.

2 All prefabricated woods are available in large sheets, sanded smooth to uniform standard thicknesses, thus no preparation is necessary and much intitial labour is saved.

3 Large sheets are always more economical in cutting, and waste factors are much lower, while quality is consistent from sheet to sheet.

4 Construction is balanced, therefore movement is negligible under normal conditions, making them ideal for large or flush surfaces. Plywood in particular possesses a natural resilience which enables it to be bent to reasonably small radii of curvature without damage.

5 The utilization of common woods in plentiful supply, which can be face veneered with decorative hardwoods, conserves stocks of the more valuable timbers which might otherwise

be insufficient to meet the demands of modern production.

There are still some lingering prejudices against the use of plywoods but they have no foundation whatsoever, and MDF particle boards are beginning to emerge, not as cheap substitutes, but as logical extensions or adaptations of wood in solid form.

Advantages of solid wood

1 First cost is often less than of plywoods, etc., in equivalent thicknesses, except for the rarer hardwoods.

2 Solid wood can be jointed with ease, shaped, moulded, carved, and bent to small radii.

3 Badly fitting joints and members out of alignment can be flushed off level after assembly.

4 Edges do not have to be protected or disguised in any way.

5 Solid wood has a natural elasticity without fatigue, thus screws and nails are securely gripped and will not work loose under normal loading. It will withstand rough treatment and can always be resurfaced. It has an effective life of many centuries.

6 It responds to careful finishing and has a depth of surface not obtainable with thinly veneered or composite surfaces.

Hints on working

Generally speaking plywoods, blockboards and laminboards should require no preliminary treatment, as they are invariably scraped or sanded on both surfaces to exact dimensions, but certain wood species, notably gaboon, often exhibit badly plucked grain which should be filled with a glue-absorbent filler (plastic wood, brummer, etc.). Particle boards and hardboards should have the glazed skin broken through with light sanding to enable the glue to take. Cheap foreign plywoods, machine-sanded with flint-papers, should be very carefully examined, sanded afresh and thoroughly dusted, for there have been several cases of embedded flint-dust setting up a chemical reaction with synthetic finishes. Cutting of some plywoods presents difficulties, and certain varieties, notably birch, tend to splinter under the saw. The remedy is either to use finer teeth to the saw, clamp a waste piece firmly under the ply to contain the splintering, or score the cutting-line deeply with a knife in advance of the cut—a preliminary trial will always show what propensity there is to splinter out. In machine-sawing, if the surface breaks out on top, increase the projection of the saw, or, if underneath, then decrease the projection, and if possible keep the board tight to the saw-table with spring arms, etc. Some panel saws now have a built-in scoring blade which finely cuts the undersurface.

4 Plastics and leathers

Despite the spectacular progress that has been made in the development of plastics, and steady reductions in the cost of their production, plastics have failed to make as much impact on the furniture industry as once seemed likely. High prices for oil and gas, the main source of raw materials, have tended to keep unit costs for plastic parts higher than those for wood-based components. The main areas where plastics have achieved dominance are in contract seating for restaurants etc., where toughness and easy care are crucial factors.

In essence, plastics are long chain molecular structures evolved from common elements and compounds—gases, lime, salt, coal, oil, molasses, cotton, wood, etc.—by chemical synthesis. Heavyweight molecules or monomers (one unit), usually but not invariably built up of carbon atoms, are linked together in long chains with or without cross-links to become polymers (many units), with the qualities of hardness, toughness, resilience, stretch, mouldability, translucence, dielectric properties, heat, acid and water resistance, etc., according to the type as determined by the molecules and their arrangement. Thus, in theory at least, the research chemist should be able to arrange the linkage of the molecules to give the physical qualities he requires, although obviously methods of achieving that linkage have to be evolved which are possible, practical and economic.

TYPES OF PLASTICS

All plastics are polymeric and all polymers may be regarded as potential plastics. Certain polymers occur naturally, i.e. casein (milk solids), cellulose derivatives (wood, cotton), etc.; all others are produced synthetically and are divided into two types, thermoplastic and thermosetting. In thermoplastic materials, the necessary degree of polymerization having been achieved, the long chain molecular structure can then be activated by heat to allow freer movement between the molecules; thus the plastic can be softened and resoftened without deformation provided the degree of heat is kept below the point of actual degrade of the material. In thermosetting plastics the polymerization has been arrested at a stage which produces relatively short chain molecules. Later application of certain simple chemicals (hardeners or catalysts) or simple heat carries the polymerization a stage further, producing cross linkages which destroy the mobility of the molecules, and the plastic sets into a hard, infusible resin which cannot then be resoftened. This latter type is usually known as 'resin plastics' (synthetic resin glues, etc.). The major thermoplastics are tough, resilient and can be given controlled flexibility either by arranging the molecular structure accordingly or by added chemical plasticizers, while the thermosets are either brittle solids which can be extended with other materials (chopped paper, wood flour, etc.) to form moulding powders, or viscous syrups for use as surfacing materials, impregnating liquids and glues, although here again the addition of plasticizers or softeners will allow a limited degree of flexibility. It should be emphasized that the chemistry of the various types of plastic is very much more subtle than this brief résumé might suggest, and readers are referred to the standard works on the subject for a thorough understanding of the principles involved. A list of the more important plastics with their applications in the furniture industry is given opposite.

Common or chemical names

Thermosetting

	Uses
Phenol formaldehyde (PF)	Wood glues, bonding agents, reinforced laminates, mouldings, etc.
Urea formaldehyde (UF)	Wood glues, chipboard manufacture, mouldings, etc.
Melamine formaldehyde (MF)	Wood glues, reinforced laminates, mouldings, etc.
Resorcinol formaldehyde (RF)	Wood glues.
Phenol resorcinol formaldehyde (RPF)	Wood glues.
Polyester	Finishes, lacquers, laminates (glass fibre, etc.).
Expoxide (epoxy resin)	Glues (metal, glass, etc.), castings, pottings, etc.

Thermoplastics (see note below)

Acrylonitrile butadiene styrene (ABS)	Drawers, doors, knobs, legs, etc.
Casein	Wood and paper glues, small moulded components.
Cellulose acetate (CA)	Sheet, film, small moulded components.
Cellulose acetate butyrate (CAB)	High impact mouldings (tool handles).
Cellulose nitrate (CN)	Finishes, lacquers, small moulded components.
Polyvinyl chloride (PVC)	Rigid and flexible sheet. Extrusions and coatings.
Polyvinyl acetate (PVA)	Wood and paper glues. Contact adhesives.
Polyethylene LD (polythene)	Low density films, packaging materials.
Polyethylene HD	High density structural mouldings.
Polypropylene	Sheet, structural mouldings and components, etc.
Polyurethane	Lacquers and finishes. Rigid foam structures.
Polyurethane ester	Flexible foam seating.
Polyurethane ether	Flexible foam seating.
Polystyrene	Sheet, film, expanded foam.
Polystyrene HD	High density sheet. Rigid foam structures.
Polymethyl methacrylate (*Perspex*)	Sheet, structural mouldings and components.
Polyacetal	Door handles, hinges, etc.
Polyamide (nylon)	Fibres, sheet, frictionless moulded and shaped components, etc.

Note: Some plastics are also thermosets. Most plastics can now be foamed.

PLASTICS APPLICATIONS

Plastics applications fall into three main categories: cast and moulded structures and components; extrusions and extruded sections; shaped forms and fabrications. The appropriate method of manipulation is determined by the plastic itself and whether it is thermosetting or thermoplastic, and the nature of the required component.

Cast and moulded structures

Thermosetting plastics

Special casting or compression moulding resins (PF, UF, MF and epoxy resins, etc.) are used. In the most simple technique a cold cure resin mix (resin syrup and catalyst) is extended with appropriate fillers and colorants and cast in metal, silicone or hot melt rubber or plaster moulds without heat. In a more sophisticated technique the resinous solution is neutralized with a suitable organic acid, dehydrated under vacuum, and poured into lead moulds which are then oven treated. A third technique using compression moulding is more widely practised in which carefully measured amounts of powder resin or resin pellets are fed into a heated mould and compressed by a heated plunger; the thermosetting plastic is thus first heat softened so that it flows into the crevices of the mould, and is then heat cured to the finished shape determined by the mould and its matching plunger. As thermosetting plastics are more brittle than the thermoplasts, all these techniques are usually reserved for heavier sections.

Thermoplastics

All types of thermoplastics lend themselves to injection moulding which is the most popular process for high-speed production of moulded structures and components. In this technique the resin chips or powder are conveyed by screw or ram along a heated barrel container which converts them into a viscous syrup or flowable solid; this is then ejected through a nozzle into a closed split mould and allowed to chill. Shell mouldings, i.e. thin-wall hollow mouldings, can be obtained by spinning the mould, thus forcing the plastic against the sides of the mould. Choice of plastic is dictated by both technical and economic factors. Press-in components which have to be compressed slightly to enter a prebored hole are formed by flexible low-density polythene/polyethylene, etc.; open components, i.e. handles, etc. of stiff plastic use polystyrene or polypropylene, or polymethyl methacrylate for transparent components. Polypropylene is also used for plastic hinges in which the actual hinging action is effected by a flexing of the material itself and not by an interlocking knuckle action, and polyamide (nylon) where exceptional strength, toughness and self-lubrication (gliders, hinges, lock components, bushes, bearings, etc.) are required.

Extrusions and extruded sections

Continuous lengths of tube, rod, sheet and various profiles are formed by extrusion processes mainly using thermoplastics, although thermosetting plastics have uses in specific cases. The resin powder or chips are conveyed along a heated barrel by means of an Archimedes' screw action which forces the softened plastic through a nozzle orifice shaped to the required profile. If a mandrel is supported in the centre of the orifice the plastic will be ejected as a hollow tube. Flexible and semi-flexible sections (wire covering, flexible edging strips, etc.) employ PVC or LD

polythene, rigid sections HD polythene/polyethylene or polypropylene. Both cellulose acetate and cellulose nitrate are also used, also nylon for strength and toughness, and perspex (polymethyl methacrylate) for transparent sections.

Shaped forms and fabrications

Vacuum forming is the most interesting technique for the furniture-maker as with this process relatively large recessed shapings can be effectively and economically produced with simple apparatus. Integral chair shell structures which are produced by the injection-moulding process require heavy and expensive equipment, but certain plastics which are not sufficiently free flowing for injection moulding lend themselves to vacuum forming. The principles involved are relatively straightforward. A presoftened sheet of suitable plastic is securely clamped round the perimeter of an open-top box containing the shaped mould or former; a vacuum is then applied to the box to pull the flexible sheet down over the former/mould and held until the sheet has chilled off and fixed the shape. Stiffer plastics may require plunger assistance, and in this system the moulding former is in the shape of a plunger which is forced down into the softened sheet, while for deep drawings a vacuum is employed to assist the deformation by helping to pull the sheet down in advance of the descending plunger. On releasing the vacuum the inherent elasticity of the sheet will pull it back against the plunger. Plastics employed in vacuum forming include polymethyl methacrylate (perspex), polyvinyl chloride (PVC), polypropylene, high-impact polystyrene and various copolymer sheet materials recently developed. In particular acrylonitrile butadiene styrene (ABS) is one of the newest and best for it can be cut, tool shaped, glued, screwed and nailed. Methods of sheet forming without pressure include powder casting with low- and medium-density polythenes/polyethylenes and PVC in which the resin powder is fed against a heated metal mould. Large surfaces can be covered in this way, as the powder softens in contact with the heated metal forming a continuous layer which can be stripped off when cold. Simple bending techniques for one-way curves can also be used as described under *Perspex*, p. 62.

Rigid foam plastics

Both polyurethane isocyanate and polystyrene can be foamed with suitable gassing agents to form rigid shell structures. If the foaming is unrestricted then it becomes open celled, but if restricted within shell moulds considerable pressures are created and the foam becomes compacted, with a hard outer skin which will conform to every fine detail in the mould. Self-supporting chair shells, imitation mouldings and wood carvings are made by these methods. The polyurethane foam is the more expensive of the two but will accept staples if upholstered, whereas polystyrene must have tacking strips applied. An example of the open-celled polystyrene foam is the lightweight ceiling tile.

Recent developments in lightweight sandwich boards use an open-celled ABS foam with outer layers of compacted foam.

Polyester resin fibre-glass laminates (GRP)

Rapid moulding techniques for the production of rigid plastic shapes or shells (chair seats, etc.) require specialist knowledge and advanced equipment beyond the resources of the small workshop, but glass-fibre laminates, familiarly known as GRP, offer a simple method of forming rigid structures whose only disadvantage is that one surface, inside or outside according to the type of former used, will be smooth and the other rough. In essence the shaped moulding is composed of laminations of chopped strand glass mat impregnated with polyester resin. The resin must be thrixotropic, i.e. it must be fluid enough for brush coats, but must be capable of building up so that it stays in position and does not creep downhill. Assuming that a simple box shape is to be moulded, then an exact pattern (Figure 27:1) must be made of timber or other suitable material, using waterproof bonding agents (*Araldite* epoxy resin, etc.), with a generous overhang all round so that the rough edges of the rim can be trimmed up afterwards. The sides of the box should be tapered if possible, as this will facilitate withdrawal, and sharp edges and internal

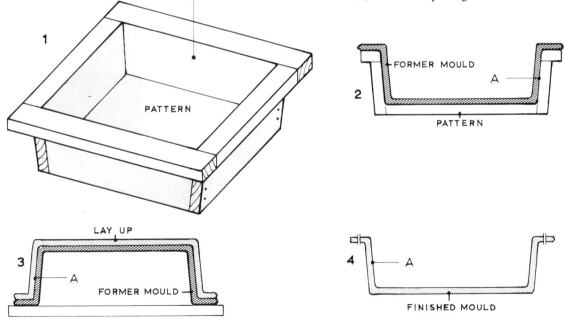

27   Fibre-glass reinforced plastic moulding

corners should be avoided, or the resin mat will tend to bulge over, leaving a void in the structure of the finished mould. The working surfaces of the mould must be filled (resin and talc, *Polyfilla, Alabastine*, etc.), sanded down smooth, lacquered (polyester wax, polyurethane, shellac, etc.), again sanded down with 400 grit wet and dry paper, and burnished with cutting-down paste to a high gloss, after which it is given a heavy coat of wax polish and left to harden overnight.

GRP former mould The *former* mould from which the finished moulding will be struck is now made up as in Figure 27:2. The wax coat is first buffed off the pattern, which is then coated with a polyester emulsion wax release, followed with an application of wax polish buffed to a high gloss, and then a layer of polyvinyl acetate (PVA) release agent applied with a sponge. A gel coat composed of polyester resin, catalyst (setting agent) and a small percentage of colour paste is then brushed on, followed by a second gel coat immediately the first has cured. The second gel coat should be of a contrasting colour, so that adequate warning is given during any subsequent rubbing down, and, when this coat has cured, a coat of catalysed resin is brushed on, and a layer of chopped strand glass worked into it, adding more resin with a stiff stippling-brush until the mat is 'wet out' or saturated. Two or more additional layers of glass mat and resin are then added, and the whole assembly stippled and rolled with a split roller to consolidate the layers and eliminate all air bubbles. The mould is then put aside to cure for at least four hours at normal room temperature, any roughness smoothed out, washed over with warm soapy water, given a thick coat of wax polish and allowed to age for a further 24 hours.

Finished mould

Exactly the same procedure is followed in preparing the finished moulding shown in Figure 27:3. The former-mould is treated with emulsion wax, wax polish and PVA release agent, then a single gel coat followed by the requisite thickness of glass mat (minimum two layers) and resin. After curing the mould is released, washed with soapy water and trimmed to exact size; it should not require any further polishing.

The method described above gives a smooth surface on one side only, marked (A) on the drawings, as the undersides will have been formed by the roller. They can be ground off smooth if necessary but will show the cut ends of the glass fibres and should be painted or otherwise protected.

Perspex

Perspex or acrylic sheet (polymethyl methacrylate) is readily obtainable in clear transparent, pastel shades, full colours, and transfusing and fluorescent colours in thicknesses from $^1/_{25}$ in (1 mm) to $^1/_2$ in (12.5 mm) in colours, and up to 2 in (50 mm) in the clear sheet. It is also supplied in clear rod and tube up to 1 in (25 mm) diameter. Although not as hard as fused glass it has the same clarity and appearance and can be cut very easily with circular saw, band-saw or very fine-toothed handsaw, using low speed and light pressure and feed. It is easily drilled with the normal twist-drill lubricated with a trace of thin oil, and can be bent to simple curves at a temperature just short of boiling water (201° F; 94° C). For accurate bending a wood form should be used, the perspex sheet heated in front of an electric plate or similar source of heat, bent over the form, covered with a cloth and held in position for from one to two minutes to cool and set. Cut edges can be bonded together with simple heat, chloroform or ether, or special perspex cement, and frameless showcases are now made almost exclusively by this method, with the meeting edges either butted and polished (wet and dry paper, burnishing pastes, etc.) or mitred together, both methods giving invisible joints if well done. There is a growing tendency also to design carcass furniture in flat sheets and simple chair forms in moulded resin, for it is an excellent structural material with outstanding qualities of clarity, strength, rigidity, stability and durability under quite severe conditions of wear, as witness its use in aircraft-work. It is, however, relatively expensive, although no doubt constant research and development, as with all other plastics, will eventually cheapen costs.

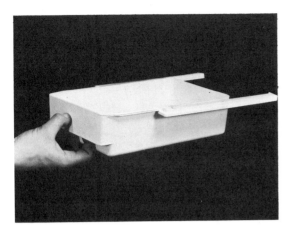

28 Drawer unit with sliders in medium impact polystyrene. (By courtesy of Prestige Caterers)

Nylon

Nylon (polyamide) has universal uses as a fibre material for it can be cold drawn to five times its original strength, thus straightening the chain molecules and imparting great strength and excellent wear resistance. It is also invaluable as a sheet material and for castings, mouldings and extruded sections for it is tough, resilient and provides noiseless and frictionless surfaces invaluable for furniture guides, sliders, rollers, etc. It is also used in knock-down fittings, while barbed or serrated nylon dowel-pegs can be glued into such loose-textured materials as chipboard to provide secure anchorages for screws. As it is a thermoplastic without the hard brittleness of the thermosetting resins it can be cut, shaped and drilled with normal hand-tools.

For particulars, manipulating data and sources of supply of other plastics readers are referred to the manufacturers concerned, lists of whom can be obtained from the various periodic journals devoted to the subject and to the standard textbooks available at most libraries.

Decorative plastic laminates

Familiarly known as *Formica, Wilson Art, Consulweld*, etc., these are composed of layers of kraft paper impregnated with phenolic resins, while the surface pattern, which can be purely decorative in an infinite range of designs or an exact simulation of real wood grains, is printed on a cover paper, and coated with a scratch-resistant surface of melamine resin. Figure 29:1 shows (A) the kraft papers, (B) the cover paper and (C) the melamine coating. Heat pressing of the assembled pack between stainless-steel platens polished to mirror finish induces a chemical change or polymerization, resulting in a homogeneous sheet possessing outstanding qualities of lightness, toughness, durability and resistance to heat, moisture, acids and alkalis, etc. Standard sheets with the pattern on one face only are usually $1/16$ in (0.062 in or 1.58 mm), but a full range of thicknesses is also available, 0.032 in (0.81 mm) for vertical facings, wall claddings, etc., 0.040 in (1.01 mm) for light use in horizontal positions, 0.052 in (1.32 mm) for post forming (heat bending), and 0.10 in (2.54 mm) to $1\frac{1}{2}$ in (38 mm) built up of separate laminations or with a sandwich core of other materials (ply, etc.). Thicknesses of $1/8$ in (3.17 mm) and over are self-supporting (29:2). A cheap-quality backing or balancing veneer composed of kraft papers only with no surface pattern is available for use on the undersides of core material to counteract the pull.

Cutting procedures

Laminated plastic veneers can be cut with circular saws, using square tipped teeth without set, band-saws with hack-saw-shaped teeth, or fine-toothed backed tenon-saws, in all cases cutting with the face side up. For machine-saws in production-work tungsten-carbide teeth should be used, for the resin content is very hard on cutting edges; while if there is any tendency for the back to chip or 'tear out' with any type of saw the teeth should be resharpened, and the plastic sheet firmly supported with applied top pressure if possible. An alternative hand method which gives no tear is to score the face with a hardened steel scraper or cutting tool—a special blade is available for Stanley trimming-knives—and the sheet will then snap easily with a clean fracture, as in glass cutting. Narrow cross-cuts, corners, etc. can be cut with a fine-toothed hack-saw, while for contour cutting portable electric sabre-saws or fret-saws with

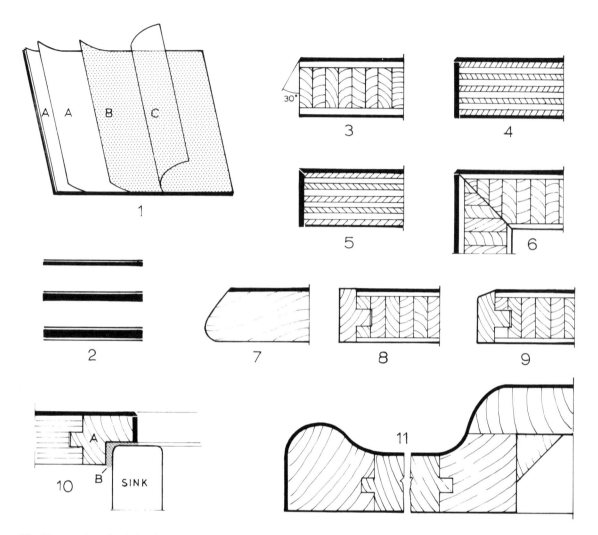

29 Decorative plastic laminate details

metal-piercing blades can be used, but support must be adequate with strips of waste material, hardboard, etc. clamped to the face to prevent chipping on the upward stroke.

Trimming edges

Cut edges can be trimmed with a heavy jack-plane, using short, quick strokes and not attempting to follow through; or with steel cabinet-scrapers, or fine-cut saw-files. If the edges require polishing a dead smooth file, or 400 grit wet and dry silicon carbide paper, will ease out the scratches, and a little fine cutting-down paste or metal polish (*Brasso*, etc.), followed up with a wipe of thin oil, will restore the lustre. Scratches on the face of the sheet can also be eased out with abrasive paste (p.86), always provided they do not penetrate to the cover paper, and matt black laminates are usually enhanced by rubbing over with finest No. 0000 steel wool, but it must be carefully done. Spilt glue, paint, etc. can be lifted with a razor-blade as in cleaning glass, and oil, greasy thumb-prints, especially on matt black veneers, eradicated by wiping over with french chalk.

Laying techniques

Composite assemblies ⅛ in (3 mm) and thicker are self-supporting; but the standard ¹⁄₁₆ in (1.5 mm) veneer requires bonding, either to a rigid framework, or to plywood or chipboard sheeting not less than ¾ in (19 mm) thick. Generally speaking, solid wood groundworks/substrates are quite unsuitable, as the laminated veneer is virtually inert and cannot move in sympathy. Additionally, the reverse side of the groundwork must also be veneered to counteract the pull as in wood veneering, unless the support is very firmly fixed. A special backing quality laminate composed of kraft papers is available, although .024 in (0.6 mm) wood veneers can also be used. Care should be taken to choose groundworks whose faces are smooth, fine grained and without strong figure such as Columbian pine, etc., otherwise the raised grain will telegraph through to the surface in time. Cross-members in made-up frameworks should not be glued together or they will also eventually shadow through.

Treatment of edges

All edges should be eased back to prevent lifting and possible impact damage (29:3). If the edges of the groundwork/substrate are also covered they should be laid first, trimmed off flush and the top applied (29:4), the front bevel being formed with a fine-cut file. Mitred edges (29:5) are possible but hardly sensible, as the resultant sharp corners positively invite impact damage, and a more satisfactory treatment is shown in 29:6. Other treatments are shown in 29:7, 8 and 9, and where hardwood lippings or edges are used they can be glued on first and the top cut to exact size and laid afterwards, or the top laid first and then the hardwood edge. Either method calls for skilful working, for the edges must be worked flush with the laminate, and the easier way is to glue on the edge and work it down to the exact projection to receive the laminate, using a loose waste strip as guide. Any fractional adjustment necessary after the top has been laid can then be done by protecting the top with a strip of cellulose tape, and sanding down the high spots. If the top is laid first and the edging after, then a slight bevel (29:9) will keep the cutting tool away from the laminate. Treatment for sinks, washbasins, etc. is shown in 29:10, where a fairly wide edge (A) is applied in case there is any water seepage which might delaminate the plywood layers, with a

proprietary mastic bedding (B) between the edge and the rim of the sink.

Gluing procedures

Several types of gap-filling rubber-based impact glues are available for hand gluing, which only require moderate pressure as they give a powerful and immediate tack. They set by evaporation or absorption of the spirit solvent, and do not attain maximum strength for at least 14 days. An advantage of this type is that they retain a certain measure of elasticity, and will thus withstand fractional movements of the base. They are, however, only heat resistant to about 140° F (60° C) and although damp proof will not stand continuous moist conditions.

In using this type of adhesive over large areas speed is essential. The groundwork/substrate must be perfectly level, dust free and free from grease, etc., while spreading with gauged metal spreader, wooden squeegee or roller should be reasonably full and even, with both surfaces coated and allowed to air dry until the glue is tacky and no longer moist. The coated sheet must be carefully positioned, dropped into place, rolled or banged down with the clenched fist to expel any trapped air, and if pre-cut to exact size then a useful precaution is to tack temporary battens to the groundwork, and use these as locating shoulders. Any spilled glue should be cleaned off with a suitable solvent— petrol, cellulose thinners, etc.—or allowed to tack off and be rolled up with the finger-tips, while rollers should be cleaned immediately. If any edge tends to lift it should be clamped down, and the assembly left for some hours before further working.

Plastic laminates can be glued with gap-filling synthetic resin glues, and this is the standard production method, although clamping pressures are necessary. One of the best glues for this purpose is *Aerolite* 306 with GUX hardener in which a proportion of glycerine has been added to the hardener to impart a measure of flexibility. Application is the same as for wood veneering (Chapter 32), but hot pressing should not exceed 160° F (71° C) with pressures only sufficient to bring both surfaces into intimate contact, and not exceeding 40 lb per sq. in (2.812 gf/cm²). This method is preferable to hand gluing with impact glues which are more suitable for on-site work, for with clamping pressures the surface will be flatter, and the glue film will be both heat and damp resistant within the limits set by the laminate itself and the groundwork/substrate.

Bending

The standard 1/16 in (1.5 mm) veneer can be cold bent to simple curves of not less than 8 in (203 mm) radius, although narrow strips will probably follow a tighter curve without fracturing. The curve should be cut very full in the length with sufficient overhang to follow the sweep, and the waste trimmed off afterwards. For more acute curves either the standard laminate must be heat softened up to but not exceeding 302° F (150° C) which is just short of the blistering point, and clamped between formers/forms, or for very acute curves to a maximum of about 1 in (25 mm) radius special post-forming grades should be used (29:11). Most manufacturers issue their own data sheets for post-forming operations, and the schedules recommended should be closely followed.

Heat-resistant qualities

Standard quality laminates are resistant against the surface temperature not exceeding 302° F (150° C) but will not resist intense localized heat, such as neglected cigarette butts, etc. Incorporating a metal foil in the laminate will tend to spread such localized heat over a wider area, and a cigarette-proof grade is available which gives reasonable protection. Such heat-resistant grades are not suitable for continuously damp situations (kitchen-sink fixtures, etc.), and will not bend so readily as the standard grades.

Real wood laminates

Plastic laminates in which the top sheet is true wood veneer instead of printed paper are available (Belfort, etc.). The sheets have the authentic depth, warmth and natural beauty of wood, although the grain is filled with resin and the natural texture is lost. In all other respects, methods of manufacture, toughness, durability,

resistance to heat, moisture, acids, stains, etc., and cutting and gluing/bonding procedures are identical, while the cost compares favourably with that of other laminates.

LEATHERS

Natural cowhides, specially dressed, and softened by a crimping action which pushes the fibres over each other so that they can slide easily giving the requisite suppleness, are extensively used in upholstery, and are commonly known as *furniture*-hides. They are slit from the tanned hides to a usual thickness of about 1/16 in (1.5 mm), pigmented or dyed, and dressed with a spray coat of synthetic lacquer.

Second quality hides are often grained between rollers. The grains can be heavy, medium or light textured, and are done either to accentuate the natural grain texture, or to even out the applied colour and to mask the inevitable defects which occur in every hide, i.e. barbed-wire weals and punctures of the 'prick' or warble fly which, it is estimated, cost the tanning industry millions each year in spoilt hides. The coloration can be an opaque dressing, sealed with a little gum arabic, or straight aniline dyes which penetrate the hide and yield a clearer finish than the heavy

30 Cowhide measurements

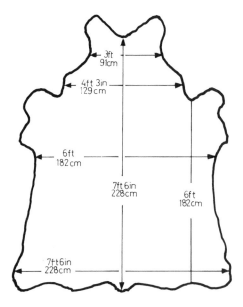

66

pigments which lie on the surface and tend to show as white cracks if the hide is heavily pulled or dressed. The advantage of leather, apart from its intrinsic beauty, is its tolerance of wetting, pulling and stretching over acute compound shapes, while it has a natural resilience which will accommodate considerable deflection. A typical cowhide will contain from 50 to 60 sq. ft (4.645 to 5.574 m^2) measured out to all edges, and Figure 30 shows the dimensions to be expected from an average hide (the standard allowance for waste in cutting to final dimensions should not be less than 60 per cent). Goat-skins—Cape Levant, Morocco, Niger, etc.—are much smaller and more expensive, and usually reserved for table linings, small seatings, etc. They are either aniline or vegetable dyed, and native skins are invariably untextured. Skivers (sheep-skin), calf-skin, etc. are rarely used in furniture as they are more delicate and wear too easily. Shagreen (shark's skin) is only used in small panels for ornamental boxes, etc.; and occasionally other exotic leathers are used as fashion dictates, but cowhide and goat-skins are the mainstays, with plastic-coated cloths (leathercloths) a fair substitute. A description of table-lining methods is given in Chapter 33.

PLASTIC COVERINGS, LEATHER-CLOTHS, ETC.

Besides the innumerable transparent or patterned sheet materials, polyvinyl acetate resins (PVC) are coated on a variety of base materials, wool (*Yana*), cotton twill and jersey fabric (*Lionide, Ambla, Flexknit*, etc.), to yield light-, medium- and heavyweight cloths which have all the advantages of true plastics, i.e. long flex life without ageing, resistance to spilt acids, stains and greases, water resistance, etc. Some are produced as impregnated woven fabrics for upholstery, etc., similar in all respects to natural woven materials, while others are close coated and grained in so exact a simulation of natural leather that it is sometimes difficult to tell the difference unless the edges are examined. These have a rapidly expanding use in wall coverings, spring and foam-covered seating, etc., with the added advantages of cheapness and continuous widths free from all defects, although they lack the beauty of the natural material, and have not the same recovery value under seating pressure as good leather.

5 Metals

METAL FURNITURE

Hitherto metal furniture was largely made of mild steel tube, hence the familiar name 'tubular steel furniture'; moreover, designers tended to think in terms of wood forms and then to translate those forms into metal sections. Modern metal furniture is now designed as such, taking into full account the qualities of stability, flexibility and hardness which allow considerable reduction in sectional dimensions over comparable wood forms. As a viable material for certain kinds of furniture, metal commends itself for its consistent quality which is of great importance in large-scale manufacture; it can be worked to precision limits and its hygienic, non-porous, smooth surfaces, toughness and great strength render it eminently suitable for hospital, kitchen, school, office and dismountable furniture.

MATERIALS

A range of solid and hollow metal extrusions is available, ranging from flat strips to complex hexagonal tube. Cast alloy parts are also made. Stainless steel sheet and tube is attractive, but its high cost and the difficulties of cutting and joining it mean that mild steel is the norm. A variety of surface treatments can be used, as a protection against corrosion and to improve its appearance. Chrome plating is inexpensive, but is prone to rust-pitting. Nickel, bronze or aluminium plating are also used. Various kinds of paints, like stove enamel, and cold-cured polyurethanes are less costly. The best results, where corrosion resistance and lasting good looks are required, are probably attained with plastic coatings. These are of various kinds, and may be chosen to suit the cost and application of the project. One of the most expensive but durable plastic coatings is applied to the clean tube in the form of a thin tubing, heat-shrunk into place. This is difficult to apply to all shapes of component, and so a variety of other methods may be employed either on the whole piece or selected components. One of the most used is powder-coating. With this technique the metal parts are pre-heated in an oven and then sprayed or fluid-bed coated with powdered plastic resin. The thickness of this coat can be controlled by varying the pre-heat temperature. The coated article is then passed through another heat cycle which fuses the powder into a smooth gloss finish.

MANIPULATION

Methods of attachment or jointing are by brazing, torch or arc welding, metal connectors or screw assemblies. Chair posts, table legs, etc. are normally fitted with protective caps of hard rubber, plastic or knock-in wooden caps cut slightly oversize and driven in wedge tight. Connection of wood members, cross-rails, etc. can be done by securing a threaded bolt to the metal section and carrying it though a prebored hole in the wood member with a captive nut in a small mortise which can be tightened up to take up the slack if the wood shrinks. Alternatively, there are knock-down fittings available. Flat strips can be bent cold round suitable forms in a bending machine, but tubes must be filled with rammed sand, steel balls, pitch, etc. and the ends securely plugged or the bending will kink the inner curve. Metal extrusion L-, T-, or U-sections, etc. are filled or packed up with thin metal strips before bending, and heavy sections may have to be heated. For methods of fabrication reference should be made to the standard books on metal-working. However, the following is a brief outline of the properties of metal and the processes involved in working it, many of which would need to be undertaken by specialist engineering or metal finishing firms.

TYPES OF METAL

Ferrous metals

Composed mainly of iron with small additions of other metals or substances, e.g. wrought iron, cast iron, mild steel and carbon steel.

Wrought iron

Iron with traces of silicate.

Properties: malleable, can be shaped or bent cold or hot, readily sawn, chiselled, filed, drilled, brazed and soldered. Rusts in exposed conditions—protect with paint, preserve indoors by waxing.

Uses: decorative work such as screens and gates.

Cast iron

Iron with small amounts of carbon, silicon, sulphur etc.

Properties: brittle, but with a very hard skin; breaks if struck hard or dropped. Can be sawn, filed or drilled, but not easily brazed or welded, rusts slowly if exposed to air—protect with paint, preferably bitumen.

Uses: cylinder blocks, piston rings, vice/vise bodies, fire backs, manhole covers.

Mild steel

Iron with up to 0.3 per cent carbon.

Properties: easy metal to work—bends, files, saws and drills well; can be soldered, brazed or welded. Rusts easily—protect with paint or indoors with clear lacquer.

Uses: general-purpose metal used in bar, rods, sheet, rolled section and angle form; nuts, bolts, screws, tubing; furniture construction.

Stainless steel

Steel with chromium and nickel. Approximately 18 to 8 per cent.

Properties: resists corrosion, although this property can be destroyed by overheating.

Tough and difficult to work; can be soldered and brazed.

Uses: cutlery, furniture frames.

Tool and alloy steel

Composition varied by addition of different elements.

Properties: harder than mild steel—difficult to file and cut. Can be soldered and brazed and hardened, to produce a strong cutting edge. Rusts easily—protect with oil or grease; paint non-cutting parts.

Uses: saws, chisels, plane irons, scissors, knives, hammer heads, springs.

Non-ferrous metals

These contain little or no iron, e.g. aluminium, copper, lead, zinc, tin.

Aluminium

Pure metal.

Properties: lightweight and corrosion-resistant; can be bent, formed, filed or sawn easily, but soldered only with special materials. Polishes to a high finish and needs no protection indoors.

Uses: kitchen utensils, furniture and fittings.

Copper

Pure metal.

Properties: can be bent and shaped easily, but may work-harden and need annealing if worked repeatedly: saws, files, solders and brazes easily. Polishes well, although colour darkens on exposure to air—protect with clear lacquer.

Uses: hot water pipes, electrical parts and decorative work.

Lead

Pure metal.

Properties: heavy, soft and malleable; cuts and works easily cold; can be soft soldered. High resistance to corrosion by weather.

Uses: plumbing, flashings, container linings, weighting objects.

Zinc

Pure metal.

Properties: fairly hard and brittle—has a 'grain' and bends more easily in one direction than another; bends better if immersed in boiling water first; can be soft soldered.

Uses: substitute for lead in flashings and linings. Perforated zinc for air vents etc.; plating.

Tin

Pure metal.

Properties: very soft and malleable; with high resistance to corrosion.

Uses: a base for alloys and a coating for mild steel; rarely used in pure state.

Alloys

Combination of two or more metals and other substances. Divided into two sub-classes: ferrous alloys (e.g. special steels such as nickel steel, tungsten steel, chromium steel) and non ferrous alloys (e.g. brass, bronze, duralumin, pewter).

Bronze

Copper with tin.

Properties: very resistant to corrosion: can be filed, sawn, bent, chiselled, soldered, brazed or welded.

Uses: pump units, marine fittings, gears and bearings.

Duralumin

Aluminium with copper and other metals.

Properties: nearly as strong as mild steel, but one-third its weight. Bends, folds and works well cold, but may need annealing; cannot be soldered by normal methods; paint for exterior use.

Uses: where high strength and light weight is important—shelving systems, chair legs, pulleys, bolts, rivets, claddings.

Brass

Copper with zinc.

Properties: sheet brass is soft and ductile—it shapes and bends easily, but work hardens and needs annealing for repeated working. Brass strip can be filed, sawn, drilled, bent and soldered easily; treat decorative work in the same way as copper.

Uses: cabinet hardware, screws, decorative work.

PROPERTIES OF METAL

Age-hardening

A slow hardening process which takes place in certain alloys, particularly those of aluminium when allowed to stand at room temperature after annealing. If you wish to work the material after it has become age-hardened, it must be re-annealed. Duralumin age-hardens after five days.

Brittleness

Liability to break under a sharp blow. White cast iron and heat-hardened high-carbon steels are extremely brittle.

Conductivity

Capacity to transmit heat and electricity. Copper, silver and pure aluminium are good conductors.

Ductility

Ability to be stretched into fine wire without fracture; copper is highly ductile.

Elasticity

Ability to regain original shape after deformation. Lead is very malleable but has little elasticity—it does not spring back when bent.

Fusibility

Property of becoming liquid when heated. Different metals have different melting points.

Hardness

Resistance to deformation, bending and cutting.

Malleability

Capacity to be extended in all directions without fracturing by rolling, hammering or beating. Gold is the most malleable metal, and can be beaten into leaf 1/25000 in thick.

Tenacity or cohesion

Resistance to a pulling force—the opposite to ductility.

Work-hardening

Hardening of metal while it is being hammered or bent. The hardening causes the metal to become more brittle, and it must therefore be annealed to prevent it from cracking.

PROCESSES IN WORKING METAL

Annealing

Heating metal to restore it to its softest possible working state.

Bluing

Treating steel to improve its corrosion-resistance. The metal is heated to create an oxide skin, then quenched in oil.

Casting

Production of metal shapes by pouring molten metal into moulds.

Drawing

Pulling ductile metals through holes in a plate, to reduce their cross-sectional areas.

Extruding

Forcing malleable materials through holes to produce bars, sections or tubes.

Forging

Shaping hot metal by hammering.

Hardening

Producing maximum hardness in high carbon steel by heating it to bright cherry red, then quenching it in water or brine. This process makes metal brittle and is usually following by tempering.

Pressing

Forming sheet metal to shape with a press tool.

Spinning

A process in which a fast revolving sheet of ductile metal is forced over a wood or metal form. Much aluminium alloy kitchenware is produced in this way.

Tempering

Removing some of the brittleness from steel after it has been hardened. The tempering is done by heating the steel, then cooling it— temperatures and speed of cooling vary with the types of steel. Steel cannot be tempered without being hardened.

METAL FINISHES IN FURNITURE PRODUCTION

Many metals and alloys readily corrode and tarnish when exposed to the atmosphere and therefore have to have a form of protective covering. These can be broadly classified as follows:

Metallic coatings

Chrome plate (the most common)
Nickel plate
Bronze plate

Silver plate
Zinc plate
Process of applying a thin coating of an expensive anti-corrosive metal. In furniture production, used predominantly on mild steel.

Non-metallic coatings

Enamelling—stove and spray—has the advantage of giving colour to metal furniture.
Lacquering—process of applying a thin transparent lacquer to decorative metals such as brass, to seal them from the atmosphere.

Plastic and nylon coating—becoming increasingly popular, especially for restaurant furniture; can be in bright colours and gives a warm feeling to cold metal.

Chemical processes

Chemical colouring—used to alter the colour of the existing metal as well as to protect it; used chiefly on brass and copper.
Anodizing—used for aluminium alloys; consists of a hard film (anobic film) which can be dyed to various colours.

6 Adhesives

All matter is composed of countless separate molecules which exert their own powerful electro-magnetic forces, and thus adhere together by mutual attraction. In theory, therefore, any two smooth surfaces should 'also adhere, and in fact will do so providing the surfaces are in reality perfectly smooth. However, these inter-molecular forces have only a very short range, and any roughness of the surfaces will prevent the molecules adhering except at local high spots. Where the surfaces are rough—and a steel plate polished to mirror smoothness will still be extremely rough by molecular standards—a bonding agent is necessary whose own molecules will flow out over the rough surfaces, and render them smooth enough to adhere together. Simple liquids such as water, which exerts considerable forces of attraction (one ton per square inch), are in effect powerful adhesives, but they have low viscosity and high volatility and are, therefore, totally unsuitable. Any good adhesive, therefore, must be not only highly mobile and free flowing, but also non-volatile, with adequate tensile strength, and with little if any propensity to shrink back as it solidifies; moreover, certain additional characteristics are necessary according to the type of material for which it is to be used. Wood, for instance, will require cheapness, ease of preparation, a measure of flexibility to accommodate residual strains and stresses, resistance to fungoid and

31 Wall fresco, Egyptian tomb (Pharaoh Rekhamen)

73

insect attack, water-resistance, acceleration of the set by heat, and absence of staining.

HISTORY OF GLUES

The first glues used were in all probability natural exudations from resinous tree-trunks, tar, bitumen, possibly animal blood and crude forms of casein glue. So-called animal glues, i.e. hide or Scotch glue, fish glues, etc. were known to the Egyptians nearly 4000 years ago, and Figure 31 shows a wall fresco in the tomb of the Pharaoh Rekhamen which depicts carpenters boiling glue over a charcoal fire, spreading glue with a spatula, and sawing and adzing wood. (The terms 'adhesive' and 'glue' have the same meaning and are virtually interchangeable, although traditional practice prefers the term 'glue' when used for bonding paper and wood, and 'adhesive' for bonding all other materials. Animal glues made from hoof, horn and hide are commonly known as 'hide' or 'Scotch' (United Kingdom only) to distinguish them from casein glue which is also animal in origin.)The glue was made much as it is today, by boiling animal skins and bones, etc., but the strained jelly had no keeping qualities, and craftsmen were always forced to make their own glue as and when required until long-storage cake glues were commercially exploited at the beginning of the nineteenth century. Later developments perfected liquid glues by lowering the gel point with acetic acid and improving the storage life in semi-liquid form with suitable preservatives (formaldehyde, etc.), and considerable quantities of this type of glue (*Croid*, etc.) are still used in industry. The greatest development has been in modern plastic glues which were first used in the 1930s, and once the commonly held belief that good adhesion relied entirely on the mechanical interlocking of porous surfaces with little dowels of glue forced into those surfaces was disproved, then enormous impetus was given to the whole field of research into the principles of adhesion.

TYPES OF GLUE

The perfect glue hardly exists except under laboratory conditions, and most professional users, recognizing the limitations of any one kind of adhesive, match the glue to the work. Generally speaking all adhesives fall within three main categories: (1) *animal* glues prepared from bones, hides, fish offal, blood, milk, etc.; (2) *vegetable* glues prepared from dextrine, rye and soya-bean flours, rubber latex, etc.; (3) *mineral* glues prepared from synthetic resins, coal-tar, crude-oil derivatives, etc. This is a good enough division, although chemists would prefer to divide them into (1) temperature-change glues; (2) solvent-release glues; (3) chemical-change glues, but as this can be confusing to the layman the first-mentioned categories are normally used in everyday parlance.

Animal glues

The universal type is *Hide* prepared by boiling bones, hides, etc. in water, and obtainable in hard cake form which must be broken up in an old piece of sacking and soaked for 12 hours before heating; in pearl, grain and bead forms requiring only a short soaking time; and in liquid glues (*Croid, Adams,* etc.) in which the addition of formaldehyde keeps the glue sweet in storage, and acetic acid lowers the gel point. Casein glues prepared from milk curds are excellent all-purpose glues requiring the addition of cold water only, but stain woods rich in tannic acid although so-called non-staining types are available. Fish glues prepared from fish offal and skins (*Seccotine*, etc.) are extremely useful for small repair-work, but lack sufficient strength for structural work. Animal-blood glues are water resistant if hot pressed and are used in cheap foreign plywoods. All these glues set by chilling or absorption or evaporation of the water content.

Vegetable glues

Dextrine (British Gum) and rye-flour glues have no application in assembly-work, and are only used for table-lining, etc. Cassava-starch and soya-bean glues are used for interior quality plywoods, while rubber glues are used in leather-work and upholstery, and also for bonding decorative laminated plastics.

Synthetic resin (plastic) glues

While a great deal of furniture is still glued with animal adhesives, synthetic resin glues are extensively used in practically every manufacturing industry, and offer unparalleled advantages in certain classes of work where ease of working, rapid setting, great strength, permanence and water-resistant properties are called for. A considerable advantage for small craftsmen is their tolerance of low temperatures, for they can be satisfactorily worked in relatively cold conditions (50° F [10° C]), whereas animal glues require heated conditions for satisfactory results. Conversely, all synthetic resin glues are thermosetting, and respond to heat which greatly accelerates the setting-rate.

The type of synthetic resin glue most commonly used in furniture-making is *urea formaldehyde* (UF), which has adequate strength, durability and water-resistance for all types of indoor-work, will set at normal room temperatures, and is relatively inexpensive. *Phenol formaldehyde* (PF) is used where great strength, durability and water resistance is necessary, but heat is required for the set and the glue-line is dark coloured, and therefore it is confined to heavy constructional work and plywood manufacture including 'exterior' quality ply. *Resorcinol formaldehyde* (RF) has outstanding durability under the severest conditions and is therefore used mainly for exterior work. Here again a dark glue-line is formed which is sometimes used for its decorative possibilities (archery bow laminations). *Melamine formaldehyde* (MF) is more expensive, and is usually employed as a fortifier of other glues and for the top coating of decorative laminated plastics (formica, etc.). *Polyvinyl acetate emulsion* (PVA) is ready mixed, requires no accelerator and is extensively used for gluing or strengthening a variety of substances, but it lacks the great strength of straight synthetics, and tends to creep from thick joints under humid conditions. (Many so-called PVA adhesives are no longer composed of polyvinyl acetate and a better term is, therefore, *emulsion glue*. They are thermoplastic, with high-tensile strength but little inherent strength in thick films and with little if any penetration, therefore they should not be used in tropical climates, for

gap-filling work or for dowelling. They are, however, useful for close-contact work with moderate pressure, and as they do not become brittle with age they can be used for laying plastic laminates. Bearing in mind their limitations they are in all probability the most popular type of glue for the small user). *Epoxy resin* glues require no volatile solvent, and are, therefore, capable of bonding non-porous materials, metals, glass, china, etc. A comparison of the various types is listed on p. 79.

PREPARATION, WORKING PROPERTIES, ETC.

Hide (Scotch) glues

Hide- or Scotch-type glues in cake, pearl and bead forms require preliminary soaking in water and heating in water-jacketed pots to not more than 160° F (54° C). Greater temperatures or constant reheating destroy much of the adhesive strength, and the heated glue should always be a dark honey colour, sweet smelling and liquid enough so that a slight rattle is heard as it runs from the brush. Components must be slightly warmed and pressure applied before the glue gels, for the chilled gel itself has no adhesive properties. Liquid hide glues only require slight warming in the tin in cold weather and give more latitude. All types are freely soluble in water and are not, therefore, resistant, but they can be reconstituted and, therefore, there is no waste. Their great advantages in some classes of work are their flexibility, and the strong tack or suck they give, so that freshly glued surfaces can be rubbed together and will grip without clamping pressure. Glued components should be left for 12 hours under normal workshop conditions, and longer if the workshop is cold or the components under strain. Clamps should be tightened up after the first 15 minutes, as absorption by the wood or squeezing from the joint edges may have reduced the pressure. If the clamps must be removed as soon as possible, a test-piece coated with glue should be laid alongside, and only when the glue-film cannot easily be indented with the thumb-nail should the pressure be released. The old craftsmen used a minimum of glue, but it is better to spread both surfaces thinly, and wipe off the squeezed-out surplus with clean rags soaked in warm water.

Hide glues can be used equally well for assembly-work and veneering, and will tolerate thicknesses of $\frac{1}{16}$ in (1.58 mm) in the glue-line. They are invaluable for antique repair-work.

Synthetic resin glues

Preparation of synthetic resin glues is more exact and the makers' instructions must be closely followed. Two types are used: (1) gap-filling assembly glues for general construction work permitting glue thicknesses of up to $\frac{1}{20}$ in (1.27 mm);(2) veneering glues which have little if any gap-filling properties, and require intimate contact between the surfaces. Some veneering glues (*Aerolite KL*, etc.) can have gap-filling properties imparted to them with suitable powder hardeners, and are thus dual-purpose glues. Additionally, synthetic resin glues are divided into (*a*) separate application glues; (*b*) mixed application glues. With the exception of polyvinyl acetate glues all synthetic resins require an acid accelerator or catalyst hardener, and set by chemical action plus evaporation or absorption of the solvent, thus they cannot be reconstituted. They have no natural tack, and require sufficient clamping pressure to bring both surfaces into intimate contact.

Separate application resin glues

All plastic (synthetic resin) glues are formed by the reaction at elevated temperatures of the components (phenol or urea, etc. with formaldehyde, for PF or UF glues). This reaction or polymerization provides resins for moulded and extruded plastic-ware, etc., but if carefully controlled and arrested, adhesives are compounded which can be supplied either as fine-grained powders or water-based thick syrups. However, the reaction cannot be halted completely, and therefore all resin glues have a limited working life only, which should always be stated on the container. To promote the ultra-rapid setting of these glues a suitable

hardener, often known as an 'accelerator' or 'catalyst', is added, which sets the glue into an intensely hard, infusible solid, and at the same time imparts water-resistant properties. Beyond that, and in the nature of all true catalysts, this hardener has no other function than promotion of the reaction, and therefore the simplest method of using resin glues is to coat one surface with the resin and the other with the hardener. In this way there is no mixing to be done, no waste, and the minimum amount of hardener is used, for all solvents used to liquify the glue so that it can be spread on the wood surfaces, and all liquid hardeners added, must disperse either by evaporation or absorption, and if present in excessive quantities will become trapped within the body of the glue during the rapid chemical set, and may eventually set up crazing or fracturing. Single application UF glues with spirit hardener of the type *Aerolite* 300 (CIBA [ARL] Ltd), and obtainable either in powder form for long storage life or as a ready-for-use syrup (effective life three to four months), are amongst the strongest in this class, and will accommodate glue-line thicknesses of up to $\frac{1}{20}$ in (1.27 mm) in assembly-work without fracturing. This type of glue cannot be used for veneering work as the application of either hardener or syrup to the veneers will immediately curl them; nor must the hardener be premixed with the syrup, as the setting is much too rapid.

Mixed application glues

With these (*Aerolite KL*, etc.) both glue and liquid or powder hardener are carefully weighed or measured in the correct proportions, and mixed together before application. They are thus ideal veneering glues whose setting time can be greatly accelerated by the application of heat. Glues are also available in which a suitable powder hardener is incorporated with the powder glue (*Cascamite One Shot*, etc.), and mixing with water releases the acidifying action of the hardener and initiates the set. These glues are principally gap-filling assembly glues, but are also quite satisfactory for veneered work, although they are not so responsive to heat as straight veneering glues. They require no elaborate weighing or measuring out, are easy to mix, and are sufficiently strong and moisture resistant for most purposes. The storage life in closed containers is the same as for most other powder resin glues, i.e. one year or more.

Miscellaneous synthetic glues

Epoxy resin glues and hardeners (*Araldite*, etc.) are in the form of stiff creams which are intimately mixed together prior to use; thus there is very little initial solvent present, and no volatile matter is evolved during the reaction. These glues have wide applications in bonding notoriously difficult surfaces, metal, glass, china, plastics, wood, rubber, etc., and with a suitable filler can be used as a waterproof mastic for bonding plastic working-tops to steel and porcelain sinks, etc. Polyvinyl acetate emulsion glues are white creams which form transparent glue-lines and set by evaporation of the water content. They are ready-mixed general-purpose assembly glues, not water-resistant but with considerable tensile strength and durability, and a curious affinity for brick, cement, glazed tiles, paint, etc. They have a tendency to creep from open joints in humid conditions, and are therefore not suitable for tropical conditions. Cellulose (vegetable) glues with added synthetic resins (quick-setting cements, balsa cement, etc.) have practical uses in the workshop, but not for general assembly-work.

So-called *impact* glues are synthetic or natural rubber latex glues in suitable solvents, and are widely used for bonding decorative, laminated plastics on site where cramping/clamping or pressing facilities are not available; the natural resilience of the rubber gives the necessary amount of flexibility between the inert plastic and the creep or movement of the wood. They are sometimes used for assembly-work and bonding small strips or inlays of veneers, but this is not their rightful function, and must be regarded as an expedient only, not suitable for permanent work.

Heat acceleration of glue sets

As already mentioned, synthetic resin glues (not impact glues) are thermosetting, and once set cannot be resoftened by heat. The acceleration of the set by applied heat is very marked, as the following tables show:

Separate application glues

Aerolite 300 or 306 Powder Glue with	Minimum setting time				
	50°F 10°C	60°F 16°C	70°F 21°C	80°F 27°C	90°F 32°C
Hardener GBQX	5-6 hr	2½	1¾	1¼	1
Hardener GBMX	—	—	3½ hr	2½	2

GBQX has an assembly time (first contact between glue and hardener) of five minutes only, therefore GBMX with an assembly time of 20 minutes is more suitable for hot-weather working.

Mixed application glues

Aerolite KL with Powder Hardener	Minimum clamping time		
	60°F 16°C	80°F 27°C	100°F 38°C
	7 hr	1½	¾

	Basic setting time*		
130°F 54.5°F 6½ min.	150°F 66°F 2¾	180°F 82°F 1¼	210°F 99°F ¼

*An additional time allowance according to the thickness of the veneers, etc. must be added to the basic setting time (see makers' instructions). Pot life of the mixed Aerolite KL glue is 15 hr at 50°F (10°C), to 1½ hr at 80°F (27°C).

PREPARATION OF SURFACES, ETC.

Timber containing a high percentage of moisture cannot be glued satisfactorily with any type of adhesive, although casein is more tolerant than other glues and synthetic resins more critical. A moisture content of 20 per cent is about the limit, and higher values lower the viscosity of the glue to such an extent that starved joints may result, and the excess of moisture may cause the glue to harden as separate particles instead of a continuous film, thus reducing the ultimate strength. For good results, therefore, the wood should be in equilibrium with the average air conditions within the range 8 to 16 per cent, and only up to 20 per cent when that happens to be the normal environmental content.

Contrary to the widely held belief, there is little to be gained by sanding or toothing the wood surfaces prior to gluing, and in fact such treatment may positively interfere with the bond. Ideally, the wood should be glued immediately after it has been worked, and there will be no appreciable difference in adhesion between planed and fine-sawn surfaces provided that blunt cutters have not burnished the wood. Where gluing has to be delayed the surfaces should be only lightly sanded, and then well dusted to dislodge the greasy dust which any unprotected surface will gradually accumulate. Teak and certain other oily and notoriously difficult woods are quite straightforward with synthetic resin and even hide glue, provided the surfaces are glued within a few hours of working, for it is the seepage of natural oils to the surface which prevents the bond. If necessary oily wood can be degreased with any suitable solvent (cellulose thinners, etc.), but never with carbon tetrachloride which is sometimes advocated, for in conjunction with cigarette smoke it can produce a lethal gas (phosgene). End grain of wood rarely permits an effective bond, and therefore sufficient side grain should always be available, but if for any reason end-grain wood must be glued it should be repeatedly sized with well-diluted hide glue (not decorators' powder glue size). Synthetic resins can also be diluted with water or methylated spirit for sizing purposes, and each successive coat should penetrate and harden before another is applied. The usual dilution for size is from three to five parts water or solvent to one part glue, dependent on the viscosity of the latter.

Glues can be coloured to match the wood, using flake-white for light-coloured woods, and gas-black, mineral-earth colours or aniline dyes for ebony, blackwood, etc. Alternatively, Salisbury or rabbit skin glue, often employed in water gilding and gesso-work, can be used for delicately coloured inlays, while PVA emulsion gives a translucent glue-line. A method often adopted by the writer in gluing up light-coloured woods—cherry, sycamore, holly, etc.—was to rub the edges of the joints with ordinary blackboard chalk before applying the glue, and this worked well with highly absorbent butt-jointed veneers. Hide glue will accept most colouring agents without appreciable loss of strength, but tests should be made with resin glues as the acid/alkali reaction is critical.

Resin glues are not so tolerant of abuse as animal glues, and all weighing and measuring must be in accordance with the manufacturers' instructions. Where the quantities of glue required are small, hand-mixing is sufficient, but mechanical mixers are imperative for large batches, for if the separate ingredients are not evenly dispersed throughout the body of the glue, patchy setting and weak glue-lines will result. In particular, scrupulous cleanliness must be preserved for resin glues, as they will not tolerate oil, grease, acid or alkaline impurities, while liquid acid hardeners must never be stored in metal containers or spread with wire-bound brushes. Separate sticks or brushes must be kept for resin and hardener, for even the slightest trace of hardener on a stick carelessly dipped into a can of resin can spoil the whole batch. A photographic rubber print roller is excellent for spreading resin glues in thin films for veneering, as they do not flow out so easily as hide glues, and bald spots must be avoided.

FILLERS, EXTENDERS, ETC.

Suitable fillers (rye and walnut-shell flour, etc.) can be incorporated with synthetic resin glues to extend and, therefore, cheapen the glue, and also to cut down excessive penetration through thin veneers. The amount of filling material can be varied within wide limits according to the type of glue, but large percentage additions will lessen the strength and water-resistant properties, and the makers' instructions should be closely followed.

GLUING DIFFICULT MATERIALS

Brass, metals, etc. Araldite epoxy resin glue in accordance with maker's instructions; hide glue with the addition of a teaspoonful of Venice turpentine per pint of glue, or plaster of Paris (alternatively rub metal with garlic).
Ivory. Coat with celluloid dissolved in ether, or glue with hide or *Araldite*.

Tortoiseshell. Araldite or UF resin glue, Salisbury glue or freshly made hide glue. Add flake-white or rouge to colour, or lay on gold-foil.

Leather, baize, etc. Casein, *Cascamite One Shot* resin glue, dextrine, thin hide glue, shoemaker's glue, etc., allowing surfaces to tack off slightly before laying, especially with baize.

Laminated plastics. Casein, *Cascamite One Shot, Aerolite* 306 with GUS glycerine-based hardener where pressure is available, otherwise proprietary impact glues. For maximum heat and water resistance use *Aerodux Resorcinal* glue (CIBA [ARL] Ltd).

Rubber to wood. Bostik glue; or treat rubber with concentrated sulphuric acid, wash, dry and glue with *Aerodux Resorcinal* glue.

Wood to glass. Araldite where strains are imposed, or *Durofix* tube cement if only for ornamentation (sham glazing bars, etc.).

Many difficult materials (metal, ivory, etc.) can be glued with simple adhesives provided both surfaces are immaculately clean. A test of the molecular attraction between surfaces can be made by scratch brushing two pieces of soft aluminium, placing together immediately and hitting with a large punch. Both surfaces will then adhere and cannot be separated, but if one surface is lightly touched with the finger it will not bond. The method usually adopted by old craftsmen for inlaying ivory, silver, etc. was to hide glue the ground or substrate, dry grind the inlay without touching the critical surfaces with the fingers and immediately place in position. Alternatively, the metal inlays were rubbed with fresh garlic, and while it was never exactly known why the garlic acted in this manner, it is possible that the garlic oil cleaned the surface and was itself so finely dispersed that it created no fresh obstacle; but no doubt the scientist could give a more valid reason.

COMPARISON OF MAIN TYPES OF GLUE OBTAINABLE THROUGH RETAIL OUTLETS

	Hide	*Casein*	*UF resin*	*PVA*	*Epoxy*	*Impact*
Shelf life	Indefinite	Long	Syrup (3 months) Powder (1 year)	Long	Long	Long
Preparation	Heat mix with water	Cold mix with water	Cold mix with hardener	None	Cold mix with hardener	None
Reconstitution (re-use)	Yes	No	No	No	No	No
Pot life	Indefinite	Short	Short	Long	Fairly long	—
Assembly time	Very short	Short	Short to long	Fairly short	Fairly long	Short
Tack or suck	Excellent	Little if any	None	Slight	Very slight	Considerable
Pressure required	Hand or cramp	Cramp	Cramp	Cramp	Hand or cramp	Hand
Creep	None	None	None	Slight	None	Slight
Strength and durability	Very good	Very good	Excellent	Very good	Excellent	Good
Elasticity	Good	Very slight	Little if any	Slight	None	Considerable
Dulling of tool edges	Moderate	Moderate	Pronounced	Moderate	Pronounced	—
Versatility	Excellent	Good	Good	Good	Excellent	Restricted
Moisture resistance	None	Good	Excellent	Little	Excellent	Fair

Definitions

Cold-setting glues. Glues which set at normal room temperatures either by chilling or evaporation, etc.

Thermosetting glues. Glues which set with, and cannot be softened by, heat.

Assembly glues. Glues capable of supporting thick glue-lines without crazing—gap-filling glues.

Close-contact glues. Glues which will not tolerate thick glue-lines, but require intimate contact throughout.

Shelf life. Storage life in original containers.

Pot life. Effective working life of mixed glue.

Initial gel. First stage in curing of mixed glue. Gel has no strength.

Hardener. Accelerator or catalyst, usually an acid salt dispersed in water or spirit, or formic acid in solution. Function of the solvent is to ensure complete dispersal of acid throughout the glue, and can be coloured for identification.

Crazing. Hair-cracks in solidified glue set up by excessive shrinkage, trapped solvent or inherent weakness in glue structure.

Extenders. Filling material used to extend volume of glue, or to prevent excessive penetration.

Pressing or cramping time. Minimum time glued surfaces should remain under pressure.

Basic setting time. Minimum hot-press time, to which must be added time allowances according to thickness of veneer, etc.

Note: All adhesives take several days to develop their maximum strength.

APPLICATORS FOR GLUE, ETC.

A special bristle brush is sold for hide glues; paint brushes are not suitable as frequent heating destroys the rubber bonding. For rubber based impact glues a tin spreader with serrated edge is supplied by the manufacturers, or teeth can be filed in a piece of waste plastic laminate—cellulose thinners will clean off waste glue if applied before the glue sets hard. PVA emulsion glues are frequently supplied in squeezable polythene containers; the same type of container (clean detergent bottles, etc.) can also be used for single application resin glues, but they will have to be washed out before the glue sets off. Bristle brushes are not recommended, for even though they are washed out every time they will eventually harden with residual glue traces, and spare lengths of stick or dowel rod with rounded or flattened ends are better.

For separate application resin glues, where resin and hardener must be kept separate, the resin can be stored for some weeks in a discarded but clean detergent bottle, thumb actuated lever pump oil can or in a plastic bottle with wide cap, through which an applicator stick, or length of $1/4$ in (6 mm) basket cane hammered out at one end to form a rough brush, is inserted and held in position with pieces of cork either side. The separate hardener, which must be kept free from any metal contamination, can be stored in a similar type bottle with a felt wick or a piece of rag bound round the end of a stick to form a mob head inserted through a cork stopper. As mentioned on p. 78 a photographic rubber roller is ideal for spreading resin veneering glues, as thick or lumpy coats will only result in excessive penetration.

Plastic sheeting is ideal for interleaving between veneer face and platen or caul in press work, for resin glues will not adhere to it. If there is much penetration with porous woods, scrape off the glazed glue patches as soon as possible. Damping the wood surface will often make difficult scraping easier.

Glue-pots

The familiar cast-iron double glue-pot with water-jacket and tinned container for use on gas-ring or Primus stove has been largely superseded by the electric glue-pot, either water-jacketed or waterless, and thermostatically controlled to give a constant temperature of around 130° F (54° C) which is the safe maximum for hide glue. The advantages of the electric pot are obvious.

7 Abrasives

Old-time cabinetmakers used sand-, brick- and stone-dust, shagreen (shark's skin) and other primitive materials for the levelling of wood surfaces, and it always appears incredible how they managed to achieve such wonderful finishes to their furniture. The manufacturing of modern abrasives is now a highly specialized field, and an enormous range of products for the surface finishing of every kind of material is available.

In all wood finishing the function of the abrasive is to wear away the wood fibres by the cutting or rasping action of innumerable sharp crystalline teeth, firmly anchored to a supporting base. The rate or speed of the cut depends not so much on the amount of pressure applied, for excessive pressure tends to defeat its own object, but on the size of the teeth, their relative sharpness, and their ability to keep their cutting edges without disintegrating. A poor abrasive is, therefore, one whose grits or teeth are relatively soft, or whose crystalline structure does not provide the requisite sharp facets, or which rapidly disintegrates either under pressure or by the heat generated by that pressure, or whose cloth or paper base fails to hold the grits securely so that they loosen easily and grind upon each other. The swirl-marks occasionally met with on surfaces finished with a machine-operated oscillating sanding pad are usually caused by these loose grits travelling round in erratic orbits. It follows, therefore, that in an age in which labour costs account for much of the expense of furniture production, it is always false economy to use the cheapest types of abrasive, for the rate of cut is slow and the sharpness of the individual grits soon wears off, crushing rather than cutting the wood-fibres.

SANDING PAPERS

Grits for sanding are deposited on the backing support either by gravity or in an electrostatic field in order that each individual grain shall be secured in an upright position, giving maximum cutting performance to the teeth. Figure 32 shows the disposition of the grains where A is the backing, B the basic adhesive coat, usually of hide glue, C the second adhesive coat of hide glue or synthetic resin and D the abrasive grain. The use of hide glue for the basic coat imparts a certain degree of flexibility to the sanding sheet, while the synthetic resin in the second coat anchors the grain in an upright position and does not soften under the heat generated by the cutting action. Generally speaking, grits anchored entirely by hide glues cut softer because the heat softens the glue, permitting the upright grain to lean over slightly, while the use of resin glues throughout gives a harder, fiercer cutting action, and will withstand the considerable degree of heat generated; therefore manufacturers use either one or a combination of both, according to the type of abrasive material and the purpose for which it is to be employed. Waterproof papers for wet sanding are anchored exclusively with synthetic resin glues.

The types of abrasive material available for wood finishing are as follows:

Glass

Originally crushed sand was used, hence the familiar name 'sandpaper', but the grit is now powdered glass, preferably from old gin or beer bottles. Slow cutting, relatively soft and soon exhausted glass is mainly used for cutting down old paint-work, although it is also used for wood finishing as it does not scratch. The flour grade 00 is still a favourite with french-polishers.

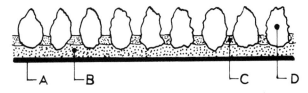

32 Abrasives (sanding paper), detail

Flint

A natural abrasive used for hand-sanding and only slightly harder than glass, it has now been largely superseded by faster materials; moreover flint-dust embedded in the grain of sanded surfaces (cheap plywoods, etc.) has been found to cause a chemical reaction with synthetic finishes.

Garnet

Crushed garnet is used almost entirely for sanding wood. It is much harder than glass or flint, cuts quicker, lasts longer, generates very little heat and consequently rarely burns the wood. It remains a favourite material among cabinet-makers, as it yields a very smooth finish.

Aluminous oxide (Aloxite)

An impure oxide of aluminium manufactured from bauxite; the purest forms yield sapphires, rubies and Oriental topaz. The toughness and hardness of this material ensure that the individual grains will not disintegrate under the considerable mechanical strains of high sanding pressures; therefore it can be used to cut harder and faster than other materials. The white is the purest form and is usually dyed orange and reserved for wood finishing, with the impure forms of brown and pink for metals, etc. Occasionally these coarse-cutting impure forms are dyed black.

Silica carbide

The hardest and most expensive grit, produced by heating mixtures of coal and quartz in an electric furnace, and commonly known as 'carborundum'. Scarcely less hard than the diamond, its sharp yet even crystalline formation is eminently suitable for wet or dry grinding, and polishing of very hard substances with a compact surface, i.e. cellulose, polyester, paint, glass, plastics, stone, non-ferrous metals, etc. It is, however, more brittle than aluminous oxide, and the latter is to be preferred for wood finishing.

Grading of papers (grain or grit sizes)

Hitherto, papers were marked with the grade only, and the principle is still employed for glasspapers which range from 'Flour', 00, to 'Strong 2'; but the grading of other papers has now been standardized to the actual mesh size per square inch for grits within the range 800, which is the finest obtainable, down to 12, which is the coarsest. To avoid confusion most papers are clearly marked with both grade and grit size, and the following table gives the various equivalents together with the approximate comparable gradings in flint- and glasspaper.

Approximate comparable gradings in flint- and glasspaper

Grit size	Equivalent grade	Flint-paper	Glass-paper
500	12/0	—	—
400	11/0	—	—
360	10/0	—	—
320	9/0	—	—
280	8/0	—	—
240	7/0	—	—
220	6/0	4/0	—
180	5/0	3/0	Flour 00
150	4/0	2/0	0
120	3/0	0	1
100	2/0	½	1½
90 } 80 }	0 }	1 } 1½ }	Fine } 2 }
60	½	2	Middle 2
50	1	2½	Strong 2
40	1½	3	—
36	2	—	—
30	2½	—	—
24	3	—	—
12	—	—	—

Both aluminous oxide and silica carbide papers are available in all grits up to 800, and garnet-paper up to 500 grit. The equivalent values for flint-papers are fairly correct, but glasspaper values are an approximation only, for it must be borne in mind that the harder the grit the sharper the crystalline facets and the quicker the cut; therefore there is no exact comparison.

Choice of types

The final quality of any piece of furniture depends in large degree on a correct choice of abrasives at all stages of manufacture. A key factor in performance is the way in which grit particles are arranged on the backing support. Densely packed grains are used to form close-coat surfaces. In theory these should give a greater speed of cut, due to there being more cutting surfaces, but close-coat papers tend to clog rapidly with dust and wood resins. This defect is overcome by spreading the grit more thinly. This type of abrasive paper is known as open-coat, and is generally less expensive and longer lasting than close-coat paper. Open-coat papers should always be specified for use when hand- or machine-sanding resinous woods, or fine sanding lacquered surfaces. Clogging of the abrasive surface with dust is also reduced by applying the grit in a pattern of small dots to the backing support. This is because dust and loose grit is able to escape into the clear spaces between abrasive patches. Stearate lubricated silicon-carbide papers are now preferred for fine sanding of polished work, since the dry lubricant is clean and convenient.

Backings

Backings or supports for grits can be either vulcanized fibre, which is ideal for disc and drum sanders where the loading is particularly severe; 'combination', comprising a heavy-weight paper laminated with an open-weave fabric, and used with floor and drum sanding machines; close-woven pure cotton fabrics in various weights and degrees of flexibility for machine sanding; and tough raw paper of high-tensile strength in a variety of weights for both hand- and machine-sanding. Cloth backs last longer but are considerably more expensive, and paper is usually suitable for most normal purposes, although a very flexible cloth backing specially prepared for hand sanding is better for pronounced contour-work. In principle, orbital pad sanders require a fairly tough paper backing usually known as 'cabinet-papers' (C or D

weight), and these are also used for hand or 'touch' sanding with a cork block in preparatory levelling off using a fairly coarse grit; but for final finishing and delicate work a lighter weight (A) is used, commonly known as a 'finishing' paper. Glasspapers, flint-papers and corundum (aluminous oxide) are usually heavy C weight papers.

Sizes, etc.

Glass- and flint-papers are only available in the standard sheet of 11 in (280 mm) by 9 in (229 mm), which is torn into four equal pieces for use with a suitable cork block; but all other coatings are available in the standard sheet, in strips for orbital pad sanders, and in an immense variety of roll sizes from which discs, belts, sleeves and drum covers are made up to special order. Belts for portable belt sanders can be made up in the workshop if necessary, but the joint should be diagonal across the belt and the overlaps chamfered off to form a scarf joint, or the double thickness will bump over the rollers. A selection of abrasive papers for general workshop use is listed at the end of this chapter.

33   Scarf joint

SANDING TECHNIQUES

Machine-sanding operators are usually skilled personnel with a sensitive touch, otherwise edges are easily dubbed over and veneered surfaces cut through to show bald patches of glue which cannot be masked with ordinary stains. Great care must also be taken with hand sanding, which should be regarded as precision work, for the pressure of the hand is inclined to vary with the movement of the stroke, and there is always a temptation to press more heavily over localized defects. At all costs sharp angles and facets must be preserved, or the effect is lost and the work assumes a woolly apearance.

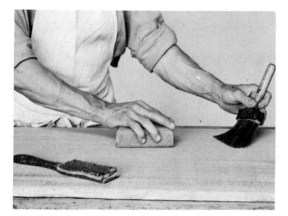

34 Sanding wood surface

Hand-sanding rubbers are usually made of cork, which gives the requisite firmness and resilience, but wood blocks covered with hard felt or rubber are suitable, and also wood alone, although it is inclined to wear the paper through more quickly. In all hand or 'touch' sanding the pressure should be fairly light but firm, as too great a thrust on the block loosens the grit and clogs the surface, while too rapid a stroke tends to skate over and crush rather than cut through the fibres. In other words, the innumerable small teeth of the grits must be given time to accomplish their task. Ideally, the wood surface should be brushed clean of dust ahead of the block for it is the loose grits grinding on their fellows which destroy the cutting action more than the actual fibres of the wood, while the sanding-block should be tapped smartly on the bench from time to time to clear the paper of accumulated dust. A fine wire card is also useful for clearing the paper. In flat work which is to be gloss polished it cannot be too strongly emphasized that the chief difficulty lies in getting rid of the imperceptible bumps and hollows which are never apparent until the mirror finish magnifies them out of all proportion, therefore the blocks should be large and the stroke as long as possible, particularly with scraped surfaces which always tend to bumpiness. Orbital sanders are excellent for this general levelling, as the size of the pad is equivalent to a half sheet of standard paper, and provided the weight of the machine itself is allowed to do the work, without bearing down, good surfaces are obtained. Belt sanders cut faster but are not so

accurate, and great care must be taken with veneered surfaces or they soon rub through. Practically all belt sanders are grossly overloaded in relation to the fractional horse-power available, and no pressure must be applied or bumpy surfaces are inevitable, and motors soon burn out. A useful precaution in sanding out to the edges of flat work is to nail waste pieces of similar thicknesses at either end, so that the sanding block or belt can travel through without dipping. For sanding curved surfaces, mouldings, etc., short lengths of thick dowel-rod or broom-handle, or shaped rubbers made out of softwood to fit the curve, should be used, and the time spent in preparing them will be well repaid in the cleanness of the final finish. This crispness is particularly important in chamfered work and in simple nosings where the curve dies away into a flat surface, for any softening of the edges or waviness of outline is immediately apparent.

CHOICE OF GRITS

For all preparatory sanding and levelling off an 80 grit firm-backed cabinet-paper is suitable, and coarse-grained woods such as oak or teak rarely require any finer treatment. For close-grained woods the first coarse sanding should be followed up with a 120 grit finishing paper, and finely veneered surfaces with 180 grit which can be used with a circular movement over mitred corners, etc. For the most delicate work and for easing down polishes a 240 grit can be used. The foregoing are, of course, only suggestions based on the practical experience of the writer, and as individual touches differ other workers may prefer coarser or finer papers. For comparable results with orbital sanders the grits can be coarser, i.e. 60 grit for preparatory work, followed up by 100 grit, and 150 grit if necessary.

Some woods are woolly textured so that the grits tend to crush rather than cut the fibres, and these should be given a very thin wash coat of white french polish or cellulose lacquer (5 parts spirit or thinners to 1 part polish), and allowed to dry hard before the final sanding. The wash coat raises the grain and sets the loose fibres in an upright position so that they can be cut off. In the best work surfaces are always 'flared off' by damping them with water to raise the grain. This flaring off can be done several times if necessary, but wherever water is used it is essential to dust the surfaces very thoroughly with a stiff brush, for if they have been scraped with steel scrapers iron mould stains may appear, which will have to be bleached out with oxalic acid. The time spent on careful sanding will be well repaid in the excellence of the finished furniture.

All abrasive papers should be stored in a dry place (ideally at 70° F [21° C] and 45 per cent humidity) and warmed slightly before use if the backing is at all damp.

Hardness of grits

Relative hardness of the various types of abrasive in comparison with the diamond which is given a MOH value of 10 are as follows:

Commercial name	Formula	Origin	MOH scale
Crocus	Fe_2O_3	Artificial and natural	5.5–6.5
Quartz (flint, agate)	SiO_2	Natural	7.0
Garnet (Almanite)	$Al_2O_3FeO_3SiO_2$	Natural	7.0–8.5
Emery	$SiO_2FeOAl_2O_3$	Natural	7.0–9.0
Aluminium oxide (corundum)	Complex Al_2O_3	Artificial	9.0–9.4
Silicon carbide (carborundum)	SiC	Artificial	9.5–9.6
Diamond (carbonado)	C	Natural	10.0

SELECTION OF HAND- AND MACHINE-SANDING PAPERS

	Bond	Paper weight	Grit	Coat	Materials
Waterproof silicon carbide paper	Resin bonded	A	600-220	Close	Metals, primers, cellulose
	Resin bonded	C	600-150	Close	
	Resin bonded	D	120- 60	Close	
For wet operations using water or other liquid suitable for hand- and machine-sanding					
Silicon carbide cabinet-paper	Glue or resin	C	240-100	Close	Metals, primers, cellulose
		D	80- 40	Close	
Dry sanding of all metal and lacquered surfaces					
Aluminous oxide cabinet-paper	Glue or resin	C	240-40	Close	Wood
			240-40	Open	
Preparatory sanding of all types of wood					
Garnet cabinet-paper	Glue or resin	C	240-100	Close	Wood
			150-100	Open	
		D	80-36	Close or open	
Preparatory sanding of all types of wood					
Flint-paper	Glue	C	220-40	Close	Wood, paint
General woodworking					
Glasspaper	Glue	C	00-3	Close	Wood, paint
General use including cleaning down old paint-work, etc.					
Silicon carbide finishing-paper	Glue or resin	A	500-60	Open	Polyester lacquers, metals, cellulose
Dry removal of imperfections in polyester and cellulose by hand or orbital sanders					

Bond	Paper weight	Grit	Coat	Materials
Aluminous oxide finishing-paper Glue or resin	A	400-60	Open	Wood
All finishing operations in hard- and softwoods and flattening cellulose with white spirit/wood alcohol				
Garnet finishing-paper Glue or resin	A	320-60	Open	Wood
Finishing of softwoods, etc.				

MISCELLANEOUS ABRASIVE MATERIALS

Wet and dry papers

These are waterproof silicon carbide papers glued with synthetic resin adhesives on a rubberized or treated backing paper. The finer grits can be used dry for flattening polyester, cellulose and catalyst finishes, but it is more usual to employ a lubricant, water and a little household soap for a fast cut, or white spirit/wood alcohol alone for a smoother, finer cut. The papers should be kept well soaked, and the sludge wiped clean ahead of the block.

Cutting-down pastes/rubbing compounds, burnishing creams, etc.

Loose carborundum powder should not be used for cutting down lacquered surfaces, as the cutting action will not be evenly distributed and deep scratching may result. Valve-grinding pastes are also unsuitable, and only proprietary cutting-down pastes specially compounded for the work should be used. If too stiff they can be thinned with water or white spirit/wood alcohol according to the makers' instructions. Most car polishes are mildly abrasive, as are liquid metal polishes, and could be used for burnishing to a high gloss. These materials should, however, be used with care since they often contain additives such as silicone oil which will cause discoloration of the surface, called 'blooming', after a few months. For this reason products formulated for use on furniture are preferred. Do not use burnishing creams or paste on any surface which has traces of open grain, since these materials will leave white deposits in the crevices which are very hard to remove. A satin matt finish on full-gloss lacquered surfaces can be obtained with either water-floated pumice powder or Silex powder, and the process is described in Chapter 49, Wood Finishing. Highly polished surfaces can be effectively dulled with No. 0000 steel wool; use wax polish as a lubricant where required. The coarser grades of steel wool are invaluable for cleaning off old polish in conjunction with a suitable stripping compound. Nylon fleece in various grades is also used for this type of work. Steel wool can be used for cleaning and dulling metals, especially chromium plate, stainless steel, aluminium, and brass. This should be carried out carefully, using strokes as in brush painting.

Recent developments include abrasive wheels made from strips or flaps of grit-coated cloth or paper. These are attached to power drills or flexible drives and may be used for rapid sanding of complex shapes. A similar idea uses rotating nylon brushes with grit-coated bristles. Stainless-steel wool is a new material which, although expensive, is a tougher, rust-free alternative to conventional steel fleece.

Part II Tools and Equipment
8 Cabinet maker's bench and accessories

CABINET MAKER'S BENCH

Good benches are indispensable for handwork; a softwood bench put together quickly from small section wood is not suitable. Cabinet-benches should be of hardwood, preferably beech, sturdy and perfectly level, because the eye will always attempt to compensate for any slope, and thus vertical cuts are likely to be out of square if the bench-top is sloping. A quick-action woodworker's vice/vise should be fitted and an end vice also. Figure 37 gives the constructional details of a standard bench with 2½ in (63.5 mm) beech top and underframing, which should not be less than 6 ft (1.828 m) long.

Instead of buying a bench, many may prefer to make their own, and all the necessary metal fittings are obtainable from specialist tool firms.

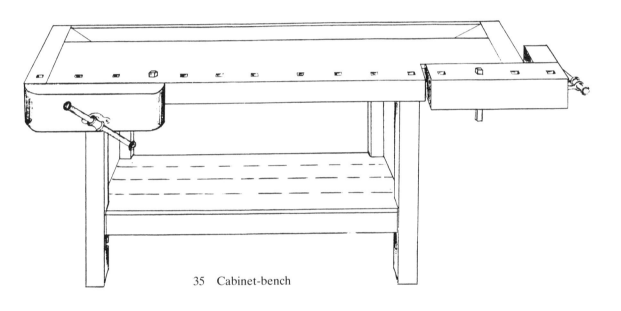

35   Cabinet-bench

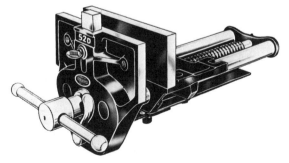

36   Woodworker's vice with end dog. (By courtesy of Record Ridgway Tools Ltd)

WOODWORKING VICES/VISES

The standard 9 in (228 mm) quick-release woodworking vice with American pattern front dog on the outer jaw is illustrated in Figure 36. The front dog is used for holding work against a batten fixed to the bench-top.

HOLDING DEVICES

Various devices are used to hold the wood or support the tool, and the test of a good craftsman is his ability to improvise. Figure 38:1

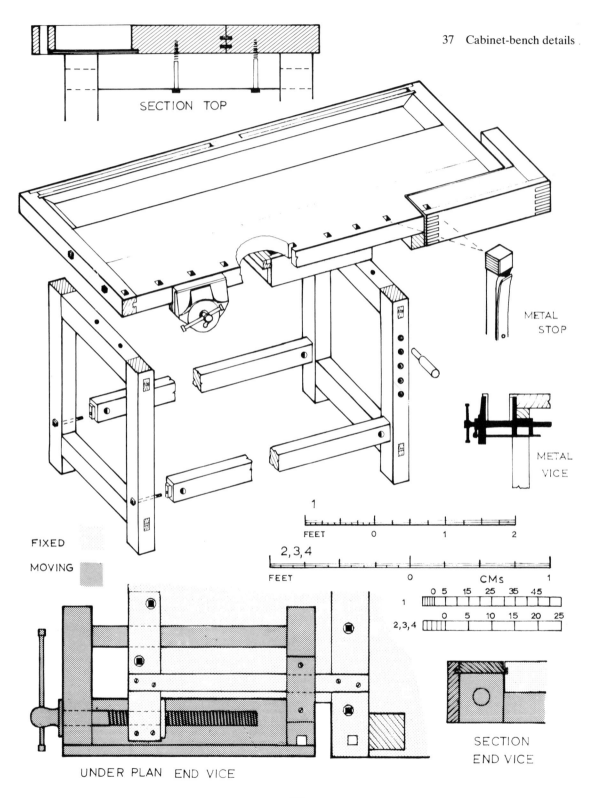

SECTION TOP

METAL
STOP

METAL
VICE

FIXED

MOVING

1

FEET 0 1 2

2, 3, 4

FEET 0 CMs 1

0 5 15 25 35 45

1

0 5 10 15 20 25

2, 3, 4

UNDER PLAN END VICE

SECTION
END VICE

88

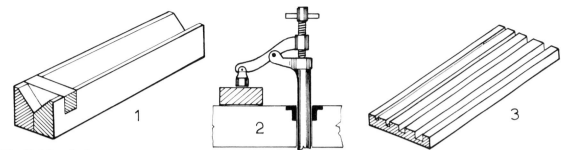

1

2

3

38   Holding devices

shows the *rounding-cradle* for supporting square-sectioned material while it is being rounded; and 38:3 a planing-board with different-size grooves for holding thin stock, etc. Figure 38:2 shows the *bench-holdfast*, which is merely inserted in a hole bored in the bench-top and will remain in any position once the screw-pad is tightened on the work, while long edges which have to be worked with a rabbet- or moulding-plane can be lifted clear of the bench by gripping them in a bar clamp G-cramped/C-clamped to the bench-top. If there is no end vice/vise to the bench there can be no possible objection to nailing battens to the bench to grip long lengths, wide panels, etc., while they are being planed, provided that only lath-nails are used, and that they are carefully withdrawn immediately after. The over-fastidious craftsman might object to this, but the important thing is the piece of work on the bench, not the bench itself.

SAWING AND PLANING APPLIANCES

Reversible *bench-hooks* are used to support small pieces while being sawn or cut, at the same time protecting the bench-top from incidental damage. They can be either bought or simply made out of hardwood about 10 in (254 mm) by 6 in (152 mm) by 1 in (25 mm) with 1¼ in (32 mm) square cleats screwed on both ends as shown (the position can be reversed for left-handed workers). Straight *shooting-boards* for the accurate squaring of ends can also be purchased or again made by the worker, preferably out of good dry beech. The bed can be in two pieces with grain direction reversed, screwed together to form a rebated bed while the headpiece should be taper housed and screwed but not glued. A shallow groove is usually provided between the two beds

ostensibly for loose dust, etc., and the headpiece or stop can be extended out, as shown by the dotted lines, to support wide boards. In making up these pieces great care should be taken to ensure that they are truly square in every detail, otherwise the whole object is defeated. An average size for normal work, i.e. squaring ends and shooting the edges of small pieces of wood with the hand plane, would be 2 ft (609 mm) long, 9 in (228 mm) wide overall of which about 3 in (76 mm) is reserved for the side of the plane, with the stop out of 1¼ in (32 mm) square timber. Larger boards up to 4 ft (1.21 m) long are also useful for trimming veneers, etc., and can be simply made from two pieces of wood, with the top board kept back to provide a shoulder for the stop to butt against, and the whole screwed together so that it can be knocked apart and lined up afresh whenever necessary, for all boards do require periodic checking.

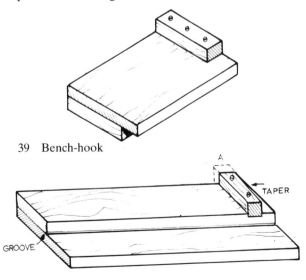

39   Bench-hook

GROOVE

A

TAPER

40   Shooting-board

9 Hand tools

The basic tools of woodwork and the elementary processes of sawing, chiselling and smoothing wood are widely known, and detailed repetition is hardly necessary. What is of concern here is the specialized application of these basic techniques to the fabrication of project components, usually of small dimension, which will eventually become pieces of furniture. Therefore, although the tools employed and the methods of manipulating them are in principle the same as for any woodworking trade, the furniture-maker must always endeavour to work to precision limits. So although he may use the same kind of saw, chisel, plane, etc. as any other woodworker, the saw will tend to have finer teeth, the chisel will be of the lighter, bevelled edged variety, the smoothing-plane will be the standard tool but it will be keener and more finely set. In the main, therefore, his tools will be orthodox but more numerous; they must be the very best of their respective kinds and he must be scrupulous in maintaining them.

MARKING, MEASURING AND TESTING TOOLS

Traditionally the furniture-maker has relied upon the standard 2 ft (609 mm) fourfold rule, the joiner on the 3 ft (914 mm) pattern, both

42 Measuring with rule

marked in eighths and sixteenths of an inch, and obtainable as standard or blindman's, the latter with extra bold figurings. For long lengths the standard boxwood rule or the engineer's long one-piece rule are preferable to flexible steel tapes which should not be used for highly critical work on the bench. Finely divided semi-flexible engineers' steel rules are very useful, also the stout square-end type not finely divided which can be used as either rule or short straight-edge, for if the edge of the rule is rubbed over the wood it will immediately highlight ridges and raised spots which are not discernible to the naked eye with a black metal shine. A useful accessory is the Stanley combination try-mitre-square and depth-gauge incorporating a sliding-rule (Figure 43:1), while the vernier caliper gauge (43:2) is invaluable for measuring exact thicknesses. These can be obtained as engineer's precision pattern, or as a more robust pattern specially designed for

41 Collection of tools

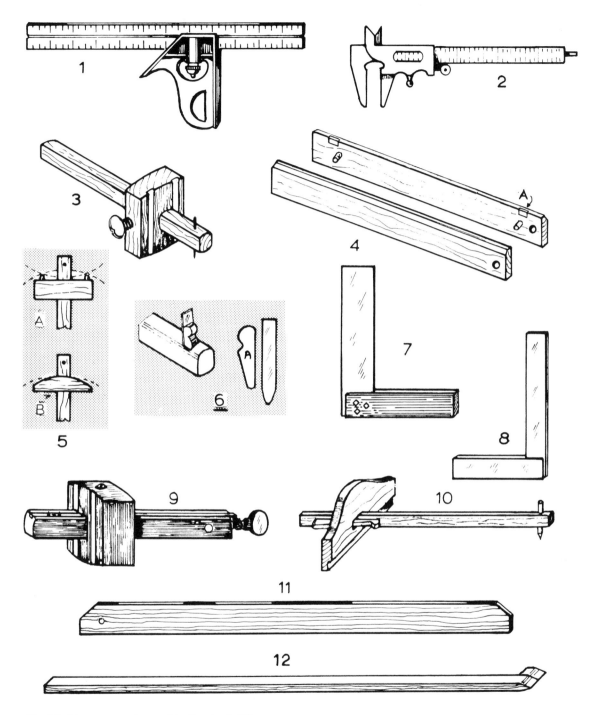

43   Marking, measuring and testing tools (1)

woodworking. All rules should be used with the markings actually touching the work (Figure 42).

Straight-edges are essential in any workshop and should be plentiful (43:11); they are usually made out of ½ in (12.5 mm) by 2½ in

(63.5 mm) mild Honduras mahogany, pine or redwood, waxed or varnished, and in a range of lengths up to 6 ft (1524 mm); while at least one metal straight-edge 4 ft (1.21 m) long or more should be provided for cutting veneers, etc.

Also necessary are *winding-sticks* (43:4) in matched pairs, usually about 2 ft (609 mm) long by 2 in (50 mm) wide by ½ in (12.5 mm) thick of good mahogany or similar wood planed truly parallel, the edges bevelled as shown and small sighting insets of white wood (43:4A) inlaid into the rear stick. Stub dowels and sockets are also provided so that the sticks can be kept together and hung from a nail, as any deviation from the straight, or uneven shrinkage across the width of either, will result in false readings. If these sticks are placed at either end of a planed-up board and sighted through from a few feet away the white wood insets will immediately confirm any slight tilt, disclosing that the board is twisted, i.e. both edges may be straight but the diagonal is curved, giving a twist or wind to the wood. *Squaring-rods* (43:12) of about 1 in (25 mm) by ⁵/₁₆ in (8 mm) straight-grained wood in various lengths and blocked and pointed at one end are used for checking the squareness of carcass openings, etc., *for it is never safe to rely upon the try-square alone over a large area* (see Carcass construction, Chapter 21).

Note: Introduction of the metric system will eventually necessitate changing the sizes of all standard tools now conforming to inch measurements. As this is likely to be a lengthy process, and as the conventional sizes to be adopted have not yet been established, all the tools mentioned in this and subsequent chapters are inch patterns with the approximate metric equivalents given in parentheses.

Gauges

Beech *marking-gauges* (43:3) are cheap enough and several should be provided, thus saving time in multiple layout work. The brass-plated variety offer no real advantage, but boxwood thumbscrews are preferable if they can be obtained as the plastic screws tend to snap off if dropped. In circular work the flat-faced gauge will give a false reading, and stubs of dowel-rod rounded over (43:5A) to give a two-point bearing are necessary, while for concave edges

one face of the gauge can be rounded (43:5B), and for pencil-use a hole can be bored in the end of the stem. Marking-gauges are primarily intended for scoring with or on the end grain; if used across the grain they will either scratch or tear unless the pins are needle sharp, and a *cutting-gauge* (43:6) is more suitable. This has a small knife in lieu of a steel pin, secured by a brass wedge shown alongside (43:6A); the knife is pointed and bevelled on one side and used with the bevel facing the fence, pulling the fence tight against the work and preventing any tendency for the knife to ride with the grain. *Mortise-gauges* (43:9) are in effect double marking-gauges with two pins, one of which is adjusted for distance by a threaded rod passing through the stem. These gauges are usually made of rosewood which is a somewhat unnecessary refinement, for the brass movement is rarely good enough to last a lifetime, and the points of the pins wear out.

All these gauges are held in one hand tightly against the edge of the wood, the fence inclined away from the body and pushed forwards so that the pin is always trailing; the movement can then be reversed to impart a rocking movement to the gauge. (It is for the individual worker to find his own particular method of handling as with all other types of hand-tools.)

The long *panel-gauge* (43:10) is used for pencil gauging panels to width; a wooden wedge secures the fence which is rebated so that it does not tip under its own weight. The stick should not be less than about 20 in (508 mm) long to take in the extreme width of an average-size carcass. Figure 44:7 illustrates the T-gauge or *grasshopper-gauge* with extra long fence for riding over projecting mouldings as shown.

Squares, bevels, etc.

Joiners' try-squares can be either all-metal, metal blade secured in a rosewood stock (43:7) or L-shaped metal blade running through the stock; it hardly matters which so long as the square is accurate and sturdy enough to stand inadvertent dropping. It is useful to have three sizes, say 4 in (101 mm), 8 in (203 mm) and 12 in (304 mm); while for highly critical work a 6 in (152 mm) precision-ground engineer's square (43:8) costs very little more than the equivalent joiner's square. A useful accessory is the *bright Mason's square* or *carpenter's standard square* with legs 24 in (609 mm) and 18 in (457 mm) long for squaring greater widths, while some craftsmen make up their own large try-square (44:8) with 11 in (279 mm) by 2½ in (63 mm) by ¾ in (19 mm) stock and 20 in (508 mm) by 3 in (76 mm) by ¼ in (6 mm) blade out of good mahogany, rosewood or ebony. A small inset stop (44:8A) is provided to support the heavy stock on the work. For setting out angles, dovetails, etc. the *joiner's adjustable level/ T-bevel* is used. The slotted screw adjustment shown in 44:1 is preferable to the brass lever

locking-nut, which often has a multi-start thread and if displaced and threaded in the wrong position will foul the work. Figure 44:4 shows a wooden template for marking out dovetails, cut out of a hardwood block about 2½ in (63 mm) by 2 in (50 mm) by 1¾ in (44 mm) overall thickness, with the sides planed to the required angle, in this case 1 in 6 (see Dovetailing, Chapter 19). Other tools in this general section include *marking-knives* with hardwood handles (44:2A), and *striking-knives* with awl ends (44:2B) for scribing. If the knife has a single cutting bevel only it can be used as an accurate trimming-knife. The *Stanley*

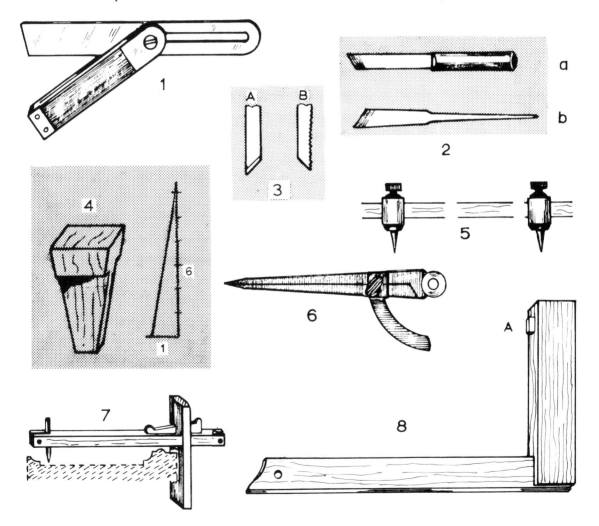

44   Marking, measuring and testing tools (2)

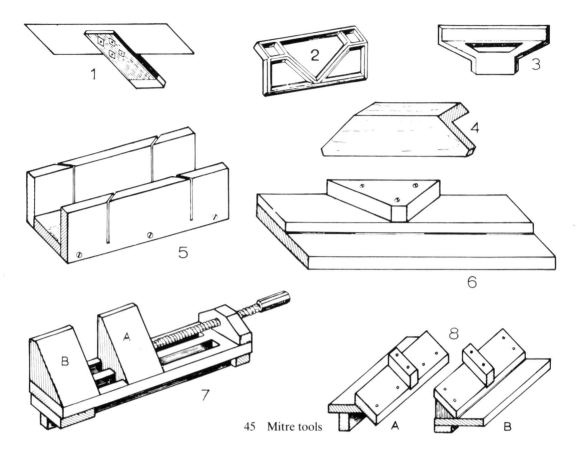

45   Mitre tools

trimming-knife is a useful all-purpose knife with a wide range of blades, including a scoring-knife for the clean cutting of decorative laminated plastics (formica, etc.). Good knives can also be made from old hacksaw blades with the teeth ground off, as shown in 44:3A, and also an excellent dovetail-marker (44:3B) which is more positive than the tip of the dovetail-saw customarily used. The *carpenter's wing-compass* with locking-screw is shown in 44:6, as ordinary compasses and dividers tend to catch in the grain and disturb the setting; while instead of the draughtsman's beam-compass, *trammel-points* (44:5) are used which slide along a suitable wooden beam. One head has a steel point and the other a socket for a pencil end.

MITRE TOOLS

Figure 45:1 shows the fixed *mitre-square* for laying out true mitres, 45:2 the combined *square* and *mitre-template*, 45:3 a brass *mitre-template* for stuck mouldings, and 45:4 a wooden version cut out of a 5 in (127 mm) by 1½ in (38 mm) square block of close-grained hardwood. Uses for these tools are described under the appropriate chapters on framed and mitred work, etc. A *mitre sawing-box* is shown in 45:5 which requires no description; it can be bought or very simply made. For the most accurate sawing of squares and mitres a *mitre-saw* is recommended which can be set at any angle by a quick-release finger-grip. Figure 45:4 illustrates the *mitre-trimmer*, extensively used by picture-framers but an invaluable tool in any workshop. Figure 45:6 shows a *mitre shooting-board* for flat material, approximately the same size as the straight shooting-board, for use where the mitre cut is across the width as in picture-frames, flat mouldings, etc. This board cannot be used for mitres in the thickness, and 45:7 shows the *mitre shooting-block* with wood or metal screw which will accommodate small box sides, plinth and heavy cornice mouldings,

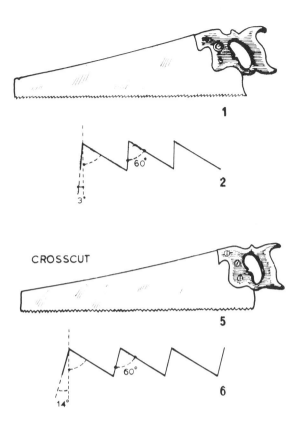

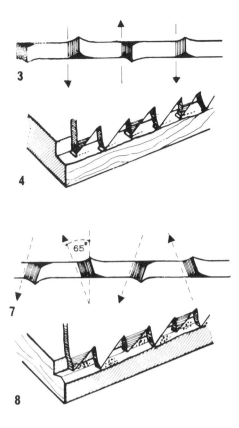

46   Handsaws: rip and crosscut

etc. The screw actuates a sliding chop or jaw (45:7A), with a fixed jaw (45:7B). The sliding jaw is retained in position by a crosspiece screwed to the prongs of the jaw under the frame, and tight enough to ensure an easy but positive slide. Both jaws should be either heavily waxed or covered with a renewable surface material, stiff cardboard, etc., to take the wear of the plane-iron, and if the back faces of the jaws are truly square the block can be used for squaring ends. The traditional *donkey's-ear shooting-board* for mitring in the thickness is illustrated in 45:8A, and an alternative form in 45:8B.

SAWS AND SAWING

A standard kit for hand work would automatically include *rip-, crosscut-* and *panel-* (small crosscut-) *saws, tenon-* and *dovetail-saws*, with *bow-, scroll-* and *pad-saws*, etc. for circular cutting. Where machinery is available

the rip and big crosscut might not appear necessary, but there will always be the occasion when it is easier to take the saw to the wood rather than the wood to the machine; therefore to some extent they are indispensable. While the rip-saw (46:1) has upright teeth (46:2) filed square to the blade (46:3)—the arrows give the filing direction—and cuts with a chisel action (46:4), all other saws are of the crosscut type (46:5) for cutting across the grain, the teeth are raked (46:6) and with the exception of the fine dovetail-saw are filed to a bevel of about 65° (46:7) so that the set of the teeth scores two parallel lines across the wood and the waste or 'kerf' between crumbles away in dust (46:8). The 'set' or alternative bending outwards of each tooth which practically every saw must have if it is to clear itself must never be more than is required to give fractional clearance to the blade as it passes through the wood, while in the case of the larger saws (rip-, large crosscut- and panel-saw) the blade itself should have the full thickness along the teeth but the back

95

should be taper ground, i.e. 'swaged', about four gauges thinner from handle to point for heavy saws, and correspondingly less for lighter saws. The blade also should be tensioned by hammering the centre of the blade to expand it, and the test of a handsaw of good-quality tempered steel and correctly tensioned by the maker is that it should neither sag nor exhibit any tendency to floppiness when held by the handle in a horizontal position. The teeth also should be of even height and shape, filed to the correct bevel, with each individual tooth set to about half its depth only, so that the kerf made in the wood is never more than about 1½ times the thickness of the blade.

A convenient size for rip- and big crosscut-saws for cabinet-work is 26 in (660 mm) long not including handle, with 4½ points (teeth) to the inch (25 mm) for the former and 7 or 8 points for the latter. The smaller crosscut- or panel-saw, one of the most useful of saws if in good condition, should be about 22 in (558 mm) long with 10 points to the inch (25 mm). Tenon-saws (47:1) and dovetail-saws (47:2), which are not taper ground, have their blades stiffened with a rib or back of steel or brass (apart from appearance it hardly matters which), and convenient sizes would be 12 in (304 mm) long with 12 to 14 points for the tenon, and 8 in (203 mm) long with 18 to 22 points (the finer the better) for the dovetail. Both these saws have a more pronounced rake to their teeth (47:4), but the dovetail teeth are so fine it is difficult to file a correct bevel, and the teeth are usually left square across their faces as in the rip. An open or pistol-grip handle is preferable for the dovetail if it can be obtained (47:2) but most manufacturers seem to regard it as just another tenon-saw, which of course it is and is not. It cuts so finely there is always the temptation to use it indiscriminately, but it should be kept exclusively for dovetails and fine mitres. An even finer saw is the *bead-saw*, sometimes known as the 'joiner's fancy' or 'gent's' saw, with bradawl-type handle (47:3), a blade from 4 in (101 mm) to 8 in (203 mm) long and with 32 points to the inch (25 mm). As it is a little difficult to file the teeth evenly it is sometimes discarded when too blunt to cut, for it is relatively inexpensive.

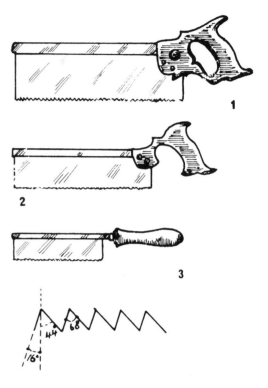

47   Handsaws: tenon and dovetail

Sharpening saws

Skilled craftsmen sharpen their own saws, using a pistol-grip saw set to bend the points, and a suitable three-cornered tapered saw-file which is gripped with both hands. For the rip-saw the file is held level as a chisel edge is necessary to the points; but for crosscut-saws the near or back hand should bear slightly downwards to form a point to the teeth. In all cases alternate teeth are filed from one side, the saw reversed and the remaining teeth filed, making sure that the 'gullet' or space between each tooth is kept constant and only sufficient metal is taken off to destroy the 'shine' which is the evidence of a blunt tooth. If the worker does not feel confident of setting and filing his saws correctly—and fair practice is needed—then they should be sent to a 'saw-doctor'.

Saw-chops/clamps

Saw-chops composed of two wood jaws held by a bolt and wing-nut and gripped in a bench-vice

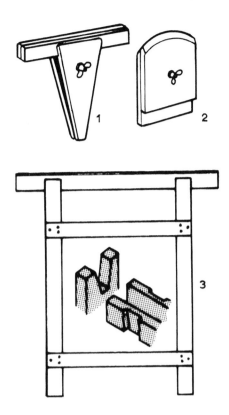

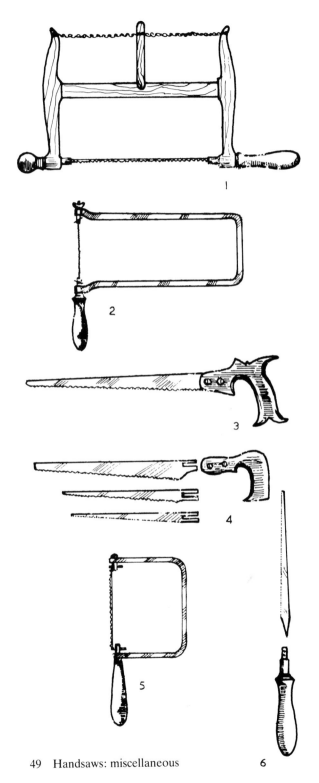

48 Saw-chops/clamps

are used for holding saws during sharpening.
Figure 48:1 shows saw-chops for handsaws and
(48:2) for circular saws. Figure 48:3 shows a
more convenient type for handsaws of all sizes,
requiring no bolt. The stand is made up of two
pieces of 2 in (50 mm) by 4 in (100 mm) deal,
3 ft 7in high (1092 mm), with 1 in (25 mm) by
2 in (50 mm) deal cross-braces 18 in (457 mm)
long nailed across either side. Taper notches are
cut in the uprights and the loose chops are also
taper housed to hold them in position and to
grip the saw firmly as they are tapped down. All
three types are usually made by the craftsman
himself.

Contour cutting

A flexible blade is necessary for contour
cutting, and for fairly wide curves the clumsy
but efficient wooden *bow-* or *turning-saw*
(Figure 49:1) is suitable. The detachable blade
is tensioned by a length of twisted blind-cord or
a wire stretcher. For smaller curves the 6 in

49 Handsaws: miscellaneous

(152 mm) metal frame *scroll-* or *coping-saw* (49:5) is useful, and both bow- and scroll-saw can be used for interior openings as the handles fully rotate, thus the blades can be detached, threaded through a pre-bored hole with the teeth pointing away from the handle, and turned to the correct angle for the cut. For openings further in than the throat of the saw will allow other means must be adopted, either by drilling a series of holes and chopping out with chisel and gouge, or if the curve is fairly easy cutting with a 12 in (304 mm) *keyhole-* or *pad-saw* (49:6) which is in effect a very narrow cross-cut-blade held by retaining screws in a slotted bradawl-type handle. Large varieties are the *compass-saw* with fixed handsaw-type open handle (49:3) or a nest of saws, *table, compass* and *keyhole*, with detachable handle (49:4). For very fine cutting in thin material the *hobbyist's fret-saw/jig-saw* (49:2) with a throat of 20 in (508 mm) and a range of wood- and metal-piercing saws is invaluable. It can be used to cut with a forward movement with the teeth pointing upwards as with the bow-saw, or downwards against a cutting-table with the teeth pointing towards the handle.

Controlling the saw

Rip- and crosscut-saws should be gripped as shown in Figure 50, with the angle of cut low to start with and raising the saw to about 45° as the cut proceeds. At the commencement of the cut the 'heel' or handle end of the saw should be placed square to the wood, and with the thumb of the left hand resting lightly against the blade to steady it. After the cut has been established with one or more upward strokes the thumb should be withdrawn and the full downward strokes commenced with moderate pressure only until the back edge of the plank has been reached; the left hand should then be brought over the front of the saw to grip the unsupported

50   Holding saw

wood which will otherwise splinter off. Some professional workers end with one powerful downward stroke which severs the remaining fibres without splintering, but it must complete the cut in one sweep and requires a little judgement. Tenon- and dovetail-saws are similarly held, with the left thumb supporting the blade on the marked line and in a truly upright position, but if the dovetail-saw has an open handle then the forefinger can lie along the top of the saw, enabling it to be pointed very accurately, pistol fashion. Some workers knock the set off the fine dovetail-saw by running a file lightly along the side of the teeth, which gives a finer cut, but the teeth must be in good condition.

Care of saws

Saws should never be allowed to rust, for microscopic pitting of the steel will prevent the formation of really sharp edges on the teeth. They should be lightly oiled from time to time, particularly the bow- and compass-saws, etc. which are not often used. The best lubricant for use during sawing is a few strokes of a candle end along the blade. If the rip- and crosscut-saws are buckled they can only be restored by a skilled saw-doctor, but slight buckling of a backed tenon- or dovetail-saw can sometimes be overcome by gently tapping the back down first at one end and then the other, thus driving the blade further into the back.

PLANES

One of the most useful of all planes is the 22 in (558 mm) *try-plane/jointer* No. 07 with 2⅜ in (60 mm) cutter. Shorter planes in this category are known as '*fore*' for general levelling, and longer planes '*jointers*' for shooting square edges, etc., but the middle size will do everything necessary. *Jack-planes* can either be 14 in (355 mm) or 15 in (380 mm) long with 2 in (50 mm) or 2⅜ in (60 mm) cutter (Nos. 05 or 05½). The name itself is probably a corruption of 'jackass' or 'Jack of all Trades' and fit for anything; it is, therefore, reserved for the rougher work although it is as much a precision tool as any other. It is often recommended that the jack-plane iron should be ground to a slight

51 Types of plane. (By courtesy of Record Ridgway Tools Ltd)

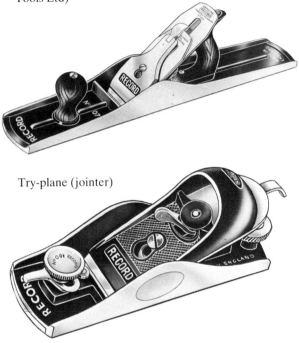

Try-plane (jointer)

Bench rabbet-plane

Block-plane

arc, but while this makes heavy cuts easier it destroys the plane's general usefulness and the cutting edge should be ground truly square, although the corners can be nicked or rounded over if preferred. Smoothing-planes for final surfacing follow the same general pattern and can be either 8 in (203 mm) long with 1¾ in (44 mm) cutter (No. 03), 9 in (228 mm) with 2 in (50 mm) cutter (No. 04) or 10 in (254 mm) with 2⅜ in (60 mm) cutter (No. 04½); the middle size is probably the most useful. Detachable cutting edges for the irons have lately been reintroduced after many years, but it is doubtful if they offer any real advantage. All the sizes and numbers quoted above refer to metal planes throughout, with screw-adjustable cutter, lateral lever-actuated depth movement for the cutter and adjustable mouth (the latter movement is rarely used as much as it should be, for a finely set iron and fine mouth are invaluable for surfacing hard or difficult woods). The merit of all these metal planes over their wooden counterparts is their ease of adjustment, but wooden jack- and smoothing-planes are still obtainable and their stouter

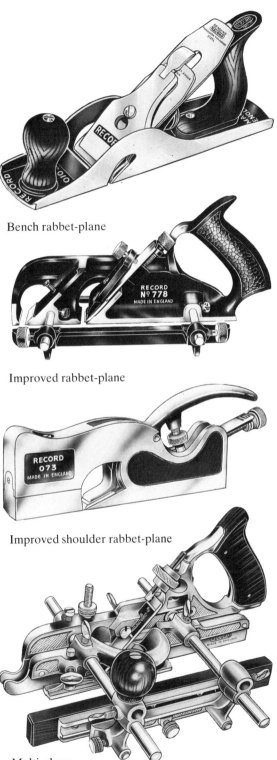

Improved rabbet-plane

Improved shoulder rabbet-plane

Multi-plane

99

cutting irons can be an advantage, as there is probably less friction between wood and wood and metal and wood. Some companies take advantage of this by supplying a pre-fabricated beech plane which embodies the easy adjustments of the metal variety.

Again, metal planes are obtainable with corrugated soles which, it is claimed, cut down friction and tend to hold the lubricant applied to the sole. This lubricant should never be oil or soft grease, but a few strokes of a hard candle end or paste wax along the sole will make an astonishing difference.

A smaller version of the smoothing-plane not available in wooden form which can be held in one hand is the metal *block-plane*, and this 6 in (152 mm) plane is best obtained with an adjustable mouth and cutter. The cheaper versions are not fully adjustable and the cutter position must be set by trial and error. For working large rebates (rabbets) in which a heavy section is to be taken out, a special *bench rabbet-plane* is obtainable, and for general light rabbeting, etc., the *improved rabbet-plane* which, if fitted with sliding fence, depth-stop and spur for scoring across the grain ahead of the cutter to prevent tearing out, becomes the *rebate-* and *fillister-plane*, although the term 'fillister' is tending to die out. (*Rabbet:* probably a carpenter's corruption of rebate [to deduct from, to diminish]. *Fillister* also means a groove or rebate.) Truing up the sides of rebates and cleaning up the shoulders of tenons, etc., can be done with the *shoulder rabbet-plane* with machined parallel sides and through cutter. This plane is worked with both hands, while the smaller, single-handed version known as the *bullnose rabbet-plane* usually has a detachable nose, distance-pieces and variable mouth for fine or coarse work. If the nose is detached it becomes a *chisel-plane*, allowing the cutting-iron to work up to the end of a stopped rebate. Both these planes should have screw adjustment to the cutting-iron which should be ground truly square to the machined body of the plane, as there is no lateral adjustment. For cutting grooves within the body of the work, i.e. away from the edge, either with or across the grain, some form of adjustable grooving-plane is necessary. This should have a sliding fence, depth-stop for determining the finished depth

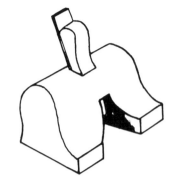

52 'Old Woman's Tooth' router

of the groove, spurs for cross grain and a range of cutters for different widths of groove. In its simplest form it can be purchased as a *plough-plane* with three cutters, as a *standard plough* with eight cutters, and as a *combination-* or *multi-plane* which will undertake rabbeting, ploughing (grooving), tonguing and grooving, beading, etc., and, if fitted with special bases and cutters, rounding and hollowing. The Record *multi-plane*, No. 405, is supplied with 23 standard cutters and a range of special-purpose bases and cutters.

The standard plough or multi-plane is usually supplied with two sets of arms permitting grooves to be worked up to 5 in (127 mm) from the edge of the wood, but for greater distances or where the groove or trench is curved on plan then a *router-plane* is necessary. This has a vertical cranked cutter, rather like a jackboot, which cuts with a chisel action, bevel upper-most, and flat to the wood; the cutter is clamped to a cutter-post and fed down by a knurled screw as the work proceeds until the correct depth is attained. As the square-edged cutter will tend to tear up cross grain a spear-headed smoothing-cutter is provided which cuts with a slicing action.

For the odd occasion a suitable chisel wedged into a block of wood on the principle of the 'Old Woman's Tooth' can be used, but the metal router with its easy adjustability will pay for its keep. Both the multi-plane and hand routers have been superseded in most workshops now by the portable power router.

A useful plane for truing up the shoulders of rebates, grooves, etc., is the metal *side-rebate* or *edge-trimming plane* whose upright sole allows it to be used in narrow spaces. It has two crossed irons allowing right- or left-hand working, detachable nose and reversible depth-stop. Here again the cutting-irons must be very carefully ground at the required angle to give equal projection of the cutting edge.

Planes for curved surfaces

Shaped edges which are convex can be worked with a smoothing- or block-plane provided the curve is not too acute, but for quick curves and concave edges a metal *compass-plane* is obtainable whose flexible spring steel face can be adjusted to any arc. This is an expensive tool proportionate to the amount of use which could be found for it, and given a true eye most curved edges can be worked equally well—but rather more slowly—with *spokeshaves* which have either a flat face for convex work or a round face for concave work. The screw-adjustable type illustrated is easier to handle than the cheaper version in which the cutter is secured with a thumb-screw and which must be set by hand. A *chamfer* version with two adjustable fences set at a true angle of 45° was manufactured until recently and is probably still available. For difficult woods there is much to be said for the wooden spokeshave illustrated in Figure 54A, in which the iron is flat to the wood, cutting bevel uppermost, and the writer has always preferred this type, although it is probably only a matter of individual preference. For rough and rapid shaping the *carpenter's drawknife* (54B) will dispose of a great deal of timber in the shortest possible time, but it must be razor sharp. In the hands of an expert it can be made to work to precision limits. It can be used bevel down for either light cutting or convex shapes, or bevel up for heavy cutting or concave shapes.

In all spokeshaving operations a slight shearing or diagonal direction to the cut will minimize any tendency to clatter or form ridges which may be difficult to eradicate.

Moulding-planes

Some types are still available although they have been almost entirely superseded by the spindle moulder/shaper and high-speed router; moreover the traditional flutes, reeds, ovolo and ogee mouldings are less used in modern work. When such work was done by hand

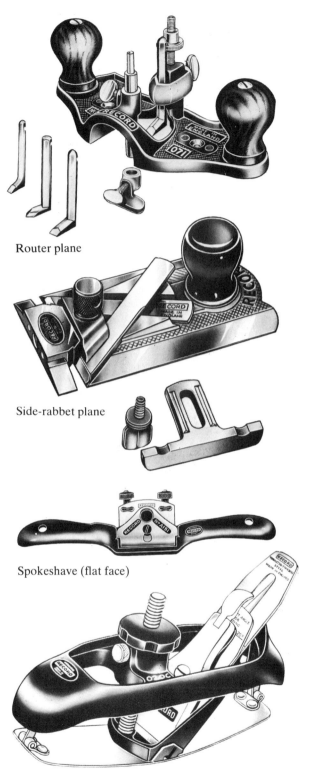

Router plane

Side-rabbet plane

Spokeshave (flat face)

Compass-plane

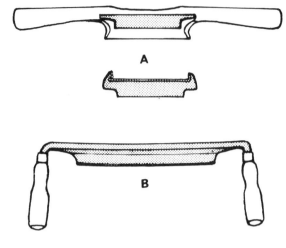

54 Spokeshave and drawknife

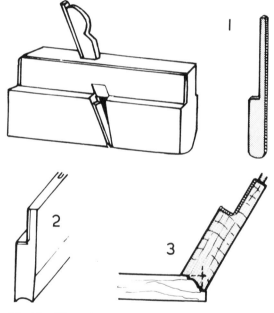

55 Moulding-planes

European pattern worked upright, the English pattern worked at an angle which was always marked on the end of the plane.

These planes are always worth acquiring whenever possible—the writer bought a full half set (18) of rounding-planes and some dozens of moulding-planes for pennies each in a junkshop just before the Second World War—for although the machine might be regarded as indispensable there will always be the time when only an odd length of a particular moulding is required. Given the necessary tool it will be much quicker to work the length by hand rather than spend an hour or more grinding a special cutter and setting up a machine. Figure 436 shows a cocktail cabinet with a fluted drawer front worked entirely with a round moulding-plane.

Scratch stocks

Without a suitable moulding-plane small mouldings were often worked with this simple tool; moreover it is still extremely useful for cutting narrow grooves for inlays, strings, bandings, etc. It is simply made from a solid block (or two pieces of suitable hardwood screwed together) with a saw cut through the arm to take a piece of old saw- or scraper-blade ground and filed to the shape required (56B), and held in the correct position by a pinch-grip with suitably placed screws (56A). The cutter can be filed, square-edged and burred/burled over as for a scraper, in which case the scratch stock is worked backwards and forwards with a rocking movement, or it can be bevel ground and burred over as for a scraper-plane iron.

exclusively it was usual for the cabinet-maker to have a half set of *rounding-planes* (Figure 55:1) for working hollows, etc., and perhaps a few *hollow-planes* for working rounds (55:2) together with several *beading-, ovolo-* and *ogee moulding-planes*, some of which he would make for himself out of short ends of red park beech always set aside for tool-making. A typical ovolo-plane is shown in 55:3 and, while the

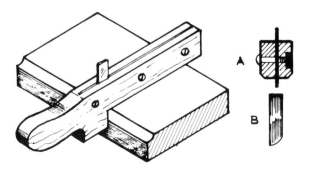

56 Scratch stock

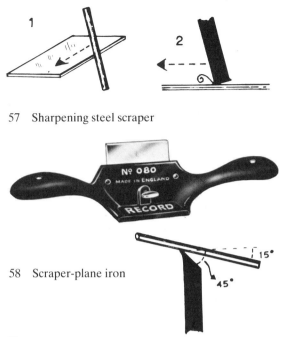

57 Sharpening steel scraper

58 Scraper-plane iron

Scrapers

One of the most useful of hand-tools is the steel *cabinet-scraper*, which is merely a blank of steel about 12 gauge in thickness, 2½ in (63 mm) wide and from 4 in (101 mm) to 6 in (152 mm) long (the 5 in [127 mm] size is most popular). The long edges must be filed flat and truly square with a mill-saw or similar file, the side burrs taken off on the oilstone and the edges honed to a mirror finish. These edges are then burred over with a ticketter (burnisher), which is nothing more than a short length of silver steel suitably hardened, and the scraper is either held upright at the edge of the bench or laid flat. A few heavy strokes of the burnisher (some workers lick the steel to give it an extra bite) at an angle of about 85° should be sufficient to raise an effective cutting burr/burl which can be restored several times without refiling simply by wiping the burr back on the flat faces and then re-forming at a slightly lower angle. The scraper is held in both hands, thumbs in the centre, with sufficient pressure to bed the steel in a slight arc, and pushed forward at an angle of about 120° to the body; the angle can be reversed and drawn towards the body if preferred.

Properly sharpened and held correctly the scraper should be capable of taking long shavings of tissue thinness from even the most difficult of woods, and it is therefore invaluable for the last fine finishing, especially of veneered work. However, in scraping out torn grain or other imperfection on surfaces which will be gloss polished great care must be taken not to localize the strokes, but to spread them over a fairly wide area, otherwise hollows will be created which will eventually show rather like a bumpy road under a car's headlights. A sound rule to follow is one stroke over the bad patch, one ahead, one behind and one each on either side. For scraping difficult surfaces, especially when they are impregnated with resin glue, the floor-finisher's trick of dampening the surface with water can be adopted, while for curved work and simple mouldings the standard scraper-blade can be ground and filed to conform to any sweep.

A good scraper in first-class condition can become hot enough to blister the thumbs and some workers pad the thumb-tips with surgical tape. Others prefer the scraper-plane in which a steel blank is set at an angle of about 10° from the vertical in a suitable handled holder, with the blade bevel-ground like a plane-iron, and the bevel burred over at an angle of about 15° from the grinding bevel. A thumb-screw in the centre bows the iron so that it cuts in the centre as in the hand-scraper, and the plane is pushed away from the body with the cutter leaning forwards.

Miscellaneous planes

Several other types of plane with occasional uses exist, some of which can be purchased, though others will have to be made. Figure 59:1 illustrates the *cooper's stoup-plane* with sole rounded in both length and width, and with the iron curved as shown; it is useful for dishing fairly large surfaces such as stool seats, etc. It can be converted from a standard wooden *smooth-* or *coffin-plane*. Another good tool is the *Jarvis spokeshave-plane* (59:2) used by wheelwrights for rounding spokes, with metal spokeshave-type flat iron ground to a hollow, and knock-in wooden wedge. Figure 59:3 shows the wooden *scrub-, rougher-* or *Bismark*-plane which is still manufactured, and is invaluable for knocking off the rough preparatory to either hand- or machine-surfacing. Also available is

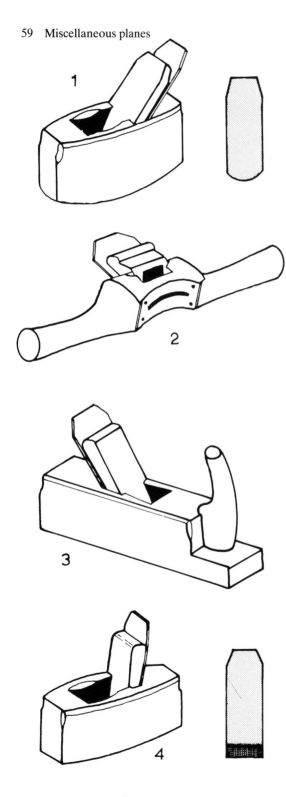

the traditional wooden *skew rebate-plane* with single iron set at an angle to give a shearing cut. Figure 59:4 shows the standard *toothing-plane* (see Veneering, etc. Chapter 32) in which a series of corrugations in the iron scores the surface of the wood. It is used for keying the groundwork preparatory to veneering with hide glue, and for levelling bumpy veneers, etc. Mention must also be made of the incomparable *Norris planes, smooth-, jack-* and *low-angled mitre-* or *piano-finishers' plane.* They are no longer manufactured, but second-hand planes in good condition command high prices and the writer counts them among his most prized possessions, not for any sentimental reason but because they happen to do their job extremely well. For the final surfacing of really difficult woods—ebony, East Indian satinwood, etc.— they are excellent, and no doubt the secret lies in the extra stout iron of first-class steel and the heavy and sturdy body which always seems to hug the wood. Before quantity production became the rule and not the exception the old craftsmen always treasured their extra long and heavy wood *jointing-planes,* and several of the smaller bench-planes they made for themselves from rough gunmetal castings; nor is there any reason why the enthusiast with some slight engineering skill should not do the same. Single and double plane-irons in all sizes are still freely available and can be ground to fit. Beech and rosewood are excellent for plane-making; the wood should not be oiled, as is sometimes advocated, but coated with shellac varnish to seal the pores.

Cutting angles

All bench-planes for general levelling, i.e. jointer-, try-, fore-, jack- and smooth-planes, have double irons (Figure 60:1) composed of the cutting iron proper and the cap-iron whose function it is to stiffen the cutting edge and break up the shaving as it is raised so that, robbed of its stiffness, it does not tend to run ahead of the cut in a series of small splits in the surface of the wood. The closer this cap-iron is to the cutting edge the sooner the shaving is bent over and broken, and therefore fine cuts or difficult timbers require a close-set cap-iron and a narrow mouth which, in the case of metal

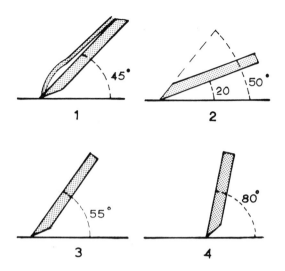

60   Cutting angles: planes

irons. Figure 60 illustrates the various pitches: 60:1 for bench-planes fitted with cap-irons whose function it is to support the cutting edge and break up the chip as it rises; 60:2 shoulder rabbet- and block-planes with bevel uppermost; 60:3 moulding-planes and 60:4 the toothing-plane. All these pitches are empirical, i.e. the result of long experience and not scientific enquiry. Whereas a good deal of research has been done into cutting angles for machine-cutters, it is a little surprising that manu-facturers of hand-tools have not experimented with variable pitch planes, in which the cutting angle can be altered for difficult woods, inter-locked grain, etc.

OTHER EDGE TOOLS

Chisels

It is hardly necessary to have complete sets of mortise-, firmer- and bevelled edged chisels for furniture-making, as the bevelled-edged will do everything necessary. Nor are complete sets of any one type essential, for there will always be three or four favourites to which the hand auto-matically turns. A first selection could be ⅛ in (3 mm), ¼ in (6 mm), ⅜ in (9 mm), ½ in (12.5 mm) and ¾ in (19 mm) *bevelled edge* (61:1A) with the addition of a ¹⁄₁₆ in (1.5 mm) *firmer* type (61:1B) and perhaps a ½ in (12.5 mm) *mortise-chisel* (61:1C), with the later addition of a long *paring-chisel* (61:4B), and a *butt-* or *sash-pocket* chisel (61:4C) for fitting work away from the workshop.

Various types of chisel handles are shown in 61:3. Figure 61:3A shows the universally popular *box* or *ash* carving handle; 61:3B the traditional round *ash*; 61:3C the oval splitproof plastic handle, either in polypropylene or the transparent cellulose acetate butyrate which is tougher but more expensive, and 61:3D the typical steel-hooped mortise handle. It is, of course, false economy to buy cheap sets of chisels, for the keenness of the edge depends entirely on the grade of steel, which varies from maker to maker, and a really good chisel should last a lifetime. A recent development is the introduction of high-speed tipped firmer and

bench-planes, is easily adjustable. Practical experience will give the best setting of the cap-iron, which may vary from a hair's breadth for the final surfacing of difficult timbers to ¹⁄₁₆ in (1.5 mm) for the first rough levelling. This use of the cap-iron means that the grinding bevel of the cutting iron must be underneath, therefore the cutting angle is dependent on the pitch or angle of the iron in the plane, irrespective of the grinding angle. Usually a compromise angle of 45° is used for bench-planes, for raising the angle gives more of a scraping action and lowering it more of a slicing cut.

In the case of metal shoulder rabbet- and block-planes which are only used for trimming and final levelling, often on end grain, the mouth must be kept as small as possible and the iron supported right up to the cutting edge to prevent clattering. As there is no room for a cap-iron the iron is reversed bevel uppermost, which in turn raises the cutting angle, therefore the pitch is lowered, giving an effective angle of about 50° which is about right for a scraping cut on end grain. Moulding-planes also cannot be fitted with a cap-iron even though the bevel is underneath, and to prevent any tearing out of the grain the angle is raised to about 55°. Toothing-planes which merely score the surface of the wood are set at an angle a little short of upright. The remarks regarding the advisability of preserving one long bevel to cutting edges advocated for chisels equally apply to plane-

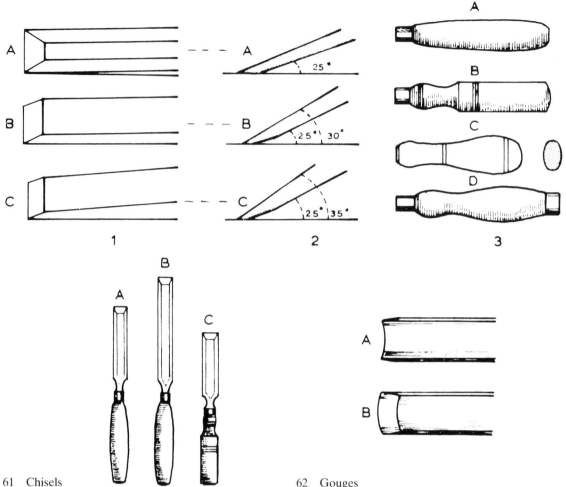

61 Chisels

62 Gouges

bevelled edge chisels manufactured by Ward and Payne Ltd of Sheffield, which the writer has tried and found excellent. They are considerably more expensive, but are capable of a fine and long-lasting edge which can be ground on the high-speed grinder without drawing the temper.

Grinding and honing angles

Most manufacturers grind to a bevel of about $22\frac{1}{2}°$ to $25°$ and advocate a secondary honing or sharpening bevel of about $30°$; but this is more applicable to stout joiners' tools, and one long bevel (61:2A) is preferable for bevelled edge chisels with about $30°$ for firmer-chisels and $35°$ for heavy mortising chisels. The long continuous bevel may be more troublesome to preserve

in honing and the actual cutting edge may not last as long as a stout secondary bevel—and in fact will tend to crumble if used for heavy chopping—but it will always be sharper and will cut more sweetly, moreover the bevel will rarely want regrinding.

Gouges

Two types are used, *firmer pattern* (62A) with cutting bevel ground on the outside of the curve and yielding a sloping cut, as the bevel tends to drive the tool out of the wood; and *scribing pattern* (62B) with inside ground bevel for upright cuts. The old-type scribing-gouge had a slightly different shoulder shape, but both firmer- and scribing-gouges are now forged to the same pattern; while it is now usual to class

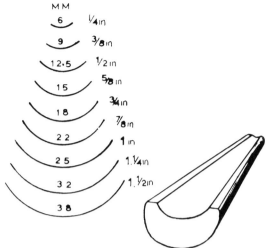

MM
6   1/4 in
9   3/8 in
12.5   1/2 in
15   5/8 in
18   3/4 in
22   7/8 in
25   1 in
32   1.1/4 in
38   1.1/2 in

63   Graduated gouge-stone

them as 'outcannelled' (outside ground) for firmers, and 'incannelled' (inside ground) for scribers, the old names will, however, probably persist.

The various curves or sweeps have also been standardized and the normal gouges are now made to one work circle only. The illustration above shows the widths available. Additional curves are only possible in the long outcannelled paring-gouges used by pattern-makers, and in the standard carving-gouges which are still made in great variety.

Sharpening

For small cutting-tools, gouges, moulding-plane irons, etc., round-edge slip-stones tapering in their thickness are used, and also a graduated gouge-stone which will fit an endless variety of sweeps. All abrasive stones must be lubricated to prevent over-heating of the steel, and to float away the accumulated sludge, but on no account should linseed or any other drying oil be used, as they will rapidly oxidize and gum up the stone. Any light machine-oil will serve, or a mixture of 1 part heavy lubricating-oil and 4 parts paraffin well shaken together will both lubricate and clear the pores of the stone. Some stones are sold oil sealed; if not they must be soaked until absorption ceases. Worn stones—and stones for chisels and plane-irons must be perfectly flat—can be

resurfaced with carborundum powder and paraffin for artificial stones, sprinkling the mixture on a flat hardwood block and rubbing the stone over it with a circular movement. Natural stones must be rubbed down on a piece of York grindstone or paving-stone, using silver sand and water only. It is more difficult to keep a long bevel in sharpening gouges, although one should always attempt to do so. Carvers' gouges, which are always outcannelled, are sometimes sharpened with an additional inside bevel, but this is not applicable to cabinet-gouges which should be kept flat on the non-bevelled inside face.

Cutting actions: chisels

The bevel of any cutting edge exercises a wedge-like action, driving the tool into the wood on its flat unbevelled side, while an easy slope to the bevel offers less resistance and gives a cleaner cut. Figure 64 gives the cutting actions. In A the single bevel lifts the chip without much tendency for the chisel to be driven into the wood, but where the bevel is steep, as in B, the greater resistance offered will either drive the chisel into the wood or split the chip ahead of the cut. In C, with bevel under, the tendency is to lift the chisel in the direction of the arrow, while in downward chopping at D the bevel tends to drive the cutting edge away from the true direction of the cut, and in order to maintain a square shoulder it is first necessary to chop away a recess as at E. Figure F shows the effect of reversing the chisel, which again does not give a square shoulder. In cutting end grain (G) there is no problem as the chip is too brittle to offer any resistance, while if a heavy chip is required along the grain it is better to reverse the chisel as at H. All cutting along the grain should always be downhill or with the grain, as at I, otherwise there is a tendency for the tool to dig in and lift the fibres. The skilled worker soon learns to 'read' the grain whether he is using a hand-tool or a machine, and it rapidly becomes instinctive. Shearing or slicing cuts where the forward movement of the cutting edge follows a diagonal path offer less resistance as the cut is spread over a greater area and the slope of the cut, governed by the combined grinding and honing angles, is reduced.

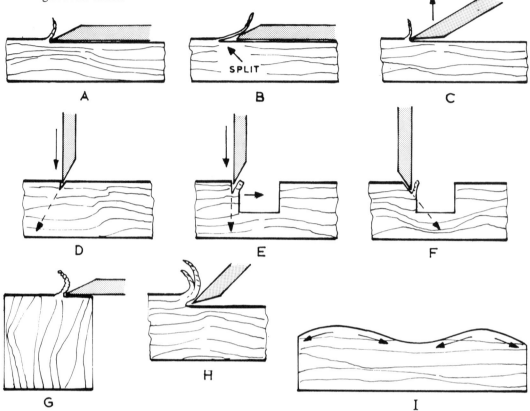

Grinding wheels

Most edge tools are now dry ground on high-speed grinders instead of the much slower cutting water-lubricated grindstone. The latter is always the better method as there is never any danger of withdrawing the temper of the cutting edge; nevertheless the high-speed grinder will give good results if care be taken. The wheels for these grinders, which can be hand- or power-driven, are either carborundum (silicon carbide) or Aloxite (crystallized fused alumina), and there is little to choose between them except that carborundum is harder and Aloxite tougher. (Generally speaking any grit-for-grit carborundum stones cut faster and wear more rapidly than the denser, tougher Aloxite stones, therefore carborundum is normally used where the stone is applied to the tool, and Aloxite where the tool is applied to the stone.) They are available in a variety of shapes and

sizes from 1 in (25 mm) diameter by ¼ in (6 mm) thickness upwards, and in a range of grits, 6 to 10 very coarse, 12 to 24 coarse, 30 to 60 medium, 70 to 220 fine and 240 to 700 very fine. They are also letter graded which denotes the strength of the bond and not the hardness of the grit which does not vary, from A soft to Z hard, with the main grades F to T. A fair average for the carbon steel used in wood-cutting tools would be about 60 grit F grade, always remembering that the softer the grit the cooler the cut. Therefore hard steels require soft wheels and soft steels hard wheels, while narrow-faced wheels cut cooler as do slow-running wheels, for less is taken off at each revolution and therefore less heat generated. Glazed wheels generate heat rapidly, and all wheels should be regularly dressed with a proper wheel dresser. To prevent burning of the tool edge, which not only draws the temper but also causes minute cracks in the bevel, the steel should be frequently quenched in cold water, with the side feed across the face of the wheel as rapidly as possible so that only a fractional amount is removed at each pass. Providing all these precautions are taken there is little danger, but careless grinding can soon ruin a good tool, and a blued edge must be avoided at all costs. The above remarks do not apply to high-speed tipped edges.

Sharpening stones

Oilstones

For the whetting or honing of ground edges (and all edge tools are supplied ground but not honed) a variety of stones are necessary. They can be either India, carborundum, or the slower cutting Washita, which is an inferior form of Arkansas, while true Arkansas is very scarce and expensive. Both India and carborundum grits are artificial, and therefore their quality is consistent, but Washita is a natural stone and can vary considerably, with an occasional piece almost too hard to cut; the best, however, will give an excellent edge. All these stones are usually bought in the standard size of 8 in (203 mm) by 2 in (50 mm) by 1 in (25 mm) for sharpening chisels, plane-irons, etc., and should be mounted in a wooden box with a lid (Figure 65), or otherwise covered when not in use.

A nail driven into the base of the box and pinched off to leave about 1/16 in (1.5 mm) protruding will prevent the box slipping on the

65   Oilstone box

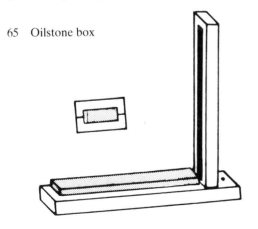

sharpening-table. For general use three oilstone grits are available—coarse, medium and fine; the coarse is for the rapid restoration of grinding bevels and the medium and fine for general honing, but for occasional use only double-sided combination stones with coarse and fine grits are obtainable. For those who tend to round their bevels over when honing on the oilstone (and the knack of working with the elbow and not the wrist takes time to acquire) a honing-gauge mounted on a ball or roller and set at the correct cutting angle is a useful accessory.

Water stones

Over the past few years a growing number of craftsmen in Britain and the USA have swung over to using inexpensive Japanese water stones. These are only available from specialist tool suppliers and, due to their extreme softness, are unsuitable for the novice or for school use. However, used with care, they cut fast, produce a near perfect edge, and avoid the use of messy oil. This latter is important as it is a basic necessity for the furniture-maker to keep his hands clean and free from grease, or he will spend half his time cleaning off dirty thumb prints.

Even their softness in the hands of a craftsman is an advantage as they can so easily be trued up by surfacing with a new coarse, but cheap, carborundum stone, thereby ensuring that one is constantly using a perfectly flat stone.

They are available in several grits; the writer manages perfectly with two only: 1200 and 1600.

Strops

An effective strop for fine cutting edges can be made out of a spare piece of cowhide, unmounted for carving tools so that it can be bent to shape, or glued to a wood base rough (undressed) side uppermost for chisels and plane-irons. The leather is dressed with oil and sprinkled with fine carborundum powder. The old school of craftsman always used the palm of his hand as a very effective strop.

RASPS, FILES, ETC.

Cabinet-rasps are very coarse files but with single pocket-shaped teeth (Figure 66A) instead of the diagonal serrations raised by the stabbing tool in file-making; they are used before the file for the preliminary rapid abrasion of the wood in shaped work. The usual sections are half round (horse-rasps are flat), with one flat side and relatively thin edges, but their use has largely been supplanted by the range of familiar *surform* tools—flat, half-round and round file, etc.—in which the chisel-type teeth are raised and perforated in a length of spring steel tensioned in file-shaped or planer-type holders. The perforations allow the sawdust to escape without clogging the work, and the cutting action is therefore very rapid, requiring care in handling, otherwise the form of the work is soon lost. Files are either single cut (66B) or double cut (66C), the former generally used for the softer materials, although steel cutting edges are usually filed with the single cut, which gives more of a true cutting rather than scratching action. They are also made in a range of cuts, rough or coarse, middle, common or bastard, second, smooth, dead smooth and double dead smooth. Probably the best type for wood is the bastard double cut, which cuts with a rasping action, and a compound movement should be used, combining a forward push with a slight rocking action which will level the inequalities left by other tools. Files for saw-sharpening are the mill saw-file for circular saws, with rounded edges for forming the gullets, and three-corner saw-files for handsaws. Band-saws require a special band-saw taper-file with more pronounced round to the edges, otherwise the acute gullet formed by the sharper edge of the ordinary taper saw-file is very liable to start small cracks in the band-saw. Needle-files are

very useful for sharpening small tools, bits, etc., and the dead smooth file for coaxing a fine finish to intricate wood edges which the scraper or sanding block cannot reach.

All files should be treated with respect and not thrown into a box with other tools. Woodworking files can be cleaned with wire file card, or if the teeth are heavily choked with resinous sawdust, gently heated sufficient only to scorch the dust, which can then be brushed out of the serrations. Files used for soft brass or aluminium alloy should be rubbed over with french chalk which helps to prevent clogging. It is not generally realized that a softish brass can blunt the teeth of a file quicker than hard steel, and render it useless for other work. Worn-out mill saw- and flat-files need not be thrown away, for the steel is usually very high quality with high carbon content and carefully hardened. Excellent tools, including chisels and scrapers for lathe turning, can be made from them by careful grinding.

MISCELLANEOUS TOOLS

Figure 67 shows the box and tap for cutting wood screws. Such screws are best made from box or hornbeam, although beech can be used if the threads are coarse enough. The screw itself is turned up to the required diameter, 1 in (25 mm), ¾ in (19 mm) etc., the end chamfered for entry, and the box or die turned round it in the usual manner to cut the threads. The hole for the tap is then bored to the exact diameter of the circle always marked on the side of the box, and the taper tap fed in.

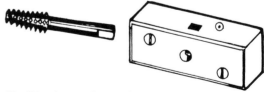

67   Wood screw box and tap

Sanding rubbers

These are blocks of resilient cork or felt-faced wood of convenient size to fit the hand, and usually about 4½ in (114 mm) by 2½ in (63 mm) by 1 in (25 mm) thick to take a quarter

66   Files

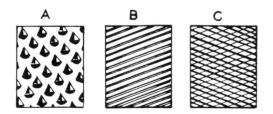

sheet of standard 11 in (280 mm) by 9 in (228 mm) abrasive paper for straight-line sanding. Shaped blocks to fit hollows, rounds and moulded sections are made from the cork blocks as required, and the use of such blocks is always to be preferred, for so-called 'touch sanding' tends to follow depressions and round over edges. For large surfaces a weighted block to take a whole sheet of abrasive paper is invaluable, as small blocks tend to linger over rough patches and create slight undulations which may not be apparent in the white, but which will show up badly under a high gloss polish.

BORING AND DRILLING TOOLS

Ninety-eight percent of all hole boring in small workshops and factories is now carried out by machine, either by a fixed pillar drill or by an electric, battery or air powered portable drill. However, there are still times when hand drilling is required, both for the safety of the work piece and for sheer convenience.

Drills and drilling

For drilling holes both the *joiner's ratchet-bit* or *arm-brace* with ball-bearing head (68:1) and the *hand-drill* (68:2) are used. The ratchet-brace is designed for slow, powerful cutting, usually with wing-bits having a square taper shank. The alligator jaws will also accept standard twist-drills with parallel shanks up to $\frac{3}{8}$ in (9.5 mm) diameter, although they are inclined to slip under load if the jaws are at all worn.

This brace can be obtained in a range of sweeps, i.e. the circle through which the arm turns, from 8 in (203 mm) to 14 in (355 mm), with the larger sweeps yielding the greater power; while for confined spaces the *electrician's ratchet-brace* with 5 in (127 mm) sweep is invaluable. The standard hand-drill (68:2) is designed for the rapid boring of small-diameter holes, and has a three-jaw chuck accepting $\frac{1}{4}$ in (6 mm) or $\frac{5}{16}$ in (8 mm) parallel shank bits and drills. For larger shank sizes up to $\frac{1}{2}$ in (12.5 mm) diameter the engineer's pattern two-speed drill with breast-pad for extra power is necessary. These hand-drills will not accept taper shank bits.

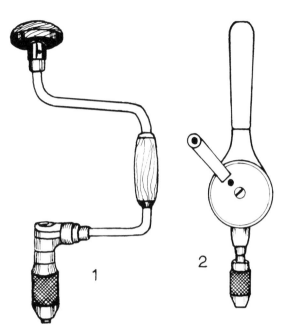

68   Boring and drilling tools

Types of bits

Bits are probably the most abused of all woodworking tools, for too often the wrong type is chosen, or the bit is incorrectly or over sharpened. The general run of bits are supplied with either square taper shanks (69:1) for use in the armbrace, or parallel round shanks (69:14) for hand-drills. A few types are also available with parallel shanks turned down to $\frac{1}{4}$ in (6 mm) diameter (69:13) for use in the standard drill-gun, and with *Morse taper* shanks for lathe heads or specialized drilling-machines. In the main, parallel shank-bits are classed as machine-bits with a constant shank diameter of $\frac{1}{2}$ in (12.5 mm), but the universally used *Russell Jenning's auger-* and *dowel-bits* are also supplied with $\frac{1}{4}$ in (6 mm) and $\frac{3}{8}$ in (9.5 mm) diameter shanks. Types of bit are as follows.

Jenning's pattern auger-bit (69:1)
The best smooth boring bit for general cabinet-work. Also available as the standard 5 in (127 mm) dowel-bit.

Solid centre auger-bit (69:2)
Extra strong general-purpose bit with greater chip clearance.

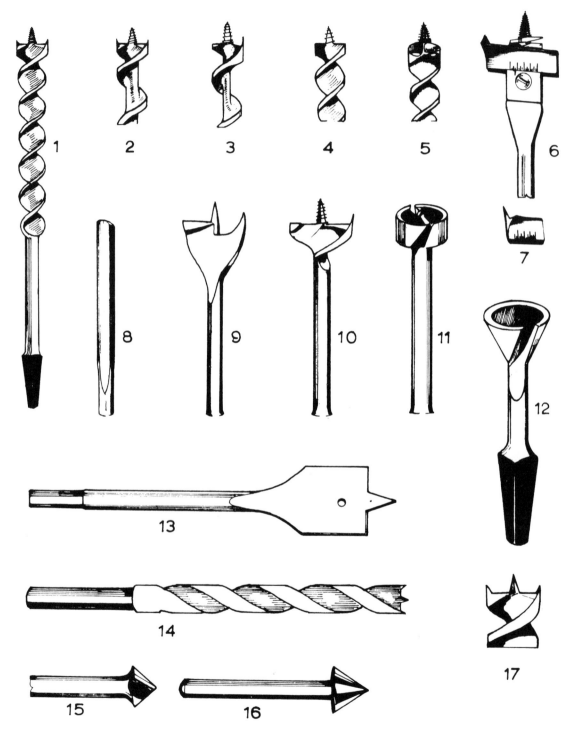

69   Wood-boring bits

Single-spur solid centre-bits (69:3)
For deep boring, also difficult or stringy wood.

Scotch square-nose auger-bit (69:4)
Designed for boring hard and rough timbers.

Solid nose auger-bit (69:5)
Unbreakable nose for tough, difficult drilling and boring at an angle.

Expansion-bit (69:6)
Primarily intended for softwoods, although it can be used in medium hardwoods provided care is taken and large-diameter holes are not attempted. Available in two sizes, each with an additional cutter (69:7) to give a range of diameters from ½ in (12.5 mm) to 1½ in (38 mm) and from ⅞ in (22 mm) to 3 in (76 mm).

Shell-bit (69:8)
For clean boring of short, small-diameter holes.

Old-type centre-bit (69:9)
Always a good bit for shallow holes, and still used as a machine-bit for large diameters. The brad-point enables holes to be bored from either side of the wood, thus preventing splintering out on the underside.

Improved pattern centre-bit (69:10)
A fast, clean-cutting bit for shallow holes.

Forstner bit (69:11)
Unequalled for boring any arc of a circle, and unaffected by knots or the run of the grain. As it is guided by its circular rim it gives a flat-bottomed hole, useful in some work.

Dowel-sharpener (69:12)
Useful for chamfering the ends of dowel-pegs for easy entry.

Flat-bit (69:13)
A revolutionary and inexpensive bit which relies on speed for its cutting ability, therefore its use is confined to hand drills and drilling machines.

Improved twist-drill (69:14)
A wood-cutting version of the standard metal-boring twist-drill.

Snail-horn countersink (69:15)
Countersink for wood, with taper shank for hand-braces.

Rose-head countersink (69:16)
General-purpose countersink for wood and non-ferrous metals, available with both taper

and parallel shanks, and in 90° and 120° included angles.

Machine bit (69:17)
With brad-point in lieu of screw lead to the nose, as the latter will snatch at the wood if driven at speed, with risk of serious injury in hand-held boards. Brad-points are not self-driving and require feed pressure, therefore they are advisable for all high-speed drilling, unless the work can be very securely clamped down.

Twist-drills
The standard jobber's twist-drill primarily intended for metal boring is also used extensively by the woodworking trades for small-diameter holes, although it will never cut as cleanly as a correctly sharpened wood bit. Moreover, it has neither screw lead nor brad-point, and is always more difficult to position accurately. On the other hand it retains its direction, and is not deflected by knots or the run of the grain. The cheaper carbon steel varieties are good enough for wood provided they are not allowed to burn. Twist-drills are not suitable for use in the ratchet-brace, as they require a higher speed than it can achieve for clean cutting.

Record Ridgway Tools Limited, who take a justifiable pride in the excellence of their products, give the following instructions for the use and upkeep of wood-boring bits:

1 A good bit should draw itself easily into the wood, cutting a clean hole without undue pressure on the brace.

2 A bit should never be used to bore a hole at one operation deeper than the length of its twist or flute. Where deeper holes are required the bit should be repeatedly withdrawn and the chips cleared as they rise.

3 Generally speaking bits are sharpened more often than necessary, and the life of the bit considerably shortened by incorrect filing.

Sharpening bits

Basic rules as laid down by Ridgway are: (1) always sharpen from the inside or underneath, never outside or on top; (2) maintain original shape and angles; (3) use suitable smooth-file, never grind and always file lightly, removing as

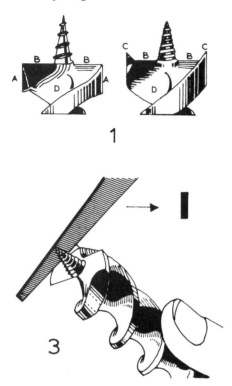

little metal as possible and preserving the balance of the bit so that each side does the same amount of work. Figure 70 gives the procedure. In 70:1, A is the side wing, B the cutters, C the spurs and D the throat. The sequence of sharpening is as follows:

Sharpening the side wings (70:2). Rest the bit in the bench with the screw lead down. File with the file working through the throat of the bit. Never file the side wings on the outside or the clearance will be ruined (the appropriate file section is shown alongside each drawing).

Sharpening the spurs (70:3). Hold the bit nose uppermost with its twist firmly against the edge of the bench. File the inside of the spurs. Never file the outside as this reduces the clearance, causing binding and clogging of the bit.

Sharpening the cutters (70:4). Hold the bit as in (70:2) and file the cutting edges on the underside only, i.e. with the file working through the throat of the bit. The cutters must be at the same level so that they cut chips of equal thickness.

Another wood-boring tool which is always abused is the common *bradawl*. It should be carefully sharpened with a fine file and finished on the oilstone, and is used for boring fine holes for nails or the threads of screws but not the clearance hole for the actual shank of the screw which should be made with a shell-bit or twist-drill. The birdcage-pattern bradawl with square shank bores with a reamer-like action, and can be used on the thinnest wood without splitting. Reamers for use in the arm-brace can also be obtained, and are used for widening existing holes.

Plug-cutters

Cross-grain pellets or plugs for filling screw-holes can be cut with Stanley plug-cutters, available in three sizes for Nos. 6, 8 and 10 screws. These are virtually hollow drills cutting a circular path, of which the core or waste forms the required pellet. Larger sizes cutting standard ⅜ in (9.5 mm) and ½ in (12.5 mm)

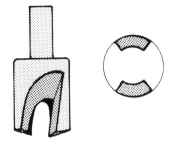

diameter plugs can be obtained for use in the drill-press or drilling machine.

STRIKING OR DRIVING TOOLS

Hammers and mallets

Figure 72:1 shows the *ash handled Warrington* or *joiner's pattern hammer* with cross pein for starting nails, etc., 72:2 the heavy *claw-hammer* with split claw for drawing nails, and 72:3 the light *pattern-maker's pin-* or *telephone-hammer*; while the *upholsterer's hammer*, which can also be obtained in magnetic form, is shown in 72:4. An average weight for the joiner's hammer would be either 10 or 12 oz (340 g) head, and 4 oz (113 g) head for the pin-hammer. The *carpenter's mallet* is shown in 72:5, and a useful size would be with head out of a 5 in (127 mm) by 3½ in (89 mm) by 2½ in (63 mm) thick beech block, and 1⅜ in (35 mm) by ¾ in (19 mm) handle 13 in (330 mm) long overall. The handle is not glued but fractionally tapered, as shown, so that the head cannot fly off. Figure 72:6 shows the *carver's mallet*, useful for light chopping, and turned out of a 4 in (101 mm) square beech block 7 in (178 mm) long, leaving 3 in (76 mm) for the mallet head and about 4 in (102 mm) for the ⅞ in (22 mm) diameter handle. Alternatively, the handle can be turned separately, taken through the head and glued and wedged.

Nail sets are shown in 72:9, type (A) for punching in larger nails, and the *pin-punch* (B) for small veneer-pins. Type (C) shows the *centre-punch*, useful for marking centres when using twist-drills, etc. The square-headed types of nail set give a greater striking surface, and are not so inclined to boss over with repeated use.

Hammer faces should always be kept clean and polished on a waste scrap of abrasive paper, otherwise they tend to bend the nails over, while the downward stroke should be directed with a slight pushing action away from the body. Screwdrivers should be cross ground to fit the screw-slot and not merely bevelled at the tip.

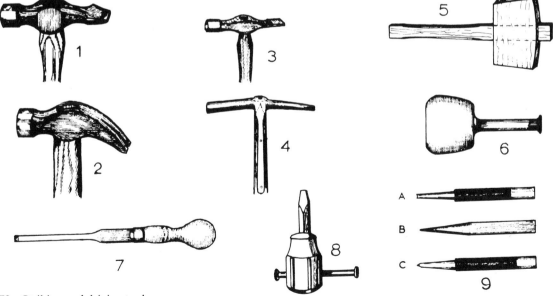

72   Striking and driving tools

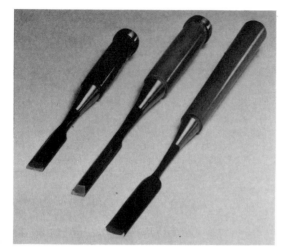

73 Japanese precision ground chisels. (By courtesy Roger's Tools, Hitchin, Herts.)

75 Japanese handsaws. (By courtesy of Roger's Tools, Hitchin, Herts.)

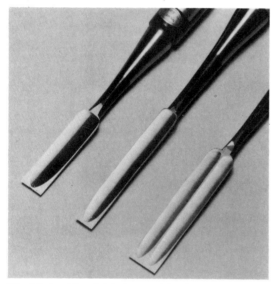

74 Underside of chisels, precision hollow ground. (By courtesy of Roger's Tools, Hitchin, Herts.)

Screwdrivers

On the production line, most screws are driven home either by pump or by powered screwdrivers, but for quality work, where one slip with a pump screw driver could be ruinous, the traditional screwdriver still has a large part to play. One should have several to fit the various screws commonly used, i.e. nos. 4 to 8 and no. 12.

All too frequently screwdrivers are dismissed

76 Detail of the precision made teeth of a Japanese tenon and dovetail saw. (By courtesy of Roger's Tools, Hitchin, Herts.)

116

as unimportant tools, but they do need to be of good quality and precision ground to fit the screws accurately. If they are not, chewed up screw-heads will mar the final piece of work.

The standard *cabinet-screwdriver* is shown in 72:7 and this is usually the best pattern for general work; and a useful *dumpy-screwdriver* with loose toggle-bar for working in confined spaces in 72:8.

JAPANESE HAND TOOLS

Since 1975 there has been a growing interest in the West in traditional Japanese hand tools. These are quite distinct from and not to be confused with the cheap reproductions of European patterns that are exported by both Japan and Taiwan.

Japan has a long tradition of working in wood, predominantly in its traditional housing, and its craftsmen have become masters in joinery construction. However, unlike their Western counterparts, they do not have a history of working at a bench in hardwoods, but on the floor, and mainly in clean, straight-grained cedar (hinoki) that cuts like cheese. This simple fact has affected the design of their tools over many centuries and thus, while we cannot fault the quality or the steel of Japanese tools, it has to be said that not all of them suit the Western way of working.

However, there are no such doubts about their inexpensive water stones which are excellent, and many craftsmen in the West now use at least some Japanese tools in their work, with chisels and handsaws being the most popular.

10 Portable power tools and accessories

All power-driven machines can be grouped within three broad classifications:

Fixed floor mounted machines.

Bench mounted machines—fixed, but not permanently so.

Portable power tools, either electric, battery powered, or driven by compressed air, the latter being more appropriate to a production workshop or factory.

There is an extensive range of power-tools available which can be used on or at the bench; and while they can never supplant the fixed sawbench, planer, spindle-moulder, etc., they are nevertheless extremely useful adjuncts and can lighten the work considerably, giving also a measure of precision which might not be attainable with pure hand methods. Various types or categories are available, viz. *light duty*, often described as 'home duty' but intended for intermittent use within the limits of the fractional horsepower available; *general duty* for tradesmen's use, and sturdy enough for intermittent but reasonably heavy work; *heavy duty*, with consistent power necessary for production work; and in some cases *super duty*, to give 'fit and forget' service over long periods.

GENERAL NOTE

It must always be remembered that woodworking machines, with their constantly varying loads as the cutters strike the hard and soft grain of wood, are gluttons for power, and that portable tools usually rely more on speed than power output or torque for their performance. They should, therefore, never be expected to undertake the heavier tasks which should rightly be given to the large fixed machines. Manufacturers give full and precise instructions and some issue their own handbooks on the techniques to be employed. They are also concerned to make their portable tools as safe as possible, but it is the rough usage to which the tools are often subjected which constitutes the

danger, and no amount of foresight on the manufacturer's part can prevent a careless worker standing on a wet floor and trailing bare wires everywhere from electrocuting himself. Given correct treatment, with the wiring periodically checked, properly earthed or grounded, and the motor itself never taxed beyond its stated capacity, the average portable tool will give good service over many years, and become essential in the workshop.

CIRCULAR SAWS

Sometimes known as 'saw cats' or 'builders' saws', and available in both general and heavy duty models, with a range of saw diameters from 6½ in (165 mm) to 10 in (254 mm)—the smallest size will cut slightly over 2 in (50 mm) thicknesses, and up to 3½ in (89 mm) for the largest. As a rule all these saws are well balanced, fully adjustable for depth and any angle of cut up to 45°, with automatic retractable lower guard and fixed upper guard, splitting- or riving-knife and ripping fence. In spite of their somewhat fearsome aspect they are safe in use, as the blade is at all times covered, and overloading merely stalls the motor. A range of saw-blades is available: combination-saws for ripping and crosscutting; crosscut for fast, smooth crosscutting and there-

77   9 in (228 mm) heavy duty portable saw

118

fore more suitable for plywood than the coarser cut combination-blade; planer-blades which give a very smooth cut and can be relied upon not to rag out the cross grain of ply or crumble particle board; flooring-blades designed for cutting through occasional nails but very suitable for resin-bonded chipboards etc., which quickly dull the edge of average saws; and a range of soft-metal cutting saws. Heavy gauge sheet-steel pedestal saw-tables or bench-stands can be obtained for these saws, but they can never have the accuracy of the orthodox table saw, and should, therefore, be regarded as a compromise solution only. Probably the chief uses for these saws in the furniture industry are the crosscutting of random plank and ripping up large sheets of plywood which cannot be handled on the normal table saw.

ELECTRIC CHAINSAWS

The lightweight electric chainsaws which have recently been introduced are a great asset to the furniture-maker. They are invaluable for roughing out large, thick boards to arrive at the sizes that can be manhandled on the normal workshop machinery. They are much safer and more versatile in use than the portable circular saws, although a little more wasteful of wood. Also, for those involved in sculptural work, heavy bowl turning or carving, they are very manageable aids to roughing out and removing waste material.

JIGSAWS

These are sometimes known as 'sabre saws', which is more correct as the term 'jigsaw' could also be taken to mean power-driven fretsaws in which the blade is secured at either end. Available in home, general and super duty, some have vertical stroke, and others have a cycloid action which keeps the teeth clear of sawdust. The no-load speed is usually around 3000 strokes per minute, with a stroke depth of from ½ in (12.5 mm) to 1 in (25 mm) and a cutting depth of up to 2⅜ in (60 mm) in softwoods and 1 in (25 mm) in hardwoods and resin-bonded ply. Various types of blade can be obtained with fine, medium and coarse teeth for sheet metal, fibreglass, plastics, wood,

78   12 in (304 mm) lightweight electric chainsaw

79   Elu ST 152 Jigsaw with two speeds

plywoods and particle boards, etc., also knife-blades for leather, latex foam and fibrous materials. As a woodworking-saw it is extremely useful for internal straight-line or contour cutting. The rate of cut is fairly slow, but the saw can be operated with one hand only, is easy to guide and can be used for bevel cuts up to 45°.

This is a specialist tool for cutting interior shapes and curves. It should not be used for heavy straight-line cutting as this soon over-

80   Jigsaw set for bevel cut

81   Portable planer used for rebating

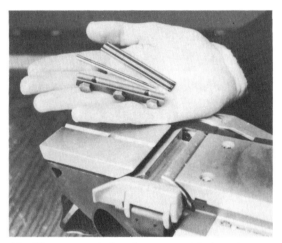

82   Planer upended to show cutter block and replaceable knives

taxes its motor; and whenever possible it is more efficient to cut exterior curves on a floor-mounted bandsaw.

PORTABLE PLANERS

These have only a limited use for the furniture-maker who, unlike the joiner and builder working out on site, has constant access to a floor-mounted machine. On occasion, however, the surface planer may not be wide enough, and then the portable is extremely useful for these extra wide boards or table tops, even though, for final accuracy, a hand plane will be needed.

It is also useful for rebating if for any reason this cannot be undertaken on either the spindle moulder or surface planer. At the cost of little more than a large hand plane, it is, therefore, a useful addition to the workshop equipment.

83   Portable planer upended in purpose-made table for use as small bench planer

HIGH-SPEED ROUTERS

These have power-driven vertical spindles on which the appropriate cutters are mounted and fed down to the work, while some models have an adjustable side swing movement enabling the width of cut to be increased or extended without moving the router-fence or changing the cutters. Usually these tools rely on speed rather than power output, therefore the depth of cut obtainable at any one setting is fairly small, but the degree of finish is quite high. Many models are available from fractional up to 2½ hp (1.864 kW) with cutting speeds up to 27,000 rpm for the lightweight models, and a range of cutters for straight-line and circular grooving, moulding, veining, dovetail cutting, rebating, slot cutting, edge trimming, etc. The router itself with double handles can be moved freely in any lateral direction, but a range of guides for straight and circular cuts, trammel-points for circles and bases for working against templates give the tool wide versatility. It can also be mounted horizontally, or turned over to act as a fixed spindle-moulder, while various dovetail guides and templates will allow box-locking, carcass- and drawer dovetailing up to 25 in (635 mm) in width. Particular care should be exercised in choosing one of these machines and the nature of the work for which it will be

85   Lightweight ¼ in (6 mm) plunging router

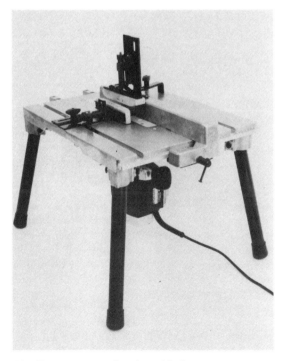

86   Router reversed under table for use as a lightweight spindle moulder

84   Heavy duty portable router

121

87 Variable speed lightweight electronic router

used fairly assessed, for while the lightweight models have ¼ hp (0.186 kW) motors and a net weight of about 3¼ lb (1.475 kg) only, the heaviest models weigh up to 26 lb (11.793 kg), all of which has to be lifted and guided on to the work by one pair of hands. There is, of course, no kick or side thrust with a good machine, but even so the heavy models do require a certain amount of effort to guide them through heavy cuts, and often the lightweight model is a more practical proposition.

Properly chosen, in good working order and with a range of cutters, it is, however, an outstandingly versatile machine in the hands of a capable operator. The cutters themselves can be purchased to fixed specifications, but some makers quote for 'specials'. Usually both high-speed and tungsten-carbide cutters are obtainable, the latter much more expensive but lasting very much longer in materials bonded with, or composed of, synthetic resin in any form. It is often more satisfactory to send the cutters back to the suppliers for regrinding, otherwise the critical profile may be lost, but some makers supply a bit- and cutter-sharpener which uses the machine itself to grind its own cutters. Typical operations performed by these machines are illustrated in Figure 90 and all

manufacturers issue fully descriptive literature covering the entire scope.

It is sometimes advisable to purchase a plunging router as it is much simpler and safer in use for some jobs, and they are now very inexpensive. However, one of the disadvantages of the standard portable router, plunging or otherwise, is that the constant high speed and accompanying high pitched whine can be distracting when undertaking delicate operations, and also renders the workshop rather unpleasant for any other occupants. A recent development to alleviate this is the variable speed electronic router, the 96E by Elu. It has five variable speed settings from 8000 to 24,000 revs, enabling very delicate work to be undertaken gently and surprisingly quietly. In addition, the electronic control prevents drop off of speed under load and also allows for a gentle build up of speed on each setting. This slower speed at the start of each cut allows for a more gradual entry of the cutter and avoids the snatching associated with high speed. The extra cost of the electronic version is soon recouped as the life of the bearings and motor is considerably extended, as for much of the time and for many operations the router can be running at quite low speeds. (In 1985 I re-equipped my workshop with the latest model, and with four people using the same workspace it has made for pleasanter working conditions for all concerned.)

Veneer-trimmer

A smaller version of the router expressly designed for the rapid trimming of veneered tops, with provision for flush or bevel trimming of laminated plastics.

Dovetailing attachment

Without doubt the most useful of all accessories for use with the ¼ in (6 mm) or greater capacity router. Accurate and tight-fitting machine lap dovetails can be cut at ¾ in (19 mm) pitch in hardwood up to 9 in (228 mm) in width in any combination of thicknesses from ⅜ in (9.5 mm) to 1 in (25 mm). Multi-pitch attachments are also available providing for additional pitches which enable the spacing of the dovetails to fit

88 Dovetailing attachment

89 Timber being positioned prior to dovetailing

within any width of material without clipping off the end pin. No marking out is necessary and both drawer front and side are cut at one operation. The attachment is complete with the necessary guides and templates. A dovetail-housing joint accessory which will cut housings in timbers up to 9 in (228 mm) wide is also marketed, but takes rather long to set up accurately and is of more interest to those who lack experience in cutting this particular joint (see also Dovetailing, Chapter 19).

BISCUIT JOINTER AND GROOVER

Although portable routers are often used for grooving, they are not very efficient except on stopped grooves, where the router cutter enables the groove to be completed in depth

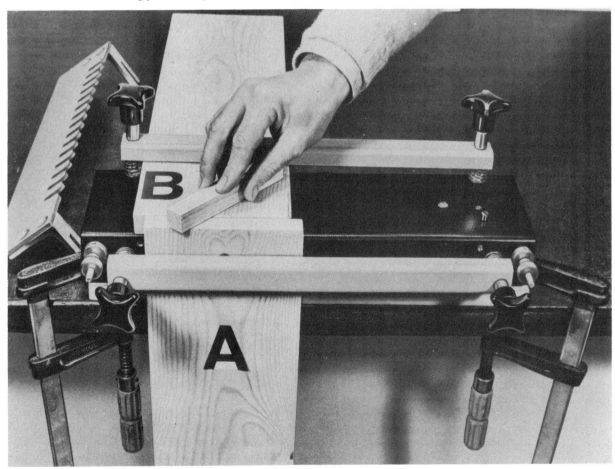

| V-grooving bit | Beading-bit (two flutes) | Rounding-over bits (two flutes) | Straight bit (single flute) |

 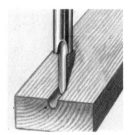 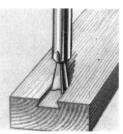 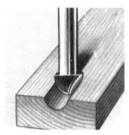

| Straight bits (two flutes) | Veining-bit (single flutes) | Dovetail-bits | Core-box bits (two flutes) |

| Cove-bit (two flutes) | Chamfering-bit (two flutes) | Rabbeting-bit (one length) | Hinge-mortising and gaining bit |

| Straight-face cutters | Concave cutter | Convex cutter | Corner bead-cutter |

90 Portable router-cutters and operations. (By courtesy of Black and Decker Ltd)

right up to the stop line. But for all through grooving and wherever any quantity is concerned, they are slow and the cutters frequently become overheated and dulled. In the absence of a spindle moulder/shaper, therefore, grooving is best carried out by a biscuit jointer and groover, a tool which cuts grooves in the same effortless way as a spindle but with the added advantage that one can operate it on the workpiece itself. Its action is the same as a very small diameter grooving saw fitted to the spindle moulder or table saw and it can simply be plunged into the workpiece at will, making an arched recess. This lends itself to its other function of making the 'biscuit joints' from which it gets its name; in these joints, oval 'biscuits' of compressed wood, which can be purchased in a variety of thicknesses to match the thickness of the cutter, are inserted and glued into the recess. In some workshops this tool is replacing much conventional use of dowelling, tenoning and dovetailing.

PORTABLE SANDERS

The perfect sander hardly exists and the ideal would probably be some form capable of 'random orbit'. At the present time the following types are used: (a) flexible disc sander grinders; (b) dustless belt sanders; (c) orbital and oscillating pad finishing sanders. Type (a) is of little interest to furniture-makers and is, therefore, not considered, while type (b) is the best compromise between disc and pad sander for the rapid removal of stock, but requires greater care in working.

Dustless belt sanders

Available in belt widths of from 2½ in (63:5 mm) to 4 in (101 mm), with belt speeds from 1000 to 1700 ft per min. (304 m to 518 m) over a pad size or effective sanding area of about 6 in (152 mm) long by the full width of the belt—the 3 in (76 mm) model is the best compromise between weight and power. The vacuum unit incorporated usually sucks about 80 per cent of the fine dust into the detachable bag, and therefore the cutting action is not impeded by the loose dust and is considerably faster in consequence. For the rapid removal of

91 Biscuit jointer in use for drawer construction, both as a groover to take drawer bottom and also to produce the biscuit joint to fix drawer sides to the drawer front (one biscuit in position)

92 One plunge of the cutter produces identical slots for the compressed hardwood biscuits

stock in wood, metal or plastics these machines can be extremely useful but care should be taken with veneered surfaces as they are inclined to dub over at the ends and cut through the veneer unless waste pieces of material are positioned at each end to prevent the belt dipping. Most models are designed to cut against the belt rotation for easier control, and the direction of the cut should be at a slight

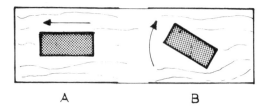

93   Portable sanders: direction of cut

angle (93B) rather than with the grain (93A). The tool works under its own weight and no bearing down to increase the rate of cut should be attempted.

A very recent addition to the range is the Elu MHB 157 Electronic. With its variable speeds it has many advantages similar to those of the electronic router in that power is always maintained under variable work loads. With the addition of the sanding frame attachment, and used at the correct speed with paper of the appropriate grit, quite sensitive sanding of veneers, for example, is now possible with safety. Although this makes the belt sander more versatile and ideal when only one portable sander can be purchased, as it can remove heavy stock and produce a fine finish, the pad finishing sanders are still preferable for final finishing of cabinet work.

94   Electronic belt sander with optional adjustable sanding frame attachment for fine sanding

Pad finishing sanders

Two types are available: reciprocating (straight-line), in which the pad moves with a backward and forward stroke to give true straight-line sanding with the grain; orbital, in which the pad is rotated in a series of small orbits of about $\frac{1}{8}$ in (3 mm) to $\frac{3}{16}$ in (5 mm) diameter. In theory at least the reciprocating type should prove more effective, but in practice there is probably little to choose between it and the orbital type, for with the speed of the cut (4000 to 5000 orbits per min.) there is virtually no scratching across the grain, and in fact a diagonal movement across the grain helps to level out inequalities in the surface. Practically the only drawback with these pad sanders are slight swirl-marks caused by loose grains from the abrasive paper, but if the surface is kept well dusted in advance of the cut they should cause no trouble. The point to remember is that applied pressure does not increase the rate of cut to any appreciable extent, and in fact heavy bearing down may result in the machine itself orbiting rather than the grit.

Various types are obtainable, differing mainly in weight and ruggedness, for the pad size is usually standardized to take a half sheet of 11 in (280 mm) by 9 in (228 mm) abrasive paper. The general pattern is a felt-faced or foam-rubber pad permanently attached to the body with an easy lock and release for the abrasive paper, but models are available in which the pad is removable for wet and dry sanding and for contour sanding with thick foam pads. Dust-extractors are fitted to some models, and at least one type has an optional adjustment for either straight-line or orbital sanding built into the machine which offers some advantage, for moulded sections cannot be sanded with the orbital action, but cork counter-profiles can be fixed to reciprocating pads.

Here again Elu have a lightweight electronic orbital model, MVS 156, with stroke speeds from 6000 to 24,000 a minute, but many may find the heavy duty single speed models more suitable. The choice depends on whether portable sanders are the only form of power sanding in a shop or merely an occasionally used addition to the much more efficient floor mounted overhead pad sander. If the latter is

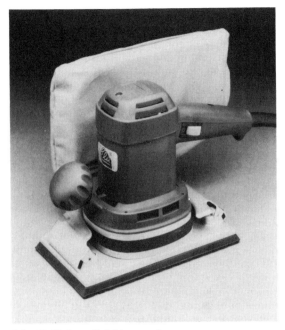

95 Half-sheet finishing sander

96 Heavy duty single speed orbital sander

the case, the lightweight electronic model is probably all that is ever needed.

ELECTRIC DRILLS

Possibly no single tool is more abused than the standard electric drill, and it is always surprising

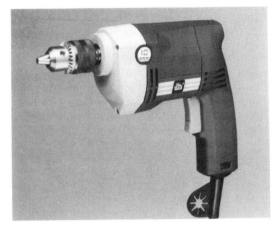

97 ⅜ in (10mm) variable speed electric drill

that it can accommodate such rough treatment. A multiplicity of types is available, from the ¼ in (6 mm) chuck capacity home model, with a chuck no-load speed of 2600 rpm, to the 1¼ in (32 mm) capacity heavy duty drill running at 275 rpm. Drills over ⅜ in (9.5 mm) chuck capacity are usually two-handed as they have low speed and maximum torque for penetrating the toughest materials, but the usual pattern for woodworking is the pistol-grip drill with a capacity of ¼ in (6 mm), ⁵⁄₁₆ in (8 mm) or ⅜ in (9.5 mm), the ⅜ in preferably with two speeds as the normal no-load speed of about 1000 rpm is on the slow side for wood. Capacities up to ⅜ in (9.5 mm) are obtainable in home, general and heavy duty drills, and for use with accessories either the general or heavy duty type should be chosen although the lightweight models will perform an amazing number of operations provided they are not sustained and the feed-rate is gentle. The heavier drills are, of course, more sturdy, usually double insulated, and some have automatic cut-outs to protect against overload. Drilling capacities are usually stated to be up to ¼ in (6 mm) in steel and ½ in (12.5 mm) in hardwood for the ¼ in (6 mm) lightweight drill, and up to ⅜ in (9.5 mm) and 1 in (25 mm) respectively for the ⅜ in (9.5 mm) model, but much depends on the type of drill and the nature of the hardwood. Stub twist-drills, jobbers' twist-drills and woodworking twist-drills up to ½ in (12.5 mm), flatbit-drills up to 1¼ in (32 mm), and Jenning's pattern dowel- and auger-bits up to ¾ in (19 mm) are all available with shanks turned down to ¼ in (6 mm) diameter for drill-guns. Great care should be taken when using auger-bits with screw-points as the snatch at high speed is very considerable, and can be positively dangerous unless the wood is securely anchored down. Speed reduction units are available, also right-angled speed-changers which will either double or halve the stated speed of the drill.

A useful development of recent years has been the cordless drill which has simply to be charged up from time to time from an outlet of the mains supply. It has transformed the noisy, fast electric drill into a lightweight, quiet, refined cabinetmaker's tool. It runs at low speeds and can be used with absolute safety for many delicate drilling operations and even as a mechanical screwdriver.

Accessories for electric drills

Numerous accessories are obtainable for sawing, rebating, jigsawing, sanding, polishing, etc., but these are, in the main, hobbyists' tools. One accessory, however, is very useful and calls for mention.

Vertical drill-stand

Vertical pillar drill-stands with spring-loaded instant-return feed and fixed table are usually available for all models of hand drills. With the gun clamped in position the stand becomes an effective vertical table-drill or drill-press for vertical drilling of wood and metal. It lacks the versatility of the orthodox drill-press but will perform most of the main functions of the heavier tool.

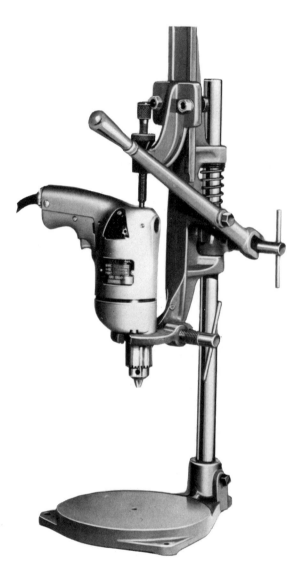

98 Pillar-stand for electric drill

11 Woodworking and allied machinery

Certain basic machines are indispensable to every workshop even where hand work predominates. These are *circular table saw; radial arm-saw; band-saw; planers; spindle moulder/ shaper; mortiser; horizontal borer; overhead table router; drill-press; bench-grinder; sanders and lathes*. If much veneer-work is done then either a screw-operated or vacuum-bag veneer-press will need a high priority, while production shops would place the dovetailing-machine and belt sander high on the list. Where it is intended to install only the most basic machines then obviously the table saw, planer and band-saw will take pride of place.

CIRCULAR TABLE SAWS

As a rough approximation it is usual to take one-third of the diameter of a circular saw as its effective cut, therefore a 15 in (381 mm) saw giving a cut of about 5 in (127 mm) would be about the minimum for general work. However, many large concerns do not use timber thicker than 1½ in (38 mm) building up for larger dimensions, and this greatly simplifies their stocks, while large-diameter saws are no

100 Startrite 9 in (228 mm) tilt arbor table saw

99 12 in (304 mm) sliding-table panel-saw (dimension saw)

101 Wadkin heavy duty 10 in (254 mm) tilt arbor table saw

102 Radial arm saw (bench model). (By courtesy of DeWalt)

103 Floor-mounted version. (By courtesy of DeWalt)

longer necessary and most of the work is done on the 12 in (304 mm) sliding-table panel-saw (45B) which is an excellent compromise if large boards of ply and chipboard are used to any great extent. Additionally it is never advisable to fit small saws for ripping out stringers and bandings, etc. to large-diameter table saws, but they could be used in the smaller saws. (Where space permits it is advisable to double up with a small 8 or 9 in diameter table saw for delicate cabinet work.) Whatever table saw is chosen it should be sturdy, adequately guarded, with an elevating spindle and tilting arbor, and with a minimum 3 hp (2.237 kW) motor for 12 in (304 mm) or 15 in (381 mm) benches.

PULL-OVER CROSS CUT SAWS (RADIAL ARM SAWS)

A heavy duty radial or swing saw mounted on a long wooden table is a regular item of equipment in most joinery workshops for the rapid crosscutting of squared up boards and timbers. It is less common in cabinet-making shops simply because waney edge boards are more commonly used. Many shops do have a lighter version, the radial arm saw, which has been particularly developed for the home craftsman and has a versatility that enables many processes from ripping to drilling to be accomplished on one machine. Its main use for the professional, though, with other machinery at his disposal, is for crosscutting and trenching/dadoing (cutting long housings) for bookshelving and similar carcass work.

It is best to purchase a heavy duty version with a standard 10 in or 12 in (254 mm or 304 mm) diameter blade.

BAND-SAW

The effectiveness of this machine is governed by the throat depth, i.e. distance from saw to body framework, and a 20 in (508 mm) band-saw will cut a width of 19½ in (495 mm) and a depth or thickness of 13 in (330 mm). The smaller machines (12 in [304 mm] throat, etc.) have small-diameter wheels imposing greater strain on the band-saws, therefore here again it should be as large as possible. All machines have (or should have) a tilting table and ripping fence,

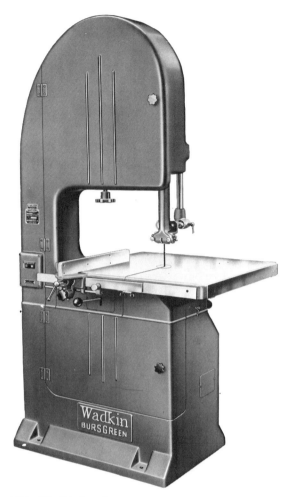

105　Wadkin band-saw

the saw-pulleys, and positive adjustment to the ripping fence.

For most hardwood cutting it is advisable to purchase skip teeth blades. These keep their edge so much longer and can be reground within the workshop on a fine grinding wheel.

PLANERS

A skilled machinist can accurately thickness a panel on an overhand surface planer/jointer but it requires practice and is dangerous. Ideally one should have a long bedded surface planer for the accurate truing of one surface and long edges, and a separate thicknesser/surfacer to reduce stock to a consistent thickness. Alter-

104　Startrite light duty 12 in (304 mm) throat bandsaw

and the larger models semi-automatic tensioning to the saw-blade, including a warning signal for slack saws, foot-brake, cleaning brushes to

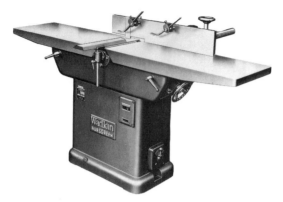

106 Surface planer/jointer

107 Wadkin heavy-duty 20 in (508 mm) by 10 in (254 mm) thicknesser/surfacer

108 Combination surface planer and thicknesser/jointer and surfacer

natively, where space and cost are crucial, a combination surface planer and thicknesser, often referred to as an over and under, would suffice.

All these machines come in a variety of cutter widths from 9 in (228 mm) up to 36 in (914 mm) with the large thicknessers/surfacers. Your choice should be governed by the nature of the work you do, for there is little point in investing large sums in a 36 in (914 mm) planer if you are never going to need to plane boards beyond 12 in (304 mm) wide.

SPINDLE MOULDER/SHAPER

The most versatile and yet the most dangerous machine in any workshop, the spindle moulder can, in the hands of the expert, almost perform miracles, but in the hands of the uninitiated it can be lethal. Instruction in its use is strongly recommended.

Not only can this machine mould virtually any shape both on straight and curved surfaces, but it can also, with the aid of templates, produce any number of identically shaped components from chair legs and curved rails to drawer handles. It can tongue and groove faster than any other machine, and with the addition of a sliding table it can cut all manner of tenon and bridle joints, dovetail housings—the list is endless.

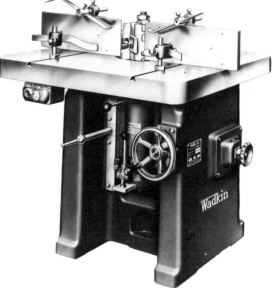

109 Wadkin single-speed heavy-duty spindle moulder/shaper

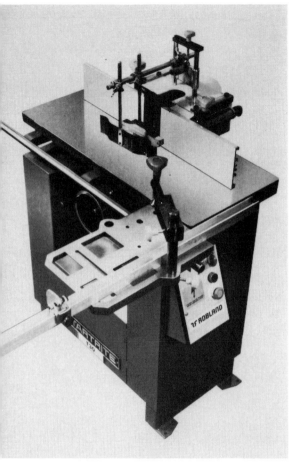

110 Startrite light-duty spindle moulder/shaper with built-in sliding table for end grain shaping and tenoning

MORTISER

This is an essential item of equipment where any production work is involved. It is possible in one-off work to manage with a hollow chisel mortising attachment fitted to a drill press, but eventually the advantages of a separate mortiser will become only too apparent.

There are two forms of mortiser: the hollow-chisel type, and the chain mortiser, which works in a similar way to the chain saw. It is chiefly the former which is used in quality craft orientated workshops because it produces the perfect square edge and square bottomed mortises from ¼ in (6 mm) width up to 1 in (25 mm) or more.

111 Hollow-chisel mortiser

HORIZONTAL BORER

The mortise and tenon joint will always be preferable in quality work to dowelling, but where economy of time is vital, the horizontal borer is an obvious alternative to the mortiser. It usually has two drilling heads side by side and an adjustable table for height.

Figure 112 shows a home-made dowel borer. This was assembled out of engineering scrap with a ½ hp (0.373 kW) motor, screw-actuated elevating, and dovetail slide horizontal movement for the working-table taken from an

112 Dowel-boring machine

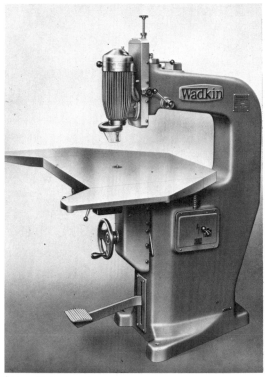

113 High-speed router

old milling-machine bought in the local scrap-yard. A ¼ in (6 mm) sliding rod under the table provided an effective distance-stop, and the ½ in (12.5 mm) capacity Jacob's chuck was mounted direct onto the motor spindle. With the table set at the right height and pushed forward by the pre-set distance against the revolving bit it gave very accurate borings, and such machines, either independent or as accessories coupled to other machines, are invaluable for accurate dowel-work. Minimum safe working distances between machines are shown in Figure 122 and where space is limited the 'in' or 'out' feed distance can often be increased by placing the machine in line with a doorway.

Both the mortiser and the horizontal borers have the advantage of operating at very slow speeds and quietly, in contrast to the overhead and portable routers which can be used in some shallow mortising operations.

OVERHEAD TABLE ROUTERS

Although these are used for general light moulding, grooving, rebating and slot mortising, they are far less efficient for this purpose than the spindle moulder/shaper or the horizontal borer and slotter in the case of slot

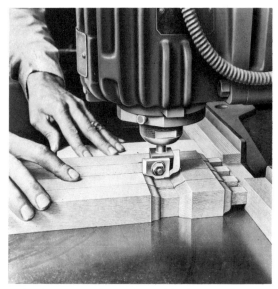

114 Square turning on legs with high-speed router

134

mortising. They are, however, excellent for recessing and cutting out complex patterns and shapes in thin material. They are ideal for following a template, and therefore for repetitive operations, but they are nowhere near as versatile in use as the portable router which can be taken to the workpiece itself at various stages of construction.

The overhead router has an additional disadvantage in that the workpiece is brought up to the cutter, unlike the portable version which runs off the surface, so any variation in the thickness of the material results in similar variations in the depths of recessing or moulding. Much will depend on the type of work you do; this is an ideal machine for quantity production work, but, for the smaller shop, a spindle moulder/shaper doubled up with a portable router would be a better combination.

DRILL-PRESS

The drill-press equipped with ½ hp (0.373 kW) motor has a range of pulley speeds for wood and metal, graduated feed, locking handle to the feed and swivelling table which can also be tilted for angle drilling. Its ½ in (12.5 mm) capacity chuck will accommodate all types of machine bits and drills, and it can be used not only for all vertical drilling operations to any preset depth, but also for veining, shallow grooving, light hollow-chisel mortising, drum sanding and polishing, etc.

Illustrated is a five-speed bench model, but these machines are also available floor-mounted with crank-up tables. Both floor and table models can have up to 12 speeds, making them even more versatile. Many imported 12-speed bench machines are surprisingly inexpensive and quite suitable provided that they are not used continuously or for very heavy work.

BENCH-GRINDER

The bench-grinder is virtually indispensable for the rapid grinding of cutting edges, moulding blanks, etc., and the various abrasive wheels are listed on p. 108.

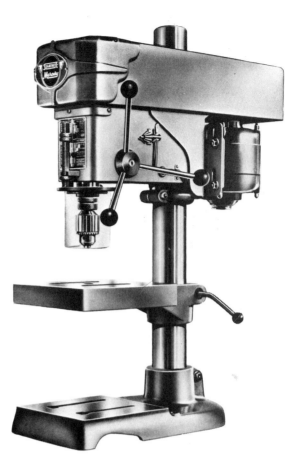

115 ½ in (12.5 mm) capacity five-speed table drill or drill press

116 8 in (203 mm) high-speed bench-grinder

135

117   6 in (152 mm) pad belt sander

119   Small bench drum sander with angled table

118   Small bench drum sander

SANDERS

The most useful sander for the cabinet-maker, if space permits, is the *pad belt sander*. This often includes a built-in sanding disc with table, and also a finishing table for sanding smaller objects. Pad sanders come in a variety of lengths and increase considerably in price with each extra foot. The belts are normally 6 in (152 mm) wide and can be made up to order to any length in a variety of grits and either cloth- or paper-backed. Adequate and separate dust collection is usually essential, since the fans that are built into many machines for this purpose are rarely adequate for full protection.

Also very useful is a drum sander for all those internal curves.

All machine sanders require garnet or aluminium oxide papers (see Abrasives, Chapter 7), and the grit used is generally some grades coarser than for equivalent work by hand methods, owing to the speed of the cut. An 80 grit aluminium oxide paper, for instance, will give a sufficiently fine finish on open-grained woods whereas hand-sanding might require 120 grit for a comparable scratch-free surface. It is possible to use four grits only: 80, 120, 180 and 240, with 180 adequate for most situations.

WOODTURNING LATHES

Most furniture-makers require turned components from time to time, from chair legs to turned drawer knobs, so it makes sense, if space permits, to undertake this within the workshop. The woodturning lathe can also be a useful source of income, and bowls and platters, often from the waste products of furniture-making, can keep apprentices and trainees gainfully employed between orders. It is preferable to purchase as heavy a machine as

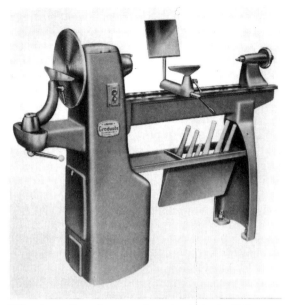

120 A medium duty wood turning lathe by T.S. Harrison & Sons

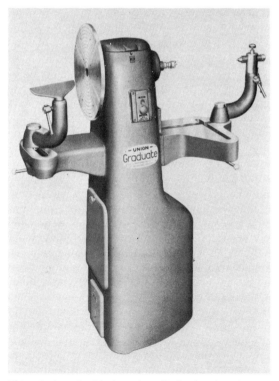

121 A short bed lathe primarily for bowl and handle making

one can afford, with a bed long enough to take dining or sidetable legs.

COMPUTER CONTROLLED MACHINERY

The CADCAM system

Computers have become well established aids to financial and stock control systems, but now they are being used to assist in the preparation of drawings and in the direct control of special types of machinery. Manufacturers who use CADCAM, or Computer Aided Design Computer-Aided Manufacture, are still relatively rare, but if computer hardware of this type continues to fall in price and increase in versatility the number of users is bound to increase. Although most large manufacturers are willing to invest in any type of technology which reduces costs and increases their production capacity, it is unlikely that the furniture industry will become totally automated while there is a growing demand for individual, craftsman-made pieces.

The electronic pencil

Computer-aided design systems are most useful where large numbers of similar drawings are used. Office and kitchen layouts, where identical items of furniture are laid out in different ways for different clients, are a good example of an area where CAD can save time and money. Outlines of the individual pieces can be stored in the computer's memory and then recalled and positioned on the display unit with ease. The designer can then move the images around on the screen until he is satisfied with the layout. The resulting screen image can then be passed to a micro-chip controlled drawing-board and turned into a high quality tracing, complete with any comments or measurements required. The electronic image of the completed drawing can be stored, recalled, and altered very easily.

More sophisticated systems are being developed where specially prepared working drawings fed into the computer can be shown on the display unit as composite images. These

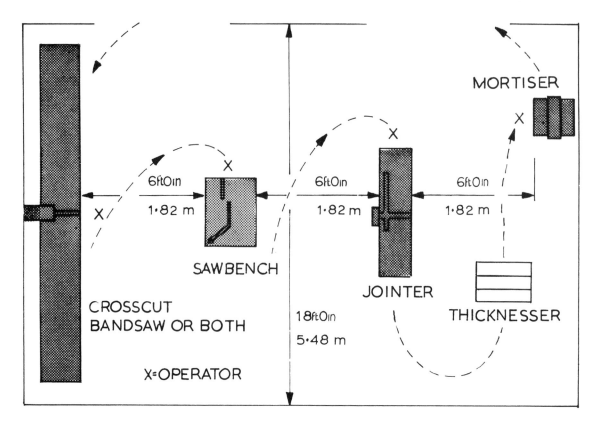

MORTISER

X

6ftOin
1·82 m

6ftOin
1·82 m

6ftOin
1·82 m

X

X

SAWBENCH

JOINTER

THICKNESSER

CROSSCUT
BANDSAW OR BOTH

18ftOin

5·48 m

X=OPERATOR

122 A very minimal woodworking shop showing a normal progression of work. What could be added beyond the mortiser is the spindle moulder/shaper with tenoning facilities, or separate tenoner in the larger workshops

composites are a good 3-D likeness of the finished piece of furniture. Solid modelling systems like this are used to assist in the development of new designs at lower cost than traditional methods.

Working robots

Computers are now being used very effectively to control other machines directly, with only limited human supervision or intervention. These machines are used for transporting work or raw materials, or for shaping, sanding or polishing the finished article. Efforts are currently being made to link the design and manufacturing stages electronically so that machines can make an article from an electronic drawing sent by wire. This method will be used only for very simple components for some time, but the possibilities will no doubt increase. One of the most widespread and successful computer controlled machines in the furniture industry is the CNC router. CNC means Computer Numeric Control, and refers to the programming language used to control the machine's operations. This control language consists of strings of numbers which, rather like map reference numbers, tell the machine where it is and where it is heading next. Information on the task the tool is to perform is fed into the keyboard attached to the router as a series of code numbers. Some of the more common operations, such as circle cutting, are built into the machine memory. This simplifies the programmer's task considerably, but even so a complex set of operations may require a fault-free program of up to 1000 lines in length. This operating software is expensive to produce, and difficult to debug if problems arise. One of the areas in which the present generation of machines can be improved is in the flexibility and power of this programming, or 'operating system'.

The hardware—the actual machinery which the software is used to control—is superficially similar to a conventional router, the differences being that the cutting head rises and falls automatically, while the workpiece is fixed to a power driven table that moves the wood past the cutter under constant control. Large machines may have mobile cutter heads in order to reduce the floor-space required for the machine. The addition of a vacuum table to the machine to hold the work down during machining reduces jig costs and improves loading times between cycles. The chief benefits of this machine are the very fine tolerances it can work to, and the consistent high speed with which it can make complicated shapes. Dimensional accuracy of the finished work is normally expected to be within 0.1 mm. Pierced and moulded chair backs are typical of the complex items that can be made. This type of machine can be fitted with several heads, so that each cycle of the main program produces two or more components. Alternatively, each cutter head may be fitted with a different type of tool, in order that the machine may perform different operations without stopping the work-cycle. This type of dual tasking is not practical using the conventional machine. Drill units can be fixed to these machines for precision boring fixing holes for flat-pack furniture kits etc.

Transfer units

Robot arms, commonly used for welding work in the car industry, have some applications in the furniture industry. More properly called *transfer units*, they may be used for moving work between machines, or in a modified form for furniture polishing work. In this application the arm is used to grip a spraygun and apply lacquer to the prepared furniture or components. The flow rate of lacquer to the gun is controlled by further automatic machinery. For these applications, the transfer unit may be programmed using the CNC system, or more simply 'led by the nose' through its appointed task. The unit is put into 'learn' mode and then an experienced craftsman sprays a sample chair with lacquer, using the gun fixed to the robot

123   CNC router

arm. As he sprays the sample each tiny movement and each change in flow rate of lacquer is stored by the machine memory bank. The robot arm is now capable of repeating the task under power as often as required to spray a whole batch of identical items. The learning process has to be repeated for each new style of chair produced. One of the benefits of this method of finishing is that health hazards are reduced, since the machines can work away from occupied areas of the plant, and tolerate high levels of air pollution without harm.

Small workshop automation

The area where CNC machines have had most impact on small workshops is in the making of upholstery and soft furnishings. CNC sewing machines are less expensive than most automatic machines and are used to speed up tasks like quilting, seam binding, and edging.

At the moment large computerized woodworking machines are too expensive to buy and programme for small workshops producing a wide range of items in relatively small amounts. For some time they will be used in bigger companies which can cover their cost. One of the ways in which the real benefits of new technology can help small workshops and individual craftsmen is by grouping small firms around a central facility equipped with automated machines of all types, capable of turning out components to very high standards. The user-group will share the costs of a central CNC facility and use its output as required. CNC machines of this kind can be used to make standard items to help small makers meet their overheads, and allow them to spend more time creating the individual items which their customers require.

A similar method of group machining was first used when power machinery was introduced and it enabled many small works to survive until machines became generally affordable. Groups of this kind are being discussed now and may be in operation by the early 1990s. Failure to use some of the advantages of economy and accuracy that robot machines bring may possibly cause contraction of the furniture industry into a small number of very large concerns, and a handful of individual designer craftsmen who survive by providing an individual service.

12   Workshop layout and furnishings

The perfect workshop hardly exists; it will always outgrow itself, or changing fashions will create other demands in working space or equipment. Ideal working conditions, regardless of expense, could doubtless be formulated; but in all professional work the overriding necessity is to keep the capital outlay within the framework of the turnover to be expected, and all the money spent on premises, equipment or materials must earn its keep if the business is to be successful.

Production-workshops

Mass-produced, i.e. quantity-production, furniture is more the result of business expertise and engineering skill than the application of fine craftsmanship, although furniture is and probably always will be a craft-based industry while it continues to use a natural and viable material. The modern factory employs machine- and hand-workers of a variety of types, assemblers, finishers, polishers, upholsterers and inspectors, etc., and, in the narrow sense, expert cabinet-makers might have no place at all in the organization. However, most large concerns keep a nucleus of skilled craftsmen for prototype-work, while all learners and apprentices do, or should receive, training in either wood machining or the basic hand-skills. In effect, therefore, a modern furniture factory which is efficient, well organized, and anxious to maintain a standard of quality is the basic handshop vastly extended, systematized and mechanized, in which the skilled fingers which once held chisels, wielded planes and coaxed satin surfaces from wood have now learned to use machines for precisely similar functions.

HAND-WORKSHOPS—PLANNING

Only general observations are possible, for there are so many factors to be considered—number of personnel; type, variety and standard of work to be produced, and amount of fixed machinery which is to be employed. In factory production the work-flow can be systematically planned from the kiln-drying units to the polishing-shop through a system of inter-communicating units. In the small handshop which caters for 'specials', 'one-off' or contract furniture, with an occasional prototype for a large concern, short runs of smaller items, coffee-tables, etc., and a certain amount of bread-and-butter repair-work, most if not all of these activities must be carried out under one roof, and compromises are inevitable.

Location of the workshop is not of paramount importance, for the handshop is not necessarily dependent on easy road and rail access or a convenient pool of near-by labour, and there have been good shops on mountain-slopes and over mill-streams. More immediate considerations are a three-phase electricity supply, good natural lighting, a dry shop and pleasant surroundings (for the psychological effect is considerable with skilled craftsmen working to high standards). Concrete, asbestos and galvanized iron for the structure should be avoided wherever possible for they all condense heavily in changeable weather, which is bad for work and tools alike. The ideal would be either cavity brick or a wood-clad structure lined with insulation board, and a tiled, slated or boarded and felted roof. Windows should be adequate to give a general flooding, for lighting from one side only can create dark shadows and dangerous twilight areas. North lighting may be cool, clean and factual, but is psychologically unhappy over long periods, while south lighting is good but must be screened in summer otherwise hot sunshine through glass can play havoc with unprotected wood surfaces. Artificial lighting should be plentiful; but while fluorescent lighting is excellent for general flooding it creates little if any shadow and it is then difficult to judge both depth and surface texture, therefore drop lights over each bench are essential if there is much working after nightfall. In particular all fixed machinery should be lit from every angle with no harsh shadows; but the quality of the lighting must be such that all moving parts are seen to be moving. Powerpoints should be numerous also, and there again hanging lights over each bench will keep the working surfaces free from trailing cables.

Suggested illumination levels are: rough sawing and bench-work, 15 lumens per sq. ft (929 cm^2); medium machine- and bench-work, veneering, etc., 20 lumens per sq. ft (929 cm^2); fine bench- and machine-work, sanding and finishing, etc., 30 lumens per sq. ft (929 cm^2). Colour matching/north-light fluorescent tubes are suitable for veneer matching, staining and polishing, etc., while the final inspection of furniture where surface perfection is looked for should be done in a light source large in size and low in brightness. The ideal is inspection on a revolving platform against a brightly illuminated screen.

If heavy machinery is included in the workshop some form of concrete raft is necessary, with the working areas round each machine heavily dressed with coarse carborundum powder in the surface screeding; but the rest of the working area is better capped with wood if possible, for bare concrete surfaces are cold, dusty, hard and tiring to work on, and inimical to dropped tools. Wooden floors should not be waxed or polished in any way for they soon become slippery, and this is the chief objection against composition floors. Heating should be sufficient to conform to the minimum requirements of the Factory Act (15° C), (60° F), and there is much to be said for the old-fashioned round coke-burning stove which radiates its heat in all directions and can also be used for burning all the rubbish. It does not consitute any additional fire risk providing it is placed on a raised concrete platform, the ashes are not allowed to accumulate, and the floors are kept free from shavings. The aim should be to maintain an even temperature—not too hot and certainly not overdry—and localized electric fan-heaters, which can be swivelled in any direction, are not the happiest solution, for if forgotten they can soon ruin uprotected work. For heating the old water-jacketed glue-pot a gas-ring is better than an electric boiling-ring, while a water service with glazed sink is essential for modern adhesives.

WORKSHOP EQUIPMENT

Storage

This can be a nightmare if unorganized and should be methodically planned. Wood in bulk can be stored in open sheds protected from the weather; but plywoods, blockboards, etc. and wood for immediate requirements should be kept in a warm store or conditioning-room adjacent to the workshop. Veneers are best kept in cool, not overdry conditions or they become brittle; but they desperately need floor space and covering cloths, for constant turning over or exposure to strong sunlight will speedily ruin them. The problem will always be short ends of valuable woods, but a balance must be struck between the intrinsic value of the wood and the cost per man-hour of unearthing a particular piece from underneath a pile of junk, therefore it will pay in the end to be fairly ruthless. Dowel-rod should be kept high up in the main shop where the warm air circulates. It is always debatable whether cupboards or open shelving are best for storing the innumerable small tools and effects which are soon collected in a busy workshop. Metal fittings, particularly screws and nails, etc., should have their own closed containers or screw-cabinet, but for the rest, open shelves collect dust especially if machines are used in the workshop, while cupboards take up valuable space and tend to hide their contents. The owner must therefore decide for himself which is more suitable, but he will never have enough shelving.

Cramps/clamps and cramping/clamping devices

Figure 124A illustrates the usual pattern *G-cramp* with swivel shoe which adapts itself to the contour of the wood, 124B the *Record spin-grip* G-cramp which can be adjusted with one hand only, and is an excellent improvement on the older type which required two hands to locate and tighten it, and 124C the *Record deep-throat*

124 Types of cramp/clamp

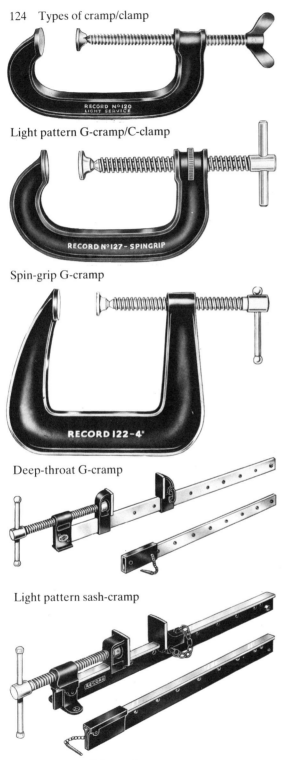

Light pattern G-cramp/C-clamp

Spin-grip G-cramp

Deep-throat G-cramp

Light pattern sash-cramp

Heavy pattern T-bar sash-cramp

Deacon patent tail slide

G-cramp. Light bar *sash-cramps* and lengthening bars are shown in 124D, and the heavy pattern *T-bar* in 124E, while 124F is the *Deacon patent tail slide*, which again is a considerable improvement over the old-type loose shoe and pin. The light bar-cramps with either ¼ in (6 mm) or ⁵⁄₁₆ in (8 mm) bar section are usually considered to be sufficient for normal cabinet-work, and the heavy T-bar for joiner's work, although lengths over 5 ft (1.5 m) are always T-bar section. In choosing the right cramp for the type of assembly a compromise must be effected between weight and stiffness. Light pattern cramps are inclined to pull the bars hollow if the strain is great, while heavy cramps may exert too great a pressure, or with their own weight pull a delicate carcass or twist framing. All cramping must, therefore, be done on a firm and level base, and the completed assembly carefully checked from every angle to ensure that there is no distortion of any kind.

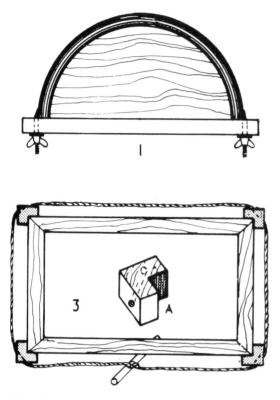

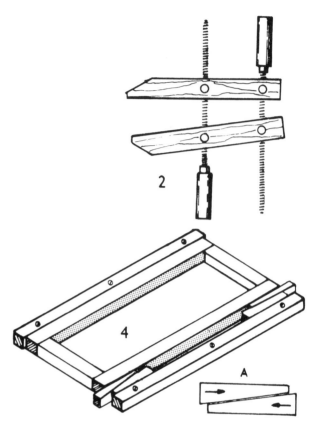

125 Cramping/clamping devices: special cramps

Special cramps/clamps

Band-cramps are used in shaped work and have a flexible steel band which conforms to the contours. Figure 125:1 shows a simple version. Figure 125:3 is the corner cramping device for mitred frames, etc., simply made out of four hardwood blocks (125:3A) threaded on a length of blind-cord and tightened with a stick; the cramping pressure is positive and considerable. Folding-wedges are shown in 125:4 and an improved version of the old wooden hand-screw in 125:2. The old type has beech jaws and hornbeam screws, but the new version has metal screws through pivoted centres, and localized pressure can be applied with the tips of the chops as far inward as the chops will reach, according to the size of the cramp. This type of cramp is particularly useful for laying blisters in veneered work, and for all gluing operations away from the edge which the standard G-cramp will not reach. It is axiomatic that no workshop ever has enough cramps of the right

kind at any given time, therefore the provision of cramping devices should be as generous as possible. Downward pressures can also be obtained with old scale weights up to 56 lb (25.4 kg), sometimes procurable at scrap prices from local dealers' yards; while a concrete brick is reasonably flat, square and weighs about 5 lb (2.26 kg), thus a fair pressure can be built up with a small pile of bricks.

In all cramping/clamping operations the working surface must be protected by padding the cramp jaws with blocks of thin wood, folded newspaper or pieces of felt or rubber, for even a lightly applied G-cramp can leave an indentation in the wood surface which may be difficult to eradicate. Pressures should also be spread with heavy blocks or bearers, particularly in carcass and framed-up work. Metal cramps should be frequently overhauled, the hard glue cleaned off and sash-bars lightly oiled, for there is nothing quite so desperate as a tail slide which refuses to move in the midst of a critical assembly. If resin glues and acid hardeners are used, metal cramps should be isolated from direct contact with the wood surface by scraps of paper, otherwise glue may interact with the steel and deeply stain the wood.

Assembly-benches

These need only be softwood and require no vices but here again they should be strong, steady and truly level. Separate benches for gluing up, especially for the hand-coating of glue on veneers, etc., are probably a luxury but well worth the extra space if it can be provided, for resin glues set glass hard and have an unholy knack of badly scarring finished surfaces if allowed to harden on working-tops. Oilstones and bench-grinders also deserve a special bench or table, preferably with metal-lined top, and placed in the most convenient position with equal access for every maker. This saves litter on work-benches and helps to keep the surfaces clean.

A long slot for hand-tools is provided at the back of the standard bench, but wall-mounted racks over the bench are more convenient and leave the bench-top free for wide work. At least two saw-horses (Figure 126) are needed for supporting planks while crosscutting, also two low stools of similar construction 12 in (304 mm) high and with 9 in (228 mm) wide tops as stands for carcasses in the making; a low platform-trolley on stout castors is invaluable for moving furniture or heavy planks. Cramping/clamping devices should be conveniently racked for immediate use, with G-cramps/C-clamps hung in graded sizes on pegs or long nails, and sash-cramps either from wall-pegs or in a special rack (Figure 127). Other items necessary will be dustsheets for the protection of finished work; softening blankets for bench-tops to protect delicate surfaces (ex-army blankets are excellent); a good pair of scales with some additional small weights for resin glues; dusting-brushes or a portable electric blower which is also invaluable for cleaning machines; rubber rollers for spreading glue; a few metal-worker's tools including an engineer's vice; innumerable

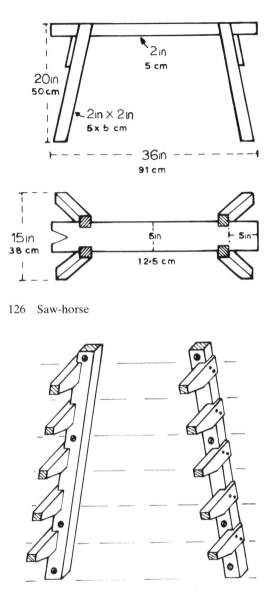

126 Saw-horse

127 Cramp/clamp-rack

small containers—tins, jars, etc.—for mixing small quantities of flue; old newspapers or cellophane sheets for press-work; soft rag . . . the list is well-nigh endless, but three months' actual working will provide the answers.

Part III   Basic techniques and joint construction
13   Wood preparation

Preliminaries to any sound construction are (1) *a full cutting list of all the pieces required*; (2) *good timber free from natural defects, accurately sawn and planed up flat, square and out of twist*; (3) *careful planning of the work ahead*, including the choosing of appropriate jointing methods, the order in which they are to be cut and the order and method in which the various pieces and parts are to be assembled in the completed carcass. This last is important and must be accurately visualized if there are to be no last-minute hitches, with carefully cut joints glued ready for assembly unable to be driven home because the direction of entry conflicts with other parts already in position.

SETTING/LAYING OUT

The wood must first be cut to approximate length, and it is always better to square off from either a sawn edge or a pencil-line along the length if the planks are waney. If an incorrect line is drawn—and all measurements should always be checked and double checked—then it should be cancelled out and a broad arrow drawn against the corrected measurement (128A). The ends of the plank should be care-

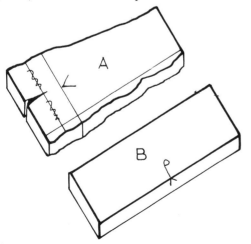

128   Marking a new line (A) and marking the trued edge (B)

fully examined for hidden splits and the first few inches of any plank which has been stored for any length of time may have to be sacrificed. Due allowance for working must be made, with 1/4 in (6 mm) on width and 1/2 in (12 mm) on the length for the first rough sawing to dimension unless the cuts are machine-made and accurate. Customary allowance for planing (surfacing) sawn thicknesses is usually 3/32 in (2.5 mm) for each wrot (finished) face.

The following is an outline of procedure using predominantly hand tools. Although many of these operations would normally be undertaken with the aid of machinery in professional shops, at some time or other, particularly on one-off, prototype or site work, every one of these hand processes might be used. Also, there is no better way of understanding the materials we work with than through a basic training in hand skills and techniques.

MARKING/LAYING OUT

Face-marks and edge-marks must be bold and should be done with a thick soft pencil. For the first approximate dimensioning of lengths, etc. a B or HB pencil can be used, but for accurate dimensions at later stages a 2H or 4H is necessary, while shoulder-lines should always be marked with a knife.

SAWING OUT

The rip-saw is used for long-grain sawing, the large crosscut or crosscut panel-saw for cutting across the grain, and the temptation to use the finer tenon- and dovetail-saws for rough work should be strenuously resisted, for more often than not the plank will be gritty. A usual tendency on the part of the beginner is to saw too fast, and in comparison the skilled worker's pace is almost leisurely, but he will cut more wood in the end and it will be accurate. Every effort should be made to saw not only on the line but also truly vertical, as this will save not only

129 Cross-cutting plank with handsaw

material but a great deal of unnecessary work at later stages. At the commencement of the cut the heel of the saw should be placed on the mark, steadied in the vertical position with the thumb and the kerf established with a few light upward strokes, not forgetting to withdraw the thumb out of harm's way before the full down-ward thrust is applied to the saw (129). A few strokes with a candle end along the saw-blade will reduce friction and lighten the work.

PLANING (SURFACING)

Either the fore- or jack-plane is used for the first rough levelling, the try-plane for true levelling and the finely set smoothing-plane for final surfacing. Contrary to the practice re-commended by some writers, the cutting edges of the irons should be square and not ground convex, although the jack-plane iron can have the corners dubbed over to prevent digging in. The set of the back iron should be adjusted to the depth of the cut required and the relative hardness or softness of the wood, for its sole function is to support the cutting iron and break up the chip, and therefore it can be set back as much as $1/16$ in (1.5 mm) for mild softwoods, but perhaps only $1/64$ (0.5 mm) for hardwoods. The projection of the cutting iron also depends on the nature of the board; it

should be fed down gradually until it gives a clean easy shaving without shuddering or digging in. The sole of the plane can be lubricated with the candle end to cut down friction.

In planing wide boards the best or face surface should first be levelled off along, across or diagonally, according to how the grain works (interlocked grain is best planed diagonally to prevent tearing out), and tested with the winding-sticks, placing one at each end and sighting through with the eye level with the nearest stick and about 12 in (305 mm) away. Any slight tilt to the further stick will then disclose whether the board is twisted, for although all edges may appear straight the diagonals may be curved. If the tilt to the further stick is, say, $1/8$ in (3 mm) then it can be assumed that the board winds $1/16$ in (1.5 mm) in its length, and about half that amount must be taken off the high further corner, and the other half from the near opposite corner by working diagonally across the board. When the board is out of wind then the try-plane should be capable of taking fine shavings the full length of the board over the entire area, to be followed up by the finely set smoothing-plane to ease out any ridges and roughened patches. During all these operations constant watch should be kept on the general levelness along the length and across the width, either with a straight-edge or the sole of the try-plane tilted on its edge. No attempt should be made to scrape or sand the surface at this stage for it is bound to attract small scratches, bruises and dents during subsequent operations, but badly torn grain should be got rid of as much as possible so that little if any thickness will be lost in the final finishing. When the surface is planed perfectly true and out of wind it should be marked with a 'face' mark (128B) which should never be omitted from any piece of prepared wood.

SQUARING EDGES

Immediately after the face surface is true, the leading or best edge should be trued straight in its length and at right angles to the face, checking carefully with the try-square all along the length; it is then known as the 'trued' or face

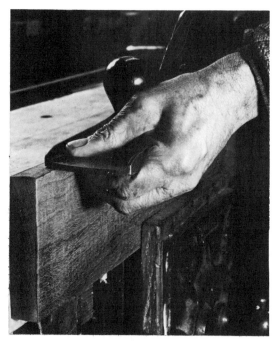

130 Correcting bevelled edge

edge and is marked accordingly. This is, perhaps, the most difficult of all planing operations, for while it is comparatively easy to plane a straight edge with a long try-plane, always remembering that pressure is applied at the front of the plane at the start of the stroke and gradually transferred to the back as the plane moves forward, it is much more difficult to keep the edge truly square to the face. If there is a tendency to form a bevelled edge, no attempt should be made to correct it by tilting the sole of the plane, but the cutting iron should be slid over to the high side with the fingers under the sole to form a guide (130) and the high edge taken down until the final shaving covers the entire width. However, should the tendency to bevel over still persist then the cutting iron should be examined for tilt, the bench top checked for general levelness with the floor, with the vice square to the bench-top and, therefore, truly vertical. The worker's own stance should also be checked, for the ability to plane a square edge must be mastered for accurate work and every effort made to achieve it.

Edging thin boards

If the edges are too thin to support the sole of the plane adequately then the shooting-board should be used. If it is too long for the board, the board should be cramped/clamped to the bench-top with a wood strip under to form its own shooting-board, and the plane slid along on its side; but the bench-top itself must be perfectly flat.

THICKNESSING/SURFACING, ETC.

Immediately after the best edge has been shot the actual thickness of the board must be gauged all round with a marking-gauge, and levelled off exactly to the gauge lines. The exact width of the board is then determined either by measuring with a rule placed on edge and not laid flat across the board (which may tend to give a false reading), or preferably marking in with a pencil-gauge, or with a panel-gauge; the edge is then trued up accordingly. If several boards have to be planed up to an exact and similar width then it will pay to cut a thin lath to the exact dimension, carefully squaring the ends on the shooting-board and using it as a trial stick or template. The lath itself should not be less than 1 in (25 mm) wide, for it is then easier to see that it is laid square across the face of the board and not at a slight angle which again will give a false reading. The length of all boards should, of course, be kept full at this stage to allow for final dimensioning. After several boards for any one carcass have been surfaced they should not be stacked haphazardly until they are needed, but should either be placed one on top of each other on a level bench and weighted down, or stood on edge with a space between so that the air can reach every surface. They should also be protected from direct sunlight and the sooner they are framed together the better, although sufficient time must be given for freshly worked timber to settle down and adjust itself to the prevailing atmospheric conditions. For this reason timber taken straight from the timber-yard is often roughly skimmed over on both faces and allowed to settle for as long as possible before the general levelling, otherwise too much thickness could be lost if the boards warp or crook in length. In machine-planing every board must be flattened on one face on the jointer to take out the wind before it is thicknessed or the pressure of the rollers will merely bend it flat while it is being cut and it will spring back to its original shape as soon as it is released.

SQUARING ENDS

The shooting-board is used for squaring ends, but if the wood is too wide or too heavy to be held on the board then the ends will have to be shot in the vice and checked against a long try-square. The practice of nicking off the far corner to prevent the grain splintering out is not to be recommended, and it is advisable to learn how to use the try-plane in both directions, leading with the left hand, reversing the plane and leading with the right. An alternative method is to cramp/clamp a block at the far corner to support the grain, and a similar scrap piece is sometimes necessary when squaring ends on the shooting-board.

TRUING OF SURFACED BOARDS

If a board does warp after it has been levelled, only experience will give the knowledge of how much it can be corrected when the construction is framed together. As an expedient, boards which warp in their width can sometimes be corrected by the old trick of wetting a level stretch of concrete floor, waiting until the water sheen dries off and then laying the hollow side downwards on the damp surface, weighting it if necessary. Alternatively, sturdy bearers can be cramped/clamped across either side, using scrap pieces to force the board over to the other extreme; but there is no guarantee that these measures will prove permanent. Thin sawn boards which are badly cupped and present difficulties in planing up can be panel pinned on the corners to the bench-top, the pins well punched in and the board surfaced, but the boards will resume their original shape once they have been released, and everything depends on whether the stiffness of the supporting framework will hold them flat without undue strain. The most satisfactory solution is to reject all boards which show pronounced movement, but sometimes it is a hard decision to take and therefore worth experimenting.

14 Jointing techniques and methods

JOINTING TECHNIQUES

The techniques of jointing sections of wood together to form rigid self-supporting and permanent structures have been evolved through many centuries to accommodate the natural movement of wood, and can rarely be improved upon. Only in the case of prefabricated boards (plywoods, particle boards, etc.), where the total movement is relatively small, have any worthwhile developments taken place (see Chapter 31 Knock-down fittings), but in the main the machine has merely adapted pure hand-techniques, simplifying them wherever possible and making greater use of the immensely strong adhesives now available, but still relying on the same fundamental principles. The best illustration of this is the dovetail joint, one of the most intricate to cut but still the best method of jointing two pieces of wood together at right angles to each other, where the machine, instead of evolving a simple worthwhile substitute—if that were possible—has accepted the joint as such, and only altered it sufficiently to allow for the rotary movements of the cutting-tool.

There are very many different varieties of joints to cover every possible contingency, but before describing them in detail some reference should be made to the function of the joints, what they have to do and how they have to do it. Glue is in itself a wonderful jointing medium, but wood imposes its own conditions. Thus two pieces of wood can be glued side by side with their grain direction parallel and will then, if properly jointed, be as strong as a single piece (131A), but the same two pieces cannot be glued end to end satisfactorily (A–B), for the cut pores of the end grain will merely suck up the glue like a sponge, preventing any permanent bond. It is true that end grain can be repeatedly sized with weak glue until the open pores are choked, and this will undoubtedly strengthen the bond, but the joint itself is still not good enough, and will always fail under any sudden impact because the natural elasticity of the long fibres lying side by side (A–A) is not there to cushion the shock; moreover, the interaction of a good glue with a wood surface is more subtle than a mere bonding skin. In the same way two pieces of wood with the grain or fibres opposed to each other (B–C) will shrink across their width in opposite directions, and *this natural shrinkage is so powerful that nothing can permanently oppose it*. Even if the junction is reinforced then the shrinkage will travel until it finds the weakest link, which will ultimately fail (131D).

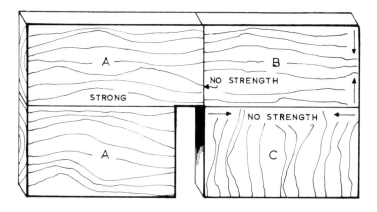

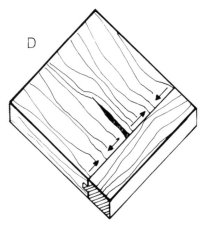

131   Jointing details

JOINTING/JOINING METHODS

Jointing methods are, therefore, designed to hold or lock pieces of wood together, either in the same plane or in opposing planes, so that the method of attachment is permanent and strong against loading stresses, thrusts, sudden impact, the wear and tear of daily use and the constant movement of the wood fibres, themselves ceaselessly moving in sympathy with the atmosphere surrounding them. All these factors must be taken into account, and whereas in heavy constructional work it is possible to calculate almost precisely the moments of compression, tension and shear to which the wood members will be subjected, unfortunately this is not possible with furniture except under controlled conditions, for although it is composed of upright piers or stanchions, bearers, cantilevers and distance-pieces as in any fabricated structure, the wood sections themselves are too delicate, the woods are chosen for beauty rather than strength, the

variety used is considerable, and the amount of use to which the piece of furniture will be put can only be broadly assessed. The cabinet-maker has, therefore, very little scientific data to help him, and he must rely almost entirely on tradition, instinct and as much practical experience as he can muster.

Methods of joining wood together can be classified under four broad headings:

1 Butted joints, either edge to edge, side to side and with or without additional reinforcement

2 Interlocking joints where one piece of wood is cut or shaped to fit a corresponding socket in the other piece

3 Mechanical joints which permit controlled movement

4 Knock-down metal or plastic fittings which secure the various wood sections together to form rigid structures.

These last fittings are described under the section devoted to metalwork, while the remaining headings tend to overlap each other, and it is usually easier to group the joints somewhat arbitrarily under their separate types or classes, i.e. edge joints, mortise and tenon joints, dovetails, mitres, housings, etc., and this is the procedure adopted in the following chapters. The basic cuts on which all jointing methods are founded are illustrated in 132.

132   Basic cuts in jointing

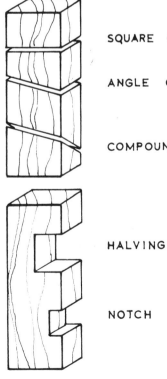

SQUARE   CUT

ANGLE   CUT

COMPOUND   CUT

HALVING

NOTCH

TRENCH

HOUSING

GROOVE   (1)

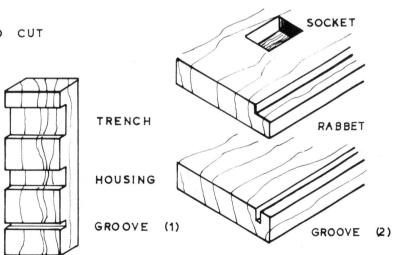

SOCKET

RABBET

GROOVE   (2)

15 Edge jointing

EDGE JOINTS (BUTT JOINTS)

These are used for jointing narrow widths, facings, lippings, glued fillets, blocks, etc., and can be either plain glued or reinforced with tongues, dowels or screws.

Plain glued edge joints

Two methods are available:
(*a*) straight shot joints coated with glue and immediately rubbed together, with the natural suck of the glue providing sufficient pull to effect a close joint, and known as *rubbed* joints; (*b*) joints planed fractionally hollow by the thickness of a piece of thin blotting-paper and pulled together with cramping/clamping actions. The advantage of the latter method is that the ends of the jointed boards are forced into compression and will not open if there is any subsequent shrinkage. Cold-setting resin glues can be used for these cramped-up joints, giving plenty of time for assembly so that boards warped in the length can be cramped at half pressure, tapped down flush and the cramps then tightened.

Rubbed joints

Assuming that several narrow boards have to be jointed together with hide-type glue, the boards should be arranged on the bench, choosing the best face uppermost, matching the grain and colour and, wherever possible, reversing the heart side so that any subsequent rounding is equalized without losing too much thickness (133:2). The boards are then marked as shown (133:1). The first board is held in the vice and the second board placed on it edge to edge and tested with a straight-edge across the total width. Any tilt either way on the top board must be corrected by replaning the edges; but if the boards have been squared on a jointer with incorrectly set fence, or on a shooting-board which is out of true, then reversing the face of

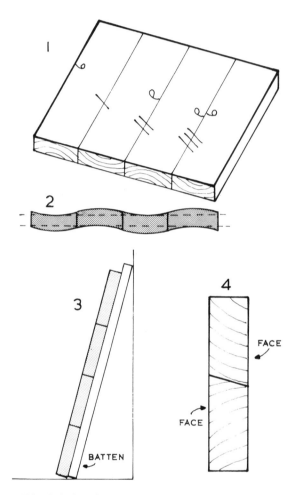

133   Jointing details

each alternative board will correct the tilt (133:4). The top board should be swivelled slightly and should bind at both ends, while finger pressure applied simultaneously at both ends will disclose whether there is any tendency to rock, denoting that the edges are twisted. After establishing that the boards seat along their entire length with their faces in one line, then the other boards should be tried in like manner until the assembly is complete.

152

Gluing up rubbed joints Hide glue should be used, thin and hot, and after slightly warming the boards the first is gripped in the vice and the next tilted against it so that the glue-brush covers both edges at one stroke. The second board is then placed in position and rubbed backwards and forwards three or four times to squeeze out the surplus glue, keeping the hands low down and at either end, if possible, to avoid breaking the joint. Joints over about 3 ft (1.0 m) long should not be attempted single handed, and in any case long lengths should be cramped/clamped and not rubbed. If the assembly is composed of several boards, they should be glued up in pairs wherever possible, and the glue allowed to harden before any further rubbing; while freshly jointed boards should not be laid flat but stood under their own weight against an inclined batten (133:3), leaving them for at least 24 hours before final surfacing.

Cramped/clamped joints

Long lengths and boards glued with cold-setting resin glues must be cramped and are first planed fractionally hollow. In theory one sash-cramp should suffice, but in practice it is better to use three or more, with one at each end underneath and one in the middle on top to counteract any tendency for the cramps to pull the assembly in warp, checking that the boards seat on the sash-bars, and testing the upper surface with a straight-edge. If resin glues are used, there will be plenty of time to adjust the assembly, tapping down any boards which are inclined to spring. In all gluing operations with resin glues containing acid hardeners, scraps of polythene should be used to isolate glue-covered wood from steel jaws or bars, as otherwise iron staining may result. Surplus glue should be scraped off, for resin glues are hard on cutting edges.

For dowelled edge joints see Chapter 18, Dowelled joints.

Tongued and grooved joints

Where there is considerable loading of the surface, as in unsupported table flaps, etc., edge joints *should* be strengthened with tongues, which increase the gluing area. Tongues can be worked in the solid (134:1) or both edges

grooved and a loose tongue inserted (134:2). These loose tongues were formerly cut from *cross grain solid wood* but plywood is now univerally used, matching the ply to the thickness of the cutter. The boards are not planed hollow, while the tongue itself, whether loose or worked in the solid, should be a hand-tight fit and no more, and slightly bare of the full depth of the groove to allow for surplus glue, allowing $3/16$ in (5 mm) thick tongues entering about $1/4$ in (6 mm) for $3/4$ in (19 mm) boards, and $1/4$ in (6 mm) thick for 1 in (25 mm) boards. Thicker boards require double tongues (134:3).

If the grooves are worked with a spindle-shaper or router they can be stopped well clear of the ends and the tongues cut back accordingly (134:5), but if worked with grooving- or combination-plane or circular saw it is more difficult to stop the grooves and they can be allowed to run through, either showing the ends of the tongues—which is not objectionable if well done—or cutting back and filling in with carefully selected end-grain pieces (134:6). Twin grooves and loose tongues (134:2) save timber width; moreover, solid tongues (134:1) worked with matched cutters in a combination-plane are not wholly satisfactory, for the carefully planed edge has to be cut back to form the tongue, and the tightness of the joint may suffer. With machine-cutters, however, solid tongues are so easily formed they are standard practice in production-work and 135 shows the variations possible.

A good tongued and grooved joint will help to pull up a warped board, but should not be relied upon to correct a pronounced problem. Faults in tongued joints are shown in 134:4 where in (A) the tongue is too long, preventing the edges meeting; (B) too thick, forcing the grooves open; and (C) too short, weakening the joint. Typical applications are also shown on this page. Figure 134:7 is a tongued and grooved table-top; 134:8, 9 show two forms of applied lippings to plywood or laminboard, etc.; 134:10 is a light framework with ply panel suitable for small doors, provided the panel is also glued into the groove; 134:11 is a carcass cheek tongued into a post or leg in preference to a series of small tenons which have to be cut laboriously by hand; 134:12 is the corner of a tongued carcass, with (A) a stronger variation as

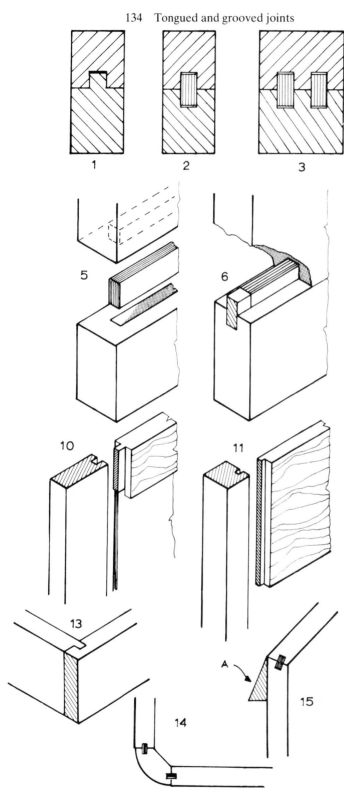

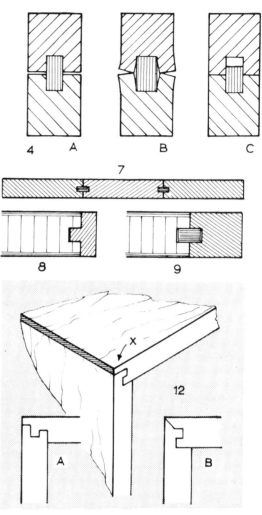

These joints should be machined, glued and assembled without a dry fit. The short grained tongues are very weak

the long lap at X is unsupported, and (B) a mitred lip and tongue; 134:13 is a simple box structure; 134:14 is a shaped carcass plinth or cornice; and 134:15 is a method of working tongues on a bevelled edge where the block (A) gives right-angled seating for the plough-plane. Other applications are shown in succeeding chapters.

Slot-screwed joints

An alternative method for strengthening edge joints is one in which the projecting head of a countersunk steel screw enters a corresponding hole and socket. The hole is bored to the diameter of the head, and the socket cut to receive the shank so that the head of the screw cuts its own path, while the bevel of the countersink pulls the edges together (136). For a tight fit the boards are first tried in position, and the top board tapped a little way home, as indicated by the arrow, to make sure everything lines up. It is then removed, the screw given a half turn, the edges glued, driven home and cramped/clamped. This joint is not now used to any extent, but may be useful for edge joints which have to be worked on before the glue is thoroughly set, and for dry jointing and secret fixings for panelling, wall fittings, etc.

Matched, cleated and battened joints

Traditional custom regards the tongued and grooved joint proper as having loose tongues glued in, and the 'matched' joint with tongues worked in the solid; but the introduction of cheap tongued, grooved and beaded or V-jointed matchings for wall linings usurped the latter term, which is now used solely to describe solid-tongue boards which are dry jointed and secret nailed or screwed to supporting battens or frameworks.

Matched boarding (137:1) has little application in furniture, although cottage-style oak furniture sometimes had doors framed together on this principle. Cleated or battened joints are jointed boards stiffened or supported by screwing ledges or battens to the back (137:2). The screw-holes are slotted as shown in the inset so that the screws can slide either way to accommodate movement, and the principle is

135   Examples of machine-jointing using standard cutters

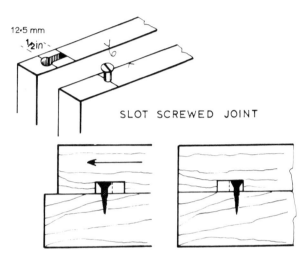

SLOT SCREWED JOINT

136   Jointing details

sometimes used for drawing boards of soft-woods, glued on the edges, deeply saw kerfed on the back to take up any movement and prevented from hollowing or warping on the face by the slot-screwed battens. An alternative method is to taper dovetail the battens (137:3) which do not need either screws or glue.

137   Jointing details

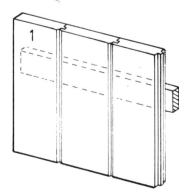

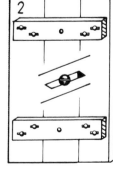

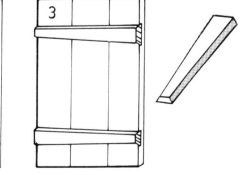

16 Housing/dado, halving and bridle joints

HOUSING/DADO JOINTS

Housings are usually taken to mean wide grooves cut across the grain to receive the full thickness of fixed shelving, drawer runners, etc., although they can also be worked with the grain. Probably the only real difference between a housing and a groove is that the latter is designed to take a shouldered tongue and not the full thickness. Trenches are usually taken to mean seatings or wide housings, but the terms are interchangeable.

Housings/dadoes for fixed shelves can be worked right through or stopped short of the front edge so that they do not show (139:1A), in which case the shelf is notched at the front to allow the remainder to enter. In working housings it is not advisable to rely on measurements exclusively, for the shelf could taper fractionally in the thickness, giving a sloppy fit if the housings were squared across and of constant width throughout. A better plan is to square a pencil-line across the cheek, place the shelf end vertically on the cheek against the pencil-line and scribe the thickness both sides with a sharp knife pressed hard against the shelf. A portable electric router can be used to cut the housings, working against a batten cramped/clamped to the work. Alternatively, if cut by hand, the correct depth is gauged on the back edge, a hole bored at the front to the correct depth, the hole cut out square, the knife-cuts deepened and a small bevel formed to act as a guide for the tenon-saw, the sides sawn down to depth and the waste chopped out with a chisel or routed

138 Working a housing/dado

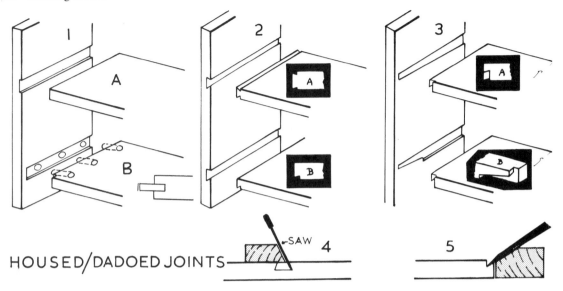

HOUSED/DADOED JOINTS

away with the hand-router (138). Without a router, or in positions where it cannot be used, a temporary depth-gauge can be made by driving a panel-pin through a block of wood with the point projecting the required depth, as shown in 138. Working the block backwards and forwards will scratch the high spots which can then be levelled.

If the sawing has been accurate the shelf will fit tightly first time, but if not then the sides of the housing/dado must be eased with an edge-trimming plane or chisel. The same setting of the marking-gauge used for the depth must be used to mark the shoulder cut on the shelf which should be sawn in fractionally short of the mark so that the shoulder pulls tight against the cheek when assembled. Housing depths can be about 3/16 in (5 mm) for normal work—and there is little point in recessing more deeply—while the set in from the front edge of the panel can be about 1/4 in (6 mm). The strength of the joint relies on the overall tightness, and a good joint will require knocking home with a hammer and block. Drawer runners in plywood panels need only be recessed about 1/8 in (3 mm) for they can be glued and screwed if necessary, and in any case the loading is up against the side and there is little strain; but drawer runners in solid timber panels will probably require a 3/16 in (5 mm) deep housing for they must not be glued across

the grain (see Chapter 21, Carcass construction).

Dovetail housings/dadoes (139:2) are used where there is any considerable side pull, as in tall cupboards, etc., where the side may tend to bow outwards in the length. They can be bareface, i.e. tapered one side (B), or double (A), with the former more usual as the bareface at the top helps to keep the shelf square. The dovetail housings are usually cut to rather less than half the thickness of the side and run right through. They can, however, be stopped about 5/16 in (8 mm) from the front edge, which is simple enough with a portable electric router and dovetail-cutter, but more difficult to cut solely by hand. A shaped block (139:4) can be used as a guide for sawing in, and another (139:5) as a seating for chisel cuts to the shelf. Such joints must be tight enough to be effective, yet free to slide across the width of the panel; and as the glue always tends to swell up the fibres, making assembly more difficult, a stopped and tapered (diminished) form (139:3) is sometimes adopted, in which the back portion is an open housing and only the front few inches (100 mm) (B) are taper dovetailed. The taper can run the full length if required (A), but here again the fit is fairly critical, and if too tight the shelf will not travel the full distance. For most normal work there is much to be said for a

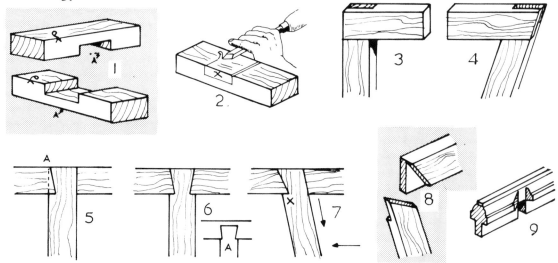

straight-sided housing, and, provided it is really tight, infinitely preferable to a badly cut, complicated joint. Simple housing joints can, in any case, be strengthened with the addition of close-fitting blind dowels (139:1B).

HALVED JOINTS

Several different forms of halving joint are used which are easy to cut and usually regarded as first exercises for students, although they have practical applications in skeleton grounds, frameworks, etc. In particular, the cross halving (140:1) gives a stronger connection than either tenons or dowels. Where the two pieces to be joined are of equal thickness, both halves or laps should be equal, the separate pieces clearly marked on the face and leading edge, and all gauging done from these, using the same gauge setting throughout so that the amount left in one piece (A) will equal the amount taken out of the other piece.

In working, the pieces should be positioned, marked in pencil either side, the cutting-lines squared across with a knife and the depths of the laps gauged in as described before. The shoulders are then sawn in on the waste, the waste chiselled away (140:2) from either side and finished off with a metal shoulder-plane. *Edge cross halvings*, i.e. halvings in the depth, are liable to fracture along the grain under any sudden impact, and an improved version is

shown in 141:1 which prevents any side give, although some strength is sacrificed. 'L' or *corner halvings* (140:3) can be cut entirely with the small tenon-saw and, if accurate, can be assembled without further treatment as the slight ribbing of a fine saw will give a key for the glue. Figure 140:4 shows an *oblique halving* with the required angle set out with the adjustable bevel, and in 140:3, 4 both pieces can be left slightly full in the length and flushed off afterwards.

'T' *halvings* are constructed in the same manner as *cross halvings*, etc., and can be straight, or single dovetail taper (140:5) and double taper (140:6) to withstand a direct pull. The dovetail rake is marked out as described in Chapter 19, Dovetailing, with the slope set in a fraction from the top corner (140:5A) to give a seating for the saw. Figure 140:7 shows an oblique single dovetail taper housing often used in gallows brackets for shelving. Any pull in the direction of the arrows is protected by the shoulder X. A stopped version of the double taper used in connecting rails in table and carcass stands is shown at 140:6A.

Mitre halvings (140:8)

These are relatively weak as the gluing area is halved (140:8), and they are, therefore, confined to light frames where the strain is negligible or where the edges are moulded and must show a mitre. Sash-bar halvings (140:9) are part cross halvings and part mitre halvings. The square recesses are cut first and the mitres after, using a mitre template for final trimming.

All halvings are glued, some can be screwed for additional strength, as shrinkage is bound to occur across the width, with rupturing of the glue-lines if the sections are wide.

BRIDLE JOINTS, ETC. (141)

Angle or *corner bridles* (141:2) are sometimes referred to as 'slot'/'open' mortise and tenon joints, and procedure is virtually the same as for tenoned work. They must be marked out with a mortise-gauge, working always from the face sides, and set to give a slot about one-third the total thickness, with equal substance left on either side. They are stronger than the corner halving as the gluing area is doubled, and the stout shoulders take the strain. 'T' bridles (141:3) form a stronger connection than 'T' halvings, and are the usual method of connecting middle legs to continuous top rails, where two short tenons would have little strength. If the top rail is thinner than the legs, the mortise-gauge must be reset accordingly (141:4), and if the rail is curved then a flat must be formed on the face of the rail so that the gauge works parallel. In cutting the slots it is quicker to saw the shoulders down to the full depth, bore a hole with brace and bit through the waste from either side (141:6) and finish off with a chisel. The slots are usually cut first and the tenon part cut and pared to fit, for it is easier to chisel across the tenon than to pare down vertically in the slot. Skew rails (141:7) cannot be bridled, and must be notched in and glue blocked from behind as shown. The rails can meet square at A if preferred.

Mitre bridles (141:5) are useful in framed-up work, mirrors, etc., and form a strong joint. Any moulding or rebating to the frame must be done first before the tenon and slot are cut. A stopped form is shown at A which is more delicate but not so strong.

141 Bridle joints, etc.

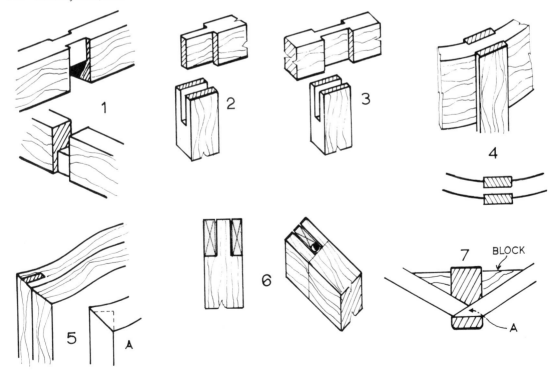

17 Mortise and tenon joints

These are probably the best known of all wood-working joints. The variations are many and only the principles and the main types need be given.

Mortise and tenon joints are usually referred to as *wedged through* (142:1) and *stub* or *blind* (142:2). The former is more applicable to joiners' work where the end grain of the tenon shows on the edge of the stile and is painted over, but as it has decorative possibilities it is included. The familiar type for furniture is the *stub tenon* with or without haunching (142:3) whose function it is to keep the unsupported part of the rail from twisting on the face.

All tenoned work follows the same general principles. The width of the mortises is slightly over one-third the thickness of the stile (142:5) but pitched according to the width of the hand- or power-chisel available. The rail width in corner mortising is also divided into three, one-third for the haunch or seating and two-thirds for the tenon, less a bare 1/16 in (1.5 mm) shoulder at the bottom edge to cover any slight gap caused by a slack tenon or bruising of the mortise socket end in levering out the waste in hand-methods. The final width of the tenon itself less the haunch becomes the length of the mortise cut to receive it. In all framed-up work it is always better to provide an extra length to the stiles to form a horn (142:1) at top and bottom which helps to prevent the splitting of soft wood while deeply mortising, and also to protect the corners from incidental damage. These horns are left on until the door is fitted.

Where the stiles and rails are grooved or rebated/rabbeted for panels the mortises are pitched to coincide with their position; they can be wider but not narrower than any groove or rebate in the rail. The mortise depth should be slightly more than the length of the tenon so that a small gap is left for surplus glue, while plenty of wood substance should be left between the bottom of the mortise and the outer edge of the stile, certainly not less than 3/16 in (5 mm) even for a small door.

HAUNCHES

Grooved frameworks will require haunches to fill them; if there is no groove a secret haunch (142:4) can be fitted; although light doors may not require haunching and the modern tendency is to omit them if possible.

LAYING OUT, ETC

Cutting lists usually take the gross length of the rails right across the width of the frame irrespective of the type of tenon. Laying out can be done entirely by measurement, but in practice it is better to mark the stiles clearly with top marks 'left' and 'right', and face marks uppermost on the inside or panel edge, and place them on the bench-top in the finished position, allowing an extra 1/8 in (3 mm) on the overall width for cleaning off and fitting. The rails are then marked and placed over the stiles also in the correct position, and allowing 1/8 in (3 mm) extra on the height. The critical positions of the rail shoulders, i.e. the net panel opening width, are then ticked, and also the opening height on the stiles. The stiles are then hand-cramped/clamped together and all the measurements—actual height of door frame (plus 1/8 in [3 mm] extra), depth of haunch or seating, position of mortise allowing for any groove or rebate in the rails—squared across and the rails similarly treated for shoulder length (width of panel opening) and length of tenon. The actual width of the tenon and the depth of the haunch can be decided later after the mortise has been cut. The mortise-gauge is then set for the width of the mortise and gauged from the face sides on both stiles and rails, after which the mortises can be chiselled, first boring out a series of vertical holes to save labour. When completed the tenons can be sawn in with the cuts always on the waste side of the marks. Figures 143 and 144 show the rail canted over first for one cut and then for the other, with the rail uprighted for the final cut. The shoulder-lines are marked with a knife and sawn through, and the tenons offered

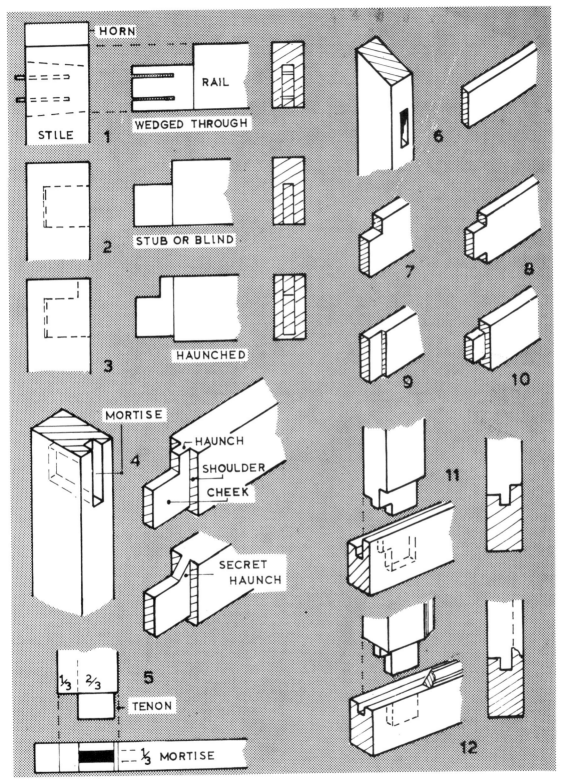

HORN

STILE

RAIL

WEDGED THROUGH

1

STUB OR BLIND

2

HAUNCHED

3

6

7

8

9

10

MORTISE

4

HAUNCH

SHOULDER

CHEEK

SECRET
HAUNCH

11

5

1/3 2/3

TENON

1/3 MORTISE

12

142   Mortise and tenon joints

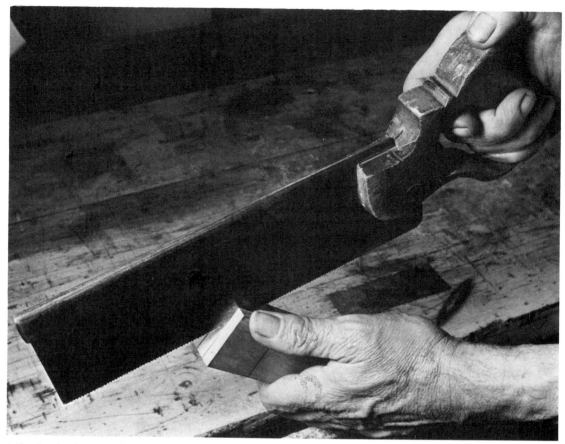

143　Sawing in tenon (first cut)

against the mortise for their final width and position of haunch. (Figure 145 also shows use of bench-hook for sawing shoulders, small parts, etc.)

TYPES OF TENONS

Several variations are possible. 142:6 is used only in the cheapest work for thin slats into thicker frameworks, such as play-pens, garden seats, etc., and the depth of the mortises must be positive as there are no shoulders on the rails to limit the depth of entry. Figure 142:7 is better as it has one cut shoulder and allows the top of the rail to be rounded over, if necessary, while 142:8 is better still as it gives a positive square location. Figure 142:9 is edge shouldered on one or both sides if the thickness allows, but no rounding of the rail is possible unless the

mortises have round ends also. Figure 142:10 is the orthodox method where the rail lines up with the face of the legs or stile and the tenon must be offset.

Wedged through mortise and tenon

This is shown in 142:1 and 146:1 and is taken through the stile with a little extra length for smoothing off, and wedged from the outside. The mortise is cut slightly full in the length on the outside to accommodate the wedges which are glued and driven home as the frame is assembled. These wedges can be at either end, which is normal for joiners' work, or darker wood is used and treated as a decoration in any of the positions shown alongside (146:1).

Stub or blind mortise and tenon

The socket or mortise is blind and, therefore,

144　Sawing in tenon (second cut)

145　Using bench-hook

hidden from the outside, and is the usual form for cabinet-work (142:2).

Long and short shoulder mortise and tenon

Figure 142:11 shows the extra shoulder length required to fill the rebate/rabbet formed to receive a panel which is beaded in from the back. The setting out of this type of tenon is described in Chapter 23, Door construction.

Moulded frame mortise and tenon

Here again the frame is rebated/rabbeted for a panel and the moulding must be cut and mitred on the face to receive the rail. If the moulded frame is grooved for the panel (142:12) and not rebated, then either both sides of the groove

163

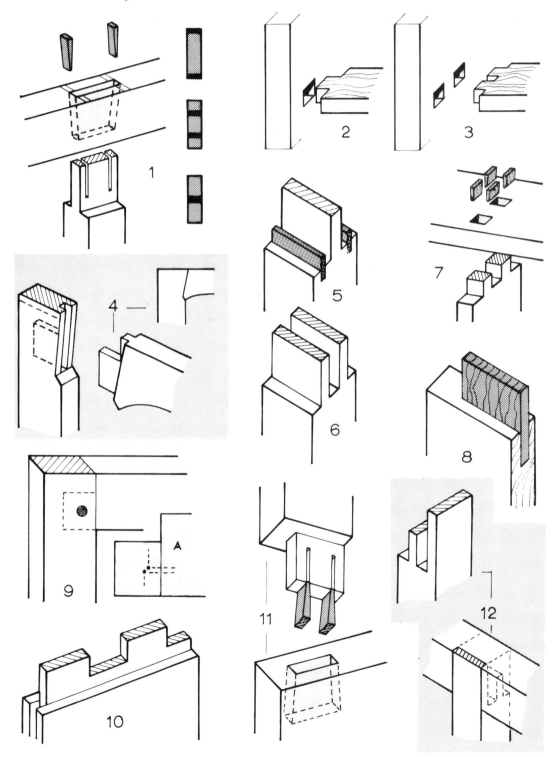

must be cut away and mitred to receive the rail, or the back shoulder of the rail must be shortened to allow for the extra width of the back stile. The positions of grooves, rebates and mouldings are marked during the critical setting out but must not be worked until after the mortises have been chiselled out; the offset of the moulding on the face must, of course, be on the same level as the depth of the rebate. Tenon cheeks are sawn in as before or the marks will be lost, but the tenon shoulders are better left uncut until the moulding has been run.

Miscellaneous tenons

Figure 146:2 shows the single stub tenon for connecting drawer rails to carcass sides, but the length of the tenon can only be a bare ½ in (12.5 mm) in a ¾ in (19 mm) carcass cheek, and double tenons are better (146:3). For instance, two ⅝ in (16 mm) wide tenons spaced apart ⅜ in (9.5 mm) in a 2¼ in (57 mm) wide rail offer nearly twice the gluing surface as compared with a single 1¼ in (32 mm) wide tenon; moreover shrinkage is less. Figure 146:4 is a mitre shoulder tenon useful where a rail meets a leg or post on a curve which would result in a feather edge at the springing-line if the normal type of square shoulder were used (see also Leg and frame construction, Chapter 22). The joint is first cut as an orthodox mortise and tenon joint, allowing about ¼ in (6 mm) of shoulder below the tenon for the mitre cut, and the sloping shoulders are then laid out and cut. A square shoulder terminating in a mitre cut can be used instead of the sloping shoulder, the only difference being in the appearance. The curve to the rail can be cut beforehand, but sufficiently full to allow final shaping to the exact curve after the rails have been fitted. Figure 146:5 is the tongued shoulder tenon useful where a heavy tenon is set back, leaving a wide shoulder; while 146:6 are twin tenons for heavy work which give a more secure fixing without taking out too much strength in a single wide mortise. Figure 146:7 shows pinning used for short uprights or divisions between drawer rails, and for partitions in large carcasses; the tenons can be wedged as shown if necessary. In modern work pinning tenons are often dispensed with, and the upright is housed/

dadoed and screwed from above, but where the rail below has to take transmitted weight, wedged pinning tenons are better.

Figure 146:8 is a false tenon either slotted or mortised into wild grain which has little intrinsic strength; it is also useful in repair work where the original tenon has snapped off, and provided it is tightly fitted there is little difference in the ultimate strength. Figure 146:9 shows the carpenter's draw bore tenon sometimes used in reproduction oak-work. The joint is cut in the usual manner, the tenon withdrawn and a waste piece slipped into the mortise socket; the hole for the pin is then bored through, the waste piece withdrawn and the tenon pushed home. If the same bit is fed through the hole to prick a position-mark on the tenon, and the mark is then moved about 1/16 in (1.5 mm) up and in towards the shoulder (A), a hole bored through the tenon will be slightly offset and will pull the parts together when a tapered drive pin is driven through the joint. Draw boring can be used in corner bridles or open slot tenons, and is an excellent way of securing these joints. Figure 146:11 is the fox wedged tenon in which the wedges are placed in position as shown, and driven in as the rail enters. This joint is of academic rather than practical interest; for if the undercutting of the shoulders of the mortise socket is too great the joint will be slack, or if not enough, then the wedges will not fully enter the saw kerfs, and will prevent the tenon from fully entering. Figure 146:12 is the combined bridle and tenon which is useful for long tables with intermediate legs and continuous rails. The position of the joint can be reversed to show either the rail butting against the leg on either side, or passing over the leg in an unbroken line. Figure 146:10 shows double tenons used in wide rails or narrow carcass cheeks into legs or posts, and divided, as shown, to counteract the inevitable shrinkage of a single wide tenon. This type is no longer used to any great extent in modern furniture, in which a continuous tongue in a shallow groove is usually sufficient to hold the joint.

LOOSE TENONS

Loose tenons for demountable structures which

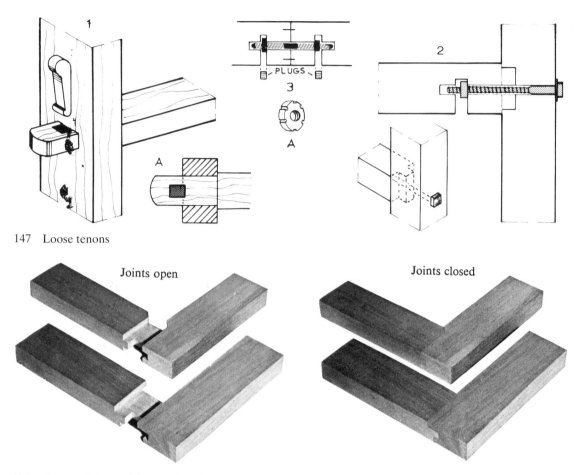

147 Loose tenons

148 Rebated/rabbeted frames showing alternative methods

are not glued together are shown in 147:1. It shows the *keyed* tenon in which a single thick tenon is taken through the post, slotted and then keyed together with a tapered wedge. The slot should pass a little way into the mortise (A) so that the wedge bears against the post. This type is used on stretcher rails in reproduction oak refectory-tables, collapsible forms, etc. Figure 147:2 is the tenon and bolt, with a stub tenon entering the post and secured with a headed bolt passing through from the outside and held with a square nut in a mortise cut to allow it to enter, but not to revolve. Another example of this technique but without tenons is the handrail bolt (147:3), used for jointing two

pieces of timber in the same plane, i.e. fireside rails, handrails, etc. A special double-threaded bolt is used with circular nuts (A) slotted to take a screwdriver-blade or stout punch. If only one bolt is used the ends should be prevented from swivelling round by short stub dowels, or more commonly with wire nails either side of the central bolt knocked in and pinched off leaving about ⅛ in (3 mm) protruding. The nuts are inserted in the mortises, the bolt fed through and the nuts tightened by tapping them round, after which the mortise holes are plugged. Examples of well-fitted mortises and tenons are illustrated in 148.

166

18   Dowelled joints

Spiral, grooved, and fluted or faceted dowel-pegs offer greater holding power than the standard smooth birch dowel-rod, and dowelled constructions are now used extensively in lieu of mortises and tenons. Providing the dowels are a good fit and enter not less that 1¼ in (32 mm) either side of the joint-line there is probably little difference in the ultimate strength. Figure 150:1 shows the standard birch dowel which should be saw-kerfed as shown to provide an escape route for trapped air and also for surplus glue; 150:2 shows the spiral grooved dowel and 150:3 the fluted dowel. Dowel-pegs can be chamfered or rounded with a dowel-rounder as in 150:4, and the seating countersunk at (B) to facilitate entry. A small gap should be left at (A, C) for trapped glue, and all dowels should be checked for diameter. If oversize they can be knocked through a dowel pop or plate (149) which can be purchased or simply made out of a piece of ¼ in (6 mm) mild steel bar, accurately bored and countersunk on the underside. Some workers keep several dowel-bits in each size, for not only do the rods vary but also the critical diameter of the bits. Dowel-rod should be kept in a warm, dry place and purchased well in advance of use.

149   Dowel pop

SETTING/LAYING OUT, ETC.

The usual diameter of dowels for normal work is ⅜ in (9.5 mm), with ¼ in (6.0 mm) for thin stock and ½ in (12.5 mm) or more for stout frameworks. At least two dowels should be used to prevent swivelling of the joint, but if a light rail can only accommodate one, then a panel-pin should be driven through the framework from the back either side of the joint-line to grip the dowel. Spacing must be accurately done with a minimum of ³⁄₁₆ in (5 mm) wood substance left either side of the dowel socket, and ¼ in (6 mm) between the bottom of the socket and the outer face, for subsequent shrinkage can shadow through if only a minimum of wood is left. Figure 150:5 shows the spacing for a normal rail 1⅞ in (47.5 mm) by ¾ in (19 mm) finish, and 150:6 staggered dowels in larger sections. Actual laying out is simple if the two members can be cramped/clamped together in the vice (150:7), with a gauge-line run down the middle of the edge, working always from the face sides, and the positions squared across. Square sections many have to be marked out with a wooden template (150:8), or a dowel-jig of the Woden type (151); while an accurate hand-method is lightly to tap veneer pins truly vertical into the correct centres in one piece, nip off the pins leaving ⅛ in (3 mm) protruding, offer up the piece in the correct position and lightly tap the other end to register the imprint of the pin ends which can then be withdrawn and the sockets bored exactly on the pricked centres. Figure 152 shows the pins cut off ready for marking.

BORING SOCKETS/DOWEL HOLES

Any expedient should be adopted to ensure truly vertical boring of the sockets. If done by hand, using a Russell Jenning's pattern dowel-bit in a bit- or arm-brace, help should be enlisted in sighting for the upright. Drilling at an angle always presents problems, for the wings of the bit tend to follow the grain, and an expedient adopted in the writer's own workshops for precision compound angle drilling was to fix the work either horizontally or vertically, thread the spindle of a ⅓ hp (0.25 kW) electric motor for a ½ in (12.5 mm) capacity Jacob's chuck (or use a hand drill), mount the motor on a baseboard running between wood guide rails securely fixed at the correct compound angle, and feed the motorized bit forward to the correct socket

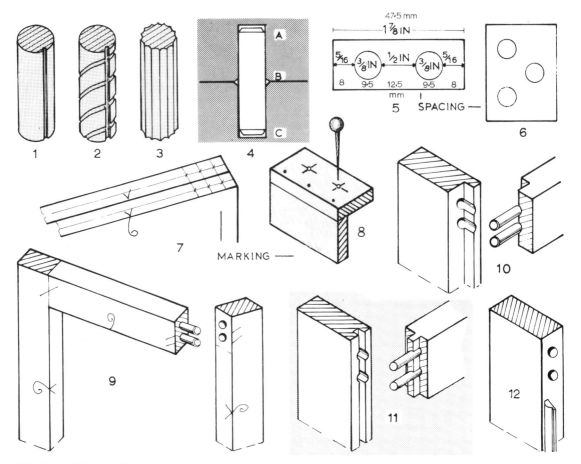

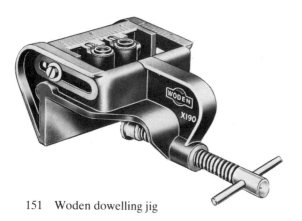

150 Dowelling practice

151 Woden dowelling jig

depth. Alternatively, the motor can be fixed and the work fed forwards. Methods such as this might appear to be unnecessarily complicated for a relatively simple operation, but with a dozen or more holes to drill much wasted time and labour can be avoided, and the motor with its threaded shaft is always a useful power source. A home-made horizontal dowel-boring machine is illustrated in 112. This included rise and fall and lateral sliding table, depth stop, etc. assembled by an engineer friend from a scrap-metal milling-machine bought from a local dealer's yard, and using the motor already described.

DOWELLED EDGE JOINTS

These are no longer used to any great extent but handworkers may find the process useful, particularly where the jointing methods must be hidden. The boards are planed slightly hollow

152 Setting/laying out dowel positions

and a marking-gauge is run down the centre of each edge; the boards are then cramped/clamped together and the dowel positions squared across. Boring must be dead accurate with a ³⁄₈ in (9.5 mm) dowel at about 5 in (125 mm) centres for up to 1 in (25 mm) boards, and ½ in (12.5 mm) dowels for thicker timbers. It is usually reckoned that dowel-pegs should enter about 1¼ in (32 mm) for maximum efficiency, with a slight gap at the bottom of the socket for surplus glue, with the dowel driven home on one edge and the projection checked with the corresponding socket on the other edge. The dowel ends can be chamfered and the sockets countersunk for easy entry, particularly

if there are slight errors in the laying out. Where boards have to be end butted to increase the overall length, dowels offer a practical method of strengthening the joint.

ASSEMBLING DOWELLED WORK

One side of the work should be dowelled, the pegs tapped fully home, surplus glue wiped off and the projection of each peg checked with its corresponding socket; it can then be dowelled into the other member without waiting for the glue to harden. If a trial assembly is made in the dry (unglued) state, spare dowels should be sanded to a loose fit and replaced with tight dowels in the final gluing up, for if tight dowels are used it may prove impossible to withdraw them without breaking the pegs. For assembly, single-application glues (hide, Cascamite One Shot, etc.) should be used and applied to the sockets only, for very liquid glues or separate hardeners applied to the pegs may swell the fibres and prevent entry. Sockets out of line or bored at an angle should be filled with glued pegs and rebored correctly, for any bending or crushing of the dowel-pegs will destroy much of the ultimate strength. Woods which split easily may have to be nipped with a G-cramp/C-clamp across the thickness if the dowel is tight and the surplus glue cannot readily escape. Sash-cramps across the assembly may be necessary to pull the dowels up.

APPLICATIONS

Typical applications are shown in 150 where two ³⁄₈ in (9.5 mm) dowels are used to each joint instead of mortises and tenons in a simple framework (150.9); long and short shoulder joint (150:10); a stub tenon and dowels for a grooved frame (the position of grooves, rebates, mouldings, etc. must be marked out first but not worked until after the dowel sockets have been drilled) (150:11); a moulded and rebated frame (150:12).

19 Dovetailing

Rapid developments in woodworking-machine techniques have evolved distinctive jointing procedures which are often as good as, and in some instances superior to, the traditional handcut joints they have replaced. An outstanding exception, however, is the dovetail, for here the handmade joint still equals and in some respects surpasses the machine-made copy. Nevertheless, even the machine joint with all its compromises dictated by the simple mechanics of power-operated tools is still a very good joint indeed, with ample reserves of strength. In short, the dovetail, whether hand- or machine-cut, is still the best method of jointing two pieces of wood together in their width and at right angles to each other.

Before describing the actual dovetailing joints and their many variations it is necessary to define precisely the various terms used, for the nomenclature as between hand- and machine-work differs radically. Thus in hand-work (15:1) where (A) is the drawer front and (B) the drawer side, (C) is the actual dovetail and (D) the pin; but in machine dovetails (153:2) the drawer front (A) becomes the female part and the drawer side (B) the male part, while 153:3D in the male part is the pin with its corresponding socket in the female part. Again, the angle or slope of the dovetail which constitutes its holding power against lateral strain is known as the 'rake', 'bevel' or 'pitch' in

hand dovetails, and is measured in terms of proportionate rise, i.e. rise of 1 in 5, 1 in 6, 1 in 7, etc., whereas the slope of a machine-cut dovetail is usually standardized at 20°, and the term 'pitch' refers to the spacing of the pins, i.e. ½ in (12.5 mm), ¾ in (19 mm), 1 in (25 mm), etc. measured from the centre of one pin to the centre of the next (153:3, 4). Other terms with different values are described under the appropriate headings, but the main structural difference between the two types is that hand dovetails can be spaced at random, whereas the spacing of machine dovetails is arbitrarily set by the machine, with the pins (male) and the sockets (female) equal in width; therefore any spacing out to fit a predetermined width of drawer side can only be done by varying the pitch.

HAND-CUT DOVETAILS

Three types are used: (a) through dovetails which show on both sides of a corner joint (154:1); (b) lapped dovetails which show on one face but are concealed on the other by a lap or lip (154:2), and (c) secret dovetails in which the joint is entirely hidden (155:2). For an understanding of the principles involved—which are intrinsically the same for both hand and machine dovetails with only the procedure

153 Dovetails

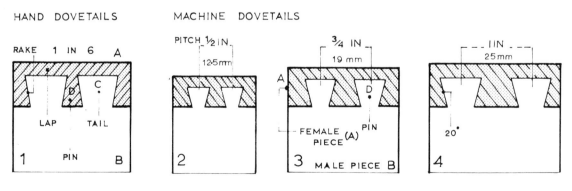

differing—it is necessary to describe the laying out and cutting of all three types in some detail.

Through dovetails

These show as end-grain wedge-shaped pins on one surface and square or oblong end-grain tails on the other (154:1). The true shape of both tail and pin resemble a dove's tail (after which they are named), and in through dovetailing by hand it is usual to make the tails at their widest part about twice that of the pins, but for extra strong work they can be equal and are colloquially known as 'cistern dovetails'. There are, therefore, no hard and fast rules regarding their width, and as with all other types a compromise is usually effected between strength and appearance.

Setting/laying out

The two sides to be joined need not be of equal thickness, but the thickness of each must be constant across the width and the long-grain edges must be parallel. It is advisable to cut the ends truly square and to the overall length, as this facilitates the setting out which must be accurately done, but a fractional fullness in the length can be left for subsequent cleaning off. Assuming that the ends have been cut square and to the true length then either a sharp marking-gauge or a cutting-gauge is set to the exact thickness of one piece (154:1A) and gauged all round the end of the other piece (B); the thickness of (B) is then similarly gauged round (A). The spacing of the separate dovetails must now be determined, and while an experienced worker might trust his eye alone the beginner should adopt the following procedure. Determine first the width of the end-grain pins (B) and, assuming that each pin is to be approximately $\frac{1}{2}$ in (12.5 mm) in width, gauge a $\frac{1}{4}$ in (6 mm) from each parallel edge of 154:6A to accommodate half a pin, and divide the space between into as many divisions as there will be whole pins. If these are, say, four then five divisions are required, and 5 in (127 mm) (or any number of inches [millimetres] easily divisible by five) is measured off on the rule and measured obliquely across the board as shown; the divisions can then be drawn in to give the exact centre of four equally spaced pins.

Dovetail rakes or bevels

The actual rake of the dovetail must now be decided. For carcass-work where strength is necessary and appearance of little consequence the slope can correspond to a slope of 1 in 5 or 1 in 6; while for show-work, drawer sides, etc., 1 in 7, and for very fine decorative dovetailing 1 in 8, can be used, always bearing in mind that the rake must not be too coarse, i.e. much below 1 in 5, or the short grain will be too weak, while too fine a pin, i.e. over 1 in 8, will have no real holding power. To set out these rakes it is only necessary to square a line across the bench-top and measure off the distances as in 154:3, setting an adjustable bevel to the rake or making up a simple wooden template (154:7). With proficiency neither bevel nor template will be required, and the eye alone will soon grow accustomed to the required slopes.

Cutting the dovetails

In practice it hardly matters whether the actual pins or the tails are treated first (although in some instances—tall carcass sides and in secret dovetails—the pins must be worked first and the tails from them), but as a rule the tail side is marked out and the pin side from it. After marking out the tail side in pencil (154:6, 7) the pin sockets or cores are sawn in with the fine dovetail saw, with the tail piece held in the vice and tilted over to bring the markings vertical (156). This sawing should be on the pencil-line, square across the edge and down to the gauge-lines, but the pin sockets should not be chiselled out at this stage—a mistake beginners often make—for the actual pins must be marked out before any chiselling away can be done. The pin piece (B) is then held in the vice (154:10), and the tail piece packed up and placed on it truly square with the edges flush (the drawing shows the positioning for a lap dovetail in which the tail piece is set back for the lap). The point of the saw is then drawn through the cuts, transferring them to the end grain of the pin piece, and once this is done then the pin sockets on the tail piece can be chiselled out, working from either side in a series of bevel cuts (154:11), so that the waste is fully supported with the last cuts vertical and exactly on the gauge-line; the end shoulders can then be sawn

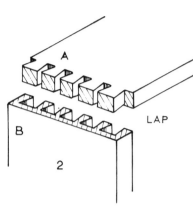

THROUGH

1

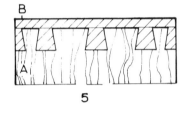

LAP

2

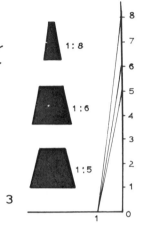

1:8

1:6

1:5

3

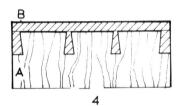

4

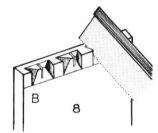

5

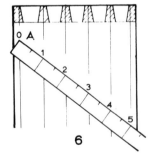

6

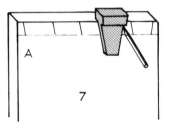

7

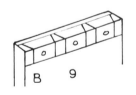

9

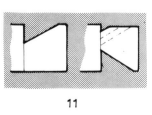

8

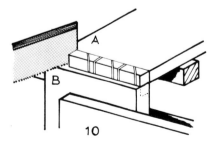

10

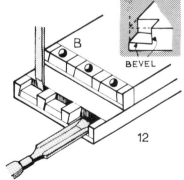

11

BEVEL

12

in with the fine dovetail-saw. Sawing in of the pins in the pin piece can now be done, again held in the vice and sawing-in as in 154:8 but down to the gauge-line on either side for through dovetails, with a centre cut in each tail socket to clear the waste. It is a useful precaution to mark this waste 'O' as in 154:9, and the sawing must always be on the waste side and alongside, but never on the gauge-marks or the pins will be too small. Alternatively, instead of sawing out small wedged-shaped pieces alongside the pins as for lap dovetails (154:8), the pins are sawn in and the waste partially sawn away with a scroll-saw. It hardly matters which, but here again a fast worker will not bother to set up another tool.

Chiselling the sockets will be done as for the tail piece, and it is customary to incline the vertical cuts through the thickness fractionally inwards towards the centre so that the bed of the sockets is undercut; but the cuts must not go over the gauge-lines on the faces. When all the cutting has been finished the dovetails can be tried together, but they should never be knocked fully home until they are glued up, for it is axiomatic that a good dovetail only fits once. Application of through dovetails is in box sides, etc. and in all right-angled framings where it does not matter if the joint shows.

Lapped dovetails

This is the usual type for drawer sides (154:4), carcass-work (154:5), etc. where one face must not show the joint and the dovetails are set back by a small lap or lip. Setting out and working is the same as for through dovetails, but the full thickness of the tail side must be gauged on the inner face of the pin side only, the width of the lap or set-back determined—$3/16$ in (5 mm) in $3/4$ in (19 mm) thickness is usual but not mandatory—the gauge reset and the lap gauged in from the inner face of the pin side and all round the tail piece. Figure 154:4 shows a typical setting out for a drawer side with two widely spaced whole pins sufficient for an average drawer up to say 6 in (152 mm) deep, and three pins for larger drawers; while 154:5 shows coarser carcass dovetails connecting, for example, a carcass top to a side. Small dovetails are provided at front and back to prevent any

twisting of the panel edges, but the main dovetails can be widely spaced with the tails about two and a half times the width of the pins as a fair average. Sawing in the tail sockets on the pin piece can be done as in 154:8, while most of the waste can be cleared with the saw or bored out as in 154:12; the remainder is then chiselled out as shown, again bevelling inwards as in the inset. In all setting out so far described for both through and lap dovetails no allowance has been made in lengths and widths for cleaning off, and this must be at the discretion of the worker. If the jointing is good only a thin shaving will be required to flush the surfaces and provide a smoothly running drawer, but if the worker is uncertain and wishes to make allowances then he must set his gauge-marks in accordingly. As with all woodworking activities the only true guide is positive experience, often bitter but nevertheless inevitable. On no account should dovetails be 'bishoped', i.e. hit with a hammer to spread the fibres and tighten up a slack fit. If there are gaps between the tails and pins—and it can happen to anyone—then it is perfectly legitimate to drive in small glued wedges of matching end grain which, if neatly done, will be invisible. Very tall carcass sides which carry the pins cannot be held in the vice for marking, and therefore the pins must be worked first and the tails marked from them with a scriber or knife point, as with secret lap and secret mitre dovetails.

Secret (double lap) dovetails

These are used where open dovetails would be unsightly, but as one lap must show end grain the jointing method could be entirely hidden with secret mitre dovetails, which are not much more trouble to cut. The double lap dovetail does, however, have certain applications, and 155:1 shows two forms: (B) side lap and (C) top lap, according to the use. In working the joint the projecting lap piece is rebated/rabbeted out (A) to the depth of the secret lap (the laps are usually made square in section). The pin piece is then set out and cut in the normal manner, and the tail piece set out from the pin piece as in secret mitre dovetailing (155:3), using an awl point as shown. A variation of this joint is shown in 155:4 where the carcass top is

1

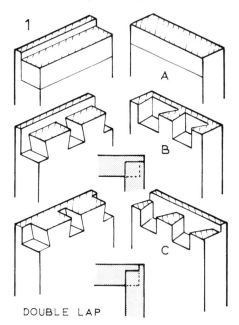

A

B

C

DOUBLE LAP

2

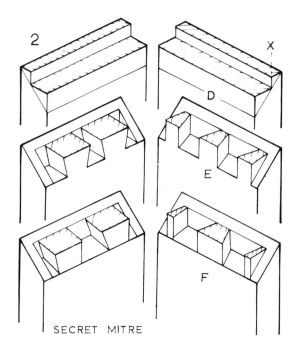

X

D

E

F

SECRET MITRE

3

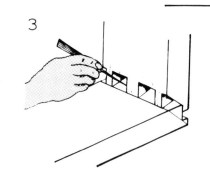

4

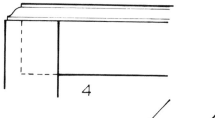

5

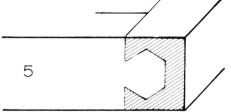

6

7

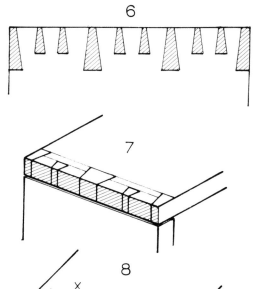

8

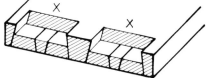

X   X

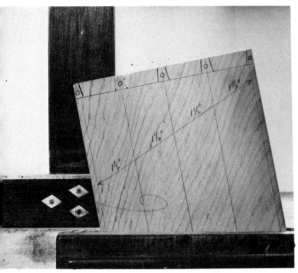

156 Cutting dovetails in drawer-work

in the rebate. Each half pin must be set in with a square cut shoulder to allow the end mitres, and at this stage these mitre cuts can be sawn in on the waste side of the line for final adjustment later. The tails are then marked with an awl (155:3) and the marks squared across the rebate. In sawing both pins and tails, which must be cut diagonally, it hardly matters if the saw kerf nicks the projecting lap so long as it is kept well clear of the outside edge, for the final mitring of the laps will clean out the nicks. When all the chiselling has been done the long side mitres are first roughly chiselled away and finally cleaned up with a finely set shoulder-plane. If necessary a piece of wood placed at a true angle of 45° can be G-cramped/C-clamped to the outer face to act as guide and bed for the plane, with a little wax rubbed over the mitre of the bed piece to prevent the plane-iron digging in. When the mitres are true throughout their length the end mitres should be pared down until they fit. A variation of this joint is shown in 155:2F where the small end pin at either side helps to prevent the end mitres opening. Plenty of long cramps and stout bearers should be available when gluing up long lengths of dovetailing in case either of the pieces have bowed slightly in the width, but no amount of cramping will close a gapped mitre which has been incorrectly cut, or whose hidden dovetails do not seat properly. This joint should, therefore, not be attempted in long lengths before experience has been gained.

Decorative through dovetails

These are used for show-work where the dovetails provide their own decorative element. In essence they are common through dovetails (155:6), with very wide tails and smaller pins introduced into the tails to hold the centres. They must be accurately set or laid out and very neatly cut or the decorative element will be lost. Marking on the face side must be lightly done, and deepened only where the sockets occur (155:7), while after the tails have been marked on the pin piece the sockets (X, X8) are chopped down from the inside to the middle gauge-line. The pin piece is then turned over and the smaller sockets chopped out from the face, with waste pieces inserted in X, X to support the cuts.

correspondingly thicker by the amount of lap, and rebated and moulded as shown to give the appearance of equal framing edges on top and side with a recessed moulding over.

Secret mitre dovetails

These are reserved for high-class work in flush carcasses, boxes, plinths, etc. where strength is essential and appearance of paramount importance. They are most useful joints and still used extensively by handworkers, but they must be accurately done or the joint will show as a gapped mitre.

The first requirement is that both top and side should be exactly equal in thickness or they will not mitre correctly. A gauge is set to this thickness and marked on the inside (155:2D); the mitre-lines are then cut in with a knife. The width of the lap should then be fixed, the gauge set accordingly and marked in from both inside faces. Where the downward projection of this gauge-line (X) coincides with the accurately cut mitre-line will lie the depth of the rebate/rabbet, which must be formed in both pieces before the dovetails can be laid out. In all cases the pins must be marked and cut first, and as the adjustable bevel or dovetail template cannot be used over the projecting lap a small cardboard template should be cut at the correct bevel to lie

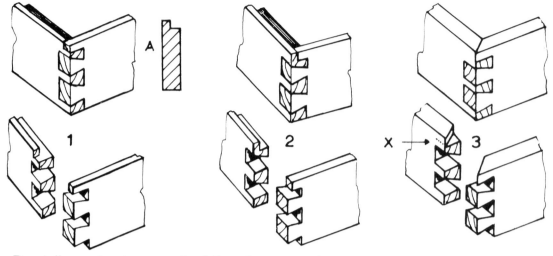

Dovetails need not necessarily follow the traditional pattern, and the writer has used other forms, of which 155:5 is an example. The dovetail is cut and trimmed and marked round for the socket in the end grain. Holding power is as good if not better than the usual form of dovetail, providing the width of the tail is not too great.

Rebated/rabbeted or mitre box corner dovetail joints

Small boxes, trays, etc. are often rebated/rabbeted for a lid (157:1A) and if through dovetailed in the normal way may show a small gap on one piece at the end of the rebate; the half pin is, therefore, laid out below the rebate, and the shoulder of the pin piece brought forward to close the gap. Figure 157:2 is an alternative form where the gap is sealed by the tail piece. If the top of the box or frame shows a mitred edge (157:3) the top pin is not cut through at X, and if the sides are rebated then the depth of the mitre should equal that of the rebate.

Canted dovetails (bevelled work)

If one piece is canted as in a drawer front, the dovetails must not be set out at right angles to the cant but equal either side of a line drawn parallel to the long edge, or weak grain will

result and loosen the joint. If the front is upright and the side canted then the tails are set out in the usual way, but the shoulders are sawn parallel to the bevel of the long side edge and not at right angles. Whichever piece is canted must be cut full to allow for the bevelling, and the bevel clearly marked or part of the half pin may be lost if the allowance is insufficient. (See also *Double bevel dovetail joints*, below, and *Canted fronts*, pp. 249-50.)

Double bevel dovetail joints

These joints are sometimes used for bevel-sided hoppers, knife-boxes, etc., and although rarely used are worth describing for the sake or the principles involved in setting or laying out bevelled work. A full-size drawing is necessary from which the true length (A) and the true width (B) can be obtained (158), also the edge bevel in the thickness of each piece shown by the arrowed line (C). All the bevels are marked and worked holding the bevel at right angles to the edges of the sloping ends and not parallel with the sides. A marking-gauge cannot be used for setting out the dovetails, and depths etc. must be marked with pencil and adjustable bevel, while the dovetails are cut to slope equally either side of lines drawn parallel with the sides (see *Canted dovetails* above), but the pins are, of course, parallel. In cutting the dovetails above the piece should be canted to bring the cuts vertical, as in 158D but marking

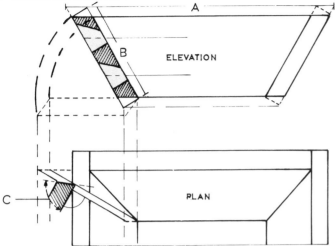

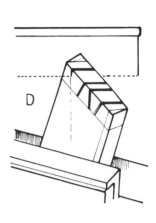

the pins by drawing the saw point through the tail kerfs is difficult owing to the slope, and therefore it is better to chisel out the dovetails and mark around them on the pin piece with an awl.

Carcass dovetails

Where a side rail is grooved or tenoned into a leg or post as in a framed-up carcass, the shoulders of the two dovetails must be offset; moreover in tenoned work the tenon and haunches must be set down by an amount at least equal to the depth of the larger dovetail. Figure 159:1 shows a typical assembly with front rail dovetailed into post and side rail. The side rail and post are assembled first and flushed off,

the thickness of the front rail gauged in the post and pencilled in on the side rail if the gauge cannot reach, and the larger dovetail set out, using the same gauging for the smaller dovetail if the shoulders line through, or resetting it if it projects (159:2). Subsequent marking is as for other forms of lap dovetail. Where the carcass panel is either solid wood or plywood, etc. a front rail (159:3B) and intermediate rails (A) are lap dovetailed in, and the latter either dovetailed as (B) or with a single large tail (A) which can be prevented from lifting by a countersunk screw. Continuous tops should be as 154:5 with a small dovetail at front and back to prevent the cheeks from curling. A suitable rake for carcass dovetails is about 1 in 5, and the spacing can be fairly coarse with the width of the tails about two and a half times that of the pins

159　Carcass dovetails

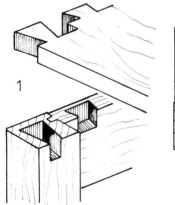

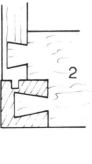

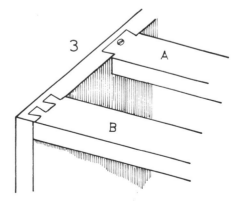

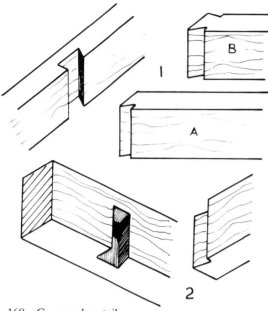

160 Carcass dovetails

(2.5:1); but there are no fixed rules, although the narrower the tails the greater the holding power.

Slot (slip) dovetails

These are cut in the width rather than the thickness and are used in stretcher frames, plinths, cornices, etc. They can be either bare face, i.e. tapered on one side only (160:1A), double tapered (160:1B) or stopped (160:2), with the last more laborious as they cannot be sawn through but must be chiselled out, and are therefore only used where the actual joints must be hidden on one face. In practice, bareface dovetails are sufficient for normal work, and they can be further strengthened with a glue block in the bareface corner.

Another variation on the slip dovetail is when stiff, usually hardwood, members are assembled unglued into dovetail slots under a solid wood table top or lid of a chest. The dry dovetailed joint allows the solid top to move freely in changing humidity at the same time as remaining flat on its top surface. Figure 161 shows such a hardwood member, one of a pair, being fitted into a wide board of Scots pine which will form the lid of a linen chest. The lid will be locked at its centre by a screw which will then allow equal movement from either edge.

161 Solid top of a Scots pine linen chest with a dry dovetailed joint

Corner lock joint

Also known as *box lock* or *finger* joint it has considerable decorative possibilities if cleanly cut in good wood. It is usually regarded as a machine joint but can be cut easily, though somewhat laboriously, by hand, for the pins must be fine (about $\frac{3}{16}$ in [5 mm] or $\frac{1}{4}$ in [6 mm] wide) as there are no bevelled shoulders to hold the joint, which relies entirely on the glue to hold it. Setting or laying out and cutting is the same as for dovetails, but the board width must be equally divided and very accurately set out. Cutting can be simplified by placing the two ends together in the vice (162:2), and offsetting one by the thickness of the saw-blade, cutting one side of each pin into the waste (W), and then reversing the offset as shown by the arrows. The pins which remain after the sockets have been cut are shaded in the drawing.

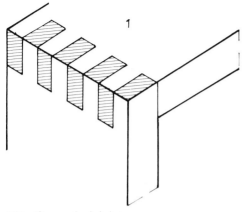

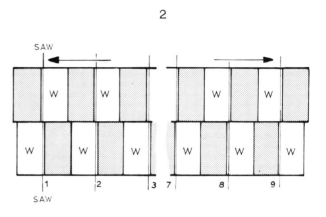

162   Corner lock joint

MACHINE-CUT DOVETAILS

Machine dovetails are easily recognizable in finished work, for both pins and sockets are equal in width and the rake is fairly coarse (20 per cent). As has already been mentioned, the hand-cut terms are transposed, and the tail (drawer side) becomes the pin or male piece entering a socket in the female piece (drawer front). In machining lap dovetails both pieces are cut together, the male vertically and the lapped female horizontally, and therefore the movement of the finger plates and the rotation of the cutters, one for each pin and corresponding socket, give a rounded base to both pin and socket. In theory this could detract from the strength of the dovetails, but with a machine of the Brookman type (163), the cutting is so exact that in all probability the total strength is as good as the average hand-cut dovetails. Disadvantages are coarseness of appearance in show dovetails, and the difficulty of fitting an arbitrary grouping of whole pins into an odd width. In handwork and with, for example, a drawer side 4⅜ in (111 mm) wide the dovetails would be spaced accordingly, but in machinework a pitch must be chosen which will best fit without sacrificing part of the shoulder adjoining a pin, a fault often seen in cheap mass-production work. The normal practice is to use 1 in (25 mm) pitch furniture-style pins, and to limit the drawer width accordingly, with other pitches for special work or where it is necessary to reduce the width and therefore the spacing of the individual pins. The actual length of the pin can be varied plus or minus 25 per cent over the

163   Brookman dovetailer

179

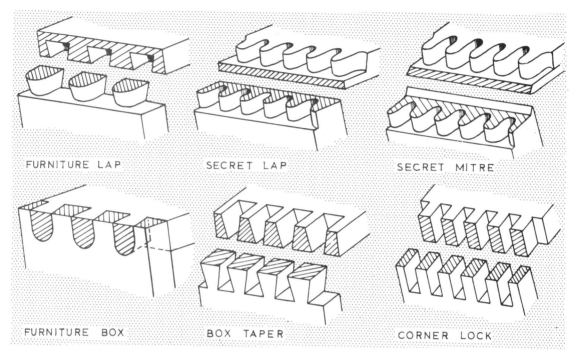

FURNITURE LAP   SECRET LAP   SECRET MITRE

FURNITURE BOX   BOX TAPER   CORNER LOCK

164   Machine dovetails

165   The Brookman 35 spindle automatic dovetailer with pneumatic cramps/clamps

normal, and thus the thickness of the female piece (drawer front) and the width of the lap are immaterial.

Figure 164 shows the various types of dovetail possible with the Brookman dovetailing machines (163 and 165), with the 25 spindle automatic version with pneumatic clamps capable of cutting two drawer sides and two fronts simultaneously. These machines can also be used for dovetailing curved drawer fronts and thus their versatility is very great.

Dovetailing accessories

Where short runs do not warrant the use of a dovetailing machine, accessories can be obtained for most types of spindle moulding/shaping machine and router (including portable routers), incorporating suitable jigs or finger plates into which the single cutter is fed. Particulars of these can be obtained from the manufacturers concerned. For the handworker not completely wedded to hand dovetailing, and lacking sufficient practice to cut dovetails as speedily as the hardened professional, a worthwhile accessory is the dovetailing unit for use with the standard portable router or hand drill (167). This gives good machine-type dovetails, but as the male pin is square and the socket slightly rounded on the base, slight gaps are visible in through dovetails, and its use is, therefore, confined to lap dovetails for drawer sides, etc. and dovetail housing.

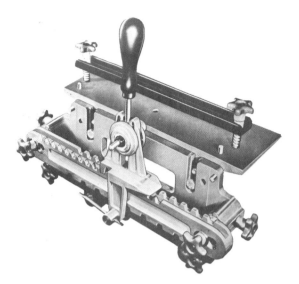

166 Arcoy dovetailing accessory

167 Cutting dovetails with Arcoy dovetailing
accessory and electric drill

20 Mitre, scribed and scarf joints

If two pieces of wood of equal section are to be joined together without the end grain showing then the mitre cut between them must halve the overall angle. Thus if they meet at 90° then the mitre cut is 45° (168:1); if 120° then 60°, etc. (168:2). If, however, the meeting pieces are of unequal section then a true mitre of 45° will result in a longer cut in the larger section, with the result as shown by the dotted line (168:3); therefore the mitre must be 'faked', i.e. the angle pitched so that the meeting cuts are equal in each piece.

CURVED MITRES

Halving the angle also applies where a curved moulding meets a straight moulding of equal section, but in order to agree either the profile of one must be altered to coincide or the mitre-line must be curved (168:4). Mouldings of the same curvature but curving the opposite way, or those in which one curvature is quicker than the other, must also have curved mitres, and the only exception is two mouldings of the same curvature and with the same direction which require a straight cut (168:4B). Methods of determining the curve are described in Chapter 40, p. 363, Workshop geometry.

MITRE JOINTS

Undoubtedly the strongest mitre joint is the secret mitre dovetail (see Dovetailing, Chapter 19, p. 175) but these are not suitable for small sections or flat frames. Various other mitre joints are shown in 168: the tongued mitre (168:5) (the tongue can be either loose or worked in the solid); the tenon and mitre (168:6); the dovetail and mitre (168:7); the keyed mitre (168:8); the dovetail keyed mitre (168:9), with the direction of entry indicated by the arrow; and the through dovetail and mitre (168:10) often used in cheval mirror-frames, etc.

Applications of mitre joints are shown in the mitre and lap (168:11), suitable for plinths, cornices or where the joint can be further strengthened by an inner glued block; and 168:12 which is a tongued version which should not require a block. A method often adopted for small boxes and frameworks, and in fact all light mitre joints, is the veneer keyed mitre (168:13), in which the sections are butt mitred, glued and assembled, and diagonal saw cuts run through the corners in which pieces of stout veneer matched to the saw kerf for thickness are glued and inserted, and cleaned off flush when dry. If well done, accurately spaced and with a carefully chosen veneer, it can be almost invisible. Figure 168:14 is the plain butt mitre with a strengthening glue block which is rubbed in position with either hide or resin glues. The joint is strong enough for most practical purposes. In all butted mitres, and particularly in 168:11, 13 and 14, the end grain should be repeatedly sized with weak glue until the pores are filled, enabling the joint to hold together while it is being further strengthened. Tongued, keyed and through mitred edges in which part of the joint is visible should not be veneered over, for the joint will inevitably shadow through the veneer in time. The only exception is the veneer keyed mitre (168:13), which will give no trouble if the slips are fairly thin.

Cutting mitres

The mitre-square or fixed mitre is used for marking true mitres (45°); the adjustable bevel for all other angles. Some jig or guide is necessary for sawing, and the simplest form is the wooden mitre box, easily made up either as a permanent tool or as and when required. A precision mitre-saw with hacksaw-type blade adjustable to any angle and extensively used by picture-framers is shown in 169, and the mitre-trimmer (170) which is also adjustable. Both these tools are virtually indispensable where there is much mitring to be done. For occasional

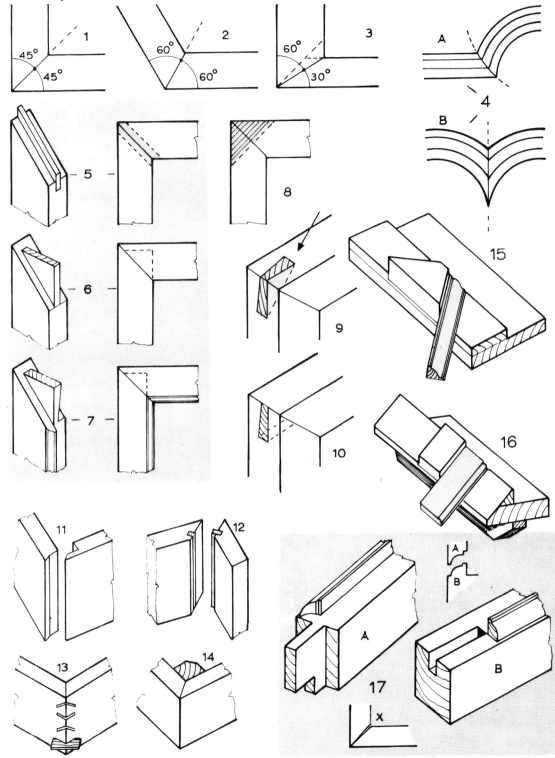

169 Cutting mitre on Ulmia mitre-saw

use the beechwood mitre shooting-block
(168:15) enables mitres in the width to be
accurately planed up, with the donkey's ear
shooting-board (168:16) for mitres in the
thickness. In cutting mitres by hand a fine saw
should be used, with the cut into the moulding
wherever possible, and not out of it, so that the
rag of the saw is at the back or bed of the
moulding and not in the face. If the tip of the
moulding tends to splinter away while the mitre
is being planed, a scrap piece should be inserted
at the back to support the fibres, with the plane
or trimmer cuts as fine as possible. Very large

170 Hand mitre-trimmer set to trim true mitre

mouldings may have to be trimmed freehand,
holding the timber in the vice and planing off
with a smoothing-plane or block-plane,
working diagonally and constantly checking
with the mitre-square. When mitring around a
carcass with front and side mouldings, complete
the front moulding first and then the two sides,
or two mitres will have to be fitted
simultaneously if the front is left to last. If all
four corners have to be mitred as with the
lippings of a panel or top, simultaneous fitting
cannot be avoided, and a waste piece is mitre
cut and used as a checking piece at each corner.
Two opposite sides are then mitred and sash-
cramped/clamped in position, checking for
correct length with the waste piece; the
contiguous mitres are then fitted. The same
procedure can be adopted in gluing up. A
simply made mitre-marking tool for sections
moulded in the thickness which are difficult to
mark with fixed mitre or adjustable bevel is
shown in 171. The suggested dimensions can be
varied as necessary.

Gluing and cramping/clamping mitred work

It is a sad truth that mitres never seem to fit so
accurately after they have been glued. In theory
they should meet exactly, but in most cases
positive pressure has to be applied. In applying
mitred edgings or mouldings to a panel the two

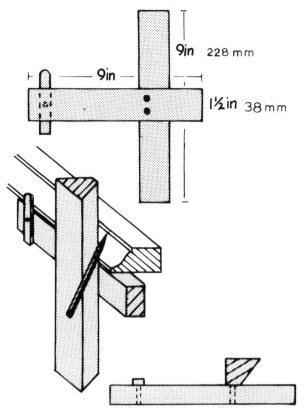

171 Mitre-marker

ends can be temporarily dry cramped in position, the sides glued and sash-cramped across from underneath, the ends then withdrawn, glued and replaced. Where, however, there is no supporting panel, as in a mirror-frame, etc., other means must be adopted, for any attempt to sash cramp all four sections together usually ends in frustration, for the glue acts as a lubricant and the mitres slide. Picture-framers' corner cramps/clamps are hardly suitable as they are only intended to hold the corners while they are being nailed, and there is no positive pressure to the mitres. Flexible band-cramps are suitable and exert considerable pressure, but they are somewhat expensive, and an excellent substitute is the old corner cramping device of four shaped wood blocks with a straining wire or cord (see p. 144). This can be simply made as needed and will pull the largest frame together provided the cord is strong enough. The wood corner blocks should be waxed or otherwise protected from the glue, and the completed frame laid out on a level base and weighted down at the corners to prevent twist, checking the diagonals of the frame for

squareness. It is advisable to size the end grain of the mitres with glue before the final assembly.

Mitre cuts for small breaks

Where the moulding to be mitred is wider than the actual break (172:1) then the points of intersection of the true mitres which halve the overall angle will lie inside the width of the moulding, and small wedge-shaped pieces must be inserted. These in turn will create new overall angles which again must be halved, as shown at 172:1A.

Mason's mitres

These are a legacy from the stonemason's craft in which simple mouldings or chamfers were worked in the solid, and the mitre return carved as shown in 172:5. A more elaborate form was known as a 'bishop's mitre' (172:6), and both are now only used in reproduction oak-work.

SCRIBED WORK

Scribing or shaping one piece to fit over another, as in a moulded and rebated/rabbeted framework (168:17), is an alternative to mitring and gives the same overall appearance; also, any shrinkage is disguised and will not show as an open gap (X) visible in mitred work. Scribes are, however, more difficult to cut and their application more limited, for external angles (172:2) cannot be scribed, nor can undercut mouldings (172:4). The inner angle (172:2) and the moulding (172:3) can be scribed.

Cutting scribes

The mortised piece is rebated/rabbeted, shaped and cut back in the normal manner (168:17B), but the moulding is not mitre cut. The tenoned piece (168:17A) is also moulded and rebated and the moulding mitred; it is then pared away exactly on the mitre-line with a suitable scribing (incannelled) gouge so that it fits exactly over the other. When assembled the general appearance will be that of an accurately fitted mitre, except for the small offset at the base of the moulding where the cut will be square.

The general term 'scribe' also means to mark

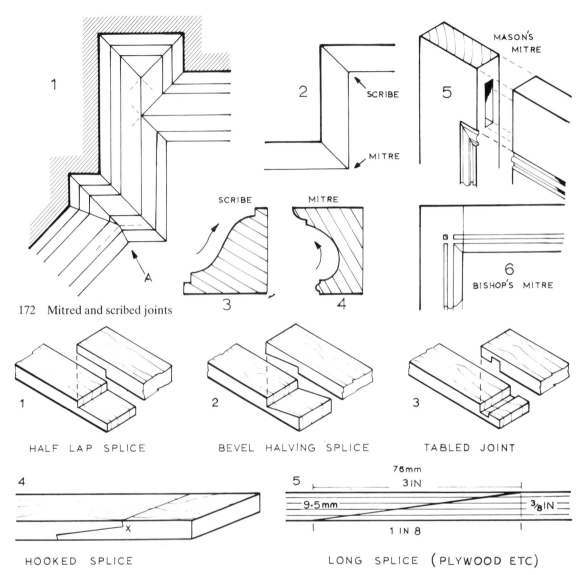

172 Mitred and scribed joints

HALF LAP SPLICE   BEVEL HALVING SPLICE   TABLED JOINT

HOOKED SPLICE   LONG SPLICE (PLYWOOD ETC)

173 Scarf (spliced) joints

or score in order to indicate the exact outline which must be followed when fitting to an uneven surface or another irregular outline. Methods of scribing are described in Chapter 36, Setting out and Cutting Lists.

SCARF JOINTS

Alternatively known as *splicing*, these joints are used to extend the length of boards and are more applicable to carpentry, although they have applications in furniture repair-work. Figure 173:1 shows the simple half lap splice,

173:2 the bevel halving splice, 173:3 the tabled joint, and 173:4 the hooked splice. Figure 173:2 and 3 will resist end pull and to some extent a side swivel, while in 173:4 less stock is taken away at the root (X) and the joint is correspondingly stronger. Simple scarfing or splicing (173:5) relies on the glue only and, provided the joint is long enough, with from eight to 10 times the thickness in thin plywoods, the union can be as strong as a single length. Solid boards are usually scarfed at nine times the thickness, but some woods will hold at lesser angles.

186

Part IV   Advanced areas of furniture construction

21   Carcass construction

GENERAL NOTE

The construction of any large carcass must provide for possible distortion, either under the weight of its own members or by applied forces—pushing, pulling, lifting, upending, etc.—or by setting on an uneven foundation such as sloping floors. The effect of any such distortion may not be detectable visually, but nevertheless doors will bind, drawers jam and connecting joints may fail; therefore overall stiffness and squareness under all normal conditions are essential. Assuming an open-faced rectangular box with top, bottom, two sides and fixed back, any force applied, no matter from what direction, will endeavour to twist the faces of the box, including the open face, which will tend to take on a diamond shape (174:1) with the corner angles greater or less than true right angles. If, however, one side of the box is so anchored that it cannot twist then all the other sides will be prevented from twisting and the opening will remain square (174:2), while if the opening itself is so stiffened with cross-bracing that the diagonals are preserved then the sides also will be prevented from twisting (174:3). Obviously, this latter method is not practicable in open carcass-work, therefore other methods must be adopted.

METHODS OF STIFFENING CARCASSES

Openings can be stiffened by applied side pilasters (174:4) and central pilasters (174:5), but the top and bottom members must be stiff also and the connecting joints as strong as possible. Other methods include pilaster attached to a stiff apron (174:6); L frame (174:7); U frame (174:8); inverted U (174:9); T frame (174:10); I frame (174:11) and H frame (174:12). Methods of increasing the stiffness of

flat panels include increasing the thickness (174:13); sandwich panel (174:14); closed box (174:15); cross-ribs reinforcement (174:16); double cross-rib (174:17) and pyramid bracing (174:18). Carcasses can also be stiffened by arbitrary fixed cross-rails or shelves or divisions, which in effect either adopt an 'H' or 'I' formation and break up the carcass into smaller boxes, with increased wood thickness relative to the opening. This method is often adopted in open bookcases with loose shelves, where one or more shelves are housed and glued into the sides to increase the stiffness, but such carcasses will still distort fractionally if stood on an uneven surface, no matter how sturdy the wood sections are, for increasing the wood dimensions also increases the overall weight, therefore some form of pilaster, stiff apron rail or box plinth is preferable. The principles of deflection and the appropriate methods of combating them are examined in detail in the *Design Manual for Cabinet Furniture* published by the Furniture Development Council.

In all carcass work it should be remembered that while a well-fitted carcass back, grooved, screwed or glued in position will help to achieve overall stiffness and squareness, it will not automatically ensure such rigidity.

MOBILITY

Large carcasses are often split vertically into two separate carcasses coupled together after erection, and *the maker should always check well in advance that stairways, elevators and door openings are wide enough for the passage of large furniture*. There is a growing practice to fit small free-running castors to heavy pieces, wardrobes, etc. and this is a sound move.

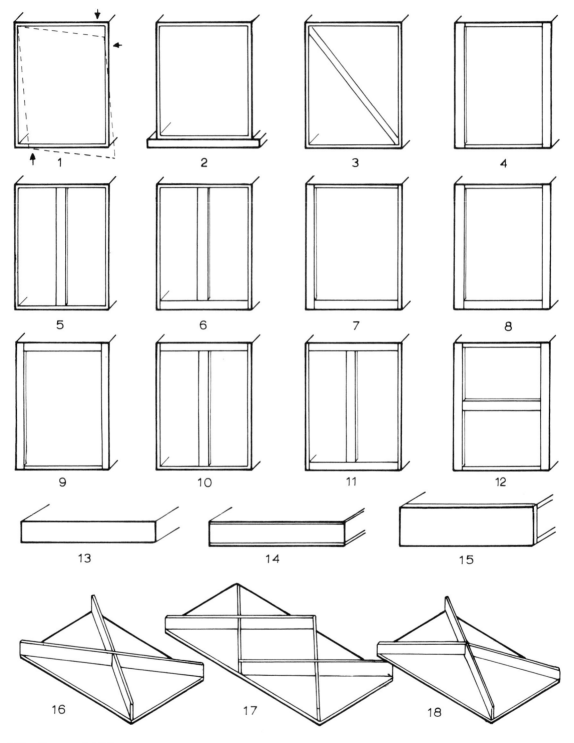

174   Carcass rigidities

MOVEMENT

Solid wood and plywoods etc. must not be mixed indiscriminately in carcass-work. For instance, solid sides and plywood tops, bottoms and fixed shelves would have different shrinkage values; so also would plywood sides and solid tops, bottoms, etc. There is, however, no objection to using relatively narrow bearer rails in solid wood to plywood sides or vice versa, as the shrinkage will be negligible. In planning any carcass construction, therefore, a moment's thought as to the probable direction and effect of the normal shrinkage of each part will usually suggest a satisfactory compromise. Framed-up (panelled) carcass sides can be treated as plywood, for here again shrinkage values are usually too small to cause trouble.

AREAS OF CARCASS CONSTRUCTION

Carcass construction can be broadly broken down into four main areas, the first being most applicable to present-day large scale production:

1 Knock-down (KD) construction using sheet materials

2 Pre-assembled carcasses from sheet materials

3 Frame and panel, or frame and thin skin construction

4 Solid board carcass construction.

KD construction using sheet materials

Most inexpensive mass-produced carcass furniture is now made from pre-finished plastic coated chipboard, either white, in colour or in simulated wood veneer. In either case, the edges are simply veneered from rolls of the same finishing material and the whole carcass is packed flat into boxes and assembled later, either in the shop or the home, with simple but ingenious KD fittings. Few people realize that of the acres of teak and mahogany furniture that fill our cheaper retail stores, much of it is no more than a paper-thick film of photographed wood protected by a clear plastic coating.

So inexpensive is this pre-finished material and the KD method of construction, that it has largely replaced the bulky and time-consuming frame and thin panel construction of a decade or so ago for most kitchen and storage furniture in the lower price ranges. Slightly higher in price, but still of the same construction, is KD carcass furniture produced from pre-wood-veneered sheets of chipboard or, occasionally, MDF. These are spray-finished after edge-veneering or, better quality still, after solid edges have been applied.

Carcass assembly with knock-down fittings

KU and KD fittings are described in Chapter 31 p. 291, and 175:1-4 shows a typical particle board wardrobe construction employing these fittings. In practice, these provide rigid fixtures; while any looseness which might develop in use can always be corrected with a screwdriver. They can be used for some solid wood carcass-work, and in fact table shrinkage plates, table brace plates and detachable leg fittings are knock-down fittings in the true sense, but the usual run of KD carcass fittings call for dimensionally stable materials.

Pre-assembled carcasses from sheet materials

In reproduction work and in quality living room and dining furniture, in particular, much is still manufactured, assembled and finished in the factory as complete items of furniture, and it is this area of industrialized construction which is of most interest to the small cabinet-maker. In this area, where veneering and surface finishing are undertaken as part of the production, MDF is fast superseding both plywoods and chipboard as the base material. Its main disadvantage (its considerably increased weight) is far outweighed by its advantages, namely:

1 its dense pre-sanded surfaces;

2 edges that for many purposes require no edging but can be sanded, moulded, stained or coloured at will;

3 no grain direction as on plywoods, so no breaking out across grain;

4 no brittleness or weakness on edges, unlike

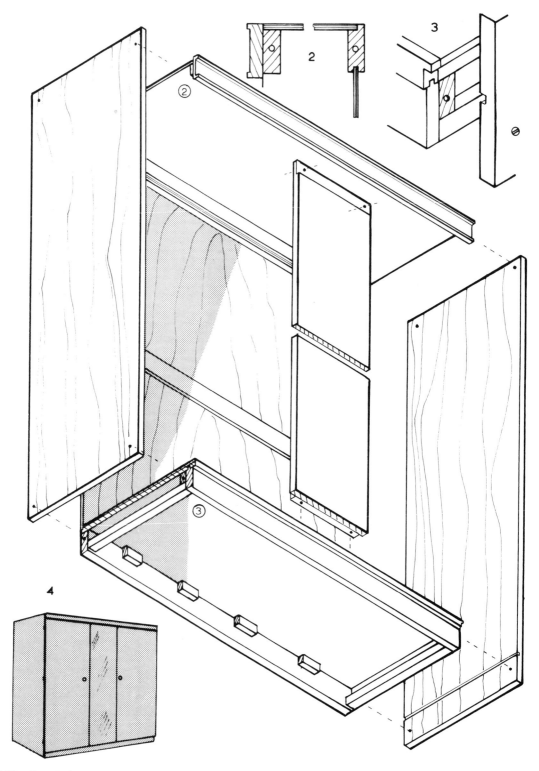

175   Knock-down carcass in particle board

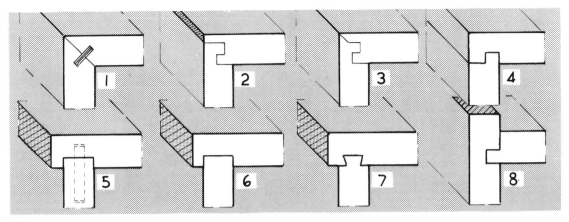

176 Jointing methods **1.** Mitre and tongue/spline
2. Tongue and lap **3.** Tongue and mitre **4.** Tongue
and groove **5.** Housed/dadoed and dowelled
6. Housed & inset tops **7.** Dovetail housing
8. Inset tops

particle board, enabling grooving, rebating/
rabbeting, housing/dadoing and edge joints to
be cut cleanly and accurately without breaking
out or crumbling.

These advantages are obviously just as
beneficial to the one-man concern as they are to
factory production.

Fig. 176 shows eight basic machine joints for
use with sheet materials from ½ in (12 mm)
thick upwards. Most could also be used, though
less satisfactorily, in solid wood instead of the
more traditional dovetailing and stub tenoning.

1-4 are all corner joints for top and bottom
fixings on flush carcasses, while 5-8 can all be
used as alternatives for jointing divisions, fixed
shelves, raised bottom panels and inset and
oversize tops. It is a matter of choice or of the
equipment available whether one stops the
joints at the front edge or merely applies solid
wood edgings after the joints have been through
cut with the spindle shaper or groover.
Naturally, the biscuit jointer and portable
router come into their own when joints are
stopped. Figure 177 shows some of these joints
in a very basic construction with an oversize top
and separate plinth.

Carcass edging

There is no structural advantage in edging MDF
and quality plywood, but particle board and
laminboard should always be edged whatever
finish is to be applied. The reason for edging
MDF and plywood is therefore largely aesthetic,
the most obvious example being in order to
match face veneers; but if the piece is to be
sprayed in colour, this is not necessary at all,
although plywood edges would need to be well
sealed to prevent the plies showing through.

Solid edges do not require tongues if they are
kept to a maximum of ⁵⁄₁₆ in (8 mm) thick (Fig.
178); anything above that should be tongued
and grooved.

Edge veneering is widely used throughout the
furniture industry, but it means near razor sharp
and vulnerable edges, and is a practice which is
incompatible with quality. It can only be
legitimately used in quality work when cross
banding is required for decorative reasons, and
then the vulnerable edges should be capped
with hardwood, either planed flush or left as
cock/corner beads.

Frame and panel, or frame and thin skin construction

Much of this method of construction is a legacy
of the utility furniture of the 1940s and early
1950s, when wood was at a premium and
components were whittled down to a bare
minimum. The extremely thin veneered
plywood skins and panels were designed to give
the appearance of solid wood construction and a
traditional feel. This method of construction,

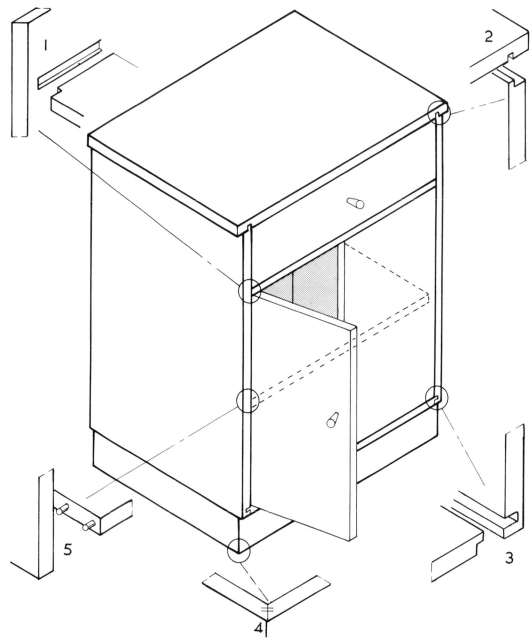

177 Basic construction showing joints **1**. Housed/ dadoed joint **2 & 3**. Tongue and lap **4**. Mitre and tongue/spline **5**. Dowel joint

with economy of material as its main aim, became standard practice for most inexpensive kitchen and bedroom furniture production. Coloured panels and plastic laminates were often used to relieve the monotony of wood veneers and to add visual interest.

This form of construction is best seen in the very inexpensive unpainted whitewood furniture so popular in the 1970s but now largely

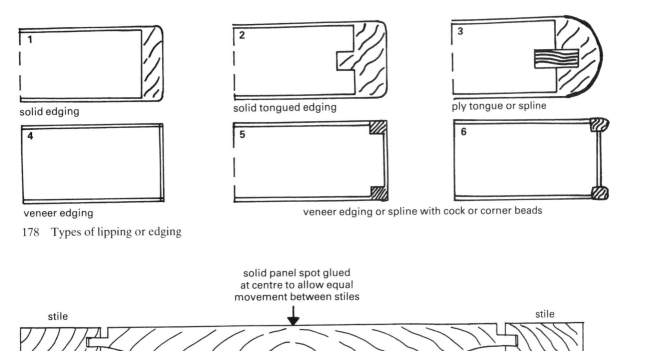

178　Types of lipping or edging

1　solid edging

2　solid tongued edging

3　ply tongue or spline

4　veneer edging

5

6

veneer edging or spline with cock or corner beads

solid panel spot glued
at centre to allow equal
movement between stiles

stile　　　　　　　　　　　　　　　　　　　　　　　　stile

179　Solid frame and panel construction

superseded by low-cost KD production. However, frame and panel construction in solid wood, as practised over the centuries, is still in evidence in high-quality reproduction work, some quality pine pieces, and in the work of the small cabinet-making shops and designer craftsmen.

A simple assembly for framed carcasses often employed in production-work is to glue and screw a fillet to the top side framing rail and screw the top frame to this, cutting it round the front post as in 181. Under-tops, fixed shelves, rails and carcass bases must be inset by the thickness of the back, and it is as well to form the groove or rebate/rabbet for these before laying out the carcass joints.

Other forms of frame construction are shown in 182. In 182:1 the panelled wardrobe or cupboard construction has side frames

180　A fine example of the imaginative use of solid frame and panel construction, this small wall-hung cabinet in walnut is designed and made by Kenneth Marshall

193

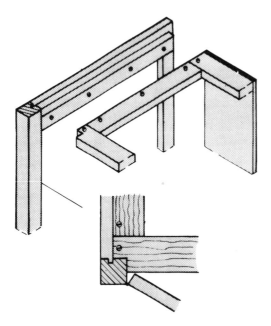

181 Simple assembly for framed carcasses

dovetailed to the top and bottom rails, and a front pilaster planted on and either tongued and grooved, as shown in the inset, or glue blocked on the inside with a small bead or vee groove at the junction with the side frames. In the chest construction (182:2) the pilasters are dispensed with; there are no middle rails to the side frames and the single ply panel is further stiffened by the drawer runners glued on. Figure 182:3 shows the junction of a top bearer rail with a post and frame construction, while in 182:4 the side frames are rebated/rabbeted for a ply sheet to yield a flush surface. This method, together with 182:5 in which the ply is press glued over the whole framework and the edges rounded over, is often used in whitewood furniture for subsequent painting. Figure 183:1 is a pedestal desk construction. The meeting of the drawer rail (183:1A) with cheeks flush with the leg posts on the inside is shown at 183:2A, and with cheeks flush with the outside at 183:3. Figure 183:4 is the junction of the base (B) stub tenoned into the post and rebated and screwed into the cheek, as carcass dovetailing cannot be used owing to the different direction of entry. Top kickers (183:1C) will be necessary, also drawer guides as shown in the dotted lines

(183:3); if the cheeks are not flush with the posts on the inside, they are merely cut in and pinned and glued to the drawer runners. Figure 183:5 is a knee-hole type desk with suspended drawer units or pedestals. The drawer bases are stub tenoned into the legs, rebated and screwed to the cheeks (183:4) and carcass dovetailed into the inner cheeks. A front apron rail in lieu of a centre drawer (which is an inconvenient place for a drawer as the sitter has to move back every time it is fully opened) is either tongued, slot dovetailed or dowelled and glue blocked on the inside. In cheap work this rail is often pocket screwed to the cheeks or sides and then glue blocked, or, if the pedestals are to be detachable, fitted with locating dowels glued into the apron rail and dry fitted to the sides with a heavy block glued to the apron rail and screwed through. The junction of two pedestals can be further strengthened with a centre bearer rail if necessary, and the top is fixed by screwing up through the top rails, pocket screwing through the apron rail, pocket screwing the back, if thick enough, or screwing up through blocks glued to the back. Figure 183:6, 7 shows the top in position, shaped or square edged.

Plywood web reinforcements

A method of strengthening light framing joints in carcass-work extensively employed in kitchen cabinet and whitewood furniture-making is shown in 184. This consists of $5/32$ in (4 mm) or $1/4$ in (6 mm) plywood webs glued and nailed as illustrated. Figure 184:1 is applicable to chairwork also, and is used instead of corner brackets, often with two webs to each corner for greater holding power, for the webs are only glued in the grooves; but this method is not recommended for quality work.

Solid board carcass construction

This method of carcass construction is rarely undertaken by large manufacturers, and, when it is, the wood is usually strip laminated for stability and uniformity of colour and grain in production. Figure 185, for example, shows a solid wood top made of 18 in (45 cm) sections glued together with a resin adhesive to form an 18 in (45 cm) board. Ercol of High Wycombe

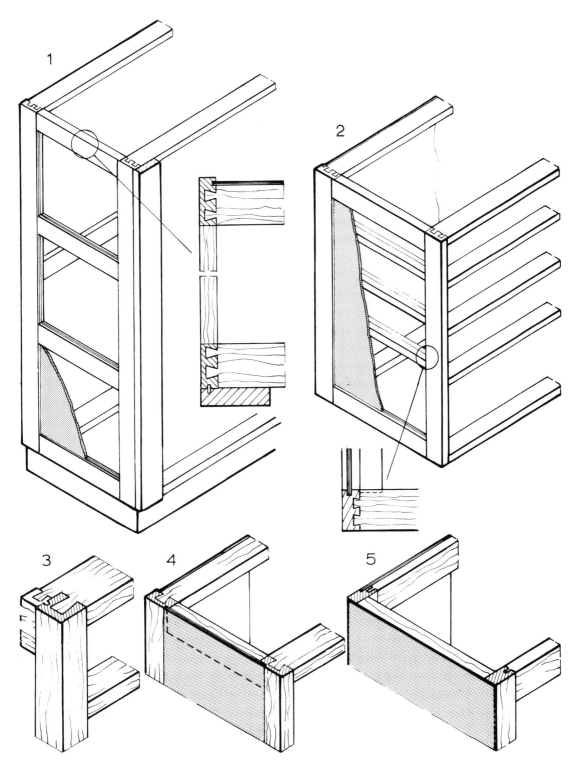

182   Framed carcasses using thin sheet material

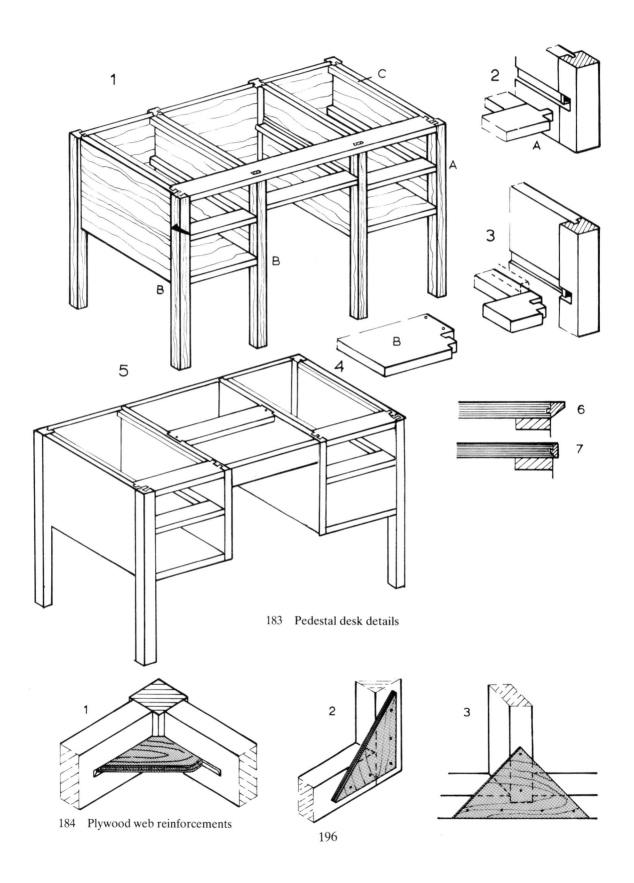

183   Pedestal desk details

184   Plywood web reinforcements

196

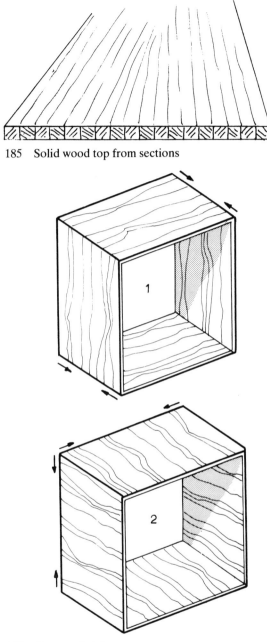

185 Solid wood top from sections

186 Carcass shrinkage

Grain direction

Carcasses built up of solid wood boards must have the grain directions continuous, with the side grains vertical and the top and bottom grains parallel to the leading edges, so that all the shrinkage across the width of the boards is from back to front, as indicated by the arrows (186:1). If the grain of the sides were horizontal, and the top and bottom from front to back as in 186:2, then a moment's reflection would show that any pronounced shrinkage across the width of the boards would lower the carcass top, close in the sides and jam the doors or drawers; moreover such cross-grain wood would have little bearing strength. Horizontal- or cross-grain effects can be achieved with plywood constructions where there is little if any shrinkage and approximately equal stiffness in either direction, *but such effects should be an integral part of the design or they will appear unnatural from the viewpoint of custom and usage.* Solid wood carcasses which are to be face veneered will have the groundwork as 186:1 and the veneers laid the same way as the grain.

CONSTRUCTIONAL METHODS

Flush-top carcasses

Where the tops are an integral part of the carcasses and not planted on as separate members, some form of interlocking joint must be used. Figure 187:1 shows a secret mitre dovetail top, and 187:2 secret lap dovetail. Figure 187:3 shows the through dovetail and 187:4 finger or box lock joint.

Separate top carcasses

Methods of constructing orthodox carcasses with separate tops attached after assembly are shown in 188. Figure 188:1 shows the usual form of carcass dovetailing for a solid under top, 188:2 front and back bearer rail, 188:3 single dovetails screwed for extra strength, and 188:4 a solid top part dovetailed and part screwed. Where the carcass cheeks/sides are connected by rails only the intervening spaces must be filled with *kickers* shown by the dotted lines in 188:2A, which are pinned and glued to the carcass sides to prevent the drawer sides kicking

are the masters of this form of construction, which they developed many years ago with the notoriously unstable wood, English elm.

Solid wood carcass construction is otherwise predominantly the province of the designer-craftsmen and the small workshops working largely on one-off commissions or small batches.

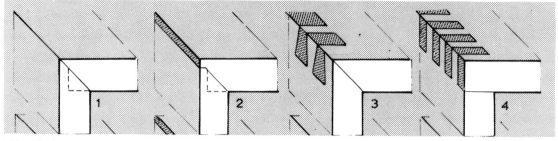

187   Flush-top carcasses

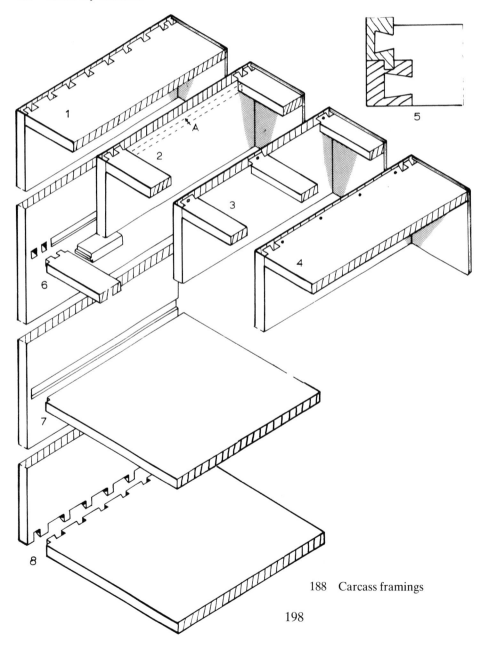

188   Carcass framings

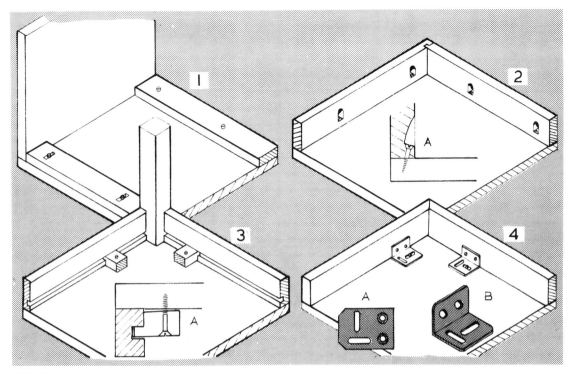

189 Fixing tops, plinths, etc.

up between the rails as the drawer is withdrawn. Figure 188:5 shows the junction of a bearer rail with square post and grooved-in side or panelled frame, 188:6 a drawer rail stub tenoned in, and the drawer runner tongued to the front rail and housed into the sides. If the carcass sides are solid boards then the runners can be glued to the front rail but must be free to slide in the housing/dado as the shrinkage direction differs, therefore they must be fitted dry and secured at the back with a screw working in an open slot. Figure 188:7 is the normal stopped housing/dado joint for shelves which is usually sufficient if the joint is tight, but dovetail or taper dovetail housings can be used if the carcass sides have to be pulled in. Figure 188:8 shows the carcass base dovetailed as in the top (188:1).

Fastening tops, plinths, etc.

Secured tops of solid wood liable to shrink across the width are fixed by screwing to the front rail (189:1) and slot screwing at the back. The centres can be held down by wood buttons (189:3A), or alternatively the centre can be screwed and the front and rear slot screwed; however, excessive shrinkage might show at the front if the top overhangs the rail to a marginal extent only. Prefabricated wood tops can be screwed direct for the shrinkage is negligible. Loose plinths are pocket screwed as in 189:2, and (A) shows the angle to the fixing screws, or they can be secured with metal shrinkage plates (189:4). Table-tops can be attached with wood buttons free-sliding in grooves (189:3A), with the thickness of the buttons slightly less than the depth below the top and the groove, so that the top is pulled down tight as the buttons are screwed on. Metal shrinkage plates can also be used (189:4), and (A) shows the flat variety which are cut in flush on the rail top, and (B) the angled form screwed on. Two slots are usually provided to each plate, and the screws must be placed so that the top is free to slide across the width (189:4).

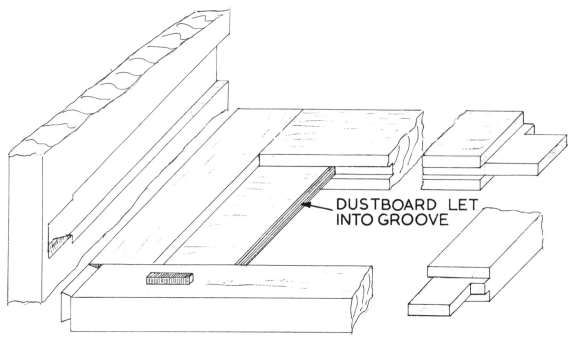

190 Dust board

Dust boards/panels

These are a refinement fitted between drawers in carcass-work to protect the drawer contents from falling dust or displaced articles. They are now only used in the highest quality work. They can be solid, i.e. housed/dadoed in shelves which act as drawer rails, runners and dust boards, or of panelled construction with the front drawer rail and runners grooved for a thin ply sheet which was pushed in from the back and held in position by a stiffening back rail tongued into the runner grooves. Alternatively, they can be made up as a complete frame with ply panels and front and back drawer rails stub tenoned and runners housed into the sides. Muntins should be provided for wide carcasses which can also act as supports for upright divisions between the rails. A cheaper compromise often seen in Victorian furniture was to glue up the carcass with grooved front rails and runners, and push in a thin ply sheet which was left unsupported at the back; however, unless the ply is sufficiently rigid it is liable to sag in time and even foul the lower drawer.

Carcass assembly

Final assembly of the various component parts is the culmination of many hours of patient work and should never be hurried. A preliminary assembly in the dry state can be made but only to establish the direction of entry and the exactness of the fit. Dowelled components can be tried with spare dowel-pegs sanded slack (tight dowels should never be used as the suction in a tight hole can hold them immovable), and there can be no objection to fully seating tenons in order to check the shoulders, but dovetails only fit once and should not be entered beyond the halfway mark. If parts of the carcass can be glued, assembled and set aside to dry well before-hand, so much the better; but the squareness must be carefully checked, and if rails or fixed shelving are first glued to the carcass sides both carcass top and bottom should be partially entered to act as spacers. All joints should be clearly marked and readily distinguishable: tenons in chalk or soft pencil on the face of the rail, mortises also numbered on the face, sides marked in bold chalk lettering 'left' and 'right', 'top' and 'base', and other parts according to their location. These precautions might seem needless in straightforward assemblies, but all tenons look alike when covered with glue, and carcass sides have a habit of transposing themselves. A stout hammer and striking-block are necessary, also a long rule for checking opening or the spread of legs, long try-square, squaring-rod for the diagonals and a pair of winding-sticks. Before

191   Solid wood carcass construction used on a simple four drawer chest by Alan Peters

the glue is mixed sufficient cramps/clamps should be assembled, tail slides set to the approximate postion and G-cramps/C-clamps likewise, with wood cross-bearers and softening pads for the cramps within reach. If hide glue is used then the component parts must be warmed slightly, but resin glues will set at ordinary room temperatures, giving plenty of time for methodical assembly. Dowelled constructions can have the pegs glued into one side, checked for length and the tops chamfered for easy entry.

Most old craftsmen only kissed the joints with glue, a dab on each tenon and perhaps a wipe across the shoulders, a brushful across the end of dovetails which were then smeared across the pin section, a trickle of glue run into the housings/dadoes. This was deliberate as it saved time applying and time in cleaning up, but the joints did fit and the glue was fairly thick; but with modern glues of low viscosity there is always a danger of starved joints if only a minimum of glue is used and the wood absorbent or the cramping/clamping pressure too great. Moreover, there is no comparison between this day and age and 80 years ago, for furniture must now withstand the ravages of central heating, and so every part should be glued thoroughly. If the surfaces are delicate then a wash coat of white shellac or cellulose can be applied up to but not over the glue-line to protect the surface, and a stick of chalk rubbed across the extreme edge of meeting joints will

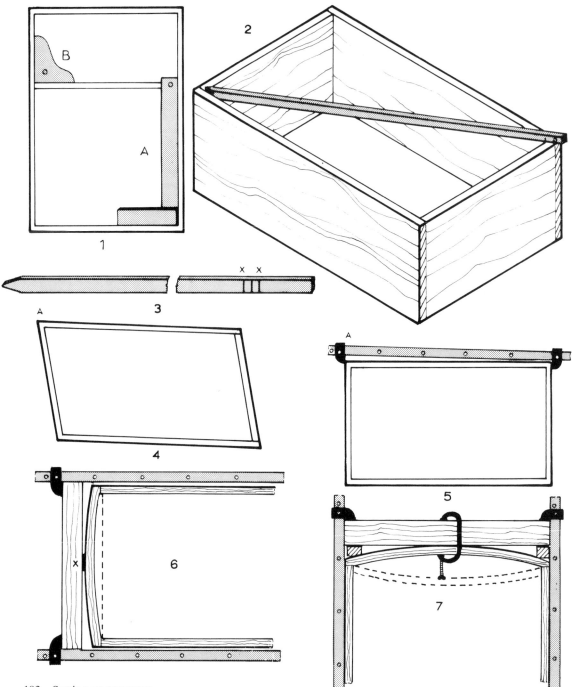

193 Setting up carcasses

prevent a dark glue-line showing on pale woods—sycamore, holly, cherry, etc. The actual assembly should be done on a firm and level foundation and the work supported so that it does not sag under the weight of the cramps. Immediately assembly is completed it should be checked and rechecked for levelness and squareness. Openings should be checked with wood try-square (193:1A) and set-square (193:1B), carcasses with the squaring-rod (193:2). If the diagonals show a difference of say ⅛ in (3 mm) (193:3) then the carcass will be

$\frac{1}{16}$ in (1.5 mm) out of square, which could be counted as negligible in a medium or large carcass, but greater disparities should be corrected by tilting the cramps (193:4A, 5A). Flat frames, drawers, etc. should be laid on a level foundation and checked for twist, and if the twist cannot be corrected by tilting the cramps then the high corner should be weighted down, packing up the other corner if necessary to force the twist in the opposite direction. If the carcass has to be cramped across the middle of the width, particularly with fixed shelvings in tight housings, heavy cross-bearers across the sides from front to back should be protected with a pad of newspaper (193:6) to apply the pressure where it is most needed. If a side or top tends to bow inwards it can sometimes be corrected by forcing it to the other extreme as in 193:7 (the distortion shown in 193:4, 6 and 7 is exaggerated for illustration purposes). A close watch should be kept that heavy cramps or cramping pressure do not bow the timber; if so it should be reinforced or the pressure eased a little. After checking from every angle the completed work should be left undisturbed until the glue has set, but heavy cramps should not be left in position longer than necessary or the carcass will tend to sag under the weight.

Carcass backs

Carcass backs can perform three functions: (1) closing in the opening; (2) adding stiffness and rigidity to the carcass; (3) increasing the back weight, thus reducing any tendency for tall carcasses to topple forward when the doors are opened. The thickness of the back and the method of construction will, therefore, depend on the degree of rigidity and the amount of extra weight required, and there is much to be said for the traditional framed-up panelled back, both from the utilitarian and aesthetic standpoints, particularly if solid cedar is used for its permanent moth-repellent properties. Sheet backs of stiff plywood or laminboard are normal and satisfactory, but thin plywood or hardboard are only used in the cheapest work. An additional advantage of the heavy back is its ability to pull a carcass square if for any reason cramping/clamping pressure has distorted it.

The usual form of panelled back is shown in

194:1, 2, while 194:3 is the flush back of ply or laminboard, etc. Backs for pedestal tables and desks can be in individual units (194:4), or taken across the carcass width in a single sheet (194:6) with a bearer rail dovetailed, dowelled or tenoned between the pedestals to support the lower edge. Figure 194:5 shows the construction of the framed back (194:2) with extra wide top rail cut to fit the shaped top; the stiles and rails are normally from 2 in (50 mm) to 3 in (75 mm) wide and $\frac{5}{8}$ in (16 mm) finished thickness, according to the size of carcass. Panels can be $\frac{3}{16}$ in (5 mm) or $\frac{1}{4}$ in (6 mm) ply, or $\frac{5}{16}$ in (8 mm) or $\frac{3}{8}$ in (9.5 mm) solid wood machined to fit the grooves. Haunching of the tenons is optional, and the framing can be dowelled together instead of the orthodox mortises and tenons. In all cases the carcass base is set back to allow the framing to pass over (194:5A). Backs for glued-on tops are shown in 194:7, with the top bearer rail set in and the stiles rebated/rabbeted into the cheeks or tongued and grooved, as in 194:9. The long edges of the stiles are beaded as shown. Where the top is mitre or double lap dovetailed or tongued and grooved to the sides, and there is no supporting bearer rail for the top of the framing, the rebate can run through (194:8A), but if the top is not mitred (194:8B) then the rebate must be stopped, or a $\frac{1}{2}$ in (12.5 mm) by $\frac{3}{4}$ in (19 mm) fixing fillet screwed to the underside of the top to form the rebate. Tongued and grooved backs (194:9) are usually rebated into the top, and fixing screws into the rebate are not objectionable if mounted in brass sockets, but the back can be pocket screwed from the inside if preferred. As mentioned before, the carcass base is set back (194:5A).

Types of solid sheet back are shown in 194:11, 12. Veneered carcasses to stand against a wall are not usually edged on the back, but if edgings are provided they must be carefully laid out. Figure 194:13A is a bad placing of the opposing grooves in which the small section beween the tongues (X) will be lost in the machining unless the edgings are glued on before the side grooves are worked, and even then there will be little strength. Figure 194:13B shows the ideal, but if narrow edges are essential they can be offset as in 194:13C and the edges applied before working the side grooves.

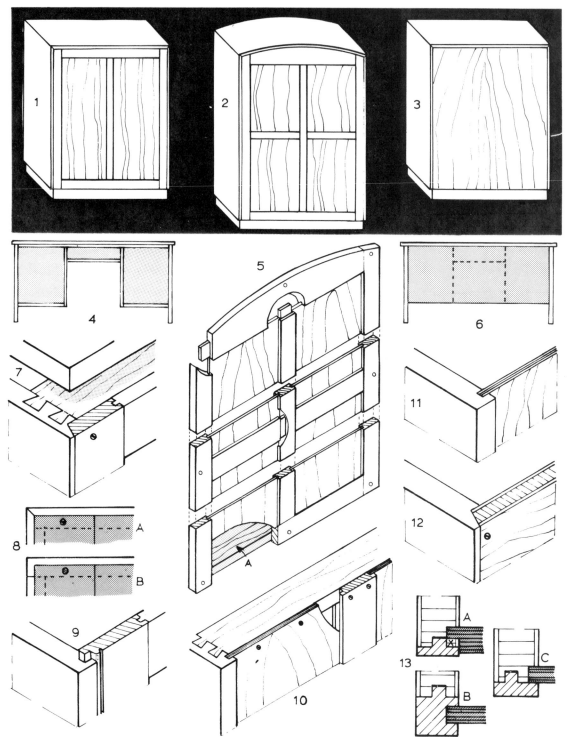

194   Carcass backs, details

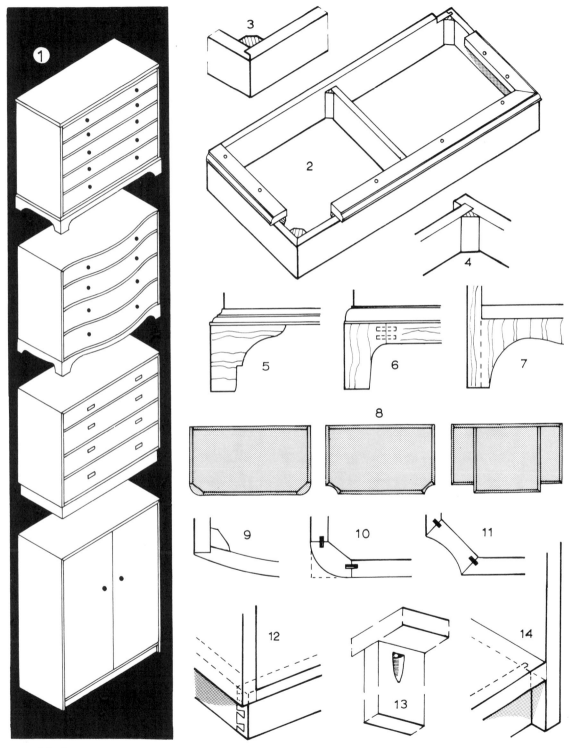

195   Plinths

PLINTHS AND CORNICES

Plinths

Plinths in traditional work were always project-ing, as distinct from recessed, the term itself meaning the lowermost square-shaped project-ing part of a base or column from the Greek *phiallos*, a brick. So-called recessed plinths are a comparatively recent development, occasioned no doubt by the necessity of evolving a base which did not require precision fitting in quantity work; moreover, such plinths are not so easily damaged and give toe room in tall cupboards and wardrobes. In the best work both types are made separately from the carcass and attached to the base with buttons, glue blocks, table plates or by pocket screwing. For accurate work the carcass should be made and assembled first, and the carcass base used as a guide for laying out the plinth.

Projecting plinths

The simplest form of projecting plinth is illus-trated in 195:1, 2 in which the front is plain mitred (195:2) or mitre rebated/rabbeted (195:3) and the corners glue blocked, with the back rail flush and lap dovetailed or tongued and grooved, or inset and housed/dadoed and blocked (195:4). Cross-bearers or stiffeners, where necessary, are housed and blocked or slip dovetailed, and a plinth moulding or capping is glue blocked to give adequate seating for the main carcass. Corner joints can be more elaborate, i.e. secret mitre or secret lap dovetailed, lap dovetails faced with solid wood (not thin veneer which will shadow the dovetails through in time) or tongued mitres, etc., but complex joints are rarely necessary, for the plinth itself is locked to the carcass and there is no side strain unless the furniture is roughly dragged over uneven surfaces. In assembling, shape the capping piece in one length, lay out the positions on the carcass base, bore screw holes for fastening, cut and glue the mitres and screw or cramp temporarily in position with scraps of paper under to prevent the surplus glue adhering. The front, sides and back rail of the actual plinth should then be assembled and glue blocked to the mitred cap moulding,

making sure that the projection of the latter is equal all round. When dry the temporary screws in the cap moulding can be released, the plinth unit cleaned off and set aside for later assembly. If the plinth is to remain detachable then locating blocks which fit inside the cap moulding are screwed to the carcass base, and the carcass will then merely rest on the plinth. Traditional bracket plinths are shown in 195:5, 6 and 7, other forms in 195:8, and the construction of shaped plinths in 195:9, 10 and 11. All these plinths can be made up of veneered ply or laminboard, etc., but wood timber is better in case of rough treatment.

Recessed plinths

These can be assembled in the same way or set out by measurement, for the position is not highly critical. Side rails can be set in say $\frac{1}{2}$ in (12.5 mm) but the front rail $\frac{3}{4}$ in (19 mm) or more to give adequate toe room, while the back rail is usually flush with the carcass. If the carcass is solid wood, fastening will have to allow for the inevitable shrinkage, either with wood buttons or metal shrinkage plates, but plywood carcasses can have the plinths pocket screwed (195:13). A fairly common way of constructing these plinths in production-work is to lap dovetail the sides (195:12), but this is done not for reasons of strength but because it is simpler to mass produce dovetails than it is to mitre saw, shoot and glue block the plinth framing.

A variation often adopted in wardrobes and cupboards is to bring the carcass sides down to floor level and tongue an inset rail under the base (195:14). This is a modern rendering of the old method of mitring in a flush front rail and masking the through housing/dado of the cupboard floor with a moulding which was returned along the sides to simulate an independent plinth. The former method (195:14) is eminently practical and reasonable, but the older method of planted mouldings was merely a sham and never really practicable, for the side mouldings were invariably knocked off in time.

Plinth stools are constructed as described in Leg and frame construction, Chapter 22, p. 208, and are made up as already described.

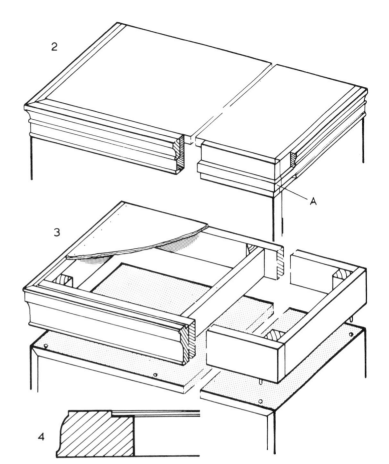

196 Cornices

Cornices

Cornices are now rarely used, but were a feature in traditional work. Strictly speaking, a cornice is the top moulding of the entablature to a column which, in Classic architecture, included frieze mould, frieze (usually ornamented) and cornice moulding; but the term *cornice* in furniture is usually taken to include all three.

Cornices can be applied to the carcass (196:2) or treated as a separate unit (196:3), and the latter is the better method. In 196:2 a solid frieze board is applied to the carcass head on the front and glue blocked to the carcass top, with the small part (A) mitred in as a separate piece to hide the end grain of the frieze board on the return. The mouldings are then applied to the frieze board and returned along the sides, but if a minimum projection only is required, they can be trenched into the frieze board as shown. Solid carcass sides may, however, present problems as the inevitable shrinkage across the width will tend to reject the long-grain return mouldings. Doors are usually overlaid (closing over carcass sides) with this type of cornice (196:2). Figure 196:3 shows a built-up cornice framed up in the same manner as a plinth, with the cornice mould, frieze and frieze moulding applied as one solid section, or as a series of independent mouldings applied to the cornice frame. Dust panels are fitted in the best work, rebated/rabbeted into the moulding and glued and pinned; while the cornice unit is positioned on the carcass top with stub dowels or locating blocks and is left detachable to allow for shrinkage in the carcass. Figure 196:4 shows a solid cornice mould mitred and glue blocked for a dust panel which is screwed up or down to the carcass top.

22 Leg and frame construction

LEGS

Cabriole legs

Perhaps no single feature in furniture has been so widely used as the cabriole leg (*cabrioler* = 'to bound or leap like a goat'). Present-day application is in reproduction furniture only, but the methods of working are applicable to other shapes.

Figure 197 shows the sequence of operations. The basic shape in profile is drawn on squared paper and a template prepared from hardboard or thick cardboard. The wings of brackets (C) are not cut out of the solid leg but are applied after. If the leg has a club, bun or ball foot, much of this can be turned in the lathe (197:2),

the outlines then marked out on the block, the cuts (A–A) on the face made first with band- or bow-saw, the waste pieces which show the side shapes clamped or pinned back in position and the cuts (B–B) made. The leg is then shaped with spokeshave, rasp and scraper, doing as much work to the lower portions as possible before the wings are added, unless a chair-maker's vice is available. In cheap work these wings are merely glued and screwed, but it is advisable to stagger dowel them (197:3C), and although the bottom dowel contributes little to the strength of the joint it prevents any tendency for the wing to twist. Figure 197:4 shows a leg with carved knee, and due allowance must be made for the extra thickness required when cutting out the shape. Between the World Wars cabriole legs

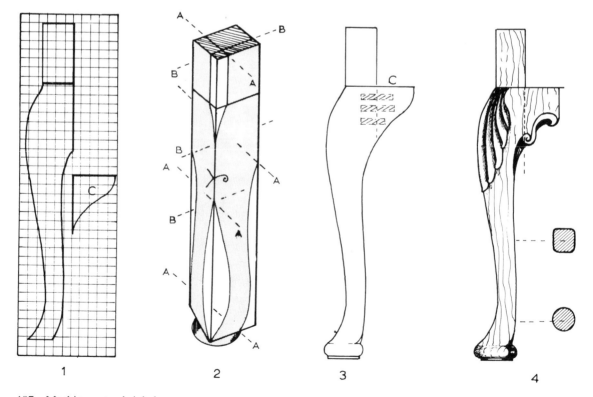

1   2   3   4

197   Marking out cabriole leg

were quantity produced on profile lathes, but all individuality was lost and the hand-carved leg is infinitely superior. If the leg terminates in a ball and claw the rendering should not be too realistic as in many Edwardian examples, for the shape of the claws is not intrinsically beautiful.

Traditional legs

Various other traditional leg shapes are shown in 198. Figure 198:1 is the plain turned Jacobean leg; 198:2 shows the twist, both of which were a feature of oak-work. Part of the twist (198:2) can be done on a slow-running lathe, but the normal procedure in handwork is to turn a cylinder to contain the twist and, while it it still in the lathe, wrap a piece of string tightly round it, spiral fashion. A pencil is then drawn along the string and the spiral sawn down just short of its greatest depth with shallow cuts either side. The hollowing is then done with suitable gouges and rasps. A typical inverted cup leg of the Walnut period is shown in 198:3 built up of sections to save wood, with the spigot ends in the thinner sections entering suitable holes in the thicker; alternatively side pieces can be glued on to a central shaft to form the cup, but the differing grain patterns will show. Figure 198:4 is the Flemish Scroll leg sawn out of the solid and cross veneered, and 198:5 the hock leg. Both types are intrinsically weak in the grain and modern practice would prefer a laminated construction, either of three equal sections glued together with grains slightly opposed, or two sections sawn from one thickness to preserve the run of the grain and a thin central veneer with grain opposed. Figure 198:6 is a typical Hepplewhite cabriole leg in the French fashion; 198:7 an eighteenth-century mahogany leg with inlaid panel of contrasting veneer edged with a boxwood line; 198:8 shows a fluted leg and 198:9 a plain recessed leg in the Adams style. Figures 198:10, 11 are both Sheraton, the former almost contemporary in appearance, and the latter turned and reeded in the cup. These curved reeds must be carved by hand, and 199 shows a similar operation to part of a mace stand made some years ago in the writer's workshops. Many of these leg patterns are still used in reproduction-work, but apart from this they can still serve as an inspiration to modern designers, for all have an intrinsic lightness and grace.

Moulded legs

Moulded legs parallel or tapered with the mouldings stopped or running through can be worked with the spindle-moulder/shaper if suitable jigs are made up, or made entirely by hand. In the case of simple flutings these can be worked first, either with a round moulding-plane or scratch stock, and the leg tapered after; although if the fluting is very shallow it will have to be deepened slightly at the tapered end or the form will be lost. It is, therefore, better to taper first and then mould, supporting the leg in a suitable cradle (200:1), with the leg wedged as in 200:2 so that the sides of the box are parallel to the main axis of the leg. It will also have to be packed up, and 200:3 shows the method of arriving at the amount of packing required. The section of the leg top (A) and the bottom (B) are drawn out full size, also the exact shape of the moulding at the top. If lines (X) are then drawn from the extremities of the mouldings to the centre point, then the intersection of these lines with the outline of (B) will yield perpendiculars to cut the arc at (C) and (D), and it is only necessary to support the leg at its lower end to this level (200:4). The moulding is then worked with a scratch stock as in 200:1, using suitably shaped scrapers to deepen the profile at the lower end, if necessary. A typical stopped fluted leg is shown in 200:5, and 200:6–9 illustrate other leg sections with the scratch-stock cutters necessary to work them. These cutters are usually made from old saw- or scraper-blades, and can be square ended and burred over, as in the standard scraper, or ground like a plane-iron and then burred, which gives a cleaner cutting action. On the other hand the square-ended cutter can be rocked slightly and will cut on both the forward and backward strokes, and may prove to be the better tool with difficult woods.

Pedestal table or pillar legs

A typical mahogany Chippendale pillar or tripod leg is shown in 201:1; 201:2 shows a

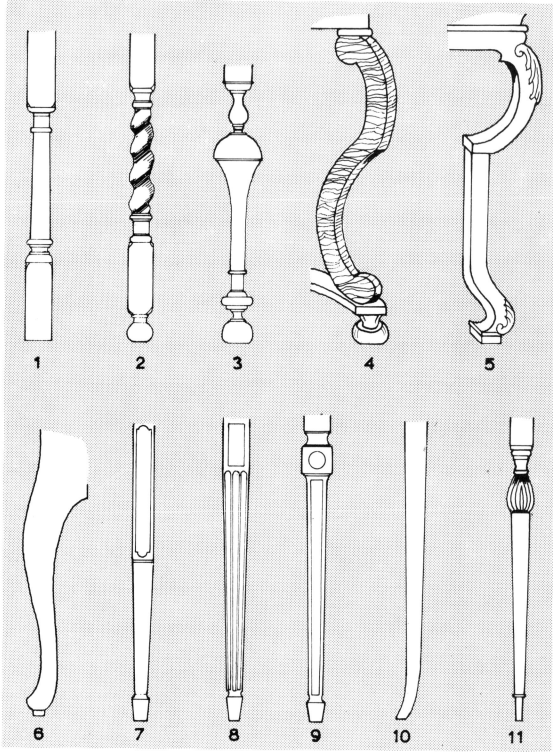

198 Traditional leg shapes

199 Carving mace stand leg. (By courtesy of Eric Coop)

Sheraton pillar table leg and 201:3 an early nineteenth-century tripod table leg with brass lion foot castor. All these legs were used in sets of either three or four according to the heaviness and type of table.

Methods of attaching shaped legs to cylindrical pillars or shafts are illustrated in 202. Figure 202:1 is the stopped slot dovetail method with either taper or straight dovetail and shoulders scribed to fit the shaft; 202:2 is a simpler method using dowels, where the shaft is flatted to receive the leg and any chamfer or moulding round the shaft is returned across the top of the leg. The dowels should be $\frac{3}{8}$ in (9.5 mm) or $\frac{1}{2}$ in (12.5 mm) spiral cut or fluted to enter not less than $1\frac{1}{4}$ in (32 mm), and 203 shows the gluing up of such a construction. An alternative

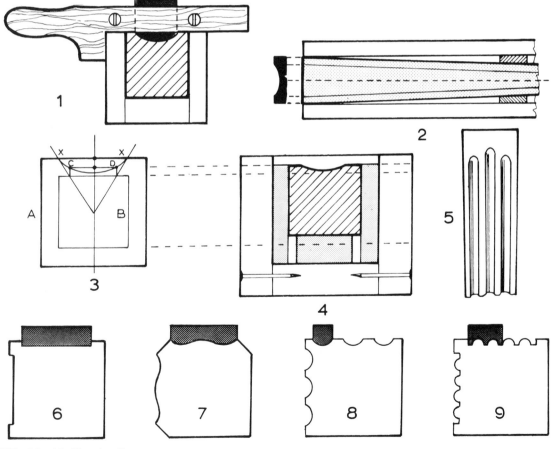

200 Moulded leg details

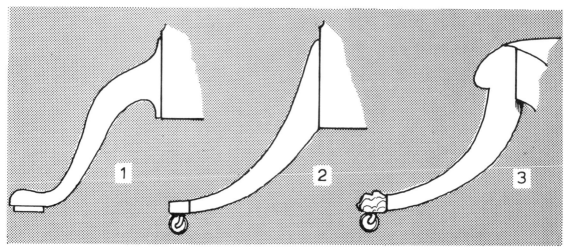

201   Tripod and pillar legs

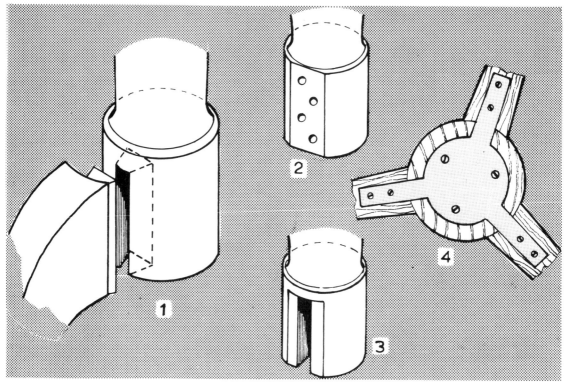

202   Pillar leg joints

method which preserves the shaft moulding intact is shown in 202:3, in which the top of the leg only is scribed to the shaft which is flattened to receive the remainder. This does away with the necessity of scribing the dovetail shoulders. As there is always a tendency for these legs to spread outward in time, no matter what jointing method is adopted, all old tables have to be reinforced sooner or later with a brass or steel plate. This is usually very roughly done, for

203   Gluing up tripod leg assembly

204   Dining-table with curved legs

most antique dealers are only concerned to have the job done as cheaply as possible, but a good plate should be set in flush and shaped as shown in 202:4.

Wood for shaped legs

Laminated constructions are often more satisfactory for curved sections, but if solid timber is used it must be carefully chosen if it is to be strong enough to support the load. Most timber

213

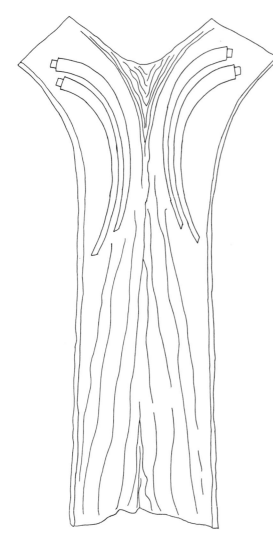

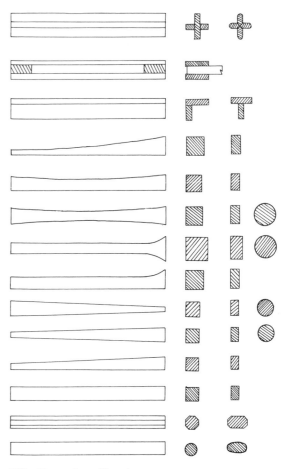

205 Curve of legs from curve of board

is cut below the first branch when felled in order to provide clear, straight logs and for convenience and economy in transport and sawing. However, the craftsman and small user can often control the felling and milling of his timber, and should always be on the lookout for those likely logs and large branches which will naturally afford a ready supply of the curved boards required for chair and table legs and other curved work.

Figure 204 shows a dining-table where the four curved legs came naturally from the curve of the board (Figure 205). With more extreme

206 Examples of leg shapes

curves one may have to compromise and aim to get the maximum strength from the grain only where it is most needed. However, in the long term, it is surprising what tight curves can be found in natural branches of trees such as oak or walnut—they just have to be rescued, along with those commercially less attractive logs, before they are reduced to firewood, usually on site when the trees are being felled.

Contemporary leg treatments

Contemporary designs are usually devoid of ornamentation and rely almost exclusively on rectangular, circular or oval sections either straight, tapered or flared. Figure 206 shows various leg shapes and sections currently used by both craftsmen and industry.

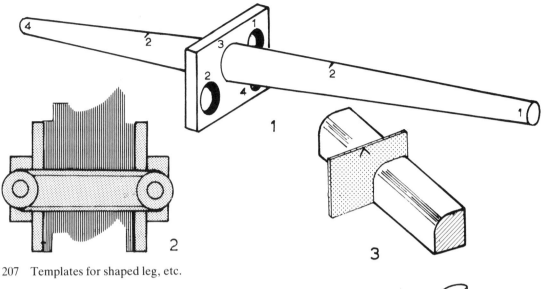

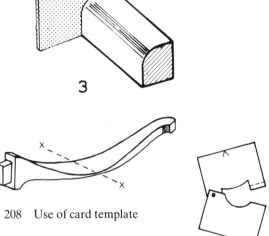

207 Templates for shaped leg, etc.

Turned legs

Round legs are more easily formed in the lathe, but if none is available they can be worked by hand. The block is first planed up to octagonal shape and the arrises so formed planed with a smoothing-plane, creating further arrises which are then taken out with hollow moulding-plane, cooper's spokeshave or curved scraper. The secret of quick and accurate work—and it is only necessary to watch a skilled joiner knocking up heavy oak cylinders with a draw shave to appreciate how quickly it can be done—is to construct a suitable cradle to hold the wood firmly while it is being shaped, and to take the cuts through from end to end every time, working the leg as a whole and not in sections. This applies equally to round taper legs which are planed square taper and then rounded. Church staves, shafts and poles usually have to be done by hand as they are too long or too whippy in the length for the average lathe, and it is always better to prepare a female template of the rounding rather than trust the eye alone. If the section varies throughout the length, i.e. the taper is a gradual swell, several templates may be necessary, and are simply prepared by arbitrarily fixing several distances along the length and boring holes of the appropriate diameters in a block of hardwood (207:1), which is offered to the work as the rounding proceeds and swivelled round to

208 Use of card template

create a telltale shine on the high spots. If the shaft or leg is oval in section then the templates can be cut out of thick cardboard (207:3), and if the shape of the wood does not permit the template being slid along from one end, then it can be hinged with a paper-fastener as in 208. Adjustable templates can be purchased, composed of thin brass strips free to slide between two rubber-cushioned locking bars (207:2). While this is an admirable tool for many purposes, i.e. complex mouldings, etc., it is usually better to use a totally enclosed template for all-round shaping.

Jointing turned and shaped legs

Mortise or dowel holes in turned legs can be marked out and cut into the square section with the holes plugged with softwood before turning in the lathe, or a simple cradle can be made (209:1) to hold the finished turning. This is an open-sided box with the bottom and sides at

215

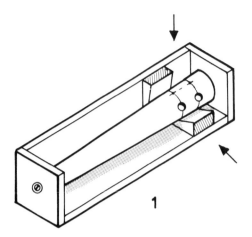

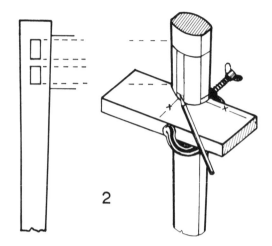

209 Marking out joint positions in shaped legs

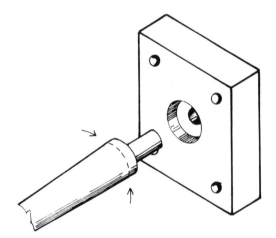

210 Fixing block for turned taper leg

true right angles, and the leg held in position by end screwing or nailing and wedging it in the fixed position. All boring out can then be done vertically on one face, the box turned over on its side and the other face also bored vertically to give a right-angled orientation. Marking out of mortises can also be done by fixing the work between the lathe centres and using the tool rest as a guide for the pencil; or right-angled marking can be done as shown in 209:2, with a shaped block on which the mortise centres (X, X) are laid out G-cramped/C-clamped to the leg. A method of attaching turned taper legs is shown in 210, with a firm tenon turned on the

leg. The shoulders of the leg are also counterbored for additional strength, and the leg is secured to the block by gluing and wedging from above, after which the block is glued and screwed to the carcass base or framing.

FRAMES

Tables and carcass stands and stools

Various forms of leg framing suitable for stands and stools are illustrated in 211. Figure 211:1 shows a typical carcass stand of four straight legs, front framing rail (211:1A), back rail (211:B) and side rails (211:1C). The joints can have mortises and tenons either mitred as 211:2A, or halved together (211:2B) which gives maximum length over half the width in each tenon. This form of construction with rails inset from the face of the legs allows the tenons to be placed in the best position, but thin flush rails necessitate barefaced tenons (211:3). As, however, there is always a tendency for this type of tenon to pull the framing out of square under cramping/clamping pressure, it is advisable to provide a small inner shoulder even if it is only $1/16$ in (2 mm) wide. There should also be a small shoulder at the base of the tenon so that any slackness in the length of the mortise will be hidden by the rail. All these tenons are not shown haunched, and there is no real necessity

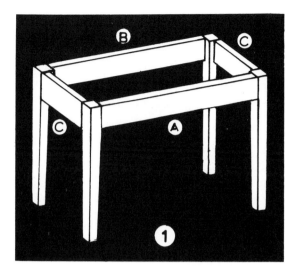

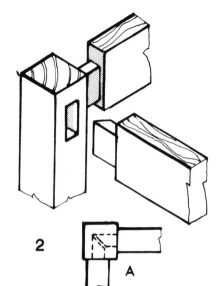

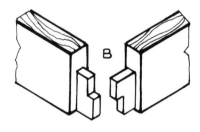

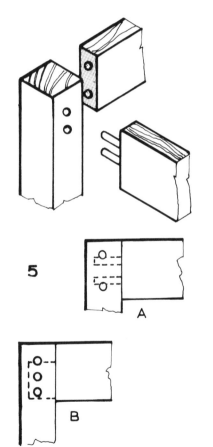

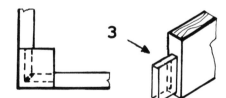

211   Table framing and carcass stands (1)

for this, for corner blocks (211:4) can usually be fitted. Figure 211:5 shows a dowelled construction which is quicker and not necessarily inferior if the dowels are of sufficient length, well fitted and their positions staggered as at (A). A composite joint with one rail tenoned and the other dowelled is shown at 211:5B which is often used in chair-work. The mortise and tenon is cut first, the rail glued in and the dowel holes then bored through the tenon. A point to watch in boring dowel sockets with screw-nose dowel-bits is to keep well clear of the outer face of the leg, and not to allow the long screw of the bit to prick through. If less than about $3/16$ in (5 mm) substance is left between the bottom of the socket or mortise and the outer face, the slight clearance always left for surplus glue has been known to show through as a faint depression even in hard oak.

Various other stand layouts are shown in 212:1–4. In 212:1 the long rails are tenoned or dowelled into the legs, and the inset cross-rails slot dovetailed with either double taper or bare-face taper (212:5, 6). Figure 212:2 adopts a similar procedure, and if there is any tendency for the stand to whip, the back dovetail slots can be reinforced with heavy glue blocks on the inside. Heavy stands (212:3) with one intermediate rail can have the rail double tenoned and wedged (212:7). A stool arrangement is often used for sideboards, where the long rails (212:8) are bridled through and the cross-rails either slot dovetailed or housed/dadoed and glue blocked on the inside.

A curved stand is shown in 212:9 and various methods of connecting the rails in 212:13. They can be either cut from the solid or laminated, dependent on the sweep. In 212:13A dowels are used to support the weak cross grain in a pronounced sweep in solid wood, and 212:13B a bridled method. If the leg has to follow the curve and lie flush with the rails then the latter must be slightly inset and the leg rounded off after assembly. Figure 212:3C is a dovetail method and 212:13D a bridle and tenon for inset legs, while 212:13E shows a tenoned construction halving the tenons, as shown by the dotted lines, for greater length. A cross-stand for small tables is shown in 212:10, 14 and if the cross is at 90° it can be dowelled together or halved, but if the crossover is at any other

angle then it must be halved as in 212:15. In 212:11 the top bearers are dovetailed as 212:16 and the long rails tenoned or dowelled in, while in 212:12 the rails are slot dovetailed as 212:17.

Shaped rails in leg framing

If the under edge of a rail is curved it will become a feather edge where it meets the leg if framed up in the usual manner (213:1A). Sugested treatments are shown in 213:1 for flush rails and 213:2 for inset rails. Figure 213:1 in particular has decorative possibilities and is a great favourite with handworkers. Figure 213:3 shows another treatment which is more wasteful of wood but equally effective. Where intermediate legs occur in long rails, as in long sideboards, they can be bridled as in 213:4. In all cases the final shaping to the curve is eased away after the framework has been assembled. Figure 213:5 is commonly known as the 'Check' joint and 213:6 shows the treatment of a rail with inset bead lining up with the face of the leg. This detail relieves the monotony of a long straight rail joining a square-shaped leg.

Sculptured joints

The term *sculptured* is applied to jointed parts fitted together and shaped to a continuous curve unbroken at the line of the joint as if the whole structure were carved out of a solid piece (although that is not the object of the technique, for the change in grain direction will always show, and the chief considerations are, or should be, flowing structural lines and smooth, unbroken surfaces with no sharp angles). This type of joint is usually confined to chair-work, although it has applications in table framing, and the final shaping must be done after the joints have been assembled. Preliminary drawings are necessary, laying out full-size plans, elevations and cross-sections, with the latter in great detail if the work is to be executed by a third person. The wood must be thick enough to take the shaping with plenty to spare, and in order to facilitate the final shaping some of the first rough cutting can be done before assembly, but wherever possible square faces should be left for laying out the joints and final cramping/clamping. Figure 214 illustrates the

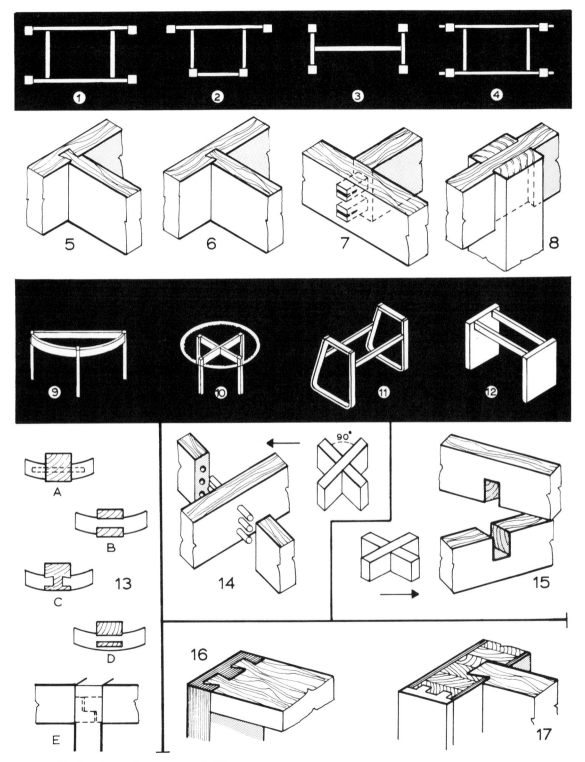

212   Table framing and carcass stands (2)

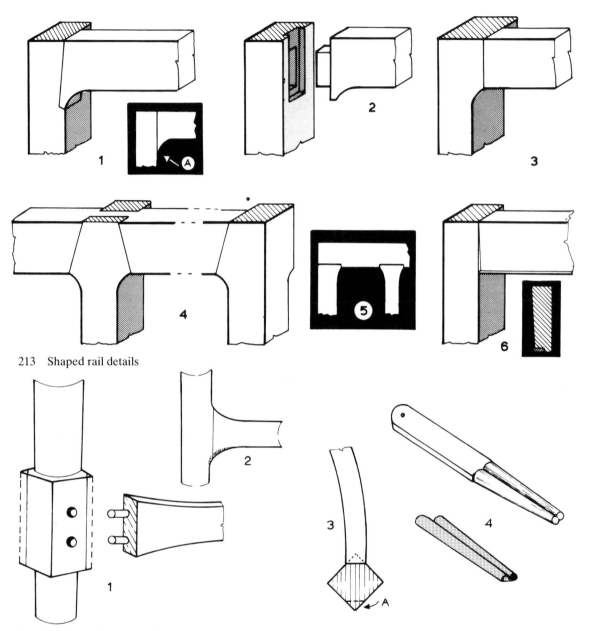

213 Shaped rail details

214 Sculptured joint details

technique, and the drawing at 214:1 shows a turned taper leg with a square block left for the jointing which is cut away on the dotted lines to give the dowel seating, and also a square face (214:3A) for a direct pull for the cramps. The completed joint is shown in 214:2, while 214:4 is a simply made rasp for final finishing made out of a two-pronged stick over which abrasive paper of the appropriate grade is wrapped. It should be remembered that the sweetness of the final curves is largely in the hands of the executant, no matter how detailed the drawings may be; therefore for very exact work a full-size model in clay or softwood may be necessary.

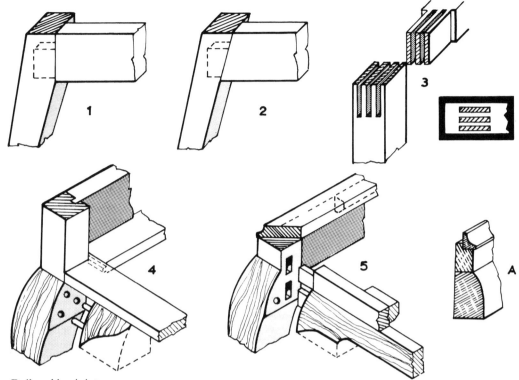

215 Rail and leg joints

Canted leg framing

These are shown in 215:1, 2 and only require laying out to the angle as shown by the drawing; but if the legs are canted in both directions (front and side) then the rails will require a compound cut although in practice an angle of a few degrees can be disregarded.

Finger joint for leg framing

Square section chair legs and arms are sometimes jointed with the finger or box lock joint (215:3). The fingers can be cut with band- or tenon-saw as described on p. 178, or a series of mortises cut by machine in both members as shown in the inset, and trimmed down to the cuts.

Cabriole leg framings

Figure 215:4 shows a bottom rail tenoned into the upper post of a cabriole leg with applied wing to the leg, and 215:5 a shaped rail in an independent stand arrangement made up of separate elements (A) to save wood. Either a plinth mould (215:5) screwed to the underside of the carcass or a cap moulding (A) is fitted, the latter forming a locating rebate/rabbet for the loose stand.

Round leg framings

The framing up of round section legs is shown in 216:3 either dowelled or tenoned as inset, and the shoulders scribed to fit the rounding; the scribing is easier with a dowelled construction. The dowels should alternate in their length (216:4), while 216:5 shows a tenoned arrangement in which a flat is formed on the leg which does away with the necessity of a scribed rail and gives the same overall appearance. Where the leg is fitted direct to the carcass and not framed up as an independent stand or stool, metal fittings can be used, either screw on or with dovetail slotted plates, and obtainable in a variety of angles for canted legs. Alternatively, a tenoned end can be turned on the leg and treated as described on p. 215.

221

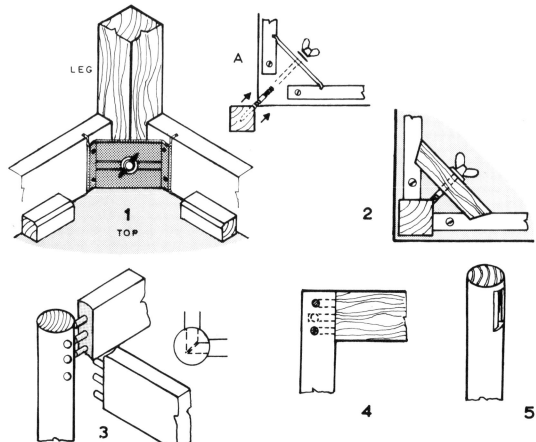

216   Table leg assemblies, etc.

Detachable table legs

Figure 216:1 shows the metal brace plate for securing legs to table-tops, etc. The rails must be securely fixed to the tops with screws and glue blocks, truly square and a tight fit against the shoulders of the legs in the fixed position. A thick screw with wood thread for the leg and metal thread for the wing nut is screwed into the leg at the correct angle and elevation (two loose nuts run on the metal screw will lock together enabling it to be turned into the wood with a spanner), and the metal plate is then notched in and screwed to the rails, the leg pushed home (A) and pulled tight with the wing nut. These brace plates can be obtained in pressed sheet steel in heavy-, medium- and lightweight sections for all types of table and stand framings, and are remarkably positive in action. For those purists who insist on handwork

throughout (and exhibition selectors of vast authority and little knowledge have been known to reject such fitting in handwork) a wooden form is shown in 216:2 which works well enough; but the metal form is preferable and can be thoroughly recommended for permanent work of the highest quality.

Stretcher rails in stands, etc.

These are used to brace or stiffen or to act as fixed distance-pieces, and the wood sections are usually kept as light as possible, necessitating skilful jointing. Figure 217:1 shows the stand in 211 with stretcher rails added for additional rigidity, where 217:1A is the front stretcher rail, 217:1B the back stretcher and 217:1C the side stretchers; while 217:2 is another layout with rails staggered in the height so that the joints do not clash with each other (217:13). As the wood sections are slight, barefaced tenons are often necessary (217:8), either shouldered at the top

222

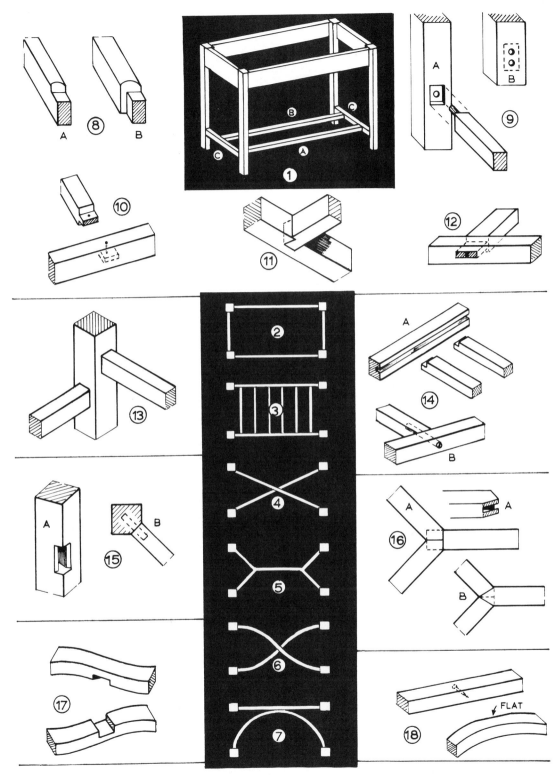

217   Carcass stands

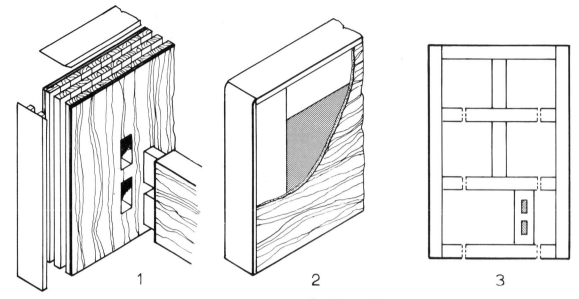

1   2   3

218 Solid stands

only (217:8A), or at the top and one side (217:8B), dependent on the thickness of the wood. If a dowelled construction is used there must be room for two ¼ in (6 mm) or ⅜ in (9 mm) dowels (217:9B), as the joint could swivel on one dowel only; but the rail could be recessed or stub tenoned in 217:9A to prevent any movement with one dowel. Very slight stretcher rails can also be tenoned and pinned from underneath (217:10) or taken through and wedged (217:12).

Other arrangements are shown in 217:3–7. In 217:3 the cross-slats are stopped slot dovetailed (217:11), or they can be stub tenoned (217:10) providing there are substantial side rails (217:1C) to prevent the legs casting or splaying outwards and breaking the joints. Magazine racks composed of many slats can be stubbed and pinned into a groove (217:14A), or with dowels taken through and wedged from the outside to form a decorative feature. Diagonal stretchers are shown in 217:4 in which flats are worked on the legs and the stretchers either tenoned, in 217:15A, or dowelled (217:15B) with a halving joint at the centre cross cover. Figure 217:5 is a double Y in which the long stretcher is either tenoned into the short stretchers (217:16A), or the short stretchers into the long stretcher (217:16B). In 217:6 the curved stretchers can be steam bent and halved together (217:17), or laminated with three or

five long strips to each stretcher, building them up to form the crossover. The curved rail in 217:7 can also be bent or laminated, with the back stretcher tenoned in between the back legs and the curved stretcher into the back of the front legs. A small flat is worked on the curved stretcher (217:18) which is glued and screwed from the back. As the two sets of tenons enter from opposing directions, a trial assembly of the complete stand should be made in the dry state to determine the sequence.

Solid stands

Solid stands are used in modern furniture for table and cabinet stands, divan-type beds and chair sides, etc. They can be of solid core block-board edged all round with hardwood and face veneered either side (218:1), or built up of light frameworks sheeted with plywood, edged and veneered (218:2). Although the finished appearance would appear to be the same for both types, nevertheless there is a subtle difference, and the former is preferable for high-class work. Solid core blanks can also be built up of plywood sheets glued together to make up the thickness, or more economically of flush-door blockwood blanks obtainable up to 2 in (50 mm) thick. A double tongue and groove for the edgings will be necessary for thickness over 1 in (25 mm) and the edgings can be applied either before or after the face

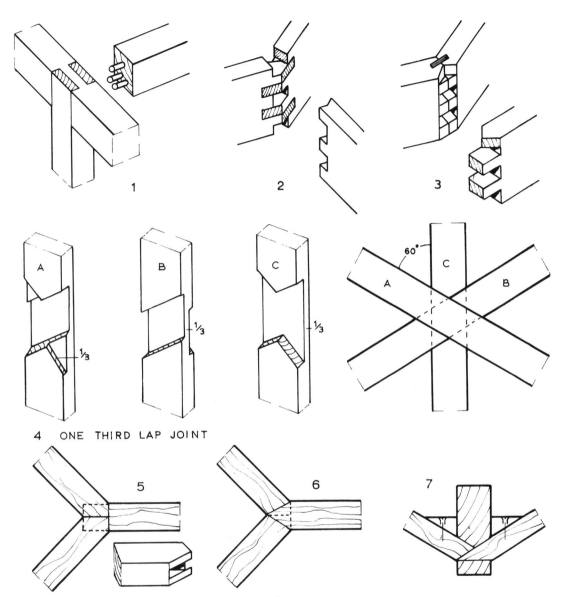

4   ONE THIRD LAP JOINT

219   Three-way joints

veneering. If applied before and veneered over out to the edges they should not be more than about ³/₁₆ in (5 mm) wide, or the junction will shadow through in time. Hollow blanks made up of light softwood framings, tenoned, dowelled or merely spiked together and overlaid with thin plywood should have additional rails and muntins for stiffness, and suitably placed uprights for any structural jointing (218:3). The vacant spaces between the framing can be filled with strawboard, fibreglass, corrugated or honeycomb paper or metal honeycomb to prevent any shadowing of the framing members through the thin plywood due to the trapped air becoming progressively drier with consequent sinkage of the unsupported sheeting material. For cheap work without filling it is customary to bore a series of holes through the framings, as indicated by the dotted lines in 218:3, which allow trapped air to adjust itself to the external atmosphere.

225

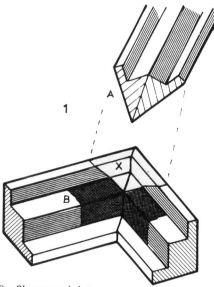

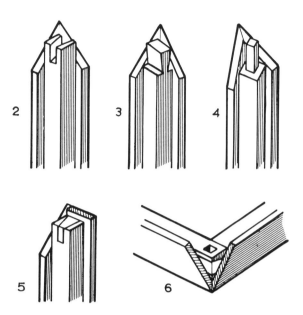

220   Showcase joints

Levelling leg framings, etc.

Some workers cut legs in framed-up work to finished length before jointing, but the better method is to leave a little waste top and bottom and trim off after assembly. The legs can then be cut to length by measuring down after the tops have been squared, or more accurately by standing the framework upside-down on a level surface (sawbench, planer-table), checking that the rails sight through and are not twisted, and then uprighting the stand and shimming up the legs until the top is level. A piece of waste wood thicker than the gap between the shortest leg and the level surface is then used as a scribing-block to mark all sides of the four legs, which are then trimmed to the marks. This method is also useful if it is required to increase the back rake or slope of a chair slightly. The front legs are supported to give the required slope to the back, and then all four legs are scribed and cut; but the alteration must not be too great or the tilt of the front legs will be noticeable, and the backward slope of the seat too much.

Three-way joints

Methods of forming three-way joints are illustrated in 219, which shows the constructions.

Showcase joints

Figure 220:1 shows the simplest form of three-way joint for glass showcase framing, in which the horizontal frame is mitre jointed together and cut away at (X) to receive the mitred vertical member (A); the joint is then strengthened with strips of fine linen canvas (B) glued into the rebates/rabbets. Constructional details of a combined dovetail and tenon joint are also given. Figures 220:2 and 3 are dovetailed together and 220:5 shows the first layout. These two members are glued together (220:6) and then mortised for the tenoned member (220:4). Both the development of light metal sections and special cements for gluing glass panels at right angles to each other have largely done away with the necessity for these wood joints, which are now of academic interest only.

23 Door construction

FRAMED DOORS

The various parts of a framed-up door, tenoned or dowelled together and with panels of ply or solid wood, are shown in 221; the horns (221:1A) are left on while the mortises are being cut to prevent the ends splitting and also to protect the heads from damage until the doors are planed to the openings. Solid panels must not be glued in but must be free to slide in the grooves, and the edges of the corners should be lightly waxed, for even a little strong resin glue squeezed out of the mortises during assembly has been known to lock a panel and split the wood; but ply panels can be glued all round and will stiffen up light frameworks. Rebated/ rabbeted frameworks for panels beaded in from the back require long and short mortise and tenon joints, and if the panels are glass the beads should be pinned only and not glued, while heavy-section glass-panelled doors may require wash-leather strips in the rebates to cushion the glass. Rebates for panels can also be formed with raised *bolection* mouldings (221:5), or panel mouldings (221:6) and both are glued and pinned to the framework only. Flush panels should be in plywood, but *fielded* panels require solid wood, while raised panels are usually solid but can be in plywood if the edges are covered and the face veneers carried over the edgings. Screwed panels in solid wood require wood buttons screwed to the back of the panel and sliding in grooves in the framework, but plywood panels can be glued direct if the seating is sufficient. The thickness of all panels entering grooves should be checked before assembly with a mullet, as shown in 222, worked with the same grooving-cutter as for the stiles and rails.

Laying out framed doors

The stiles are first cut full in height, and the rails the full width including the width of the stiles. Assuming that the door is rebated/rabbeted for a panel then the stiles are first gauged from the face edges with the width of the rebate, and on the backs with the depth of the rebate; they are then cramped/clamped together (223:1) and marked in pencil with the actual door height (A), face width of rail (AD), width of haunch (AB), width of tenon (BC) and depth of rebate (CD). They can then be separated, the mortise thickness gauged on, the mortises chiselled out and the rebates worked. The haunch socket sides (223:4) can now be cut with a dovetail-saw and chiselled out, using a piece of wood equal to the thickness of the tenon and the length of the haunch as a trial template. In marking out the rails (223:2), gauge in the rebates using the same setting as for the stiles, cramp together, mark the overall door width less the width of the two stiles on the faces, and outside these mark the rebate depth to give the shoulder size on the backs. The rails can now be separated and the marks squared round with a knife, taking care to mark the short shoulder on the face (223:3) and the long shoulder on the back, after which the tenons can be sawn down, the rebates worked and then the tenon shoulders sawn in. Fitting the joint is shown in 223:4. The tenon is marked for width against the mortise, and the length of the haunch from the depth of the haunch socket. The mortise depth is also checked, and the length of the tenon is marked fractionally short to allow for surplus glue, after which the cuts can be made and the tenon test fitted. If the tenon shoulders do not line up then they must be checked for squareness, also the squareness of the rail with the stile (223:5), and the overall squareness of the frame opening, using a diagonal squaring-rod or long rule. The old carpenters' trick of dry cramping a frame together and getting rid of any shoulder gaps by running a fine saw through the shoulders on either side is certainly efficacious, but hardly to be recommended in fine cabinet-work. Mortise sides which are out of square with the face (223:6) must be trued up with a chisel, badly sawn tenons corrected with a shoulder-plane and thickened up by gluing on a slip of veneer to the side (223:7). The completed joint should be

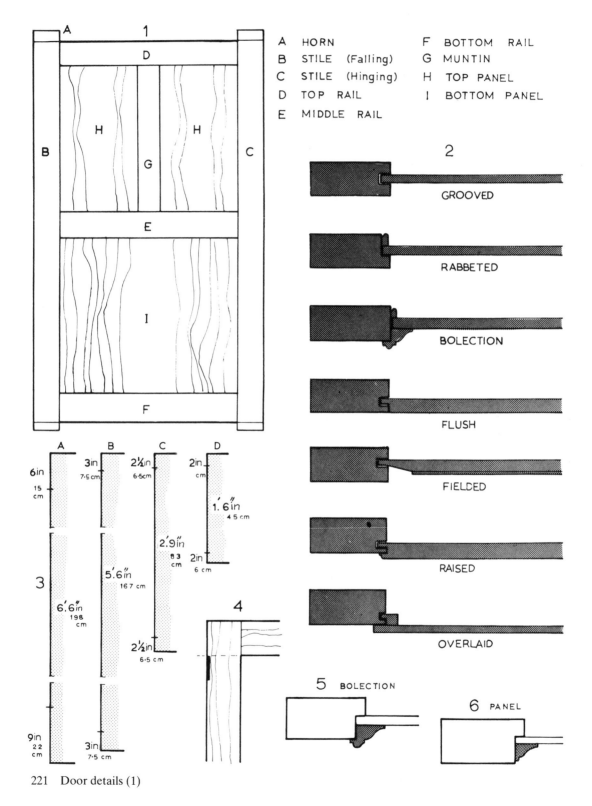

A HORN	F BOTTOM RAIL
B STILE (Falling)	G MUNTIN
C STILE (Hinging)	H TOP PANEL
D TOP RAIL	I BOTTOM PANEL
E MIDDLE RAIL	

2

GROOVED

RABBETED

BOLECTION

FLUSH

FIELDED

RAISED

OVERLAID

5 BOLECTION

6 PANEL

221   Door details (1)

a smooth, reasonably tight fit not requiring excessive cramping pressure, and should be assembled on a level surface, checking the completed frame with winding-sticks.

Grooved and moulded frameworks

Grooved frameworks present no special features. The width of the rail tenons will be less the depth of the groove and also of the haunch, which is essential to fill the groove in the stile, and the joint should be cut first and the groove

worked afterwards. A typical example with raised panels is shown in 226:1. In rebated/rabbeted frameworks with stuck moulding, i.e. mouldings worked in the solid and not glued on as separate pieces, the rebate is worked as before, followed by the moulding which must be to the same depth, while the cutting away of the

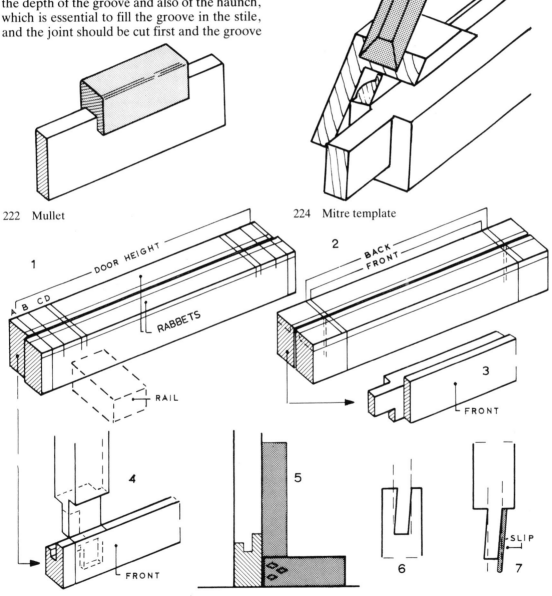

222　Mullet

224　Mitre template

223　Door details (2)

229

moulding on the stile and the mitre junction on the rail is left to last. The mitre cuts are made with a brass or wood mitre template as in 224. (See also Mortise and tenon joints, Chapter 17.)

Dowelled constructions can be used for all framed doors in lieu of mortises and tenons, and adequate strength will be attained if the seating of the dowel-pegs is not less than 1¼ in (32 mm) either side of the joint.

Muntins

Vertical divisions between the rails are known as *muntins* (vertical sash-bars in windows which fulfil the same function are known as *mullions*). Their object when fitted is to stiffen up the panel area by dividing it into smaller sections, and also to increase the overall rigidity of the framing, but they are often used purely for visual effect. As they are distance-pieces—keeping the rails apart rather than pulling them together—they can be stub tenoned and glued into the grooves of the rails with a fine pin through the back of the rail to keep them in position, or if the frame is moulded and rebated/rabbeted, cut in and mitred on the face. Muntins in heavy frameworks may require tenoning in as for the rails, but the tenons should be kept as short as possible, for there is little point in weakening the rails with deep mortises. It is customary to make the width of the muntins the same as, or slightly more than, the width of the rails, but if they are shaped the width should allow for the double moulding and should show the same amount of flat (this also applies to intermediate rails). Examples of muntins occur in framed carcass backs, drawer bottoms and panelling, etc.

Framed bow doors

Framed-up bow doors, either dowelled or tenoned together, in which the panels are grooved into the stiles and rails and assembled within the framework at the time of gluing up, present no difficulty. But where loose panels of either wood or glass enter from the back and are secured with loose beads, the rebates/rabbets in the stiles must not be radial to the curve, but parallel to the outer edge of the stile, or the panel will not enter (225:1, 2). In cramping/

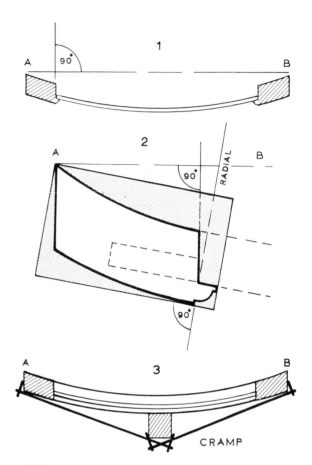

225　Bow doors: laying out and cramping/clamping

clamping up these doors sash-cramps across the back of the box (225:3A–B) will pull the joints open on the face, therefore the cramping pull must follow the arc, and a sturdy block should be laid across the face for the cramps to pull on (225:3). If there is any tendency for the face cramps to flatten the bow then a cramp across the back will correct the distortion.

FITTING DOORS

The bottom edge should be levelled first and held in the carcass opening, checking that the hinging stile is square with the carcass side, and correcting if necessary. The other stile is then tried and planed to the opening, and lastly the top of the frame is levelled to fit the opening, with a final shaving from both top and right stile to give the necessary clearance.

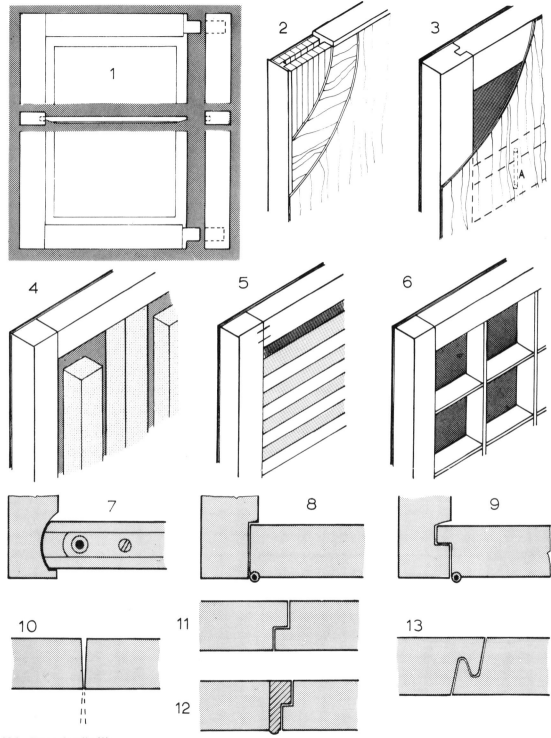

226   Door details (3)

Hinge positions

No precise rules can be laid down and appearances must be studied. Joinery pattern doors are usually hinged 6 in (152 mm) down and 9 in (228 mm) up from the bottom (221:3A), and wardrobe and cupboard doors as 221:3B, with an additional centre hinge or hinges equally spaced if the door is heavy or bowed in the length. Light cabinet doors are shown in 221:3C, D, while framed doors are often hinged to line up with the inner edges of the rails (221:4). It is usual to trial fit the doors in with one central screw to each hinge, and a piece of thin cardboard under the bottom rail to give the necessary clearance, while steel screws should be used throughout if the wood is hard and then replaced with brass screws in the final assembly. If brass screws are used from the onset a head may easily twist off, and the whole screw will have to be bored out with a Torus reamer or fine drill. (See also Hinges and hinging, Chapter 27, p. 267).

FLUSH DOORS

Light pattern flush surface doors for cupboards, wardrobes, etc. are usually made of ply, blockboard, laminboard or particle board covered on the edges (226:2), with the edgings sturdy enough to support the hinge screws. Heavier doors can be made up of plywood sheets glue pressed to supporting softwood frameworks with crossrails as 226:3. As the strength of these doors is almost entirely dependent upon the thickness and rigidity of the ply faces and the glue bond to the framework, the frame itself acts as distance-pieces only, and in theory at least can be light in section and jointed together in the simplest possible manner, i.e. tongued into the grooves (226:3), butted (226:4, 6) or stapled together (226:5). If, however, the intermediate rails are widely spaced, there is always a danger that the framework will show through under a high polish, owing to the suction of the trapped air in the interior; and an alternative sometimes adopted is to bore holes through the bottom and all interior rails (226:3A) to allow the air to circulate. It is, however, more satisfactory to fill the interior spaces with any convenient material—strawboard slats (226:4), horizontal

softwood battens closely spaced (226:5), wood or metal honeycombing (226:6), or even softwood shaving curls placed on edge—but such doors are only economic if produced in quantity, and when the number required is small, solid cores are more practicable for all but the thickest doors. With framed skeleton doors appropriate lock rails and hinging blocks must be incorporated.

Dustproof doors

Modern practice rarely provides for dustproof doors, although it was common practice in traditional furniture, presumably because sweeping rooms by hand raised dust whereas vacuum-cleaners are now universal. However, the technique is sometimes useful and the illustrations in 226 give representative examples. Figure 226:7 shows a door hung on centre-pin (pivot) hinges, 226:8 a rebated/rabbeted carcass side, and 226:9 a grooved carcass side with allowance for the radius of the curve as the door swings open. Meeting doors must be bevelled slightly to prevent binding (226:10) which further increases the gap; but the doors can be rebated together (226:11), or a parting bead glued and pinned on 226:12, while 226:13 shows a machined joint formerly worked by hand with special moulding-planes. The obvious disadvantage of rebated door stiles is that the right-hand door must be opened first and the left-hand door closed first, and for this reason (226:10) are not now common practice.

Shaped flush doors

Curved doors, *bow* (227:1), *serpentine* (227:2), *ox bow* (227:3), etc., can be built up by traditional methods out of solid wood veneered on the face and back. The slats can be coopered (227:4) and then smoothed to the curve, or offset (227:5), or built in sections (227:6) and shaped with stoup-plane, round Surform tool, shaped scraper, etc. The slats need not be tongued together, as in 227:4, 5, and a simple cramping/clamping device is shown in 228 composed of sawn bearers with a packing piece (A) and folding wedges (B) which are driven to cramp the sections together. Modern methods form shaped doors out of thick constructional

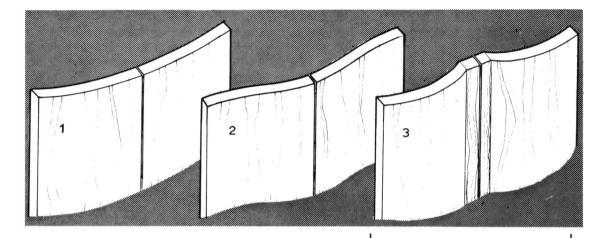

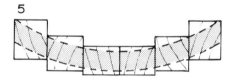

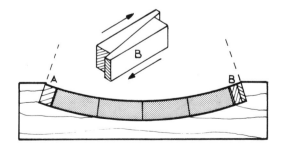

227 Shaped doors

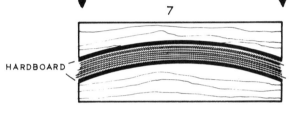

HARDBOARD

RUBBER

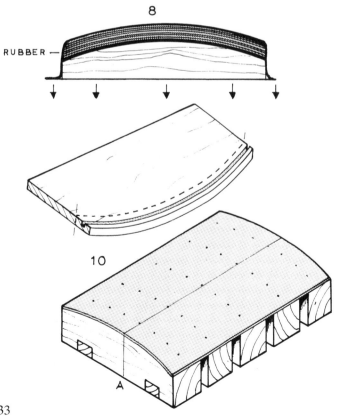

10

228 Cramping/clamping built-up doors

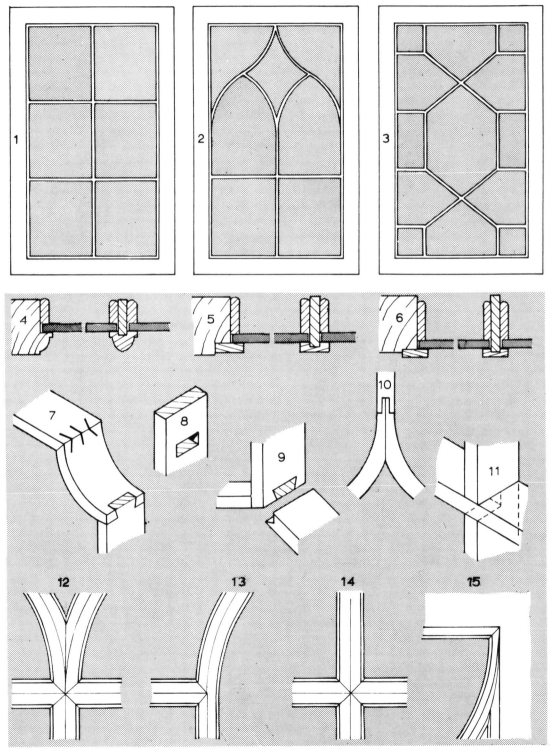

229 Barred door details (1)

veneers or thin sheets of plywood pressed between male and female forms/formers (227:7), or over a male former only in a vacuum-bag press (227:8). In constructing matched formers allowance must be made for the thickness of the assembly, as the radius of the curves of inner and outer faces is not identical. The former (227:10) can be constructed of softwood pieces accurately band-sawn to the curve and faced with hardboard, well waxed to prevent the veneers sticking. Resin glues should be used for cold pressing, or if hide glue is used then heated cauls of heavy sheet zinc or hardwood must be introduced into the assembly. Hand-cramping pressure should be applied to the centre-point, working outwards to each end.

Edging shaped doors

Solid wood will not require edgings, but veneeer assemblies will need the usual form of applied edges. In very shallow curves it may be possible to bend the edging to the shape, first saw kerfing the tongues if they are worked in the solid; if not the edging must be machine-moulded or formed with a portable router or scratch stock on a wide board (227:9), with each length of edging cut off as it is worked and the sawn edge reshaped for the next. Grooves in the door will have to be worked with a suitable cutting-gauge with rounded or dowel-stubbed stock (see Hand tools, Chapter 9) or with veneer or plywood assemblies it may be possible to cut and assemble the individual plies so that the groove is formed in the process. The completed assembly should be glue pressed, left under pressure for as long as possible and given plenty of time to set before face veneering. Any assembly which twists during this period should be rejected, for it is never worth the trouble of trying to correct the twist, nor can the edgings, however stiff, be relied upon to pull it back to shape. As the same formers or forms will be used for the face veneering, a centre-line should be drawn on the former (227:10A), and marked on the assembly before it is withdrawn so that it can be accurately repositioned in all subsequent operations.

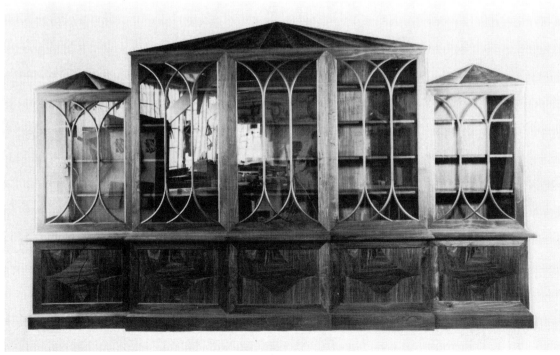

230   Breakfront library cabinet in American black walnut, by Rupert Senior and Charles Wheeler-Carmichael

BARRED GLASS DOORS

Traditional barred doors are illustrated in 229:1–3 and rely for their appeal on the delicacy of their treatment. Contemporary examples sometimes apply a cut-out pattern or jointed face mouldings to a single sheet of glass with Araldite or Durofix cement, but apart from the sham element the glass cannot be replaced without sacrificing the mouldings, and in the best examples the sash-bars are composed of a face moulding and a separate stiffening rib grooved in to form rebates/rabbets for the glass which is beaded or puttied in (229:4, 5, 6). These face mouldings must be of the same shape and section as the moulded edge of the stiles and rails or the mitres will not meet. Various methods of jointing the ribs are practised: veneer keyed with a dovetail joint for curved sections (229:7); straight mortise and tenon (229:8); angle joint in which the third rib is forked over the other two (229:9); two curved

ribs spliced together and slotted into the upright (229:10); and a simple halving joint for crossovers (229:11). The mitred junctions of the face mouldings are shown in 229:12–15.

Sash-bar assembly

Two methods are available. In the simpler the ribs are merely butted together between the framing rebates, and the joints strengthened with glued canvas in the same manner as the strengthening of a crossover (232). The better method is to joint the ribs as already described, and stub tenon them about $\frac{1}{8}$ in (3 mm) deep into the framing (231:1, 2). Curved ribs can be simply formed by pressing three or more thick veneers between sawn formers or forms (231:3), and the face mouldings worked on a wide board (231:4). The mitre cuts can be made with the help of a wooden template (231:5), with a waste piece inserted into the groove as a

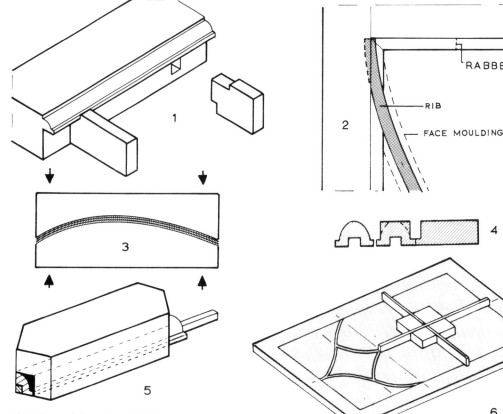

231   Barred door details (2)

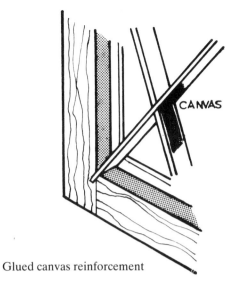

232 Glued canvas reinforcement

support. Assembly is made on a board (231:6) on which the layout is accurately drawn. The ribs are cut, dry jointed and kept in position with blocks nailed to the baseboard; the door-frame is then placed over the assembly, the shoulders of the tenons marked and the position of the mortises in the rebates/rabbets also gauged. The rib assembly can then be glued together (reinforcing with glued canvas if necessary, as shown in 232), for it will spring sufficiently to enter the mortises, the door-frame is replaced on top and the mitre cuts marked, and then sawn in with a small allowance for final trimming. The rib assembly can then be glued in its final position in the frame and the face mouldings trimmed and glued to the ribs. When complete the glass panes are cut with a slight clearance all round and beaded or puttied in.

If the finished work is to be gloss polished the face mouldings are often polished in the length before they are cut, but this calls for clean and accurate working.

SLIDING FLUSH DOORS (WOOD)

Sliding actions for light flush doors suitable for sideboards, free-standing cupboards, etc. are shown in 233. The doors are usually composed of laminboard, particle board, etc. edged with hardwood all round (the top and bottom edging can sometimes be omitted in laminboard without detriment) and face veneered in the

usual way. Figure 233:1 shows a two-door layout, 233:2, 3 alternative placings for three doors and 233:4 four doors; the arrows give the direction of travel. It will be noticed that in every case the doors overlap by the minimum amount necessary, from 3/4 in (19 mm) to 1 in (25 mm), otherwise the openings to the cupboards are restricted; while the gap between the doors in the thickness is kept as fine as the type of track and the projection of whatever handles are chosen will allow. Grooves about 3/16 in (5 mm) deep are also cut in the carcass sides to receive each door in its closed position, but these are often omitted in cheaper work. The layout for this type of door should be done full size, and the open and closed position of the doors carefully studied. In 233:1 the doors are equal in width, but the edge of the front door does not line up with the centre of the carcass. If the width of this door is made equal to the opening beside it then the the rear door will be correspondingly larger, which will automatically restrict the cupboard opening. In practice, the unequal appearance of 233:1 in a fairly long carcass is not noticeable with fairly quiet straight-grained face veneers, but might pose problems with very ornamental veneers, and a compromise will have to be made. Additionally, the position and projection of the handles will have to be watched. In light free-running doors it hardly matters if the rear door is masked by the front door in the open position, for the rear door can still be moved with light pressure of the finger-tips, but the handle-grips must be unobstructed in heavy doors. Buffer stops may also have to be fitted for very heavy doors otherwise pinched fingers may result.

SLIDING ACTIONS

Various sliding actions are illustrated. Figures 233:5, 6 show the standard fibre track composed of a strip (A) and a nylon or plastic slider, two of which are mortised up into each door groove. The door tops can be held in position with lengths of fibre track or hardwood strip fed into the grooves. The rear track is fitted first, fed in with the door in position and lightly pinned, followed by the front door. Figures 233:7, 8, 9 show an improved method which slides more easily as it is top hung. Two forms of slider,

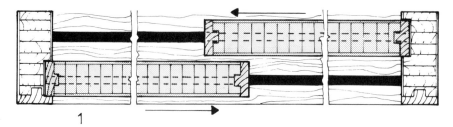

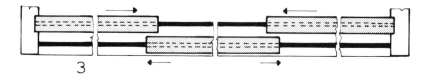

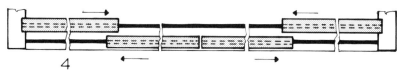

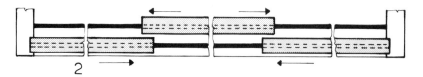

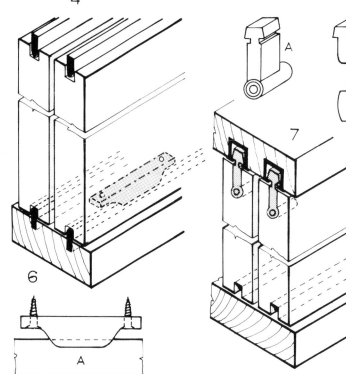

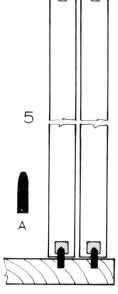

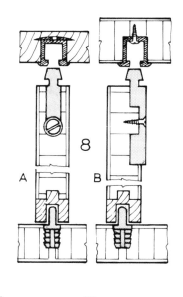

233　Sliding doors (wood)

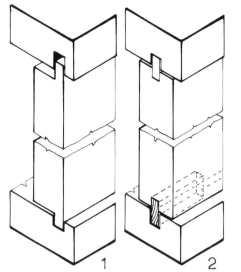

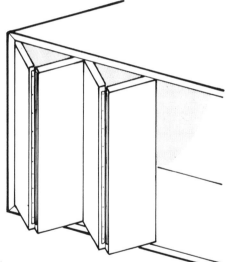

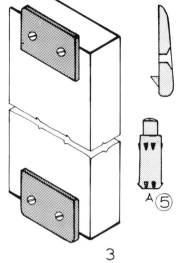

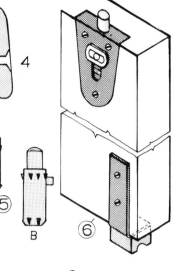

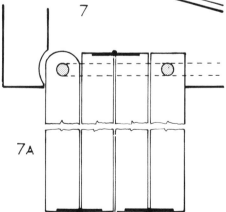

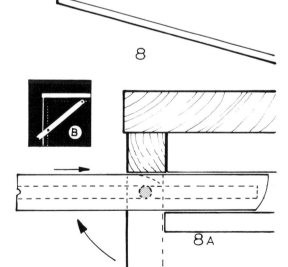

234 Sliding, concertina and raised flap doors

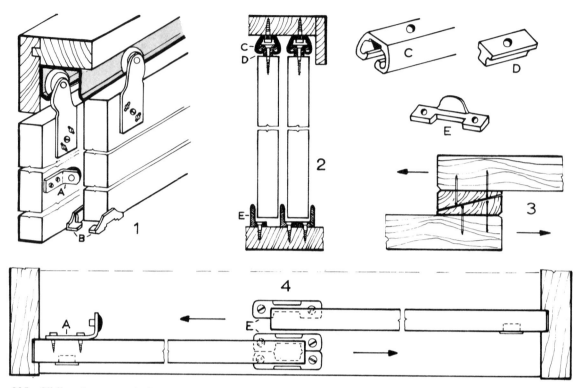

235   Sliding doors: wardrobes, etc.

233:7A mortise, and 233:7B face fixing, are shown, also two forms of top channel (233:8). The door bottoms are held in position by nylon studs (233:9) located in the centre of the carcass opening, and leaving a flush floor surface. Other methods are shown in 234. In 234:1 the doors are tongued to slide in grooves with sufficient extra length in the top tongue for it to be lifted up and dropped down into the bottom groove. Figure 234:2 uses hardwood strips in lieu of fibre track, 234:3 plastic or metal plates screwed on at the back of each door; 234:4 the section of another type of plastic plate rounded at the tip for easy travel. Pivot pins which are recessed into the door thickness and also slide in grooves are shown in 234:5, with 234:5A a spring type in which the pin is depressed and clicks into position and is intended as a semi-permanent fixture, and 234:5B with a projecting lug which enables the pin to be depressed, thus releasing the door from its groove. A pivot bolt which works on the same principle is shown at the top of 234:6, together with a plastic slider which rides over the base track without the necessity of mortising in the slider as in 234:6. Other uses for pivot pins and bolts are shown in 234:7 and 7A, which illustrate a concertina door with pivots top and bottom sliding in grooves in the carcass, and the separate leaves linked with brass piano hinges, and in 234:8, which shows a lift-up sliding flap. An enlarged detail 234:8A shows the pivot pin mounted on the carcass sides, engaging in grooves in the flap. In the inset (234:8B) two pivots either side are used, preventing any side rock as the flap is raised up. The grooves for the pivots must be stopped at the top and the flaps slid in from the back of the carcass.

Sliding wardrobe doors

Heavy doors, or tall and narrow doors in wardrobes and cupboards are always more satisfactory if they are top hung, and typical

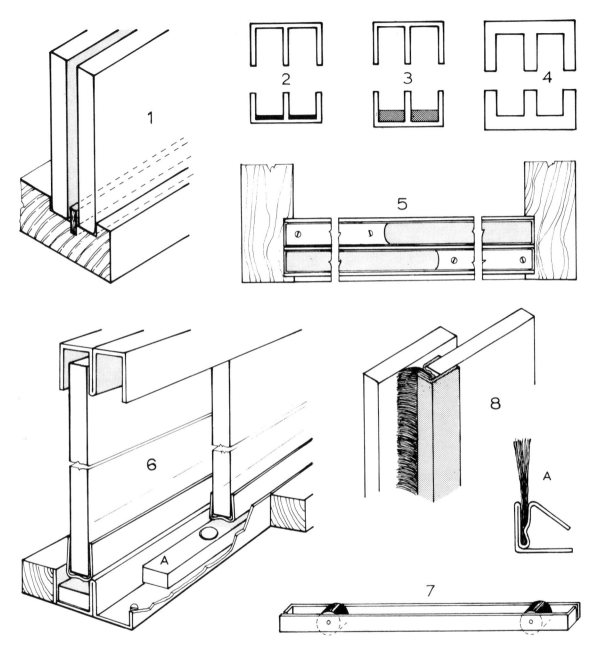

236   Sliding glass doors

sliding actions are illustrated in 235. Figure 235:1 is one type of track for doors up to 60lb (27.210 kg) weight, using steel top channel and two nylon pulleys per door screwed to the back, while 235:2 is a different track for doors up to 25 lb (11.330 kg) weight with nylon sliders (235:2C,

D) instead of pulleys. There is no bottom channel with either type, thus preserving a flush surface for easy cleaning, and the doors are held in position by metal or nylon guides (235:1B, 2E) which are screwed to the centre of the carcass base (235:4). As there is a fair gap between the doors, a buffer-stop is necessary (235:1A, 4), or pinched fingers will result. The doors can be made dustproof by fitting bevelled strips (235:3) which are glued and pinned to the leading edges, and the necessary clearance is obtained immediately a door is moved.

Sliding glass doors

The general principles are the same as for sliding wood doors. Figures 236:1, 5 show a pair of glass doors which can be either 3/16 in (5 mm) or 1/4 in (6 mm) plate, depending on the overall size, and with all edges rounded and polished. These slide in twin channels or grooves at top and bottom of the carcass opening, either worked in the solid or with one wide groove divided by an inset hardwood strip; or various channel sections can be fitted (236:2, 3 and 4). Figure 236:2 is the standard brass channel velvet lined for easy running, as bare metal alone gives a somewhat hard and gritty action; 236:3 is a metal channel with inset plastic strip, and 236:4 a plastic or fibre channel. The last is somewhat clumsy in appearance but offers little friction. All these channels are let in flush, and in every case the top channel is approximately 3/8 in (9.5 mm) deep and the base channel 1/4 in (6 mm) deep, for assembly is effected by pushing the doors up into the top channel and

letting them fall into the base. In effect, therefore, the overall height of the doors will be the exact size of the opening plus 1/4 in (6 mm) for the bottom channel, and a bare 1/8 in (3 mm) for the top. As these measurements are fairly critical it is rarely safe to order by measurement alone; moreover the carcass may not be truly square, therefore it is a wise precaution to cut sheets of plywood or hardboard, test that they enter and run freely in the channels and use these as templates for purchasing the glass.

An improved sliding action for glass doors is shown in 236:5, 6 which offers definite advantages. Top and bottom metal channels are provided, also a sprung U section for the bottom of the doors and a metal carriage (236:6A) with inset metal or nylon balls. As this carriage is free to travel independently it must be longer than the width of the door or the latter will tip off, and assuming a 3 ft (914 mm) wide carcass opening with two doors, then the top and bottom channels will be 3 ft (914 mm) long, the U channel two lengths 18 in (457 mm) long, and the carriage two lengths 2 ft 2 in (660 mm) long. Here again the doors are lifted up into the deeper groove of the top channel and allowed to drop into the lower. This fitting is an improvement on the older type of carriage (236:7) in which small vulcanite wheels were used.

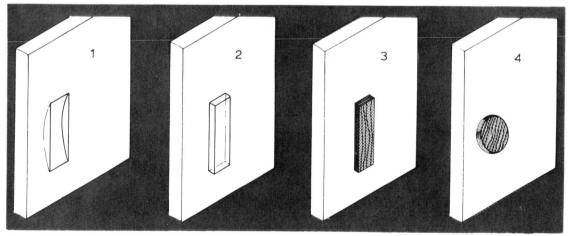

237 Glass door grips

Handles for glass doors

Cheaper doors have oblong finger-grips of about ⅛ in (3 mm) thickness glass cemented to the plate (237:2), but undoubtedly the better method is a cut finger-grip (237:1) which is run in with a grinding-wheel. Alternatively, thin sections of wood, preferably built up of several sheets of veneer to overcome shrinkage, can be glued to the glass with Araldite cement (237:3, 4), and in the writer's experience have proved satisfactory in use, although obviously they will not stand hard knocks.

Dustproofing glass doors

As with wood doors the carcass sides should be grooved to form a dust seal, while the actual gap between the doors can be closed with an available bristle fitting as shown in 236:8, 8A. The bristle assembly clips over the edge of the glass and requires no other fixing. The impact of a free-running glass door against the sides of a carcass can be fairly considerable, and the grooves should be lined with velvet, or small felt, leather or rubber buffers can be fitted to absorb the shock.

It should be stressed that, as with all types of flush sliding door, if the carcass is made up of laminboard, particle board, etc., the hardwood covered edges should be wide enough to accommodate all the groovings, or the ragged core will be visible when the doors are slid open. This hardly matters if the grooves are cased in, but in any case the tongues of the edgings should be placed well away from the grooving, and care in laying out will be amply repaid.

24 Drawer and tray construction

DRAWERS

Various types of drawers are shown in 238. Figure 238:1 is a sectional elevation of an orthodox inset drawer sliding on front drawer rail and side runners; 238:2 an onset drawer which fits under the carcass top but over the side ends, with the drawer rails set back to give a flush front to the carcass; 238:3 a rebated/rabbeted and moulded drawer front for easy fitting, and 238:4 an inset drawer with set-back front rail allowing the bottom (or top) edge of the drawer front to overhang and act as a pull. In 238:2 the front drawer rails can be dispensed with if necessary, and the drawer hung on side runners; while the rebated front in 238:3 requires no very accurate fitting and no drawer stops, therefore it is widely used where cheapness of production is the main consideration, as in kitchen cabinets, whitewood furniture etc. Alternative methods of construction are also given. Figure 238:5 is the orthodox lap dovetailing to the front and 238:9 through dovetailing to the back; 238:6 a slip or slot dovetail for rebated fronts with either single or double taper as shown; 238:7 a tongued front and 238:8 a star tonguing applicable to quantity production, although it could be done on a small sawbench if the setting out were very accurate. An alternative method of jointing the back with a full thickness housing/dado into the sides is shown in 238:10 which is satisfactory if the housing is really tight, for there is no strain across the width of the drawer to pull the joint apart. Figure 238:14 is the old method of attaching the bottom, where a quadrant drawer slip is glued and pinned to the drawer side thereby increasing the wearing surface, and 238:15 a flush slip instead of quadrant which gives a neater appearance, with 238:10A the modern method of grooving into the sides. In old work the bottom was solid wood, as in 238:14, 15, and the drawer sides kept as fine as possible (5/16 in [8 mm]) but modern sides are up to 1/2 in (12.5 mm) in thickness, and unless the bottom happens to be solid cedar as in 238:14 for moth-proofing, plywood is invariably used which can be glued all round if necessary. Drawer fronts are usually standardized at 3/4 in (19 mm) thick; they can be thicker at 7/8 in (22 mm), but should not be under 3/4 in (19 mm) for good work. In factory production the drawers are made slightly slack in the openings to save labour in fitting, which can be a costly business if individually done. There is, however, nothing to equal a well-made hand-fitted drawer, for it will continue to slide like silk, giving satisfaction to its owner over many years. A good test is whether the act of shutting one drawer puffs out all the others in the carcass, and although this can be cured very easily by boring a few holes in the back of the carcass to relieve the air pressure, the writer has yet to meet a proud owner who would allow this to be done.

Materials for drawer-work

Drawer fronts can be solid wood, which is preferable, or laminboard or ply, for both can be lap dovetailed if care is taken; particle board is unsuitable. Drawer sides should be in hard good-wearing wood, with oak the favourite, but teak and prime quality mahogany are good and agba a fair substitute if a pale wood is necessary. Soft hardwoods such as obeche, etc. should not be used, while common pine wears quickly (unless it is very resinous) as old examples show. Backs are usually 1/4 in (6 mm) or 5/16 in (8 mm) thick and can be in any common timber, although here again oak is used in the best work. Solid bottoms can be in English cedar or oak about 5/16 in (8 mm) thick and mulleted into the grooves as in 238:14, but 5/32 in (4 mm) good-quality plywood, preferably limba, oak, gaboon or birch, is usual. The grain of solid bottoms must, of course, run from side to side or shrinkage will pull them out of the side grooves; they can be glued to the front groove

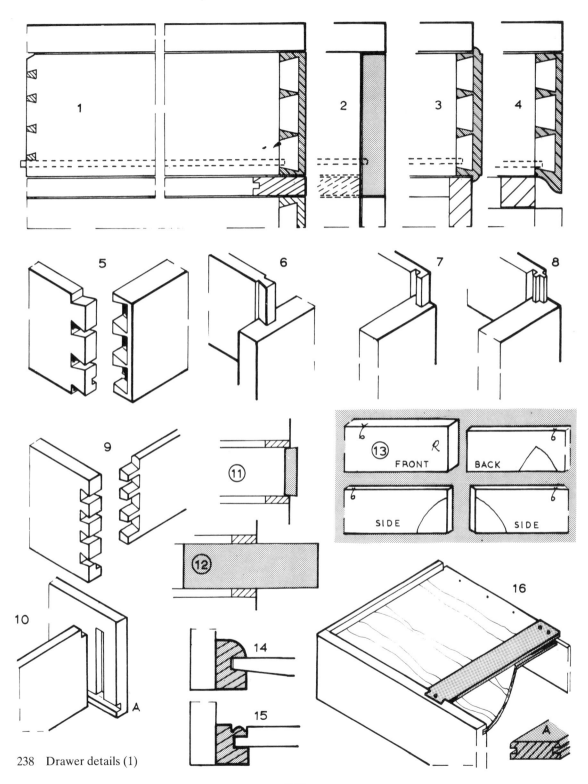

238   Drawer details (1)

and should override the back by about ¼ in (6 mm) to which they are open slot screwed. The grain of plywood bottoms can run either way, but custom and usage usually dictates from side to side. Wide drawers may need thicker plywood, but it is more usual to support the bottom with a centre muntin about 2 in (50 mm) wide by ⅝ in (16 mm) thick, lap dovetailed at the front and rabbeted and screwed to the back (238:16).

Laying out and machining drawers

The drawer front is first cut roughly to size with the long edges parallel, and cut fractionally bevelled on all four edges so that it fits the opening half-way (238:11). The drawer sides, which must be of constant thickness, are also cut to the opening, fractionally sloping in the length so that they slide in half-way (238:12). This is the ideal to work for in hand-fitted work, and assumes that the worker is prepared to spend the time necessary to secure a perfect fit. The sides are then cut to length, allowing for the front dovetail lap and the necessary clearance at the back of the carcass, and the ends are cut truly square. The back is cut correspondingly narrower to allow for the plywood bottom to pass under, with a set down from the top of about ³⁄₁₆ in (5 mm) for clearance; the drawer front is placed on it and the length marked with a knife. The ends are then cut square, leaving the knife-marks on the wood to give just that fractional fullness in the length. All the parts are clearly marked in pencil as they are fitted, the front with face and edge marks and left and right, the back with a triangle on the outside, and each side with a quadrant (238:13). The grooving for the bottom in the front and sides is gauged in before the dovetails are set out, or part of a pin may be lost, showing an unsightly gap. Dovetails are at the discretion of the maker, very fine (1 in 8) as in the best traditional work, or the firm 1 in 6 for modern work. Purists may insist that they should be as fine as possible, but drawers are not left open for the dovetails to be admired, and the first consideration must surely be the strength of the joint. If the front is slip dovetailed (238:6) or rebated/rabbeted (238:3), setting out for the carcass opening will have to be done by measurement; although with the latter it is possible to through dovetail and apply a false front after to form a rebate, but the practice is not to be recommended if it can be avoided for the false front could be thrown off in time under repeated impacts.

Assembly

Drawer dovetails should never be completely fitted before assembly as they only fit once, and the worker should have enough confidence in his jointing to accept that they will fit. Some craftsmen use only a minimum of glue, thickly coating the ends of the sides and wiping them across the pins on the assumption that as the dovetails are mostly end grain there is little point in gluing every socket. However, it is better to have too much glue than too little, providing it is thin enough to be squeezed out. One drawer side is laid flat on the bench, the front and back pushed home, the other side placed in position and tapped down with a mallet using a block of wood to cushion the blows. A sash-cramp/clamp should be kept handy in case the drawer needs a pull across the width or from front to back, but it should not need much cramping, and if a cramp does have to be left on while the glue sets, the drawer should be set on a level surface free from twists. After wiping off the excess glue with a clean wet rag (some workers give the insides a coat of polish before assembly to prevent the glue staining), the drawer is checked for squareness with a rod and left undisturbed until the glue has set and the bottom can be cut and fitted. If the drawer is fractionally out of true the bottom can be cut to pull it square, but it is rarely possible to correct a twist.

Fitting drawers

Any protruding pins are planed off and the back of the drawer is fitted to the opening. From then on it will be a question of gently easing from back to front until the whole drawer enters sweetly. Chalk-marks along the sides and edge usually disclose high spots, and if the carcass back can be left off, a light can be shone through to show up any tightness. At this stage the bottom is in position to support the drawer, but it is not finally fixed until last, running a little glue into the front groove to hold it, and either screwing or pinning at the back, unless it is a solid bottom in which case it should be open slot screwed so that it is free to move. Drawers which run harshly can be lubricated with a candle end (not soft waxes which quickly pick up dirt), although a well-fitted drawer should run sweetly enough without the need of lubrication.

Drawer stops

Drawers must not hit against the carcass back or they may force the back off in time, quite apart from the noise of the impact. It is, therefore, usual to allow a generous clearance, say ½ in (12.5 mm) at the back, and fit stops to prevent the drawer entering too far. The drawing (239) gives the usual type, two of which are pinned and glued to the front rail. They can be of hardwood or plywood, fractionally thinner than the set-up of the drawer bottom; the thickness of the drawer front is gauged in on the rail, the stops glued and temporarily veneer pinned in position and the drawer pushed home. If the position is not correct the stops can be tapped over, the pins hammered in flush and the glue left to set. Drawer fronts are often fractionally inset (bare ⅓₂ in, 1 mm) as this enhances their appearance, but if flush they should be really flush and not slightly proud.

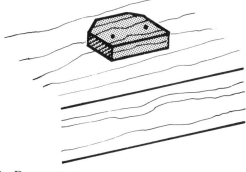

239   Drawer stop

Side-hung drawers

Drawers can be side-hung by screwing 1 in (25 mm) by ¼ in (6 mm) fillets to the carcass sides, and corresponding ¼ in (6 mm) deep grooves in the sides. The principle is an old one revived; it gives fractionally sweeter running for

the drawers as the bearing surface is reduced, but wear on the fillets and in the housings/dadoes may cause the drawers to drop and foul the fronts below. However, the method is often used, for it saves both space and time fitting drawer rails, although the carcass must be stiff enough to stand on its own without cross-ties, and in tall carcasses it may be necessary to fit at least one intermediate drawer rail to hold the sides in. The screwed fillets should be in a hard-wearing wood and the drawer sides also, and 240:1A shows the usual form, with a machined groove in the drawer side and the side fillet rounded to fit, which automatically becomes the drawer stop. Figure 240:2 is a hand method with the groove running through the length of the side and stopped by an extra wide pin in the front, but this method should not be used for heavy drawers unless front rail stops are also fitted, or the front may be forced off in time. Figure 240:3 shows the application to a plan chest, with 240:3A a cover board screwed to the sides to prevent plans riding up over the drawer back.

Extension drawers

Metal extension slides for filing-drawers are available in a variety of supporting weights (240:4), enabling a heavily loaded drawer to be withdrawn to its full extent easily and without tipping; the larger slides include a quick-release trigger enabling the drawer to be released from the carcass channel. This outer or case channel (240:5, 6) is screwed to the carcass side and the inner drawer channel to the drawer side, which must be set in by the amount of clearance necessary according to the track. The slides are bought in pairs, right and left hand, and in a limited range of lengths, while some can be cut to suit most carcass depths. Fitting the tracks is fairly critical, for the whole of the weight is taken by the slides and the drawer sides are kept just clear of the front rails (no runners are necessary) so that there is no rub. If the carcass back can be left off it will help the positioning, and if a dummy drawer side is cut from waste wood, the drawer channel screwed to the board, the board run in and planed off on the bottom edge until it is just clear of the rail when it is slid into the case channel, it will serve as an accurate

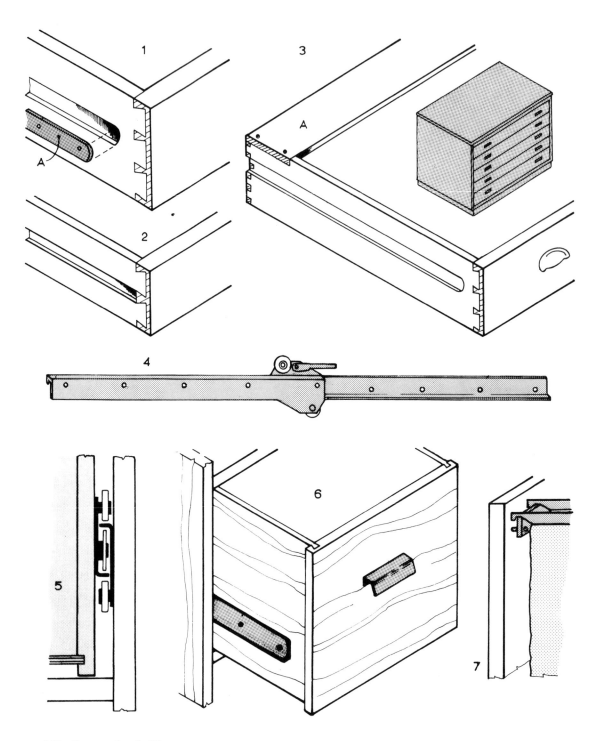

240   Drawer details (2)

template for the final fixing. Filing-drawers are usually fitted with hanging pocket-type files, and 240:7 shows a $5/8$ in (16 mm) by $1/8$ in (3 mm) brass strip runner which is screwed to the front and back (or both sides according to how the files run) with brass screws and distance-collars.

Drawer positioning and depths

There are no strict rules regarding the number, dimensions or positioning of drawers in carcasses, although the old custom was to graduate the depth of the drawers with the deepest drawer at the base to allow for visual foreshortening, while deep drawers were never placed at the top as they tend to look somewhat overbalanced. These refinements are often neglected but always worth considering for good proportionment, moreover drawers should never be too deep or they tend to hide their contents and are heavy to pull out, while over-wide drawers are inclined to rock as they are pushed home especially if they are a little slack in the openings. Drawers in cabinets and chests can be from 3 in (76 mm) deep outside measurement up to say 9 in (228 mm) deep, always remembering that a good $1/2$ in (12.5 mm) is lost from the inside depth. Filing-drawer dimensions will be governed by the standard size of the file hangers used; plan-chest drawers should fit the standard paper sizes, allowing 3 ft $6^{1/2}$ in (1.08 m) by 2 ft $6^{1/2}$ in (774 mm), 2 ft 11 in (889 mm) by 2 ft (609 mm), etc. and 3 in (76 mm) deep, all inside measurements. In old work of very high quality both carcass and drawer backs were made fractionally wider than the fronts so that the drawers automatically tightened up as they were withdrawn, but it is doubtful whether anything is gained by working to such precision limits.

Shaped drawer fronts

Traditional shaped drawer fronts (bow, serpentine, etc.) can be cut out of the solid (241:1), built up in brick formation (241:2), or laminated from thin plywood sheets or constructional veneers (241:3). Figure 241:1 is only suitable for very slight curves or the short grain will be too

weak and will not support the dovetails, therefore 241:2 is better for pronounced curves, for the separate blocks can be cut, fitted and glued together to contain the shape; but the modern technique of laminating is undoubtedly the best. Figure 241:4 shows a more intricate shape which in old work was built up on a solid base (241:4A), worked with moulding-planes and richly veneered. A softish pine was used for the applied strips, and although any shrinkage across the depth of the drawer front could cast off the strips, furniture was not subjected to central-heating conditions, moreover the face veneers were thicker and any blistering not unduly evident. Here again, therefore, a laminated base is the only satisfactory solution under modern conditions, and the same principle of applied moulded strips can be used providing the wood is amenable. Face veneering can be done either with a vacuum-bag press or by the traditional method of laying the acute curves with heated sandbags, trimming back and hammer veneering the straight sections. In old examples the veneer was either laid diagonally to counteract the shrinkage of the solid base, or soft, flexible burr/burl veneers were used, immersed in boiling water to soften them, and then laid with very thin hide glue, repeatedly hammered down until the veneer stuck. In laying out shaped-fronts the ends must not be shot square to the bow but to the base or chord of the bow (241:5) and a convenient method is to cramp/clamp the shape to a board and use the try-square as shown, while a small flat is worked for the drawer sides (241:5A). Laminated build-ups will have to be covered on the edges or cock beads applied. With the former, the dovetail lap edges need not be covered if the constructional veneers are fairly thick, for they will hardly show when polished.

Canted fronts

Slight cants (241:6) can be worked in the solid, but if steep then the whole front must be canted (241:7), and the dovetails laid out on lines drawn parallel to the long edges of the drawer sides. Laying out the pins square to the canted front as in 241:8 would result in short grain at the points (X, X).

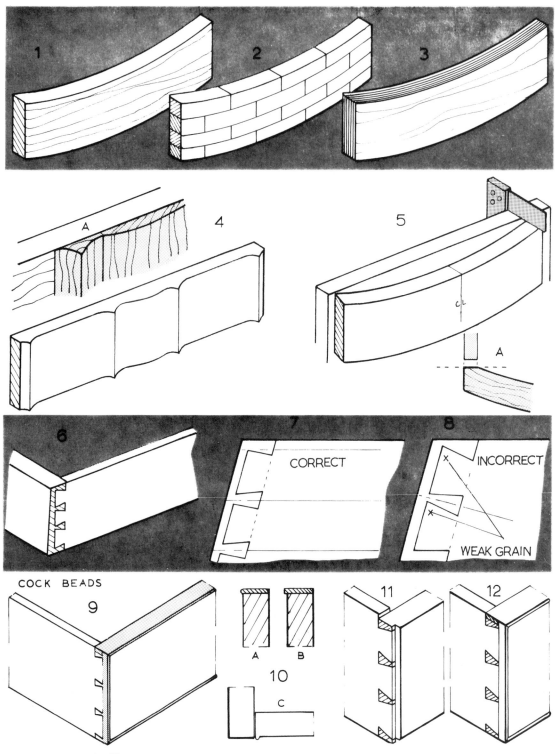

COCK BEADS

CORRECT

INCORRECT

WEAK GRAIN

241   Drawer details (3)

242   Cock beads to drawer front

Cock beads

Any bead which stands raised from the surface as distinct from flush or sunk is known as a 'cock bead', but the term is usually taken to apply to small beads or edgings to drawer fronts and cupboard doors (241:9, 242). The usual form is a raised bead (241:10A), but it can be square (241:10B). Both should be kept as fine as possible, say a bare ⅛ in (3 mm) in width for a normal drawer, and fractionally above the carcass edge (241:10C). The top bead usually covers the thickness of the drawer top (241:9), with the sides rebated/rabbeted to the pins and the bottom a similar amount, mitring the corners all round. The rebates should be worked after the drawer has been fitted to the opening, and while some workers might set the top edge down for the bead beforehand, the former method of fitting as for a plain front and then gauging in the exact thickness of the cock bead all round and rebating is more accurate (241:11). A point to watch is the provision of a wider half pin at the top (241:12) to accommodate the bead.

Modern furniture is made with all the drawers in a chest the same height. This is fine for low cost production in a fully mechanized factory, but any item too large for one drawer is also too large for any other. If the drawers are of graded heights the piece is more versatile and the appearance improved.

To lay out graded drawers:

1 Measure the total height of the drawer space.

2 Decide on the number of drawers required.

3 Decide on the scale of graduation.

4 Calculate as in example below.

Drawer space 36 in (92 cm)
Number of drawers 4
Scale of graduation 4, 5, 6, 7
Add together the numbers in the scale of graduation = 22

Drawer heights will be:

1st drawer $\dfrac{36}{22} \times 4 =$ approx. $6\frac{1}{2}$ in (165 mm)

2nd drawer $\dfrac{36}{22} \times 5 =$ approx. $8\frac{1}{4}$ in (210 mm)

3rd drawer $\dfrac{36}{22} \times 6 =$ approx. $9\frac{3}{4}$ in (248 mm)

4th drawer $36 \times 7 =$ approx. $11\frac{1}{2}$ in (292 mm)

This makes no allowance for the thickness of the drawer rails.

Drawer rails, runners, kickers and guides

A typical carcass framing for a chest is shown in 243:1, with (A) the top bearer rails dovetailed into the sides, (B) the lower drawer rail twin stub tenoned in, (C) the central division, (D) drawer runners, and (E) kickers, whose function it is to prevent the drawer sides kicking up as the drawer is withdrawn. In solid work the drawer runners (3D) are stub tenoned and glued into grooves in the front rail and housed to the sides, but the housing/dadoes must not be glued, and the runners are secured by open slot screwing at the back. Plywood or laminboard sides have the runners housed and glued with a small pin (4A) driven in at an angle to hold the runner flush with the front rail. The centre division (C) has a front upright tenoned and wedged to top and bottom rails, and a long-grain division tongued in with a wide double runner (D) screwed up. An alternative method of forming the centre division is shown in 243:5,

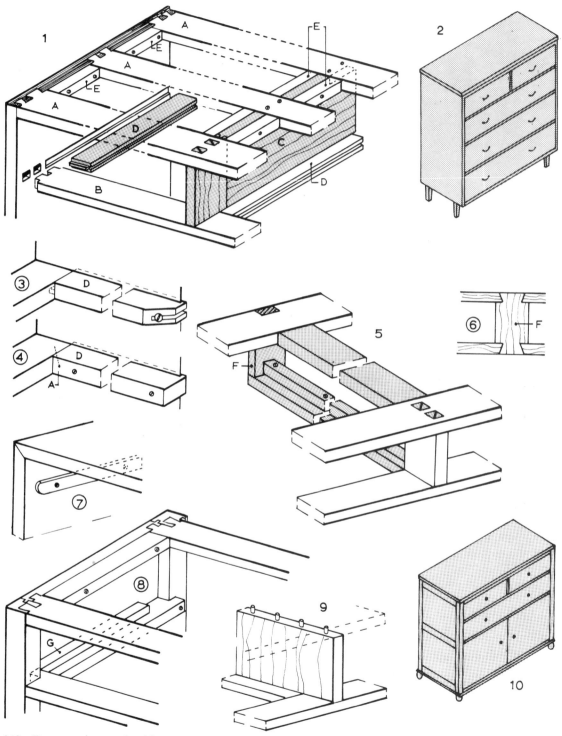

243   Drawer runner and guides

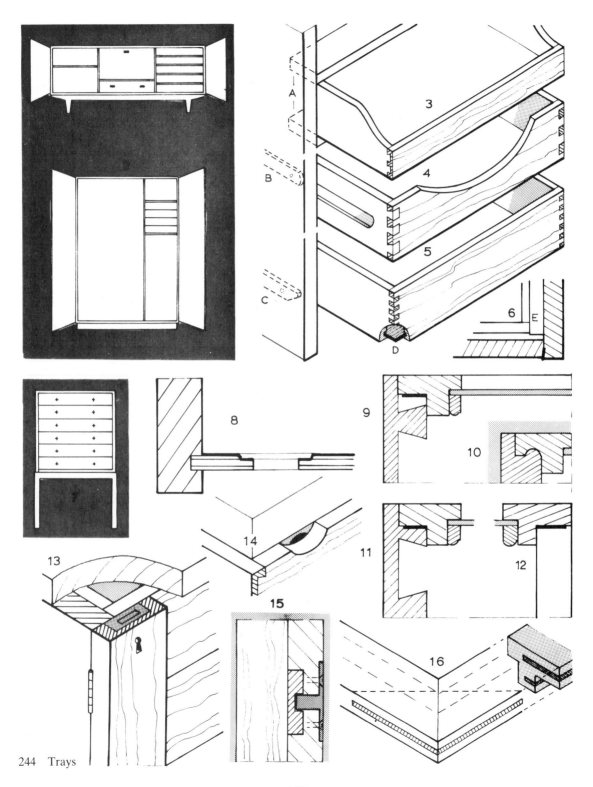

244 Trays

253

and is supported by a dovetailed hanger at the back (6F). Figure 243:9 shows another method suitable for flush-top carcasses, with the division dowelled or dovetail housed to the top, housed and screwed to the front rail, and the drawer runner stub tenoned to the front rail. Fillets for side-hung drawers are shown in 243:7, while in 243:8, where a framed carcass construction (243:10) is used, drawer guides (G) glued to the runners are required.

TRAYS

Sideboards and wardrobes (244:1, 2) often include interior trays for storage. These can have shaped fronts in which the contents are visible, or flat fronts, which are suitable for cutlery, etc. Construction can be lap dovetails (244:3), through dovetails (244:4) or box lock joint (244:5), and in all cases the plywood bottoms are grooved in as shown in 244:5. The trays can run on the usual type of drawer rail (244:3A), side hung on guides screwed to the carcass sides (244:4B), or sliding on screwed guides under the trays (244:4C); the latter is useful for trays which have neither shaped fronts nor handle grips as sufficient space is left between each tray for finger-grip. In all cases the trays are a fairly slack fit and slide easily. Where the carcass doors are inset, as in 244:6, and hung on standard butts, a false side (E) must be fitted which allows the tray to clear the door as it is withdrawn. Figure 244:5 can also be used as a filing-tray for office purposes, and sizes range from 2½ in (63 mm) to 3 in (76 mm) deep by 14 in (355 mm) to 15 in (381 mm) long and 10½ in (266 mm) to 12 in (304 mm) wide, with the back, sides and front of equal thickness and about ⁵⁄₁₆ in (8 mm) or ⅜ in (9.5 mm) thick. The plywood bottoms need only be about ⅛ in (3 mm) thick.

Trays for specimens

Specimen cabinets and trays (244:7) fall into two classes; (a) those intended for reference and research purposes where the individual specimens can be removed for first-hand inspection; (b) those intended for viewing only, with air-tight, dustproof and/or thief-proof protection in museums and public galleries. The latter are special fittings calling for precision manufacture, and 244 refers only to those normally made by furniture-makers for private collectors, or the occasional 'one off' for special display purposes. Whichever type they are, however, the trays should be close fitting as in drawer-work and interchangeable throughout.

Coin trays

These are made up in the usual manner with grooved-in plywood bottoms which are velvet-lined. Separate recesses for each coin are bored with a suitable expansion bit, and a smaller hole bored through the centre to allow the finger-tip to be inserted from underneath to tip the coin out of its recess (244:8). If the recess is shallow the velvet will usually stretch sufficiently to fit the depression, with the centre hole trimmed out with a sharp knife after the glue has set. The velvet can be laid with shoemakers' paste or other suitable adhesive as described in Table lining, Chapter 33, taking care to use only a minimum of glue and allowing it to set partially before the velvet is smoothed down. Cabinets for precious coins are normally provided with locking doors or hinged cover fillets at each side which can be locked in position (244:13).

Entomological trays

Trays for insects, etc. should be provided with glass dustproof covers which are made up as separate frames, veneer keyed at the corners (244:16); the inset shows the section. A rebate/rabbet is worked on the tray sides (244:9), with a velvet puff or strip to form a dust seal, or both rebate and frame shaped as at 244:10. If the front and sides of the tray are of equal height a stopped rebate will be necessary at the front unless the dovetails are laid out as in 244:9, commencing with a half tail instead of a pin; but the tray sides can be lowered, the dovetails laid out in the usual manner (244:11), with the frame overhanging the sides as in 244:12. If the glazed frame is sunk all round, as in 244:9, finger-nail grips will have to be provided as 244:14. The beds of the trays are covered with a suitable antiseptic material, prepared peat or treated cork, etc., to allow the insects to be pinned

245 Coin collector's cabinet in Bombay rosewood and mahogany. Designed by H.S. Slan

through, and the glass frames screwed down in the rebates if necessary.

Cabinets for specimen trays are not normally fitted with individual drawer rails if the trays are shallow and numerous, and the tray sides can be grooved for side guides (244:4B). Tie rails may, however, be necessary at intervals of about 2 ft (609 mm) to prevent movement of the carcass sides in tall cabinets. Some method of stopping the individual trays from being fully withdrawn may have to be included, either as a precaution against loss, or to prevent a tray tipping out and spilling its contents. If the glass frames are screwed down in the tray rebates/rabbets the stopping mechanism will have to be installed from the back, with the carcass back either treated as a hinged door or easily removable, with small bolts screwed to the tray backs working in stopped slots grooved into the running guides. If the stopping mechanism can be fitted inside the trays then a simple brass pivot and screw plate can pass through the tray side to engage in the stopped slot (244:15). Rubber buffers may also have to be fitted to the back of the cabinet to cushion the shock of free-running trays. As already mentioned, the trays should be interchangeable, calling for very careful layout and assembly, and it is advisable to make up various jigs for cutting to length, jointing, etc. Assembly of both trays and frames can be done on a flat board, with another board screwed to it which is the exact inside dimension of the tray or frame. If the component parts are closely fitted to the inner board, and the material has been accurately machined, all units should be identical.

25 Fall flaps, secretaires, cylinder falls and tambours

FALL FLAPS

Fall flaps for writing bureaus and cabinets where it is essential to preserve an uninterrupted flush writing surface are hinged with back flap hinges, and can be rebated/rabbeted over the carcass sides, as in the traditional sloping-front bureau, or inset between the sides, which is the usual method for modern bureaus, writing desks, cocktail cabinets in sideboards, etc. If the front is rebated (246:1) and the rebate worked along the front and down both sides (but not at the bottom), then a gap will show at the hinging point which was usually concealed in older examples by a shaped wing-piece glued to the carcass edges, as shown by the dotted line X. A better method is to stop the rebate as illustrated in the main drawing (246:1) and the inset (246:1A). Inset flaps are hinged with a rebated fall flap joint (246:2), and the inset (246:2A) shows the flap in the lowered position. An additional bearer rail is provided under the flap, hollowed to receive the swing of the fall. Alternative methods of hinging are (246:3) pivot hinges described in Chapter 27, with the slight gap at the end of the recessed hinge not visible in either the open or closed position, and the patented stopped pivot hinge in 246:4 which supports the flap in the open position. This is only obtainable in mild steel, and, while it is strong enough for small flaps, would require additional stays for very heavy flaps. Figure 246:5 shows a method sometimes adopted in sideboards and wall fittings, using either butt or piano hinges, but the flap falls below the level of the inner base and is unsuitable for writing surfaces unless the flap is very deep. Chapter 27 should also be consulted for hinging methods.

SECRETAIRES (SECRETARIES)

These provide useful writing space and storage for papers in the top drawer of a chest or cabinet (247:1). The drawer front is a simple fall flap rebated/rabbeted as shown (267:2) to give a flush surface, hinged with brass back flaps and supported on brass quadrant stays which are recessed into the thickness of the drawer sides. It is obvious that the design of the chest must allow for the standard writing height of 2 ft 5 in (736 mm) or 2 ft 6 in (762 mm). As the hinged drawer front gives no support to the drawer sides a thick bottom must be provided, lap dovetailed into the sides, although the back portion can be of lighter plywood to cut down weight, grooved into the thick sides. The drawer front is held in the upright position by link plates at either end which engage in spring-loaded push-button catches recessed into the sides, both of which must be pressed simultaneously to release the front (247:3). As the drawer sides must be relatively thick the stationery divisions or 'pigeon holing' can be grooved in or built up as a separate unit. A wooden stop is fitted to the bottom of the drawer preventing it from being pulled out beyond the half-way mark, which can be adapted from the old method of secret joining shown in 248, in which a thin, springy lath was attached to the drawer bottom and engaged against the front drawer rail. To release the drawer the hand was inserted under the rail and the lath pressed up. Secretaire drawers can be adapted for toilet articles etc. in a man's dressing-chest and some examples have a hinged mirror which lifts up and is supported at the correct angle by a simple wooden strut. Brass catches and quadrants for secretaires are still obtainable.

CYLINDER FALLS

These are rigid falls travelling in a circular path and are more wasteful of space than a tambour front, and are therefore rarely, if ever, used in modern work. The construction is worth recording, nevertheless. A typical example is shown in 247:4, and in designing these falls proper allowance must be made for the method of assembly. In 247:5, where the fall is

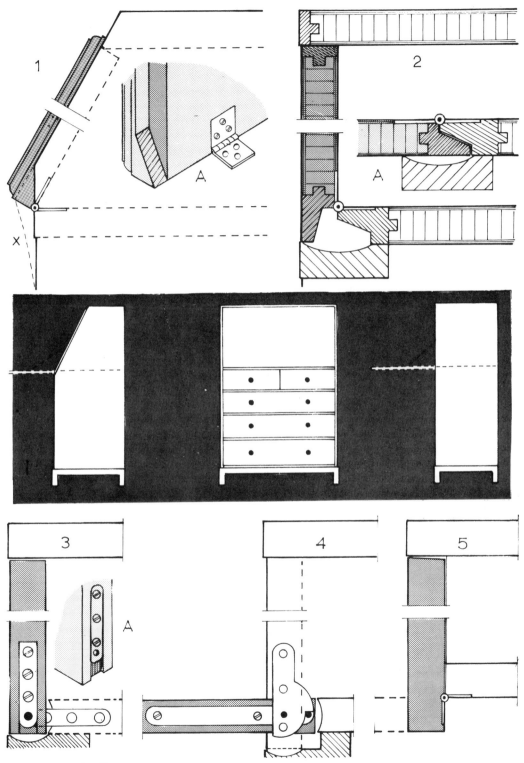

246   Fall flap details

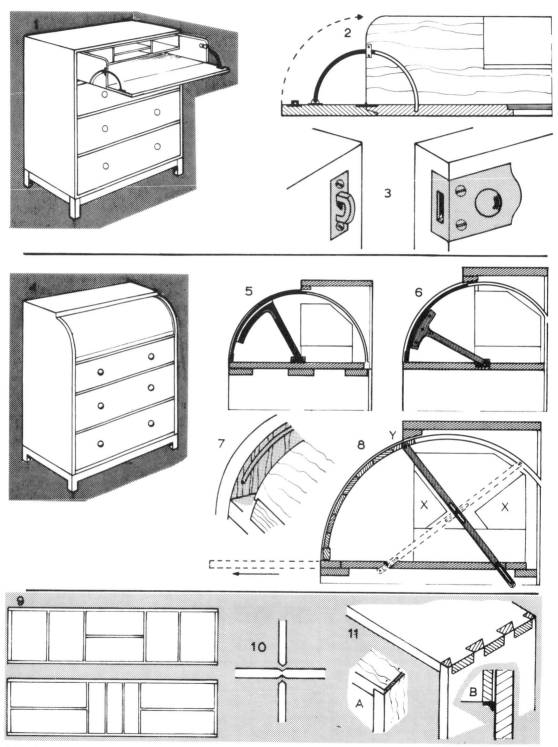

247   Secretaires, cylinder falls, and stationery cases

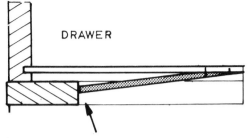

248   Drawer stop

approximately half the total depth of the carcass, the top containing the fall must be made up as a separate unit so that the fall can be entered from the bottom, while in 247:6, where the fall is less than a true quadrant, entry can be from the back. In both cases the thick lock rail, which can have a shaped or recessed handle grip, is tongued to receive the cylinder fall and is glued in position after assembly. The fall itself can be constructed of laminated veneers or two sheets of thin 1/8 in (3 mm) plywood pressed between sawn formers/forms, or coopered as in 247:8. The latter method is probably more positive, although difficult to make, for it will keep its shape, whereas laminated falls tend to spring back a little after release from the cramps/clamps and the flattening of the curve must be established by trial and error. Face and balancing veneering can be done either between shaped cauls or formers or in a vacuum-press, or more simply by the traditional hand method with hide glue. In the best work the fall is tongued at the sides to engage in a circular groove worked in the carcass sides (247:7), with 3/16 in (5 mm) or 1/4 in (6 mm) falls entering the full thickness, and the lock rail can have shallow tongues or can be cut back as shown. If the fall is not grooved into the sides there is always the danger of the end rubbing and scarring the polish, for it is virtually impossible to prevent a certain amount of side play in the quadrant arms, but a curved cover fillet can be fitted on the outside to cover the rub. Methods of swivelling the fall are shown in 247:5, 6 which will have to be specially made out of sheet brass or steel, pivoted to a screw plate and either flanged for screwing to the fall, or side screwed to a shaped block glued to the fall. Figure 247:8 shows a slotted bar movement cut from 3/16 in (4.5 mm) mild steel which pulls the writing-top

forward as the fall is raised. The bar is screwed to the fall but free to rotate and slide on a centre pivot screwed to the carcass side and another pivot on the writing-flap, and the length of the slots which control the movement can only be established by making full-size drawings of the closed and open positions. With all these movements the stationery case must either have independent sides set in to allow free passage of the metal arms, or distance-pieces (247:8X, X) for the slotted bar movement. A closing fillet (Y) can also be fitted to close the gap at the top. The locking rail can be fitted with a box or piano lock. Antique examples of cylinder falls show the falls coopered up out of very thin stock, reinforced with glued canvas at the back.

STATIONERY CASES

Often called 'pigeon holing', these are designed to hold the usual stationery sizes, and 247:9 shows typical examples. They are best made up as separate units, through dovetailed together (247:11) or rebated/rabbeted, glued and pinned (A), with a slight clearance for easy entry, screwed to the carcass sides and the gaps sealed with a cover moulding (B). In fine work the main elements are either 3/16 in (5 mm) or 1/4 in (6 mm) thick, with the divisions no more than 1/8 in (3 mm) vee grooved (247:10), glued, and veneer pinned together. The vee groove can be cut with a sharp knife against a bevelled block, and the divisions polished before assembly.

TAMBOURS

Tambours are flexible screens composed of narrow slats of wood mounted on a silk, canvas or leathercloth backing, and running in grooves which control the travel. The system originated in France in the seventeenth century, was introduced into England in the eighteenth century, fell into disuse in the Victorian era, was popularized by the American pattern roll-top desk and has since been firmly re-established, forming as it does an admirable space-saving method of closing carcass openings. Tambours can be vertical, rising or falling (249:1, 2) or horizontal, moving from side to side (249:3, 4), and can be secured with a bird's beak, sliding door or box lock. They can be built up of solid slats, shaped, chamfered or rounded on the edges, or veneered in simulation of a solid sheet.

Vertical tambours

These can open from the top (falling, 249:5) or at the bottom (rising, 249:6) and require careful planning for there are certain pitfalls in this type as distinct from the horizontal form. If the vertical opening is tall (249:1) then a falling tambour could rattle down under its own weight immediately the lock is released, and if the carcass is shallow in depth it could partially return from the fully opened position if most of the weight is transferred to the back. On the other hand, a rising tambour requires more physical strength to lift it from a low position, and if very tall could either rattle down at the back as it opens, or down at the front as it is closed. This is assuming a sweet, free-running tambour (as it should be), and methods of restraining the unwanted movement, which can be pronounced in long tambours of heavy wood, include coil springs recessed into the carcass sides, with the locking rail attached to nylon cords; lazy-tong springs housed at the back of the carcass to absorb the downward movement, and felt restraining pads recessed into the sides of the grooves which grip the tongues of the slats and slow down the movement. These are compromises, however, and it is usually better to avoid large and heavy tambours or to split them into two wherever possible. These objections do not apply to wide but shallow tambours fitted to roll-top desks, or small vertical tambours in writing-cabinets and wall cabinetry.

Horizontal tambours

These can open from one side or the other (249:7, 8), or two separate tambours can meet in the middle (249:9). They should not be too tall in relation to their width or they are inclined to shake.

Laying out

A full-size drawing must be made, and the requirements of a successful tambour are that it should have a truly square carcass with opposite ends or sides parallel, and accurately positioned grooves of constant depth to take the slats—which are always shouldered in the best work—sweetly round the curve. Attached guides or fillets (249:11A) to form the running groove can be used, with a tongue worked on the thick locking rail, which simplifies the installation, but it is better to work grooves in the solid (249:10A), and extra wide edging should be provided in laminboard carcasses or the core-work will show in the grooves, and the travel will not be so smooth. From 250 it will be seen that the grooves are radiused at the corners to carry the tambour round and out of sight, and slightly widened at the bends to prevent the slats jamming. This can be accurately detailed in the drawing by using a cardboard template cut to the shouldered section of the slat, and trial worked round the bend; while the cover fillet (250:2F) which hides the slats as they commence to open on the bend must be set to give sufficient clearance, for any rub-marks on the face of the tambour must be avoided. If the grooves are formed by attached guides the completed tambour shutter can be placed in position and the guides screwed on, but for grooves worked in the solid provision must be made for running the tambour in from the back (250:2, 3), and the groove is run out either as 250:1A or B. If the run out at 250:1A is adopted then it must be filled in with a shaped piece screwed on after the tambour has been installed. The locking rail, of which various forms are shown in 249:13A, B, C, prevents the tambour from passing behind the front cover guide (250:2F), but as it is of thicker section it cannot be entered from the back and must be sprung in from the front after the tambour has been finally run in, with the flexible backing glued on or taken into the rebate/rabbet and held with fine screws through an attached bead (249:13B, C). A false top or bottom for vertical tambours, or false sides (250:1D) and back (250:1E) for horizontal tambours, must be provided, not only to hide the movement but also to prevent the contents of the carcass from interfering with the travel. In all detailing it is wise to provide for withdrawal of the tambour at any future date without unduly interfering with the carcass-work, therefore the back should be fully detachable.

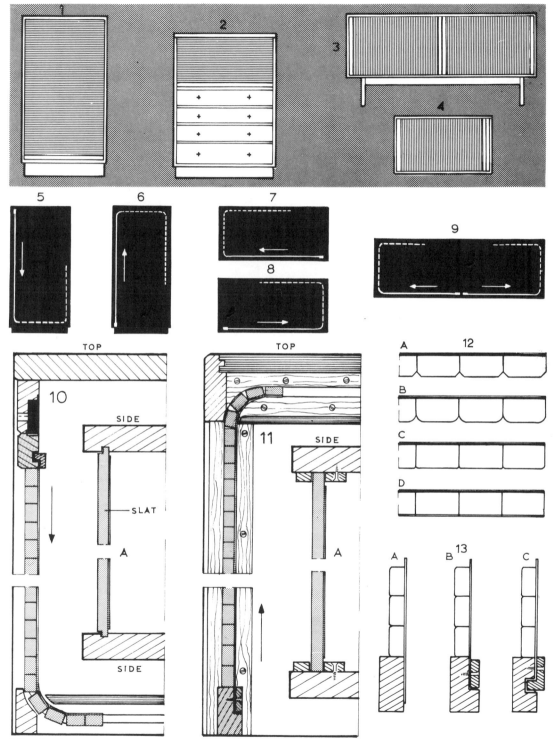

249 Tambours

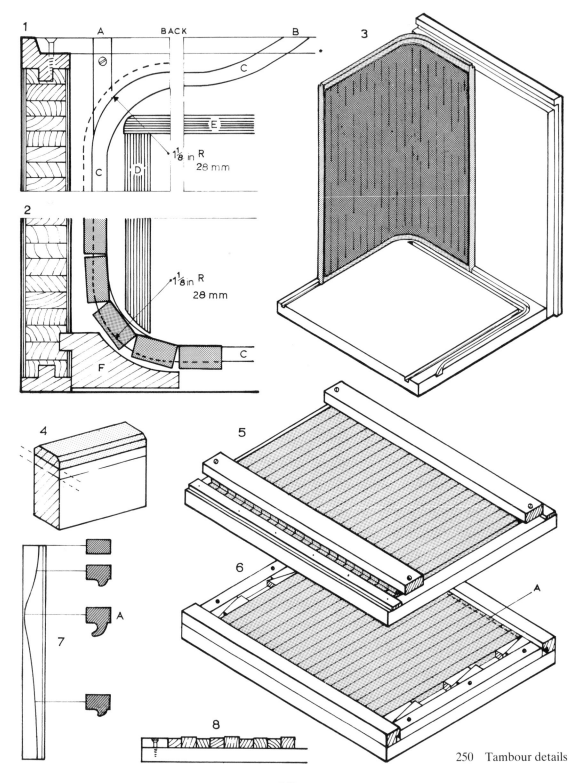

1

A   BACK   B

C

E

C   D

$1\frac{1}{8}$ in R
28 mm

2

$1\frac{1}{8}$ in R
28 mm

C

F

3

4

5

6

7

8

A

A

A

250   Tambour details

Working procedures

The individual slats can be ¼ in (6 mm) wide for small delicate tambours, up to ¾ in (19 mm) wide for large carcasses, with ½ in (12.5 mm) or ⅝ in (16 mm) about the usual. Thicknesses of the slats can be from 3/16 in (5 mm) for small work, up to 5/16 in (8 mm) for average shutters, with a 3/16 in (5 mm) tongue on the latter running in a ⅛ in (3 mm) or 3/16 in (5 mm) deep groove. Total overall length of the slats will be the exact opening plus the depth of the two grooves and minus a bare 1/16 in (1.5 mm) clearance, and the net length between the shoulders of the tongues pitched to give a clearance of 1/32 in (0.75 mm) either side or top and bottom, so that the slats ride in the grooves on the ends of the tongues and not on the shoulders. These tolerances may prove too tight in practice, but it is better to start with a tight tambour and ease the shoulders, for loose-running tambours are always noisy. Grooves which are sunk and not formed by attached guides must be accurately worked to a constant depth throughout, either by plough-plane on

the straight and chiselling out for the bend, or with hand or portable electric router against a suitable template, with a trial slat prepared and put in place to test the travel. This trial slat can then be used as a pattern for all the other slats, which must be accurately sawn and planed to finished dimension, with a generous allowance for rejects. Figure 250:4 shows a method of working chamfered slats by hand from a solid width, and 250:8 levelling off to thickness by cross-planing on a supporting board. When sufficient slats have been prepared they are assembled on a flat surface, sprung slats rejected, the remainder matched for colour and grain, spreading any pronounced differences over the total width and then numbering them in the exact order in which they are to be assembled. The tongued ends can now be spindled, or the lasts laid out and firmly held in position with covering battens (250:5) exactly on the shoulder-lines and the shoulders cut with

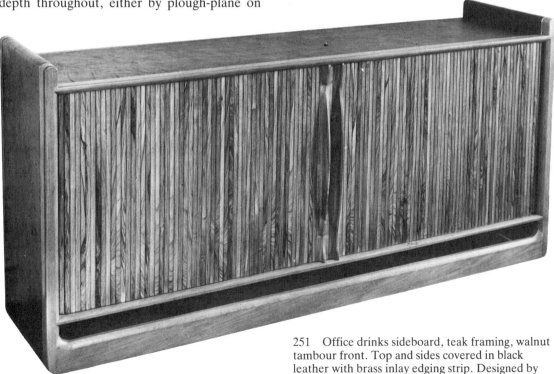

251   Office drinks sideboard, teak framing, walnut tambour front. Top and sides covered in black leather with brass inlay edging strip. Designed by William Mitchell Des.RCA and Ernest Joyce MSIA. Made in author's workshop.

a fine dovetail-saw, and then planed off with a metal shoulder-plane, working to a template pinned alongside to yield a constant thickness of tongue throughout. After checking that the shoulders line up and the net shoulder length is constant throughout, the faces are sanded, the slats turned over and the backs sanded. The slats can also be polished on the face and the edges also sealed, as this will prevent surplus glue from adhering and will make the final finishing much easier. The flexible back can now be glued on, the slats firmly held by rebated/rabbeted battens (250:6) with folding wedges top and bottom to drive them together. This backing can be silk for delicate slats, fine linen canvas, reinforced if necessary with three webbing straps spaced apart and tacked over the glued canvas, or preferably a good quality leathercloth with a closely woven twill backing. It should be long enough to cover the locking rail, and any semi-flexible glue which will not crack at the joints can be used (hide, PVA, etc.), rolling it evenly over the back of the slats and smoothing down the cloth with hand pressure. The flexible backing should be kept back from the edges (250:6A) about ⅜ in (9.5 mm) on either side. Very oily timbers—teak, rosewood, etc.—may have to be degreased for increased glue adhesion, using cellulose thinners or methylated spirits, and not carbon tetrachloride which is often advocated and which can be highly poisonous under certain conditions. When the glue is dry the tambour can be rolled and unrolled a few times to make it flexible, the tongued ends rubbed over with a candle end and fed into the grooves. The locking rail is then sprung in, the flexible backing temporarily attached and the tambour tried. Only when it is sweetly running should the backing be anchored with screws and a few dabs of glue. Locking rails can be shaped to form handle grips by running a length of moulding as in 250:7A, and then cutting and rounding as shown in the sections, and can be made wide enough to accommodate a suitable lock, or the lock can be mortised into a pilaster or apron rail.

Veneered tambours

Tambours can be veneered over (249:12D), and if the slats fit tightly the effect will be that of a single sheet of veneer. Timber for the slats should be of approximately equal colour to the veneer; they are finished to dimension, cramped/clamped together faces uppermost, veneered with a single sheet or matched pattern, and then carefully knifed through from the back on a fractionally curved surface to open the joints sufficiently for the passage of the knife. Some veneers may need scoring on the face before cutting and the edge sanding should only take off the whiskers or the cuts will show. Backing veneers are not necessary as the flexible backing will act as balancer. In a well-fitted veneer tambour the joints should not be visible.

Part V Metal fittings/fasteners and their application
26 Screws, nails and pins

WOOD SCREWS

Conventional wood screws commonly used are the *Countersunk/flat head* (252:2A), *round head* for attaching metal to wood (252:2B), and *raised/oval head* (252:2C), obtainable in brass, steel, japanned (round head), coppered, chrome, BMA finish, etc. according to the type. The length of a screw is taken as all that part of the screw concealed by the wood, thus the length of a countersunk screw will be the overall length (252:1), round head from under the head, and raised head from the junction of the raised head with the counter-sinking. The diameter of all screw-heads is twice the diameter of the shank, the angle of the countersink 45° to the central axis, and the length of the actual thread three-fifths (0.6) of the stated length. A useful formula for the determination of the stated gauge number is: diameter of head in $\frac{1}{32}$ in $-3=$ screw gauge number; thus diameter of head $\frac{13}{32}$ in $-3=10$ which is the gauge number. The diameter of the shank can be calculated from the gauge number by taking the known diameter of a No. 1 screw as 0.066 in with an additional 0.014 in for each subsequent increase in the number of the gauge; thus a No. 8 screw will be 0.066 in (No. 1 screw) $-7(0.014)$ or 0.164 in diameter. This will be the size of the hole required for a No. 8 screw shank, but as drill sizes are in $\frac{1}{64}$ in the nearest approximate size will have to be used, and the

formula commonly adopted is to add 3 to the gauge number to give the size of the drill in $\frac{1}{64}$ in. Thus No. 8 screw plus $3 = 1\frac{1}{64}$ in which is 0.172 in in diameter. The table gives the usual drill sizes for the shank or clearance hole, and for the hole to receive the thread.

RECESSED HEAD SCREWS

These are available in countersunk/flat, round head and raised/oval head forms, and have a cross slot in lieu of the single slot which gives less tendency for the screwdriver to ride up axially as torque is applied, and therefore less danger of marring the work if the driver slips. Special shaped screwdrivers are required and advantages claimed are more positive engagement of the driver in the slot, easier alignment of the screw and the work, particularly at difficult angles, increased speed of driving and more power. This type of screw has almost universal application in production-work with power screwdrivers for rapid assembly, but the conservative craftsman still clings faithfully to the conventional screw, and on balance the single-slot screw would appear to be more decorative, although this may well be the prejudice of ingrained habit.

As every workshop inevitably collects an assortment of odd screws over the years, a useful screw size gauge can be made by inserting a large-diameter screw in a piece of scrap wood, nipping two short lengths of brass strip round

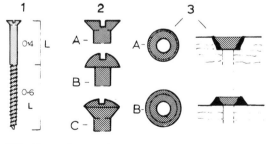

252 Screw types, etc.

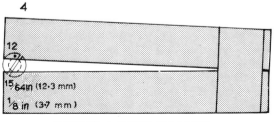

SCREW SIZE GAUGE

the shank with panel-pins either side, and soldering on a brass cross-piece. Screws of known gauge number can then be slid between the strips, the exact position dotted with a centre-punch and the gauge number and drill sizes scratched on the brass. Figure 252:4 shows the gauge with a No. 12 screw so marked.

Screw No.	Clearance Hole in	Drill Hole in
0	$1/16$	$3/64$
1	$5/64$	$3/64$
2/3	$3/32$	$1/16$
4	$7/64$	$5/64$
5	$1/8$	$5/64$
6	$9/64$	$5/64$
7	$5/32$	$3/32$
8	$11/64$	$3/32$
9	$3/16$	$1/8$
10	$13/64$	$1/8$
11	$7/32$	$1/8$
12	$15/64$	$1/8$
14	$1/4$	$5/32$

Metric values for all the above quoted inch sizes will depend on the units ultimately adopted by the International Standards Organization, as there are many different units quite unrelated to each other in use throughout the metric world at the present time.

SCREW SOCKETS AND CUPS

Some confusion often exists between the two types, and the writer has sometimes bought gross packets clearly labelled 'screw cups' which were in fact 'screw sockets'. The socket type 252:3A is recessed flush into the wood with a countersink bit, while cups (252:3B) lie on the surface and require no sinking. Both types are used for countersunk/flat head screws which may have to be withdrawn at any time, and also for neatness of finished appearance. The sockets are preferable but must be accurately fitted, and 253 shows the difference between screws carelessly placed and sunk, and those neatly fixed in sockets which are sanded off flush after the screws have been driven home.

NAILS

Apart from panel and veneer pins the furniture-maker has little use for nails except for softwood work, etc., but in passing it should be noted that oval wire nails have less tendency to split the wood than the round variety. Nevertheless, they bend more easily, and the lost-head or finishing nail, which is a larger version of the panel-pin, is usually preferred, with the screw nail which has a twisted, as distinct from a cut, thread having greater holding power in particle board. Special panel pins or nails with hardened tips are also available for hardboards as it is difficult to break the hard glazed skin of the boards with the ordinary type which often bend. Some workers give either a pushing or pulling action to the hammer-head when driving a nail (254:1), and this certainly reduces any tendency for the nail to bend under the impact of the head. In all probability this slight swing to the hammer keeps the hammer-head flat to the nail-head, while a direct vertical swing may tend to offer it at an angle (254:2). The hammer-head must be clean and kept polished on a piece of used abrasive paper, as a pitted or dirty head will usually bend the nail.

253   Spacing of screws

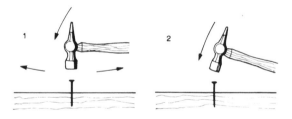

254   Impact of hammer stroke

27 Hinges and hinging

Rapid assembly of furniture components in production-work calls for face-fixing hinges, or hinges which can be sunk in circular recesses, drilled or routered out instead of a hand-cut oblong recess; and many new types have been developed with this in view. These new hinges do not, however, supersede the traditional types but complement them, and for the handworker the familiar types of square or oblong, cast or extruded brass hinges remain viable.

BUTT HINGES

Steel hinges are used in joinery and brass in furniture. The standard brass butt is shown in 255:1, with 255:1A the section of the solid drawn type, and 255:1B the cheaper pressed or folded pattern. Plastic hinges are also available, suitable for light work. The width across the plates (leaves or flaps) is governed by the overall length, which is the listed size, and four ranges are usually available—*narrow suite, broad suite, strong suite* and *extra-wide broad suite*, with lengths rising in ¼ in (6 mm) for 1 in (24 mm) to 2 in (50 mm) long, and in ½ in (12 mm) increases after. Variations of this type of hinge are: *lift-off butt* (255:4) for doors which have to be removed from time to time without disturbing the setting; *strap hinge* (255:3) for narrow sections; *loose pin hinge* also known as *ball-tipped hinge* (255:5), where it is required to throw the door clear of the carcass frame with the whole of the hinge knuckle protruding. Figure 255:6 is the *stopped hinge* opening through 90° only for box lids, etc.; 255:2 is the *back flap hinge* with wide plates for table leaves and rebated or rabbeted fall flaps; 255:8 is the *clock case hinge* with one plate wider to allow for a projecting door (255:17), and 255:7 the *piano hinge* in continuous strip form for supporting long lengths, supplied in either drilled and countersunk or undrilled blanks. Figure 256:1 is the *rule joint* or *table hinge* with an extra wide plate to clear the hollow in a moulded rule joint, and with the knuckle on the reverse side to allow a full 90° drop (256:2).

HINGING BUTTS

So long as the hinges amply support the door or flap, the actual positions are not critical, although appearance must be studied and reference should be made to Door construction, Chapter 23. The plates can be recessed equally (255:9), or the total thickness of the hinge cut into either the door or the carcass (255:10), for it is the position of the knuckle which governs the throw of the hinge. If cut in as 255:9 a well-fitted door flush with the carcass edge might tend to bind on the corners, while with an inset door the knuckle would cut across the projection; therefore on balance the method shown in 255:10 is usually adopted, as this gives a neat finish and allows the stile to clear the carcass end immediately it begins to open. It is, however, necessary to take the strain off the screws by recessing both carcass side and stile, tapering the recesses as shown, and a marking-gauge is first set to the total thickness at the knuckle and gauged on the face of the stile. The width of the hinge to the exact centre of the pin is then gauged on the edge of the stile and the recess cut from the full thickness at the front to the thickness of one plate at the back. The hinge is then screwed to the stile using one centre screw only, placed in position in the opening, a piece of thin cardboard placed under the door to provide the necessary clearance, the position of the hinge marked on the carcass side, the gauge reset to the width of the hinge and marked accordingly, and the recess cut from nothing at the face to the thickness of one plate at the back. The door can now be tried in with another centre screw and the setting adjusted if necessary. The full complement of screws should only be used when the setting is correct, and steel screws should be used for testing, eventually replacing with brass. In very hard woods, oak, etc., it is advisable to run in steel screws throughout and then replace with brass in the final assembly, for it is very easy to scar a slot or twist off the head of a small brass screw in difficult woods. If a screw hole has to be moved fractionally a piece of matchstick inserted in the

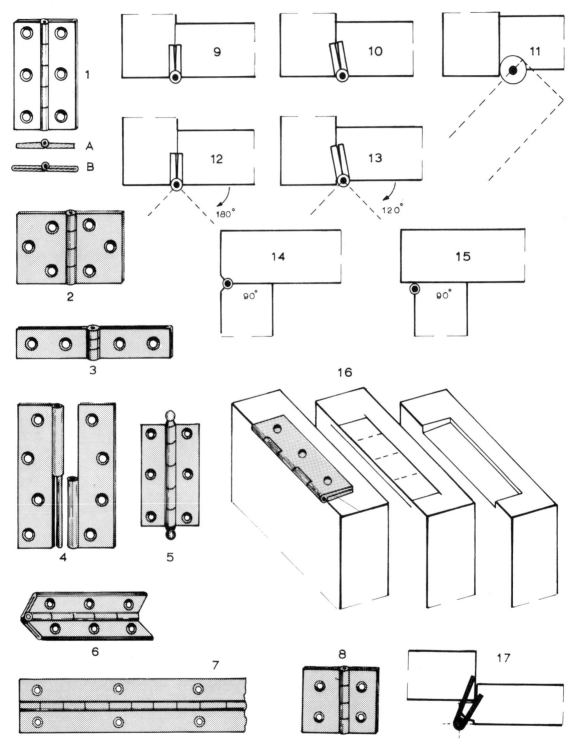

255 Hinges (1)

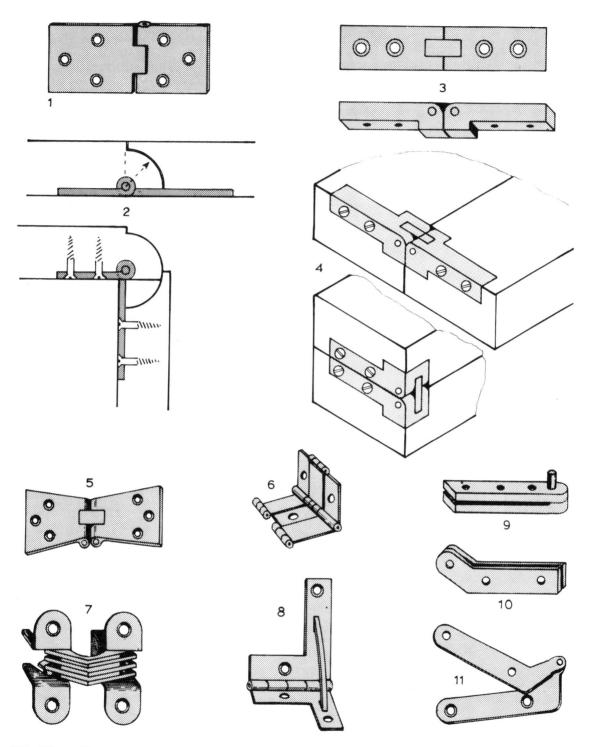

hole will usually provide sufficient bite, while empty cigarette-cartons are useful for shimming up hinges.

As already mentioned, it is the position of the knuckle which determines the throw of a hinge, and a preliminary test can be made by drawing a plan of the fixed section on drawing paper and the moving part on tracing paper; a pin driven through the position of the hinge-pin centre will then allow the tracing to be rotated, showing the extent of the throw. Figures 255:11-15 give various knuckle positions and the angle of opening to be expected (the hinge proportions are exaggerated for illustration purposes), and 255:16 shows the various stages in cutting in and marking out. The positioning of clock-case hinges is illustrated in 255:17, where the centre of the pin must lie on the extreme edge of the moulding with the knuckle clear of the latter.

RULE JOINT HINGE

Figure 256:2 shows the layout for the rule joint hinge used for fall flaps on gate-leg tables, etc. in which the countersinking is on the reverse side of the knuckle, with the pin centre placed in the centre of the quadrant describing the moulding. In practice, the pin is moved very fractionally to the right to give a slight clearance, or the mouldings will grind against each other.

COUNTER FLAP AND CARD-TABLE HINGES

Counter flaps which lift up and over need hinges without projecting knuckles, and 256:5 shows a common type with double pin and connecting link let in flush. The same principle is applied to card-table hinges, either top face fixing (256:3) or edge fixing (256:4), both of which allow the table-leaf to move through 180°. As the hinges are handmade and vary slightly in dimension, each hinge must be gauged for separately.

CENTRE AND PIVOT HINGES

Centre hinges either straight (256:9) or necked (256:10) have one loose plate with steel pivot pin and raised seating for clearance, and the other with socket hole for the pin. Figure 256:11 shows the necked pivot hinge in light steel strip. The name *centre hinge* is usually reserved for the original hand-wrought cast brass hinge, still obtainable, but all too often of appalling quality and finish as compared with earlier examples; while machine-stamped hinges with either fixed or loose plates and generally of good quality are commonly referred to as *pivot hinges*. As the action is the same throughout, subsequent descriptions will refer to both types as *pivot hinges*.

Attaching pivot hinges

Straight pivot hinges are used where the centre lies within the wood thickness (259:1), necked or cranked hinges where it is necessary to throw the door clear of the carcass (259:5), or through an angle of 270° as in the fold-back doors for television cabinets, etc. Various applications are also shown which are self-explanatory. In fitting these hinges a working drawing should be made to determine the exact position of the pivot (259:2). It is a matter of choice which part of the hinge, pin or socket is fitted to the door, but in practice it is easier to attach a pivot plate to the bottom of the carcass and the other pivot plate to the top of the door. All the recesses are first cut, the bottom pivot plate and socket plate screwed in position, the top socket plate screwed to the carcass, the door tipped on the bottom plate, the top pivot plate placed on its socket plate and the door head slid on and attached. It is evident that the recess for the top door plate must be carried out to the edge of the stile to allow the hinge to be slid on (259:1). *Recesses* for *necked hinges* are cut round the hinge (259:5), whose shape usually permits a swivel entry, but it is advisable to check this before assembly, and if the hinge plate will not slide easily into the cranked recess then part of the plate should be filed away rather than cutting out the recess and leaving too little wood substance. If the gap left for the passage of a straight plate would be visible—although it is normally hidden—then the attaching procedure can be reversed or the gap filled in with a glued strip (259:1). These hinges are sold in pairs, right and left hand, and are not suitable for tall wardrobe doors which usually require a third centrally placed hinge to keep them from

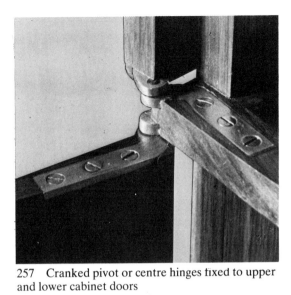

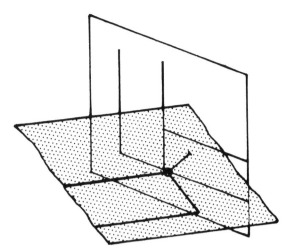

257 Cranked pivot or centre hinges fixed to upper and lower cabinet doors

258 Finding hinge position

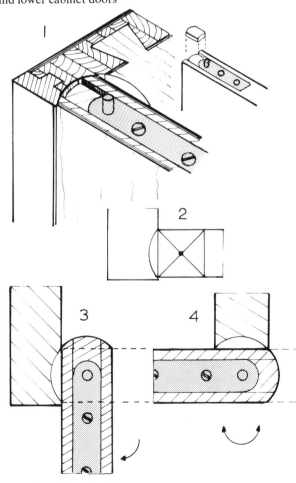

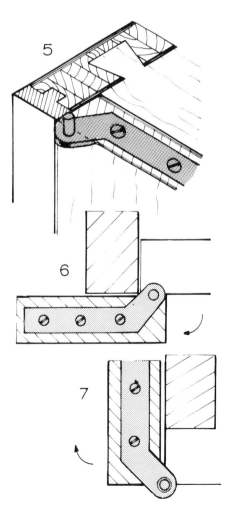

259 Pivot hinge details

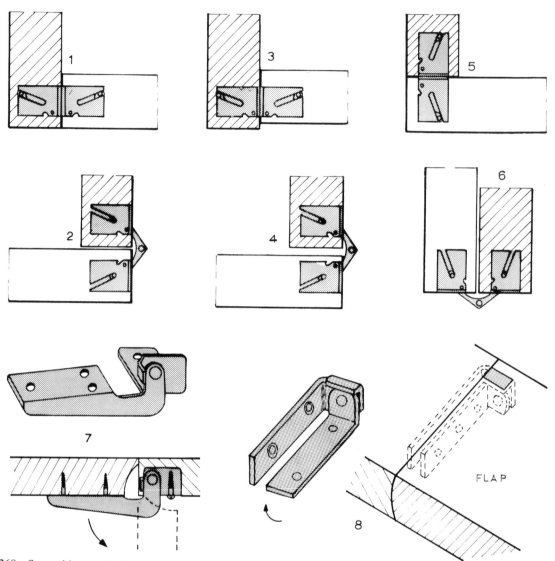

260   Secret hinges: attaching positions and table-flap hinges

bowing. They can be used for fall flaps (Chapter 25) in which case the socket plates are screwed to the carcass sides, the pin plates placed in the sockets and the flap slid on in the horizontal position.

MISCELLANEOUS HINGES

Figure 256:8 shows a secretaire combined hinge and stay for light flaps, and 256:6 the *reversible*

screen hinge which allows the separate wings of a screen to fold either way. With these the screen thickness must not be more than the distance between the knuckle centres, while if it is less the movement will not be affected but the wings will show a gap. A type of invisible hinge is shown in 256:7 and attaching positions in 260. In 260:1, 2 the hinge is centrally placed, while 260:3, 4 show an inset door with hinge off centre, and 260:5, 6 an onset door. These hinges

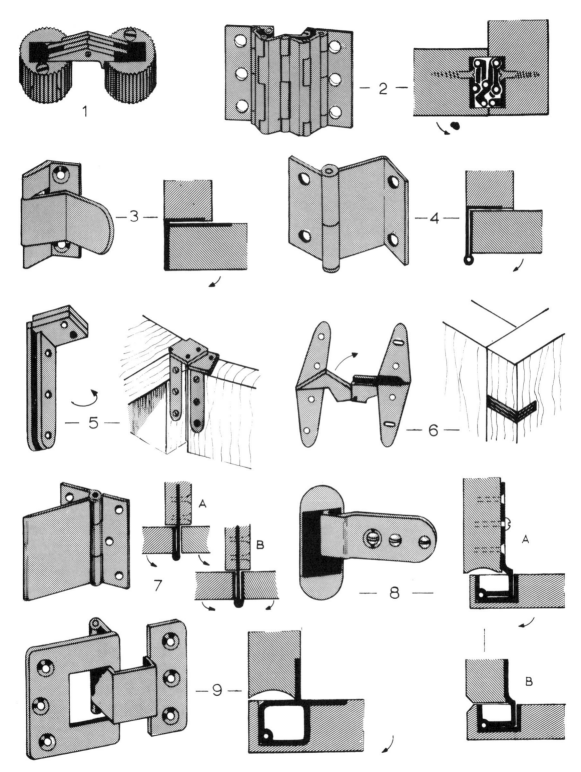

261   New-type hinges

are made in a range of sizes for different door thicknesses and are usually placed centrally in the door thickness, although there is some latitude as shown in 260:3, 4, and a trial assembly in waste wood may be necessary, for mortises once cut cannot be shifted, as with the screw holes of a butt hinge.

NEW HINGES

The necessity for rapid assemblies in production-work has brought about a minor revolution in hinging techniques, and new types of hinge are continually appearing, mostly from European sources. Some show boldly and can be featured, for the finish is usually excellent, while others are partially or wholly hidden. It should be borne in mind, however, that imported hinges which call for machine-drilled or routered recesses are made in metric sizes only, therefore standard inch bits and drills will not fit exactly, and the recesses will have to be enlarged by hand.

Figure 261:1 shows the *cylindrical door hinge* for secret installation which gives a full 180° opening and only requires the boring of two holes. The main body is split, and tightening the set screws exerts a tightening action within the hole. This type is not suitable for anything but light pattern doors or flaps, as any strain on the hinge can pull it bodily from the hole unless it is anchored by a side screw passing through the thickness of the wood. Figure 261:2 is an *invisible hinge* with seven steel pins and full 180° opening, very positive in action and an improvement on the hinge illustrated earlier for heavy doors, as the latter can exhibit a fractional drop when first fitted which is difficult

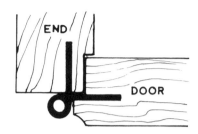

262   Hinge slots

to correct. A single-door high-quality decorative *cranked hinge* is shown in 261:3 which gives an opening of 270°, and 261:4 a decorative *lift-off hinge,* while 261:5 is a *door and flap hinge.* A *pivot hinge* for overlaid (onset) doors is shown in 261:6 in which a ¼ in (6 mm) groove is cut to receive the knuckle which is flush with the face and edge of the door. This type is suitable for tall wardrobe or cupboard doors which require an additional central hinge. Figure 261:7 is a *semi-mortise hinge* with either two or three leaves (261:7A, B) for single or double doors hinging from one central division, and 261:8 a *concealed hinge.* This type can be positioned as shown at 261:8A or 261:8B, but a dummy run should be made for the position of the hinge can be varied within narrow limits, and final adjustment after assembly is made with the set screw provided. Figure 261:9 is a *semi-invisible hinge* with concealed pivot point. An improved *table-flap hinge* is shown in 260:7, and 260:8 shows a *semi-secret pivot hinge* for fall flaps.

Certain types of hinge require very narrow slots (262) and these can be worked by hand with a hinge-slotting tool.

28 Locks and locking actions

The Victorians fitted locks to everything, even their whisky (hence the whisky tantalus), but the modern tendency is to dispense with them wherever possible, while the cheap pattern single-lever pressed-steel locks often fitted to mass-produced furniture can only be regarded as catches or securing devices, for they offer little or no protection. Thus if locks must be fitted for protection they should be the best of their respective kind.

Locks are made to require different keys by increasing the number or the position of the levers or gates which must be lifted by the key before it will shoot the dead bolt; by enlarging the diameter of the pin; and by shortening the pin socket in the key. Thus four good four-lever brass locks taken from the same dozen box and requiring different keys can often be adapted to accept one master key by rearranging the order of the levers, or drilling out the socket in the key to fit the different pins; and as delivery of special 'differs' or master keying can often take up to 12 months, some adaptation (including taking out one or more levers if they do not fit) is sometimes necessary, although not to be recommended if it can possibly be avoided. Purpose-made individual locks of beautiful workmanship can still be obtained and, although obviously much more expensive than the one-, two- or four-lever brass lock with cast riveted cap, are not out of proportion to the total making cost of a good piece of furniture. If maximum protection is required *Yale*-type locks with projecting cylinder nozzles can be obtained from stock which will give an infinite number of differs, with master keying up to 200 differs if required.

TYPES OF LOCK

Figure 263:1 shows the *straight cupboard lock* screwed to the inner face of the door, and with a through bolt shooting right or left as required; 263:2 shows the *cut cupboard lock* which must be bought right or left hand, as the case is, cut into the door and the bolt can only shoot one way; 263:3 is the *mortise cupboard lock*, again in right and left hand versions. The standard *cut till* or *drawer lock* is shown in 263:4, also obtainable in mortise form, while two- or three- way keyholes as 263:6, 8 are often obtainable in both cupboard and till locks, which give a measure of changeability. Striking plates as 263:6, 7 are standard throughout and usually bought separately, but the *box lock* (263:5) requires its own striking plate as the twin bolts shoot up and sideways to lock the lid. Figure 263:6 is the usual form of mortise-type *sliding door* or *hook lock*, again right or left handed, and also obtainable as a cut lock, while 263:7 is another type in which the hook dead bolt is at the back of the case and can be used in the centre edge of the outer sliding door instead of separate locks to each door. A cheap alternative often fitted to production furniture with sliding doors is the cylinder type (263:9), in which the key and barrel shown at the back of the lock are inserted into the cylinder to engage in a socket in the rear door, and turning the key releases the barrel which remains in the body of the lock. A combined *latch* and *dead bolt lock* suitable for roll-top desks and known as such is shown in 263:8, while 264:1 is the brass *piano mortise lock*, and 264:2 the *link plate lock* for doors closing over the cupboard sides (A). A typical *slam* or *spring lock* and striking plate are shown in 264:4, 5 which can be closed without a key but requires unlocking to open it, while 264:3 is a *till lock* with projecting nozzle which forms its own escutcheon plate. The fitting of the latter requires very careful laying out, as a suitable hole for the nozzle must be bored through the face of the work exactly of the right size and in the correct position, and the laying out should be done from a cardboard template. The traditional *bird's-beak lock* beloved of the old school of craft examiners, which was used for roll-top desks, has lately been reintroduced in a

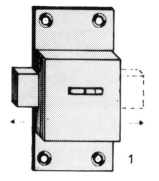

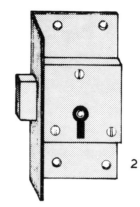

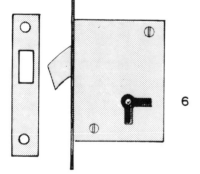

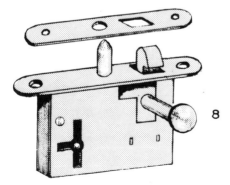

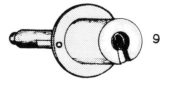

263   Locks (1)

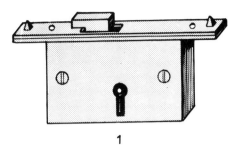

1

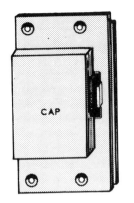

2

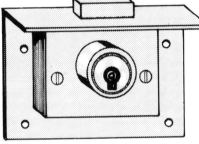

3

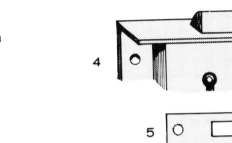

4

5

6

7

264   Locks (2)

streamlined form for television and radio cabinets. With this type (264:6) twin bolts shoot out either side to engage in the striking plate. Figure 264:7 shows the usual form of lock chisel for cutting in bolts, etc.

FITTING LOCKS

The cutting in of a typical till or drawer lock is shown in 265. The dimensions of the face plate are first lightly set out and gauged on the drawer top as 265:1, and the recess cut, keeping well inside the lines in case the face plate is slightly

out of square. The position of the case is then marked and sawn as 265:2, and then cut out slightly full so the body of the lock can be placed in position and the face plate checked against the layout marks on the top edge. These are then corrected, recessed out, the lock offered up as 265:3 and the back plate scribed round to be recessed as 265:4. A slight tap on the lock will then register the position of the projecting pin, a hole is bored through to the face, and the keyhole cut from the face side with a small block in the cap recess to support the wood; the lock can then be screwed in position as 265:5. To mark the position of the striking plate rub a little lampblack or dirty grease over the lock bolt,

277

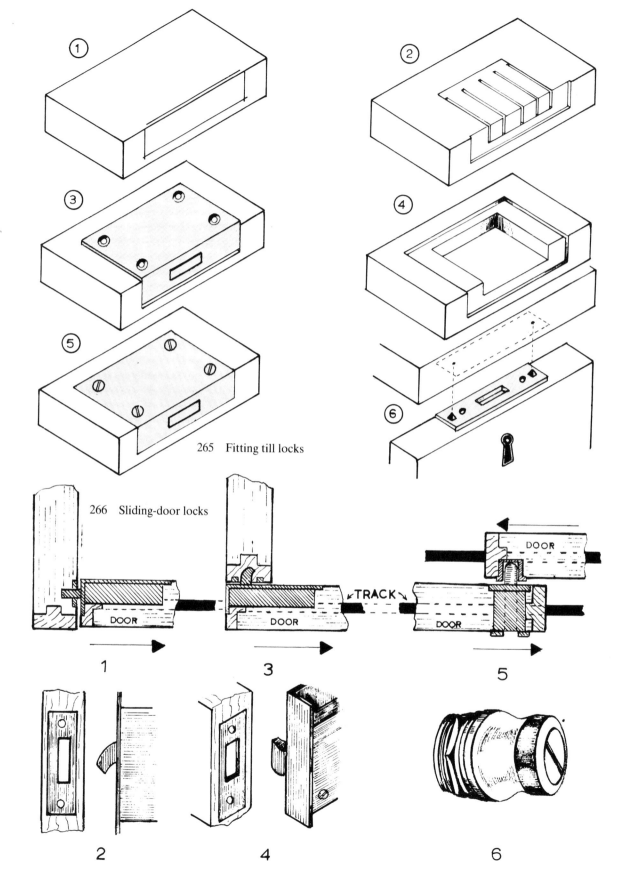

265 Fitting till locks

266 Sliding-door locks

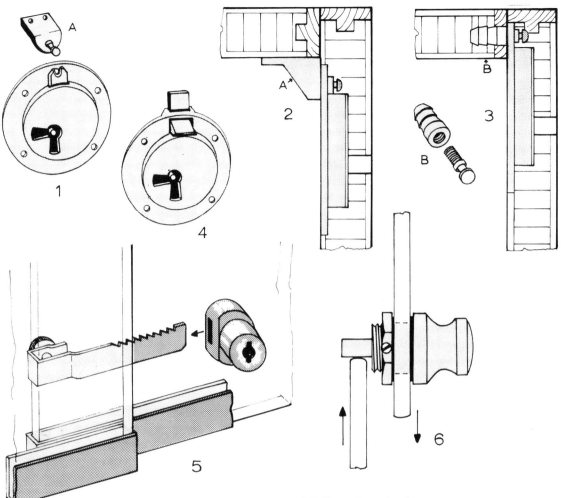

267   Fall flap and glass door locks

turn the key quickly to register the bolt position on the underside of the lock rail and then cut away for the plate. If there are many locks with striking plates to be fitted (the plate is often omitted in cheaper work) it will be worth acquiring a lock chisel (264:7). Striking plates for box locks have projecting nibs (263:5), and the plate is placed in position over the bolt, the lid shut and the marks transferred with gentle pressure. As already mentioned, some locks with their own integral escutcheon plate must be precision fitted, where the pin is dead centre with the back plate, but it is offset in most types of lock and this does simplify the layout, which should be done with a cardboard template.

Sliding door locks

Fitting is as for till locks, and 266:1, 2 shows the hook lock for inset sliding doors, 266:3, 4 the back hook lock for onset doors, and 266:5, 6 a cylinder lock primarily intended for glass doors which can be adapted for use provided the cylinder is long enough for the door thickness.

Fall flap locks

Fall flaps which are inset, i.e. closing within the carcass framing, can be secured with standard till or drawer locks, but lay-on or onset flaps closing over the carcass framing require either purpose-made locks, link plate locks or special flap locks of which the type shown in 267 is a typical example. This lock can be used with striking plate 267:1, 2A for both inset or lay-on flaps, and with threaded bush and collared pin

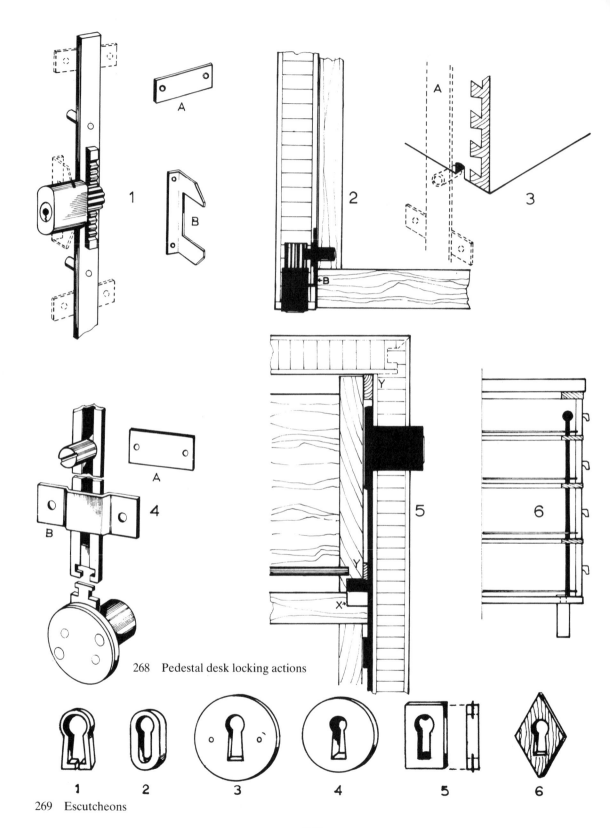

268   Pedestal desk locking actions

269   Escutcheons

(267:3B) for lay-on flaps only. Figure 267:4 is another variety for inset flaps in which the bolt shoots up into a standard striking plate.

Sliding glass door locks

Methods of locking sliding glass doors are shown in 267:5, 6. Figure 267:5 is a *ratchet-bar lock* for glass thickness from $5/32$ in (4 mm) to $5/16$ in (8 mm), and requires no drilling as the ratchet bar assembly is thumb screwed to the leading edge of the rear glass in any convenient position. The detachable lock is slid on to this bar and prevents either door being moved. Figure 267:6 is a plan drawing of a cylinder type which passes through a hole drilled in the front glass and is secured with a nut and set screw; the projecting circular bolt shoots out to bear against the edge of the rear glass, thus preventing any movement of either.

PEDESTAL LOCKING ACTIONS

Locking actions for pedestal drawers, in which the locking of one drawer—usually at the top—automatically secures all the other drawers in the pedestal, were usually effected by incorporating a spring-loaded vertical sliding bar at the rear of the carcass. Arms or pegs were attached to the bar which engaged in slots cut in the drawer sides, and a sloping ramp cut into the top drawer side automatically raised all the pegs and thus released all the other drawers as the top drawer was partially withdrawn, while if the drawer was pushed fully home then a back spring attached to the bar pulled the pegs down into the slots. The disadvantages of this older method are obvious, and improved types are shown in 268 in which the throw of the desk lock itself actuates the pegs. Both are particular types of pedestal locking actions. 268:1 shows one variety in which the throw of the lock rotates a cog which engages in a metal rack so that the slider with its pegs (268:3A) is forced downwards, releasing the drawers. The cylinder of the lock is mortised into the edge of the carcass side (268:2) and held in position with a pronged plate (268:1B) mortised in from the side, while the metal slider moves freely behind

two or more metal strips (268:1A) which are recessed in and screwed to the inner carcass face. Slots are cut into the bottom of the drawer sides (268:3) and corresponding slots in the drawer rails (X) in the elevation (268:5) to accommodate the travel. The exact position and number of the pegs must be clearly detailed when ordering as there are no standard dimensions. For the small user not ordering in quantity the other lock (268:4) is more suitable, as the pegs are freely adjustable and can be fixed at the required distances by turning the slotted heads. This particular type of lock is mortised into the knee-hole side of the pedestal at a convenient distance under the top (268:6). Both these locks must be ordered right or left hand, and in both also the metal slider (268:1A, 4A) can be recessed in flush as 268:2, or face screwed as 268:5 in which case drawer guides (Y, Y) must be fitted to fill the gap. As with all fittings of a specialist nature the unit should be designed round the fitting rather than the fitting laboriously altered to fit an arbitrary design. Other types of these locks are available, and the designer should consult the catalogue of his usual supplier for further details.

ESCUTCHEONS (KEY-PLATES)

Constant use of a key in a lock can scar the wood surface and escutcheons are, therefore, both decorative and utilitarian. Figure 269:1 shows the usual pattern thread escutcheon split at the base and pressed into an appropriate hole in the drawer front; the slight spring offered by the split grips the wood, and the shape of the hole can be marked out by placing the escutcheon in position and smartly tapping with a hammer. Figure 269:2 is a heavier type with a fine hole in the base for a fixing pin; 269:3 the disc plate for surface fixing with brass escutcheon pins; 269:4 the disc plate with screw-in thread, and 269:5 an oblong plate. The cheaper varieties are stamped out of sheet brass, sunk flush and glued with Araldite epoxy glue, but the better patterns have either pin fixings, screw-in threads or small metal tongues (269:5) which are knocked into the wood thickness. Plates can also be formed from ebony, rosewood, box, bone or ivory, etc. (269:6) cut to outline, recessed and glued, the keyhole cut and sanded off flush.

29 Stays, bookcase fittings and castors

STAYS

Wardrobe, flap and fall stays are shown in 270. Figure 270:1 shows the *wardrobe stay* used to limit the swing of a door or to support a fall flap, 270:2 is the *quadrant stay* and 270:3 is the *rule joint stay* also for flaps and supplied right and left handed. The latter has been almost entirely superseded by the improved *fall flap stay* (270:4) with silent nylon glide (270:4A) which can be used in either the vertical or horizontal position. A combined *pivot hinge and stay* for flaps is shown in 270:5, and a slotted version in 270:6 which lifts the flap clear of the framing rail. Both types are made in mild steel brass plated for greater strength. Figure 270:7 is the *radiogram lid stay* with adjustable friction

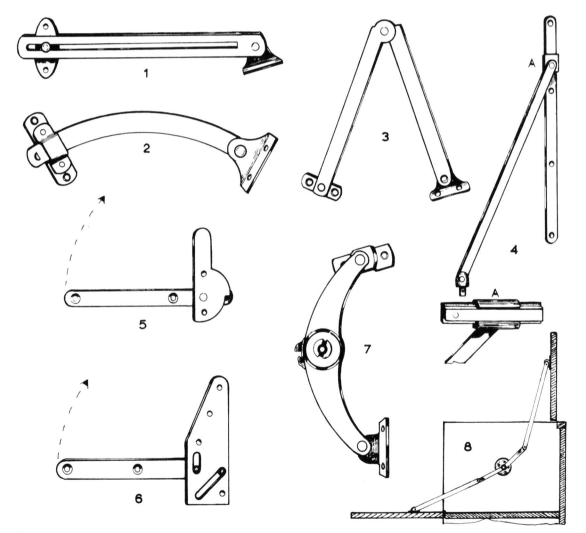

270 Stays

282

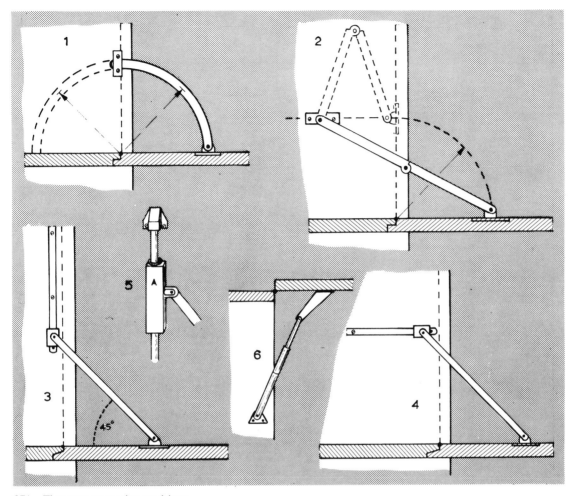

271   Flap stay mounting positions

movement, and 270:8 one type of *cocktail cabinet stay* which automatically lowers the flap as the lid is raised. The fixing position for this type of stay must be found by trial and error with a bradawl driven through one of the screw holes into the carcass side, and the centre plate is large enough to cover several trial holes which may be necessary before the critical centre is located. Fixing positions for quadrant, rule joint and improved fall flap stays are shown in 271:1, 2, 3. In 271:2 the flap plate is fixed at a distance from the hinge knuckle equal to half the length of the stay measured from pin to pin. The carcass plate must then be fastened on a line drawn parallel to the base as shown.

As with most other hardware items the traditional types have remained unchanged for many years, but modern production methods and the increasing use of particle board with its reduced holding power for screws, etc. call for constant innovations. Figure 271:5 shows a *varioscope fall flap stay* with adjustable brake which retards the downward movement, thus there is no danger of a heavy chipboard flap tearing out the fixing screws if allowed to fall. A stay for upward flaps (271:6) is also shown, with a stopping device which holds the flap either side of the horizontal according to the adjustment. A slight upward lift beyond the automatic stop releases the catch and allows the flap to be lowered. Figure 271:4 shows the improved *fall flap stay* (270:4) mounted in a horizontal position.

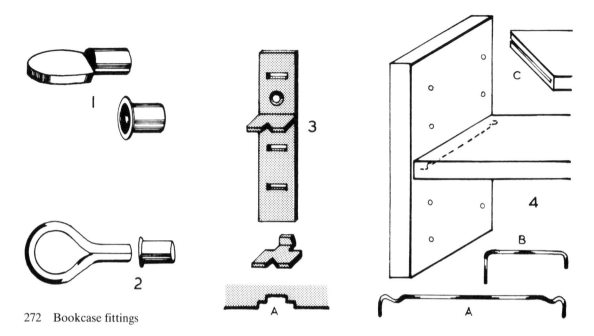

272   Bookcase fittings

BOOKCASE FITTINGS

Loose shelves in cupboards and bookcases can be adjusted at various heights by several methods. Studs and sockets (272:1, 2) require holes to take the sockets drilled at regular intervals in the carcass sides back and front. Positions can be squared across the matched carcass sides and drilled before assembly, and if they are very numerous it will be convenient to prepare a wood or metal template bar bored out at the correct intervals—1 in (25 mm), 1½ in (38 mm) or 2 in (50 mm) etc. according to the estimated use—which can be G-cramped/C-clamped to the carcass sides and the holes rapidly bored with a drill and bit, limiting the depth with a stop or a small block of hardwood on the drill. Figure 272:3 is the bookcase strip which requires grooves worked at two levels (272:3A), while 272:4 is the *magic shelf wire* which is completely invisible when assembled. Holes ⅛ in (3 mm) diameter are bored to take the wires at a distance apart (front to back) fractionally less than the overall length of the wire (272:4A) which is sprung in position with a corresponding stopped groove (272:4C) worked at each end of the shelf. The wires are obtainable in various lengths or in short sections (272:4B), two of which will be needed per shelf end. The system is very positive in action, and the wires cannot be displaced with the shelf in

position as there is only sufficient play in the groove depth to ensure an easy sliding fit.

CASTORS AND GLIDERS

Castors and wheels are available in great variety from light pattern swivel castors for tea-trolleys/carts, etc. to heavy-duty ball-bearing castors for mounting machinery. Figure 273:1 shows a fixed wheel castor, 273:2 the orbit swivel castor, both with mounting plates either square, oblong, round or shaped for corners, while 273:3 illustrates the grip-neck method of fastening in which the socket with its pronged base is hammered into the leg and the peg pushed home, and 273:4 the wood screw type. Metal thread screws for metal are also available. Before choosing the type, usage and working conditions must be allowed for, and if maximum manœuvrability is required then four swivel castors should be used; but for heavy loads and long runs two fixed and two swivel are better, with the trolley pushed from the swivel end. Cast-iron wheels are suitable for concrete and rough, gritty surfaces, while indoor use calls for hard- or soft-tyred rubber or plastic, or cast brass or brass-plated steel for the smallest types. The castors can be hidden behind a curtain rail (273:7), but the trolley must be wide enough to permit the full swing of the castor within the

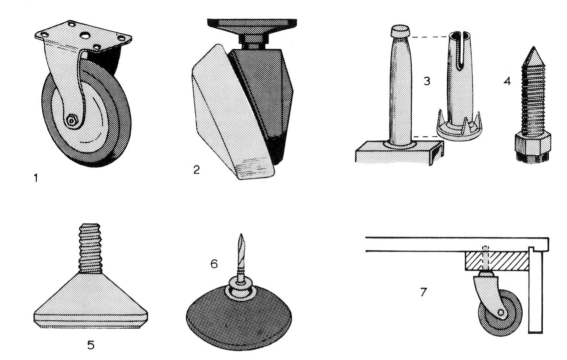

273   Castors and gliders

curtain without sacrificing overall stability.

Gliders or floor protectors are suitable for furniture which is not often moved. With their greater bearing surface there is less indentation or wear on floors and coverings; moreover, it is not advisable to fit very free-running castors to chairs or divan beds, particularly if used by old people or invalids. Types vary from the simple knock-in nickel-plated furniture glide, to the more sophisticated pattern shown in 273:6.

HEIGHT ADJUSTERS

These are often essential for four-point contact on uneven surfaces (three-point contact will automatically adjust itself). Figure 273:5 shows one version, which is screwed into a tapped socket mounted in the leg; but for heavy desks and tables, etc. either the stem should have a hexagonal nut or a small hole be bored through for a tommy bar so the adjuster can be raised or lowered under load.

285

30 Catches, bolts and handles

CATCHES

Magnetic catches with *ferrite* or *ticonal* nickel alloy magnets (the latter have greater holding power in small diameters) have a practically unlimited life with a probable strength loss of not more than 1 per cent over ten years. Figure 274:1 is the smallest type for gluing in with a pull of about 2½ lb (1.134 kg) and suitable for very light doors and flaps; 274:2 is a stronger type with ribbed brass or nylon case and about 4½ lb (2.041 kg) pull, and 274:3 is a face mounting type in a range of pulls from 4½ lb (2.041 kg) to over 40 lb (18.143 kg) according to the size. A mortise version suitable for light doors, etc. is shown in 274:4. All these catches require intimate contact with the metal striking plate, and are therefore not suitable for bowed or warped doors which require a more positive catch to pull them in. In fitting, the magnet catch is fixed first with the striking plate placed in position on the magnet. The back of the plate is then rubbed over with chalk and the door pressed against it to register the position. To check that both magnet and plate are in perfect contact throughout, a trace of oil is smeared over the magnet face, and if the oil fails to register exactly to the ends and sides of the plate, it should be shimmed out accordingly.

Ball, bale and double ball catches are shown in 274:5, 5A and 6; the double ball type is useful for the heavier type of door or one which has bowed slightly, for the compression on each spring-loaded ball can be adjusted by the retaining screws. Single ball catches, either barrel (274:5) or plated (bales, 274:5A), can be fitted at top or bottom or on the side, and either to the door or to the carcass framing. However, with the striking plate (274:5) and ball on the door, the edge of the carcass will be crushed with the passage of the ball, while the lip striking plate (274:5A) can be cut off flush with the outer edge and gently tapped down to lead the ball into the socket. Alternatively, the ball can be located in the carcass framing, but here

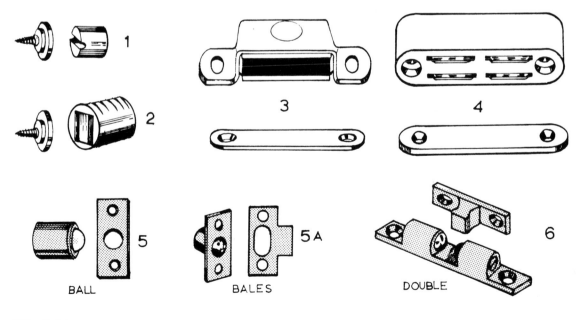

BALL   BALES   DOUBLE

274 Catches

again a slight depression must be gouged out under the striking plate to receive the ball and this will be noticeable on the door edge if below eye level. In effect, therefore, the position of ball and plate should be chosen to give the neatest appearance. As to whether one or two ball catches are necessary per door (at top and bottom) depends entirely on the size and power of the ball ($\frac{3}{8}$ in [9.5 mm] is a good average), the size of the door and whether it requires pulling in. However, doors in slight twist are usually corrected by moving out either the top or bottom hinge, and generally speaking a perfectly flat small- or medium-sized door will only require one catch. In attaching ball catches the barrel should be a reasonably tight fit in its prebored hole and tapped home with a hammer on a wood block to protect the ball. Normally, the projecting rim is hammered flush, but some woods tend to crush badly and it is advisable to score the exact diameter of the rim with the wing tip of a sharp bit before the hole is bored for the barrel.

BOLTS

Cabinet bolts can be flush sunk or the open type screwed to the face, with the latter either necked or straight. Necked bolts (275:1) are used where the door fits against the shoulder of a rebate/rabbet (275:1A), but the flush type or the extruded open-face fixing type (275:2) are usual for light cabinet-work. Various forms of automatic self-closing or self-aligning bolts are

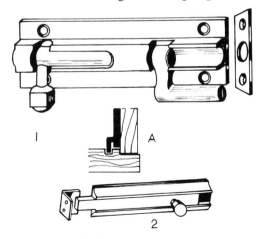

275   Cupboard bolts

available and manufacturers' catalogues should be consulted.

HANDLES, KNOBS AND PULLS

It is axiomatic that handles can make or mar a piece of furniture. The first essential is that they should provide the necessary grip, strong enough for a direct pull on heavy drawers or doors, but discreet enough not to usurp more than their fair share of visual interest. There are no golden rules and good taste alone must decide their selection and placing. A flamboyant piece of furniture might require flamboyant handles, or handles so unobtrusive that they are hardly noticeable; plain, utilitarian furniture, utilitarian handles or some added richness to relieve stark surfaces. One thing only is certain: the designer must visualize the handles as part of his total conception; they must grow out of and not be added to his design merely as an afterthought.

Number and placing of handles

Here again there are no rules. If one handle will open a drawer without having to rock it from side to side so much the better. If two handles are necessary, they can be placed in the usual positions, i.e. on the quarter and three-quarter division marks in the drawer width and central in the depth; but this is not compulsory and the placings can be symmetrical on the quarter lines or asymmetrical, if the design composition calls for it, always providing the handles perform their proper function.

Wood handles

Hitherto bought wooden handles were invariably clumsy and in stained common woods, but ornamental knobs and pulls in palisander, teak, walnut, mahogany, etc. are now obtainable, or they can be very easily turned on a suitable lathe. Kingwood is beautiful for turned knobs, if it can be obtained, but ebony, rosewood, satinwood, Indian laurel, walnut and box are all excellent. Sycamore can also be used, but care must be taken and the knobs gloss polished on the lathe immediately after the final sanding or the end grain (all

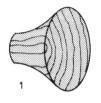

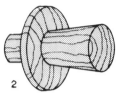

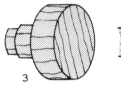

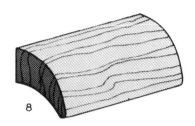

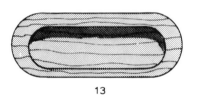

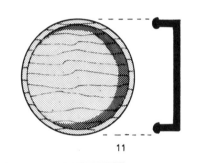

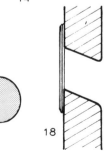

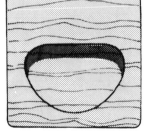

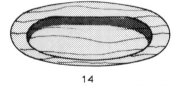

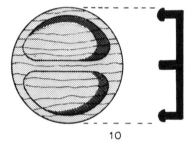

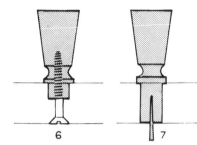

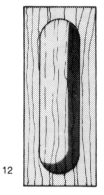

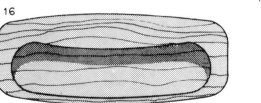

276   Wood handles

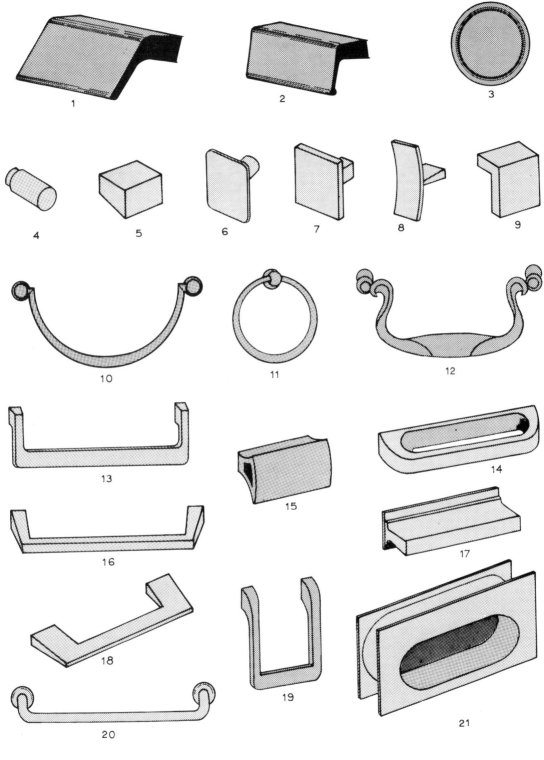

277 Metal handles

knobs are turned out of long-grain stuff) will take on a grubby appearance.

Representative examples are illustrated in 276:1, 2 and 3, while 276:4, 5 are hand turned. Methods of fastening are shown in 276:6 where a pilot hole is drilled for the screw, and the short stub dowel inset into the drawer front prevents the knob splitting as the screw is driven home; while in 276:7 the dowel-pin is taken through the thickness of the drawer front, saw kerfed and wedged from the back. Large wooden knobs can have the dowel or spigot threaded with tap and die as in much Victorian furniture, but the methods already described can be as effective. Figures 276:8, 9 are wood pulls worked in the length and cut off as required; they are screwed from the back. Figures 276:10, 11 are typical sliding flush door pulls, the former routered out, but the latter can be turned in a lathe, while 276:12 is an oblong routered version. Recessed cabinet handles for door and drawer fronts are shown in 276:13-16, while a simple method of forming a grip recess to a drawer front is shown in 276:17, 18. Overlapping holes are bored at an angle, cleaned up with file and abrasive paper and backed with a piece of thin veneered plywood glued and screwed on (276:18).

Metal handles

Reproduction brass handles of good quality are obtainable at most architectural ironmongers. The back plates of these are usually pressed, as distinct from cast in the best antique examples, but the similitude is fair enough. Modern handles in brass, alloy, electro-plated plastic, clear perspex, etc. are available in bewildering variety and some manufacturers' lists contain many hundreds of varieties. In selecting these handles for hand-made furniture it is advisable to exercise restraint, for the more elaborate examples can advertise the fact that they are production-made by the very excellence of their finish, thus destroying the subtle appeal of an individually made piece of furniture. Representative examples are shown in 277. Figures 277:1 and 2 are extruded metal alloy pulls, 277:3 a spun-metal pull for sliding doors, 277:4-20 various types in brass, alloy and plated plastic. Figure 277:21 is a flush pull in two parts recessed into the door or drawer and screwed together from the back. Types of finishes for all these handles vary with the pattern, and the particular catalogue from which some of these examples have been chosen lists no less than 95 distinct finishes, from 'polished continental silver anodised' to 'matt black coated plastic'.

31 Knock-up (KU) and knock-down (KD) fittings

Both are mechanical means of assembly employing a variety of metal or nylon fittings which replace standard jointing procedures. Knock-up fittings are those designed for the speedy erection of structures providing permanent fixtures which will not be dismantled; knock-down fittings speed erection plus the ability to dismantle, i.e. knock down, at any time and for any number of times. In theory, at least, manufacturers can produce with these fittings standardized components which can be stored and transported flat for erection later by the retailer or customer in his own home. In practice, many retailers are reluctant to undertake the erection (which is simple enough in all conscience and usually requires only a screwdriver or spanner); they often insist upon delivery in the assembled state and the main advantage is lost, for full knock-down assemblies often cost more to manufacture unless full advantage is taken of systematized production on a large scale. However, many manufacturers do use one or other forms of KU or KD assembly for very cogent reasons: (*a*) a large proportion of present-day furniture is composed of veneered particle board which does not lend itself to traditional jointing methods; (*b*) machining processes can be simplified with less handling of components; (*c*) the spray coating and surfacing of flat components is easier and cheaper than handling bulky items of furniture.

The basic requirements of good KU or KD fittings are that they should (*a*) positively locate the joint; (*b*) ensure a tight joint when correctly assembled and tightened; (*c*) distribute the load evenly throughout the structure. Many different types are available which satisfy these requirements and which can be divided into three categories:

1 threaded fittings in which a suitable receiver or bushing is onset or inset on one component and the other component locked to it with a barbed dowel or metal screw;

2 interlocking fittings in which both components have screwed-on parts which lock together either with screws or by knocking together;

3 cam action fittings onset or inset, in which a hook fixed to one component engages in a cam-operated fitting in the other and is tightened by operating the cam with a screwdriver.

The most usual form in the cheaper ranges of furniture, particularly with the use of particle board, is the threaded fitting, but the fixing is usually visible on the face of the work either as a screw head or a metal or plastic cover plate. Interlocking fittings are usually surface mounted, therefore they are confined to hidden interiors, and while very easy to attach, for there is no machining to be done, they are not so strong or so positive as the cam action fitting which is the method usually adopted for better class work. Representative examples are shown in 278. Figure 278:1 is the barbed dowel and glued-in nylon bush/bushing; 278:3 a shorter version with twin bushes suitable for KU assemblies, and 278:2 a KU and KD form using a shake-proof screw in lieu of dowel which is, however, visible on the face of the work, although detachable brass cover caps are available. Figure 278:4 is the slotted plate for connecting flat panels; 278:5 a corner version; 278:6 a plastic dovetail fitting; 278:7 a bush and screw, easy to fix and with brass cover plate for screw, and 278:8 the mortise type, very neat in appearance and with adequate strength for all normal carcasses. Applications for these fittings are shown in 278:9-17. A typical cam operated fitting is illustrated in 279. This is composed of a plastic cover (279:7A), metal socket (279:7B), connecting screw (279:7C) and eccentric wheel (279:7D). Figure 279:1 shows a corner connection with two wheels; 279:2 a side connection with fluted metal socket and cover screw; 279:3 a slim fitting for carcass thicknesses down to ½ in (12.5 mm); 279:4 a double way with two connecting screws and fluted screw

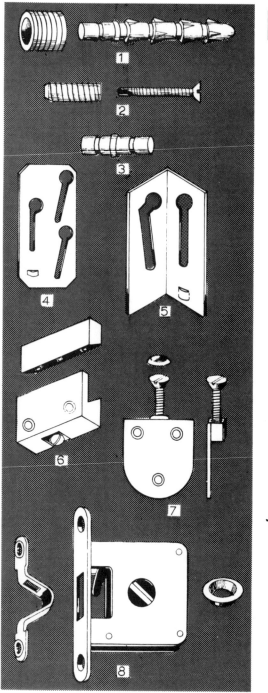
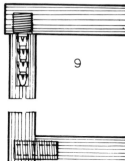

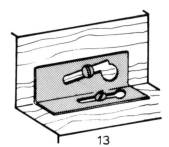

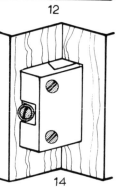
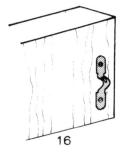
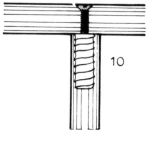
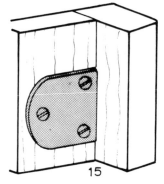
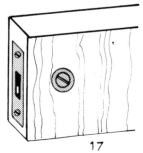

278 Knock-up and knock-down fittings

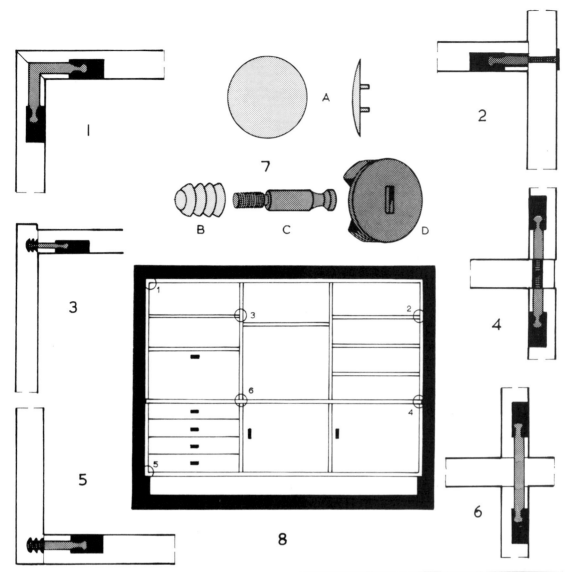

279 Knock-down fittings

socket; 279:5 the standard version of 279:3 for thicknesses down to ⅝ in (16 mm) especially in particle board, and 279:6 a double way with two wheels and double-ended connecting screw. Applications are shown in a typical large wall unit composed of upper and lower units (279:8), and assembly is effected by insetting and gluing in the metal socket, screwing in the connecting screw to the correct projection to allow the collared head to engage in the eccentric (cam operated) wheel, and turning the wheel clockwise with a screwdriver to engage the cam, after which the plastic cover can be pressed in position over the wheel. Figure 279:9 shows a two-way fitting in particle board, and all the fittings are remarkably strong and positive in action, but as with all other mortise types of KD fittings the holes and recesses must be accurately positioned and machined to a constant depth.

Part VI   Advanced techniques
32   Veneering, marquetry and inlay

The art of veneering—and there is or should be considerable art in the selection and matching of veneers—is over 4000 years old; it is not in any sense a method of covering up shoddy workmanship or materials, as the strict dictionary definition would imply (to veneer: to gloss over, to cover up). Many rare and costly woods with wild, distorted or intrinsically weak grain cannot be used in solid form; moreover, the ever-increasing demand for carcass furniture would very soon deplete if not totally exhaust even the most common decorative hardwoods if they were consistently used in any thickness.

PREPARATION OF GROUNDWORKS OR SUBSTRATES, ETC.

Either solid or prefabricated woods (plywoods, particle board, etc.) can be used for veneering provided they are stable, mild mannered, not too coarse in the grain and free from defects, although heated animal glues (hide glues) should not be used for particle boards as they tend to swell up the surface chips. Very absorbent woods should be sized before laying, defects cut out and filled with plugs cut to follow the grain (280:1); holes and depressions filled with plastic wood, wood-dust and glue, or plaster of Paris and glue (not wax-based stoppers or putty). The usual advice given that the groundwork should be well scoured with a toothing-plane to roughen up the surface as a key for the glue is not strictly accurate. The old toothing-plane is undoubtedly an excellent tool for the general hand-levelling of bumpy surfaces, but glue sticks by molecular attraction, although some degree of mechanical attachment is usually present, therefore keyed surfaces are not really necessary (and might even interfere with the bond). Provided the surface is reasonably absorbent and not glazed with age or dirt, or with a very hard burnished grain, a light scouring with abrasive paper followed up with a thorough dusting is all that is necessary, and this applies to veneers also.

These should be laid 'with the grain' on solid boards which are liable to shrink across the width, but 'across the grain' of prefabricated boards if these are already faced with knife-cut veneers, as the innumerable stress cracks caused in the cutting will only augment those in the facing veneers if they are both laid together with grains parallel (see Veneers, Chapter 2). End grain should be repeatedly sized with weak glue to lessen the absorption, but even this is a risky procedure and end-grain veneering should be avoided wherever possible. Veneering over surface joints, lap dovetails, tenon shoulders, etc. should also be avoided, for they will eventually show through as definite sinkages or stressmarks in the face veneers (287:1, 2).

HAND-VENEERING WITH HIDE GLUES

Almost without exception all veneering of new work is now done with modern synthetic resin or casein glues—the latter may be considered a natural plastic—using cramping/clamping pressure. However, the traditional hand method of employing hot hide (Scotch) glue and a heated household iron is still extremely useful in the repair of valuable antique furniture and in situations where no cramping facilities are available, therefore the process is described in some detail, for in capable hands it can be done quickly and cheaply and its permanence is beyond question. Basic requirements for hand-laying are: freshly made glue, thin and as hot as possible (animal glues must never be boiled), plenty of clean hot water (not taken from the iron glue-pot), clean rag, thin absorbent paper for taping, veneer pins, a fairly heavy Warrington pattern hammer, household iron and heating stove, or heavy-weight electric iron, and veneering-hammer. Figure 281 shows the simply made veneering-hammer with brass tongue (steel rusts badly with hide glue). An average size for the head will be about 4 in (101 mm) by 4 in (101 mm) by 7/8 in (22 mm) with a 3/4 in (19 mm) dowel rod taken through and wedged. If there is much hand-veneering to

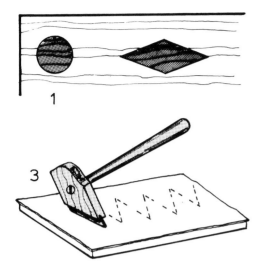

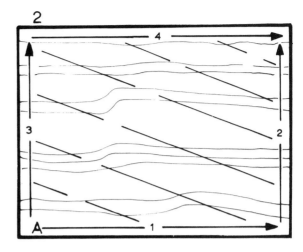

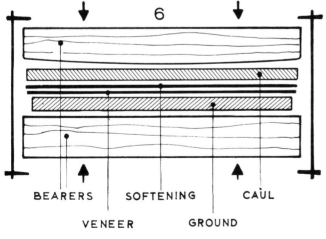

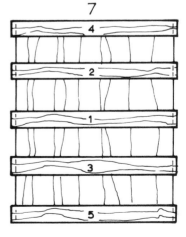

BEARERS   SOFTENING   CAUL

VENEER   GROUND

280   Veneering details (1)

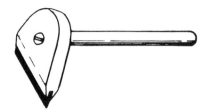

281 Veneering hammer

be done smaller hammers are useful for inlays, cross-bandings, etc. A heated room or workshop is necessary, and in the old workshops veneering by hand methods was never attempted in cold or humid weather or until the workshop had been warmed up after the day's start.

Hand laying veneers

The veneers must be laid one sheet at a time, for built-up patterns taped together cannot be laid by this process, as will become evident. A fast worker could no doubt lay a sideboard top without using the heated iron, but the veneer sheet would have to be very amenable, and it is wise not to attempt large areas without the iron until proficiency is achieved. The usual practice is to coat the groundwork or substrate evenly with thin glue, swab the outer surface of the veneer sheet with hot water to prevent it curling up once it touches the glue, add a few dabs from the glue-brush to lubricate the heated iron, lay the veneer on the glued surface, smoothing it out from the centre to exclude the air, and heat a section with the iron, lightly swabbing the veneer to prevent the iron sticking. As the glue starts to flow with the heat from the iron the surplus must be squeezed out towards the edges with the veneering-hammer, but the iron must not be too hot or steam will be generated and the veneer will stretch. A good test is to hold the iron an inch or so away from the cheek where it should feel hot but not uncomfortably so. There is no one method of handling the veneering-hammer: it can be held in one hand or two, pushed or pulled, but the movement should be zigzag (280:3) and wherever possible away from the centre. The amount of pressure applied will, of course, depend on the type of veneer, for thick spiteful veneers may require two-handed pressure and mild veneers only light pressure

282a Holding the veneering hammer with one hand

282b Holding the veneering hammer with both hands

with one hand, but the strokes of the hammer must always overlap and must be repeated until each patch or section has cooled off and bonded before moving on to heat and press the next section. It is a good plan to lay a sheet of used abrasive paper on the bench near by, for the iron will rapidly blacken with burnt glue and should be cleaned on the sheet from time to time. Figures 282A, B show methods of holding the veneering-hammer, and a commonly adopted procedure of laying is depicted in 280:2, starting at A and following in the order

296

shown, 1, 2, 3, 4, etc., working with the grain as much as possible, for hammering across the grain will stretch the wet veneer and subsequent shrinkage across the width will be considerable. Figure 280:3 shows another method favoured by some workers, working from the centre outwards, but here again there are no strict rules and much depends on the nature of the veneer and the speed of the worker. Excessive use of water should be avoided, with enough just to keep the veneer supple and the iron from sticking. Small local patches or blisters which refuse to stick can often be persuaded with a weight applied, covering the blister with a scrap of paper to prevent the weight sticking. Persistent blisters can be detected by tapping with the finger-nail; and if the glue has set the blister should be slit with a sharp knife along the grain, fresh glue inserted, covered with a scrap of paper and weighted down. If veneering is done without the aid of a heated iron the groundwork should be warmed, the veneer swabbed with hot water, the groundwork quickly spread with thin glue, the veneer applied and smoothed over with the palms to exude the air, and hammered down as already described. When the panel is dry, and 24 hours should be allowed for this, it should be closely examined for blisters, either tapping with the finger-nail or sweeping the finger-tips over the surface, when the presence of blisters will be indicated by a slight whisper. The pein of a Warrington pattern hammer can be used for narrow widths or small patches which require extra pressure.

Protection of edges

Edges of veneers laid with hide glue have a tendency to lift or splinter out particularly in the long grain, and they are, therefore, protected either by applied mouldings or edges, or, as in traditional work, with narrow crossbandings of veneer. The process is described on p. 305-7. The shrinkage pull of face veneers as they dry out must be compensated for by a corresponding balancing veneer applied to the underside of the panel, and this is also described later. Veneer edges laid with resin glues do not need protection (287:3, 4), but balance veneering is also necessary.

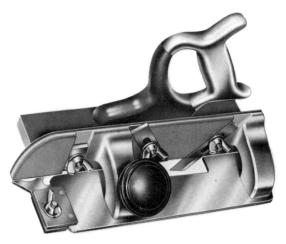

283   Veneer trimmer

Trimming edges

Veneers should be laid with a generous overlap all round in case they slip during laying, and should not be trimmed back until thoroughly dry. Cross-grain edges may have to be knife cut across the face before trimming back with chisel and finely set plane, although veneers laid with resin glues have not the same propensity for splintering out. An excellent veneer-trimmer is illustrated in 283 which cuts the overhang tight against the edge even across the grain, and is invaluable if there is much trimming to be done.

Jointing veneers (hide glues)

If the veneer leaf is insufficient to cover the width, one leaf is laid as already described and the next with a 1 in (25 mm) overlap (280:4). The centre-line of the overlap is then cut through with a sharp knife, working against a straight-edge, the edges carefully lifted, fresh glue inserted if necessary, the area reheated and hammered down, and the joint taped with paper to hold the edges together while the glue sets. If the joint subsequently opens it is usually a sign that either too much water has been used or too much pressure applied across the grain, stretching the moist veneer. Built-up patterns, matched curls, etc. are laid in the same way, centre- or guide-lines drawn across the groundwork/substrate and marked on the edges, the first sheet laid to overlap the guide-line, the second sheet laid and knifed through (280:5). Diamonds and quarters, etc. can also be treated in this manner, taking care to cut them the same overall size and positioning them with equal laps so that the grain matching is not lost; but they are better laid as taped patterns between cauls. Burrs, burls and curls with violently contrasted grain which have buckled badly should also be laid with cauls, but the veneers must be flatted or flattened before laying (see *Flattening veneers*, p. 300). Here again an experienced worker might prefer to soak the burrs in very hot water, using the thinnest possible glue and repeatedly hammering down until the veneer sticks.

Caul veneering (hide glues)

In this method the veneers are cut square, taped together and laid as a single sheet without preliminary dampening. This eliminates stretching, and the method is always used for laying thick saw-cut veneers, complicated patterns and marquetry-work where any swelling of the individual pieces would inevitably ruin the design. The groundwork/substrate is glued and allowed to cool off, the veneer assembly laid on the guide-lines and held in the correct position with staples or fine veneer pins tapped in and pinched off level. It is then covered with a heated caul of softwood or thick zinc sheet with an interleaving of newspaper to prevent the caul sticking, and pressure is applied with cross-bearers and cramps/clamps (280:6). The bearers should be fractionally rounded in the length to spread the pressure from the centre outwards, and the cramps tightened in the order shown (280:7). Softening, composed of several thicknesses of newspaper, thick felt or rubber sheeting can be used to even out any irregularities, but they must be warmed throughout or the glue will not flow. Modern veneering practice follows the same principles, but cold-setting resin adhesives have eliminated the necessity for heated cauls, although they can be used for great acceleration of the setting time.

PRESSURE VENEERING WITH RESIN GLUES

Resin glues offer very definite advantages , for the glues set at ordinary room temperatures and the application of heat is optional according to the required rapidity of the set. As the veneers do not have to be dampened no water is used except as a solvent for the glue, therefore expansion and subsequent shrinkage is negligible; moreover, there is or should be little, if any, penetration to the wood surface, the pores of the wood are not choked with glue, and all the lustre is retained. Edges do not have to be protected as with hide glues, and in fact veneered surfaces can be shaped, moulded and run out to a feather edge without the veneers lifting, while the surfaces are harder, with greater wear resistance, and are impervious to moderate heat and moisture. Lastly, veneers can be cut square, assembled in complex patterns, taped together and laid as a single sheet with the certainty that if properly prepared there will be no gapping of joints, with a good joint in straight-grained boards almost invisible to the naked eye.

Pressure is always necessary with synthetic resin glues for they have no natural suck (impact glues suitable for laying formica, etc. are quite unsuitable for permanent veneer-work), but it need only be sufficient to bring both surfaces into intimate contact and to maintain that contact until the glue has set. Various forms of veneer-press are used and Figures 284-6 show representative examples. The principle is the same throughout, i.e. to maintain sufficient positive pressure to bend or flatten the veneer onto its former or groundwork (form or substrate); excessive pressure over and above the minimum requirements should be avoided or glue-starved joints will result. A thin skin only of glue should be used, and the object, therefore, is not to squeeze out the surplus glue as in hand-veneering but merely to establish the requisite intimate contact. Some form of veneer-press is virtually indispensable for every trade-shop no matter how small, for it will soon pay for its keep, and one of the most suitable for the general run of work is the hand-operated screw veneer-press (284) with open ends. With this type extra-long work beyond the capacity of the standard daylight press can be veneered in sections, or the overhang at the ends clamped between bearers and G-cramps/C-clamps. Alternatively, very long panels can be slit into convenient sections in the long-grain direction

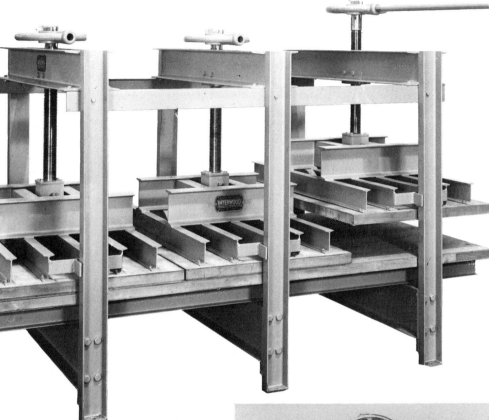

284   Quick-acting hand-operated screw veneer-press with open ends.   (By courtesy of Interwood Ltd)

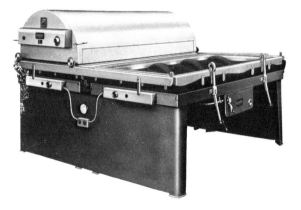

285   Twin vacuum shapers and veneer-press with mobile dome.   (By courtesy of Interwood Ltd)

286   FS.1 Single platen manual veneer press.   (By courtesy of Interwood Ltd)

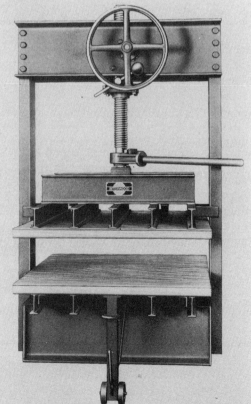

of the face veneers, grooved for loose tongues and each section veneered and then assembled. The process is simple enough and highly effective, but the grooving must be very accurately cut if the veneered surfaces are to line up. Failing any kind of press large areas can be satisfactorily veneered with nothing more elaborate than heavy cross-bearers and sash-cramps as in caul veneering, but some local blistering must be expected which, incidentally, is not as difficult to lay as some writers would make out. A simple way of checking that the cross-bearers are exerting full pressure in the centre of the panel is to slip tags of newspaper under the bearers at intervals. A slight pull on the tags will disclose whether the pressure is uniform throughout.

Preparation and laying (resin glues)

The groundwork/substrate is prepared in the same way as for hammer veneering, laying the veneeers 'with the grain' on solid wood and 'across the grain' of plywoods, etc. The surfaces should not be roughened or keyed except for a light sanding to break through any surface glazing or grime, followed by a thorough dusting to clean the fibres. Any general-purpose single-application resin glue can be used for cold pressing at room temperatures, but special veneering glues such as *Aerolite KL* (CIBA (ARL) Ltd) with gap-filling powder hardener are preferable. The glue should be mixed exactly in accordance with the maker's instructions and applied to the groundwork in a thin coat, spreading it evenly with spatula or palette-knife, or more satisfactorily rolling it out with a photographic rubber roller or trough hand spreader, carefully checking for bare spots, as there will be no surplus glue to level them out in the pressing, and allowing a few minutes air drying according to the make of glue. Cramping/clamping pressure in handwork can be as for caul veneering with hide glue, but the bearers need not be rounded, always providing that they press in the centre, and a good test of this is to insert tags of newspaper under the bearers which should be firmly gripped when the cramps are tightened. As there is plenty of time for assembly both face and counter (backing) veneers can be laid at the

same time with an interleaving of paper, cellophane, or waxed hardboard to prevent the veneers sticking to the cover boards or cauls. Setting time will be according to the type of glue and the working temperature, but work under strain should have more than the minimum before the cramps are released. For more detailed information as to working procedures, reference should be made to the printed instructions of the manufacturers concerned.

BALANCING VENEERS

Veneers laid with hide glue will pull even the thickest groundwork/substrate into cup as it dries out, and even resin glues with their reduced moisture content will cause slight warping. If the groundwork is firmly anchored to a heavy supporting frame or locked in a carcass construction it may not call for additional treatment, although solid wood bases should always be veneered on the heart or rounded side to equalize the natural pull (287:5, 7); but in all unsupported work the reverse side must be treated with a balancing veneer (287:8). Ideally, this balancing or 'backing' veneer should be of the same thickness and of similar or comparable species as the face veneer, but in practice balancing veneers are usually makore (cherry mahogany), African mahogany, sapelewood, etc. They are laid with the grain direction similar to the face veneers, but the joints need only be cut and fitted together without matching unless the work is visible. Balance veneering is sometimes referred to as *Counter veneering*, but it should not be confused with the latter which is a distinct process described on p. 307.

FLATT(EN)ING VENEERS

Only experience will tell whether a buckled veneer can be laid satisfactorily without preliminary flattening. A good veneer-press, whether screw operated, hydraulic or vacuum, will flatten most stubborn veneers, but it may be at the expense of extensive splitting and cracking; therefore badly crumpled or spiteful veneers should always be flattened, using either water alone or a weak solution of glue size (one part glue to five parts water). The veneers

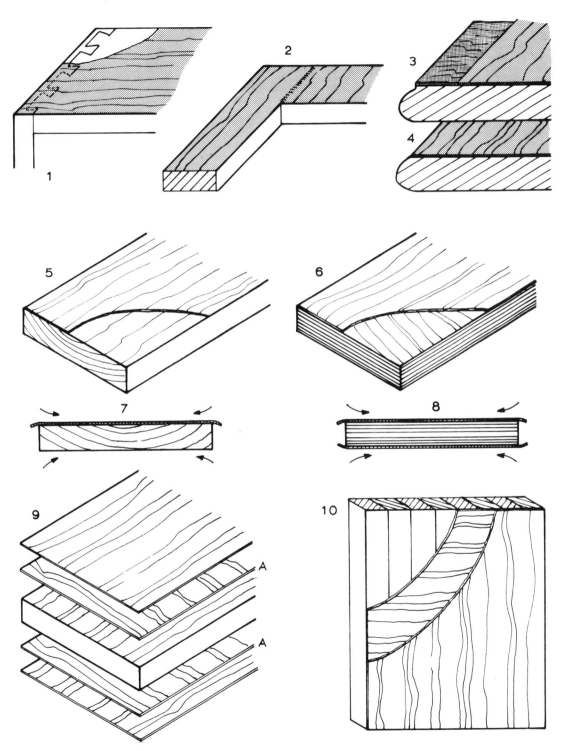

287 Veneering details (2)

should be thoroughly moistened and flattened between warm boards with light cramping/clamping pressure or weighted down. They should be turned occasionally to prevent them sticking, and pressed individually and not in a pack unless interleaved with cellophane or waxed hardboard. Oily woods such as rosewood and satinwood do not require moistening and can be flattened with heat alone. Either hide glue or a very weak mix of resin glue and water can be used for size, for resin glue will take over either, and the flattened veneers must be dried thoroughly before laying, keeping them between weighted boards until ready for use. If the veneers have split open during the flattening—and strong burrs and curls are sometimes prone to this—only actual experience will tell whether the split can be pulled together and taped in position. Usually it is advisable to accept the split, slit the sheet through and joint together or patch the gap, for if a stubborn sheet is arbitrarily pulled together it may buckle further up during the pressing. If the splits are wide open they can be covered with gummed paper strip on the face and filled on the underneath with Brummer stopping, which will prevent the glue forming a glass-hard filling in the crack. The Brummer can then be scraped out in the final finishing, and the crack patched or filled with suitable filler.

REPAIRING BLISTERS

Blisters and loose patches can be located by tapping with the finger-nail to disclose a hollow sound, or the fingertips brushed rapidly backwards and forwards which gives a slight whisper over the hollow places. Contrary to the general idea, blisters in veneers laid with resin glues are by no means difficult to repair. The veneer should be slit with a razor-blade or sharp knife along the grain, fresh glue inserted, rubbed hard with the pein of a hammer to expel the surplus glue, taped with paper or cellulose tape, covered with a warmed steel scraper or wood block and weighted down for a moment or so. A soldering-iron or electric iron can be used, but all the excess glue must be squeezed out first or the heat will fuse it into a solid lump under the veneer. If blisters occur in very pale or delicate woods, a piece of white blackboard

chalk rubbed along the edges of the cut will help to disguise the scar, and in fact all joints in pale woods can be treated in this way, keeping the chalk to the outer edges of the joints only. (Hide glue mixed with flake-white and Salisbury glue [rabbit skin glue] were used for delicate inlays in traditional work, and both types are still obtainable.)

VENEERING PARTICLE BOARD

Chipboard (particle board) should be veneered with synthetic resin glue, for hide glues may or may not take over the resin impregnated surface and water-based glues tend to swell up the chips. If resin glues are not available the outer skin of the board should be broken through with coarse abrasive paper and a test for adhesion made, or the manufacturer of the board consulted. Synthetic resin glues adhere perfectly and give no trouble. If the boards are supplied already veneered with a common backing quality veneer, usually agba (tola) or African mahogany, the decorative face veneer should be crossed as usual, as this locks the minute cracks always present in knife-cut veneers. Furniture quality particle boards with fine chips in the surface layers should not require counter veneering with backing quality veneers, but if the coarse particle boards (building boards) are used then they should be double veneered (see *Counter veneering*, p. 307).

JOINTING VENEERS

The trimming and jointing of narrow veneers to form larger panels is done by special saws or power-operated guillotines in production-work, but knife cutting by hand is rarely satisfactory and the veneers should be worked as in jointing narrow boards. Single leaves can be planed up on the shooting-board (293:1) if adequately supported as shown, or a pack of veneers can be cramped/clamped between two wood straight-edges and either held in the vice (288) or passed over the jointer. If the veneer edges tend to splinter out or crumble they can be supported with strips of adhesive tape while they are being planed. After planing, the edges

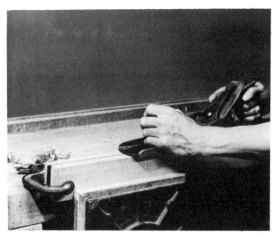

288 Planing edges of veneers

289 Taping veneers

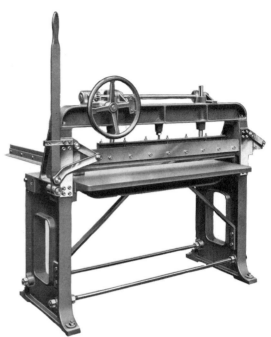

290 Hand-operated veneer-guillotine. (By courtesy of Interwood Ltd)

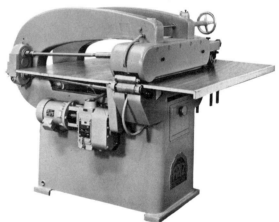

291 Automatic veneer-splicer. (By courtesy of Interwood Ltd)

are taped together with adhesive tape, with a final strip along the entire length of the joint (289), and while gummed paper tape is normally used, clear cellulose tape has very definite advantages, even though it is more expensive, for the joints can be examined for tightness against the light and the tape is more easily peeled off after pressing. Tape-splicers in production-work apply mechanical methods to the same principle, and the two leaves of veneer are pushed together by angled rollers while a continuous strip of gummed paper tape is wetted and pressed down by a front roller. With tapeless splicers the veneer edges are first coated with a mixture of hide glue and formaldehyde and allowed to dry. A heated roller in the splicer then liquefies and sets the glue as the two edges are fed together, with sufficient strength of bond which enables the veneers to be handled as a single sheet.

Wedge jointing (finger jointing) veneers

Short veneers which are merely butt jointed together end to end to increase the overall length show the joint as a hard line saturated with glue no matter how skilfully they are laid. While this is acceptable in matched curls (297:4) it can be objectionable in long runs of straight-grained woods. Finger or wedge jointing will, however, provide an almost invisible match

303

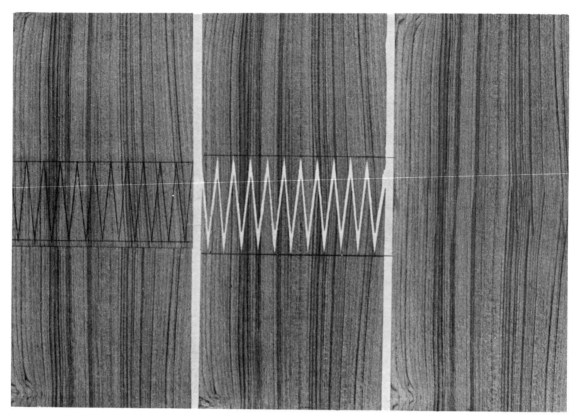

292   End jointing veneers with finger joint

with the grain of the separate veneers merging into each other.

Laying out finger jointing

The veneers chosen should be reasonably straight grained and not too pronounced in figure. The butt ends of the matched veneers taken in strict order from the bundle should be overlapped by the amount required for the fingering, always remembering that the longer the fingers the more they will approximate to the direction of the long grain and the less evident they will be when laid. A small allowance, say ⅜ in (9.5 mm) over and above the length of the fingers, should be made at each end to support the cuts, and two lines should be squared across the top veneeer ⅜ in (9.5 mm) from the end of the top veneer and ⅜ in (9.5 mm) from the position of the end of the under

veneer. Within this box parallel lines should be drawn and the position of the fingers marked in with a hard pencil; the fingers are then cut in with a sharp knife, the waste lifted and the two veneers pushed tightly together and taped in position. Figure 292 illustrates the various stages, and the completed finger joint, which was not 'faked' in any way, shows the joint as a slight deviation only in the grain direction on the right-hand side of the completed panel. The method can also be used in random lengths of veneers, providing the grain is reasonably uniform throughout the several sheets.

Finger jointing is a traditional hand process, but wedge joint veneer shaping machines working on the principle of a small fly-press are now available with up to 12 right-hand and 12 left-hand knives to cut joints up to 14 in (355 mm) in width. The principle is also employed in the scarf jointing of heavy construction timbers, but precision machines are required as the fingering cannot be sawn by hand accurately enough to give the required tightness at the tips.

CROSS VENEERING

All veneers laid at right angles to the grain direction of the groundwork/substrate are classed as cross veneers, but more specifically the term *cross veneering* is applied to narrow widths laid across door-frames, mirror surrounds, etc.; *border crossbanding* to narrow edge borders on panel- and table-tops; *crossbanding* (*counter veneering*) to an under veneer laid on groundworks and then covered with a face veneer, and *balance* veneering to compensating veneers laid on the underside of groundworks.

Cross veneering of door stiles and rails can be done with hide glue using either hammer or caul techniques, or with cramping/clamping pieces or veneer-press using cold-setting resin glues. Assuming that the door-frame shown in 293:2 has to be veneered on the face and back only, there is no problem and the operation is straightforward; but if the door edges are veneered also then the framed-up door must first be planed to the opening with due allowance for the veneer thickness plus the necessary clearance all round, for there can be no adjusting to fit afterwards. Probably the surest method is to trial fit the door, tape small pieces of the actual veneer either side of each corner, hinge with one steel screw in the centre of each plate and then adjust as necessary. If the door is slack in the opening then one stile and one rail can be double veneered on the edges, for the veneer edges will be covered by the face veneers. The edge veneers can run with the grain but the face veneers are cut across the veneer sheet (or from running sheets if matching veneers are required), keeping the same faces uppermost throughout to prevent some strips appearing darker as the light catches them, and cutting the strips rather full in width. If the corners are butted together as in Elizabethan walnut-work the edge to each corner must be planed on a shooting-board and lined up on the inner edge of the frame (293:2X), but for mitred work (293:2A) it is only necessary to pencil in the mitre-line and fit the corners accordingly. It hardly matters if all four corners are done first, working in to the centre in each case, or the strips laid in sequence round the frame, but in practice it is easier to fit two straight ends at the centre rather than one straight end and one mitre simultaneously. With hide glue narrow strips hardly need wetting before laying, and this should be avoided wherever possible as it only swells up the strips, nor need the strips be laid with an overlap for it is simple enough to cut each strip exactly square, glue, hammer in position and tape the joint with a temporary weight placed over it to keep it from curling. If cramping techniques are employed it is better to use resin glue, fitting, gluing and cramping each section in sequence, for there will be ample time to fit the joints; while for press-work with either hide glue and cauls or resin glue and veneer-press the strips can be assembled, taped and laid as a whole, driving in fine veneer pins and pinching off the tops to prevent the veneers floating in the press. The glue should be thoroughly hard before the surplus edges are trimmed back, and care should be taken not to hit or round over the faces when cleaning up. In fact, it will always pay to tack waste pieces of the same thickness as the frame to the bench to act as an overhang for the plane, scraper or sanding block.

Cross veneering moulded frames

Wherever practicable frames moulded on the inner edges should be put together dry, planed off smooth, face veneered and then moulded and assembled. Alternatively, the moulding can be worked in strips and glued on. If the framework must be moulded and assembled before veneering, endeavour to keep the veneer flush with the inside edges of the frame and clear of the moulding which can have a coat of polish to prevent the surplus glue adhering. While it is always risky to veneer the frame sections first and then cut the joints, the expert worker might not hesitate to do so.

Border crossbandings

Various treatments are shown in 293:3–6 with (3) against an inlaid boxwood or ebony line, (4, 5) shaped bandings and (6) a shaped panel. In all handwork the central panel is laid first, trimmed back with a cutting-gauge or against a template, the inlaid line or banding fitted, glued and held in position with either cramping/clamping blocks or veneer pins driven in

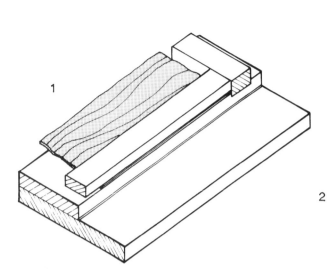

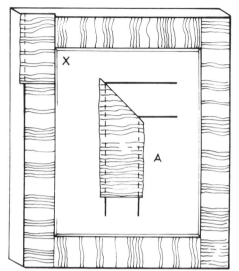

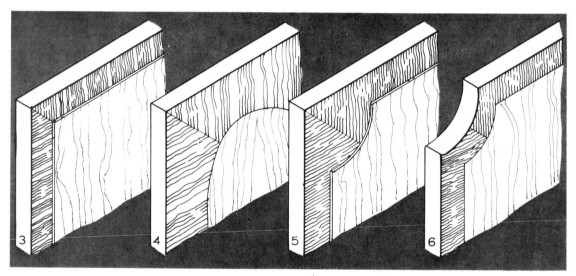

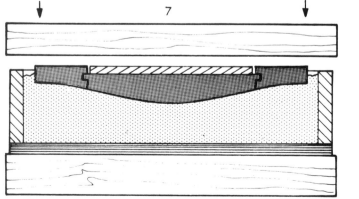

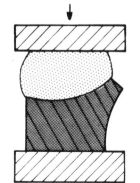

293   Veneering: crossbanding, etc.

294   Crossbanding table edge

alongside, and the crossband then cut, fitted and laid. If the crossband is fairly narrow the separate pieces cut from the veneer sheet can be rubbed glued in position and then taped, or cellulose tape can be used with resin glues as it has a certain degree of elasticity and can be stretched tight to give sufficient pressure (289). Press-work will either call for dry fitting of the whole surface securely taped together and laid in one operation, or two or more pressings of central veneer, inlay banding and cross-banding. A method often adopted by the writer for this type of work was to press the centre first, trim back, dry fit both banding and crossbanding with cellulose tape, leaving the straight joints untaped, and then fold back the bandings with the tapes acting as hinges, glue the groundwork/substrate, tape the straight joints and press. This method is, of course, not possible with curved bandings, and the cellulose tape cannot be used with animal glues as it will not stick to wet surfaces. If the bandings are thicker than the central veneers and the panel is pressed between cauls or cover boards, softening material (newspaper, felt, rubber sheeting, etc.) will have to be used to accommodate the differences, but rubber bag (vacuum) presses will automatically do this.

Crossbandings were first used as safe edges for veneered work, for long-grain veneer has a tendency to lift or splinter out at the edges if laid with animal glues. Resin glues seal the edges effectively and require no crossbands, but the method is still used in reproduction furniture and as a form of surface decoration.

Crossbanding (counter veneering)

Both terms are synonymous and refer to a crossband underlay laid at right angles to the grain direct of the groundwork/substrate (287:9A), and then veneered over with a face veneer with the grain direction again recrossed. Thus in unsupported work two balancing veneers on the underside of the groundwork will be necessary to counteract the pull of the crossband and face veneer, and the assembly will be in effect a five-ply construction counting the panel as one ply. The process is useful for groundworks built up in segments (287:10) or surface joints which might shadow or telegraph through a single face veneer, and for the coarser grades of particle board. If solid wood is counter veneered, which was often done in richly veneered traditional furniture, the core panel must be a mild amenable wood, thoroughly seasoned and bone-dry, or shrinkage of the core will buckle or stress the veneers.

Yorkite crossbanding veneer

A recent development is the use of a manufactured pure wood cellulose fibre sheet in lieu of a natural wood veneer, produced by the NVF

Company of Wilmington, Delaware, and marketed in the United Kingdom under the brand name of *Yorkite*. This material resembles a very stiff brown paper (it can also be obtained in white for pale woods), and as it is a tough, dense, resin-free sheet of uniform thickness and obtainable in continuous rolls up to 54 in (1.371 m) wide, it offers definite advantages. It is particularly useful as an underlay for spiteful curls and burrs which otherwise have a tendency to crack and craze over a period of time, and as a preventative against the telegraphing through of coarse chip particle boards, etc. Additionally the grain direction of the face veneers can be in any direction irrespective of the groundwork/substrate. A range of thicknesses is available, of which 1/64 in (.39 mm) is the most popular.

SANDBAG VENEERING

If a vacuum-bag press is not available, shapes of double curvature can be veneered with the traditional sandbag techniques. Either a canvas bag or sandbox filled with coarse silver sand is used, and an example of the latter is shown in 293:7. Assuming that a *bombé* shape has been constructed either of segments, wood bricks, or, in the traditional examples of *bombé* commodes, a solid panel tongued to a jointed framework and shaped to the curves with plane, floats (coarse files) and scrapers, the box is filled with sifted sand and the shaped groundwork/substrate to be veneered tamped down until it fits exactly. Register-marks should be made on the groundwork and also on the edges of the box so that the curves of the shape will be exactly located in the depressions in the sand, for the sand, being inert, will not slide under pressure. The groundwork is then carefully withdrawn and the veneers fitted, tailoring them if necessary and taping them firmly together to form a self-supporting shell. If hide glue is used the groundwork is then glued and allowed to cool off, the veneers placed in position and held with staples or pins in the waste edges, the sandbox thoroughly heated and the groundwork with its covering of veneers exactly located in the box. It is then cramped down with suitably shaped cauls, applying pressure in the centre first and then both edges simultaneously or the shape will rock over. Resin glues can be used instead of hide glue, and in fact the heat of the box will accelerate the set, although in this case the sand should be warm rather than hot or precuring will result before the cramps are in position. Canvas bags filled with sand (293:8) follow the same principle and are thumped down over the glued assembly and either cramped or weighted.

RUBBER BAG VENEERING

A method of veneering curved work and forming laminated shapes which has supplanted the traditional sandbag technique, except for occasional work, is the rubber envelope which can take the place of the vacuum-bag press if necessary. Some form of vacuum extraction is

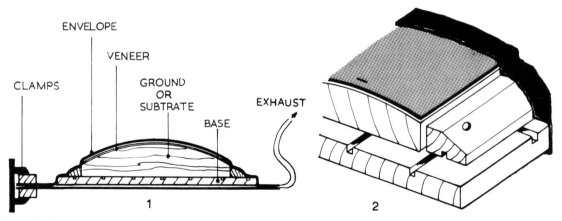

295   Rubber bag veneering

required, either a suitable vacuum pump, the intake side of a standard compressor, or the slip side of a blower motor. The household vacuum-cleaner is not suitable as a vacuum of 26 in (660 mm) of mercury must be induced. The envelopes are procurable from 4 ft (1.22 m) by 3 ft (0.91 m) up to 12 ft (3.65 m) by 5 ft (1.52 m). The work to be veneered is placed on a suitable flat baseboard or support with loose flaring pieces either side to even out the pull on the rubber, and the whole assembly placed in the envelope, the open end of which is sealed with cramped/clamped battens. It is advisable to run crossed shallow grooves in the baseboard and flaring pieces with vertical holes at the intersections to allow the air to be withdrawn evenly. The usual precautions must be taken, i.e. formers, forms, etc. must be waxed to prevent adhesion or the veneers covered with waxed paper, with the veneers stapled through the waste to prevent displacement. Figures 295:1 and 295:2 show an enlarged diagram of a section of the assembly. The envelope can be used for flat-work, curved work and compound shapes with equal success, but the bag must be smoothed out and the shapes under held down as the air is withdrawn, to prevent the rubber drawing under the veneers.

PATTERN VENEERING

Considerable artistry is called for in the selection and matching of veneers for pattern-making, for the results can be beautiful or truly horrible, according to the skill of the operator. Modern furniture does not make use of patterned effects, although even a plain front does require careful matching of the individual leaves, therefore the techniques, as far as it is possible to describe them, should be fully understood even if the art is indefinable. One golden rule should always be observed, however, that of restraint, for a richly figured pack of veneers is an open invitation to flamboyance.

The various methods of matching veneers using two or more leaves taken in strict order from the bundle are as follows:

Balanced matched General term meaning consecutive leaves of veneer of uniform size and matched for grain.

Book form or side matched (297:1) The first leaf of the bundle opened out as in turning the pages of a book, and matched at the sides with its fellow.

Running (297:2) Consecutive leaves laid out side by side as they rise from the bundle.

Random matched (297:3) Assorted leaves not matched for grain and not necessarily of the same width.

End or butt matched (297:4) The top leaf folded down as in book form matching.

Diamond quarter (297:5) Four consecutive leaves cut diagonally and side and butt matched.

Reverse diamond (297:6) As for diamond quarter.

Quartered (297:7) Four consecutive leaves side and butt matched.

Herringbone (297:8) Two consecutive leaves cut diagonally and side matched.

Inverted herringbone (297:9) As for herringbone.

The running pattern (297:2) is usually adopted for contemporary designs as against the traditional book form pattern. Diamond and herringbone patterns are cut from successive leaves and not from a single sheet, for any slant in the grain will give a twisted effect as shown in 298B. Card templates cut to the required shape can be laid on the veneer and each section cut through to be planed square and matched with its mate. The first cutting out should be generous to allow for trimming so that the grain markings register with each other. As it is sometimes difficult to pick out the best section from a sheet of wild grain, a cardboard window the size of the template can be cut, placed over the leaf and the best section chosen and marked in pencil. When the first section has been cut the remainder of the leaf can be used as a window for successive sections. To judge the effect of book form matching of sections which are to be cut from large sheets of veneer, a piece of unframed mirror glass should be placed at right angles to the chosen area and the effect of doubling viewed in the glass, and this will

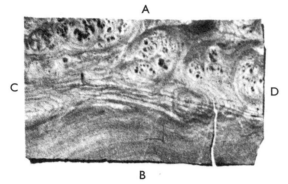

1 Single leaf of veneer before trimming and laying

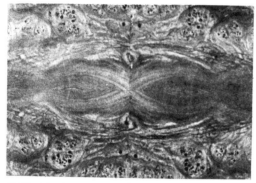

2 Matched veneer panel with sides B to B and ends C to C

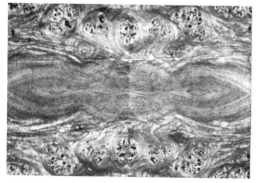

3 Matched veneer panel with sides B to B and ends D to D

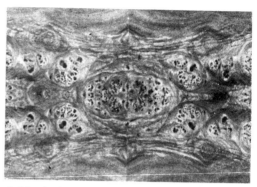

4 Matched veneer panel with sides A to A and ends C to C

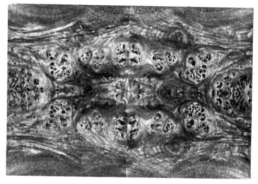

5 Matched veneer panel with sides A to A and ends D to D

prevent bad errors of choice. A point to watch in all veneer matching is how the pores of the wood run, for if the sheet is cut with the pores diagonal with the thickness, folding the sheet over in book form fashion will reverse the inclination of the pores, and the play of light over the surface may strike correspondingly darker in opposing sections, particularly in coarse woods such as African mahogany curls or burls. The effect can be pronounced enough to ruin the appearance of side or end matching in vertical surfaces, but it can be observed before laying by opening out the leaves, wetting them on the face surfaces, standing them upright and viewing them from a distance.

Built-up patterns of various shaped sections —and the variety is endless—should be assembled on a base-plan drawn on stiff drawing paper and each piece cut to shape, taped to its mate and pressed. Complicated patterns which cannot be cut with knife and straight-edge will have to be sawn out with a fret-saw as in marquetry cutting. If the veneers are cupped they should be flatted before cutting, and if boxwood stringings, bandings and thick inlays are included they can be cut in and the difference in thickness compensated for

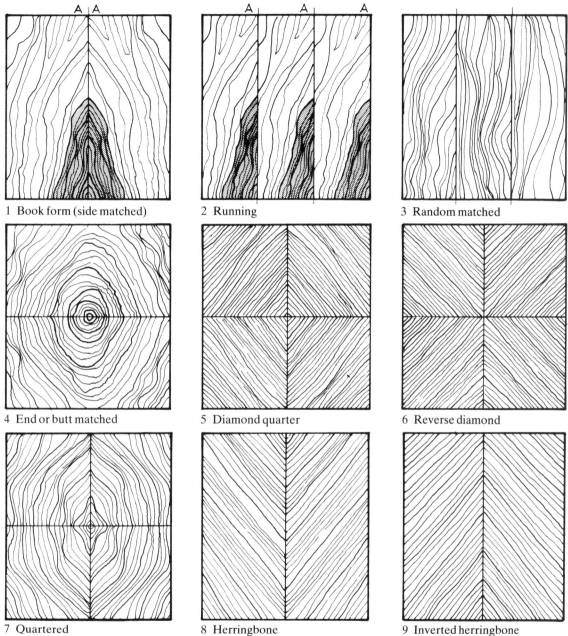

1 Book form (side matched)

2 Running

3 Random matched

4 End or butt matched

5 Diamond quarter

6 Reverse diamond

7 Quartered

8 Herringbone

9 Inverted herringbone

by layers of softening in the final pressing, but usually it is more satisfactory to tape the various veneer sections together, lay them and then incise for the lines or inlays and re-press (see *Inlay lines, bandings, etc.*, p. 316). For examples of intricate pattern-work the reader is referred to the innumerable encyclopaedias of furniture and to museum-work. No matter how complicated the assembly may appear in the finished work it is always basically as already described, although certain precautions may have to be adopted according to the nature of the veneers. If individual .pieces or sections refuse to lie flat on the base-plan preventing

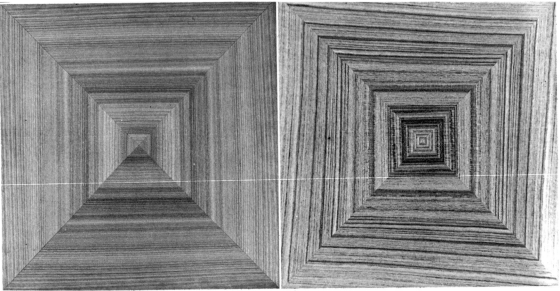

298a   Diamond quartered panel (correct)   298b   Diamond quartered panel (incorrect)

accurate fitting, it may be necessary to paper tape the plan to a supporting base and glue each section down with dabs of hide glue, Seccotine or Balsa cement weighted in position until set. The whole assembly is then covered with a glued cover paper, and when thoroughly dry split away from the plan with a sharp knife and the back cleaned off, using as little water as possible (Balsa cement will have to be sanded off). Fragile veneers cut to sharp points may have to be reinforced with a glued cover paper before they are cut, and time spent on such preparation will be amply repaid. All cover papers and backings should be glued with thin hide glue in preference to resin adhesives, and in no circumstances should impact glues be used as they are extremely difficult to clean off.

Cleaning off patterned work

Complicated assemblies of different kinds of veneer or veneers with wild fluctuations in grain should be left for as long as possible under pressure. Even when released they should be kept between weighted boards whenever they are not being worked on, for it will take some time for veneers and panel to adjust themselves to the varying stresses, particularly with

synthetic resin glues which delay but do not finally inhibit the absorption or evaporation of moisture in accordance with the prevailing atmospheric conditions. Thick saw-cut veneers can be levelled off with a finely adjusted smoothing-plane, and the Norris plane is admirable for this, but thin knife-cut veneers will have to be treated very much more gently with sharp scraper and abrasive paper. Resin glue assemblies are more laborious to clean off, for any glue that has penetrated to the surface will be glass hard, but they can be repeatedly swabbed with water which will not only lift the glued cover paper but will ease considerably the scraping of very hard woods if done while the surface is still wet. Tests should be made, however, for the colours of some veneers leach out and may discolour paler inlays. Even the final sanding may present difficulties, and in the finishing of the Bombay rosewood petals in the bird's-eye maple pilaster illustrated in 299 no water could be used, and it was found necessary to seal the maple with several coats of thin white polish (french polish) before the panel could be sanded, to keep both colour and dust from the very dark rosewood from spreading into the pale ivory-coloured maple grain. Water also must be used very sparingly on hide glue

299 Inlaying rosewood motif in veneered pilaster

assemblies; while raised or fluffy grain will have to be sealed or 'flashed' with dilute white polish, usually known as a 'wash coat', to raise and set the fibres in an upright position so that they are stiff enough to be cut off by the abrasive paper. Where the grain directions conflict, as between the individual pieces of veneer, the final sanding with 180 or 240 grit abrasive paper will have to be done with a circular movement, and an orbital pad sander is recommended for this.

Column veneering

A traditional and effective method of veneering small circular columns and half columns, which does away with the necessity for shaped cauls, is to glue the column with hide glue and allow to cool off, cut the veneer with a generous overlap in the width, pin one long edge (if necessary damping it so that it lies flat), wrap the veneer round the column and bind it with a 2 in (50 mm) continuous calico strip which has been well wetted so that the whole of the area is covered with the strip. The column is then gently heated over a flame or other source of heat until the glue runs, the webbing again wetted with warm water and then reheated to shrink it and force out the surplus glue. After the glue has set the webbing is removed, the overlap joint cut through, the edges warmed, fresh glue inserted, hammered down and strapped with tape. Jointed up or fragile veneers which do not bend easily may have to be reinforced with a glued paper cover before wrapping, while intricate inlays and built-up patterns of small elements may have to be glued firmly to a supporting base of thin fabric which must be dampened slightly before bending and gluing in position. (Subsequent cracking, crazing and lifting of highly figured or spiteful veneers [mahogany curls, rosewood, etc.] can often be prevented by the traditional method of backing the veneer with glued muslin prior to laying. See also *Yorkite crossbanding veneer*, page 307). Large columns of either coopered or laminated construction can be made in convenient sections, each section hammer or caul veneered and then reassembled with either tongued and grooved or rubbed joints; but such work belongs more properly to specialized joinery and advanced techniques are employed for repetition work, although the occasional 'one off' usually has to be made up by traditional methods improvised to suit. One thing is very certain, that no matter what new shape is evolved which would seem to call for revolutionary methods it has usually been done before by primitive but essentially practical methods. To state it fairly, the old cabinetmakers knew every worthwhile trick, and the study of antique furniture is the study of man's mastery over his material. The heavily shaped *bombé* commode with its flashing richness of intricate veneer-work may look almost impossible, but it was done with primitive planes and scrapers, a pot of home-made glue and a lump of heated iron. No doubt the old craftsmen had more time in which to develop their skills and we are in too much of a hurry, but in the end they achieved more than we can usually show. The moral, therefore, must surely be 'make haste slowly'.

Diaper-work

Typical examples of these entrancing patterns of repeat squares, diamonds, lozenges and foliage in contrasting woods are shown in 300 and methods of construction in 301. The

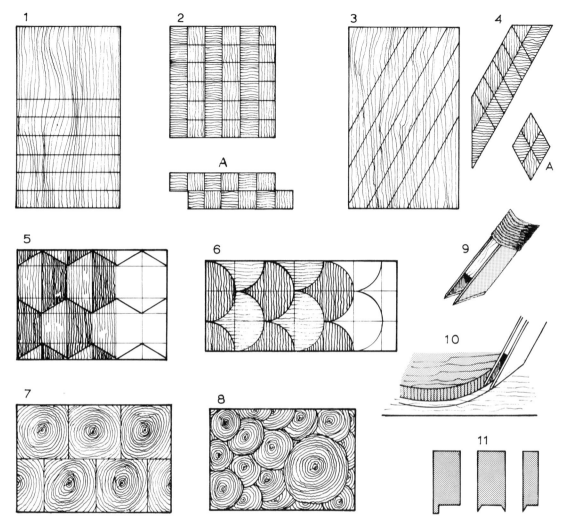

301   Veneering: parquetry, etc. (2)

contrasts between the various woods should not be too abrupt except in very small sections, and strong figure markings rather than violent alterations in colour or tone, with a good play of light and shade as the direction changes from vertical to horizontal, should be used or the charm will be lost. A full-size plan should first be made on stiff drawing paper and the pieces fitted to it. Figure 301:1 shows the build up of a square pattern in which strips are cut across and along the grain of two separate sheets of veneer, the edges planed and taped together (301:2). Strips across the composite sheet can then be built up on the base-plan as shown (301:2A). In diamond-work the strips are cut at an angle (301:3) and assembled as in 301:4A. If boxwood

lines are incorporated (300:4) they can be glued in between the strips and again across the composite strips, and bandings treated similarly. The first cutting of the strips must be very accurate and the widths identical using a sharp cutting-gauge, but the composite strips can be laid against a straight-edge and corrected if necessary. Transparent cellulose tape is invaluable for building up the strips as the joints can be watched for alignment at every stage. In 300:3 strips are cut the width of the separate diamonds and cut to the diamond shape against a template or in a jig; every square is then assembled with its banding and matched against its mates. The three-dimensional cube effect (300:5), which was always a great favourite, is

315

cut in a jig or from a template using strips of three contrasting woods of identical width, two strips along the grain and one at an angle of 30°. Figure 301:6 is, strictly speaking, marquetry-work, with separate sheets of veneer pinned together or interleaved with glued paper, marked with a template and cut with a saw and then fitted to the pattern, and eased with fine files where necessary. It takes much longer to assemble but is remarkably effective if the woods are well chosen. Figure 300:1 shows the chess or chequer-board pattern; 300:2 is a square pattern to give a diamond quarter effect; 300:3 has an inlay banding diagonally across the squares. Woods generally used for diaper-work were Macassar ebony, Rio and Bombay rosewoods, Cuba and Honduras mahoganies, satinwood, kingwood, tulipwood, walnut and box, etc., being woods with strong markings or stripes. Boxwood, holly and stained blackwood (pearwood) were used for lines and stringings with insets of bone, ivory, tortoiseshell, mother-of-pearl, brass, pewter, etc.

INLAY LINES, BANDINGS, ETC.

It is a little sad that inlaid lines and bandings are no longer used in modern furniture, for they add great richness and a touch of welcome colour. Figure 302:1 shows various traditional examples, and 302:2–5 the method of assembly in which composite blocks are built up of layers of contrasting woods and veneers and then sliced as in 302:3, with a special planer or swage-set circular saw projecting only sufficiently above the saw-table to cut the thickness. Reproduction-work still makes use of these bandings, and those usually available from marquetry and veneer suppliers include $1/16$ in (1.5 mm) boxwood and blackwood strings, $1/8$ in (3 mm) boxwood, blackwood and rose inlay lines, three-line bandings box/black/box and box/rose/box, and some patterned bandings, viz. dentil, check, rope, domino, feather, herringbone, diamond and chevron in combinations of box, blackwood, mahogany, rosewood, tulipwood, satinwood and walnut, etc.

Lines and bandings can be incorporated in the veneer pattern at the time of assembly and laid as a single sheet; or the veneers can be taped together, laid and then incised for the lines which are cut in with a cutting-gauge or scratch stock working from the edge, or knifed against a template; or, if in circles or circular sweeps, a waste block can be cramped/clamped or paper glued to the surface, with a stub dowel in the centre working in a hole in a straight bar which has been part saw kerfed and screwed together to form a scratch stock. Various forms of cutters for use in scratch stocks are shown in 301:11, while 301:9 illustrates a simply made double knife from old hack-saw blades for use against a template (301:10). If the veneer has been laid with hide glue the waste can be lifted with the heated tang of a file, and eased out with a narrow chisel; but resin glues will require cutting out with the bevel of the chisel flat against the groundwork/substrate. If the grooves are fairly tight the line or banding can be glued with hide glue or Seccotine, pressed into position with the pein of a hammer and weighted down if necessary, or taped in position for cold-setting glues and re-pressed. Complicated assemblies may require several such pressings, working from the centre outwards, although it is possible to lay thin strings and bandings with resin glues and a soldering-iron or electric iron which will set the glue instantaneously, but there must be no surplus of glue or it will harden into lumps before it can be pressed out. Where the line is fitted against a central veneer with a cross-banding to the edges of the panel, the veneer should be cut and trimmed to shape, the line glued and held in position with veneer pins until set, and the crossbanding then fitted and glued, taping it down with cellulose tape tightly stretched to hold it firmly in position. Figure 294 shows the crossbanding of a circular table-top done in this way. Square lines rebated/rabbeted into the edge of a top are also anchored in this fashion and cleaned off flush when dry. It is essential that inlaid lines and bandings should be allowed plenty of time to settle, for the contraction of the glue will pull the inlays below the surface if they are cleaned off level too soon. Work containing inlaid brass lines should be brushed over with dilute polish to protect the grain against fine brass-dust, while the lines can be scraped flush with a steel scraper and polished with finest silicon carbide paper.

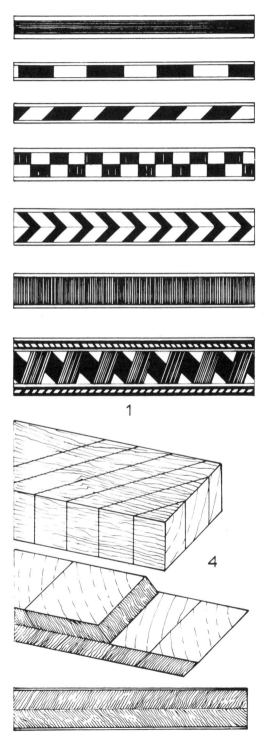

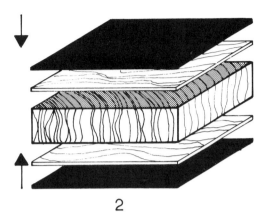

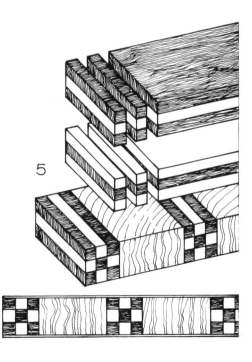

302 Building up bandings, etc.

INLAY-WORK

The general term *inlaying* covers the practice of inletting any one material into another material of different colour or composition, but more specifically *wood inlaying* is divided into *intarsia*, in which relatively thick sections are set into suitable depressions cut in the groundwork/ substrate, and *marquetry*, in which the pattern is built up of veneers or materials in veneer thickness and applied to the groundwork as an overlay. Confusion often persists between the two terms, for marquetry pictures which adopt a naturalistic approach are sometimes known as 'intarsia pictures', but in practice it is better to confine the term *inlay* to intarsia or cut-in work, and marquetry to veneered work.

Intarsia-work

Originally developed in the fourteenth century this process uses separate inlays of wood, ivory, bone, tortoiseshell, mother-of-pearl, brass, silver, etc. cut to shape, laid on the ground/ substrate, the outlines traced with a fine point and the appropriate recesses cut in with wood-carving tools, slightly bevelling the shoulders of the cuts to give a tight fit. Wood thicknesses are usually from ⅛ in (3 mm) to ¼ in (6 mm) thickness and can be levelled off flush after laying, but the more precious materials in thin sheets are laid on a bed of plaster of Paris and hide glue suitably coloured. Metal insets can be laid with hide glue if the surface is first rubbed with a slice of garlic to destroy the grease, or preferably with epoxy glue. The original intarsia-work employed arabesques and elaborate perspectives.

Marquetry-work

This was a later development of true inlay or intarsia-work, and the rendering was always much freer with scrolls, bunches of flowers, etc. covering the ground/substrate. Veneers or materials in veneer thickness are used, the pattern cut out, assembled and laid as a single sheet on a suitable ground. Professional cutters have evolved their own methods for the work is highly specialized, and while a good general craftsman could no doubt easily master the techniques of cutting and laying, the art lies in the preparation of the design and the selection, matching and shading of the veneers.

Cutting and laying marquetry-work

A full-size drawing of the design is necessary, done with a continuous fine line and coloured to represent the actual veneers used. Working copies of the drawing can be prepared either by tracing through with carbon paper, or more accurately by the traditional method of closely pricking through the lines with a fine needle. Several copies can be pricked at the same time, or the design can be printed through the perforations with a pounce-bag filled with finely powdered asphaltum which must then be heated to fuse the deposited powder, or rubbed through with a pad soaked with heelball and methylated spirit. If the design allows of it, two or more sheets of the materials to be used can be pinned or glued together with a waste sheet of veneer under to take the rag of the saw, and the printed design pasted on the top sheet. The whole of the pattern can then be cut out either on a marquetry-cutter's donkey or with the usual form of fret-saw, working on a V-notched table fixed to the bench. The finest jeweller's piercing saws with from 40 to 80 teeth to the inch (25 mm) according to the grade can be used, and wherever possible the saw cuts are made outside the line of the insets, and on the line of the background; the sheets are then separated and the complete pattern assembled on the master drawing, covered wtih a surface paper and laid in the usual manner. If, however, the design contains many separate pieces of different woods and differing grain directions, then each piece of veneer must be treated separately, the outline transferred to it, the piece sandwiched between waste veneer if there are delicate fibres to be supported, the piece cut, numbered and either taped to the surrounding pieces, or butt jointed with quick-setting Balsa cement or PVA glue. When the pattern is complete all traces of glue must be removed from the under face before laying, and some professional workers fill up slight gaps with a mixture of glue and veneer-dust. Local shading of the individual pieces to give chiaroscuro is achieved by scorching the wood in heated silver sand before they are assembled,

303 Marquetry panel in entrance hall of
Gallaher Ltd, London

but it must be skilfully done to be effective. As
the veneers are $\frac{1}{16}$ in (1.5 mm) or less in
thickness, the completed surface must be
carefully scraped and sanded with a circular
motion, and delicate insets may have to be
protected from the coloured dust of other insets
by coating with white french polish before
sanding.

A superb example of modern marquetry-
work which must surely equal the best examples
of any previous age was to be seen in the
reception hall and main entrance of Gallaher
Ltd's former offices in London. Figure 303,
kindly lent by Gallaher Ltd, can give only an
approximation of the wonderful richness of this
panel which is 16 ft (4.87 m) long and 3 ft
(0.91 m) high and composed of 70 native and
exotic timber species in 20,000 different pieces.
The selection, matching and cutting of the
veneers was carried out by Mr A. Dunn to
sketch designs prepared by Mr George Ramon
and drawn in detail by Mr F. Bellan. No staining
of any kind was used, and local shading was
done by the traditional hot-sand method.

Sand shading (marquetry-work)

The delicate shading often seen in traditional
marquetry-work is done by scorching the
veneer in a tray of hot sand. Each piece of
veneer is dipped for a few seconds only, and the
sand must be clean, sharp, fine silver sand
(obtainable from pet shops), uniformly heated.
For island shading within the body of the veneer
the sand should be heated in an old spoon and
poured on repeatedly from both sides, again for
a few seconds each time. After shading the
pieces should be moistened on the surfaces and
dried under a weight.

Parquetry-work

Geometrical patterns, squares, rectangles,
lozenges, etc., either inlaid, veneered or
overlaid, are known as 'parquetry-work',
typical examples of which are chessboards and
parquet flooring. The treatment is the same as
for any other inlay- or marquetry-work.

Boulle-work

Marquetry patterns comprising sheets of brass
and tortoiseshell in elaborate scroll-work and
foliage are known as Boulle-work (Buhl-work)
after the celebrated French marquetry-cutter
André-Charles Boulle (1642-1732) who
perfected the process. Thin sheets of
tortoiseshell and brass or silver, or boxwood

304 Box with veneered laburnum oysters with sycamore edging. Designer and maker: Richard Fyson

and blackwood-veneers, were pinned together with a waste veneer under to take the rag of the saw; the design was then glued to the top sheet and the whole pack cut at one operation with a very fine saw in a marquetry-cutter's donkey. The sheets were then separated and the components fitted together. As all the cutting was done simultaneously the waste of one sheet could obviously fit the waste of another sheet; thus in a simple assembly of, say, boxwood ground/substrate and blackwood scroll-work there will be a complete sheet of boxwood ground and black scroll-work, and another of black ground and box scroll-work. Antique examples exist in which one side of the cabinet is black on white and the other side white on black, and this economic use of the waste was known as *Boulle* and *counter Boulle*, although it was never practised in the finest work. In fact, although Boulle carried this composite cutting to perfection, skilled marquetry-cutters considered it greatly inferior to the traditional method of cutting each piece separately whereby the grain direction could be varied at will.

OYSTER-SHELL VENEERING

Thin slices about $\frac{1}{16}$ in (1.5 mm) thick cut transversely from the branches of lignum vitae, olive, laburnum, mulberry or walnut to yield an oyster-shell effect were often used in traditional furniture. The oysters can be cut and stacked with wood spacers between and weighted down, or short lengths of branch wood buried in dry sand, but the seasoning must be very gradual and prolonged if splitting and casting are to be avoided. They were either trimmed square or to an octagonal shape, carefully matched, coated with glue size to stop absorption, with a glued cover paper over to prevent them curling, and laid between cauls. Figure 301:7 shows the usual method of matching up but there is no reason why oysters of different sizes should not be laid in a random build-up (301:8). A modern example of oyster-shell veneering is shown in the photograph of a large cigarette-box in 304 designed and made by Mr Richard Fyson, which shows to advantage the careful selection, matching and patching of inevitable defects necessary in the finest work.

OVERLAY-WORK

A material which is laid *on* and not *in* another material or ground is known as *overlay*, and typical examples are the applied frets on solid groundworks or substrates in Chippendale cabinets, and the lavishly applied overlays of ebony and ivory in Italian and Dutch period work. In applying these frets the groundwork must not be glued for it would be impossible to clean off the surplus glue between the frets, therefore the glue is rolled out on a flat surface, the fret pressed on the glue, quickly transferred to the ground, pinned and weighted down.

Overlays of boards thicker than a veneer and applied to a ground of common boards to save valuable material are usually referred to as *facing-up* work, or *facings*.

MISCELLANEOUS MATERIALS

Mother-of-pearl can be obtained prepared for use in various qualities and colours, blue, pink and green being the most expensive. It can be cut with a jeweller's piercing saw and filed to shape, but should be backed with a temporary veneer or sheet of paper before cutting as some varieties are very brittle. If laid with hide glue it should be roughened with a file and any slight curvature taken up with plaster of Paris mixed in the glue. Very little pressure must be used, sufficient only to press the shell home flush with the surface, and final finishing is done with 10:0 grit abrasive paper, from which the fierceness of the cut has been knocked off by rubbing two sheets together, followed up by pumice powder and rottenstone. The pearl can be engraved by brushing over with warm wax, scratching through the wax when cold and pouring nitric acid into the scratches, after which mastic suitably coloured is run into the lines to complete the design. Tortoiseshell can be cut and laid in a similar fashion to pearl, and can be cleaned off by scraping and papering and then polishing with dry whiting or rottenstone. It is usual to colour the ground under the shell, or insert gold-foil underneath to increase the brilliance. Ivory is obtainable in fairly large pieces and can be turned, cut and shaped with normal woodworking tools, laid with normal glues and the surfaces flushed off with scraper and file followed up with fine paper and pumice powder, and polished with whiting on a chamois-leather buff. Bone and horn are fair substitutes in small sections but lack the wonderful depth and ripple of real ivory, while white plastics are only poor imitations, although valid materials in their own right if treated as such.

PLASTIC INLAYS

A method of inlaying wood, metal and other hard materials in a groundwork/substrate of suitably coloured polyester resin, first developed by William Mitchell at the Royal College of Art in London, is illustrated in the coffee-table shown in 305. The table, which was one of a series designed by the writer especially for this inlay, had the wood top inset 3/16 in (5 mm) in the yew framing. Cross-sections of various short ends of wood in the workshop—laburnum, Indian laurel, acacia, yew, grey sycamore, oak, brown oak and rosewood—were then sawn 1/4 in (6 mm) thick, broken up at random, spaced out on the ground/substrate and anchored with a little of the polyester resin used. A mix was then made up of resin, accelerator, hardener, and thixotropic medium, which allows a build up without creep or slide, coloured pale green with polyester pigments and poured over the assembly, working it into the gaps with a pointed stick. After hardening, the surface was levelled off flush with scrapers and belt sander, polished with silicon carbide paper and the whole table then sprayed with a clear catalyst finish. The completed table is successful because it treats the plastic as a material in its own right and not as a substitute for other materials, and although it has seen hard service over many years shows no signs of cracking, lifting or failure of any kind. Very oily woods (rosewood, etc.) should not be used for this type of inlay as the natural oil may inhibit the setting of the polyester resin. A photograph of the table-top with a broken-up laburnum oyster as a central motif is also shown (305B).

STORAGE OF VENEERS

All veneers should be stored flat in a dry, even atmosphere and protected from the light. Decorative veneers, curls, feathers, etc. intended for pattern-making should be numbered with chalk (not wax crayon) in the exact order of cutting and the ends taped to prevent splitting. Repeated handling of veneers should be avoided as much as possible, for they tend to become brittle with age and the wastage caused by careless storage and handling can be greater than the wastage incurred in laying.

Moisture contents

Moisture content at the time of laying should be the same as the groundwork/substrate, ideally in the neighbourhood of 8 per cent, but higher contents are not necessarily harmful provided both groundwork and veneer are equal and plenty of time is allowed for the completed surface to settle down.

305A   Coffee-table in English yew with mosaic top designed by William Mitchell Des.RCA.
Table designed by Ernest Joyce MSIA

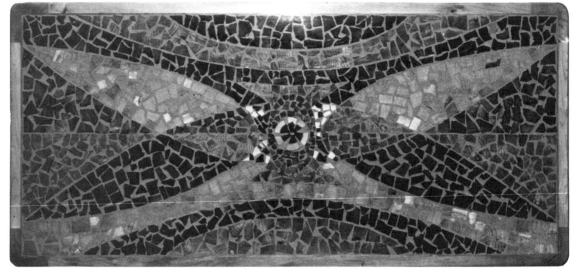

305B   Detail of mosaic top

33 Table lining

Hitherto a separate craft, the lining-in of inset leather or baize surfaces to table- and desk-tops was usually passed over to small specialist firms who also gold blocked the borders. The actual laying of the leather, etc. is now often done by the furniture-maker, with any gold border blocked in by a specialist. It should be pointed out in this connection that most leathers are now heavily dressed with synthetic resin lacquers during finishing which may or may not take the leaf or foil, and this should be established before laying.

Inset leather-tops are laid against a shoulder and flush with the surface (they can be very fractionally below but never above). The shoulder was originally formed by gluing on strips of saw-cut veneer, but as plywood tops are now usual a raised edge is used instead (306:1). Two methods of laying are practised: (*a*) the leather is cut oversize and laid from the centre outwards, using a felt-faced pad to smooth out the air pockets. The shoulders are then scored in with the back of a knife or the thumb-nail and the leather cut against a metal straight-edge. This method is very quick in the hands of an experienced worker who will often only score with the nail and trim off the surplus by eye alone. (*b*) The inset surface is carefully

measured, or if not truly square a stiff paper template is fitted and used as a pattern. The actual leather panel is then cut fractionally full in size, say ⅛ in (3 mm) over the length and the width of an average desk-top. Actual laying requires two pairs of hands, one to locate one end of the sheet in the exact position, the other to hold the other end of the sheet and gently lower it into place. It is then smoothed out from the centre, the edges tucked in tight against the shoulders and any surplus width gently eased away back towards the centre. This method is slower but has more chance of a neat finish if table lining is only occasionally done. If any edge tends to fly leaving a slight gap it can be pulled back into position, and held with fine steel dressmaking pins until the glue has set.

GLUING THE GROUNDWORK/SUBSTRATE

Hide glue, shoemakers' paste, dextrin, casein and *Cascamite One Shot* glue can be used for laying leather, leathercloths and baizes, while wood glue is useful for edges. Animal and paste glues call for very quick working, while if the surface is a large one it may be necessary to glue and lay half the sheet at a time. If the ground-

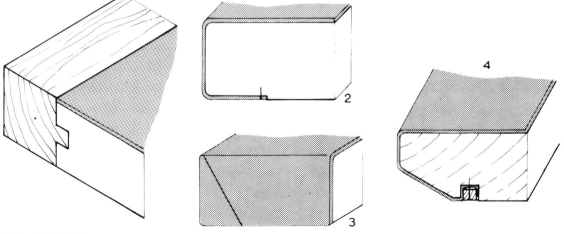

306   Table lining

work is aborbent it should be sized with weak hide glue, while casein and resin glues should be fairly thin and allowed to air dry until they have begun to tack before laying. Particular care must be taken to dust the work thoroughly with a stiff brush before spreading the glue which must be free from lumps or gritty particles, and to work the glue well into the shoulders of the inset. If air bubbles cannot be smoothed out before the glue finally tacks off, prick the bubbles with a needle and cover with a padded weight. Where the leather has to be worked over and round the edges (306:2) glue and lay up to the edges, glue the edges and coax the leather over, stretching it gently and evenly and temporarily securing it with fine pins. Rounded edges tend to puff or belly out, and the edges should be repeatedly smoothed over with the thumb. A flexible leather will probably flow over well-rounded corners, but sharp edges are always difficult and the leather will have to be cut. Figure 306:3 shows the most satisfactory method with the cut at an angle and not on the edge of the corner; while 306:4 illustrates a neat method of finishing off underneath, using a hardwood strip which is glued in after the leather has been fixed and allowed to dry. Leather can be worked round acute bends if it is first dampened, but the grain texture is lost and the colour may be affected, therefore it should be avoided if possible.

PVC leathercloths are laid in exactly the same way, but they must be cut to size if method (*b*) above is adopted as there is not the same measure of elasticity, while rounded corners will have to be tailored. Baize is also laid in similar fashion but certain precautions must be taken: there must be no surplus glue and pressure must be very gentle or the glue will soak through, leaving hard white patches which cannot be eradicated. Cheap quality cloths may also shrink back considerably as they dry, and a preliminary test should be made to determine the extent, if any, of the shrinkage.

34 Mouldings and lippings/edgings

The decline in the popularity of moulded sections dates from the introduction of plywoods and machine techniques, and is a good example of new materials and their manipulation influencing design. Mouldings are, however, both decorative and utilitarian, for subtle curved surfaces catch and reflect the light giving warmth and feeling, while softened angles are less easily damaged and more comfortable to handle. Current architectural styles worship severe functional restraint, but while rich mouldings may be temporarily out of fashion, they usually survive periodic neglect.

Traditional mouldings are developed from Greek examples based on ellipses and Roman examples on circles, but the classic geometric shapes are better suited to bold architectural features, and small-scale furniture mouldings are happier if drawn freehand, with due regard for the type of wood of which they are composed. For instance, fine-grained woods, mahogany, walnut, etc. call for delicate treatment, while coarse Gothic details would look ridiculous in any but strong, open-grained woods such as oak, chestnut and the like. In designing such elements, therefore, certain rules should be observed: (*a*) the sections must be in scale, i.e. in proprotion to the type, size and overall appearance of the carcass; (*b*) mouldings above eye level should protrude (307:20A), and below eye level recede, otherwise the effect will be lost, while undercut mouldings (307:21) should be boldly profiled; (*c*) composite mouldings (307:22) should be built up of alternate convex and concave profiles. These arbitrary rules can of course be broken, but only with discretion; and an example of bad profiling is the coarse reeded legs of some Victorian furniture in which the bold convex profiles of the reeds are placed side by side with no relieving flat between.

TYPES OF MOULDING

Traditional shapes are illustrated in 307 with alternative names inset in the sections where applicable. Certain details regularly occur and an astragal or nosing (5) becomes a torus bead with one flat (10), and a bead moulding with two flats (13), while a succession of parallel beads becomes a reeding (19), and a large flute (15) becomes a hollow (16). A flat is the slight member between two opposing curves (22), and a quirk (shift or turning) a right-angled projection (6, 10, etc.). Additionally, an astragal composed of two ellipses meeting at a point becomes a quirked bead because the two curves do not flow into each other.

CROSS-GRAIN MOULDINGS

One of the delights of antique walnut furniture is the rich cross-grained mouldings usually found in the best work. Some 30 years ago the fashion was revived, using cross-grain veneers over a solid core; but these mouldings, known as *waterfall*, obviously could have no sharp arrises, and the total effect was invariably third rate. Genuine cross-grain mouldings can be worked by hand and even by spindle-moulder/-shaper, provided the cutters are sharp and the feed-rate modest. Well-seasoned richly grained wood should be chosen; strips are then cut across the board, the ends matched up, cut square and hide glued to the edge of a waste board with a layer of thick paper between (307:23). The moulding can then be shaped in the usual way, adopting the normal precautions for cross-grained work, the glue-line split in the thickness of the paper, the paper soaked off and the moulded sections butt glued in their permanent positions, or, if practicable, the strips can be glued direct to the groundwork/substrate and then shaped. In theory, such mouldings should shrink and split open, but provided thoroughly dry wood is used and the sections are not too wide, the cross grain will accommodate a certain measure of shrinkage without parting at the joints.

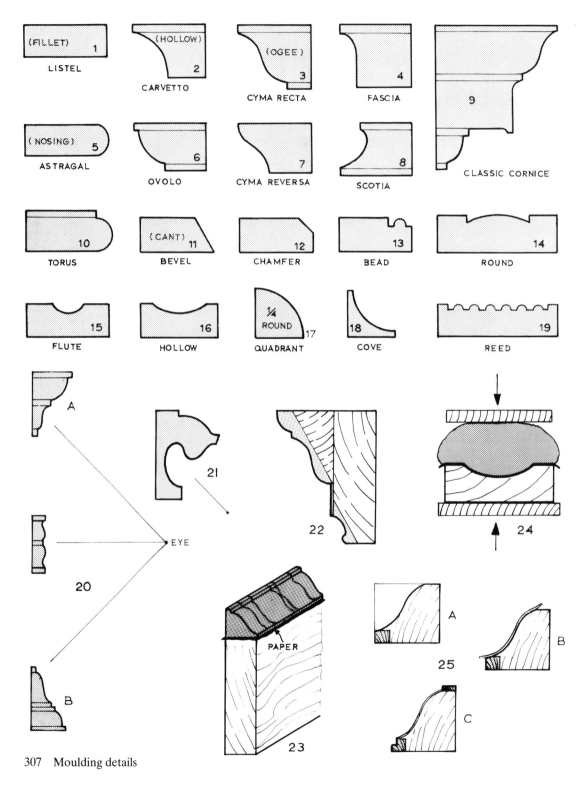

307 Moulding details

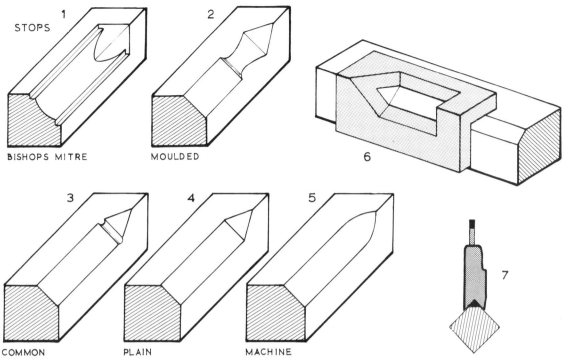

STOPS

1

BISHOPS MITRE

2

MOULDED

6

3

COMMON

4

PLAIN

5

MACHINE

7

308   Chamfers

COMPOSITE MOULDINGS

Faced-up mouldings of richly figured wood in antique furniture were usually wide in section and glued to a pine core (307:2), no doubt to save valuable wood but also to cut down shrinkage in sections worked cross grain.

VENEERED MOULDINGS

Where veneered mouldings have to be veneered and a vacuum-bag press is not available, the traditional sandbag method can be employed. The bag should be made up out of twill or coarse linen sturdy enough to withstand pressure but supple enough to follow the curves, and filled with fine dry silver sand which has been thoroughly sieved or screened. If hide glue is used the bag must be warmed throughout to the melting temperature of the glue, or used cold for synthetic glues, carefully positioned with a generous overhang and packed down. If there is sufficient volume of sand the weight alone may be adequate, although resin glues

may require a flat board laid along the length and cramped/clamped in position (307:24). Hide glue is very suitable for veneered flutings which are stopped at each end, as the heat and moisture will soften the veneer sufficiently to follow the compound curves. If a moulding to be veneered has sharp corners or arrises then a composite assembly should be adopted, and 307:25A, B, C show the stages.

CHAMFERS

Chamfers must be scrupulously laid out and cleanly worked if they are to be effective. They should be gauged in pencil, allowing for an equal amount of wood to be removed from both sides of the corner, worked with bullnose rabbet-plane, chamfer or flat-faced spoke-shave, scraper, flat file, etc. and checked in the length with a metal straight-edge. The ends are usually stopped and various forms are illustrated in 308:1-5, while 308:6 shows a simply constructed hardwood template which will give a constant angle to the slope of the stops. An old-type wooden chamfer-plane is shown in 308:7 which can be made up out of a

327

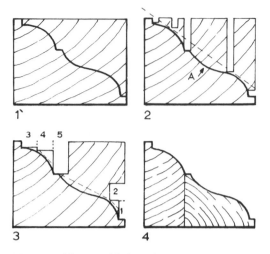

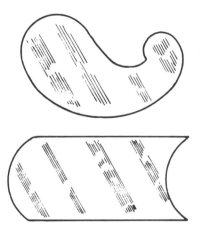

309 Working moulded section

310 Shaped scrapers

beech block about 5 in (127 mm) long and 1 in (25 mm) thick, or a standard wood rabbet plane can be converted. A square edged iron is used which is set to project to the depth of the chamfer, and the strokes must be gentle or the iron will tend to dig in. This type of plane can only work in the middle of the length of a stopped chamfer, but is useful for establishing the cut which can then be extended to the stops with a bullnose rabbet-plane.

WORKING MOULDINGS

Some form of spindle-moulder/-shaper or high-speed router is almost indispensable in any trade workshop, but where such facilities do not exist or the length of moulding required hardly justifies grinding a cutter blank and setting up a machine, then hand methods must be used. Very few craftsmen now own a set of moulding-planes, nor are they freely obtainable, while the scratch stock is hardly suitable for deep mouldings. In working the moulding shown in 309:1 much of the rough work can be done by making a succession of saw cuts (309:2) and then planing off to the dotted line; or working a series of grooves (309:3) in the order stated, as a firm shoulder must be left for the plough-plane fence. If the capacity of the plane allows it additional grooves can be worked, but the number shown will probably be the limit, and here again the waste is planed off as in 309:2.

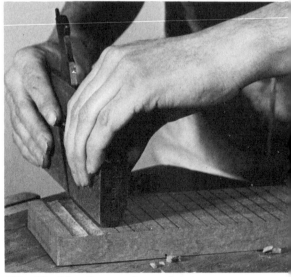

311 Sanding edge with shaped rubbing block

312 Moulding flutes to drawer front

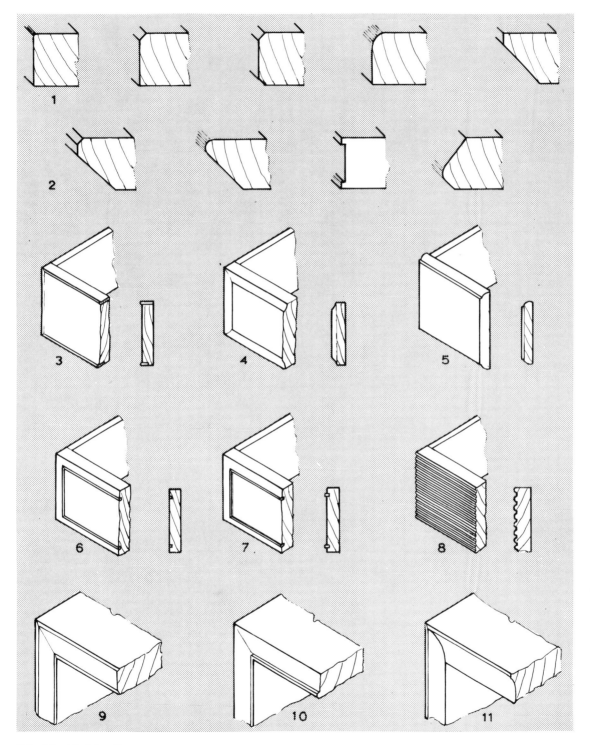

313 Moulded details

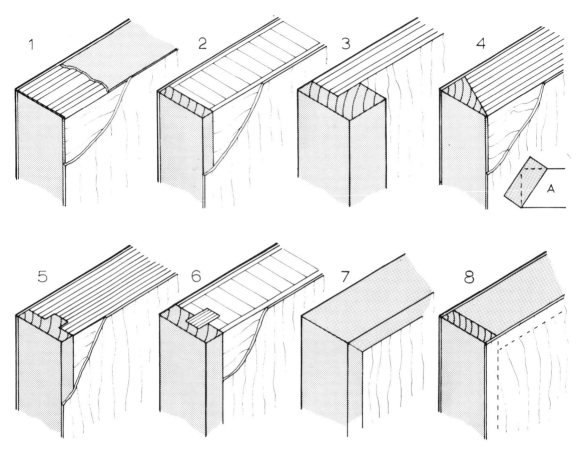

314 Lippings/edgings

Final shaping will have to be done with bullnose rabbet- or shoulder-plane, chisel or scraper, and the hollow (309:2A) worked with a gouge or scraper ground to a suitable curve, shown in 310, while it will pay to make shaped rubbers out of pine blocks for final sanding (311). If a spindle-moulder is used it will be more usual to form the moulding in two sections (309:4), thus avoiding heavy cuts.

FLUTINGS, REEDINGS, ETC.

Flutings can be worked with a scratch stock if small in section (see *Moulded legs*, p. 209), but wider flutings must be cut with a gouge or formed with a suitable round moulding-plane if available, and 312 illustrates a typical fluting worked cross-grain on a drawer front by the latter method. If necessary, battens can be cramped/clamped across the face of the work to

form a guide for the plane, but the example shown was worked entirely without guides. The flutes were laid out with pencil, the cross-flutes worked first and the half-fluting to the surrounds worked afterwards to take out any chipped edges.

Various moulded details are illustrated in 313: 1-2 are carcass or table-top treatments; 3-8 show drawer fronts and 9-11 carcass edges.

LIPPINGS/EDGINGS

Exposed edges of plywood, laminboard, chipboard, etc. must be masked or edged, although in the cheapest work such edges are sometimes filled and stained or painted with water-based pigments (poster paint, etc.) and then polished. The usual procedure in medium-quality work is to use edgings of veneer (314:1), adopting some form of strip heating to set the glue rapidly, and relying on the face veneers to clip the edges of the edge veneers, but these are not altogether satisfactory, for the fractional creep of the alternate grain in plywood laminates will tend to throw off the veneer, which will then blister and chip over a period of time. Solid edgings relying only on the glue to hold them on plywood constructions are also subject to the same defect, for although not so easily damaged they are more liable to split off as they do not have the elasticity of thin veneers. However, solid edgings applied to the long grain of laminboard cores or to particle board edges are relatively permanent (314:2). Where a thin plywood top has to be reinforced a thick solid edge can be rebated/rabbeted over (314:3), and the increased gluing area will hold it in position. An alternative solid edge is shown in 314:4, with the inset (A) the method of working, but the advantages are only minimal and admittedly the best methods are tongued edges worked in the solid (314:5) or with loose plywood tongues (314:6). These can be veneered over (314:5) provided the width of the edge on the face is not more than about 3/16 in (5 mm) (for wider edges will shadow or telegraph through in time), or left to show as a border (314:6). They can be mitred as in 314:7, which is the neatest finish, or allowed to run through (314:8), in which case the end edgings are glued on first and the side tongues trimmed back to fit.

Edgings which are to be veneered over present no problems in working for they can be fitted and worked off level with the ground-

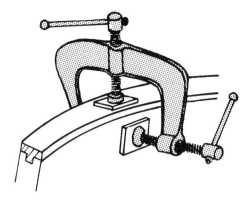

315   Edge cramp/clamp

work/substrate when dry, but they should be given plenty of time to settle as the water in the adhesive may cause temporary swelling up of the edges which will sink back later. On the other hand border edgings will have to be accurately worked, fractionally full and with the tongues truly central. The proud edges on the faces will then have to be eased back very carefully with a finely set try-plane working diagonally from the centre of the panel outwards to avoid digging in to the veneered faces, and the last tissue-thin shavings removed with a steel scraper. This method of planing outwards to the edges and not inwards will also prevent any dubbing over of the edges, as the body of the plane will be well supported on the flat panel. A useful cramp/clamp for applying solid edgings is the edge cramp (315).

35 Curved work

Permanent curves in wood can be achieved by the following methods:

1 Cutting to shape from the solid timber
2 Steam bending
3 Coopering
4 Saw kerfing
5 Laminating thin sections together

CURVES FROM SOLID WOOD

The process of finding wood with grain that naturally follows the curve required goes back centuries. It was this tradition that led to the oak forests of Britain being scoured for timber which would naturally supply the structural curves which were necessary for roof stresses and boat building. Sadly, because of industry's demand for straight-grained, easily worked wood, it is more difficult today to find these natural curves. It is this shortage of naturally curved timber that has led to an increase in the use of the other methods, and laminating is now the main technique used to achieve curved shapes, especially where any quantity is required.

STEAM BENDING

Any piece of wood bent or bowed within the limits of its normal stress range, i.e. where the neutral axis between the stretched convex face and the compressed concave face is roughly equal (316:1) will revert to its normal shape immediately the strain is released, owing to the natural elasticity of its fibres. If the limiting stress according to the wood species is exceeded (316:2) some permanent deformation will occur, but there is always a danger that the fibres will be disrupted (316:3). If, however, the wood is rendered semi-plastic either by heating it with live steam or immersing it in boiling water or heated wet sand, its compressibility ratio will be greatly increased, and provided it is locked in position until the fibres have cooled

and dried it will set rigid to the desired curve. There will be some recovery as the created internal stresses equalize themselves, but while this slight tendency to straighten out cannot be precisely calculated, a test-piece in the same species and of the same dimension will usually show the extent of the movement.

In practice prolonged immersion in boiling water or heated wet sand is never as efficient as steam bending, and the latter is to be preferred. The technique is straightforward and all that is required is a sufficient head of steam at atmospheric pressure to heat the wood thoroughly to 212° F (100° C), and to maintain that temperature for at least 45 minutes for every inch of thickness, i.e. a 1¼ in (32 mm) section will require approximately one hour's steaming. A simple apparatus using a large kettle or oil-drum, a source of heat (Primus stove, coke fire, etc.), a length of rubber hosepipe and a wooden box or metal or earthenware pipe sealed at each end with wooden bungs is shown in 316:4, and is quite sufficient for the occasional bend. Production in quantity would, of course, call for more sophisticated methods if consistent quality with low waste factors are to be achieved.

Bending methods

Immediately the wood is soft enough, i.e. uniformly heated throughout, it is taken from the steam chest and bent by hand, or by mechanical means if of heavy section, round a suitable former or form. A rough and ready method is to use sturdy pegs driven into a board, but this is inclined to bruise the wood, the bend may not flow easily between the pegs and the ends are inclined to split as they dry. A more sophisticated method is shown in 316:5 in which an 18 swg spring steel strap, slightly wider than the wood section, greatly minimizes the actual disruption of the fibres in the stretched convex face, permitting bends of much smaller radii. The strap is firmly anchored to heavy wood or metal back plates which prevent the ends

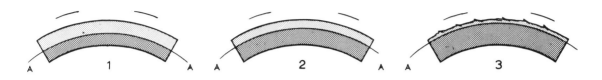

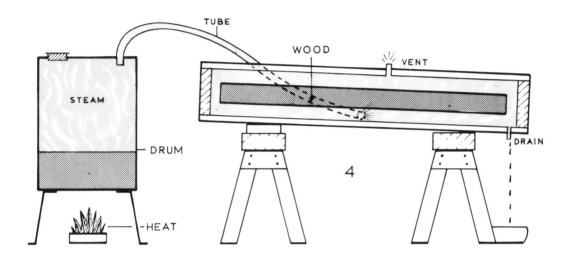

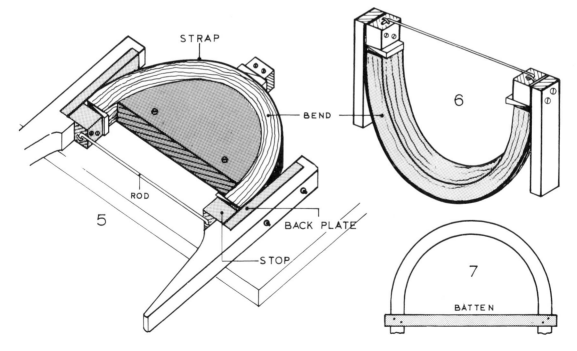

316   Solid wood bending

swivelling, and if oak or other acid timber is to be bent then the strap should have an interleaving of thin aluminium sheet or other protective material. End stops fixed to the back plate are also necessary to keep the strap tight against the bend; they should be spaced to allow a certain fractional creep in the bend length (not exceeding 2 per cent) with the slackness taken up with wooden wedges.

Detachable handles can be clipped or bolted to the back plates, or the plates can be extended to form handles for easy manipulation, and once the bend is completed it can be anchored by a tie-rod and lifted from the former. It should then be placed in a dry heated atmosphere to set for about 12 hours, after which it can be freed from restraint and allowed to settle naturally for about 2 weeks. With acute bends it is always better to leave the metal strap and tie-rod in position during the actual setting time (316:6), but simple bends may need only a batten nailed across (316:7), thus releasing the strap for further use.

Bends of fairly large radii usually tend to straighten out a little after they have dried. The recovery movement is not calculable, and it is usual to bend to slightly smaller radii to allow for the movement, but bends of small radii may tend to turn inwards, although they should not move once they have set. Very green timber will obviously bend more readily than dry seasoned wood, although hydraulic pressures induced in the moisture-choked cells may cause extensive rupturing, while old dry wood is usually too stubborn or too brittle to bend well; therefore the ideal is probably partially seasoned wood with a moisture content of around 25 per cent which the steam heating and subsequent drying will further season to within acceptable limits. Shaped, moulded or round section timber can be steam bent, but some deformation of profiles and slight flattening of rounded faces against the strap must be expected, therefore it is better to bend first and profile after whenever possible. Woods vary greatly in their bending properties, with elm outstanding and home-grown ash, beech and oak fairly equal. Comparative minimum radii of curvature in inches to be expected from (*a*) supported and (*b*) unsupported sections 1 in (25 mm) thick are as follows:

MINIMUM RADII OF CURVATURE

Timber	With supporting metal strap		Without strap	
	in	mm	in	mm
English ash	2.5	63	12.0	305
English beech	1.5	38	13.0	330
Imported birch	3.0	76	17.0	432
Dutch elm	0.4	10	9.5	241
English oak	2.0	50	13.0	330
Honduras mahogany	12.0	305	28.0	711
Burmah teak	16.0	406	28.0	711
European spruce	30.0	762	—	—

No precise data are available for English walnut but the writer has always found mild, straight-grained walnut roughly comparable to oak or beech, ebony fairly malleable and even oily rosewood capable of simple curvatures if taken in several stages. The quoted figures given in the table are taken from the Forest Products Research Laboratory data.

317   Chair in steam bent ash by David Colwell

334

COOPERING

This traditional method of building curves or cylinders is best illustrated by the traditional beer barrel. The basic method involves bevelling sections of wood to form curves, and it has been undergoing quite a revival in small workshop production. Many of James Krenov's designs incorporate coopered doors.

Bevelled and coopered joints

Bevelled joints are edge joints at any preset angle other than 45°, at which angle they are termed *mitre* joints, while coopered joints are usually taken to mean several bevelled joints assembled together, as in coopered barrels. Both terms are, therefore, in essence synonymous. Their application is in splay corners and in cylindrical falls, bow fronts, pillars, columns, etc. built up from solid sections and rounded to shape. They can be tongued together, but are more often merely glued, butted together, rubbed or cramped/clamped and later reinforced with glue blocks, although good joints should not necessarily need them. The usual difficulty is to plane the edges at the required angle. It can be done easily enough on the overhand-planer or jointer with the fence set to the required angle, but hand-planing in a vice and using an adjustable bevel instead of a try-square for testing presents some problems, for it is very easy to lose width if both edges have to be bevelled, thus forming a taper section. A good method is to use support pieces cut at the correct angle temporarily nailed to the planing-board. If the angle of the splay or bevel required is 67½°, as in building up an octagonal column, then the support pieces must be 22½° to make up the required 90° at which the plane works (318:3). (Six sides will require angles of 60° and 30°, ten sides 72°

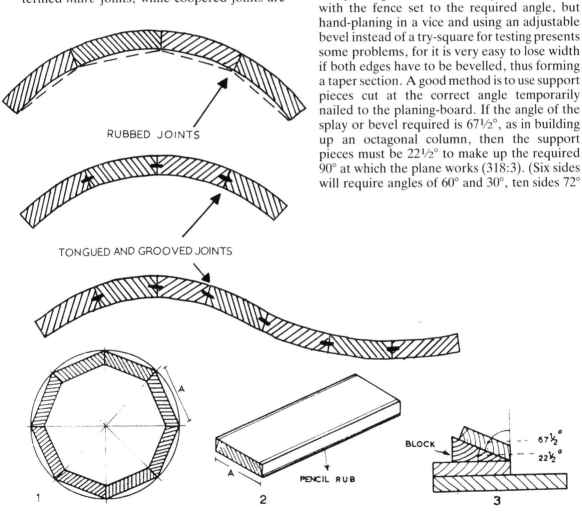

RUBBED JOINTS

TONGUED AND GROOVED JOINTS

BLOCK

67½°

22½°

1   2   PENCIL RUB   3

318 Bevelled and coopered joints

and 18° and twelve sides 75° and 15°). In order to obtain the correct angle of any splay it is first necessary to draw an end view full size (318:1) and set the adjustable bevel, template or protractor accordingly. Having ascertained the correct angle it should then be drawn at each end of the board to be bevelled, and the pencil should also be rubbed along the leading or base edge (318:2). Each section must be to exact width and truly parallel, and the last fine shaving taken off should just—but only just— take out the pencil-rubbing on the base edge, leaving only a darkened arris or corner.

Rubbed joints glued with hide glue present little difficulty, and in building up an octagonal column the eight pieces are first glued in pairs and carefully stood on end or otherwise supported, so that there is no strain on the joints while the glue sets. The quarter sections are then connected into half sections, and finally the two halves are glued together, first trying them in the dry state, for fractional errors do creep in and some adjustment may be necessary. If the bevels are to be glued with resin glue, supporting cradles may have to be used for cramping/clamping up, or the pieces temporarily held with adhesive tape, bound with thick string and wedges driven under the twine to pull the assembly up. A fairly slow-setting glue should be used, for with all the pieces assembled together at the same time the final adjustment must not be hurried, and the cross-distances between the internal flats should be carefully checked. If the column is to be rounded a cardboard circle to the exact finished shape should be used for marking out the ends.

An alternative method of cramping/clamping up splay corners sometimes advocated is to glue temporary wood lugs or blocks to the outer faces at such an angle that the cramp gives a direct pull without slip, but it is a laborious and somewhat uncertain process, and should only be adopted as a last resort. Much can be done with thick blind cord or twine, looped round and twisted with a stick (see Mitre, scribed and scarf joints, Chapter 20) for the pull exerted is fairly considerable. Pads of thick rubber or felt will sometimes prevent a metal cramp slipping on an awkward slope, and it is always worth trying an assembly in the dry state to see whether the cramps will bite.

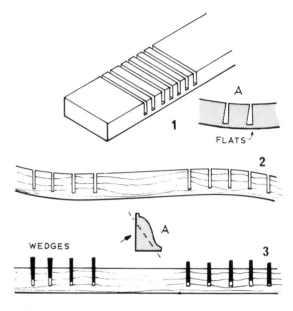

319   Saw kerfing

SAW KERFING

This traditional method is not now used to any great extent in production furniture-making, but it still has an important role in smaller workshops, as it is often a more economic method in one-off work than laminating. In practice a series of saw cuts are run down to within about ⅛ in (3 mm) of the outer face (319:1) according to the wood species, and the closer the cuts are the easier the wood will bend, with hard oak requiring a spacing of ¼ in (6 mm) or less. There is a tendency for the bend to form a series of small flats at (A) not discernible in the white but magnified under a gloss polish, therefore highly finished surfaces should not be bent by this method. It is, however, useful for bending sheets of stiff plywood or laminboard and 319:2, 3 show its application to lengths of very hard English maple moulding (A) which warped badly after they had been worked. Saw cuts were run in 319:2 down to the dotted line (A), the moulding G-cramped/C-clamped down to a level surface and small glued wedges inserted as 319:3. Plenty of time was allowed for the glue to harden and the straightened moulding gave no further trouble. (See also Restoration, repairs and wood finishing, Part X).

LAMINATING

LAMINATED BENDS

Thin strips or laminations of wood glued and bent to a curve will not revert to their former shape because each strip is in effect concentric and of fractionally smaller radius than its immediate neighbour which the adhesive will lock firmly in position. Here again practical application is straightforward and equally applicable to fairly large surfaces, door and drawer fronts, etc., or to square sections as in chair-work. The thickness of the individual laminae must depend on the limiting radius of curvature of the particular timber employed, but as a general rule thickness should not exceed $1/8$ in (3 mm). Thinner laminae of veneer thickness $1/32$ in (0.7 mm) and up will yield stiffer, heavier laminations but will take much longer to build up and require more glue. Gap-filling adhesives should be used, preferably synthetic resin, although animal glues (hide, casein) are dependable but more troublesome. The laminae are not crossed as in plywood manufacture for maximum strength is required in the long-grain direction, but are laid the same way and in the same strict order as cut from the log (321:1) with the grains exactly matched as far as possible. If the grain directions in the individual sheets are allowed to cross as in 321:2, the glue will inhibit any actual shrinkage movement as indicated by the direction of the arrows, but the latent opposing forces will endeavour to exercise a turning movement, subjecting the assembly to torsion, and twisting or warping may result. In theory, and provided the grains are straight and matched throughout, it hardly matters whether the number of plies is odd or even, but in practice an odd number of laminae, 9, 11, 13, etc., dependent on the required thickness is generally used, and some slight shrinkage across the width must be allowed for as with solid wood.

Curly grain veneer should be avoided, for the completed assembly will tend to curve with the curvature of the grain, and spiral grain to twist badly. For this reason a predominantly ductile wood like elm is rarely used because of the wildness of its grain, while beech with its straight and even fibres is a firm favourite. As

320   Chair made in laminated ash from one shaped former/form only, by John Varley

337

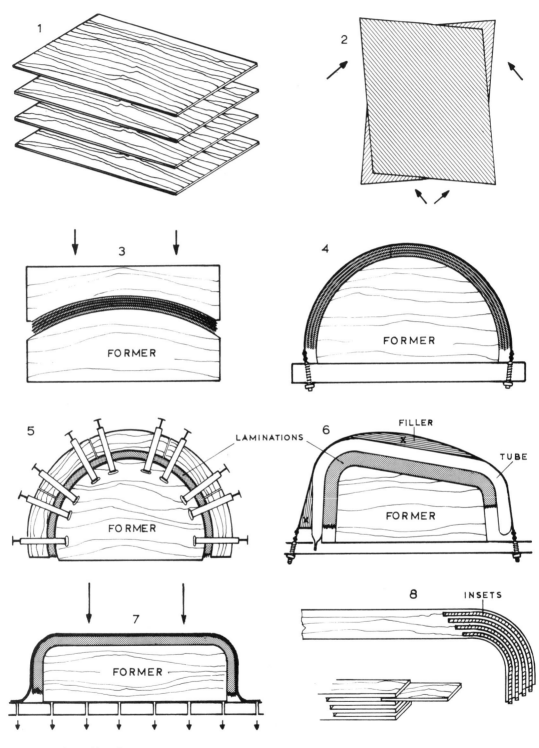

321 Laminated bends

with plywood and laminboard, etc., sheets and square sections will be stronger and stiffer than solid boards in the same thickness.

Laminated insets

Where the required wood member is for the most part straight with a curved portion at the end, the bend can be achieved by saw kerfing the timber and inserting glue-coated laminae of the exact thickness to fill the gaps. The saw cuts should be staggered in the length and spaced within the capacity of the separate tongues to bend to the desired radius. Figure 321:8 makes the process clear.

Laminating compound spapes

Thin malleable veneers will sometimes conform to very shallow curves in two directions, as on the surface of a large sphere, and such double curvature can be assisted by pre-moistening and pressing between heated cauls or formers/forms, but the amount of stretch must be within the elastic limits of the wood plies otherwise the veneers will crease and crumple like a sheet of stiff paper. In traditional compound work soft burr veneers, notably burr walnut, were first soaked in boiling water and laid with the hammer, using very thin hide glue and going over the work repeatedly until complete adhesion was achieved. Stiffer veneers or more acute curves require actual tailoring of the sheets to fit, and in one method the veneers are either cut into strips or 'fashioned' to fit the curve so that the butt edges of the cutout notches fit exactly. The first sheet is then stapled down to a wooden former, the next sheet glued and applied, removing the tacks in the first sheet and restapling through the top sheet. Each tailored sheet is treated similarly, removing the tacks and restapling, and leaving the tacks in the last sheet until the glue has set. In another method each sheet is fashioned as before, and the tailored cuts soldered together with hide glue and formaldehyde, using a heated iron to set the glue. Cold glues are used for assembly and the top sheet is strapped with adhesive tape. Templates can be used for cutting the veneers, but several will be required as each sheet will differ fractionally and the tailored cuts should be staggered wherever possible.

Heat setting of bends

A range of slow hardeners is available for synthetic resin glues which will allow plenty of time for complex assemblies in handwork. For production-work low-voltage strip heating is used extensively to accelerate the setting time, and this releases the formers/forms for rapid turnovers.

Continuous strip laminations

In quantity production such work is usually undertaken by specialist firms using sophisticated processes and considerable technical know-how. Figure 323 shows a range of production bends.

Bending plywoods, etc.

Fairly stiff resin-bonded plywood to WBP specification can be bent more readily if one side is wetted, or conversely the other side heated. Much depends on the thickness and number of plies, the direction of the bend in relation to the grain direction of the stout hearted core, and to the timber species of which the plywood is composed, therefore actual tests are necessary. If the plywood sheet is too stiff to take the curve two or more sheets of thin plywood to make up the thickness can be glued and bent between simple formers/forms or merely stapled together as practised in boat hull building, for each sheet becomes concentric and the adhesive will lock the fibres and hold the curve. An admirable plywood for this purpose is $1/16$ in (1.5 mm) birch three-ply, readily obtainable, which can be rolled up like a sheet of thin cardboard. Heat softening of wood was well known to traditional craftsmen, who bent their boxwood lines for delicate inlay (purfling) by repeatedly passing them over a heated metal pipe or rod.

PRESSING METHODS

Thin sheets or veneers can be pressed in simple male and female formers/forms (321:3), or over

322   Dining chairs by Robert Williams of Pearl Dot. The graceful backs to this design are tapered in thickness as well as being laminated

323　Finishing laminated shapes at the factory of Alesbury Brothers Limited.　(By courtesy of CIBA [ARL] Ltd)

324　Bending beech chair backs.　(By courtesy of Ercol Furniture Ltd)

a male former only in a vacuum-bag press (321:7). Square section laminations can be bent and pressed with metal straps terminating in screw bolts over a male former (321:4), or with segmented female formers G-cramped/ C-clamped in position as 321:5 which will pull the ends in to the curve. Pressure should be applied from the top centre outwards. An inflatable rubber hose can also be used (321:6), but where a straight section meets a curve there is a tendency for the straight to puff out at (X,X) and shaped wood fillers should be used.

One of the best examples of laminated work is the grand piano, which must be made to exacting standards, be immensely strong, rigid and unaffected by the severest climatic conditions. The craft is highly specialized but in essence the case-work is pure cabinet-making. The heart of the piano is the soundboard of quarter sawn Sitka spruce dried to a moisture content of 6 per cent and then planed to thickness, tongued and grooved, glue jointed,

sanded to final dimensions and then stored in a kiln at 100°F (38°C) for two weeks. It is then cut to shape, shrunk in an oven at 150°F (66°C) for up to three hours, which slightly bows the board, before gluing on the ribs which are pressed into position with lance-wood 'go-bars'. The bridges of quarter sawn beech are then added, and the completed soundboard is then glued to the supporting belt or inner rim composed of eight $\frac{3}{16}$ in (5 mm) Parana pine laminations curved in a shaped 'buck' or jig. The separate shaped outer bend or rim, which is the chief external feature of the piano, consists of six $\frac{1}{8}$ in (3 mm) laminations veneered both sides; while sides and top are of mahogany core with $\frac{3}{32}$ in (2 mm) obeche strapping veneers and face veneer over; bottom of three deal laminations $\frac{5}{8}$ in (16 mm) thick; and panels in veneered particle board for greater dimensional stability. Keyboard cover or 'fall' is composed of solid mahogany strips turned to shape and veneered in a vacuum-dome press, while the heavy legs and head blocks are built up of seven thick laminations double veneered. The wrest plank which receives the tuning pins is made up of three transverse and two longitudinal laminations of quarter sawn beech or Rock Maple dried to 6 per cent. Resin glues are used throughout, e.g. Aerolite R with CHW hardener and L48 gap-filling hardener, and Aerolite 301 with GBPX hardener. Prior to the advent of synthetic resin glues pianos for export to tropical countries were composed of solid woods elaborately screwed together.

HEAT ACCELERATION OF GLUE SETS

While all types of glue set faster in warm atmospheres, thermoplastic glues, i.e. heat-melting glues such as hide glue, will soften or liquefy under pronounced heat; but thermosetting glues will cure much more rapidly either by quicker evaporation of the moisture content, as in modified animal glues, or by a definite heat reaction in the case of synthetic resin glues. As this rapid acceleration of glue sets is of great importance to furniture-manufacturers seeking quick release of expensive tools, jigs and equipment, considerable research has been directed into the study of the most effective methods of applying heat without scorching the wood or disrupting its fibres, and various processes have been perfected which are now used extensively in industry for edge banding, laminating, scarfing, veneering and general assembly-work. It should be pointed out, however, that while the various processes are simple enough to operate, the more sophisticated methods require the initial services of skilled electricians and expert jig-makers, and as such are only applicable to production in quantity. It is, therefore, proposed to refer to them in broad outline only.

Various methods of applying heat to glue-lines are practised: (a) space heating of the surrounding air by any convenient heat source (hot-air blowers, radiant heat sources, etc.) which relies upon the conductivity of the warmed-up wood to transmit sufficient heat to cure the glue; (b) contact heating, also actively heating the wood substance either by hot cauls, steam or electrically heated platens or strip heaters (low-voltage heating). (Low-voltage

heating of glue-lines was first perfected by Aero Research Ltd [now CIBA/ARL Ltd] in 1939, and was used extensively in the production of war-time *Mosquito* aircraft, gliders and assault craft). (c) radio-frequency heating, whereby the wood molecules are actively distorted and rotated, thus causing friction and inducing heat according to the electrical resistance of the materials (wood and glue).

Of these methods only low-voltage and radio-frequency heating require further explanation.

Low-voltage (LF) heating

This method relies upon the conductivity of the wood to transmit heat from the contact elements to the glue-line. The actual elements can be 26 gauge stainless steel or mild sheet steel plated against corrosion, and are heated by low-voltage high-amperage currents from a suitable stepdown transformer giving a range of tappings of low voltages suitable for normal work. The heat is generated by the resistance of the metal sheet to the passage of the current, and while stainless steel has more resistance and therefore more heat generated for a given power-supply, mild steel is cheaper and more readily obtainable. In practice, therefore, narrow elements up to 6 in (152 mm) wide used for edge banding, etc. are generally in mild steel, while wider elements are made of stainless steel, otherwise the amperage required to attain the degree of heat necessary to cure the glue would probably be in excess of the capacity of the transformer.

The metal sheets or 'elements', which can be either flat or curved to conform to whatever shape of jig is used, are laid in contact with the work, and it has been established in practice that various power ratings per square foot are necessary for differently shaped elements.

It follows, therefore, that as the amperage increases rapidly with the width of the element, some means must be adopted of reducing the amount of current required, and two standard methods are used. As the voltage requirements are low the length of the element can be increased at the expense of the width, either by (a) connecting a series of narrow strips of identical width with brass plates, nuts and bolts (325:1) so that the square element now becomes a continuous ribbon, or (*b*) cutting slots in a square sheet alternately from each side to form the continuous ribbon (325:2). If the latter method is adopted the ends of the cuts must be pronged as shown in 325:4 with each prong one-third of the width (W) and at an angle (A) of 90° to each other, or local hot spots will occur and the end of the strip will be much cooler. For all practical purposes method (*a*) is better, but whichever is used the strips must be identical in width, and cable connections, brass plates, bolts, etc. clean and firmly seated. Measurement of the effective temperature in any part of the continuous strip can be made with a thermo-couple; while paints and crayons which change colour when the temperature reaches certain values are obtainable.

Jigs and platens for LF heating

Narrow strip elements can be laid directly against the veneer or laminate in edge banding, etc. but some softening is often necessary to absorb inequalities. If a strip of old bag press rubber is available this can be placed either between the element and the veneer or against the pressure member, with a thin piece of heat-resistant material to conserve the heat. Figure 325:3 shows a typical disposition. Continuous strip elements (325:1, 2) in panel form cannot be laid directly against the veneer as there are gaps between the strips, and in order to spread the pressure a sheet of 20 gauge aluminium is often used with an interleaving of ¹⁄₁₆ in (1.5 mm) laminated plastic to insulate the strips. The elements can be attached to the wooden pressure former with again a thin layer of some type of heat-resistant material to conserve the heat, and a softening pad if necessary (325:5). Platens or jigs can be made of plywood or blockboard on a rigid softwood foundation, and shaped to fit for curved work. Pressure must be positive and of the order of 50 lb per sq. in (3.515 Kgf/cm²), for inadequate pressures will allow thick glue-lines to form which will boil under heat, forming an air-filled froth which will eventually collapse. Raising the pressure naturally raises the boiling-point of the glue, and if 50 lb per sq. in (3.515 Kgf/cm²) cannot be attained then the amount of heat will have to be reduced well below the boiling-point

of the glue at the particular pressure applied, with consequent longer pressing times. With the working temperature of the element within the range 212°F (100°C) to 230°F (110°C), which is well below the scorching temperature of the wood, a normal synthetic resin glue will set in about 30 seconds plus the time taken for the heat to travel from the element to the glue-line. A general rule for this heat transfer is 1 min. per mm of thickness separating the element from the furthest glue-line up to a total of 6 mm, and 1½ min. per mm for thickness up to 12 mm; therefore a built-up lamination 12 mm thick with core veneers 2 mm thick and face veneer 1 mm thick will take 11 × 1½ = 16½ min., plus the actual setting time of the glue. For thicknesses over 12 mm it is better to place elements on either side of the lamination, in which case the time is calculated for only half the thickness. In constructional work where there is a considerable thickness of timber in the joint it may only be necessary to cure the glue part way into the joint before it is removed from the jig or press, and to allow residual heat to set the remainder, always providing no great stresses are involved, otherwise the joint will spring. Care must be taken in the choice of glue for all low-voltage heating, for a very fast-working glue may have a tendency to precure before the pressure has built up sufficiently, particularly with hand-operated screw presses or jigs, and in case of doubt the advice of the manufacturers should be sought.

Although low-voltage installations are inexpensive and very economical in power they are, as already mentioned, more applicable to quantity production, for individual elements will have to be made up for each particular platen or jig, calling for the services of both jig-maker and electrician; but a heated platen for a standard single daylight screw-operated veneer-press can easily be made which will give all the advantages of a hot press for flat veneering in a small workshop. Another technique is the incorporation of a length of resistance or *Eureka* wire in a tongued and grooved joint during assembly, which when coupled to a step-down transformer will heat the glue sufficiently for the cramps/clamps to be withdrawn within a few minutes; the ends of the wire are then snipped off with the length embedded in the

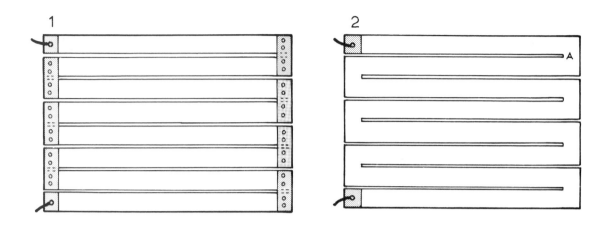

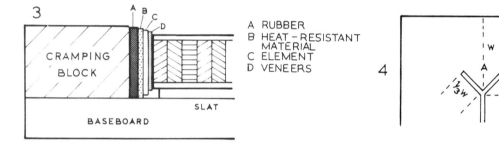

3

CRAMPING
BLOCK

BASEBOARD

SLAT

A RUBBER
B HEAT–RESISTANT
MATERIAL
C ELEMENT
D VENEERS

4

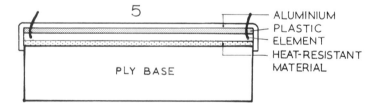

5

PLY BASE

ALUMINIUM
PLASTIC
ELEMENT
HEAT-RESISTANT
MATERIAL

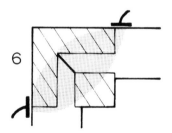

6

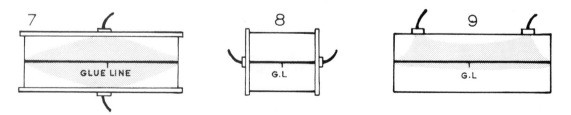

7

GLUE LINE

8

G.L

9

G.L

325   Glue-line heating

joint unnoticeable. The voltage requirements will depend upon both the thickness and the length of the wire, and must be either calculated by a competent electrician or arrived at by trial and error. Mention should also be made of flexible heating mats after the style of electric blankets which run from standard voltages and do not require transformers, but as the wiring elements are very thin they will not stand rough usage, nor can the mats themselves be cut to shape.

Radio-frequency (RF) heating

In this process a suitable generator will take current from the mains and transform it into very high frequencies which, when transmitted to the work via suitable platens or electrodes, will excite the molecules of the material which is being glued, distorting them and causing them to rotate, and thereby causing friction and inducing heat. The amount of heat generated depends upon the electrical properties of the material, and the poorer its insulating properties the more heat will be generated. Thus the actual glue itself, which must be of the heat reactive (synthetic resin) type, is purposely made more conductive than the wood (which is a good insulator and, therefore, a poor conductor) and will absorb more energy and, therefore, generate more heat.

Three basic methods of applying RF heating to a glue-line are practised: (a) through or transverse heating; (b) glue-line heating; (c) stray field heating. In 'through' heating metal platens are applied on either side of the work (325:7), and the whole mass of wood is heated in order that the glue-line itself can reach the required temperature for a rapid set. This method is generally adopted for laminated bowed doors, etc. in either plywood or constructional veneers, where pressure can be applied on either side by male and female formers/forms which have been lined with non-ferrous metals (copper, brass, aluminium, etc.). These form platens which act as electrodes for the high-frequency voltages to pass through the total thickness of the laminates, dependent of course on the power of the generator and the

rapidity of the set required. As with low-voltage heating, pressure must be positive and high enough that the glue-lines will not foam, otherwise lower temperatures and consequent longer setting times must be tolerated. With 'glue-line' heating (325:8) the electrodes are placed on either side of the glue-line, thus allowing most of the energy to be concentrated in the glue itself and ensuring a faster setting time for the same power, but in practice the glue-line must not be more than about 3 in (7.5 mm) wide, therefore the technique is confined to butt joints, edgings, etc. On the other hand 'stray field' heating (325:9) is usually adopted when neither 'through' heating nor 'glue-line' heating are feasible, and in all cases where it is physically impossible to place the electrodes on either side of the glue-line. The main disadvantage of this method is the longer setting time required, for there is no heating directly under the electrodes but only in the field between the electrodes, therefore the heat generated within the field must be given time to penetrate to the glue. The greater the thickness of material and, therefore, the greater the required heat penetration, the greater the distance there must be between the electrodes; nevertheless faster sets than with most other methods can be obtained, and in complicated assemblies all three techniques can be adopted through the same jig (325:6).

While the operation of RF heating does not call for electronic skill, a thorough knowledge of the basic working priciples is called for, and as the equipment itself (generator, co-axial cable, etc.) is relatively expensive to install only high outputs in quantity production will justify the cost, moreover the generator must be as close to the jig and, therefore, to the method of pressing as possible. Portable outfits for spot setting of small areas of glue are available but their application is fairly limited, for instance in spot tacking veneers in position before pressing. Where large outputs are called for, however, RF heating is probably the cheapest and most efficient process in the long run.

Figure 326A depicts a dielectric RF generator for continuous operation; 326B is an RF carcass press with a small mitred corner open carcass being pressed and cured; 325C is an LV heating unit comprising step-down transformer and

326a   Dielectric RF generator

326b   RF carcass press

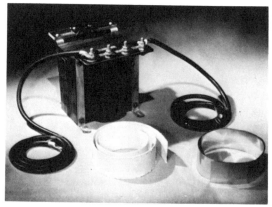

326c   LV heating unit

326d   RF stray field platen (Figs 326a-d by courtesy
of Pye Thermal Bonders Ltd)

leads, mild steel heating strip and heat-resistant strip for softening; 326D is a stray field platen in which the electrodes are placed at an angle of 45°, thus the RF field extends over the full area of the platen and can be used for sub- assemblies, fastening tops, etc. The platen is covered with silicone bonded glass-cloth to yield a smooth surface, and mounted on a 2⅜ in (60 mm) insulating plywood base with a plastic shield base for the electrodes.

Part VII   Setting out and cutting lists

36   Setting out and cutting lists

SETTING OUT

Full-size drawings or rods are necessary for setting out the work, showing the exact dimensions and constructional methods to be employed. Normally, design-drawings do not show the constructional methods unless they are of an unorthodox nature, and it is generally assumed that the furniture will be made in accordance with established custom; therefore the setter-out must decide the kinds of joint which will ensure adequate strength and rigidity in the construction, within the framework of the price factor and the designer's clear intention. In other words he must be a sympathetic interpreter, but at the same time completely practical in his approach.

Working drawings can be on paper, on sheets of plywood or on rods. The rods were almost invariably used in joiners' shops, and the lines were broken to condense the overall dimensions into a narrow pine rod about 9 in (228 mm) wide and ½ in (12.5 mm) thick. The method is useful for tall fitments, large bookcases, fitted wardrobes, panelling, etc., but a full-size drawing which is unmistakably clear is always simpler in the end. Figure 437 shows a fairly typical example of a full-size working drawing (reduced in scale for reproduction purposes only) of the cocktail cabinet described in Chapter 42. Figure 437:1 shows the front elevation, 437:2 the side elevation, 437:4A and B the plan halved on the centre-line to show the lower framing and the upper carcass with shaped interior shelf. Working details of the carcass construction, leg framing and lower shelf are shown in 437:6, door construction in 437:5, and drawer details in 437:7. Alternative methods of carcass construction and applied edgings are illustrated in 437:3, but in actual practice only one method need be shown.

In preparing working drawings the scaled dimensions of the original design-drawing must be followed and no allowance made for fair facing, etc. Thus a section shown as 3 in (76 mm)

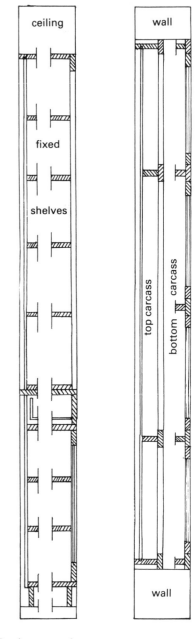

327   Laying out rods

thick must be taken as 3 in (76 mm) thick finished section; whereas in joinery practice it is taken for granted that a specified dimension will conform to the standard sawn sizes for softwoods, or if shown as, say, 3 in (76 mm) by 2 in (50 mm) will in reality be ex sawn 3 in (76 mm) by 2 in (50 mm) or approximately $2\frac{3}{4}$ in (70 mm) by $1\frac{3}{4}$ in (44 mm) net finished thickness, unless expressly stated to the contrary.

CUTTING LISTS

Cutting lists are prepared from the full-size drawings and rods and precisely enumerate all the individual pieces of wood required. They can be dead nett or finished dimension,

allowing only for jointing, or including the standard allowances for cutting, etc. $\frac{1}{2}$ in (12.5 mm) on each length and $\frac{3}{16}$ in (5 mm) ($\frac{3}{32}$ in [2.5 mm] per wrot face) in the width (thicknesses are always actual). The finished-dimension list is probably less confusing, while each piece can be easily identified on the drawing. Where tenons, dovetails or housings, etc. occur it is easier to measure right across the carcass or framework, not just the shoulder length of the bridging-piece plus the length of the tenons, etc. A specimen cutting list for the cocktail cabinet illustrated in 436 and 437 is shown below. The dimensions are net throughout with allowances for jointing. Requisitions for brasswork and ironmongery can be made on the same list or on a separate schedule.

Cutting list

Sheet No. 1

Job No. . . . .
Cocktail Cabinet—English Walnut
Customer . . . .

Order No. . . . .
Date . . . .

Mark	Description	No.	Length		Width		Thick		Wood	Notes
			in	mm	in	mm	in	mm		
	Carcass									
A	Top	1	30	762	$17\frac{13}{16}$	452	$\frac{3}{4}$	19	Solid	
B	Base	1	$29\frac{5}{8}$	752.5	$17\frac{13}{16}$	452	$\frac{3}{4}$	19	Solid	
C	Sides	2	$26\frac{13}{16}$	681	$17\frac{13}{16}$	452	$\frac{3}{4}$	19	Solid	
D	Fixed shelf	1	$28\frac{7}{8}$	733.5	$17\frac{3}{4}$	452	$\frac{5}{8}$	16		Not edged
E	Back	1	$26\frac{5}{8}$	676	$29\frac{5}{8}$	752.5	$\frac{1}{4}$	6	Plywood	Rebated
F	Adjustable shelf	1	$28\frac{1}{2}$	724	6	152	$\frac{1}{2}$	12.5	Plywood	
G	Shaped shelf	1	$28\frac{1}{2}$	724	$16\frac{1}{2}$	419	$\frac{1}{2}$	12.5		
H	Front edgings		10 ft	3048	$\frac{3}{4}$	19	$\frac{3}{16}$	5	Solid	No tongues
	Doors									
I	Stiles	4	$20\frac{7}{8}$	530	$1\frac{11}{16}$	43	$\frac{3}{4}$	19	Solid	
J	Rails	4	$14\frac{1}{4}$	362	$1\frac{11}{16}$	43	$\frac{3}{4}$	19	Solid	
K	Panels	2	$17\frac{7}{8}$	454	$11\frac{1}{4}$	286	$\frac{5}{8}$	16	Solid	
	Drawer									
L	Front	1	$28\frac{1}{2}$	724	4	102	$\frac{7}{8}$	22	Solid	
M	Sides	2	17	432	4	102	$\frac{1}{2}$	12.5	Oak	
N	Back	1	$28\frac{1}{2}$	724	$3\frac{1}{4}$	82.5	$\frac{1}{2}$	12.5	Oak	
O	Bottom	1	$27\frac{7}{8}$	708	17	432	$\frac{1}{4}$	6	Plywood	Limba
	Stand									
P	Legs	4	$21\frac{1}{2}$	546	$1\frac{7}{8}$	48	$1\frac{7}{8}$	48	Solid	Tapered to 1 in (25 mm)
Q	Long rails	2	$29\frac{1}{4}$	743	2	51	$\frac{7}{8}$	22	Solid	Tenoned
R	Side rails	2	17	432	2	51	$\frac{7}{8}$	22	Solid	Tenoned
S	Shelf rails	2	$17\frac{3}{8}$	441	$1\frac{1}{4}$	32	$\frac{3}{4}$	19	Solid	Tenoned
T	Shelf	1	29	737	$12\frac{1}{2}$	317.5	$\frac{3}{8}$	9.5	Plywood	Veneered
U	Shelf edgings	2	$28\frac{1}{2}$	724	$\frac{5}{8}$	16	$\frac{1}{2}$	12.5	Solid	
V	Shelf veneers	2	29	737	$12\frac{1}{2}$	317.5	—	0.7	Walnut	
	Brasswork									

4 brass handles; 2 pairs 2 in (50 mm) brass butts and screws; 8 shelf pegs brass; 36 sockets for pegs; screws for ply back

Note: Metric conversions are approximate only.

JIGS

Jigs are work-holders or guides for shaping; thus the bench-hook is a simple form of jig to support small sections of wood during cutting. They are widely used in machine-work, particularly in spindle moulding and routering, and the reader is referred to machine-handbooks for details. The term 'jigsaw' is an abbreviation of 'jigger' saw and has no connection.

TEMPLATES

Templates or patterns will be required for curved and shaped details, mouldings, etc. These can be cut from thick card, .06 in (1.5 mm) ply or zinc sheet according to the amount of use; while the outlines can be traced with carbon paper, by rubbing the back of the drawing with a soft lead pencil and then tracing through, or by pricking through with a needle. The templates must be dead accurate and carefully sanded or filed to the correct outline, with the position of any abutting member, i.e. rail to leg, pencilled in. A simple card template for a shaped leg is illustrated in 328, and careful setting out will save valuable wood as shown.

MEASURED WORK

Where new work has to be fitted to existing work or built to specific dimensions, as, for instance, built-in cupboards or panelling, on-site measurements must be taken. Assuming that an interior has to be measured (329:1), individual details should not be measured separately, but a running total should be preserved. Where corners or angles occur then templates should be made up from slat-wood (329:2), screwed together and carefully numbered; they can then be unscrewed, bundled and reassembled in the workshop. Curves or irregular shapes can be scribed by fitting a waste piece of plywood, etc. up against the curve and scribing with a pair of wing-compasses, small block or the workshop rule, or a piece of stiff brown paper can be slit as shown in 329:3, the paper pushed against the curve and the strips bent back as in the dotted line. The approximate outline is then transferred to a piece of plywood and corrected as necessary.

328 Laying out with card template

For small details the Maco brass template shown in 207:2 is invaluable. Cupboards which have to fit existing openings must either have scribing fillets planted on or extra wide stiles or marginal moulds which are scribed and cut to the opening on the site. It is never wise to assume that plastered walls will be straight, corners square or floors level, for they rarely are.

COPYING DETAILS

Impressions of carvings, mouldings, etc. are taken with artist's modelling-wax, hot paraffin-wax or dental quality plaster of Paris obtainable at most pharmacies. Plaster will give the cleanest impression providing there is no under-cutting and the original is heavily waxed to facilitate release. From this first impression a mould can be struck, again with plaster of Paris, which can be used as a pattern for metal casting. More permanent moulds can be formed with resin-impregnated glass fibre (see also p. 00) and for small work with intricate detail Araldite epoxy cement with or without reinforcement.

Details of flat relief carvings, frets, etc. can be obtained by laying a sheet of paper on the carving and rubbing over with heelball or soft-lead pencil. Inlays and marquetry-work can also be rubbed in this way, for there is usually sufficient proudness or recession of the individual pieces to give a reasonable impression which can be sketched in more firmly.

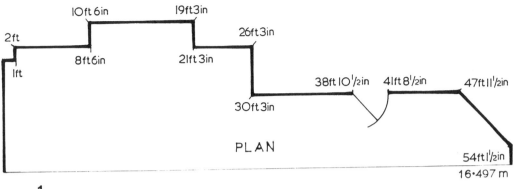

PLAN

2ft

1ft

10ft 6in

8ft 6in

19ft 3in

21ft 3in

26ft 3in

30ft 3in

38ft 10½in

41ft 8½in

47ft 11½in

54ft 1½in

16·497 m

1

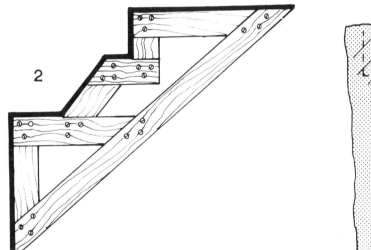

2

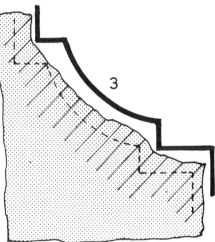

3

329　Site measurements and templates

351

Part VIII Draughtsmanship and workshop geometry

37 The drawing office

Technical drawings are the link between the designer and the producer (even if they are the same person).

1 They force the designer to make a clear statement of what he really has in mind.

2 They force the craftsman to decide exactly how the components of the construction are going to be put together.

3 As the drawings are made they point to problems before expensive materials are cut or time is wasted on unsatisfactory construction.

4 By the drawings the whole production routine can be planned before work starts.

EQUIPMENT

Modern practice is to use transparent plastic, fibre, or aluminium for T-square blades. For use in the workshop, and for 'full sizing' on sheets of plywood, a fibre bladed T-square, such as sold for school blackboard use, is ideal.

Clear plastic set squares have the advantage of the draughtsman being able to see what has already been drawn beneath them. A large adjustable set square is expensive but well worth the outlay. When buying or ordering remember that most manufacturers quote the hypotenuse of the closed set square as its size.

The same advice is given with regard to compasses. Cheap 'school' compasses are a frustrating nuisance. A large, well-engineered instrument of good quality is well worth the expense. Multiple outfits in velvet lined cases, or 'drawing sets' containing such items as ruling pens and ruling nibs for compasses are of little use in the workshop.

Circles under 2 in (50 mm) diameter are best dealt with using a circle template, the most practical being made of transparent plastic with a graded series of holes punched through them. They are accurate when used with a sharp pencil

or a stylus pen and in the smallest sizes of circle are more comfortable to use than any pair of compasses.

For the drawing of curves, a set of large french curves makes a useful addition to the workshop, also a set of boat curves or railway curves which may well be picked up from junk shops. The latter are Victorian or Edwardian in origin, made of pear wood, and are frequently in well-constructed boxes. For the drawing of long sinuous or continuous curves a spline made from thin plywood, cut so that the grain of the outer skin lies across the width of the spline, is indispensable. It is a two-man job to use it.

Good quality HB or F pencils will give a thin and dark line, while a Japanese Pentel enables drawing office standard drawings to be made with a propelling pencil, the lead being half a millimetre in diameter. Should the drawing need to be reproduced, modern pencils and reprographic machines can make a very satisfactory copy without recourse to ink.

DIMENSIONING

Apart from the setting out on the paper, putting on the dimensions is the most difficult aspect of technical drawing. Figure 330A illustrates some of the drawing conventions recommended.

If should be noted that:

1 Dimension lines are placed well clear of the part dimensioned.

2 The figures read straight down from the top, or from left to right.

3 Smaller dimensions are shown inside larger dimensions.

4 Except where unavoidable, no dimensions appear on the actual piece drawn.

Three recognized conventions to indicate the limits of any dimensions are shown:

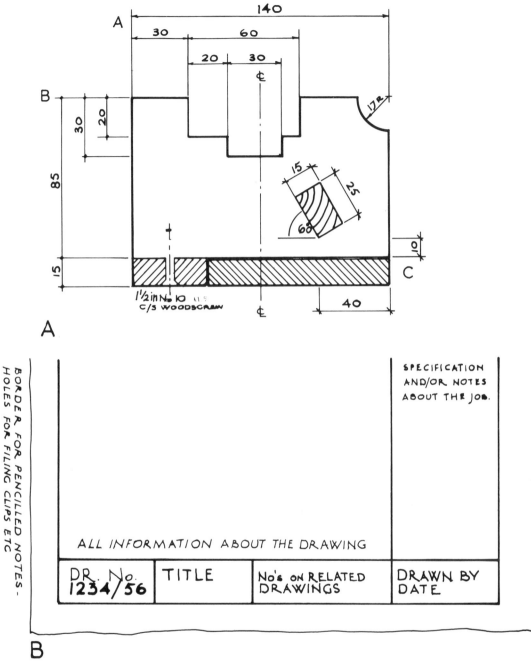

A

B

PERMANENT, FILED DRAWINGS FOR OFFICE USE ARE
SOMETIMES INK ON TRACING PAPER, HELPFUL WHEN
DYELINE COPIES ARE TAKEN

330   Dimensioning and dimensioning systems

A Arrow heads at the end of the dimension line.

B A dot where the dimension line and the limit line cross.

C A short line at 45 degrees instead of a dot at the intersection.

A convention to show a wood screw is also shown.

A further convention is used on the section in that a double line is used to indicate that the joint between the two pieces is a sliding fit.

Figure 330B shows an inked-in drawing which is to be kept permanently in a drawing/production office. This is also useful if the drawing is going to a client or a contractor, and therefore likely to be reproduced many times on a dyeline machine.

If the drawing number, which is also the job number, is clearly set out in heavy type at the same place on each drawing it makes for quick and convenient sorting and retrieval from the filing system.

It should be emphasized that to make a beautifully finished ink drawing on strong tracing paper, solely for use in the workshop, is a waste of time and materials.

Scale drawings

As already mentioned scale drawings prepared by the designer are not concerned with visual aspects (perspectives, etc.), but with the accurate outline representation of the object to be made, drawn to a representative fraction of the full size.

38   Projections commonly used

ORTHOGRAPHIC (ORTHOGONAL) PROJECTION

The standard method of representing a three-dimensional object in two-dimensional form, i.e. as a scale drawing on one plane, is by orthographic projection in which related views give the various aspects, viz.:

Plan   Representation of the object on the horizontal plane, i.e. looking down.

Front and side elevations   Representation of the object on the vertical plane, i.e. level with the eyes.

Section   The object cut through either on the horizontal or the vertical plane to show details which would not be visible in simple outlines of plan and elevation. Vertical sections are usually included in a side elevation projected from the front elevation, and horizontal sections included in the plan, although if the object is complex several such sectional drawings may be necessary.

All these drawings are to a convenient scale, but full- or half-size details are necessary for free-hand curves where a compass radius cannot be stated, or where the particular detail calls for amplification.

They can be projected from either the first dihedral angle (first angle drawings) or the third dihedral angle (third angle drawings), and 331:1 gives a typical layout using the first angle and drawn to a scale of ⅛ (1½ in to the foot) or to metric scale. The details given show, at 331:1B, the front elevation of a simple wooden plinth with a circular recess on the face for an inlaid metal plaque; 331:1A is the plan of the plinth showing a stepped housing for a statuette; and 331:1C a vertical side section on the centre-line XY (331:1A). Full-size details of the stepped housing and the circular recess are shown in 331:1D and 331:1E and no further information should be necessary. Where the drawings are of complex objects, however, it may be necessary to add a three-dimensional project for clarification.

First-angle projection

Where a horizontal plane intersects a vertical plane (VP) dihedral angles are formed, of which both the first and third angles are used in orthographic projection. Where the first dihedral angle is used (332:1) the object is placed between the observer and the vertical plane (332:2), thus the front elevation is seen first (the arrow points the direction), the side elevation is projected from it by folding back the side vertical plane on the vertical trace (VT), and placing it alongside the front elevation. The horizontal plane is then folded down on the horizontal trace (HT) XY, known as the XY line, and therefore appears below the front elevation.

Third-angle projection

This method is becoming increasingly popular, although it hardly matters which method is adopted provided the drawing is quite clear as to what it is intended to represent. In third angle projection the object is placed behind the vertical plane (332:3), the plan is seen first, the front elevation below it, and the side elevation projected alongside the front elevation.

OBLIQUE PROJECTION

The elevation of the object is drawn to scale and parallel to the observer, as in orthographic projection, but receding lines, i.e. the sides of the plinth not visible in 331:1, are drawn at a convenient angle 30°, 45°, or 60° according to the set-square available. Figure 331:1 shows the plinth side drawn at an angle of 45°. If the receding lines are short the angle should be fairly large; if they are long the angle should be acute, otherwise an exaggerated effect is produced. Figure 333:2 gives the effect achieved by drawing the side to half the scale of the front, which gives a more pleasing appearance, but a warning notice should be

1

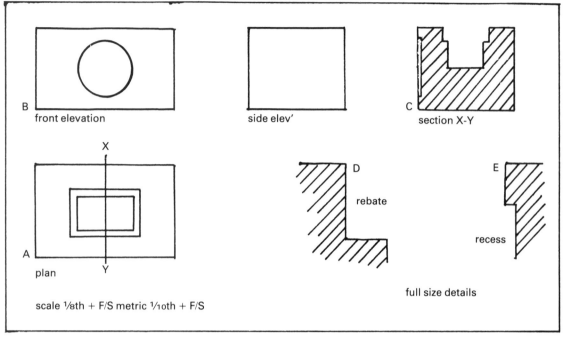

B   front elevation

side elev'

C   section X-Y

X

A   plan   Y

D   rebate

E   recess

full size details

scale ⅛th + F/S metric ¹/₁₀th + F/S

first angle

2

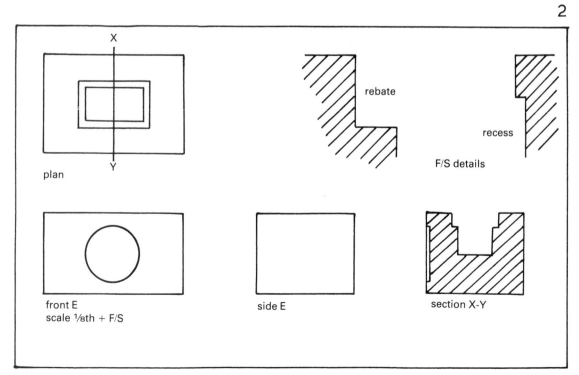

X

plan   Y

rebate

recess

F/S details

front E
scale ⅛th + F/S

side E

section X-Y

third angle

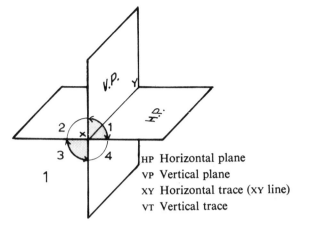

HP Horizontal plane
VP Vertical plane
XY Horizontal trace (XY line)
VT Vertical trace

included in the drawing if this method is adopted. Circles and parts of circles can be drawn with the compass in oblique projection, and the method is invaluable for showing details of constructional jointing, etc.

ISOMETRIC PROJECTION

Isometric is a simple and mechanical way of producing a pictorial representation. Orthographic projections of one kind or another make the most efficient type of drawing from which to work, but the final appearance of the completed piece is often somewhat hidden. This method gives a closer approximation to the visual appearance (333:3). For normal work the sides are inclined at an angle of 30° using the 30° set-square, but the angles can be varied within wide limits, using, for instance, 20° for the front elevation, and 40° or 50° for the side elevation—actual experience alone is the only true guide to the most satisfactory angle of representation for any particular view. Isometric scales proportionate to the true scale were formerly used, but the practice has now been abandoned, and the drawings are made to the true scale.

The method of drawing curves or irregular shapes is shown in 333:5 and 333:6. A plan of the curve is first drawn and included in a square. Ordinates (*ordinate*: half the chord of a conic section in relation to the diameter which bisects it) are then drawn in 333:5, and the square with its ordinates is then drawn in isometric projection 333:6, and the critical distances for the curve plotted off. In the example given the circle becomes an ellipse.

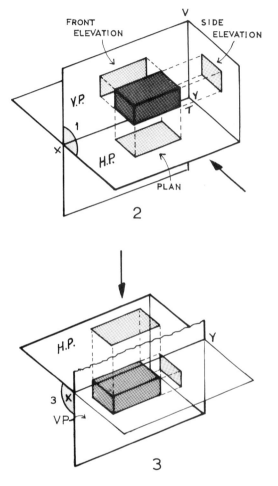

AXONOMETRIC PROJECTION

This is a variation of isometric projection, sometimes known as 'bird's-eye' perspective, as it gives more of a downward view (333:4). The true plan is first drawn to scale at angles of 45° and 45° or 30° and 60° to the horizontal, and the verticals projected from it. This projection is chiefly used for interiors, and it is interesting to note that the base of the socket housing in the plinth only becomes visible with this method.

Distortion is great and obvious. This projection is sometimes refered to as isometric.

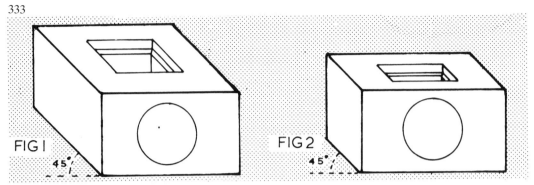

FIG I

45°

Oblique projection

FIG 2

45°

Oblique projection

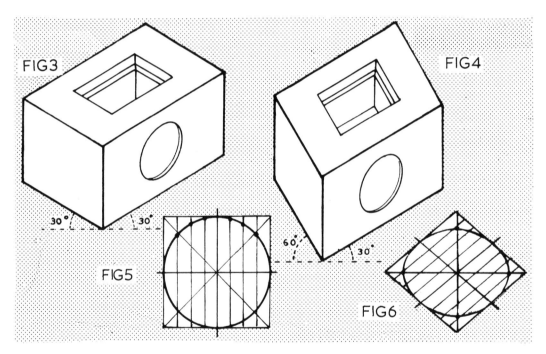

FIG3

FIG4

30°   30°

FIG5

60°   30°

FIG6

Isometric projection

Axonometric projection

39 Perspective drawing

Perspective drawings are used to illustrate the appearance of the object so that it is completely understandable to a third person. Actual measurements are not taken from such drawings, as they are only concerned with the mechanics of vision in which receding lines appear to converge and diminish. Various methods are used, many of which are highly technical and require special study, but 334 shows a simple compromise which should be sufficient for most practical purposes. Figure 334:2 shows the elevation of a simple chest of drawers, and in 334:1 the plan ABCD is drawn to scale at an angle to the horizon (eye-line) dependent on the viewpoint required (in this

case 45°). The station point (SP) is placed to represent the eye of the beholder, and only trial and error can give the most satisfactory position. While the angle or cone of vision represented by lines drawn from the extremities DB of the plan ABCD to the station point (SP) should be between 40° and 60° for a normal aspect (the normal camera lens takes in about 55°), a narrower angle, even though it increases the distortion, helps to contain the vanishing points within the drawing, as a little experiment will show. Lines are now drawn to form a right angle at SP and cut the horizon at VP1 and VP2, which are the vanishing points to which all receding lines converge. A base- or ground-line

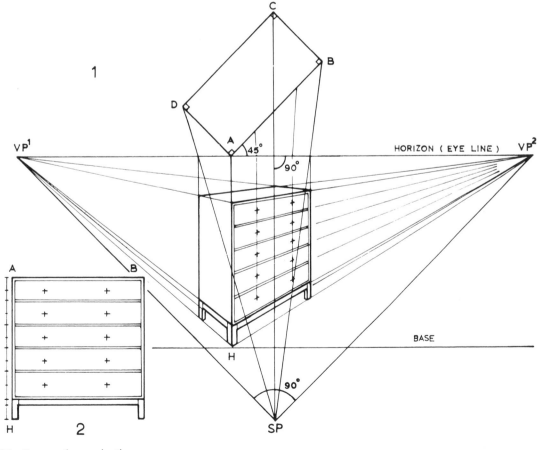

334   Perspective projection

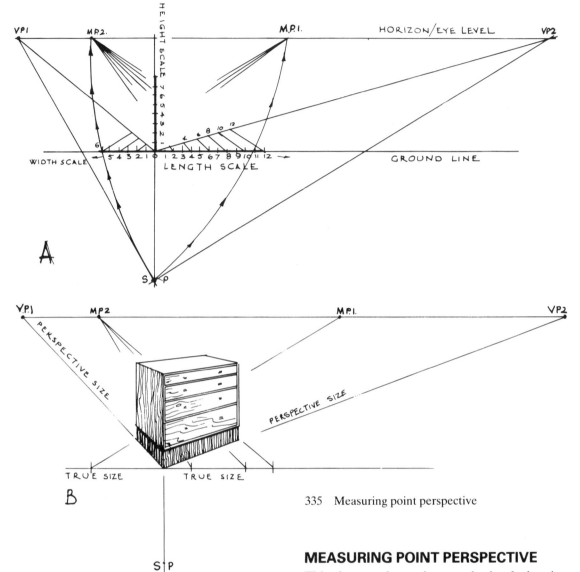

335 Measuring point perspective

MEASURING POINT PERSPECTIVE

This is an alternative method of drawing perspective which has the advantage that no plan has to be drawn. If the sizes are known, they can be used directly on the horizontal and vertical scales and a perspective drawing produced. Once the SP has been used to fix the measuring points (335:A) it can be ignored.

Remember that the measuring points fix measurements of length and width, read off directly from the height scale, the lines from which are taken to the vanishing points.

As the object of such a perspective drawing is to convey the visual appearance only, and not to

is drawn approximately 5 ft (150 cm) scale measurement below the eye-line or horizon, while a perpendicular dropped from A to H will provide a height-line on which all significant measurements can be transferred from the elevation (334:2). Lines are then drawn from all the salient points on the plan ABCD to the station point SP, and from where they cut the horizon verticals are then dropped as shown. If from the line AH (334:1) the various heights are connected to VP1 and VP2 the completed drawing will then be automatically developed.

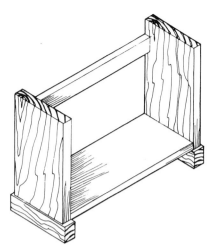

336 Isometric projection

serve as an accurate scaled representation from which critical measurements can be taken, small details should be drawn free-hand rather than rigidly adhering to mechanical projection with its inevitable distortion. Curves are also better drawn as free-hand ellipses after plotting the general position.

WORKING DRAWINGS AND SETTING OUT

The book rack set out in isometric projection (336) is turned into an orthographic drawing. A system is used that employs the under-mentioned basic principles.

1 Most furniture is symmetrical about an axis, normally the centre line. Therefore often one half only will provide sufficient information.

2 Where a piece has a feature repeated more than once, to draw in full detail once is sufficient.

3 The craftsman's prime interest is how the component parts are joined together. Provided the length of the component is clearly indicated, it is the joints and the intersections between pieces that really matter.

4 A drawing such as figure 337 is intended for workshop use only, and can be written on, sketched on, and used as a visual diary of ideas.

5 Where the drawing is made in the workshop by the craftsman for his own use (337), labelling and lettering can be kept to a minimum.

On the example shown (337), the draughtsman should proceed as follows:

1 Draw a full size front elevation in outline, symmetrical about a centre line.

2 Using the heights already indicated, draw the end elevation in the position shown.

It is now possible to measure from the drawing the following information:

1 Overall length(s)
2 Overall height
3 Height of end
4 Width of end
5 Position of back rail
6 Width of back rail
7 Thickness of bottom
8 Thickness of ends
9 The length, width and thickness of foot.

By turning the end elevation into a section the thickness of the back rail can be indicated.

If the right-hand end of the drawing is left as it is, it will show the front elevation as it will be seen.

If the left hand of the elevation is referred to as the view from the back it can be shown how the back rail is joined to the ends.

Information is needed on the joint between the ends and the bottom. By superimposing part of an inverted plan on the end, the setting out of the joint involved can be shown.

The positions of the slot screws retaining the feet are also shown.

The three colour convention

These drawings, using views and sections that are superimposed, gain enormously in clarity and ease of reading if the front elevation(s) and sections are left black, side elevations and sections are drawn in blue, and anything that is plan or part plan is drawn in red.

True coloured pencils and not crayons (even if they are encased in wood) should be used and kept sharp.

When the drawing is on paper or plywood the use of this system is well worthwhile. Colours do not come out on dyeline machines (on some machines the blue or the red does not come out at all).

Figure 338 is the same drawing figure as 337, but is finished for another craftsman to make. Its dimensions are given and it is labelled to make it clearer to read. It is also dimensioned in millimetres which has the advantage of avoiding the use of fractions of an inch. Once the common sizes are memorized and immediately related to a specific length, width or thickness, it becomes a most convenient system to use.

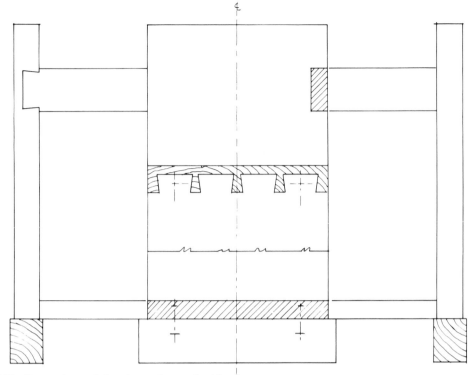

337 Drawn in workshop by craftsman for his own use

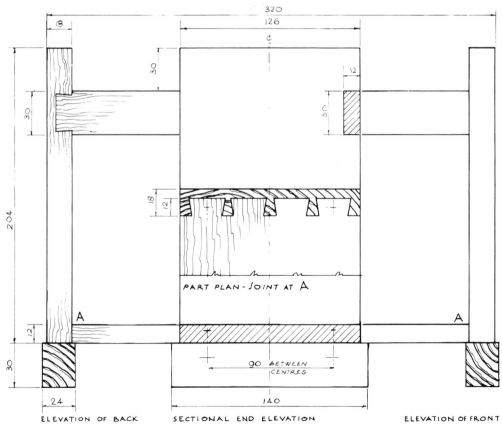

PART PLAN - JOINT AT A

ELEVATION OF BACK　　　SECTIONAL END ELEVATION　　　ELEVATION OF FRONT

338 Drawn to give instructions to craftsman

40 Workshop geometry

Some knowledge of elementary geometric drawing is necessary for the preparation of workshop drawings or 'full sizings', which are, in effect, accurately drawn full-size outlines of the object to be made, prepared from the smaller scale drawings of the designer. No elaborate equipment is necessary, nor need the setter-out be a skilled draughtsman, but he should understand the principles involved.

EQUIPMENT

Drawings can be made on narrow rods (see Setting out and cutting lists, Chapter 36), on plywood sheets, or on a drawing-board which can be a piece of good-quality ply or laminboard with an outer facing of close-grained timber, planed up truly square on all four edges. A 30 in (762 mm) T-square is necessary which the craftsman can make for himself (339:1), using 1/8 in (3 mm) finish straight-grained mahogany for the blade, which should taper from about 4 in (101 mm) at the heel to 2 in (50 mm) at the tip, and a 12 in (304 mm) by 2 in (50 mm) by 1/2 in (12.5 mm) stock secured to the blade with short brass screws and a small dab of glue in the centre only. The stock is usually edged with a darker wood, ebony or close-grained rosewood, bevelled off as shown at 339:1a and b, and the blade is similarly treated, with the edge tongued. A hole is bored at the tip for the square to be hung under its own weight, and the wood is sealed and polished with shellac varnish or cellulose. Set-squares are also required, both 60° and 45° and up to 12 in (304 mm) in length

(the key-jointed mahogany square edged with ebony [339:2] is excellent for workshop use), also a long wooden straight-edge, adjustable set-square or protractor, scale rules, dividers, pencil-compass and a beam-compass or set of trammel-points for large sweeps. Pencils should be HB, H and 4H of good quality, sharpened to a long point with about 1/4 in (6 mm) of lead exposed. Paper when used need only be the cheaper detail paper obtainable in widths of up to 5 ft (150 cm), or rolls of good-quality paper-hanger's lining paper which can be taped together to form larger sheets. Drawing-pins are now rarely used, and the paper can be taped to the board with draughting or cellulose tape.

DRAWINGS

Drawings should be lightly done at first, using a medium hard pencil and boldly outlining when correct, while a 4H pencil should be used for critical measurements. Moulded sections should be heavily outlined to show the correct profile, and all end-grain sections cross-hatched for easy identification. Curved lines should be drawn first and straight lines carried into them, while tracing through to another sheet or to the bare wood can be done with carbon paper or rubbing the back of the drawing with a very soft pencil and then tracing through from the face. Both plans and elevations can be superimposed on one sheet, outlining them in different coloured crayons, but to avoid confusion it is better to keep them well apart wherever possible.

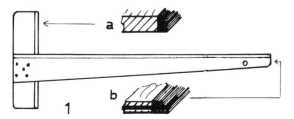

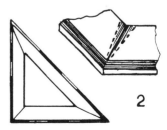

339   Drawing instruments: T-square and set-square

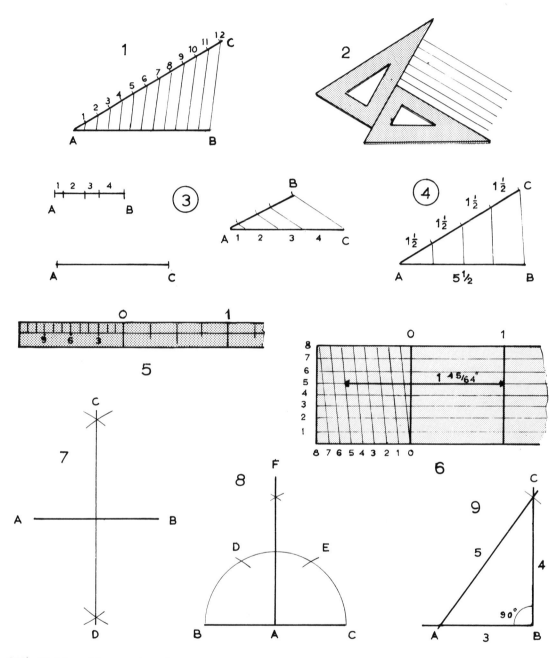

340 Division of lines, scales, etc.

SCALES

Design-drawings are made to a fixed scale or representative fraction, with special features—mouldings, free-hand curves in which the radius is not constant, etc.—drawn full size. Inch scales can be $\frac{1}{12}$ (1 in representing each actual foot in length), $\frac{1}{4}$ (3 in to each foot) and $\frac{1}{2}$ (6 in to each foot). The latter set are more easily translatable in the workshop for each $\frac{1}{8}$ in on the full-size workshop rule is then equivalent to 1 in on the $\frac{1}{8}$ scale drawing, with $\frac{1}{4}$ in or $\frac{1}{2}$ in equivalent to 1 in on the larger scales. Metric scales are usually $\frac{1}{1}$ m (full size), $\frac{1}{2}$ m (1 m= 2 m or 1 cm = 2 cm, etc.), $\frac{2}{5}$ m, $\frac{1}{5}$ m, $\frac{1}{10}$ m,

364

¹/₂₀ m, etc. The larger scales are divided into centimetres and millimetres and the smaller into centimetres only, except in engineers' precision steel rules which can show very fine millimetre divisions. If other scales have to be constructed then it is necessary to know how to divide a given line into any number of equal parts and 340:1 shows the procedure where AB is the given line, AC another line drawn at any convenient angle and marked off with the workshop rule or dividers into the exact number of parts required: if B and C are then joined and parallel lines drawn from the upper marks with two set-squares (340:2) then AB will be similarly divided. Any scale, therefore, can be constructed on this principle, and assuming that an ¹/₈th scale is required then the base-line AB (340:1) is drawn exactly 1¹/₂ in long to represent 1 ft of actual measurement, with AC divided into 12 equal parts; and metric scales are constructed in the same manner with AC divided into tenths. In some scales showing very fine divisions only the first whole unit is subdivided and marked 0, as in 340:5, and the scale is then read from right to left. Finer scales can be constructed on the diagonal principle to mark any number of divisions, but they must be very accurately drawn and 340:6 shows the method of construction where each base-line division is ¹/₈ in and each upright division ¹/₈ of ¹/₈ equalling ¹/₆₄. To read the scale add the number of base divisions to the number of vertical divisions; thus in the illustration five base divisions at ¹/₈th+five vertical divisions at ¹/₆₄=⁴⁵/₆₄. Metric scales showing divisions up to 100ths can be similarly constructed.

PROPORTIONAL DIVISION

Lines can be divided proportional to each other in the manner described above and 340:3 gives the details where AC is to be divided in the same proportion as AB. The method is also useful in dividing a given line into any number of equal parts (as in setting out dovetails) where AB (340:4), which is assumed to be 5¹/₂ units (inches or millimetres) long, has to be divided into four equal parts. AB is first drawn the correct length and AC any convenient length easily divisible by four. Parallel lines from AC will then equally divide AB.

Where a line has to be divided into two equal parts, i.e. bisected, then 340:7 shows the method in which arcs with equal radii are struck from A and B to intersect at C and D, and a vertical line drawn through CD will then bisect AB. This method can also be used for striking a perpendicular to a given line, and 340:8 shows the method in which a semicircle is described from point A on BC, and using the same radius throughout describing arcs D and E from B and C and intersecting arcs from D and E to F; a line drawn from F to A will then be truly perpendicular. If compasses are not available then perpendiculars can be drawn using the theorem attributed to Pythagoras (scale of equal parts) in which the square on the hypotenuse of a right-angled triangle is equal to the sum of the squares on the other two sides. Thus in 340:9 if AB is drawn 3 units long, then measurements of 4 units from B and 5 units from A (or any multiples of all three measurements) will only coincide at point C on a line which is at true right angles to A.

ANGLES

Angles are formed by the convergence of two straight lines, or more precisely by the rotation of a straight line about a fixed point, and the method of bisecting them is shown in 341:1 where an arc is struck from centre A and further equal arcs from B and C. From the point at which these two arcs intersect a line drawn to A will bisect the angle. This method can be used to strike all the commonly used angles, e.g. a right angle of 90° can be bisected to produce a true mitre of 45° and again bisected to produce a half-mitre of 22¹/₂°. Angles of 60° can be struck by describing an arc BC from A (341:2) and a similar arc AC from B. If lines are drawn from C to A and B then the figure thus formed will be an equilateral triangle with all sides and all angles equal. As the sum of the angles contained in a triangle must equal 180°, then each angle will be 60°, and bisecting them further gives angles of 30°.

TRIANGLES

Triangles are shown in 341:3. Right-angled triangles (A) have two sides at right angles to

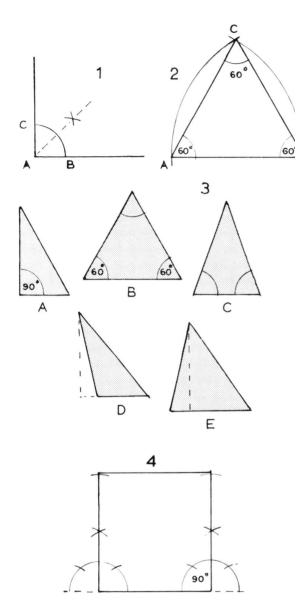

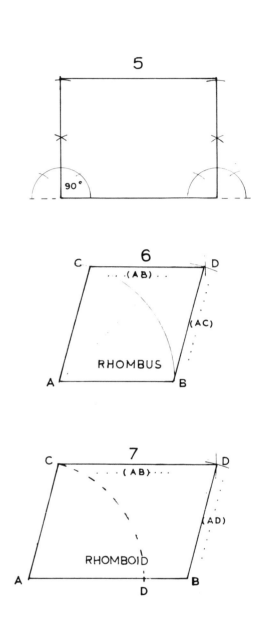

341   Angles, triangles and parallelograms

each other, the third side is known as the 'hypotenuse' and the angles so formed by this line are equal in sum to one right angle, i.e. 45° each. Equilateral triangles (B) have three equal sides and therefore three equal angles of 60°. Isosceles triangles (C) have two equal sides and two equal angles, and scalene triangles—acute scalene (D) and obtuse scalene (E)—have three unequal sides and therefore three unequal angles.

PARALLELOGRAMS

Parallelograms are quadrilaterals with opposite sides equal and parallel to each other, therefore the opposite angles are equal, the diagonals bisect the figures into similar triangles and also bisect each other. They are simple to construct as shown, where 341:4 is a square, 341:5 a rectangle, 341:6 a rhombus and 341:7 a rhomboid.

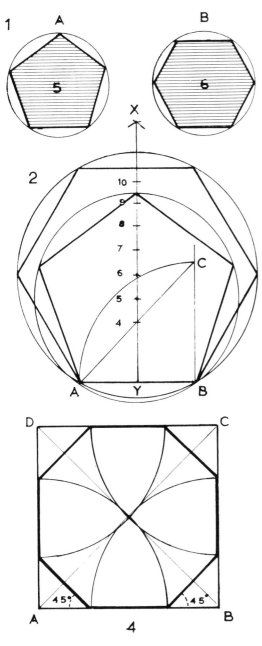

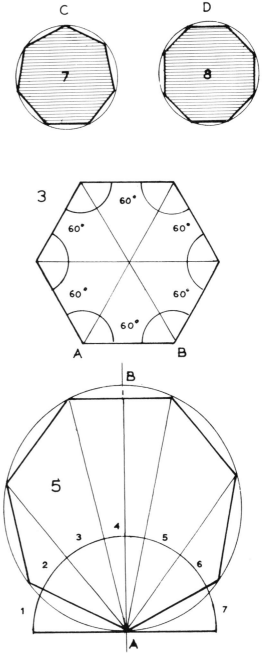

POLYGONS

Regular polygons—a pentagon has five sides (342:2A), a hexagon six sides (1B), a heptagon seven sides (1C), an octagon eight sides (1D), etc.—have more than four sides, the sides are equal and the angles also equal. All the corners must, therefore, lie on the circumference of the

circumscribing circle, and given the circle it is only necessary to divide the circumference into equal parts representing the number of sides required. Alternatively, any regular polygon can be drawn on a given base-line AB (342:2) by erecting a perpendicular BC equal in length to AB and joining C to A. AB is then bisected at Y

367

and a perpendicular XY of indefinite length erected which bisects the diagonal AC to yield the centre of a square raised on AB. If a quadrant (quarter-circle) is now drawn with centre B and radius AB, then where it cuts the perpendicular XY will lie point 6 which is the centre of a circle circumscribing a hexagon, while midway between points 4 and 6 the point 5 will give the centre of a pentagon, and similarly placed points 7, 8, 9 and 10, etc. the centres of other polygons. Other methods of drawing regular polygons are also shown. In 342:3 a hexagon on the given side AB is simply drawn with a 60° set square forming six equilateral triangles, while 342:4 illustrates the construction of an octagon within a given square ABCD. The diagonals of the square are first drawn, then with radius equal to half a diagonal arcs are drawn from centres A, B, C, D giving points of intersection with when joined become the sides of the octagon. Figure 342:5 shows the construction of a regular polygon within a given circle. The circle is first drawn with diameter AB, and a semicircle of any convenient radius with centre A. If this semicircle is divided into as many parts as the required polygon is to have sides—in this case a heptagon—then radials extended from A through these points will cut the circumference and give points of connections for the base-lines of the required figure.

CIRCLES

The various terms used in connection with circles are illlustrated in 343. *Arc*, any part of a circumference; *chord*, any straight line shorter than the diameter terminated by the circumference at both ends; *diameter*, a chord which passes through the centre of a circle; *radius*, a straight line drawn from the centre of a circle to the circumference and therefore half the diameter; *normal*, a straight line drawn from any point on the circumference radial to the centre; *tangent*, a straight line touching the circumference at any one point at right angles to a normal at that point (343:1). *Quadrant*, a sector which is a quarter of a circle; *semicircle*, a segment which is a half of a circle; *minor segment*, part of a circle contained between a chord and its arc and less than a semicircle;

major segment, part of a circle greater than a semicircle; *minor sector*, part of a circle contained within two radii and less than a semicircle; *major sector*, part of a circle greater than a semicircle (343:2). Additionally 343:3 shows *concentric circles* having the same common centre but different radii, and 343:4 *eccentric circles* each of which has a different centre.

The circumference of a circle is approximately 3.1416 or $3\frac{1}{7}$ times the diameter, usually expressed by the Greek letter π (pi). Thus the circumference is $\pi \times d$ (diameter), while the area is πr^2 (radius). In practice, the development or length of the circumference can easily be found by dividing it into any number of equal parts which are then plotted as straight lines and measured off, but the method is not strictly accurate as the plotted units are in reality chords of the circle. Alternatively, dividing the diameter into seven equal parts and adding one part to three times the length of the diameter will give a reasonable approximation.

Methods of describing circles to pass through given points, between converging lines, tangential to each other or inscribed within two equal arcs, are used in the full sizing of *fan* (Gothic) *tracery* and are illustrated in 344 and 350. Figure 343:5 shows the construction of a circle about the fixed points A, B, C, where AB and BC are each bisected and the intersection of the perpendiculars at O will give the centre of the required circle. Where a circle has to be inscribed within a triangle (343:6), as the circle will be tangential at points B and C which are equidistant from A, a perpendicular erected on B will provide one radius, and the bisection of the angle at A another, while the point at which they intersect at O will thus be the centre of the required circle. If a series of circles has to be inscribed tangential to two converging lines (344:1) then the angle BAC is first bisected and the first circle drawn as already described, after which the angle BOD is bisected and from centres E with radius EB an arc is described to cut AB at F. A line drawn from F parallel to BO will give the centre of the next circle, and centres for succeeding circles are found in like manner. If a circle has to pass through a given point X (344:2) and touch a line AB at a given point Y, then erect CY perpendicular to AB. Join XY and construct the angle DXY equal to

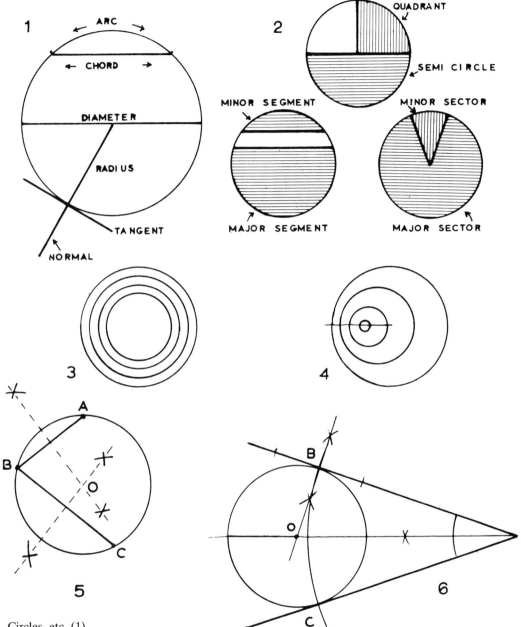

1 ARC CHORD DIAMETER RADIUS TANGENT NORMAL

2 QUADRANT SEMI CIRCLE MINOR SEGMENT MINOR SECTOR MAJOR SEGMENT MAJOR SECTOR

3

4

5 A B O C

6 B O A C

343 Circles, etc. (1)

the angle CYX. At the point of intersection of DX with CY the point E will now form the centre of the required circle as EX and EY have equal angles and are, therefore, also equal.

Where three equal tangential circles have to be inscribed within two equal arcs as in a trefoil to a pointed arch (344:3), an equilateral triangle ABC is first drawn, and three circles with radii

equal to half the length of the sides are described with centres A, B, C. A horizontal line is then drawn tangential to the base circles and where the bisectors of the angles BAC, BCA intersect this line will lie the points X, Y which are the centres of the arcs. A method of inscribing any number of equal circles within a given circle is shown in 344:4. First divide the

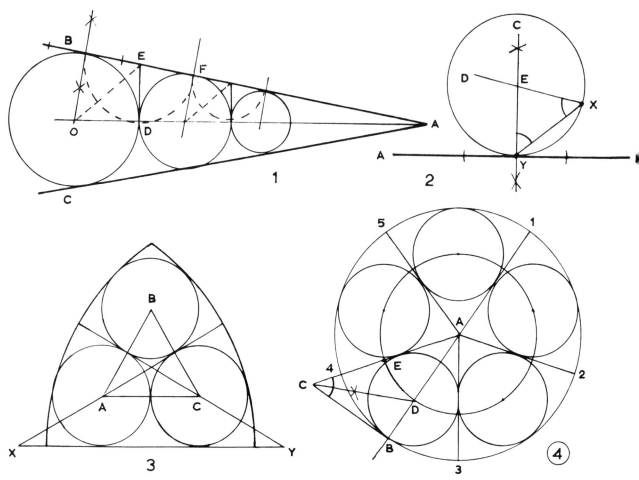

344 Circles, etc. (2)

circumference of the given circle into the same number of equal parts as the number of circles required, and join each division to the centre. One of the sectors so formed is then bisected at AB and a tangent is drawn passing through B and extended (developed) to meet the sector division AC. If the angle ACB is then bisected and extended to meet AB at D it will give the centre of the first circle with radius DB. A circle is now drawn from centre A with radius AD, and the centres of the remaining circles found by stepping off distance DE from the intersection of the inner circle with the radius of each sector.

CONIC SECTIONS

A *cone* is a pyramid with a circular base (345:1), and a vertical cut through the axis will yield a section which is a *triangle*, parallel to the axis a *hyperbola*, and parallel to one of the sides a *parabola*. If the cut is parallel with the base then the section will be a circle (345:2), and inclined to the base an *ellipse*. Of these conic sections the ellipse is of considerable importance in the setting out of oval-shaped work, gate-leg tables, etc., and although it can be drawn by hand it is more satisfactory to construct it geometrically.

Ellipses

Several methods are available of which the *foci* method (345:3) is the most common. The major axis which is to be the larger diameter of the ellipse is drawn first, and the minor axis at right angles to it. Focal points (foci) are then found by taking half the length of the major axis, and from point A on the minor axis striking an arc to cut the major axis at the foci F1 and F2. If pins

370

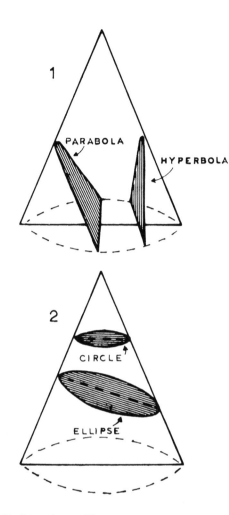

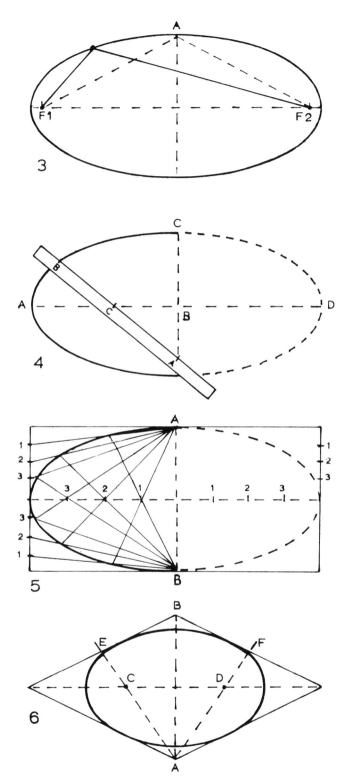

345 Conic sections, ellipses, etc.

are inserted at A, F1 and F2 and a length of string stretched taut round them, with pin A removed and replaced by a pencil the curve can be traced by keeping the pencil taut against the string. Another familiar method (354:4) uses a trammel composed of a thin lath or strip of stout paper. The major and minor axes are drawn as before, the trammel is then marked with half the length of the major axis AB and half the minor axis BC, and if the point C is kept on the former and the point A on the latter then the point B will trace out the ellipse.

Ellipses can also be constructed by the rectangle method (345:5), in which both major and minor axes are divided into the same number of equal parts, and lines drawn through each division will yield points through which the

371

ellipse can be drawn. Where, however, a geometric ellipse gives too elongated a shape, an approximate ellipse of four arcs corresponding to the isometric projection of a circle can be used as shown in 345:6. First construct a rhombus whose sides are equal to the diameter of the circle which is to be the basis of the ellipse. Draw in the diagonals and from point A bisect two sides of the rhombus at E, F. With radius CE and centres C and D describe the smaller arcs, and with centres A and B the larger arcs.

DEVELOPMENTS

Compound shapes cannot be measured accurately from a two-dimensional drawing of elevation and plan, and require development, i.e. the parts opened out and flattened on one plane. Figure 346:1, 2 illustrates a typical hopper with all sides splayed, from which it will be seen that the elevational outline is correct, but the given width of both sides and ends do not allow for the actual splay or leaning outwards towards the observer which cannot be shown. To develop these true measurements first draw the plan ABCD (346:3), extend as shown by the dotted lines, draw AB, BC, CD and DA parallel to the plan at a distance equal to X and Y in 346:1, 2 and complete.

SURFACES OF DOUBLE CURVATURE

Surfaces of double curvature (domes, etc.) cannot be developed with complete accuracy, nevertheless the method illustrated in 347 is sufficiently accurate for most practical purposes. Assuming that a hemisphere has to be developed to provide the exact shapes of the constructional ribs and of the covering veneers, first draw the elevation and divide horizontally into any number of zones A, B, C, D, E, F, etc. The outer circumference of the dome is then drawn on plan, and the zones in elevation projected downwards to the corresponding circles on the plan B, C, D, E, and F. The circle on plan is then divided into any number of equal parts 1, 2, 3, 4, 5, etc., and the radii drawn in. To develop any one zone in the elevation, for instance the zone contained within the horizontal lines C and D shaded on the drawing,

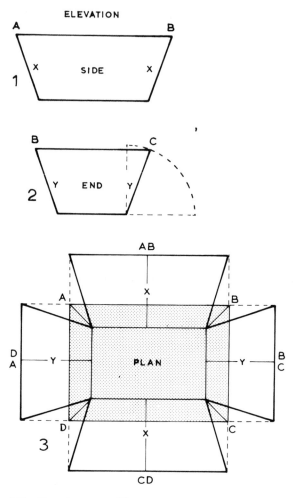

346   Developments (1)

draw a straight line CD through C and D from point O to meet the central axis R extended, and with centre R and radii RD and RC describe arcs. These arcs are then plotted off to correspond with the division of the appropriate circles D and C on plan and numbered similarly (the drawing shows part of the development only and 12 divisions will be required to plot the exact circumferential length of the zone).

To plot the shapes of the individual gores or lunes draw verticals from the points of intersection of each individual circle on plan with any two adjacent radii, and where these verticals intersect the horizontal limits of each zone will lie points through which smooth curves will define the gore. The true approximate shape of

372

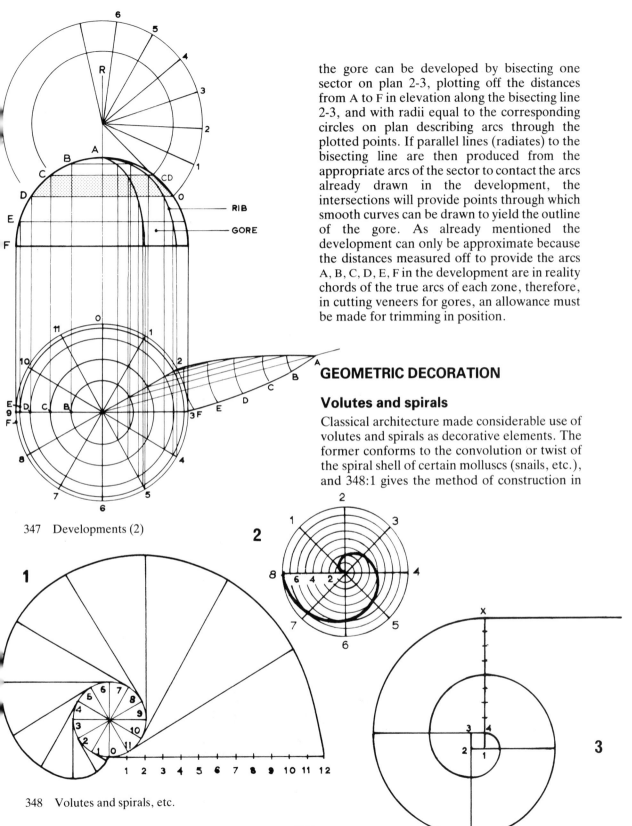

the gore can be developed by bisecting one sector on plan 2-3, plotting off the distances from A to F in elevation along the bisecting line 2-3, and with radii equal to the corresponding circles on plan describing arcs through the plotted points. If parallel lines (radiates) to the bisecting line are then produced from the appropriate arcs of the sector to contact the arcs already drawn in the development, the intersections will provide points through which smooth curves can be drawn to yield the outline of the gore. As already mentioned the development can only be approximate because the distances measured off to provide the arcs A, B, C, D, E, F in the development are in reality chords of the true arcs of each zone, therefore, in cutting veneers for gores, an allowance must be made for trimming in position.

GEOMETRIC DECORATION

Volutes and spirals

Classical architecture made considerable use of volutes and spirals as decorative elements. The former conforms to the convolution or twist of the spiral shell of certain molluscs (snails, etc.), and 348:1 gives the method of construction in

347   Developments (2)

348   Volutes and spirals, etc.

which a circle is first drawn and divided into any number of equal parts, in this case 1 to 12. A tangent is then drawn at O equal in length to the circumference of the circle and similarly divided. If further tangents are drawn at each point of the circumference progressively increasing in length according to the number of divisions on the first tangent, i.e. from point 1 one part, point 2 two parts, etc., they will yield points for the free-hand drawing of the curve.

Spirals are shown in 348:2, 3. In 2 the containing circle is divided into any number of equal sectors (eight are shown). One radius (radius vector) is then divided into the same number of equal parts, and concentric circles described through each division. The spiral is then unwound from point O at the centre of the circle, gaining one division as it travels through each sector. If necessary the number of divisions in the radius vector can be doubled, i.e. 16, and the curve will then travel twice round the containing circle to form a double spiral; while the spiral need not start from the centre of the circle but from any point on the radius sector provided the divisions 0, 1, 2, 3, 4, 5, etc., are marked off from the commencement of the spiral and not from the centre of the containing circle.

Spirals of constant pitch built up of quadrants are constructed as shown in 348:3. A square 1234 is first drawn and a perpendicular X erected equal in height to eight times the side of the square. The arcs are then drawn from centre 1 with radius one part (one side of the square), centre 2, two parts, centre 3, three parts, centre 4, four parts, centre 5, five parts, etc.

Entasis

Tapered shafts or columns with straight sides give the optical illusion of curving inwards, therefore classical architecture gave a slight outward swelling (entasis) to counteract the tendency, and to convey an impression of the weight-bearing function of the column. Various methods are used of which 349 gives one of the simplest and most satisfactory, for the curve must be subtle or the effect becomes exaggerated. The height of the column AB is first drawn, also the top EF and bottom diameters CD. Semicircles with centres A and

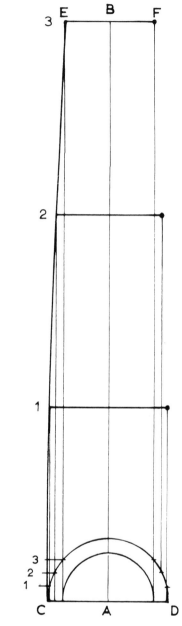

349   Entasis

radii AC and BE are then drawn, and perpendiculars erected from the smaller semicircle to cut the larger semicircle at 3. The arc C3 is then divided and from points 1, 2 perpendiculars are erected to cut corresponding divisions in the height of the column, yielding points through which the curve CE can be drawn.

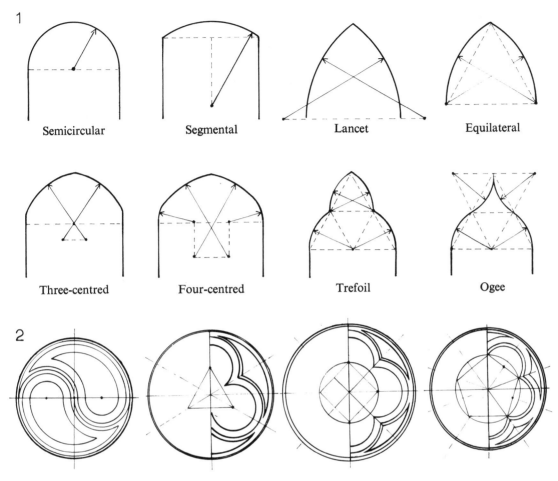

350 Gothic details: arches and tracery

Arches

Various forms of arch are shown in 350:1 together with the geometric construction. The points from which the curve of the arch springs are known as the *springing-line*, the exterior curve the *extrados* and the interior curve the *intrados*.

Tracery

Gothic tracery used as infilling or 'foliation' in window arches, etc., and still called for in traditional church-work, is based on geometric principle, and 350:2 gives various examples with their constructions. Where there is a demand for this type of work, local church examples should be examined.

Repeat patterns

Practically all decorative patterns, whether carved, moulded, inlaid or applied, have a geometric basis, and are in essence composed of curved or straight lines repeated in regular sequence. Even representations of fruit, flowers, shells, etc. are stylized to fit within circles, squares and diamonds, etc. Once the principle has been established it is relatively simple to break down the pattern into its component parts, and thus establish the structure on which it is built up.

PROPORTIONAL REDUCTION AND ENLARGEMENT

The principles of reduction and enlargement are based on the properties of a triangle in which there is a progressive diminution from base-line to apex (the proportionate division of

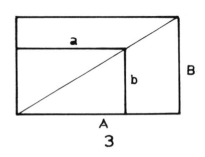

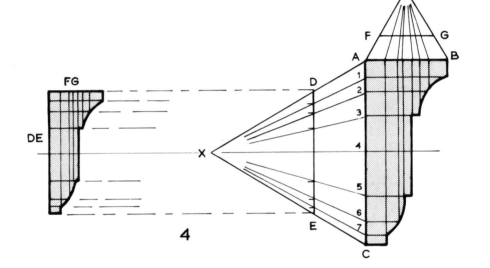

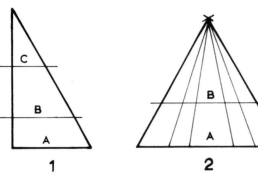

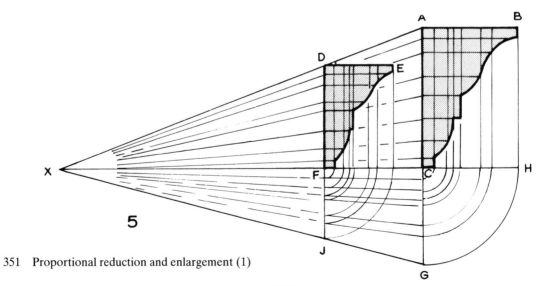

351   Proportional reduction and enlargement (1)

lines described on p. 365 is founded on this principle). Any line, therefore, drawn parallel to the base of a triangle (351:1) will form another triangle either smaller or larger, of similar angles and therefore of similar shape. If a series of lines are drawn from points on the base of a triangle (351:2A) to the apex they will cut any other parallel line (351:2B) in exactly the same proportion. The triangle can be of any shape, but in practice either equilateral or right-angled triangles are normally used.

Where the figure to be reduced (or enlarged) is a rectangle it is only necessary to draw the diagonal (351:3) to create two triangles in which the smaller rectangle (ab) is in strict proportion to the larger (AB). If a given moulding has to be reduced in section, for example to two-thirds its original size, then the procedure is shown in 351:4. The full-size section CAB is first drawn, and at a convenient distance the required height of the reduced section DE. A triangle AXC is then drawn on base-line AC to enclose DE. If DE is placed centrally as shown then the triangle will be equal sided, but if DE is placed on a horizontal line drawn from C it will be a right-angled triangle. Salient points of the moulding 1, 2, 3, 4, etc. are then drawn from the profile outline to the bed AC, and from there diminished to X, cutting DE in exactly the same proportion. The thickness of the reduced moulding section FG is then enclosed in a similar triangle erected on AB and additional salient points produced and diminished to Y, yielding points on FG which can be stepped off on the reduced section DE, FG. Alternatively, the reduced thickness can be plotted as shown in 351:5, where salient points in the thickness are drawn to the base-line CH and from centre C swung round to AC extended to G, and from there diminished to X, cutting DF extended to J. From DJ with centre F they are swung back to plot the reduced thickness of the required section FDE. In all cases the procedure can be reversed for the enlargement of any given section, and if the moulding section FDE (351:5) is to be enlarged to CAB then FDE is drawn first and the enlarged section developed from it.

The application of these methods to turned-work (balusters, table legs, etc.) is identical, and it is only necessary to draw an axis or centre-line and treat one half of the turning as a flat-bedded moulding as described above. If reeded or fluted columns in tapered legs or pilasters have to be reduced then the simpler method shown in 352:1 can be used. The thickness of the reduced section EF can be determined by describing an arc from centre C with radius BC in the section ABCD, and describing a further arc with centre F and radius taken from F to the plotted point to yield the proportionate thickness FG. If the moulding arcs are compass drawn and must also be proportionately reduced in depth (352:2), then draw in the centre-line EF for the radius centres of the arcs, and with centre D and radius DE describe an arc to DC, and from there diminish to G to give the required arc to H, which in turn will yield the compass line HJ.

Where a moulding has to be reduced in width but not in thickness, then it can be done by drawing the normal section BAC (352:3) and the reduced width AD at any angle from A. Salient lines are drawn parallel to AB as shown and swung from centre A to CA extended to D, while salient lines in the thickness which is not to be reduced are drawn horizontally. It should be pointed out that in all the foregoing examples the greater the number of salient points the more accurate will be the plotting of the required curves in the altered profile.

INTERSECTION OF MOULDINGS

Raking moulds

Where two mouldings of unequal width intersect on one plane then the junction is a bevelled mitre as distinct from a true mitre of 45° (see Mitre, scribed and scarf joints, Chapter 20); but where two mouldings of equal width intersect then the mitre lines on each must be the same length, therefore the angles must be equal, or, as commonly stated, the mitre must halve the overall angle. Figure 351:4 shows the correct mitre line of two pieces of equal width meeting at an angle, and the dotted lines the effect of unequal angled cuts, where the cut (A) is longer than the cut in the opposite member. This halving of the overall angle is not possible in raking moulds in cornices, pediments, etc. as the side or return mould must have a right-

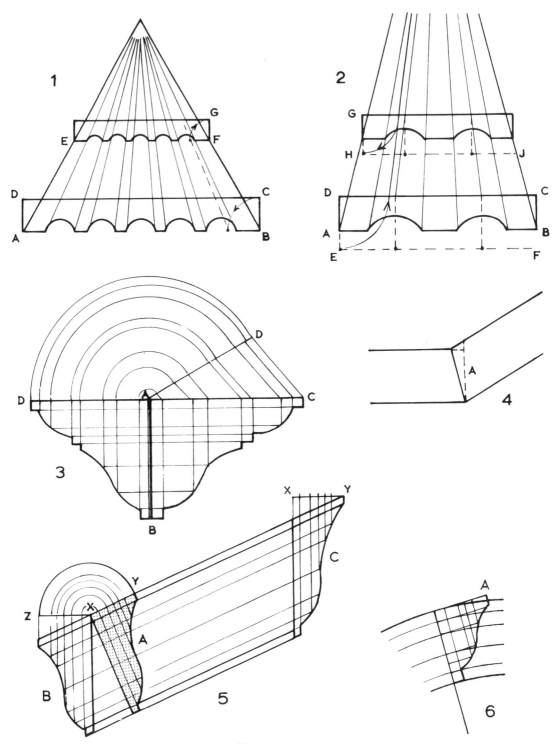

352 Proportional reduction and enlargement (2)

angled cut, and the raking or face mould an inclined cut vertical to the side of the carcass or door framing, as shown in the dotted line at A (352:4).

It is necessary, therefore, to alter the section of either the side mould or the raking mould so that they correspond, and 352:5 shows the method. As the raking mould is normally to a fixed section this is drawn in first and the profile added as A. Lines are then drawn through salient points parallel with the slope, and from the points of intersection other lines at right angles to the slope. From point X draw a true horizontal XZ equal in length to XY which is the thickness of the face mould, and on the centre X describe arcs as shown, dropping verticals from XZ to meet the lines drawn parallel to the rake. The points of intersection will then enable the profile of the return mould to be drawn in B. To ascertain the profile of the top return mould (C) it is only necessary to transfer XY with its plotted points to the horizontal plane and drop verticals to give points of intersection as with B. If the raking mould is curved (352:6), the arbitrary lines through the salient points of the profile A must be drawn at right angles to the bed of the mould, and should not follow the axis of the sweep.

Curved mouldings

The junction of a curved and straight moulding, or of two curved mouldings of dissimilar sweep or direction, is not in a straight line, therefore either the profile of one must be altered or the mitre line itself must be curved. Obviously the latter method is always simpler and the drawing below shows the procedure. Arbitrary lines are drawn either from the salient points of the profile 353A or, if the moulding is composed of one large member only, at any convenient spacings, and the curve is then drawn through the points of intersection.

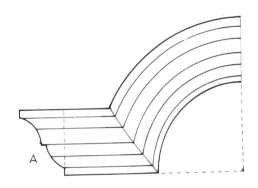

353   Curved moulding mitre-line

379

Part IX   Furniture designs and constructional details

41   Tables and desks (domestic and office)

The general term 'furniture' has wide meanings, but from the standpoint of the cabinet-maker its range will be limited to four main classes as follows:

Supporting units	Tables, trolleys/carts, desks, writing fitments, working tops, etc.
Seating units	Chairs, stools, settees, etc.
Reclining units	Beds, divans, daybeds, etc.
Storage units	Cabinets, chests, sideboards, wardrobes, bookcases, wall fitments, etc.

Additionally there will be miscellaneous items including mirrors, occasional furniture, some kinds of wall panelling and small articles of woodware commonly known as *treen* which do not fit readily into any of the above categories. Obviously only a fraction of all these can be included, nor is it necessary to describe in detail a great number or variety of furniture examples, for the underlying principles of construction remain the same throughout, and all that is needed is the application of basic techniques already described under the various chapter headings. In all probability the only real difference between a good cabinet-maker and an indifferent one will be the former's ability to think for himself and to apply his knowledge.

TABLES

General note

The normal height for any working-top in the seated position is now accepted as between 28½ in (72 cm) to 29 in (73.5 cm) with chair seats 10½ in (27 cm) to 11½ in (29 cm) lower. Elbow-room, i.e. width around the perimeter of the table for each sitter, should be not less than 23 in (58 cm). Normal width of table-tops is taken as 30 in (76 cm), but if there are flower-bowls, candles, etc. then 34 in (86 cm) will be required. A square table for four people should be 40 in (101 cm) by 40 in (101 cm), while six can be accommodated at a rectangular top 60 in (152 cm) by 30 in (76 cm). Circular tops 44 in (112 cm) in diameter will seat four, and 48 in (122 cm) six. Table legs should not interfere with sitters, and 20 in (51 cm) clear space between legs is required for each.

Types of table

Boardroom and conference tables: very large tables usually composed of smaller units linked together.

Refectory tables: long narrow trestle-type tables with fixed tops, so called after the monks' refectory or dining-room in the Middle Ages.

Extending tables: incorporating some form of lengthening the top for additional sitters, of which the oldest type is the *draw leaf* extension table dating from the fifteenth century and still one of the most popular forms.

Drop-leaf tables: in which the side leaves hang vertically in the closed position and are supported by brackets, sliders, or, in the case of the *gate-leg* table, by a hinged leg or leg frame.

Double top tables: in which the top leaf or leaves fold over and are supported by brackets or by pivoting the top.

Pedestal tables: usually circular or D end and supported by a central podium or pillar terminating in three (tripod) or four legs.

Pembroke tables: small rectangular tables with drop leaves on the long sides supported by brackets, and an end drawer or drawers.

Sofa tables: rectangular tables with drawers on the long side and small flaps at the end supported by brackets.

Side tables: generic term usually referring to all types of occasional table placed against a wall, writing-tables, hall-tables, console-tables, serving tables etc.

Coffee tables: originally small circular tables with tray-type tops, but now embracing a wide range of low occasional tables.

Nest of tables: usually three small tea- or occasional tables diminishing in size and nesting together.

Boardroom and conference tables

Normally this work is undertaken by the larger contract furniture manufacturers, but increasingly over recent years the designer craftsman has been getting involved. There is still, however, a natural reluctance on the part of companies, institutions, architects and interior designers to place this important and often quite prestigious work with smaller workshops. They have an understandable fear that the conditions of manufacture will not be adequate, that delivery dates will not be kept,

and that craftsmen generally are not business-like enough to undertake work of this nature. Edward Barnsley proved long ago that all this need not be so, and demonstrated also with his table for Courtaulds (354) in 1963 that veneered construction, so necessary with tables of this size and complexity, could be exploited in an honest way. All too often boardroom tables have meant acres of exotic veneers laid in a manner to simulate solid timber, the sole feature distinguishing them being their monotony, equalled only by the wood veneered panels that usually clad the walls. There is a huge potential here for imaginative designers and craftsmen to create environments that are unique and individually designed for the companies and institutions involved, but they have first to be persuaded that quality and individuality are both worth waiting for and worth the slightly higher cost.

354   Directors' dining-room furniture in rosewood for Courtauld Ltd. Designed by Edward Barnsley CBE, made at Barnsley workshops

355 Eight-foot diameter table in solid English oak
with central motif in marquetry. Designed by Jon
Barnsley and made by George Taylor in the Edward

Barnsley Workshops, 1984. (Photo by courtesy of
White Eagle Lodge)

356 Boardroom Table commissioned in 1978 by the
Oxford Centre for Management Studies. Overall
diameter 12 ft 6 in (3.8 m). Surface width 2 ft 6 in
(0.76 m)   Made in eight sections, constructed from
1 in (25 mm) birch ply with plain sycamore veneer on

horizontal surfaces and red stained sycamore veneer
on the verticals. Cross bracing structure in stainless
steel wire and tensioning devices. Designer and
maker: Fred Baier

357   Boardroom table and chairs in olive ash for
PosTel Investment Management Ltd, King William
Street, London. 1985, by Alan Peters

358   Table and chairs in cherrywood leather and   by John Makepeace MSIA
cane for Toynbee Hall London. Designed and made

359   Linking boardroom tables in sycamore with 56   Brokers' Association, Bevis Marks, London, by
chairs. Designed and made for the British Insurance   Rupert Williamson

360 Dining table and chairs in olive ash for BIBA House, Bevis Marks, London. Winner of Design Competition, 1985. Seen fully extended to seat 18. Designer and maker: Alan Peters

361 Alternatively, end sections can be removed either for use as sidetables, or linked together to make a six-seater square table, while the centre section will seat eight. The illustration is of a one-eighth scale model

362 Simple, robust, solid wood refectory tables to seat eight, 10 or 12. Treske (Workshops) Ltd

363 & 364 One-quarter scale winning entry in the open design competition for the High Table for Pembroke College, Oxford, 1983. The 22 ft (6.7 m) long table top was eventually made from two single planks of English oak. Designed and made by Richard La Trobe Bateman

Refectory tables

This old type is still popular and large numbers of reproduction refectory oak tables with solid tops are made. Figure 365:1 shows a representative example and 365:2 the method of construction, with 363:3 another form with square column and shaped brackets tenoned or dowelled to the column, and tenoned, dowelled or screwed to the foot. Figure 365:4 shows various table-tops: solid timber rub jointed or tongued and grooved (4A); solid planks with end clamps (4B); flush panelled (4C); plywood or laminboard, etc. veneered and edged (4D) with a double-tongued edge for thick tops (4F); and thin plywood, etc. with wide rebated/ rabbeted edging in which the increased gluing area will hold without the necessity of tonguing (4E, G). Other examples of this type appear in 366. In 366:1, carried out in English cherry with 1 in (25 mm) finished thickness jointed top, the

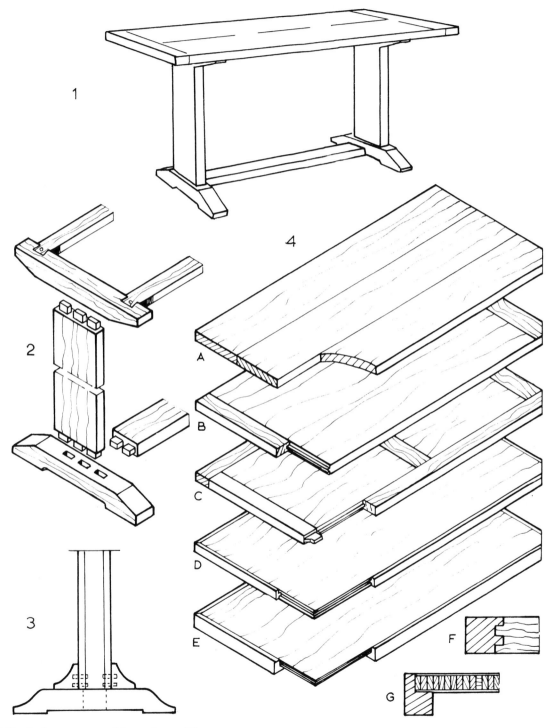

1

2

3

4

A

B

C

D

E

F

G

365 Refectory-type tables and tops (1)

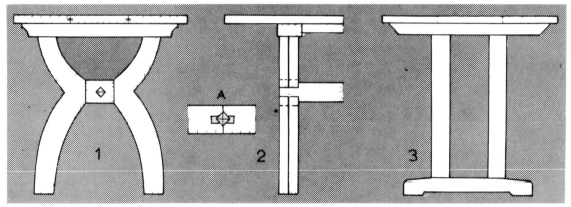

366   Refectory tables (2)

3 in (76 mm) legs are formed of two thick laminations (the 3 in [76 mm] plank cut through the centre) and glued together with a veneer thickness between to hold the short grain (366:2), and the centre block dowelled in on either side. A top stretcher rail is dovetailed and screwed to the ledges or top bearers, and a lower stretcher rail diamond tenoned through the leg blocks and wedged as 366:1. The jointed boards of the top are tongued together, with the ends of the tongues cut back and decorative insets of contrasting wood inset as 366:2A. Figure 366:3 shows a table end with turned twin columns.

Fastening tops   Solid tops must be fixed with slot screws, wood buttons or metal shrinkage plates (see also *Flush-top carcasses*, p. 197) to allow for shrinkage; the centre is permanently fastened and the outer edges free to slide. Plywood and laminboard tops can be fixed with metal shrinkage plates, or screwed through the stretcher rail and top bearers without fear of movement.

Extending tables

These are two types: *telescopic* in which dovetailed or keyed sliding frames fit within each other, and are pulled out as with a telescope to receive extra leaves which must be stored elsewhere; and *extending leaf* tables in which the stands are fixed and only the leaves slide open, with the extra leaf or leaves stored within the framework of the table. Figure 367:2 shows the principle of the telescopic tables with frames extended; 367:1 the table closed, 367:3 the separate frames sliding on sturdy tongues with cross-rails dovetailed on, and 367:4 dovetail keys which do not require connecting rails across the frames if the keys are sturdy enough. Tables of this description were often actuated by a long quick-thread screw working in a tapped barrel, and actuated by a detachable handle at one end; but as there was always a tendency for the separate frames to sag in the open position, a middle leg was often fitted, and the frames themselves were planed in rounding on the top edges by as much as ⅜ in (9.5 mm) over the length of a long table. This extending system was a great favourite in large Victorian and Edwardian households, but has now been superseded by the smaller types of sliding-leaf extending table, while large boardroom- and conference-tables are now usually made up of smaller units coupled together as required.

Fixed stand extending tables   Figure 367:5 shows the simplest type with loose centre leaf stored within the framework of the legs. Rebated/rabbeted sliders or lopers are secured to the underside of the outer leaves, and engage in corresponding rebates worked in the side rails screwed to the table rails (367:6), with 367:7 showing the detail of the rebates and the end table rails notched out to allow the sliders to pass through as the outer leaves are pulled apart. Locating pins or keys and matching sockets must be provided in the leaf edges for location (see also p. 391); also stub dowels let

388

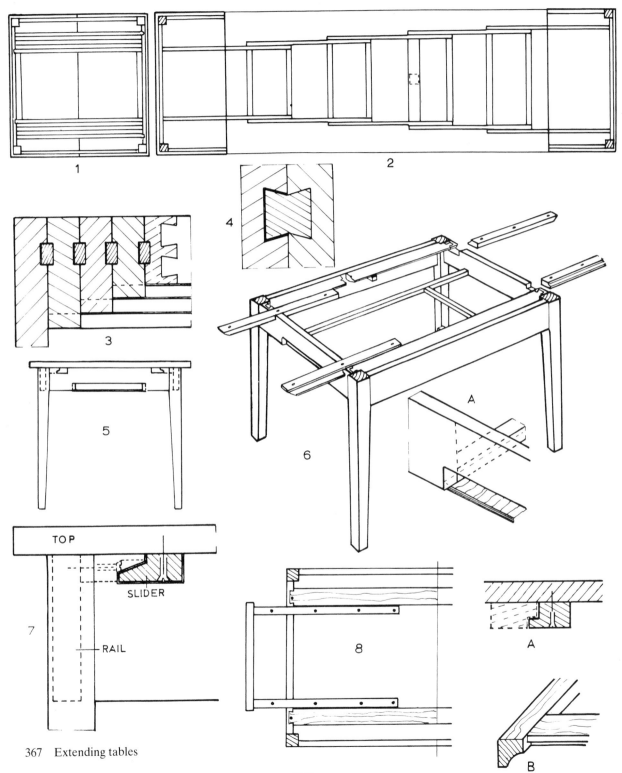

TOP

SLIDER

RAIL

A

B

367 Extending tables

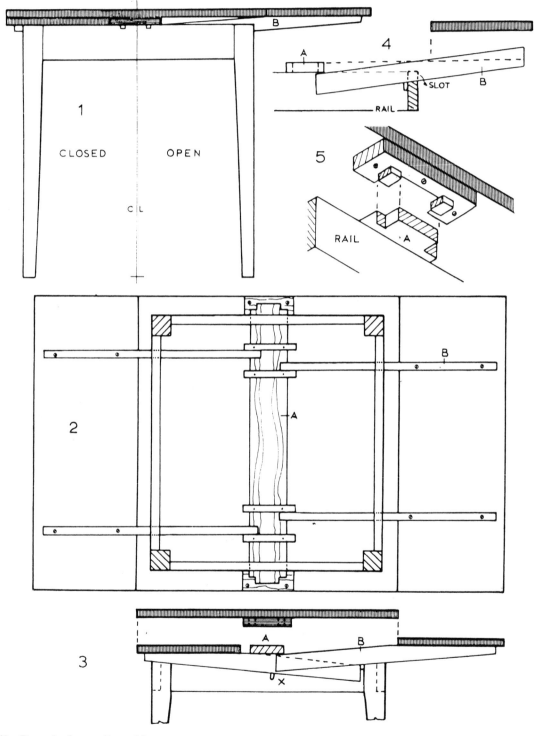

1

CLOSED   OPEN

C L

4

A

SLOT

B

RAIL

5

RAIL   A

B

2

A

B

3

A

B

x

368   Draw-leaf extending table

into the underside of the sliders to limit the travel, and centre stops to prevent the leaves passing over the halfway mark. The loose centre leaf can be stored underneath, with a ¼ in (6 mm) ply tray bottom screwed to bearers dovetailed to the end rails, one of which has an opening cut to receive the leaf (367:6A). A half-moon hand hole should be cut out of the ply bottom, and a slight scoop cut in the underside of the leaf sufficient for the tips of the fingers. Another version of the sliding action is shown in 367:8, where the sliders are rebated as 367:8A and screwed to the outer leaves with a moulded bar-handle grip (367:8B). This type of slider is also used with drop-leaf tables where the centre leaf is fixed to the table framing, and the sliders are made up as complete frames which are pulled out to support the drop leaves in the raised position.

Draw-leaf tables   This is the most popular of all extending table movements, and details are given in 368. Figure 368:1 shows the elevation divided on the centreline (CL) to show the closed and open positions of the leaves, which should be of identical thickness as the main top. Figure 368:2 is the underview plan with the bearer rail (368:2A) of the same thickness as the leaves, and firmly screwed to the table framing. Cross-guides are screwed to the bearer rail, and the diminishing sliders (368:2B), whose width should be twice the thickness of the tops, are firmly screwed to the two leaves and free to slide between the cross-guides, with a dowel-peg (368:3X) to limit the travel. Slots equal in depth to half the width of the sliders are cut in the end framing, and the angle at which the sliders are cut to diminish is shown by the dotted line at 368:4B. The main top is not fixed, for it has to be raised slightly to allow the leaves to be pulled out and slid back, and it is held in position by shaped blocks (368:5) glued and screwed to the underside, with small locating blocks screwed to the main block to guide the top into the correct position over the notched bearer rail (368:2A). As a refinement card-table pivots or coach bolts welded to a fixing plate are screwed to the underside of the main top, passed through the bearer rail and set to allow the required upward movement, but these are hardly necessary unless the table is frequently upended. Baize

strips glued to the top edges of the end rails provide a sweet sliding action to the leaves as they are withdrawn.

Flip-top (up and over) extending tables   With this type the centre leaf is in two halves hinged together with Soss-type invisible hinges (373:1, 2), and pivoted at the sides to cross rails so that the complete hinged leaf can be folded up and swung down within the table framing (373:3); the outer leaves are then slid back to close the gap. These outer leaves have sliders attached, with worked tongues sliding in grooves in the sides of the table, and the cross rails must be notched out to allow their passage. The sliders can be kept short, in which case the leg shoulders will act as stops limiting the travel (373:6, 8), but the tops will be unsupported at 373:8X and careless handling could place too much strain on the short lengths of tonguing. If, on the other hand, they are extended out almost to the edges of the leaves (373:5), then either the side rails must be flush with the legs on the insides or filler pieces must be inserted (373:7) to take the grooves. The grooves must also be worked across the inner faces of the legs, and the end rails notched out as for the cross rails. Short stub dowels must be let into the grooves on the halfway mark, and also on the under edge of the sliders to limit the travel in either direction. Locating pins or keys must be fitted to the leaves; either short dowels entering corresponding sockets on the opposing edges or inset oblong keys of hardwood tapered in all directions (373:5), with appropriate mortises cut to receive them. If the sockets are placed either side of the centre leaf and keys on the outer leaves the positions must be offset, and each outer leaf must have both keys and sockets; but if they are fitted in sequence, i.e. key on outer leaf, socket on centre leaf, key on centre leaf, socket on outer leaf, then the keyed edge of the centre leaf must be set back from the cross rail by moving the pivot plate over to allow the key to clear the cross rail as the leaf is swung down. The position of the hinged centre leaf in the closed (under) position is not critical provided it does not foul the table sides, and the approximate position can be found on the drawing by placing the folded leaf in a central position, and placing the pivot point (373:9X)

369 Extending circular table with flip-over centre
leaf and chairs. Designed by Philip Hussey for
production by White & Newton

370 John Makepeace: a special commission in burr
elm, the 6 ft (1.8 m) diameter top of this table is
supported by 12 laminated legs clustered into four
carved feet. 1982

392

371 & 372   This 6-seater oak table extends in four stages to seat a maximum of 14 people. Chairs are the now famous plank back. All designed by Robert Williams and made by Pearl Dot Workshops

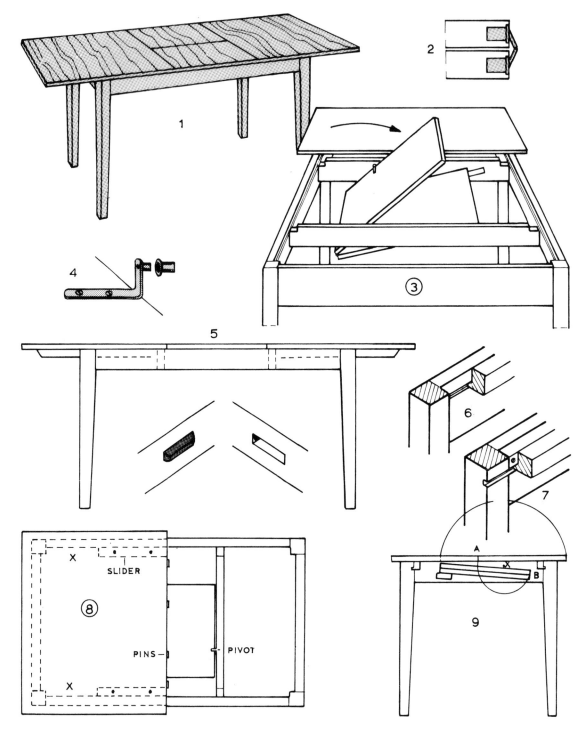

373   Flip-top (up and over) extension table

Within the figure:
2
1
3
4
5
6
7
8
9
SLIDER
PINS
PIVOT
X
X
A
B
X

374 The Kingsclarg dining/boardroom range. An industrial design of 1968, this extending table has a centre automatic flip-over leaf and extends from 6 ft 6 in (2 m) to 10 ft (3 m)

on the centre of an arc swung from the edge of the folded leaf to the outer edge of the table. The placing of the pivot point itself is, however, highly critical, and it can best be done by holding the folded leaf between the cross rails of the stand in the approximate position as indicated by the drawing. The pivot point will lie on a vertical line drawn halfway between the exact centre of the table framing (A) and the hinged side edge (B) of the leaf; and it is then only necessary to lay the centre leaf face downwards on a flat surface, register the stand in the correct position with the centre of the stand corresponding with the hinged joint of the centre leaf, place the pin of the pivot plate on the vertical line, prick through for the exact centre, bore and fit the socket, insert the pivot pin and screw the plate down to the leaf; it will then swing on the arc (A-B). The illustrations show a table 6 ft (183 cm) long in the extended position, with outer leaves 2 ft 3 in (68.5 cm) and centre leaf 1 ft 6 in (46 cm), closing up to 4 ft 6 in (137 cm) overall. Table widths can be 2 ft 6 in

375   Underneath view of draw-leaf table with panelled top showing one leaf fully opened

376   Swing leg, fall-flap table in solid English walnut with walnut platters and bowl.   Designed by Ernest Joyce MSIA. Silverwork by Leslie Durbin MVO. Author's workshops

(76 cm) to 2 ft 10 in (86 cm) or wider if necessary, and the tops can be solid timber if very carefully chosen, although veneered laminboard is better. The grain of the tops should run across the width, and it will be necessary to fit either a cross-bar or screwed brackets to the cross rails, set at an angle to support the centre leaf and to direct the movement upwards (373:9). Pivot plates can be bought as cranked pivot hinges or as a special pivot-plate assembly for this type of table (373:4).

Gate-leg tables

These superseded the draw-leaf type in the sixteenth century, but their popularity has greatly declined in recent years. They are a useful form for small rooms, and a wide range of tops can be attached—square, rectangular, circular, elliptical, D ended, serpentine, etc.— but the additional legs of the gates are somewhat inconvenient for sitters. The principles of construction are simple: the tops can be double and folded over, or fall leaf and lifted up, to be supported by a swing gate or gates pivoted to the main framing. These gates can be single (377:1, 2), double, which is more usual (377:3), twin for large leaves (377:4), while a semicircular side-table with double top and single gate is shown in 377:5. Figure 377:6 shows the basic framework with gate open, 377:7 an elevation of a typical elliptical top table with turned legs, and 377:8 a top and bottom plan. From these drawings it will be seen that the side framing rails must be wide or locally increased in width to receive the pivots of the gate framing (377:6, 8), and also where the gate leg is notched over (377:13). The rails of the gates can be relieved slightly (377:7A) to prevent them grinding on the table rails as they are pushed home. The actual pivots can be thick hardwood dowels, $\frac{3}{8}$ in (9.5 mm) iron rod or brass tube, etc. with the bottom pivot kept short and tipped on, and the upper pivot taken through the top rail and tapped home after assembly (377:12). A little candle grease rubbed over the dowels or rods will prevent squeaking and the sockets should be an easy but not slack fit. Figure 377:10 shows the bottom end rail set in for knee-room, and 377:9 the

small stops screwed to the underside of the tops to limit the travel of the gates, while 377:14 is an end-fixing card-table hinge for square-edge double tops, 377:15 is a back-flap hinge for square-edge fall-leaf tops, and 377:16 the moulded rule joint often used. The top ovolo moulding can be carried round the perimeter of the table, and this was usually done in typical examples (377:7). The legs of the gates can be shortened fractionally to accommodate metal gliders (377:11) for easier sliding over hard floor-coverings.

Pembroke tables

Figure 378 is an isometric sketch of a Pembroke table with fall flaps on the long sides, the support brackets (either one long one or two short ones according to the size of the flap) knuckle or finger jointed as described. One or two end drawers were provided in old examples, and if only one long drawer was fitted then the other end was treated as a dummy drawer front complete with ring or knob handle. The flaps were either square edge on butt-type hinges, or with table hinges and rule joints as for the sofa-table (379). Average sizes of traditional examples were about 39 in (99 cm) long, 19 in (48 cm) wide, with 10 in (25 mm) flaps either side, and a 2½ in (6.5 cm) deep drawer, but the measurements can be varied within wide limits.

Finger joint and knuckle joint Swing legs for card and occasional tables, etc. were hinged to the underframing by either the finger or knuckle joint, and while they have been largely superseded by metal fittings, there is no doubt that a pivoted wood joint correctly made will give good, if not better, service over a period of years. Figure 380 shows the finger joint, which is simpler to cut as all the work can be done with saw and chisel, with A as the fixed part screwed to the table framing and B the moving part or wing. The notches are cut at an angle of 45°, both parts secured with a central metal pin, the moving part (B) opened out in stages, and the rounding gradually chiselled away. Figure 388:1, 2 is the knuckle joint of more refined appearance, and here again A is fixed and B free to move through 180° if necessary. The circles

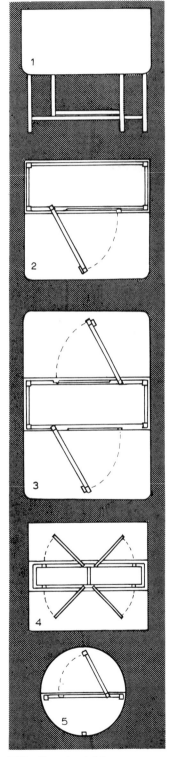

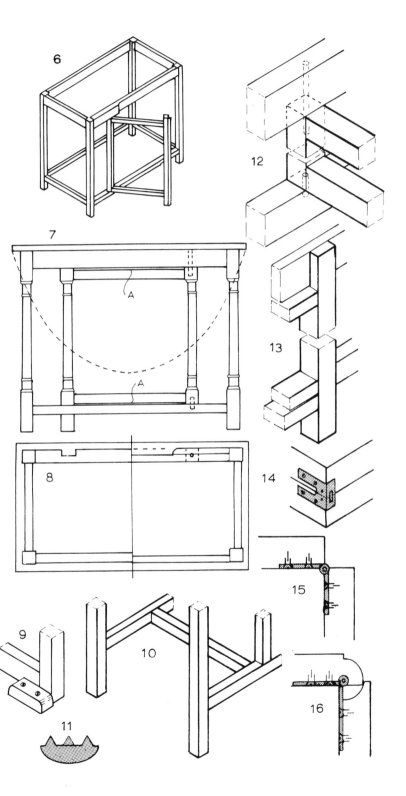

377   Gate-leg tables

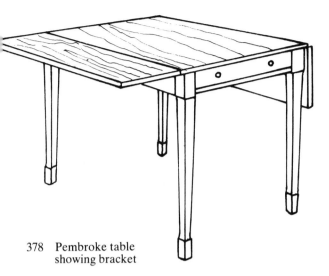

378 Pembroke table
showing bracket

and diagonals are laid out as in 388:2, saw cuts run in at the necks (X), the shapes worked and the shoulders cut. The knuckles are then laid out, usually five or more in number, and allowing two projecting knuckles in the fixed piece A and three in B. Sawing-in must be done on the waste side shown unshaded in the inset drawing (388:3), the unwanted knuckles sawn out, and the interiors hollowed with a scribing-gouge to take the swing of the opposing protruding knuckle. When the two parts can be fitted, waste pieces are cramped/clamped on either side to keep them together with a sash-cramp across the length to pull them tight, after which they can be bored through either end in the exact centre for a suitable metal pin, which can be ³/₁₆ in (4.5 mm) steel rod or a large french nail. The joint can be lubricated with candle grease and should be reasonably tight but smooth in action. The stopping angle of the wing can be adjusted by altering the angle of the diagonal shoulders, and a good medium hardwood should be used, preferably not beech which is very prone to worm, with ⁷/₈ in (22 mm) finished thickness for light brackets in Pembroke-type tables, etc., and 1¹/₈ in (28.5 mm) for heavier swing legs.

Concertina-action double-top tables

Figure 381 shows the side elevation with double top and end-fixing card-table hinges. In 381:2 the back legs (hinged side of top) are not

379   Rule-joint table top

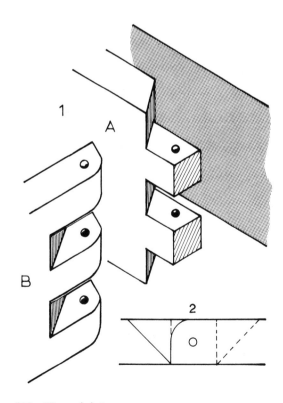

380   Finger joint

399

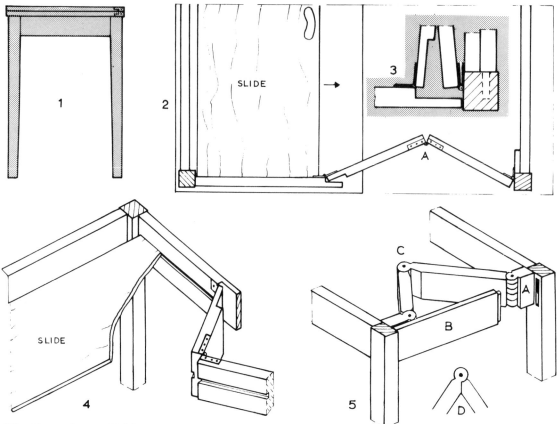

381 Concertina card-table

connected to the table frame, but to hinged rails extending as 381:2 and closing up as 381:3. Figure 381:2A shows a special top-fixing hinge often used in old examples, but back flap or piano hinges can be used. The frame when opened is kept rigid by a sliding shelf pulled along the grooves worked in the rails (381:4), and the top is then folded over. Figure 381:5 shows an improved version more rigid in performance, in which stub rails (381:5A) are barefaced tenoned into the legs and a show rail (381:5B) tenoned and glued to the front leg and glued to the adjoining stub rail, and tenoned but not glued to the other leg. The stub rails are knuckle jointed to the hinged rails, which are also knuckle jointed at 381:5C with extra long shoulder bevels to allow the joint to close at the acute angle (381:5D). A cabin hook and eye can be fitted to keep the frame rigid in the open position, as a groove for a slide (381:4) cannot

be worked across the knuckle without seriously weakening the joint. The method usually adopted for keeping the back legs in the closed position was to recess a $3/16$ in (5 mm) wood spring into the underside of the top, with a projecting knob which clipped over the rail as shown in the drawing (382).

Envelope-top card-tables

In this variation of the double-top table the upper top, which must be square, is divided into four triangular sections (383:1) hinged to the under top with centre card-table hinges. The under top is pivoted with a card-table pivot, known as a 'table swivel plate' and still obtainable as such, and a stop (383:3) which allows a movement through 45° in a clockwise direction (383:2). As the top flaps are flush, some method of raising them must be provided,

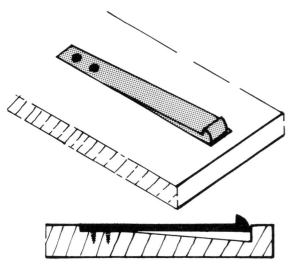

382   Wood spring catch

and in traditional examples a wood or metal dowel was inserted in a socket hole bored through the under top about 2 in (50 mm) in from one corner (383:2X). A ³⁄₁₆ in (5 mm) wood or thin metal spring was fitted over the dowel-peg (383:4A) pressing it up as the top pivoted over the table rail, thus raising the flap by a fractional amount which tipped the point of the flap clear so that it could be raised with the finger-tips. The method was crude enough; nevertheless it worked extremely well in practice, and more sophisticated methods

sometimes adopted in modern examples of this type of table are not necessarily more efficient.

Swivel-top tables

This method is more practicable than either the concertina or envelope-top card-table and is used in contemporary designs. Figure 384:1 is a pedestal type with double top hinged with counter-flap hinge or the more decorative mangle-top hinge, while 384:4 gives details of the framework and 384:5 the pillar fixing to the cross rails and the feet (384:3). The lower top is pivoted with a card-table pivot or table swivel plate (384:2) taken through a cross-bearer in the framing, and is free to move through 90°. The exact position of the pivot is fairly critical, and is found by drawing a plan of the table in the closed position (384:4A), and an outline of the open position (384:4B). A line at 45° is then drawn through the centre point, and the centre between the points where this line intersects the outer edges of the pivoted top in the closed and open position will be the pivot point (X). The extent of the travel is shown by the dotted lines swung from this centre, and a small stop is screwed to the top to limit the movement. Baize insets glued to the top edges of the framework will ensure an easy sliding movement. The most satisfactory format for a table of this type is square, as shown in 384:4, but rectangular

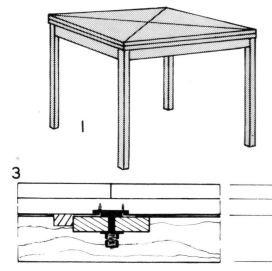

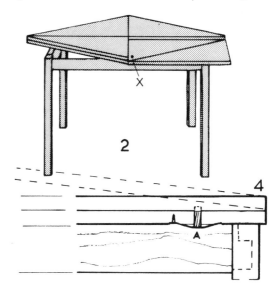

383   Envelope top card-table

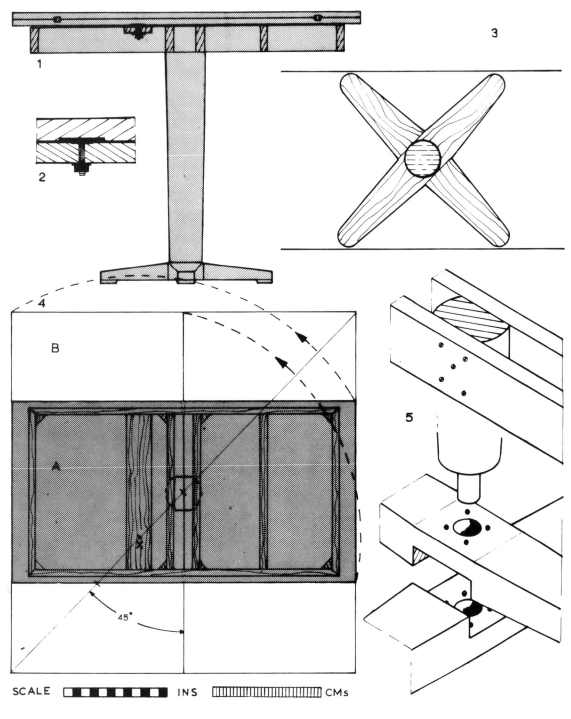

1

2

3

4

B

A

45°

SCALE ▪️⬜▪️⬜▪️⬜▪️⬜ INS 〔⫿⫿⫿⫿⫿⫿⫿⫿⫿〕 CMs

5

384 Pivot-top table

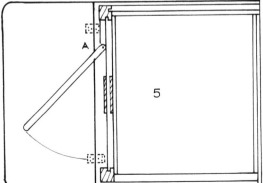

shapes are feasible within certain limits, always provided that the width of each leaf is more than half the length of the rectangular framework, or the opened leaves will not cover. A scale drawing will show the permissible variations, and the extent of the overhang, which should not be too great in either length or width or the table will be unsteady. Framed-up table stands can be used instead of the pedestal stand shown.

Sofa tables

Traditional forms have side drawers and end flaps, but without flaps this type of table can easily be adapted for use as dressing or occasional tables, etc. Figure 385:1 shows a

385   Sofa-type table

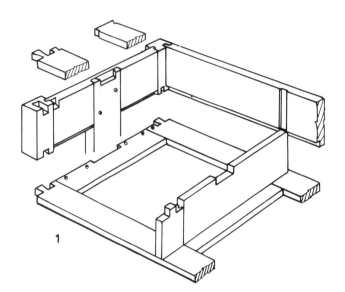

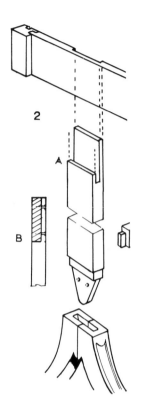

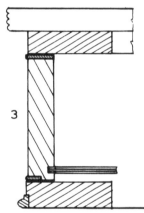

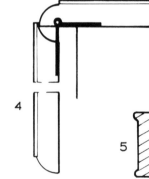

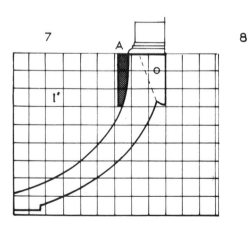

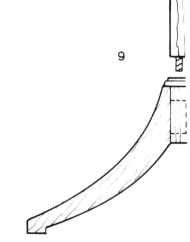

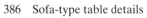

386 Sofa-type table details

387 This fine table in solid walnut makes good use of the traditional knuckle joint. Designer/maker: Peter Kuh

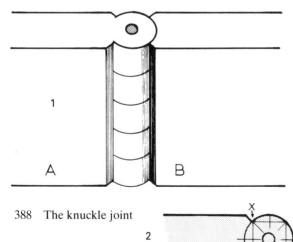

388 The knuckle joint

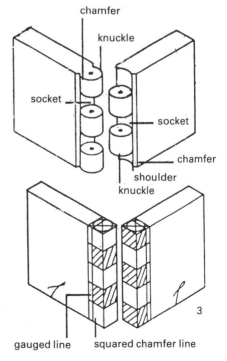

table without flaps, 385:2 the sectional elevation and 385:3 an isometric projection of the overall appearance. Figure 385:4 is the usual table with end flaps supported by swing knuckle-jointed brackets as in Pembroke tables, etc., and 385:5 an under plan showing the flap in the raised position. Constructional details are given in 386 with 386:1 the carcass framing, 386:2 leg details from which it will be seen that the side rail is bridled over the upright or standard, with the outer side of the latter cut back as at 386:2A to allow the bracket to fold back. If flaps are not fitted as 386:1 then the outer side can be carried up to the top of the rail, or more neatly finished by setting the rail flush with the legs on the outer face and grooving and screwing the standard (386:2B). The shaped legs are set out full size as shown in 386:7, with the shaded portion left on to facilitate cramping/ clamping up and then cut off after asembly, butt jointed and glued together and mortised for the triangular-shaped tenon of the standard (386:2) which is glued and screwed from the inside. Figure 386:3 is the sectional elevation of a typical drawer front with cock beads, also a reeded edge to the table-top and a small base moulding rebated/rabbeted in, while 386:4 is the rule-joint assembly for the flap, and 386:5 the moulded section of the stretcher rail between the two leg frames. The standard is usually rebated out for an inset capping moulding mitred all round (386:6), while 386:9 shows an alternative method of framing the legs which are tenoned into a block, with a separate moulded capping piece glued on and the standard dowelled in.

Sunderland tables

These worked on the same principle as the Pembroke table, but the tops were narrow and the flaps much deeper, with the result that the tables were not as stable as the Pembroke and, therefore, not so popular. A compromise between the two was sometimes made with large flaps supported by swing legs on the gate-leg table principle.

Side tables

This typical side table (389:1) was originally made up as a teak display-table for a very valuable and heavy Tang dynasty pottery horse, but is equally suitable as a serving- or library-table, etc. Figure 389:2 gives the detail of leg, tenoned-in rail and attached top, showing the chamfers worked to relieve the otherwise plain design. The original top was 1½ in (38 mm) blockboard (obtainable as flush door blanks) veneered and edged, but 389:3 shows an alternative construction with ⅝ in (16 mm) plywood and wide edging, and middle stiffening rail glued on. On practical grounds it can be argued that there is little intrinsic difference between a solid and a built-up top, provided the ply is heavy enough, and the outward appearance must be the same; nevertheless, there is a very subtle difference which the expert eye will be able to detect.

Coffee and occasional tables

The coffee or occasional table as an item of furniture has no parallel in past centuries in the West, although low tables, used mainly for dining purposes, have been in use for many centuries in the Far East. The low table has, therefore, no need to reflect the images of past centuries and can thus afford the designer considerable scope, and has become an item of furniture much favoured by the designer-maker and amateur alike.

As a result, in recent years the coffee table has developed for beyond being a mere surface from which to serve tea or coffee to become an important focal point in many interiors. To meet this new situation, low tables are now often quite large, bold items of furniture, as able to accommodate the buffet supper, large bowls of fruit or flowers as the delicate tea or coffee service. They are increasingly becoming more artistically designed, devised to be looked at and admired in a static position, almost items of sculpture in their own right, rather than flimsy articles to be picked up and used in a flexible way. Flexibility, however, is still an important requirement in many households, particularly in smaller rooms, and hence the popularity of *the nest of tables*. These tables are light enough to be picked up with one hand and used individually by guests when necessary, but for most of the time they take up very little floor space against a wall.

1

2

$1\frac{1}{2}$in 38 mm

$2\frac{7}{8}$in 73 mm

2 in 50 mm

L	48 IN	122 cm
W	20 IN	50 cm
H	30 IN	76 cm

3

389   Side table

Construction and materials   The constructional methods employed on these tables often echo those of taller dining, writing or side tables. The main point to remember is that, unlike many items of furniture, there are no rules that apply to low tables. They can be circular, square, rectangular or free-formed; the height can be 10 in (25 cm) or 20 in (50 cm), and the top almost any size; the top surface can be of glass, slate, marble, leather, wood or plastic, and it can involve intricate veneer or inlay work, bold use of colour, or simply be a slab of unadorned solid wood; and the possibilities for the structure that supports the surface are endless. The following pages of line drawings and photographs illustrate the wide variety of possible interpretations.

390   Small side table using contrasting coloured veneers. Designed and made by John Coleman

A table with interior illumination (397) is included to show the principles involved. Figure 397:1 is a plywood box jointed by any suitable method and edged on the top with wider boards (397:4). The sides of the box are cut away at the base as 397:1 to provide ventilation, and an obscured glass inner top is held in position by wood spacers (397:3, 4) to allow for free circulation of air, for most light fittings emit some degree of heat. The 12 in (300 mm) strip light is fixed to a cross-bearer across the centre of the box (397:2, 5), and hidden by the

391   Coffee table in Zebrano veneer, 4 ft 3 in × 1 ft 6 in × 1 ft 2 in (1300 × 450 × 375 mm) high. Designed and made by John Coleman. Photo by Tim Imrie

obscured glass inner top. The main top is 6 mm or 9 mm plate glass with four shallow recesses drilled out to provide seatings for the stub metal locating dowels (397:4). The light can be coloured by using any stained glass for the inner top.

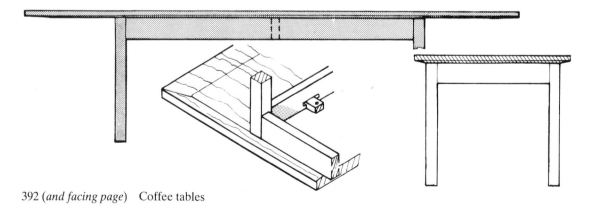

392 (*and facing page*)   Coffee tables

Dining table, Edward Zucca, U.S., 1982. Mahogany, maple, satinwood and ebony.
30 x 42 x 78in (76 x 107 x 198cm)

Writing desk, designed and made by Rupert Senior and Charles Wheeler-Carmichael, U.K. Wenge

Detail of the sycamore chest, seen from above

Chest of seven graduated drawers, Ashley Cartwright, U.K. Sycamore with coloured lacquer in handle recess

Yellow table, Hugh Scriven, U.K., 1983. Sycamore, stained and painted. The sides are 24in across x 14in high (600 x 365cm)

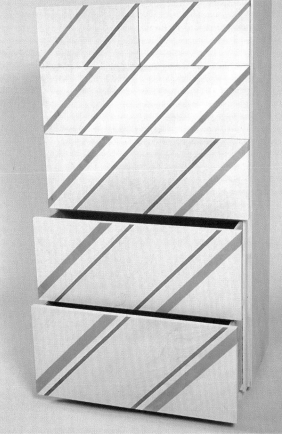

Chest of drawers, John Coleman, U.K. Sycamore and coloured veneers. Access to the drawers is by rebated finger pulls on the outside edge of each drawer

Tapered chest of drawers, 'The Great Art Deco Explosion', John Cederquist, U.S. Bird's-eye maple and colorcore. 64in high, 40in wide, 14in deep (163 x 102 x 36cm)

Table, Edward Zucca, U.S., 1984. Maple and mahogany. 34 x 62 x 18in (86 x 158 x 46cm)

Little white desk, Garry K. Bennett, U.S. Colorcore, wood and gold-plated brass. 60in wide x 24in deep x 29in high (153 x 61 x 74cm)

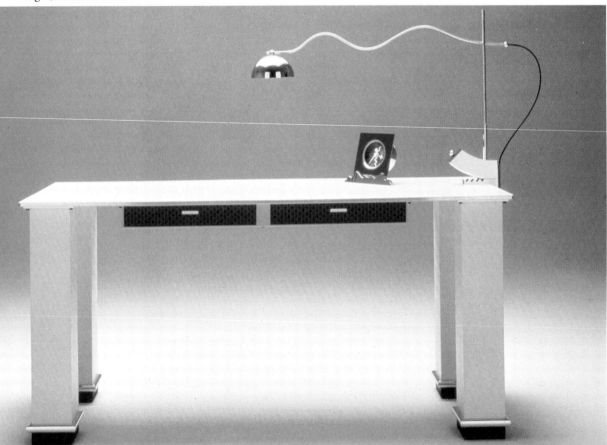

Mirror, John Coleman, U.K. The frame incorporates dyed veneers

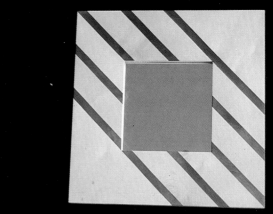

Corner shelf, Hugh Scriven, U.K., 1980. Stained and painted sycamore. The outside edges are 22in (56cm)

Saw tooth bench, Garry K. Bennett, U.S., 1984. Automotive lacquer, ebony and colorcore. 62 x 32 x 15in (158 x 81 x 38cm)

Continuous arm chair, Thos. Moser, U.S. The seat and chair back are cherry, the spindles and legs white ash.
41in high, 23in wide, 17in deep (104 x 59 x 43cm)

Ball and cone chair, Norman Petersen, U.S.
Purpleheart wood, lacquered wood, gold and
aluminium foil, painted leather. 33 x 22 x 21in
(84 x 56 x 53cm)

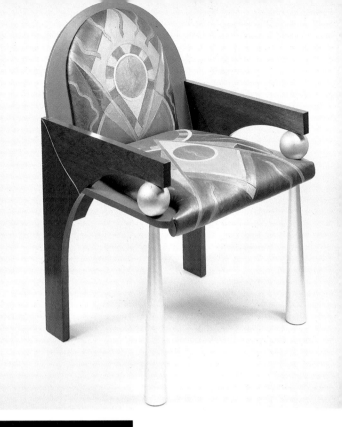

Lady's workbox, designed and made
by Edward Hopkins, U.K. Solid pine

Fan-back Windsor arm chair, Michael Dunbar, U.S. Three coats of paint aged to simulate an antique finish

393 & 394   These two large tables were designed
and made by Jeremy Broun. The top one has an
interesting and intricate top surface built of thin
strips of Columbian pine bonded to a fixed core.
Simple black inlaid lines complete the design. The
one below, in contrast, is of solid wood construction
throughout but uses narrow sections glued together,
a method that has been exploited in the bold corner
and centre joints.

410

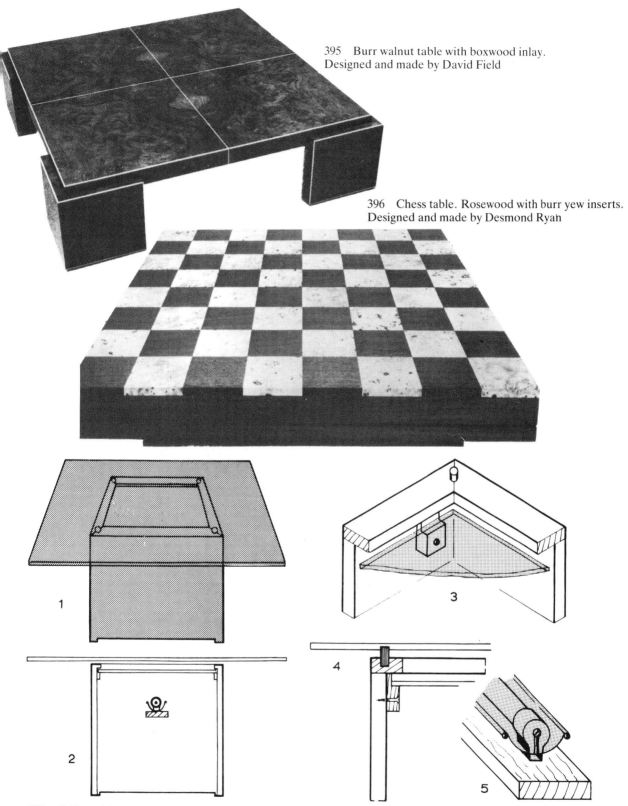

395 Burr walnut table with boxwood inlay.
Designed and made by David Field

396 Chess table. Rosewood with burr yew inserts.
Designed and made by Desmond Ryan

397 Coffee table with glass top

411

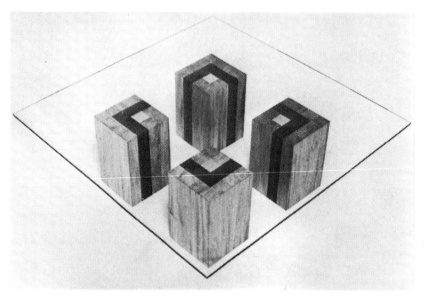

398 Glass top on pedestals of mahogany and Indian laurel. Designed and made by Martin Grierson

399 Display table in natural and stained sycamore. Designed and made by Neil Henderson

400   Table in solid oak by Desmond Ryan

401   Circular table in solid cherry with five veneered
panels. Designed by Robert Williams for Pearl Dot

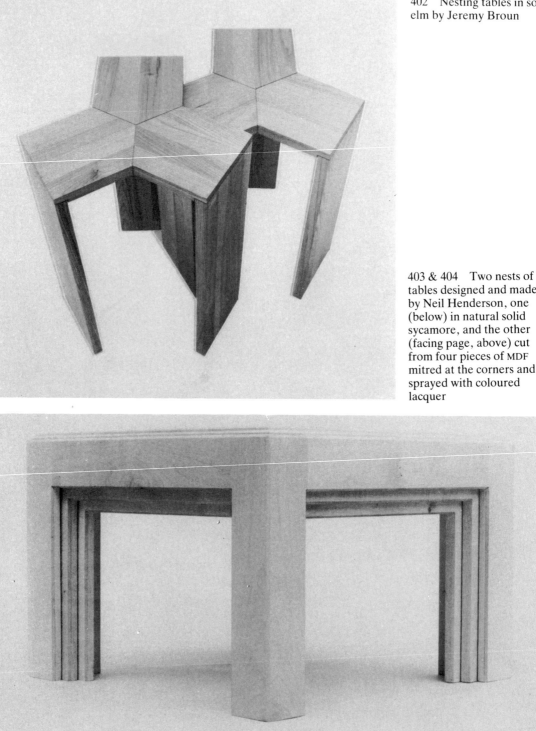

402 Nesting tables in solid elm by Jeremy Broun

403 & 404 Two nests of tables designed and made by Neil Henderson, one (below) in natural solid sycamore, and the other (facing page, above) cut from four pieces of MDF mitred at the corners and sprayed with coloured lacquer

404　Neil Henderson – Linear '3 in 1' set of tables.
Semi-matt coloured lacquer with contrasting line
around legs

DESKS

Writing desks

The writing desk in English walnut (405) was
designed on a series of golden sections for a
special client. The canted pedestals are attached
by screwing through the bearer rails into the
1¼ in (32 mm) blockboard top, and therefore
no stiffening rail is required. The main
construction is in ¾ in (19 mm) veneered
laminboard, with agba framing rails, etc. and
walnut edgings mitred at the corners and
chamfered all round (406:6). Figure 406:1
shows the elevation, 406:2 the side sectional
elevation with the small pen-drawer on
orthodox runners, and the other drawers with
grooved sides and side runners. A deep filing-

405　Walnut writing desk with canted front

drawer is provided for foolscap hangers (see
Chapter 24). Figure 406:3 shows the cant of the
pedestals, 406:4 the constructional details,
406:5 a section of the legs which are shaped to a
round at the base and tenoned up through a
double rail thickness as shown, while 406:7

415

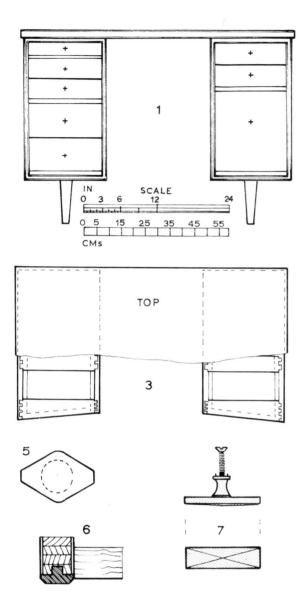

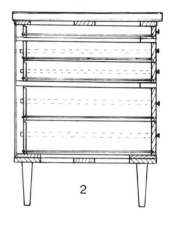

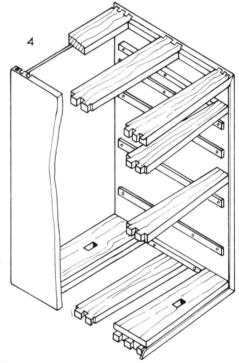

406   Writing desk details

gives details of the purpose-made brass handles with turned stems and brazed-on plates out of $3/16$ in (5 mm) brass, with the facets filed away and machine buffed. Two steel pins are drilled in either side of the screw tapped into the stem to prevent the handle turning. The final polish to the desk shown was one coat of hard lacquer steel-wooled and matt waxed.

Office desks

With the exception of senior executives' desks, which are purposely more ornate for prestige purposes, office desks are simply constructed and to a fairly standard pattern. Figure 407:1 gives a representative example with the flat side frames of 2 in (50 mm) by $1\frac{1}{8}$ in (28.5 mm) or $1\frac{1}{4}$ in (32 mm) stock, mortised and tenoned or dowelled together, with a $\frac{3}{4}$ in (19 mm) stretcher rail stub tenoned in. The stout top of $1\frac{1}{8}$ in (28.5 mm) solid blockboard, or $\frac{5}{8}$ in

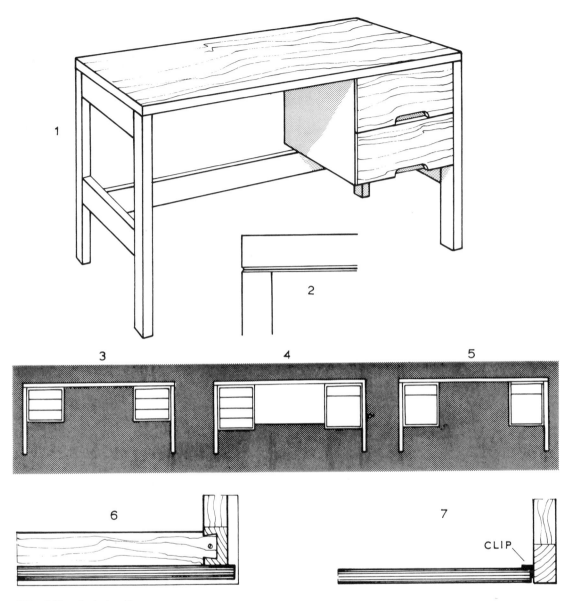

407   Office desk details

(16 mm) plywood thicknessed up on the outer edges, is secured to the frames by gluing and screwing; while the separate pedestal unit with ¾ in (19 mm) sides, recessed top, bottom and drawer rails, etc. and onset drawers, firmly screwed to the side frame and the top, is usually sufficient to ensure overall rigidity. A small vee or double chamfer can be worked round the top lower edge and edge framing as 407:2. Standard sizes for this type of desk are usually 4 ft (122 cm) by 2 ft 6 in (76 cm) wide and 2 ft 5 in (74 cm) high, while 407:3, 4 and 5 show 5 ft (152 cm) long variations. As these latter have double pedestals the lower stretcher rail can be dispensed with provided the top is strong enough to prevent any sagging action. Executive desks standing isolated usually have an apron front to hide the knees (407:4), which is merely a sheet of veneered blockboard, etc. either overhanging the frames or inset between them (407:6, 7), and screwed in position through the back of the pedestals.

408   Print chest with adjustable top covered in black leather. Chest in Rio rosewood with two drawers. (HRH Duke of Edinburgh's Prize for elegant design 1962.) Designed by R.D. Russell RDI. Author's workshops

409 & 410 (*left & below*) Writing desk in solid rosewood and cherry. Designed and made by Desmond Ryan

410 (*left*)   Desmond Ryan's writing desk, seen from the front

412 & 413 (*opposite*)   A quiet but distinctive piece in applewood with sycamore interior. Writing bureau, designed and made by Christopher Faulkner

411 (*above*) A desk and chair in cherrywood and
green leather. Designed by John Makepeace

414 A detail shot illustrating the type of recessed
finger pull also used for the flaps and drawers in the
writing bureau by Christopher Faulkner on the
previous page

415 Writing table and boxes, 1985. Natural and
ebonized ash; ebony details. By Rod Wales

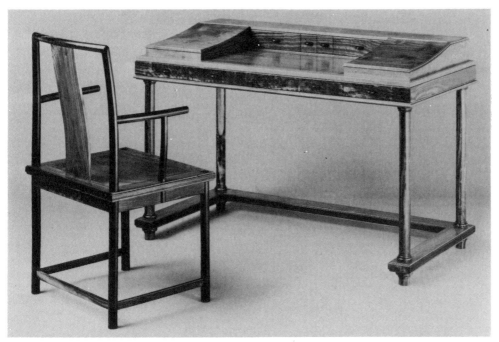

416 Writing desk with chair. Size 4 ft × 2 ft × 2ft 8 in (1200 × 600 × 812 mm) high. Frame and drawers in macassar ebony with tops and stretcher frame in American black walnut. Drawer and box interiors in Canadian Rock Maple. Made in Martin Grierson's workshop by Robin Furlong

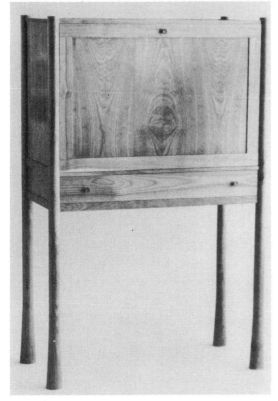

417 Drop front bureau in cherry. Designed and made by Michael Yeomans, Shrewsbury College of Art and Technology

418 Roll top bureau in mahogany with sycamore interior. Designed and made by Paul Morgan, Shrewsbury College of Art and Technology

42   Chests, cabinets and sideboards

CHESTS

Chests, man's oldest furniture, continue to have a place in modern households, being used chiefly for the storage of blankets and linen, but not exclusively so, as the cedar one in 419 by David Savage illustrates. They often double up as occasional seats, and the contoured tops as used by David Savage and Alan Peters (421) help to facilitate this as well as to provide visual interest.

419   Chest in solid cedar by David Savage

420   Chest in solid Scots pine with through tenons
and padauk feet, by Alan Peters

421   Specially commissioned chest in ash for
Kirkham House, Paignton, by Alan Peters

CABINETS

Corner cabinets and cupboards

Corner cabinets are useful for display purposes, also for conversion into cocktail cabinets, but are unsuitable as general cupboards, bookcases, etc. owing to the wasted space. Figure 423:1 shows a typical example of a glass door corner cabinet, and 423:2 a single-door corner cupboard. If tall cabinets are built-in it is usual to make the side pilasters extend beyond the sides and scribe to fit the walls, while the angle of the cupboard plan should be slightly more than a right angle as it is never wise to assume that plastered walls will be plumb or the corners at true right angles to each other. Such precautions hardly matter with free-standing cabinets (423:1) as the skirting boards will throw the carcass clear of the walls, but may be necessary with the wall cupboard.

Construction of corner cabinets, etc.

Tall cabinets can have separate top and bottom carcasses, with the sides made up of top and bottom framing rails and grooved-in plywood panel grooved into the front pilaster and back post (423:3), or solid laminboard sides grooved together (423:4). In 423:3 the back post will continue down to floor level, but 423:4 will require a stump leg added. Tops and upper carcass bottom can be framed in as 423:5, dove-tailed to the pilasters and either rebated/rabbeted into the side rails or screwed to fixing fillets, or tenoned (423:6) and screwed from the outside; while the lower carcass bottom will have to be housed/dadoed in as 423:10 or treated as the tops (423:11). The pilasters are usually set at right angles to the sides, but this is not obligatory and the angle or splay can be flattened slightly if necessary, but the doors should enter as 423:9 with the appropriate angles taken from a full-size layout. (See also *Canted dovetails*, p. 176.) Drawer arrangements are shown in 423:7, where in 7A the length and width are greatly restricted if orthodox runners are used, whereas in 7B a larger drawer is possible if a centre muntin is provided dovetailed as shown in 8A to fit in sliders (8B) screwed to the carcass bottom. A typical base

carcass assembly is shown in 423:10 in which the sides are carried down to floor level, and 423:11 where an independent plinth or leg framing is added.

422 Rupert Williamson: this corner cabinet has its roots in tradition and yet possesses a freshness and speaks to us as a piece of the late twentieth century. Note how the extremely delicate glazing lines extend visually through the door stiles

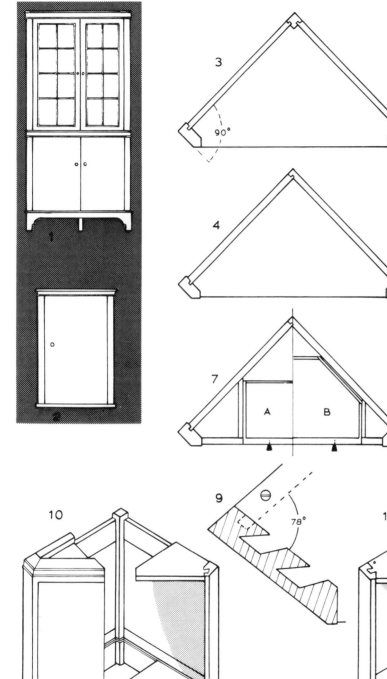

3

90°

4

7

A B

5

6

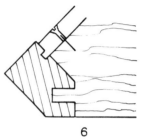

A

B

⑧

9

⊖

78°

10

11

423   Corner cabinets and cupboards

424 & 425   Jeremy Broun: an ingeniously simple
and yet distinctive design in yew with no visible
handles, merely a tilting centre panel that allows
access to the interior and provides strong visual
interest

426 (*above*)   David Savage: a quiet piece in pearwood, this display cabinet cleverly makes use of the wooden shelves to create a well-proportioned front elevation as seen through the four plain glass panels

427 & 428   Display cabinet in ash (*above right*) and detail of doors (*below*). Designed and made by Fred Perry, Shrewsbury College of Art and Technology

427

428

429 (*left*)   A fine cabinet in South Indian satinwood, with a green burnished lacquer interior, containing 13 satinwood drawers lined with green cotton velvet. Ivory handles.

The main cabinet stands on an elevated plinth supported on 12 cylindrical legs. The sides, back and doors of the cabinet are made up of book-matched saw-cut veneers, each joint broken by a semicircular fillet, with a green line of lacquer inset. The top of the cabinet, framed in solid timber around a quartered veneered panel, incorporates a concealed catch, and pivots for the doors which swing against the sides when fully open. The interior is made up of compressed hardwood panels, lacquered and burnished before assembly, except those areas facing drawers, which are velvet. The drawers are through dovetailed and radiused in plan to produce a highly decorative detail. Other parts of the lining provide a variety of vertical, square and horizontal pigeon holes for storage and display. Designed by John Makepeace and made in his workshops by Andrew Whateley, Alan Amey and David Pearson. 1980-1982

430 (*right*)   This elegant display cabinet in ebony makes intelligent and honest use of veneered construction without any attempt to imitate solid wood. Note the angle of the grain on the side panels and the subtle shaping on the solid edging. Designed and made by Martin Grierson

429

431 Edward Barnsley: a sophisticated bow-fronted cabinet which demonstrates the finest traditional cabinet-making skills and meticulous attention to detail. Note the carefully matched walnut door panels

Wall units

Figure 432:1 is an example of a backless wall unit incorporating writing-top, stationery case, cupboard with sliding doors and adjustable shelving for china, books, etc. Construction can be with knock-down fittings (see Chapter 31), or lap dovetailed if the top is above eye level, and the base housed/dadoed into the ends with a heavy support rail tenoned through and wedged. Methods of supporting the adjustable shelving are described in Chapter 29, but it is always advisable to include one or more dovetailed or plain housed fixed shelves for overall rigidity, and to hold the ends in case they are inclined to bow out under central heating conditions. Wall units can be built on site to fit alcoves or arbitrary spaces (432:4) or constructed on a modular basis, i.e. multiples of a constant measurement, 4 in (10 cm), 6 in (15 cm), etc., or constant width, 21 in (53 cm), 24 in (61 cm), etc. with the separate units brought to the site fully assembled and coupled together by screwing through the sides (432:5). The interior units, writing compartment, drinks cabinet, etc. can also be built in as part of the structure, or as separate boxes which can be adjusted to any height by screwing through the sides into the main divisions. In 432:1 the base shelving is raised up to allow for easy cleaning, but if toe-room only is provided (432:2), then the support rail should be brought forward to seal off the gap. Suggested measurements are shown in 432:3, with space above about 63 in (160 cm), which is the eye level and maximum reach height for the average person, treated as 'dead storage' area for occasional access only. If the units are made up to ceiling height any slight gap should be covered with a scribing fillet cut to the ceiling-line, and either glued on as 432:6 or set in and pinned from the back (432:7). The latter also shows an inset side scribing fillet, as plaster walls are rarely plumb. Tall units can be anchored with glass mirror plates, or with battens screwed to the underside of the top shelf and plugged and screwed to the wall.

Wall cabinets attached direct to the wall have obvious advantages in small rooms as there is no wasted leg space. Figure 433:1 shows a writing cabinet, 433:2 a cupboard with shelf with either glass or laminboard doors, and 433:3 an open

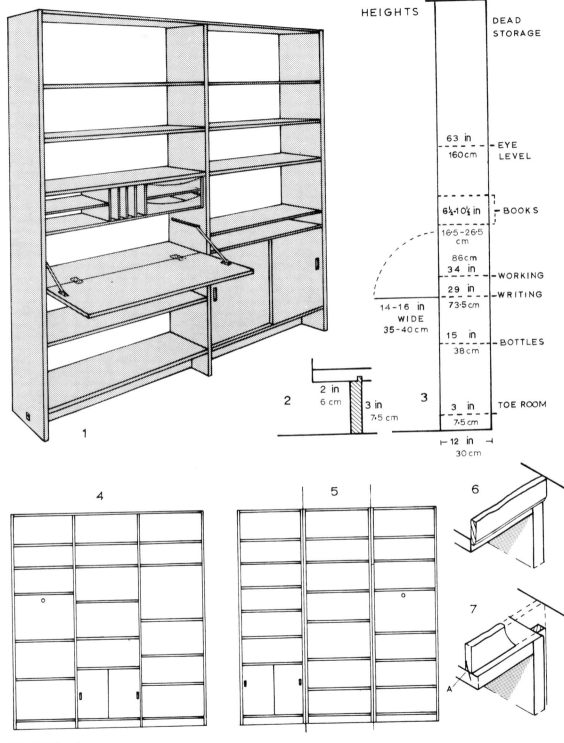

HEIGHTS

DEAD STORAGE

63 in
160 cm — EYE LEVEL

6½-10¼ in — BOOKS
16·5-26·5 cm

86 cm
34 in — WORKING
29 in — WRITING
73·5 cm

14-16 in
WIDE
35-40 cm

15 in — BOTTLES
38 cm

2 in
6 cm

3 in
7·5 cm

2

3

3 in — TOE ROOM
7·5 cm

⊢ 12 in ⊣
30 cm

4

5

6

7

A

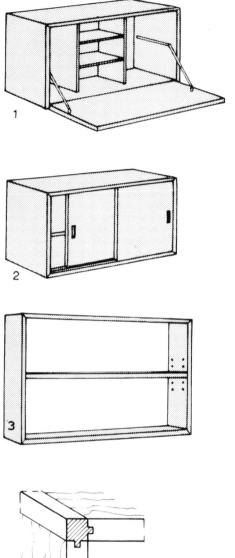

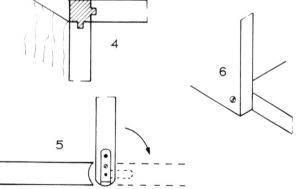

433 Wall cupboards and shelving

434 Wall hung display cabinet in sycamore by John Elbert

bookcase on similar lines. Acceptable dimensions could be 8½ in (21.5 cm) deep and 20 in (51 cm) high for the bookshelves, and 14½ in (37 cm) deep, 15 in (38 cm) high and 32 in (81 cm) wide for the cabinets. Larger sizes are possible providing the fixings are adequate. Construction of the small cabinets shown can be with any orthodox jointing method, mitre dovetails, through dovetails, etc. or tongued as shown in 433:4, while fall flaps can be hung on pivots (433:5), or merely pivoted through the sides with brass screws and sockets (433:6). Figure 435 shows a method of wall mounting in which the cabinet is hung from a bevelled rail securely plugged and screwed to the wall, with a corresponding bevelled rail attached to the back of the cabinet that hooks over it. This top hanging method will support considerable weights, but if there is any tendency for the carcass bottom to sag it should be stiffened with an inner rail, or an under batten should be screwed to the wall. Small cabinets can also be made with glass mirror plates. The slotted variety are easier to attach as the wall screws can be aligned and driven home, and the carcass with its plates dropped in position.

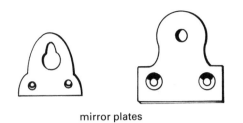

mirror plates

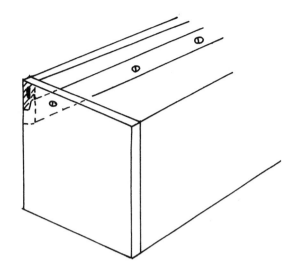

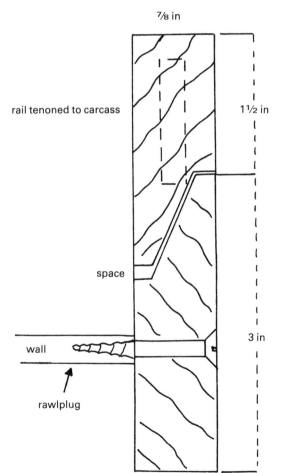

7/8 in

rail tenoned to carcass

1½ in

space

3 in

wall

rawlplug

435   Wall mounting using bevelled rails

Cocktail cabinets

Figure 436 illustrates a cocktail cabinet in English walnut, composed of carcass and separate stand with built-in shelf. Figure 437:1 shows the elevation and 437:2 the side sectional elevation. The carcass is in ¾ in (19 mm) laminboard with exterior veneered walnut from one wide leaf of sufficient length to yield continuous grain throughout, and interior in Nigerian pearwood, with the carcass mitre tongued and grooved at the top, and lap tongued and grooved at the bottom. Alternative methods of jointing are shown in 437:3, with 3A tongued and grooved for solid timber, 3B tongued and grooved with lap set back and an edging strip inserted for laminboard, etc., and 3C secret mitre dovetailed for solid wood or laminboard, etc. In both 3A and B the fronts are edged with the corners mitred, as this enables the tonguing to run through for ease in working. Figure 437:4A shows the plan of the leg stand with the veneered and edged plywood tray grooved into the side rails, and 4B the plan of the carcass with the lower shelf cut away to accommodate tall bottles. The upper shelves are fully adjustable on shelf pegs or *magic* wires, and the lower shelf, which forms the top of the drawer division, is housed/dadoed into the sides. The doors are framed up out of solid walnut mitred and tongued as shown by the dotted lines in 437:5, with the raised plywood panels edged, tongued into the framing, shaped on the face edges and veneered over the edging with

436 Cocktail cabinet in English walnut with fluted drawer front. Designed by Ernest Joyce MSIA. Author's workshops

matching veneers. Figure 437:6 is the detail of the taper legs with curve formed in the leg and not out of the rail which would result in a feather edge at the junction, while 437:7 shows the handworked fluting to the drawer front, and the turned knob handles which were also used for the doors. Figure 438 shows a similar fluted front being worked with round moulding-plane, guided only by carefully marked-out pencil-lines. This measure of accuracy is only possible with a plane-iron whose profile has not been distorted by careless sharpening.

SIDEBOARDS

Sideboards can be tall and fairly narrow or long and low, dependent on the size of the room. Most types provide storage space for bottles, glasses, china and table linen, etc., with orthodox drawers or interior trays, adjustable shelves, fall flaps or tambours or side-hung doors. Attached legs or independent stools or stands are favoured, as there are obvious disadvantages in taking cupboards down to or a little above floor level on a shallow plinth. Reference should be made to Part IV which details stands and stools, carcass constructions, tambours, fall flaps, etc.

A sideboard in Rio rosewood is illustrated in 439 and 440. Dimensions are 5 ft 6½ in (169 cm) long overall, with separate carcass unit 2 ft 1 in (63.5 cm) in height and 18 in (46 cm) deep, and stool 11¼ in (28.5 cm) high. The sideboard is divided into three compartments, with double tambours to the middle section, and inset doors on butt hinges to the outer sections. Figure 439:1 shows the elevation, 439:2 the sectional side elevation through the tambour section, and 439:3 a plan section of the tambour and shutting edge of the right-hand door with shaped handle grip. Carcass construction is in ¾ in (19 mm) veneered laminboard, doors 1 in (25 mm) laminboard edged all round, tambours, show rails, edgings and stool assembly, etc. in solid rosewood. The top is secret mitre dovetailed, and the long rails which take the tambour grooves top and bottom are inset 3/16 in (5 mm), with the doors rebated/rabbeted over 439:4 and the door corners slightly rounded. Figure 439:5 shows the leg assembly, 439:6 sections through the handle grips shaped in a continuous length, and 439:7 the moulding to the carcass edges. The interior is fitted with trays in the right-hand division and adjustable shelves to the remainder, while the tambour division has false sides and back to hide and protect the travel. As the rosewood was exceptionally richly marked, varying from purple-black to light tan, and as the photograph had to be taken with only normal workshop lighting, much of the detailing has been lost and the handle grips are barely discernible, but both tambours and both doors have grips running the full height of each.

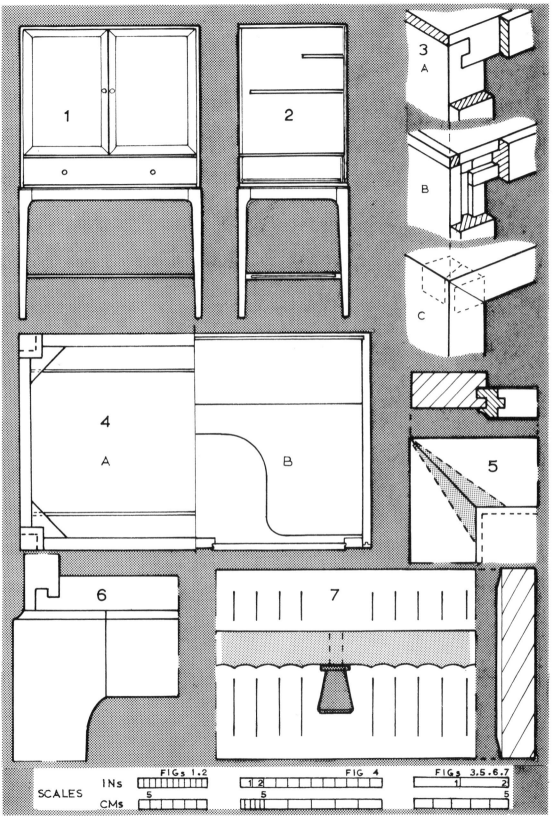

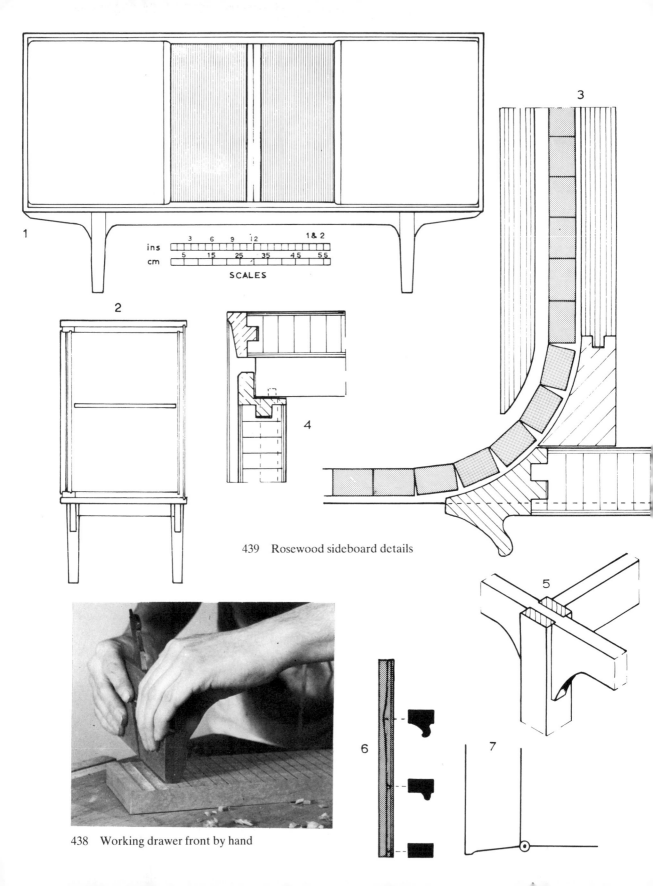

ins

cm

SCALES

3   6   9   12   1 & 2

5   15   25   35   45   55

1

2

3

4

5

6

7

439   Rosewood sideboard details

438   Working drawer front by hand

440   Sideboard in Rio rosewood with centre
tambours. Designed by Ernest Joyce MSIA.
Author's workshops

441 & 442   Two examples
of good quality industrial
cabinet work of the late
1960s designed by Philip
Hussey for White &
Newton, Portsmouth,
England. The piece on the
right is in European oak
with sea-grass panels, the
one below is in Burmese
teak veneers and solids

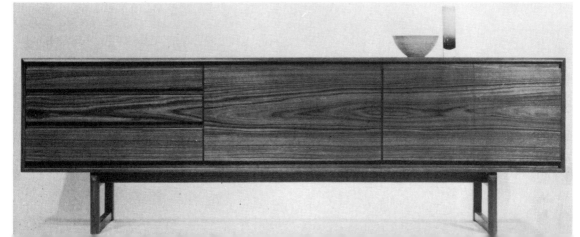

443 Desmond Conlan: woodturning plays a large
part in this simple cottage piece in solid Irish chestnut

444   Lucinda Leech: designed as part of a special
dining room commission, this piece in solid ash has
touch catches to the doors and the cabinets are
screwed to the wall

43 Bedroom furniture

Increasingly, clothes storage is being catered for either by permanent built-in units installed by the builder, or by KD linking wall units that arrive in flat boxes ready for DIY assembly. These often replace not only the traditional wardrobe but also the chest of drawers and dressing table as well. For this reason, and because the general public is less willing to spend the equivalent amount of money on bedroom furniture as they do on their sitting room, dining or kitchen requirements, bedroom furniture is an area less frequently undertaken by the craftsman. The exception to this is the chest of drawers, which can have a more general application than strictly bedroom use. However, the following information may still be useful and relevant as small workshops do get involved from time to time in the construction of built-in units, and free-standing bedroom furniture is still a requirement in many older houses.

WARDROBES

Even when these are designed as free-standing items of furniture, they are increasingly being produced in KD form to facilitate transportation and access to bedrooms, often up many flights of stairs. So, whatever the design, it is obviously desirable that it should dismantle easily.

Sizes

Wardrobe sizes are determined by fashions in clothes, and modern designs are usually 5 ft 10 in (178 cm) overall height, 20 in (51 cm) to 22 in (56 cm) deep for clothes hung sideways, and with widths of 5 ft (152 cm), 4 ft (122 cm) or 3 ft (91 cm) according to the type. Hanging wardrobes are shown in 445:1, 2, 3, while 445:4 is a fitted wardrobe with shelves or trays, and 445:5 a combination robe. Figure 445:6 gives a larger view of the latter, with half the width allocated to full-length hanging space, and the other half

divided into short-length hanging space or shelving and four drawers under. Figure 445:9 is a different arrangement with full-length doors, hat shelf and interior trays. Large wardrobes are often known as 'double', and provide a full-length mirror either on the centre pilaster between the doors, or fixed to the interior of one door.

Construction of all types of wardrobe is as for typical box structures already described under Carcass construction, Chapter 21, but in planning such large carcasses without fixed centre divisions or cross shelves due regard must be paid to the overall rigidity, and some method of stiffening must be incorporated with either reinforced head, plinth or central pilaster, and sturdy well-fitted back. Such reinforcements to prevent 'diamonding' have already been discussed (p. 187), but even with these there is always a tendency for large carcasses to rick slightly on uneven flooring, therefore they should be shimmed up level or flush doors will bind. Partially for this reason manufacturers favour overlaid doors closing over the carcass sides, as any slight rick to the carcass does not upset the hanging to the same degree. If flush doors are fitted (445:7), then false sides (7A) will be necessary to prevent the trays fouling the doors in the open position, but with overlaid doors (445:8) there is no difficulty, as the drawing shows. Trays (445:9, 10) are usually cut away boldly at the front so that the contents, shirts, underclothing, etc. can be plainly seen. They can be grooved for side runners or with bottom runners (445:10), and this latter method is preferable as it gives about ¾ in (19 mm) clearance between the trays which is usually necessary for soft, fluffy articles. Hanging rods for coat-hangers are ⅝ in (16 mm) or ¾ in (19 mm) brass-cased steel tube mounted in screw sockets fixed to the sides for clothes hung sideways (445:9, 11). For shallow wardrobes which will not accept the full width of the coat-hanger, short rods from front to back

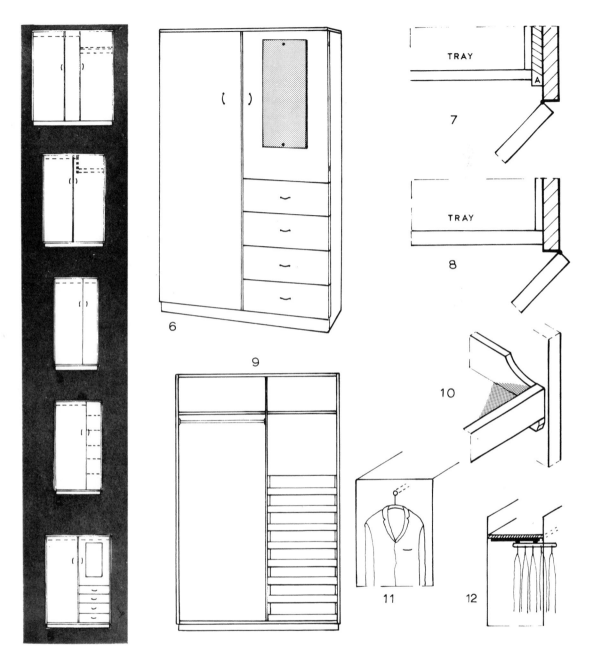

445 Wardrobe details

are held by socket hangers screwed to the underside of the shelf or top, or pull-out rods or sliders (445:12) can be attached which enable the hanger to be pulled forward clear of the carcass.

DRESSING-TABLES

Dressing-tables vary from around 27 in (68.5 cm) to 29 in (73.5 cm) high exclusive of mirror, or around 48 in (122 cm) high including mirror, with carcass lengths from 36 in (91 cm) to 60 in (152 cm) and an average depth of 18 in

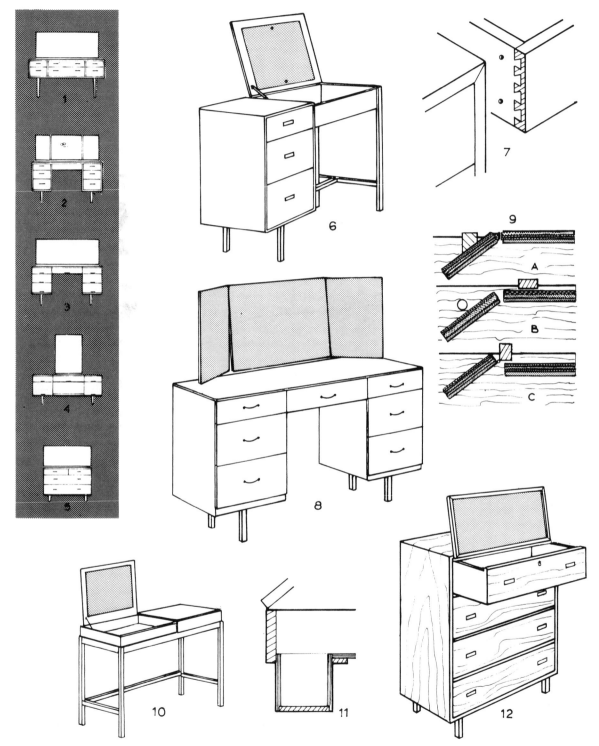

446   Dressing-table details

(46 cm). Low dressing-tables about 21 in (53 cm) to 24 in (61 cm) high without knee room, and therefore needing low stools to match, are also popular. No hard and fast rules apply to sizes for designs change frequently. Various types are shown in 446. Figure 446:1 shows a chest type 4 ft 10½ in (148.5 cm) long and 4 ft (122 cm) high overall with single mirror; 446:2 a 4 ft 6 in (137 cm) kneehole pedestal type with wing mirrors; 446:3 kneehole with centre drawer and single mirror; 446:4 a low type with three-quarter-length cheval mirror; and 446:5 a 3 ft (91 cm) dressing-chest. A dressing-desk with lift-up flap and interior mirror is illustrated in 446:6. The pedestal containing three drawers is made up separately, with legs attached either by tenoning into blocks screwed to the base or tenoned through the carcass base and wedged from the inside. The dressing-box and leg frame is a separate structure with the lower rails tenoned in, and the problem here is to form a strong joint between the box front and back and the pedestal side. They cannot be slot dove-tailed in, and while stub tenons might be strong enough a more practical way is to fit an inside side to the box (446:7), lap dovetailed to the front and back and screwed to the pedestal sides. This also serves as a support for the lid, which is hinged to the back and closes over the framework. Another type is shown in 446:10 where the two units rest on a separate frame-work and are screwed together as in 446:7. A plywood box for tall scent-bottles is incorporated in the dressing-box (446:11), and in both examples the brass mirror stay is fixed so that the mirror is stopped at the angle most convenient to the user in the seated position. Figure 446:8 is a pedestal type table with attached top and overlaid drawers closing over the carcass ends, with the drawer rails inset accordingly. If preferred, a front or apron piece can be substituted for the centre drawer which is not altogether convenient, for the user must lean back every time the drawer is opened to its fullest extent. This apron piece can be dovetail housed/dadoed, tongued in, or dowelled and glue blocked from the inside, and gives a strong junction between the two pedestals. The frameless mirrors can be treated in various ways. In 446:9A the wing mirrors are permanently fixed to hidden pillars, and the

447   Dressing table and stool by designer/craftsman Robin Nance, *c*.1955

centre mirror pivoted to the wings with friction plates blocked out to the required angle. Figure 446:9B shows each mirror pivoted on independent hidden pillars, and 9C hidden pillars so placed that the wing mirrors can be butt hinged to the pillars. The various types of mirror fixing are shown in 448 and 451. Figure 446:12 shows a man's dressing-chest of the military-chest type with or without brass corner plates and flush brass handles, in which a bearer rail is screwed to the top drawer sides and the mirror fixed to this with a length of piano hinge. The drawer sides must be set down by the thickness of the mirror frame plus the protruding knuckle of the hinge, and the drawer is stopped so that the mirror inclines slightly off the vertical, and is supported by the edge of the carcass top in the fully open position.

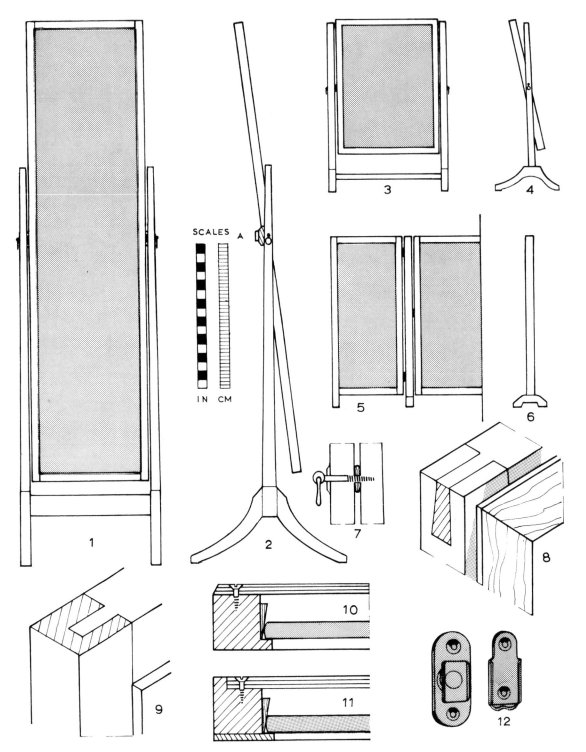

SCALES A

IN CM

448 Mirror details

444

MIRRORS

Mirrors are usually ¼ in (6 mm) first-quality polished plate glass silvered and protected. Frameless mirrors should have all edges ground and polished, but framed mirrors need only ground edges. Rough cut edges should not be used even in framing, for the sharp edges of the fractures will be clearly visible from the sides, and even with ground edges it is usual to matt black the frame rebates/rabbets to cut down unwanted reflections.

Framed mirrors

Frames need be of light section only, for the glass itself will keep the framework square and rigid, and the plywood back will strengthen the jointing. A typical cheval mirror glass with stand is shown in 448:1, 2 with 1 in (25 mmm) by 1 in (25 mm) frame jointed as 448:9. The stand (448:1) has a bearer rail tenoned into the tapered standards, and the legs are dowelled on 448:2. Small blocks are screwed to the standards (448:2A), and a thin lath fixed across the width to tie the standards in, while the mirror frame is mounted with drop or ring handles screwed through, with a wood button spacer as shown in

448:7. The friction created by giving the drop handles half a turn is usually sufficient to keep the heaviest mirror in the desired position. The mirror glass itself is cut about ¹⁄₁₆ in (1.5 mm) shy all round, and held in position with small softwood wedges glued and pinned (440:10, 11), while the plywood back can be attached (440:10) or let into a rebate/rabbet (448:11). It should not be glued in case the glass has to be replaced at any time, but should be brass screwed at frequent intervals. Figure 448:11 also shows a method of forming the frame rebate by gluing on an ⅛ in (3 mm) facing piece, often cross-grain saw-cut veneer in old work. Figures 448:3, 4 show a small toilet mirror with stand, with the standards sloping fractionally, and the mirror frame also attached by small drop handles. If wings are added to these toilet mirrors (448:5) the bearer rail shown in 448:3 can be omitted, and the spread of the feet reduced (448:6), as the angle of the wings will support the complete mirror. The framing need only be jointed as 448:8, with a facing thickness to form the rebate, and the wings attached to the standards with brass butts or back-flap hinges. Drop handles cannot be used for this type as they would foul the wings, and a friction-plate assembly is used of which

449   Wall mirror designed and made by John Coleman in sycamore and pearwood

450   Walnut table mirror by Alan Peters, c.1965

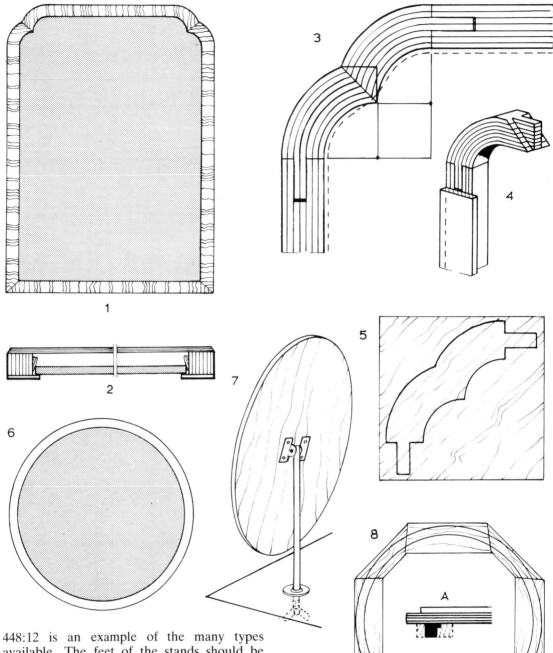

448:12 is an example of the many types available. The feet of the stands should be tipped with felt or baize to prevent scratching polished surfaces when the mirror is moved.

Shaped mirrors

Figure 451:1, 2 shows a wall mirror with shaped head. The frame can be band-sawn out of solid

451   Shaped mirrors

stock, jointed together as in old examples, but a better method is to laminate as in 451:3, tenoning the various sections together as 451:4, and facing with ⅛ in (3 mm) stock to cover the laminations and form the rebate/rabbet. An alternative method for small mirrors is to build up a laminated block with the double curve cut out in one piece as 451:5. The cross-grain tenons might appear weak, for the grain directions forming the lamination are not crossed as in plywood, but in practice the glue-lines hold the fibres together and the strength is adequate. Straight members jointed to curved members can be cut out of solid stock, but in principle it is better to use laminations throughout so that the shrinkage values are identical. Circular mirrors can be spindle shaped or turned on the face plate of a woodturning lathe, building up blocks to form the ring as 451:8, mounting on a plywood disc with a sheet of thick paper glued between, and centring the disc on the metal face plate (451:8A). The individual blocks should be cut and jointed to give as long scarfing joints as possible, and well sized before gluing together; but large mirrors may require the segments jointed together with veneer tongues as in mitre-work, or the face and back of the frame veneered to hold the joints. If the face of the frame is shaped then the back of the frame will have to be glued to the plywood disc and the glass rebate formed with a turning tool. After turning and sanding in the lathe the frame is separated from the paper interleaving in the usual way, and the back (or face) cleaned off. A standard tilting pillar fitment for mounting circular mirrors on dressing-tables is shown in 451:7, which is taken through the top and secured.

Frameless mirrors

Frameless mirrors with all edges polished are supported by a sturdy plywood back, and held in position with chrome-plated clips as inset. Figures 452:2, 3 are bevel shaped all round, while 452:4 is mounted on a veneered board and held by special fixing screws with heads tapped for chrome-plated domes (452:5). The screws should be an easy fit in the glass holes, and must not be screwed down tight; moreover if there is the slightest suggestion of bumpiness in the

ground, rubber washers (W) should be used to isolate the glass, which could crack if any local strain is imposed.

Hidden pillar mirrors

Small mirrors fixed to dressing-tables will only require one pillar (452:6) screwed to the carcass back, with the mirror supported by a friction stay. The mirror can be released by pressing the forked arms (452:6A) together, and lifting the top plates off their pivots. Larger cheval-type mirrors will require two pillars (452:7), with a stronger stay (452:8) in which the wing arm is secured with a wing nut. The edges of the plywood backs used for mounting these mirrors can be masked with thick poster paint, coloured to match the wood finish and then polished in the usual manner.

CHESTS OF DRAWERS

Chests can be 2 ft (61 cm) to 3 ft 9 in (114 cm) wide and up to 4 ft 6 in (137 cm) high with a fairly standard depth of around 18 in (45 cm). Tall narrow chests or those composed of two separate carcasses are usually known as *tallboys*. Chests can be placed on plinths or stump legs 4 in (10 cm) to 5 in (12 cm) high, or on stools up to about 10 in (25 cm) to 12 in (30 cm) high; the latter is more convenient for drawers in constant use. All these measurements are the generally accepted standard and in no sense obligatory.

Seeking alternatives to applied handles can in itself provide a strong design element, as can be seen in many examples of modern design.

Designed by Philip Hussey for White & Newton Ltd in 1977, these honest, functional chests (Figures 455 and 456) in cherry veneers and solids have all their drawers the same depth for convenience and economy in mass-production, in contrast to the graduated drawers produced by individual craftsmen. Note, however, the careful grain selection on the drawer fronts and the generous solid wood edgings and plinths. Sadly, White and Newton and their quality modern furniture were forced out of business in 1984.

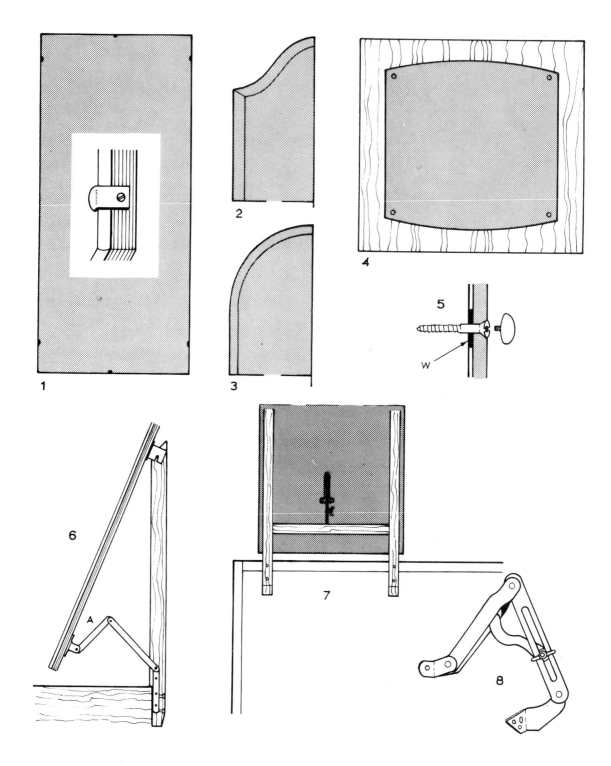

452   Frameless mirrors

453 Bow-fronted chest of drawers in makoré with inlays of ebony and sycamore. Designed by Edward Barnsley CBE. Barnsley workshops

455 Chest of five drawers in American cherry finish, introduced Feb. 1977

454 Chest of four drawers in solid afrormosia. Designed by George R. Ingham Des. RCA. (By Courtesy of Pedley Woodwork Ltd)

456   Chest of six drawers in American cherry finish, introduced Feb. 1977

457   Christopher Faulkner: this simple but well-proportioned ash chest is considerably enhanced by the clever detail of the finger recesses

458   Detail of chest in 457

Serpentine-fronted tallboy

This tallboy (459) was primarily designed as a contemporary interpretation of a traditional form and has been on permanent exhibition since first made in 1951. Figure 460:1 shows the elevation and 460:2, 3 the side sectional elevation. As can be seen the tallboy is composed of two separate carcass units with attached top and plinth stool. Carcass top and sides are ¾ in (19 mm) finish first-quality solid African mahogany cut from flat planks over 4 ft (121 cm) wide; sub tops, bases and solid divisions between drawers are ⅝ in (16 mm) selected western hemlock lipped with mahogany; while the ¾ in (19 mm) finish serpentine drawer fronts were made up from nine ³⁄₃₂ in (2 mm) gaboon constructional veneers pressed between male and female formers/forms in a screw-press and veneered with striped sapelewood. Drawer sides are ⁵⁄₁₆ in (8 mm) English oak, flush drawer bottoms and backs ⁵⁄₁₆ in (8 mm) English cedar, also the panelled backs with 2 in (50 mm) by ⅝ in (16 mm) stiles, rails and muntins, and ⁵⁄₁₆ in (8 mm) panels mulleted in. The panelled backs are rebated/rabbeted into the carcasses with a flush bead at the meeting edges, and all the drawers have a ¹⁄₁₆ in (1.5 mm) mahogany cock bead. Carcass tops and bottoms are carcass dovetailed, drawer divisions stopped housed/dadoed into the sides, upright centre division housed and screwed top and bottom. The plinth stool is built up of the same mahogany, with 2 in (50 mm) stump feet and serpentine-shaped rails out of 2½ in (63.5 mm) square stock tenoned in. Plinth capping moulding and lower carcass moulding are ⅞ in (22 mm) and ¾ in (19 mm) thick respectively by 2½ in (63.5 mm) wide stock, mitred and screwed in position, and all the mouldings were handworked throughout with small hollow and round planes shaped in the length to fit the curves. The serpentine shape is shown in outline in 460:4, while 460:5 is the top moulding, 460:6 the lower carcass capping moulding, and 460:8 the plinth moulding. The drawer knobs are turned from kingwood, dowelled in and wedged from the back. It is interesting to note that a second chest made to this design in 1952 and in daily use by the writer is still completely mothproof, as the solid cedar linings have not lost their pungent, aromatic scent.

459 Serpentine-fronted tallboy in African mahogany with drawers veneered in sapelewood and kingwood handles. Designed by Ernest Joyce MSIA. Author's workshop

BEDS

Bed sizes

Ideally, single beds should be as wide as the out-stretched elbows of the sleeper and certainly not less than 2 ft 6 in (76 cm) wide, with 3 ft (91 cm) more convenient. Double beds should be not less than 4 ft (122 cm) wide, with 4 ft 6 in (137 cm) or 5 ft (152 cm) preferable. Mattress lengths are usually standard at 6 ft 3 in (190 cm) for people up to 6 ft (183 cm) tall, but can be supplied up to 7 ft (213 cm) long. For easy making, heights should be about 20 in (508 mm)

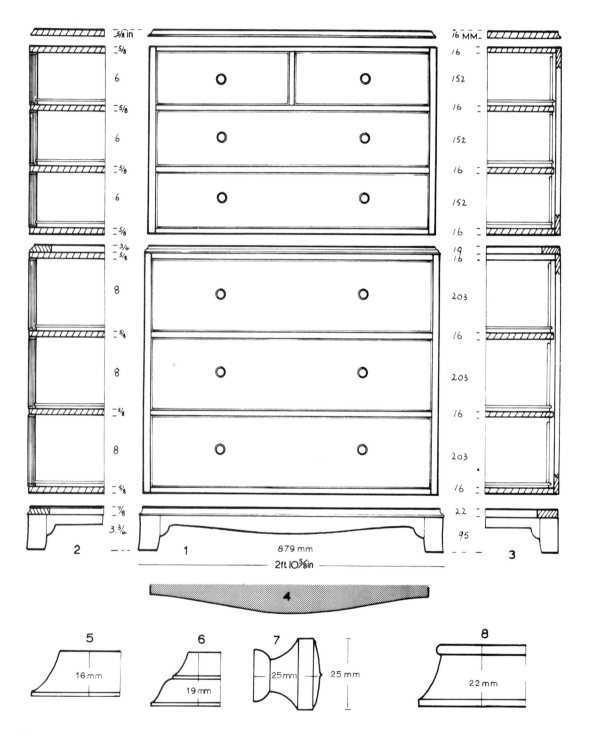

460   Serpentine-fronted tallboy details

461　Simple solid oak bedhead and footboard by
Edward Barnsley *c.*1940

to the top of the over-mattress but the modern
tendency is to place divan beds either on or
about 6 in (152 mm) from floor level, which is
not so hygienic and more difficult for the
bedmaker.

Beds take different forms of which the most
popular are:

1　legless sprung-base supports with either
steel channel or wood framing for connection to
orthodox bedsteads (bedhead and foot), and
with spring or foam over-mattresses;

2　divan beds in which a wood-box framework
on stump legs is sprung with metal mesh or coil

springing covered with fabric, on which a
sprung or foam over-mattress is laid, and with a
headboard screwed to the box framework. Both
forms are specially made, and the furniture-
maker is only concerned with the provision of
bedheads and feet or divan headboards.

Bedsteads

A typical sprung-base support bedstead with
detachable bedhead and foot is shown in 462:1.
Figure 462:2 shows a corner of the framework
mitred and tenoned, and with glued-in plywood
panel. This panel can be covered with material
(grass matting, etc.) in which case the covering
is glued on with a suitable adhesive (wallpaper
paste, shoemakers' paste) and glued and pinned

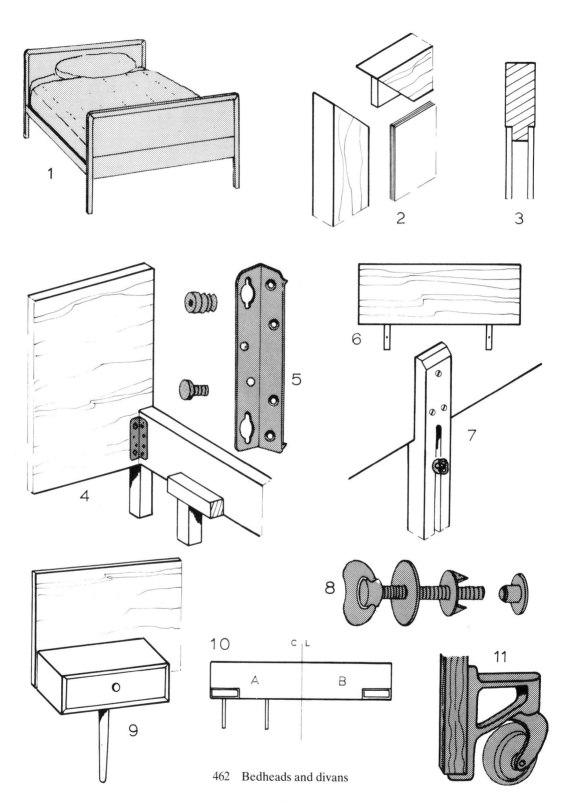

462 Bedheads and divans

454

through the weave of the material to a suitable rebate/rabbet worked in the framework (462:3). The framework can also be caned if it is rigid enough to support the pull of the caning, which is fairly considerable over a large area. A shallow rebate is worked on the face, ½ in (12.5 mm) wide and sufficiently deep to take the thickness of about three layers of cane, with ⅛ in (3 mm) holes bored at ⅝ in (16 mm) centres. The inner face of the bed foot framework can be sheeted in with a plywood panel set in a corresponding rebate to hide the rough back of the caning. It is usual to make headboards about 6 in (150 mm) to 8 in (200 mm) higher than the foot to allow for the pillow, etc. Patent screw fastenings or locking plates are used to connect the wood side rails with the head and foot, and 462:4, 5 show a typical assembly in which the corner plate is screwed to the side rail, and slotted over special screws or nylon bushing let into the head and foot.

Divan headboards

As the divan base is equipped with its own stump legs a headboard only is necessary (462:6), either screwed direct to the box frame of the divan or anchored with special screw-plate assemblies (462:8) through screwed-on supports (462:7), which can be slotted to allow the headboard to be adjusted to the correct height. Continental-type headboards for double divan beds (462:10) are usually about 7 ft 9 in (236 cm) long overall, and carry drawer fittings on either side so placed that there is sufficient space to allow the bed linen to be tucked in during making. These fittings are made up as independent backless boxes firmly screwed in position from the back of the headboard; they can have central leg supports (462:9, 10A), or if the headboard is fixed to the wall with mirror plates both they and the central supporting struts (462:10B) can be dispensed with. Ideally the top of the fitment should be about 4 in (10 cm) higher than the top of the mattress, and this also applies to separate bedside cabinets or tables. The actual headboard is usually a single sheet of ⅝ in (16 mm) or ¾ in (19 mm) veneered plywood, laminboard or particle board, edged on the outside, but it can be framed up, or caned or upholstered. A secret castor fitting for beds, divans, etc. is shown in 462:11, in which case long divan headboards with drawer fittings

463 Divan bed with under drawers in natural pine. (By courtesy of Price Brothers Co. Ltd)

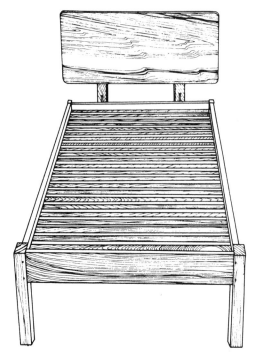

464   Inexpensive solid wood beds by Treske (Workshops) Ltd

should be fixed to the wall and not to the divan. The castors should have hard polished wheels for carpets, but soft rubber ones for slippery tile and linoleum or the divan will move too easily and could be dangerous for invalids or the elderly.

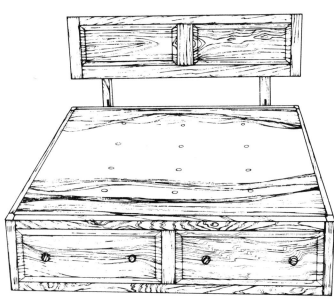

465 (*facing page*)   Headboard and matching bedside chest of drawers using dyed and natural sycamore and dyed green veneers. Designed and made by Lucinda Leech

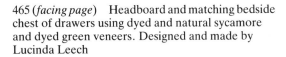

44 Seating and upholstery

CHAIRS

General note

Chairs of compound curvature and subtle shaping require the application of special skills, and in many richly ornamented traditional examples the designer prepared his sketches, leaving it to the actual maker to choose the wood and methods of jointing. As it is difficult, if not at times impossible, to plot all the curves of an elaborate chair in two-dimensional drawings only, the final result was dependent in great measure on the skill and sensitivity of the individual craftsman, and such chairs were highly expensive to manufacture, requiring the wasteful use of heavy wood sections which were rough shaped, jointed and assembled and then sculptured and carved, using special chair-makers' tools. Modern designs employ straight sectioned stock wherever possible, and steam bending or laminating for curved work, thereby effecting considerable economies in both time and materials. Such chairs are relatively simple to make, and do not require the same measure of special skill.

Chair sizes

Much research has been done into the principles or restful sitting, but while it should be possible to construct the perfect seating medium for any particular user, the average chair is designed for unseen customers, male or female, tall or short, fat or thin. Thus careful calculations based on the law of averages should be approached with caution. For instance, the standard height of a table-top, now usually accepted as 29 in (735 mm), calls for a chair seat height of 17 in (430 mm) to 17½ in (440 mm), but this is still too high for many people, and too low for some. What is badly needed, and will no doubt be evolved at some future date, are tables and chairs which can be adjusted at a touch to any individual requirement. In the meantime the measurements given below must be regarded as guidelines only.

Generally speaking the backward slope of the seat should not produce a knee angle of less than 90 degrees with the feet flat to the floor, while the elbow angle at rest on the side arms should not force the shoulders up. If the back is curved then the arch of the curve should be a bare 8 in (200 mm) above the seat, and the seat should be as deep as possible but not greater than the length of the thigh measured from the fold of the knee to the back. Easy chairs should not be so low or the backward slope of the seat so great that it requires physical leverage against the arms to lift the body from the seated position, and due allowance must be made for the extent of the compression or 'bottoming' of thick foam cushions under load.

Chair construction

Traditional chairs were normally framed together with mortise and tenon joints, for dowel-pegs had to be hand-shaped and boring-bits were primitive. Modern chairs rely more on dowelling techniques, and there can be no valid objection to this providing the pegs are of sufficient length to hold the joint. The usual procedure is to make up the front and back frames first, and then connect with the side rails unless a knock-down assembly is used. All chair-work requires accurate full-size drawings from which the correct angles and bevels can be taken, and more elaborate chairs really need a full-size working model or prototype in softwood which can be tested and altered as required.

Chair joints

Top back rail joints are illustrated in 466. Figure 466:1 is a tenon on the rail, 466:2 shows a tenon on the post, and 466:5 a dovetail bridle joint. Where the wood sections are very slim (466:6) the joint can be reinforced by forming a step to

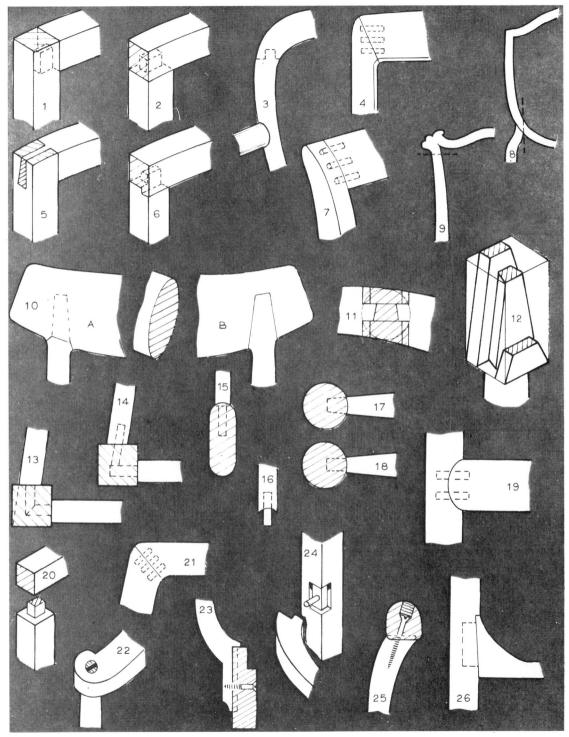

466   Chair joints

support the back thrust and increase the gluing area. Figure 466:3 shows a shaped post and top rail mortised and tenoned together and rounded after assembly. In 466:4 the top dowel has no real holding power but does prevent the top twisting out of line, while dowels are also used in 466:7 where it might be difficult to accommodate a tenon in the curve of the back post. The shield back chair in 466:8 and Chippendale carved chair in 466:9 are shown as a matter of interest only, for the heavy carving usually disguises the line of the joint, as shown by the dotted lines. A modern treatment in which a bowed, tilted and rounded back rail meets turned back posts is shown in 466:10-12, with 466:10A the front view and 466:10B the back view. Figures 466:11, 12 show the actual joint and the amount of material left on to accommodate the dovetail. The joint must be carefully laid out and worked with the final rounding and shaping done when the rail is fully assembled. This type of construction is very expensive, therefore, and confined to the best handwork only. Figure 466:13 shows a mortise and tenon joint at the junction of front and side seat rails with the front leg. Either a canted tenon or a canted mortise is necessary for the latter; therefore it is more usual to tenon the front rail and dowel the side rail (466:14), in which it is comparatively simple to bore the leg at the correct angle obtained from the full-size drawing. The outer face of the leg is usually planed off after assembly to the line of the rail, as indicated by the dotted lines in 466:13. Back seat rails are normally tenoned into the back posts. Where a rail meets a rounded leg (466:15) a small flat can be worked for square-cut tenon shoulders, but if the rail is also rounded then the leg recess must be scribed to fit. Here again it is simpler to use dowels, cutting the rail end square, marking and boring for the dowels and scribing the rail shoulders to fit the leg before the dowels are glued in (466:16). Figure 466:17 shows a turned spindle entering a round leg, and if a bung borer (taper bit) is available then the spindle is turned to fit the taper, taking care to ensure that the socket depth is correct, for there will be no shoulder to limit the entry. Parallel-sided sockets bored with standard bits will require a turned shoulder on the spindle and a small flat formed on the leg, but in cheap work

the taper spindle is merely driven into the parallel hole, with the result that it only bites at the neck. In 466:19, where a pronounced hollow is formed in the leg, it will be easier to use dowels, marking, boring and then fitting the rail to the leg before the dowels are inserted. An improved method of jointing side rails to back posts sometimes adopted in Scandinavian furniture is shown in 467 but it is essentially a machine operation.

The junction of arm rests with leg posts is shown in 466:20 where a small stub tenon can be used, although a single dowel is often effective, for the strain is upwards and not sidewards. Traditional chairs with turned legs and flat arm rests employed a spigot end to the leg taken through and wedged from the top, as 466:22, while 466:21 is the jointing of a typical modern framework where the overall angle is halved and dowelled together. Figure 466:23 is the juction of arm post with side rails in conventional armchairs, with the arm post housed/grooved in and screwed from the inside, and 466:24 the connection with the back post with stub dowel to take the pull. Older examples were often housed in and screwed and pelleted from the back (466:25), while 466:26 is the junction of a downward curved arm rest tenoned in and housed at the top to avoid a feather edge in the final shaping after assembly.

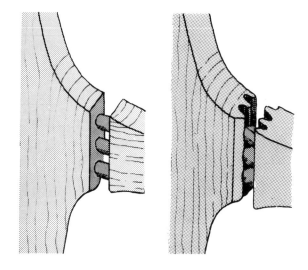

467   Chair rail joint

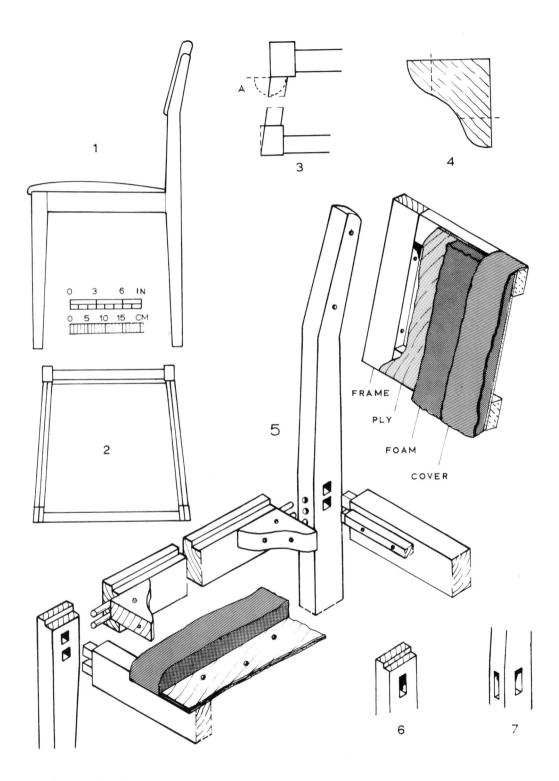

1

3

4

0   3   6 IN

0 5 10 15 CM

2

5

FRAME

PLY

FOAM

COVER

6

7

A

468   Dining-chair details

469   Timeless dining chairs by Gordon Russell Ltd, first designed in 1953

Simple dining-chair

The illustrations in 468 show the construction of this type of chair. Figure 468:1 is the side elevation; 468:2 the seat plan; 468:3 the angle of the rail joints taken from the full-size drawing, and 468:4 the heavy corner blocks which are glued and screwed into each corner of the seat frame to increase the overall rigidity of the chair. Figure 468:5 is an exploded diagram of the construction, with the front rail kept down flush with the rebates/rabbets in the side rails, with a supporting fillet screwed to the back rail for the plywood base of the seat. This plywood base should be bored to allow the air to escape from the foam-rubber seating, especially if impervious top coverings (leather, plastic cloth, etc.) are used. Figures 468:6, 7 are alternative mortise and tenon joints for front and back posts. The padded back is screwed to the back posts from the inside, and the top cover carried over to hide the framing, or alternatively 6 in (152 mm) taper dovetail slide connectors can be obtained in which the female part is screwed to the back post, and the male part screwed to the back rest slid down into position after the upholstery is completed. Chairs of this description can have webbed and upholstered drop-in seats as shown later in this chapter, in which case the front rail is flush with the side rails and the ⅝ in (16 mm) rebate continued round to receive the seat frame. Figure 496, for example, shows a typical seat frame for webbing which can either be dowelled, or half lapped and screwed. Suitable dimensions for average seat frames can be 2 in (51 mm) or 2½ in (63.5 mm) wide stuff, ⅝ in (16 mm) or ¾ in (19 mm) thick, and are usually made of beech, which will take closely spaced tacks without splitting. There is usually a rebate in the chair rails, allowing about ⅛ in (3 mm) clearance all round for the thickness of the covering materials.

Turned rush-seated chair

Traditional examples of this type of chair often used coppice ash for the back posts, which merely required soaking in hot water to enable the bend to be formed. It is usual to turn first and then bend, although there is always some danger of crushing the rounded surface of the wood if the bend is acute. Modern examples of these chairs are often stained with clear penetrating dyes which do not choke or disguise the grain of the wood, but to avoid uneven coloration the whole chair should be dipped.

The chairs by John Makepeace and Rupert Williamson illustrated on the following pages show clearly the work of the modern artist-craftsman. All four pieces are extremely complex feats of woodworking skill and are designed to be made without compromise. Production would be near impossible by machine production methods.

The pieces by John Makepeace are achieved partly by the careful laminating of thin strips cut from the same piece of timber, then numbered, so that when reassembled in the mould the joints are nearly invisible to the naked eye. Rupert Williamson employs more traditional forms of construction, but the skill and patience of the hand craftsman are clearly seen in these highly intricate backs.

In contrast, 476-478 show the work of crafts-men when they are not designing for a unique situation but for relatively inexpensive batch production. These chairs could possibly be mass-produced, but the fact is that they are not; they are all made to a very high standard within each craftsman's workshop.

470　Ash chair with rush seat made by Neville Neal, 1983. Design based on traditional country chairs as revived by Ernest Gimson c.1890

463

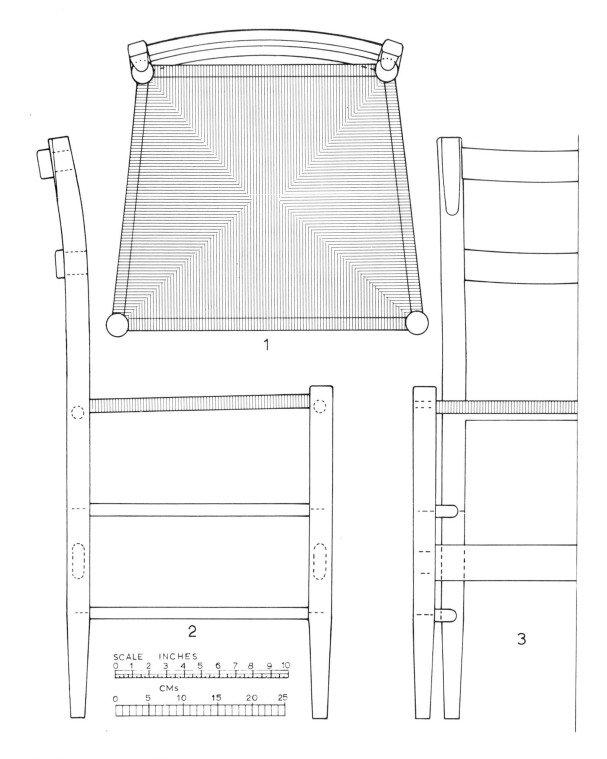

1

2

SCALE INCHES
0 1 2 3 4 5 6 7 8 9 10

CMs
0   5   10   15   20   25

3

471   Turned rush-seated chair

472   John Makepeace: chair in solid and laminated ebony with woven nickel seat and back

473   John Makepeace: part of a special commission in oak for dining table and chairs designed to reflect the surrounding woodland as seen from the dining room

465

474 & 475   Rupert Williamson: dining chairs in
sycamore with inlay and edging of rosewood

Richard La Trobe Bateman's chair (476) is ideally suitable for this form of workshop production, relying as it does on simple square-edged wood and machined joints. However, being a craftsman, he is not content with that, so the seat is carefully contoured to the body and those two harsh-looking back planks spring to provide unexpected comfort.

David Colwell (p. 468) uses steam bending and turning and low technology to produce his visually simple and appealing chairs which are made in considerable quantities for retail distribution.

Lucinda Leech's chaise longue and armchair, designed for garden, patio or conservatory, use a combination of simple square framed joinery and laminated construction so straightforward and cleverly designed that only one mould is used for each piece. For clarity, both pieces are illustrated here without the cushions designed to go with them (479 and 480).

Easy or lounge chairs

Figure 482:1 shows a lounge chair of knock-down construction, using tenoned or dowelled side frames and separate back frame and front apron rail connected with suitable slot-headed screws engaging in sunk nuts. There is no seat frame as such, and resilient rubber webbing is used for the suspension, anchored with metal clips as shown at 482:1A, A, top rail 482:2A, A, and front rail 482:2B, B. The front rail (482:2B) should have locating stub dowels either side of the central screw to prevent it twisting. Figure 482:3, 4 is another framed-up chair with finger-jointed arm rests and tenoned or dowelled front, side and back rails, with the back frame screwed from the inside into the arm and lower rails. Here again suspension is with resilient webbing.

Swivel chair

A typical swivel-chair action is shown in 485:1, together with 485:2 swivel metal chair action, and 485:3 matching metal settee support. This type of chair should have a fairly firm seat, and the foam padding can be placed on a plywood base. Sturdy cross-bearers are fixed under the seat to take the swivel arms.

476 Richard La Trobe Bateman: dining chair in brown oak

477 & 478   David Colwell: folding chairs and matching foot stool in steamed and turned ash

479 (*left*) Lucinda Leech: chair of solid and laminated yew. Tie-on cushion and back rest are available

480 (*below*) Lucinda Leech: chaise longue in laminated oak. The wide flat arm rest is designed for drinks etc.

481 Rod Wales: two-seater settee in figured sycamore with cushions upholstered in cotton chintz

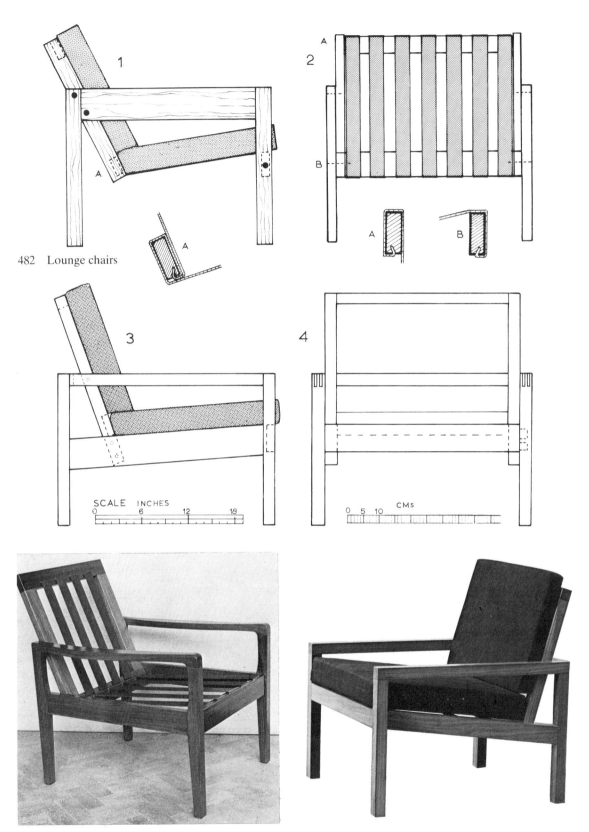

482 Lounge chairs

SCALE INCHES
0   6   12   18

0 5 10   CMs

483 Lounge chair in American black walnut.
Designed by T.A. Marsh, Brighton College of Art

484 Easy chair in afrormosia. Designed and made
at Brighton College of Art

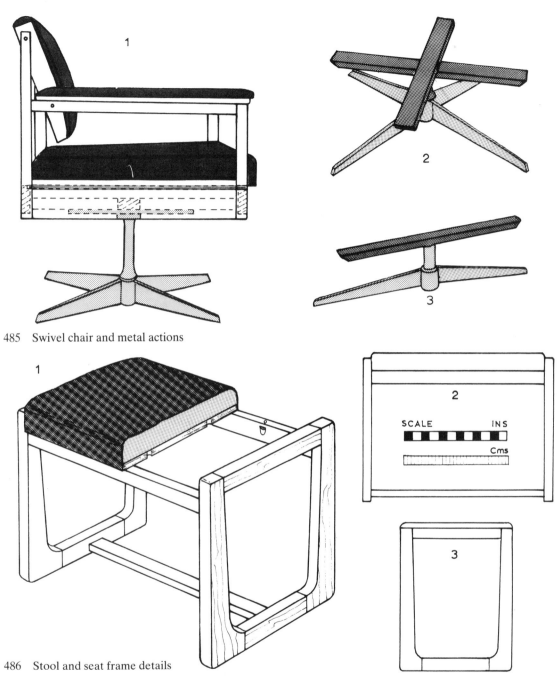

485   Swivel chair and metal actions

486   Stool and seat frame details

STOOLS

Figure 486:1, 2, 3 shows a low fireside- or dressing-stool, with foam upholstery on a plywood base pocket screwed to the framework which can be tenoned or dowelled together.

In 487, one of a set of twelve stools, the solid seats out of 3 in (76 mm) African walnut were dished by hand using spokeshaves and improvised wooden planes with curved soles. The foam padding was glued to the seat and the leather to the foam padding with rubber cement (upholsterers' rubber glue), with the leather eased and stretched round the sharp corners with a minimum of tailoring.

487 Bar stool in Rio rosewood, solid seat dished and shaped, covered foam pad and leather. Designed by R.D. Russell RDI. Author's workshops

488 & 489 Sturdy seating in stained ash designed for permanent use in the Bluecoat Gallery, Liverpool, England, but suitable for many other uses. Height of each seat is 18 in (45 cm). Designed and made by Hugh Scriven

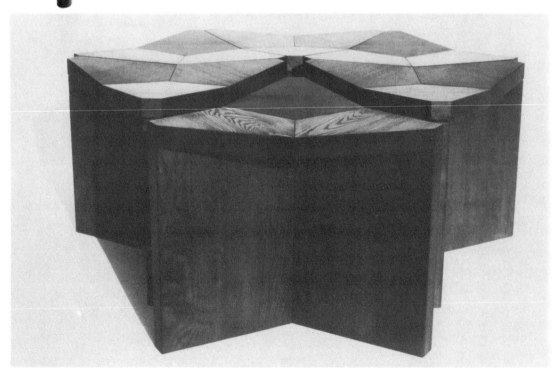

490-492 Folding stool designed by Adrian Reed at the Royal College of Art, 1982. The photographs show examples (*left*) in natural ash and (*below*) finished with coloured lacquer. Over the page are some of the working drawings

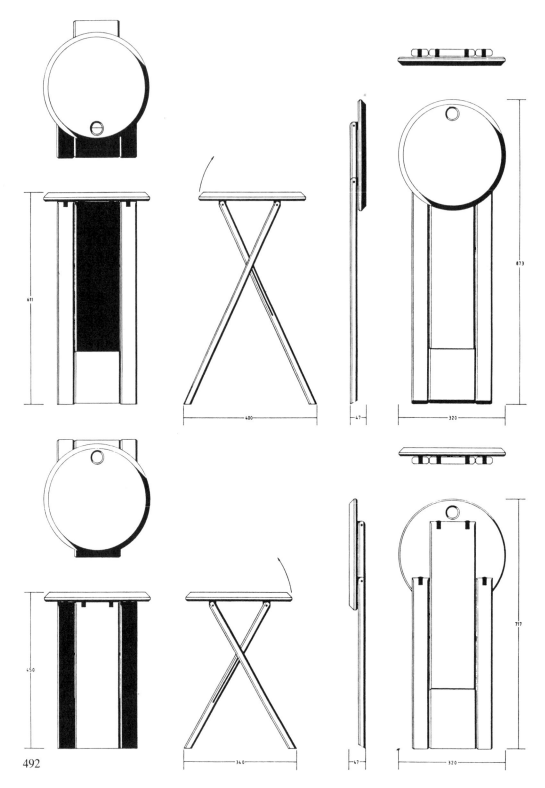

492

474

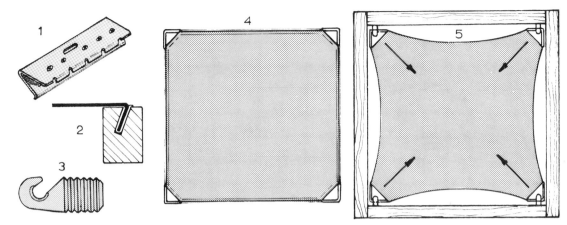

493 Upholstery details, resilient rubber springing, etc.

UPHOLSTERY

This again is a specialist craft, for a good upholsterer capable of stuffover-work, shaped work and deep buttoning in a full range of materials including leather must be part tailor, dressmaker and leather-worker. However, the introduction of foam pads and resilient rubber webbings has vastly simplified the usual run of upholstery in dining and easy chairs, which is now well within the scope of the average workshop.

Resilient webbings

Invented in 1953 by Pirelli Ltd of Italy, these consist of resilient rubber tensioned strips of attractive appearance, and have almost entirely superseded the jute webbings of traditional upholstery. The advantage of Pirelli webbing is that it can be used without sub-frames or springing, and need not be hidden for it is obtainable in various colours and in four qualities for different seating requirements. The webbing is composed of a rayon fabric bonded in rubber and has proved extremely tough, durable and elastic, with negligible loss of recovery over long periods. It is secured by tacks or staples, as with jute webbings, or with special patented metal clips with serrated edges (493:1) clenched to the ends of the strips and slipped into a sawn groove (493:2) in the framework (another form of wire clip is available for metal framing); and it must be tensioned by stretching to a fixed percentage of its original length (plus 5 to 10 per

cent) in accordance with the makers' recommendations. The strips can be placed 2 in (50 mm) to 3 in (76 mm) apart and need only run one way, with cross-weaving (as with jute webbings) unnecessary except over large areas. Full details, fastening instructions and samples can be obtained from upholstery suppliers.

Four-point platforms

Another development of Pirelli is the resilient rubber diaphragm with triangular steel loops (493:4) engaged in metal bosses screwed to the

494 Detail of chair seat for loose cushion with resilient webbing straps secured by metal fasteners in grooves sawn into rails

475

framework of the chair (493:3). They are used instead of webbing for loose cushioning, and the four-point diagonal anchorage eliminates distortion of the side rails, hammocking and localized areas of wear in the cushions (493:5). The diaphragms must be tensioned from 8 to 15 per cent maximum, and a simply-made metal stretching device is obtainable for quick assembly work. They are available in a range of seat sizes from 15¼ in (387 mm) to 22½ in (571 mm), and therefore the chair must be designed accordingly, though the square format can be stretched to fit square, rectangular or tapered seat frames within the maximum permissible tensioning.

In designing chairs and settees, etc. with resilient webbing or platform suspension in mind, both initial and depressional tension must be considered, with wood sections sufficient for the loading. The position of the webbing strips is also important, whether from side to side or back to front, and here again there must be specific understanding of the tensions involved. Booklets are available from the suppliers giving the relevant details.

Foam padding

The original and familiar latex rubber foam was first developed by the Dunlop Rubber Company in the early 1930s, and completely revolutionized upholstery techniques, to be followed later by polyester and polyether synthetic foams. Apart from differences in performance, latex rubber sponge is foamed by chemical additives (originally soap solutions); therefore the cushions can be shaped or moulded at the time of manufacture, while synthetic sponges generate their own carbon dioxide which blows the liquid, and self-foaming is generally too rapid for satisfactory moulding techniques, although recent developments have overcome this disability to some extent. In practice latex foam is more expensive but more efficient, and does not lose its sponginess unless exposed to damp conditions or direct sunlight. On the other hand, synthetic foams are tougher but yield (bottom) more rapidly under pressure and the recovery is slower; therefore the effect is a little dead in comparison. Of the two forms of synthetic

495   Rubber diaphragm seat for loose cushion, showing method of fixing

foam, polyether is more rubber-like and is the form usually adopted for work.

Both latex and synthetic foams can be obtained in sheet form (solid foam) and with cavities which cut down weight and give increased softness, and in a range of thicknesses up to 12 in (305 mm) according to the type. They are also obtainable in a range of densities corresponding to soft, medium, and hard for traffic seating (railway, bus seating, etc.). Pad thicknesses can be built up with rubber adhesives (Bostik, etc.) and can be cut with shears, corrugated kitchen scissors, sharp knives or on the band-saw. They can be glued direct to solid plywood bases or placed direct over resilient webbings. Adequate ventilation must be provided, and if covered with impermeable materials—leather, leathercloth and PVC-coated fabrics—solid bases must be pierced with ¼ in (6 mm) holes at 3 in (76 mm) centres, and loose cushions provided with brass eyelet holes sewn in, or potential users will suffer serious embarrassment, as the effect is that of a joke cushion. It is usual to cover foam padding with under-covers of coarse calico if the top covering is leather or PVC, etc. owing to the difference in the recovery rates, but these are unnecessary under open-weave materials except as an added refinement protecting the inner pad from wear.

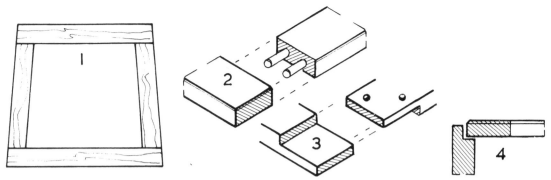

496   Construction of loose seat frame

497   Fixing Pirelli webbing

498   Hessian or burlap cover tacked in position

499　Installing foam pad

500　Tailoring corners of leather top cover

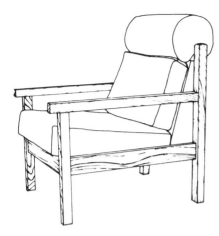

501　Light style armchair with head cushion

502 (*right*)　Chancellor's chair, Keele University, in English oak with upholstery in red Niger goat-skins. Designed and carved by Professor D.W. Pye ARIBA, FSIA. Author's workshops

503 (*below*)　Chairs for St Saviour's Girls' School in 1983 of laminated sycamore with upholstered sides, seat and back with the school emblem embroidered on the backs. Made at Bim Burton's workshop

Figures 497 to 500 show the various stages in the upholstery of a drop-in seat for a dining-chair, using resilient webbing, latex foam padding and top leather cover. Figure 497 shows the installation of the webbing with each strap stretched to the pencil-mark and secured with three ⅝ in (16 mm) improved tacks, while in 498 the under-cover of coarse burlap is folded to allow for deflection of the webbing and secured with ⅜ in (9.5 mm) or ½ in (12.5 mm) improved tacks. In 499 the foam padding has been cut to shape, the edges roughly chamfered with a ¼ in (6 mm) overhang all round, and secured in position with upholsterers' adhesive tape firmly tacked to the framework. The final covers are then stretched evenly over the pad, working from the centres of each side out to the corners and temporarily tacking with ⅜ in (9.5 mm) or ½ in (12.5 mm) fine tacks which are not driven home until the stretching and shaping is correct. A little horsehair stuffing can be worked in to the under top cover to raise the dome and increase the firmness of dining-chair seats. Figure 500 shows the leather cover cut to fit.

45 Church furniture

GENERAL NOTE

Fixed church work—pews, pulpits, stalls, chancel screens, etc.—is usually regarded as a form of highly specialized joinery-work, and as such beyond the scope of the average furniture-maker, who will be called upon to provide only the occasional piece of movable furniture—litany desks, lecterns, altar-tables, bishop's chairs, etc. All too often the work has to match in with existing furnishings, such as Victorian Gothic, etc., heavily carved and moulded, and opportunities for imaginative work are confined to the very few new churches and church halls which are built from time to time. Where such opportunities exist, church authorities will usually consider veneered work and other woods besides the traditional oak in the contemporary idiom, but the accent will mostly be on the traditional approach, for the study of which the student has only to visit a local church. The illustrations following are, therefore, intended more as guidelines for average sizes than any detailed treatment of the subject. Constructions are usually orthodox and the accent on sturdiness, with moulded members boldly pronounced, for the setting is so much vaster and the viewing distances considerable. For ease in manufacture heavy wood sections are built up, and while oak is still a prime favourite there is a growing tendency to use ash, and afrormosia, etc. Problems of over-heating and consequent shrinkage do not usually arise, except in church halls which are used for other purposes, therefore moisture contents need not be so critical as with domestic furniture, although thoroughly seasoned wood

504   Solid oak pews and frontals for St John's Church, Coleford, Gloucestershire, England; designer-maker: Kenneth Marshall

ALTAR TABLE

C L

505   Altar table in ash for the Swiss Catholic Mission Chapel, Westminster, London, England, by Alan Peters

506   Box construction altar table

CHOIR STALL
FRONT

C L

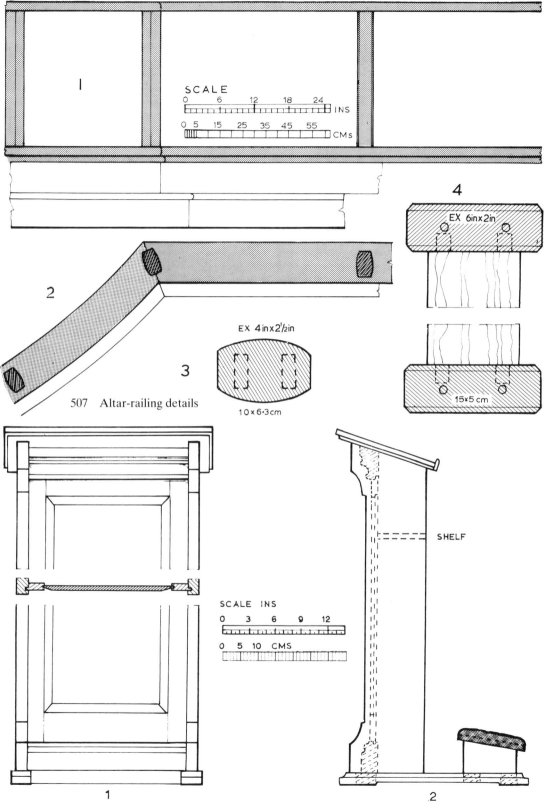

SCALE

0   6   12   18   24   INS

0 5   15   25   35   45   55   CMs

4

EX 6in×2in

2

507   Altar-railing details

EX 4in×2½in

3

10×6·3cm

15×5 cm

SHELF

SCALE INS

0   3   6   9   12

0   5   10   CMS

1

.2

508   Litany desk with fixed kneeler

509 Litany desk with hinged kneeler details

must be used. Particular attention should be paid to sharp edges which should be well rounded or eased back, especially in the more splintery woods, and polishes should be hard, avoiding sticky waxes or soft varnishes.

ALTAR-TABLES

Altar-tables can take several forms. At their simplest they need be no more than a solid slab of prime wood resting on two rectangular columns of stone, brick or wood; or they could be just the very simplest of tables draped with cloth or with side curtains. Alternatively, they may be complete box forms with all four faces elaborately moulded or carved.

Figure 505 shows a box construction that merely uses simple frame and panel construction throughout and rests on a separate plinth; 506 shows a similar construction used on choir stall fronts.

ALTAR-RAILS

These are wide in section and assembled on site, using handrail screws (507:4) to connect the lengths. Figure 507:1 gives the elevation, 507:2 the plan, 507:3 a cross-section of the uprights tenoned in, and 507:4 the handrail and base rail. Sweeps are cut from the solid as the sections are usually sturdy enough to support the short grain on the curve.

510 Litany desk in brown oak with hinged kneelers, designed by Ernest Joyce MSIA. Author's workshops

511 Simple litany desk for Bullwood Borstal Institute Church, England.

LITANY DESK

A litany desk with fixed kneeler is shown in 508, while 509 gives a side elevation of the desk illustrated in 510, with a collapsible kneeler upholstered with foam rubber on a plywood base and covered with cowhide. This memorial desk 2 ft 6 in (76 cm) wide, 1 ft 5½ in (44 cm) deep and 3 ft (91 cm) high was made at the request of a client who asked for a primrose and ivy carved decoration to be incorporated for remembrance. Details of the St Mark's lion are shown in 509. As the central aisle of the church was fairly narrow the lectern was fitted with hidden ball-type castors so that it could be wheeled to a side aisle when not in use.

512 Oak litany desk with pull-out kneeler. Designed by Ernest Joyce MSIA. Author's workshops

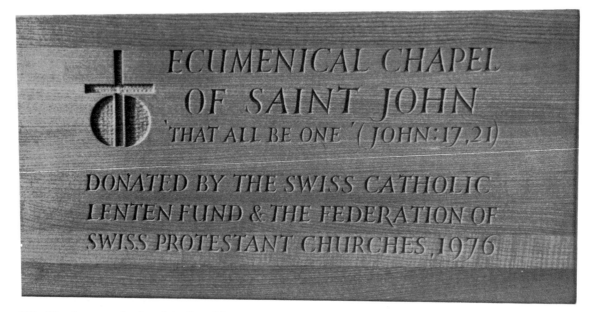

513   Fine letter cutting in ash by Ronald
Parsons FSD-C

Construction was in natural brown oak of
outstanding hue, polished with hard (carnauba)
wax polish to preserve the great beauty of the
wood.

CLERGYMAN'S DESK

Figure 514 shows a clean, timeless example in
solid English oak designed and made by
Kenneth Marshall for Pauntley Church,
Gloucestershire, England. 515 illustrates a
similar design but uses solid frame and panel
construction for the ends.

Solid wood must always be considered the
right and appropriate material for church work,
and anything else but a poor substitute,
particularly in older buildings.

LECTERNS

Two forms of lectern are shown in 516, while
517 gives details of adjustable lecterns where
both the height and the angle of the top can be
varied. Figure 517:1 shows a variable height top
with a boxed-up standard and a $1\frac{1}{4}$ in (32 mm)
central shaft a sliding fit. The movement is

controlled by a brass spring plunger engaging in
a series of brass sockets let into the central shaft
at $1\frac{1}{2}$ in (38 mm) intervals. In 517:2 the
counterweight principle as applied to sliding
sash-windows is employed for larger lecterns.
The central shaft is slotted to pass freely over a
small $\frac{1}{2}$ in (12.5 mm) pulley fixed to a spindle
which rides in brass socket bearings let into the
sides of the standard. A length of piano wire is
attached to the base of the shaft, looped round
the pulley and secured to a suitable weight
below. These cast-iron cylindrical sash weights
are obtainable in a range of weights, but a more
exact method is to weigh the complete top and
shaft and cast an equivalent amount of scrap
lead in a suitable container, embedding a metal
hasp for the piano wire at the time of casting.
This gives finger-tip control, but the movement
must be capable of being locked in any position
by inserting a length of metal strip in the side of
the shaft, with a brass thumb-screw passing
through the side of the standard. A series of
holes can be drilled in the metal strip to form
locations for the screw. Figure 517:3 shows an
adjustable hinged top with the angle of tilt
controlled with two brass stays and locking wing
nuts.

514   Priest's chair and desk, Pauntley,
Gloucestershire, England; designer-maker: Kenneth
Marshall

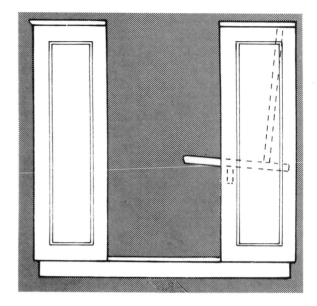

515   Clergyman's desk details

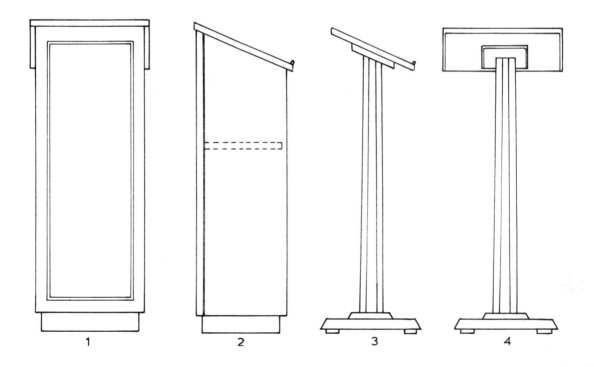

516   Lecterns

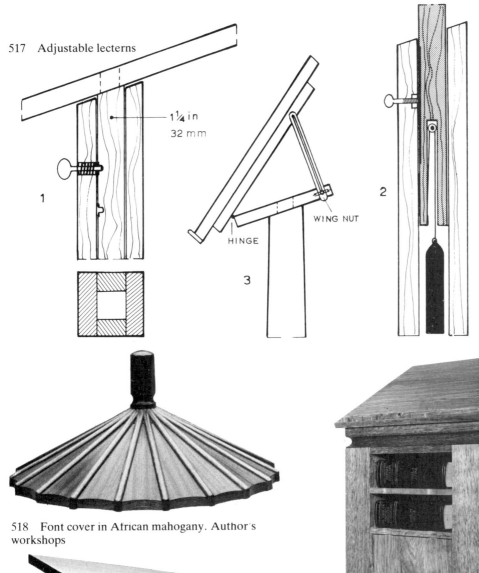

517 Adjustable lecterns

1¼ in
32 mm

WING NUT

HINGE

1

3

2

518 Font cover in African mahogany. Author's workshops

519 Adjustable table lectern with centre pillar. Author's workshops

520 Lectern in English brown oak for Liberian Senate House, Monrovia (1952). Designed by Ernest Joyce MSIA. Author's workshops

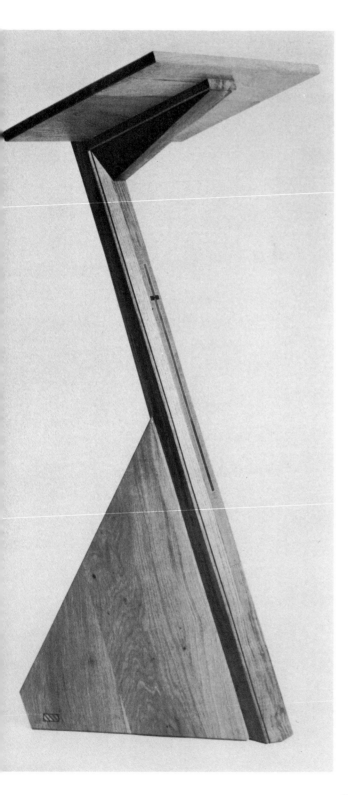
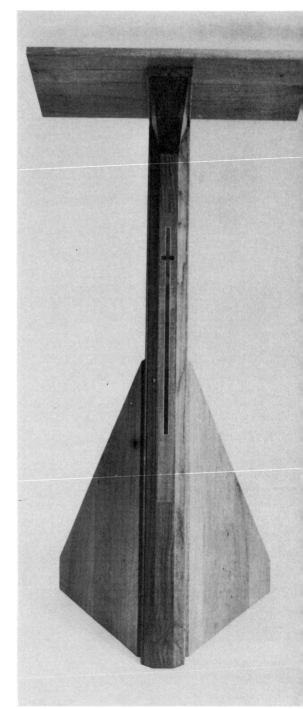

521 & 522   Lectern in oak and ebony with sycamore inlays for St Stephen's, Old Ford, Bow, London, by David Field; photos by Frank Thurston

490

523 & 524 A pair of oak doors and frames for a
Devon church, under construction in the workshop
of David Savage, 1986

491

46　Miscellaneous furniture

TEA TRAYS

Tea trays

A simple tray which illustrates the technique of preforming is illustrated in 525 to 528. This was originally designed some years ago, but is still in demand owing to its exceptional lightness (1 lb 2 oz [510 g]) combined with the overall rigidity, absence of whip under load and great strength which the curved bottom imparts to it. It is made up from a sheet of $\frac{1}{16}$ in (1.5 mm) birch plywood veneered both sides and cold pressed with resin glue between two formers/forms, either in a press or between G-cramps/C-clamps. Grooves are worked in the $\frac{7}{8}$ in (22 mm) by $\frac{5}{16}$ (8 mm) sides cut from the solid, and in the moulded end-grips into which the shaped bottom is glued. The glue joint between the sides and end-grips is further reinforced

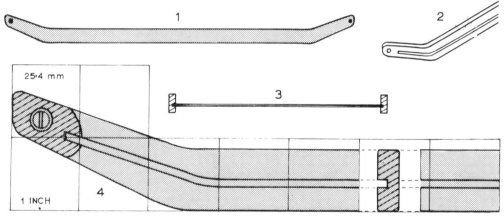

525　Preformed tray details

526　Pressing plywood base in simple formers/forms

527　Five veneers pressed together to form ply base

with brass screws in neat brass sockets sanded off flush. A convenient size is 20 in (508 mm) long by 12½ (318 mm) wide overall.

Butler's trays

This old form of carrying tray was usually made in two forms: a tall variety on X legs with a turned centre spindle connecting the legs, and the low stool variety illustrated in 529. The

528   Preformed tray with bent plywood base and solid sides and ends. Designed by Ernest Joyce MSIA

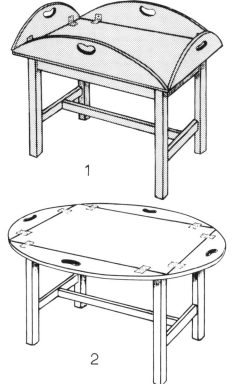

529   Butler's tray

former were about 29 in (737 mm) high and the latter 18 in (457 mm) high, with an elliptical top about 39 in (981 mm) by 30 in (762 mm) when fully opened. The fixed top was usually panelled to prevent casting, but modern versions are veneered plywood, etc. with the wings in carefully matched solid wood. The ellipse should be laid out as described under Workshop geometry, Chapter 40, and the wings are connected with ordinary back flap hinges. If the hinges work too easily, allowing the wings to fall from the upright carrying position, they can be set very fractionally askew to stiffen the movement. The stool is framed up in the orthodox manner and the top secured with shrinkage plates. Figure 529:1 shows the tray in the carrying position and 529:2 with the wings down.

TEA TROLLEYS/WAGONS

Tea trolleys usually vary from about 28 in (71 cm) to 30 in (76 cm) high, 22 in (56 cm) to 27 in (68 cm) long and 14 in (36 cm) to 18 in (46 cm) wide, with wood sections as light as possible consonant with overall rigidity. If the corner posts are square section (531:1) then the rails can be tenoned in as 531:3, with the ¼ in (6 mm) veneered plywood trays grooved into

530   Tea trolley/wagon in Australian walnut. Author's workshops

493

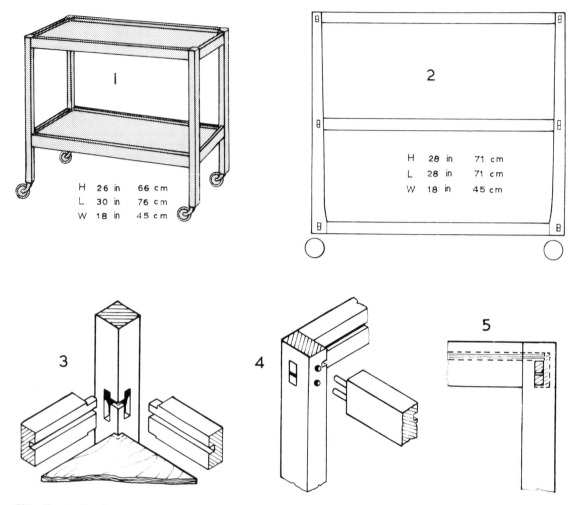

H 26 in 66 cm
L 30 in 76 cm
W 18 in 45 cm

H 28 in 71 cm
L 28 in 71 cm
W 18 in 45 cm

531 Tea trolleys/wagons

the rails and posts. Thinner posts (531:4) may require the end rails tenoned through and wedged, and the long rails dowelled in. The trolley ends should be glued up first, the grooves extended into the posts, the tray bottoms cut and a trial assembly made to see that everything fits. In the final assembly a little glue run into the grooves will increase the overall rigidity of the completed framework. Trolleys can have a top and bottom shelf, or an intermediate shelf, and one end rail can be flush with the top shelf for easier cleaning.

LIBRARY STEPS

The library steps shown here are 18 in (46 cm)

wide, 18 in (46 cm) deep and 30 in (76 cm) high, which is sufficient for normal requirements. Figure 533:2 shows the layout; a mortised and tenoned construction is used, with the treads not less than a full inch in thickness for a stiff hardwood such as oak. The curved rails are band-sawn out of solid stock, while the posts can be continuous and housed/dadoed, screwed and pelleted if flush with the edge of the treads (533:3), or built up of sections, grooved, mortised and tenoned together if slightly inset (533:4). Castors can be fitted but are dangerous if very free running, and it is probably safer to tip the posts with hard rubber insets or dome gliders.

532 Drinks cart in sycamore, black ash, black laminate and rubber. Designed and made by Rupert Senior and Charles Wheeler-Carmichael

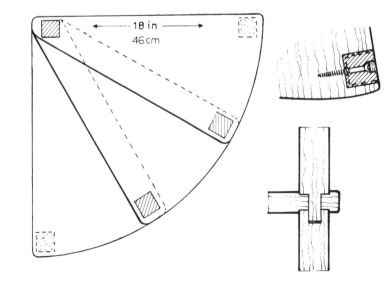

495

533 Library steps

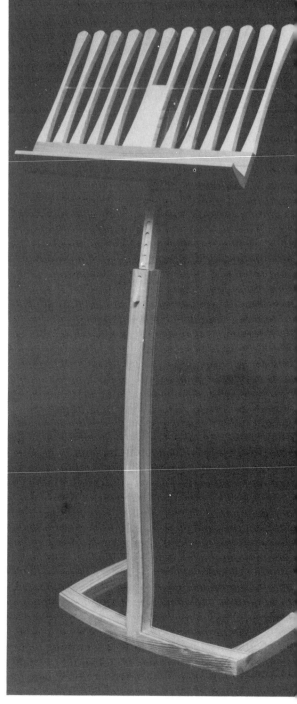

534   Library steps in Zambesi redwood by Alan Peters

535   A delicate adjustable music stand in yew with ebony inlaid stringing. Designed and made by Peter Kuh

FURNITURE FOR OUTSIDE USE

It is essential that the right materials are used for outside work, and this applies not only to the choice of wood but also to the choice of hardware and adhesives. If the appropriate materials are used, then outside furniture will give years of maintenance-free service.

Of the home-grown species oak, macrocarpa, yew, cedar of Lebanon and sweet chestnut are all ideal; similarly from the imported timbers, Burmese teak, iroko and Western red cedar are eminently suitable. They can be left with no finish whatsoever and they will mature over a period of time to a lovely silver grey. Alternatively, if it is felt desirable to preserve the richness of colour of the original wood, it is advisable to use only cedar type preservatives

536   A sturdy music stand/reading lectern of rippled sycamore. Designed and made by Rod Wales

537   Garden or patio tables in various diameters in dyed and natural oak. Designed and made by Lucinda Leech

497

which enable the timber to breathe, and to avoid varnishes and polyurethanes which require regular maintenance. There is, however, no need to use a preservative as such unless the wood itself is not naturally resistant, for example, normal construction softwood.

All glues used should be of the waterproof resin varieties favoured for boat-building, and all screws and hardware should be corrosion resistant.

These two visually striking tables and matching benches in elm illustrate that preciousness and fine cabinetwork are not the only areas of interest for the furniture-maker. Designed and made to commission in both cases by Ashley Cartwright, 539 shows a 6 ft (1800 mm) square table for the English National Trust, and 540 a 9 ft (2750 mm) table and chairs for a private client.

538   Circular bench with laminated curved rails commissioned by Gray's Inn, London, England. Designed and made by Luke Hughes

539 (*facing page, above*)   Large outdoor table made from elm, with metal understructure. Four cantilevered legs provide support for four separate top surfaces. Size 6 ft (1800 mm) square. Made for the English National Trust by Ashley Cartwright

540 (*facing page, below*)   Large rectangular table and benches in wych elm. Size 9 ft (2750 mm) long. Made by Ashley Cartwright

PART X Restoration, repairs and wood finishing
47 Structural repairs

The repair of modern everyday furniture usually calls for cutting out and replacing broken parts, fixing false tenons or dowels to fractured joints, strengthening joints with metal straps, insets or angle pieces, renewing whole members where necessary, and in general applying normal cabinet-making skills. Valuable antique furniture repairs require expert know-how with carefully matched old wood, scraps of old saw-cut veneer, and a keen appreciation of period, colour and patina, together with considerable skills in carving, veneering, inlaying, marquetry cutting, staining, polishing and lacquering, etc. Any such antique repairs should not be undertaken without considerable experience of the particular type of work, for repairs inexpertly done or out of period can detract from, or even destroy, the market value.

Generally speaking, where structural joints have failed, part or all of the construction will have to be taken apart, for there is little point in squeezing glue into the shoulders of a loose tenon and expecting it to hold. Most old work can be knocked apart fairly easily, although a firm but not necessarily heavy hand may be needed. However, modern adhesives may resist parting, and discretion is, therefore, necessary. Joints filled with old hide glue, usually in thick layers, will have to be cleaned out with repeated applications of hot water; they can then be packed up with veneer slips to make up the slackness, and reglued with either hide or synthetics. If the furniture is antique and valuable, great care must be taken to disturb as little of the existing surfaces as possible, and to incorporate only the minimum of new wood, for extensive renovations will always detract from the value. Worm-eaten timbers must be treated if the worm is still active, crumbling parts cut away or built up as described later. If the joints are broken altogether, either dowels or false tenons can be fitted, or new sections scarfed in (see *Scarf joints*, p. 186). Figure 542:8 shows a

false tenon fitted; 542:9 a new section of rail inserted and strengthened with a pad or web if it is load-bearing, while 542:7 is a long scarf joint to a broken chair leg which will need gluing only if the scarf is long enough.

A recent development in the repair of valuable antique furniture has been the use of Araldite epoxy resin adhesive (CIBA [ARL] Ltd) with suitable reactive diluents, fillers and colorants. This type of glue has excellent adhesion to wood, high moisture resistance and, most importantly, negligible shrinkage in curing, so that it can be built up into solid sections without the usual cracking, crazing and disruption of normal adhesives which will only permit thin lines of glue. In particular, worm-eaten timbers can be repaired, restored and strengthened by surface application or penetration, and 541 shows a French marquetry cabinet richly veneered with marquetry patterns of kingwood, ebony, tortoise-pewter and staghorn which was recently restored in the Department of Conservation of the Victoria and Albert Museum in London. In this case parts of the stand seriously ravaged by wood-worm were cleared away and then made good with a liquid Araldite formulation. Plastic wood formulations can also be used with Araldite to build up missing parts, and the techniques are applicable to a wide range of materials, metal, wood, plastic, terracotta, etc. The CIBA (ARL) Ltd technical bulletin *Araldite in the Restoration of Antiquities* gives specific examples.

WARPED TOPS

Badly warped tops can often be corrected by saw kerfing, provided the under surface is not visible in the fixed position. A series of parallel cuts are run in with the circular saw, ¼ in (6 mm) apart and to within a full ⅛ in (3 mm) of the upper surface. The board is then cramped/clamped down to a level surface, and softwood wedge strips or strips of veneer glued into the

541　Seventeenth-century French marquetry cabinet under restoration at the Victoria and Albert Museum, London, using Araldite epoxy resin cement. (By courtesy of CIBA [ARL] Ltd, and the Trustees of the Victoria and Albert Museum)

cuts. The wedges must not be too tight or they will force the warp over in the opposite direction, and plenty of time should be allowed for the work to settle before the cramps are released. Badly warped table-tops in which both surfaces show, as in double-top tables, are almost impossible to correct by any known method to give permanent results, and the only alternatives are to renew the top or slit the existing top into two or more pieces, reversing the strips and re-thicknessing, neither of which would be acceptable in antique-work. This shows that the craftsman must resist the invitation to accomplish the impossible by those who do not appreciate what wood really is and how it behaves.

DRAWER REPAIRS

Wear is inevitable in all moving parts, and drawers and drawer runners may require extensive renovation, especially if the drawer sides and runners are of soft pine. Figure 542:2 shows a typical old drawer with missing cock beads, dovetails loose, drawer sides worn and solid bottom split and shrunk out of its groove. The sides will have to be cut back (542:3, 4) and fresh pieces glued on. Solid bottoms which have split can be shot and reglued, with the joint toped with glued coarse canvas if necessary, and the width extended with a new piece to take the slotted screws. Loose dovetails will have to be knocked apart and reglued. If the drawer rail and runner are badly worn (542:5) and the existing runner cannot be removed and replaced, then it may be necessary to work a trench in the old runner and glue in a fresh slip of hardwood, covering it with a neat patch on the rail. The trench will have to be chiselled out or worked with a bullnose rabbet-plane, and as a preliminary step a small spur-cutter from a metal plough-plane or a piece of scraper steel can be screwed to a suitable block (542:6) and worked backwards and forwards to cut the side of the trench. In all old work strict watch should be kept for nails and rusty screws from previous repairs which will wreck a cutting edge. Carcass backs which have shrunk may require glued canvas over the splits, and side pieces glued on to make up the width.

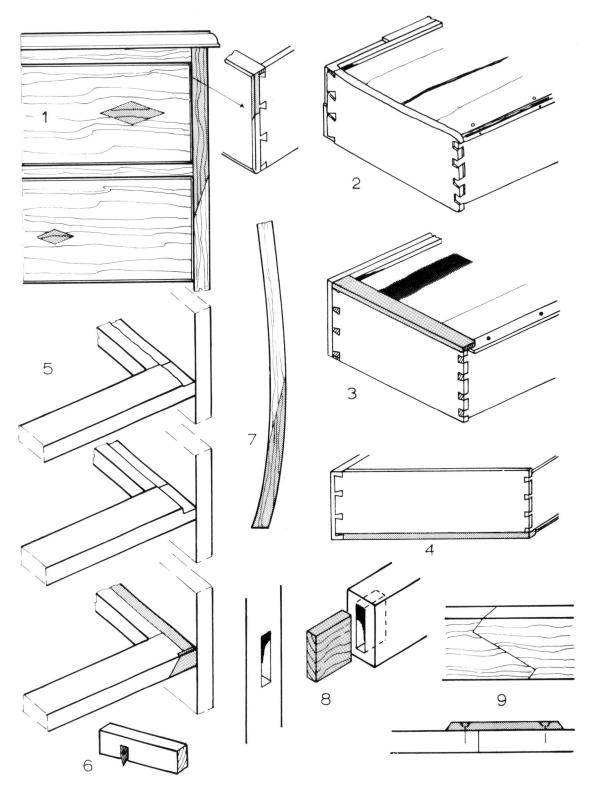

542 Furniture repair details

48 Surface damage

Slight bruising of surfaces where the actual fibres are not fractured can often be lifted by the repeated application of a heated iron tip through a wet cloth, creating sufficient steam to swell the fibres up. Bruises in bare wood can also be lifted by flooding the bruise with methylated spirit and setting fire to it, but the wood must not be scorched. There is no guarantee that the bruises will be eradicated entirely, for much depends on the elasticity of the wood fibres and their ability to recover, but it is always worth a trial. Deeper scratches, dents and bad bruising will have to be cut out and plugged with wood or filled with hard stoppers, plastic wood, etc. coloured to match the finished work. If wood plugs are used they should be cut to an elongated diamond shape with the grain direction carefully matched, placed on the damaged surface, scribed round and the recess cut; the plugs should be slightly bevelled in the thickness for a close fit. All possible help should be given to the polisher by choosing wood of the same species and grain configuration, preferably from old sources in the case of antique furniture, for while he will be able to match colours he cannot change or disguise the texture of a wood. Before gluing in the diamonds a piece of white chalk rubbed round the edges will often hold back a dark glue-line in light-coloured timbers. Slight depressions in work polished with nitrocellulose or synthetic finishes can sometimes be filled by pouring a little of the mixed lacquer into a tin lid and leaving it to set until it gels; it can then be worked into the depressions like putty, allowed to harden thoroughly and then cut off. Figure 542:1 shows various surface repairs to a veneered chest with all cuts tapered as mentioned above.

BLISTERS, etc.

Blisters in modern work can usually be pricked or cut with a knife along the grain and relaid (see Veneering, marquetry and inlay, Chapter 32) but large blisters in old thick saw-cut veneers may not readily respond to treatment. If the whole of the veneered surface has to be lifted off and replaced on a fresh groundwork, it may be possible to lift the veneers by steaming or repeatedly swabbing with hot water. Some veneers may be too tough or too brittle for this treatment, and the whole of the ground may have to be planed off down to a level at which the water will soak through the back and loosen the glue. This latter method is only worth the very considerable labour involved if the top surface is especially valuable, and the patina of age must be preserved.

INLAY REPAIRS

Figures 543-5 show the extensive renovation and repair of a set of six Regency-style chairs carried out by Mr C.M. Lacey of Brighton, England. (The appellations 'Genuine Antique', 'Genuine Regency' etc., etc., cannot be applied to any furniture made after 1830, which is the fixed datum line. As it would be impossible to distinguish between furniture of the same type or style made in, say, 1820 and 1840, any claim to genuineness must be supported by an original bill of sale or other trustworthy documentary evidence. The terms 'Antique Style', 'Regency Style', etc. therefore mean exactly what they say, i.e. 'in the style of . . .'. They could be genuine antique but are not claimed as such). The chairs in question were beech framed stained in imitation of rosewood, with a beautifully executed Boulle inlay of brass and rosewood veneer on the curved back rails; as there was no point in using old beech, even if it could be obtained (beech is highly susceptible to woodworm), new wood was used throughout. As some of the Boulle inlays were damaged and others althogether missing, rubbings of a complete inlay were taken, a clear tracing made and glued to sheet brass of equivalent thickness and colour (brass is obtainable in several tones and colours according to the composition), and

543 Renovating Regency-type chairs

544 Brass inlay part cut

the brass sheet then glued to a thick rosewood veneer. The pattern was then cut out with a fine jewellers' piercing saw, the parts assembled and glued to the rails with shaped cauls and G-cramps/C-clamps. All new work was then stained, the rosewood markings drawn in with Indian ink, which was the usual practice of the time, and french polished. It was then distressed by the usual methods, i.e. beating with rubber or hide hammers, hammer-heads covered in sacking, barbed-wire wrapped round a stick, round pebbles, etc., and scratched with the milled edge of a new coin, with parts which would be expected to show wear rasped or sanded away. No attempt was made to fake or deliberately deceive with the inclusion of worm-eaten timber or simulated worm holes, and the distressing was only carried out sufficiently to fade in the new work with the old. The completed chairs were then sold in good faith and to a reputable dealer as 'Regency Style, extensively renovated'.

545 Brass inlay completed

49   Wood finishing

The craft of staining, matching, hand and spray finishing is highly specialized and forms a separate trade; the following notes are therefore for general guidance only, and the reader is referred to the standard textbooks on the subject.

GENERAL NOTE

Furniture in general use must be polished to seal the pores of the wood, protect the surfaces, accentuate and enhance the beauty of the figure, create highlights and provide as much resistance against heat or spilt liquids as possible. Earliest polishing materials dating back to the time of the Pharaohs were probably nut, poppy and linseed oils, gums, resins, etc., and it was not until 1820 that the familiar french polish was introduced into England from France. Prior to that Evelyn's Diary refers to the practice of 'Joyners' laying walnut boards in an oven or warm stable, and when the furniture was completed polishing it over 'with its own oyl, very hot, which makes it look sleek and black', while Sheraton advocated using a mixture of soft wax and turpentine. (Furniture was originally made by carpenters and later by joiners who were given exclusive entitlement in 1632 to 'make all kinds of furniture, mortice, tenoned, dowelled and pinned, glued but not nailed together . . .'. Later specialization produced the cabinet-maker exclusively concerned with furniture). Favourite materials for cabinet-makers of that period were linseed oil for furniture, stained with alkanet root (which yields a permanent red dye) and mixed with brick-dust to produce a polishing putty under the polishing cloth; and hard wax (beeswax, turpentine, copal varnish and yellow ochre) for chairs. Modern practice uses a plethora of materials, natural and synthetic, whose aim it is to hasten, cheapen and give added protection, all of which is achieved to a very marked degree.

It is very doubtful, however, whether any modern method can match the old processes for sheer beauty, for the secret lay in the patient hand-rubbing over long periods whereby the polish was forced into the pores of the wood, and not applied merely as a surface coating.

POLISHING MATERIALS AND PROCESSES

Wax polish

This is one of the oldest and probably the most beautiful of all finishes, as the softened wax penetrates the wood surface and enhances the figure, giving it great depth and warmth. A semi-matt surface with distinctive patina is cheaply and easily achieved, but several applications are required over a period of time for good results. Pure waxes have good moisture resistance but are very easily marked, with little or no heat resistance dependent on the particular melting-point of the wax. Commercial polishes with or without silicone additives for greater protection are usually composed of soft waxes (paraffin, etc.) and are not suitable for first coats on bare wood, although excellent as revivers in finished work. The best mixture for first coats is the old tried formula of pure beeswax and turpentine (1 lb [0.450 kg] wax to ½ pint [280 ml] turps) dissolved in a water-jacketed pot, and thinned with additional turpentine as necessary. A teaspoonful of pure copal varnish can be added for increased toughness and wear, also carnauba wax (Brazilian palm wax) for hardness and shine. Application should be made with a fairly sloppy paste, rubbed in and stroked off along the grain as in painting with No. 0000 steel wool, and then set aside to harden before burnishing with soft dry cloths. Matt waxes suitable for finishing over thin base coats of cellulose or synthetic lacquer, etc. are composed of soft paraffin-wax and synthetic micro-wax, and do not buff to a gloss finish. A fairly recent development is teak paste reinforced with ethyl cellulose for increased resistance. One of the chief virtues of all wax finishes is their easy renewal.

Oil polish

Linseed oil alone will give moderate heat and water resistance with high gloss if applied sparingly over a period of several months. Each separate application must harden by oxidization, and 5 per cent white spirits and 5 per cent terebene can be added for easier working, but at least 12 coats will be necessary. This method was often used for dining-table tops but it is much too slow for modern requirements, and sophisticated penetrating oils, teak oil etc., have been developed, incorporating rapid oxidizing agents capable of achieving a sufficient build-up in two coats only. These new oils are used extensively in modern teak and afrormosia furniture, but the resultant finish hardly compares with the older process. As with wax, oil finishes are easily renewed, which is one of the chief advantages.

French polish

This is a specialist craft and should not be attempted without proper training, for the whole secret lies in the minimum and not the maximum amount of polish applied for a full gloss, and thick coats unskilfully applied are no better than cheap varnish. It is often said that a good french-polisher is born and not made, and that not only can he equalize the colours of mixed woods but can actually make some pieces appear lighter by regulating the thickness of polish and therefore the refractive index. Commercial brands of polish incorporate various gums and synthetics for quick drying and build up, also increased heat and water resistance which is usually poor with straight french polish, but the most beautiful finishes are still obtained with the older method, using flake-orange or garnet shellac dissolved in industrial alcohol (methylated spirits, methylated finish, etc.). The best results are only obtained over long periods and 12 months

546 Applying rubber in french polishing a table top

was considered usual for the German vitriol finish on grand pianos. The polish as such is now little used in production work for it is essentially a hand process, but modified polishes are available for spray finishing.

Nitro-cellulose lacquers

These are composed of nitro-cellulose, alkyd resin and castor oil or glycerine plasticizers, etc. dissolved in various aromatic hydrocarbon solvents according to the type. Originally developed some 40 years ago to replace french polish they have good heat-, water- and spirit-alcohol-resistant properties, and in spite of fierce competition from harder and more resistant synthetic lacquers, still account for about 70 per cent of the total output, presumably because they are familiar, can be used straight from the can and have an unlimited shelf and pot life. Obvious advantages are a very quick drying rate giving dustproof coats in a matter of minutes, high transparency, an exceptional even flow and good gloss together with satisfactory amalgamation of successive layers, as with french polish. This last factor is of considerable importance, for each coat applied partially redissolves the underlying coat, and therefore any subsequent damage is more easily repairable than with synthetic lacquers, which set by polymerization so that the separate layers do not amalgamate and any renewal usually necessitates stripping down to the bare wood.

Normally, all cellulose lacquers are compounded for spray application and have a solids content of around 34 per cent with low viscosity and a flash point of 32° C (90° F); they are therefore subject to the requirements of a number of workshop regulations. However, full gloss lacquers can be obtained with a flash point of over 32° C (90° F) which are outside the regulations, but owing to the slower solvent evaporation-rate they do not have the rapid set-up of normal lacquers. They can, however, be brush coated, which is satisfactory for thin coats but rather more difficult for a filled grain full gloss over large areas. Cellulose lacquer can be 'pulled over' as in french polishing, with a chamois-leather pad soaked in pull-over solutions composed of high-boiling retarder thinners; recent developments include straight cellulose lacquers for pad polishing, high solids content lacquers for quick build-up, and scratch-resistant lacquers with resistance to bruising without fracture, which was one of the disabilities of the older, more brittle formulas.

For those who do not have spraying facilities and prefer soft shine with reasonably good protection, a proved specification is as follows:

> One coat or more well-thinned clear cellulose lacquer, brushed on, allowed to harden thoroughly, and then wire wooled (grade No. 0000) and waxed, preferably with the lacquer-maker's own matt wax formula.

This treatment yields an acceptable finish for the general run of handmade furniture, but will not give full protection on dining- and coffee-table tops. Either white french polish or polyurethane lacquer can be used for the base coats in lieu of cellulose; but whichever lacquer is used some judgment is needed, for if the coat is too thin rubbing down will strike through to the bare wood in places and show as bald patches under the wax, while too thick coats will merely lie on the surface and show the brush-marks.

Synthetic lacquers

These include cold acid catalyst, polyurethane and polyester lacquers, all of which have greatly increased heat, water and spirit resistance, tough films and high gloss, particularly the latter which is extensively used for wireless and television cabinets as there is little if any sinkage, and the gloss is comparable with a vitriol (German) piano finish. Polyester lacquers are, however, unsuitable for small turnovers, for they require dual-feed sprays for intimate dispersal of the catalyst hardener throughout the lacquer, and the resin-dust in surfacing can be an industrial hazard if suitable precautions are not taken.

Acid catalyst lacquers

Originally phenolic resins were used, but modern formulas include urea formaldehyde, melamine and epoxy resins with alkyd plasticizers for increased resistance to wet, heat, etc. A two-pack lacquer is the norm,

547 Portable rotary vane air compressor. (By courtesy of A. Bullows and Co. Ltd)

composed of lacquer, syrup and separate acid catalyst, often hydrochloric acid, which must be mixed with the lacquer in the stated proportions. Setting is by polymerization, but the mixed lacquer has a pot life of several hours and enough can be mixed for the day's work. *A one-solution pre-catalysed form* is now available with a shelf life of about six months, but the pre-catalysation is obtained by lowering the solids content, and therefore the build-up is less rapid.

Polyurethane lacquer

The isocyanate cured polyurethanes were at one time toxic but are now controlled and are outstanding for adhesion, flexibility, gloss, water and chemical resistance. Originally in two-can form with separate hardener, they are now obtainable in one-can pre-catalysed solutions. The usual application is by spraying apparatus, but they can be brushed more easily than cellulose lacquers, and pad-application

french polish type polyurethane lacquers are available for pure hand methods.

Both acid catalyst and polyurethane lacquers are very suitable for dining-table tops, etc. and a full gloss polish is possible with the use of appropriate grain fillers, sealers and base coats, etc. flatted with wet and dry silicon carbide paper moistened with either white spirit or water (the latter gives a fiercer cut, and the surface should be lubricated with a little common soap), followed up by cutting-down pastes and burnishing creams. They can also be used for thin finishes showing the grain, with the dust nibs cut off with 7/0 abrasive paper, or steel wooled and waxed. The secret of applying these lacquers is to complete the required number of coatings as quickly as possible, for if each coat is allowed to set glass hard then any build-up will lie as separate layers, and any chance cutting through of the top layer in sanding will show up as a blue blaze. With rapid coating (three in one day) each layer tends to soften up the under layer, and some degree of amalgamation is achieved.

Dulling methods

Contemporary finishes usually call for an egg-shell, matt or semi-matt surface in preference to a choked-grain full gloss. Most lacquers are available either as full gloss (burnishing lacquers), matt or semi-matt finishes, the matt appearance being obtained by incorporating silex powder of other additives to scatter the light. These matt finishes do, of course, cloud the wood to some degree, and in fact all dulled surfaces cannot be expected to show the clarity of a high gloss which acts as both mirror and magnifying glass. The after-dulling of gloss surfaces for an egg-shell gloss effect can also be done with finest grade steel wool, which must be skilfully applied to be effective, or with french-polishers' pumice and petrol/gasoline. A handful of water-floated pumice powder (or fine silex powder) is stirred into a cupful of petrol and swabbed over the surface, keeping the mixture constantly agitated. Any degree of dulling can be achieved by using a special soft dulling brush kept exclusively for the purposes, and sweeping the brush backwards and forwards as in painting until the petrol has evaporated and only the dust remains. Silex powder need not be graded, but all powdered pumice should be water-floated by stirring it into a large bowl of water, allowing a little time for the larger grains to settle, and then decanting the liquid, letting it stand overnight and pouring off the clear water. The degree of fineness of the floated powder will depend on how long the coarser grains have been allowed to settle before decanting, and the process can be repeated several times if necessary.

Satisfactory egg-shell gloss surfaces can only be achieved by carrying out to a full gloss polish and then dulling, and there are no short cuts. The dulling of thin finishes with unfilled grain should not be attempted with the above method or the surface will show white deposits.

Spraying equipment

Production-work uses air or airless sprays in vacuum exhaust or water wash booths, etc. but small portable spray outfits are obtainable which will support one gun with pressures up to 60 lb per sq. in ($4.218 \, \text{kg/km}^2$), and sufficient for all but the heaviest materials. These can be the compressor type or fully portable rotary vane type (547), relatively inexpensive and efficient in use. Light pattern spray outfits for the handyman are hardly suitable for serious work, as there must be sufficient pressure and feet cube (m^3) air delivery per minute fully to atomize the spray or extensive spitting, blobbing, tear runs and orange-peel effect will result, and rubbing down will be as difficult and as tedious as with brush-work. Some form of moisture extractor should also be incorporated in the compressor, or as a separate unit installed in the pipeline, or 'blooming' will result. Even with fully efficient moisture extraction—and the very act of compressing air squeezes out the moisture always present—some blooming must be expected on humid days. This can be controlled by adding anti-chill thinners to the lacquer, which retard the evaporation and thus allow the suspended moisture to escape before it is trapped by the setting film, or by over-spraying the lacquered surface with thinners, but the gun must be good for this and the application skilful. Regulations regarding the storage and use of inflammable materials are fairly stringent, but non-regulation materials are available which are not subject to the legal requirements. Small outfits in which the air is delivered direct from the compressor unit to the gun do not need periodic testing, but air receivers, i.e. storage tanks for air under compression, require safety checks at regular intervals. In estimating for spray work it should not be forgotten that on average one-third of the material is lost.

Wood finishing production methods

Present-day techniques include spraying, hot lacquer spraying, airless spraying, dual-feed spraying for polyester, electrostatic deposition, roller coating and reverse roller coating for sanders and sealers, curtain spraying for gloss finishes and roller printing of wood patterns on chipboard and hardboard. Methods are geared to flow-line production to yield printproof surfaces in the shortest possible time, and call for sophisticated techniques and equipment which become obsolescent almost before they are installed. The small tradeshop cannot hope to keep pace with this mounting tide of new ideas, new approaches and new materials, and it

548 Spraying-booths. (By courtesy of Aerograph de Vilbiss Co. Ltd)

will continue to use traditional methods, hand-polishing and simple spraying, and taking advantage where it may of worthwhile developments. In the meantime, the perfect finish has yet to be evolved.

In conclusion it should be stressed that no matter what method and what material is used the final polish will only be as good as the ground it is laid upon, for no amount of after finishing can ever disguise poor workmanship and shoddy materials. The thick, heavy gloss of cheap furniture is there for a purpose—it masks the imperfections which a clear finish would only magnify. An illustration of this is the superlative finish achieved by the professional gun-stock maker. The completed walnut stock is sponged with clean water to which a little oxalic acid has been added, dried rapidly with a blow-torch or over a gas-ring and sanded immediately. This process is repeated several times with an occasional rubbing over with very fine pumice powder to burnish the wood and seal the grain, and the wood surfaces can be further burnished by 'boning', i.e. rubbing with a block of the same wood. The resultant surface is dead smooth and velvet to the touch, moreover any subsequent exposure to damp conditions will not raise the grain.

WOOD STAINS

These rightly require a complete textbook devoted to their manipulation, and therefore only general observations are possible here. Of the three categories, water, spirit/alcohol and oil, the water stains are most troublesome to apply but penetrate fairly deeply and yield the clearest finishes; they are therefore firm favourites with the hand-worker. The old tried recipes are still viable, i.e. vandyke brown crystals dissolved in hot water with a little 0.880 ammonia to bite into the wood and a teaspoonful of household detergent to break down surface tensions; mahogany crystals for red staining, water black aniline dye and potassium bichromate. As all photographers will know the last is light sensitive, and an aqueous solution of the orange crystals obtainable at most pharmacies will yield any shade from fierce red-brown to light tan on certain woods after exposure to light. The concentrated solution should be stored in brown or covered bottles, diluted and tested on scrap wood, for the results are never predictable. Both oak and mahogany are affected (some African mahoganies do not respond), and the results are fairly permanent although inclined to fade somewhat in strong light, as will most other stains. Other shades of brown are easily obtainable with mixtures of red, yellow and black anilines with the addition of a little blue for coldness. Modern anilines are reasonably fast to light and some pronouncedly so.

Before applying water stains the work should be flashed off with clean water, dried, sanded and the dust cleared from the fibres with a stiff brush. Even staining without streakiness is facilitated if the surfaces are first lightly swabbed with water; moreover this dilutes the stain and gives more time for levelling off. Two coats are always better than one, for one strong coat may strike too dark in places; moreover, a first coating gives another opportunity to ease off upraised fibres. The stained surface can be coated or finished with all types of polishes.

Painted work

So-called painted work—bedroom and living-room furniture, kitchen furniture, etc.—are spray coated with pigmented nitro-cellulose, acid catalyst or polyurethane finishes available in gloss and semi-matt formulas. The build up is the same as for clear lacquer finishes, with appropriate pigmented grain fillers, sealers and base coats, etc. and the final surfaces flattened with wet and dry silicon carbide paper, cutting down pastes and burnishing creams. Brush coating can be attempted but is likely to fail on large surfaces, for it is the dead smoothness of this type of finish which constitutes much of its charm.

Compatibility in wood finishes

As so many types of wood finish are now used it is useful to know which finishes will take over each other and which will not. The list below gives the average behaviour:

Oil finish will accept french polish, polyurethane or wax.
French polish will accept cellulose, polyurethane, oil and wax.
Cellulose will accept polyurethane and wax.
Polyurethane will accept oil and wax only.
Polyester will accept oil, polyurethane and wax.
Wax will accept none.

Discretion must be exercised, for whereas the solvent used in cellulose finishes will soften if not actually dissolve french polish and permit the partial fusion of the two coats, the methylated spirit solvent in french polish will not dissolve cellulose and both coats will remain separate; moreover, any oil used with the french polish will be prevented from soaking down into the wood and will inhibit final hardening. It should be noted that wax is inimical to all other finishes, and must be completely removed by stripping, scraping, sanding and degreasing before attempting any other form of finishing.

Safety precautions

Modern spray booths will ensure a fume-free working atmosphere in properly organized factory work, but the hand-maker using a portable spray outfit without fan extraction should watch not only the fire risk but the health hazard. Many of the synthetic finishes and solvents used today are highly toxic, and their inhalation over a period can do active damage to the lung tissue and to the nervous and digestive systems. An efficient respirator or face mask should always be worn while spraying, and this also applies to brushwork if working in a confined space. To quote only one illustration, the popular polyurethane lacquers are isocyanate cured and are therefore capable of releasing hydrogen cyanide and carbon monoxide if they catch fire.

Appendix: Costing and estimating

Costing is the pricing of completed work taking into account not only all the direct expenses—materials, wages and insurances, fuel and power, machining costs, workshop expenses, etc.—but also a fair proportion of the indirect expenses—salaries, office expenses, rent, rates, depreciation, interest on capital, etc.—expressed as a percentage addition to the workshop cost. Estimating is the intelligent anticipation of what the total cost is likely to be, and as such must have a basis of actual costing experience. In other words good estimating is the product of sound judgment and careful appraisal of the amount of labour involved in the proposed work, in the light of past experience of other comparable work.

In costing and estimating for quantity production the work can be broken down into a sequence of bulk operations, and accurately priced by cost accountants and experts in work-study. Where large runs are contemplated, or where a totally new design is to be introduced, a finished prototype will be made by skilled craftsmen, knocked down into its component parts, further simplified or systematized for repetition machining, and then costed either with trial-runs of the individual components or recorded costing of other similar operations. This measure of accuracy, often carried to decimal points per item, is not attainable in hand-production for most of the work will be continually breaking fresh ground, therefore the estimator must rely on his own good judgment, building up as he goes his own personal file of cross-reference. There are, however, certain guiding principles which, while they will not solve his equations for him, will at least suggest a method.

COSTING FOR HANDWORK

The cost of any piece of woodwork will consist of several factors, each of which must be independently valued. Some, if not all, of these costs are always present in any analysis or build-up, and should be itemized as follows.

Materials

Wood, plywoods, veneers, etc.: actual net bulk purchase or replacement cost, whichever is higher, including haulage, stacking, weathering, etc., to which must be added the appropriate wastage factors.

Brasswork, ironmongery, etc.: cost of screws, nails, brasswork, special fittings, etc. at purchase price or replacement value.

Sundry materials: all other miscellaneous materials, including glue, glasspaper, polishing materials, etc., directly chargeable to the work. As it is sometimes difficult to assess the amounts of such items as glue, sanding and polishing materials, etc. consumed in any one job, the total cost over the year is sometimes expressed as a percentage addition, but the system is likely to be unfair to some classes of work, and it is better to itemize wherever possible.

Timber calculations

In calculating the timber content of a cutting list for costing purposes the appropriate wastage factors must be added. Whereas softwood in scantling dimensions may need from only 5 to 10 per cent addition, square-edge hardwoods will require 15 to 20 per cent, and most waney or wane edge boards and planks 60 per cent, with the exception of certain wasteful timbers—walnut, rosewood in the log, etc.—where the true waste factor may be as high as 200 per cent. Plywoods, blockboards, etc. bought carefully to suit the dimensions needed may only require 10 per cent, but an average 20 per cent is safer, while most veneers will need at least 50 per cent. Where there is any doubt it is always better to debit the whole planks, sheets or leaves to the job and credit back the usable surplus, not including rippings and offcuts.

Costs of man-hours

The total cost of man-hours at the rates paid, plus overtime rates where applicable, plus health insurance, pensions, paid holidays, etc.

have to be considered. Here again these may be added to the hourly rate, or as percentage additions to the wage total. Strictly speaking, either method is not really accurate, for most of the charges remain the same whether a man works 40 or 60 hours a week; but the percentage addition is the simplest method.

Machine costs

The cost per running hour of each machine is arrived at in accordance with the following example:

Sawbench	
Initial cost	400
Estimated life 20 years, depreciation per year	40
Interest at 15 per cent per annum	60
Annual value	100
Annual cost of maintenance and repairs	30
Annual electric power consumed	40
Annual saw replacements, sharpening, etc.	40
Annual cost	210

(The figures quoted are purely hypothetical for illustration purposes only.)

Assuming that the average use of the sawbench is 20 hours a week for 50 weeks in the year, then the hourly rate will be 210 (the annual cost) ÷ (20 × 50), exclusive of the machinist's wages. If the use is only 10 hours per week then the hourly rate will be doubled, or, if more, reduced accordingly. Where, however, the machine or machines are only used intermittently and by several craftsmen instead of one particular machinist, which is more often than not the usual practice in small workshops, then it may be difficult or impossible to keep accurate records, and the only method which can be adopted is to value the machines as above, and to include the total costs of all machines, not including craftsmen's wages, in workshop overheads. The latter method was used by the writer in his own workshops, and worked reasonably well over a number of years.

ESTIMATING THE COST OF MAN-HOURS IN HANDWORK

Where no previous records are available the proprietor must assess his own capabilities and those of his employees. Common joinery items are usually in softwood of fairly large dimensions, with no careful selection of materials and no elaborate detailing. In furniture, hardwoods require from 10 to 20 per cent more time to work, more time to cut the smaller joints, more time to finish off; and a cabinet-door only a quarter of the size of a standard softwood door might take twice as long to make. The only practical method, therefore, is to see the work as a whole and attempt an assessment of the hours required to make it in terms of one man's working time; then to itemize the various operations, i.e. making working drawings, setting out, preparation of jigs and templates, getting out material (plenty of time should be allowed for this as it entails careful selection), sawing out and planing up for carcass, jointing carcass, getting out drawer material, framing drawers, fitting drawers (again allow plenty of time), etc., etc., timing each operation individually and thus arriving at an alternative total. With a little experience and given the normal perspicacity the two totals should not be far apart and the average reasonably accurate. Points to watch will be (1) a general tendency to underestimate for small work, particularly where there is fine detailing; (2) failure to allow for the extra working time involved in lifting, handling and helping to set up large and heavy work, which may necessitate the help of several craftsmen as the work progresses; (3) failure to allow for mistakes in setting out, or defects in material which develop in the making.

One thing is reasonably certain, the average newcomer will usually underestimate the amount of work involved, for it is a perfectly natural failing to overestimate one's own speed and accuracy. In the first few months of working, therefore, the time allowance should be generous, for again the newcomer will be frightened of allowing too much, and will often quote at uneconomic prices in his anxiety to secure the work.

Percentage additions

To the cost of working time, materials and machine costs, etc. must be added a fair proportion of the workshop overheads and other indirect expenses. Workshop overheads will be all the indirect costs incurred by the workshop which cannot be debited entirely to one particular job, i.e. foreman's time in general supervision, heating, lighting, maintenance and repairs, carriage of goods 'in' and sundry materials, etc., but not including rent, rates, insurances or interest on capital. Indirect expenses will be salaries, rent, rates, insurances, office expenses, car expenses, depreciation, audit fees, interest on capital, profit, etc. Both workshop overheads and indirect expenses will be expressed as percentage additions to the direct cost of the work.

Where the business has been in existence for some time accurate assessment of all indirect expenses can be made, but new businesses will have to estimate for them until sufficient data have been accumulated. A typical costing

Estimated total yearly wages paid say	20,000	
Estimated insurances, paid holidays, pensions, etc. say 10 per cent	2,000	
		22,000
Estimated workshop overheads at 40 per cent on 22,000	8,800	
		30,800
Estimated materials consumed at cost	10,000	
15 per cent profit	1,500	
		42,300
Estimated indirect expenses at 20 per cent		8,460
Estimated total turnover		50,760

where many of the factors are still unknown could be as follows:

From the above example it will be seen that out of the total estimated turnover the cost of the workshop overheads plus the profit on materials would be available for all the indirect expenses of the workshop, and an additional 20 per cent of the estimated indirect expenses to provide for all expenses incurred in running the business, including the owner's own remuneration and profit over and above the wages he would pay himself if he also worked at the bench with his craftsmen. Working masters who do not employ craftsmen often price their work at the standard craftsman's rate per hour plus 50 per cent, plus the bare cost of the materials used, but they will usually find that they are either grossly underpaying themselves or rapidly drifting into bankruptcy.

Subcontractors

Where fixed sums for specialist subcontractors have to be included in an estimate, i.e. prime cost sums where the exact cost is known, or provisional sums to cover the probable cost, it is usual to add a 5 per cent charge for handling.

Carriage of goods

If the proprietor maintains his own transport for the conveyance of finished furniture, the cost per running mile must be arrived at and added accordingly; or if transport is to be hired on each occasion then the estimated cost can be added before or after indirect expenses have been included in the final estimate.

Index

ABRASIVES, *see also sanding materials* 81
  choice of grits 84
  choice of types 83
  comparable gradings 82
  hardness of grits 85
  miscellaneous 86
  sanding papers 81, 85
  wheels, etc. 86
Adhesives, *see also glues* 73
Altar-rails 484
  tables 484
  Angles 365
  Arches 375

BALANCING VENEERS 300
Bandings 316
Beads, cock 251
Bed sizes 451
  types 453
Bedsteads 453
Belt sanders, dustless 125
  pad 136
Bench, cabinet maker's 87
  -drill 135
  -grinder 135
  -holdfast 89
  -hook 89, 163, 350
Bending plywoods 52, 339
  wood 332
Bevelled joints 335
Bird's beak lock 275
Biscuit jointer and groover 123
Bits, wood 111
Bleaching stains 31
Blisters, repairing, etc. 297, 302, 503
  in plywoods 55
Blockboard 53
Bolts, cabinet 287
Bookcase 432
  fittings 284
Borders 305
Boulle-work 319
Box lock joint 178, 221
Bradawl 114
Bridles 159
Bureaus 256
Burls/burrs 25
Burnishing creams 86
Burrs/burls 25

CABINET MAKER'S BENCH 87
Cabinets 424
  cocktail 433

corner 424
display 424
wall 430
CADCAM system 137
Carcass assembly 200
  backs 203
  construction 187, 189
  dovetails 177
  edging 191, 203
  flush top 197
  frame construction 191, 195
  KD construction 189
  MDF 189
  preassembled 189
  rigidities 188
  solid board construction 194
  stands 216, 223
  stiffening 187
Case hardening 26
Casting, warping 149
Castors 284
Catch, wood spring 400
Catches, ball, etc. 286
  magnetic 286
Caul veneering 298
Chain mills, portable 7
Chainsaws, electric 119
Chairs 458
  construction 458
  dining 462
  lounge 467
  rush-seated 463
  sizes 458
  swivel 458
Chamfers 327
Chests 422
  coin 254
  of drawers 447
  print 418
  serpentine-fronted 450
Chipboards, *see also particle boards*, 54
  edging 330
  veneering 302
  working properties 54
Chisels 105
  cutting actions 107
  grinding and honing angles 106
Choir-stall fronts 484
Church furniture 481
Circles 368
Circular saws 118, 129
Clamp, *see cramp*

Clergyman's desk 486
Cock beads 251
Column veneering 313
Combination plane 100
Compound shapes 372
Computer-controlled machinery 137
Conic sections 370
Contour cutting 97
Coopering 335
Copying details 350
Cornices 207
Costing and estimating 512
Countersinks 113
Counter veneering 307
Cramp/clamp rack 145
Cramps/clamps and cramping/clamping devices 142
Crossbanding 305, 307
Cross-grain mouldings 325
Cross veneering 305
Cupboards, corner 424
  wall 430
Curvature 334, 339
  double 372
Curved wood 214, 332
Cutting angles, chisels 106
  planes 104
Cutting-down pastes 86
Cutting lists 349
Cylinder falls 256

DEHUMIDIFIERS 13
Desks, clergyman's 486
  litany 485
  office 416
  pedestal 194
  writing 415
Developments 372
Diaper-work 313
Dimensioning 352
Divan headboards 455
Divans 455
Door panels 227
Doors, barred glass 236
  concertina 240
  dustproof 232
  fitting 230
  flush 232
  framed 277
  framed bow 230
  hinge positions 232
  raised flap 240
  sliding 237, 240

sliding glass 242
Dote 27
Dovetailing accessories 180
  attachment 122, 180
  machines 179
  practice 170
Dovetail joints 170
  marking 171
  rakes 171
Dovetails 170
  box 176
  canted 176
  carcass 177
  decorative through 175
  double bevel 176
  double lap 173
  hand-cut 170
  lapped 173
  machine cut 179
  rebated/rabbeted 176
  secret mitre 175
  slot 178
  through 171
Dowel pop 167
Dowelled joints 167
  applications 169
  assembly 169
  setting out 167
Dowelling jig 168
  practice 167
Dowels 167
Drawer positioning 249
  rails, runners, kickers and
    guides 251
  repairs 501
  sliders, polystyrene 63
  stops 247
  -work, materials for 244
Drawers, assembly 246
  construction 244, 246
  extension 247
  filing 247, 249
  fitting 246
  plan 247, 249
  shaped front 249
  side-hung 247, 254
Drawing, geometyric 363
  instruments 352, 363
  perspective 359
  scale 354
Dressing-tables 441
Drill-guns 127
  accessories 128
Drill-press 135
Drill-stand 128
Drills and drilling tools 111
  cordless 128
  electric 127
Drying kiln 12

oven 13
times 12
Dulling methods 509
Dustboards/panels 200, 207

EDGE TOOLS 98
  chisels 105
  gouges 106
  planes 98
Edging, carcass 191
  thin boards 148
Edgings 325, 330
  shaped door 235
Electric tools, portable 118
  chainsaws 119
  drills 127
Electronic pencil 137
Ellipses 370
Entasis 374
Epoxy resin glues 77
Equilibrium moisture
  content 9
Escutcheons 281

FALL FLAPS 256, 432
  hinges for 270, 272, 274
  locks 279
Falls, cylinder 256
Fibre boards 55
Files and rasps 110
Finger jointing 303
Finger joints 178, 397
Fire resistance of wood 22
  risk 142
Flatt(en)ing veneers 300
Flutings 209, 330
Foam padding 476
Font cover 489
Formica 63
Four-point platforms,
  upholstery 475
Frames 216
  mitre keyed 182
  rebated/rabbeted 159, 163, 166,
    185, 194, 227
French polish 506
Furniture repair work 500

GAUGES 92
  honing- 109
Geometry in workshop 363
Glass fibre plastic mouldings 61
Glasspaper 81
Gliders 285
Glue, heat acceleration of
  setting 342
  -pots 80, 142
  spreader 300
Glues, see also adhesives 74

applicators 80
comparison of various
  types 79
hide 74, 294
impact 77
preparation of 75
preparing surfaces for 77
resin 75, 298
types of 74, 79
working properties of 75
Gluing difficult materials 78
Go-bars 341
Gothic tracery 375
Gouges 106
Grasshopper gauge 92
Grinding and honing angles,
  chisels 106
  wheels 108
Grits, abrasive 84

HAND TOOLS, see also tools 90
Handles 287
  glass door 243
  metal 290
  wood 287
Handrail bolt 166
Hand saws 95
Haunches 160
Height adjusters 285
Hide glue 74, 294
Hides, leather 66
  measurement of 67
Hinge, mangle top 401
  slotting tool 274
Hinges, butt 267
  centre and pivot 270
  counter-flap and card table 270
  miscellaneous 272
  new 274
  rule joint 270
Hinging 267, 270
Holdfast, bench- 89
Holding devices 87, 89
Honing angles 106
Horizontal borer 133

IMPACT GLUES 77
Inlaid lines 316
Inlay repairs 503
  -work 316, 318
Inlays, plastic 321
Intarsia-work 318

JAPANESE HAND TOOLS 117
Jigs 168, 255, 343, 350
Jigsaws 119
Jointing details 150
Joints, bevelled and coopered 335
  bridled 159

chair 458
'check' 218
cleated and battened 155
corner lock 178
cramped/clamped 153
dadoed/housed 156
dovetailed 170
dowelled 167
dowelled edge 168
edge or butt 152
finger 221, 397
glued 152
halved 158
housed/dadoed 156
knuckle 397
machine 153, 179, 191
matched 155
mitred 158, 175, 182
mortise and tenon 160
rubbed 152
rule 397, 406
scarf 186, 304
scribed 185
sculptured 218
showcase 226
slot-screwed 154
three-way 226
tongued and grooved 153

KERF, KERFING 95, 336, 500
Key-plates, *see escutcheons* 281
Keyed joints 166
Kiln drying 12
Knobs, *see handles* 287
Knock-down (KD) fittings 189, 291
Knock-up (KU) fittings 291

LACQUERS, *see also wood*
  finishing 505
  acid catalyst 507
  matt finish 509
  nitro-cellulose 507
  polyurethane 508
  synthetic 507
Laminated bends 337, 339
  continuous strip 339
  insets 339
Laminating compound shapes 339
Laminboard 53
  edging 330
Lathes, woodturning 136
Leather 66
  for table lining 323
  upholstery 480
  waste factors 67
Leathercloth 67
Lecterns 486
  adjustable 486
Legs, cabriole 208

canted 221
circular or oval 214
contemporary 214
detachable table 222
framing 216, 221, 226
jointing methods 215, 218, 226
levelling framings, etc. 226
moulded 209
pedestal, tripod or pillar 209
rectangular section 214
shaped, wood for 213
traditional 209
turned 215
Library steps 494
Lining, table 323
Litany desk 485
Lock chisel 277
Locks, fall flap 279
  fitting 277
  pedestal 281
  sliding door 279, 281
  types of 275
Locks and locking actions 275
Low-voltage (LF) heating 342
  jig and platens for 343

MACHINE LAYOUT 134
Machinery, computer controlled 137
  portable 118
  running costs 513
  woodworking 129
Manufactured boards,
  advantages 56
  quality 55
Marking out 146
Marquetry-work 298, 316, 318
Mason's mitres 185
Measured work 350
Medium density fibreboard
  (MDF) 50
  carcasses 189
Metal extrusions 68
  finishes 71
  fittings 265
  furniture 68
  glues 75, 78
  handles 290
  properties 70
  sections 68
  types 69
  working processes 71
Metrication 44
  conversion factors 45
  conversion tables 44
Mirrors, cheval 447
  framed 445
  frameless 447
  hidden pillar 447
  shaped 446

supports for 443, 447
Miscellaneous materials 321
Mitre, curved 182
  cutting 182
  gluing and cramping/clamping 184
  halvings 158
  joints 175, 182
  template 94, 230
  tools 94
Moisture content 9, 12, 322
  meter 15
Mortise and tenon joints 160
  long and short shoulder 163
  moulded frame 163
  stub or blind 162
  wedged through 162
Mortiser 133
Moulded details 329, 330
Moulding-planes 101
Mouldings, chamfers 327
  composite 327
  cross-grain 325
  curved 379
  intersection of 377
  types of 325
  veneered 327
  working methods 328
Moulds, raking 377
Multi-plane 100
Multiply, *see plywoods* 50
Muntins 225, 230

NAILS 266
Nylon 63

OIL POLISH 506
Oilstone box 109
Oilstones 109
Outdoor furniture 497
Overlay-work 320
Oyster-work 320

PAD FINISHING SANDERS 126
Padding, foam 476
Painted work 511
Panel-gauge 148
Parallelograms 366
Parequetry-work 314, 319
Particle boards, *see also*
  chipboards 54
  uses 55
  veneering 302
  working properties 54
Pattern veneering 309
Pedestal desk 194
Pencil gauge 148
Perspective drawing 359
  measuring point 360
Perspex 62
Piano manufacture 341
Pilasters 187

Pins 266
Planers 131
  portable electric 120
Planes 98
  cutting angles 104
  moulding-plane 101
  toothing- 294
Planing 147
  appliances 89
Plastic coverings 67
  inlays 321
  laminates 63
Plastics, applications 59
  types of 58
Platens 343
Plinths 206
  fixing 199, 206
Plug-cutters 114
Plywood, advantages of 56
  bending 339
  bending properties 52
  dimensions 52
  edging 330
  grading and classification 50
  manufacture 50
  properties compared with solid
    woods 56
  web reinforcements 194
Plywoods 50
  defects in 55
  hints on working 57
Polishing materials and
    processes 505
Polyester resin fibre-glass laminates
    (GRP) 61
Polygons 367
Polyvinyl acetate glues (PVA) 75
Portable electric tools 118
Power-tools 118
Prefabricated wood 50
Pressing 298, 300, 307, 339
Projections, axonometric 357
  isometric 357
  oblique 355
  orthographic (orthogonal) 355
Proportional division 365
  reduction and enlargement 375
Pulls, see handles 287

RADIO FREQUENCY (RF) HEATING
    345
Raking moulds 377
Rasps and files 110
Reedings 330
Relative humidity 9
Repeat patterns 375
Resin glues 75
Rigid foam plastics 61
Robots 138

Router cutters and operations 121,
    122
Routers, CNC 138
  hand 100
  overhead table 134
  portable electric 121, 191, 263
Rubber bag veneering 308
Rule joint 397, 406
  hinge 270

SAFETY PRECAUTIONS 511
Sandbag veneering 308, 327
Sanders, electric 125, 136
Sanding materials, see also
    abrasives 81
  operations 81
  papers 81, 85
  rubbers 84, 110
  techniques 83
Sand shading, marquetry 319
Saw-chops/clamps 96
Saw-horse 145
Sawing and planing appliances 89
Saw-kerfing 336, 500
Saw-milling 7
Saws and sawing 95
  care of 98
  power 118, 129
  radial arm 130
  sharpening 96, 110
Scales and scale drawings 354, 357,
    360, 364
Scarf joints 186, 304
Scotch (hide) glue 74, 294
Scrapers, cabinet 103, 327
Scratch stock 102, 209
Screwdrivers 116
Screws, placing of 266
  recessed head 265
  size gauge 265
  sizes 266
  types 266
  wood 265
Scribed joints 185
Sculptured joints 218
Seasoning wood 9
Seat frames 460, 471
Secretaires (secretaries) 256
Setting out 146, 348, 360
Shakes in wood 23, 40
Sharpening edge tools 107
  stones 109, 117
  wood bits 113
Shooting boards 80, 95, 148, 184
Showcase joints 226
Shrinkage in solid wood 15, 16, 244
  in carcasses 189, 197, 199
  plates 199
Sideboards 434

Site measurements 350
Sliding actions 237
Spindle moulder/shaper 132
Spokeshaves 101
Spraying equipment 509
Squares and bevels 92
Squaring rods 92
Stains in wood 30
Stains, wood 510
Stands, carcass 216, 222
  solid 224
Stationery cases 259
Stays 282
  fixing positions 283
Steam bending 332
Stickers 10
Stools 471
Storage units 430, 434
Straight-edges 91
Stretcher rails 222
Stringings 316
Strops 109

TABLE FRAMINGS 216
  lining 323
  tops, fastening 222, 388
Tables, altar- 484
  boardroom and conference 381
  coffee and occasional 406
  concertina-action 399
  draw-leaf 391
  envelope-top, card- 400
  extending 388
  flip-top 391
  gate-leg 397
  mosaic top 321
  outdoor 498
  Pembroke 397
  pillar 401
  refectory 386
  side 406
  sofa- 403
  Sunderland 406
  swivel-top 401
  types of 380
Tallboy, serpentine-fronted 450
Tambours 259
  backings for 264
  veneered 264
Tea trolleys/wagons 493
Templates 350
Tenons, types of 162
Thermoplastics 59, 60
Thermosetting plastics 59
Tools, boring and drilling 111
  cramping/clamping 142
  drills and drilling 111
  driving and striking 115

grinding and honing 107
holding devices 89
Japanese 117
marking, measuring and
  testing 90
miscellaneous 110
mitre 94
planes 98
portable chain mills 7
routers 100, 121, 134, 138, 191,
  263
saws 95, 118, 129
squares and bevels 92
wood bits and braces 111
Tracery 375
Trammel points 94
Transfer units 139
Trays, butlers' 493
  coin 254
  entomological 254
  storage 254
  tea 492
Triangles 365
Try-square 90, 92

UPHOLSTERY 475

VENEER EDGES 297, 302
  guillotine 46, 302
  jointing 297, 302
  presses 298, 300
  splicer 303
  thicknesses, table of 47
  -trimmer 122, 297
Veneering, caul 298
  chipboard 302
  column 313
  counter 307
  cross 305
  crossbanding 305, 307
  diaper-work 313
  edge 191
  -hammer 294, 296
  hand- 294
  particle board 302
  pattern 309
  practice 294

preparation 294, 300
pressure 298
reasons for 294
rubber bag 249, 307, 308
sandbag 308, 327
with miscellaneous materials 321
Veneers, balancing 300
  coloured 49
  flatt(en)ing 300
  man-made 48
  manufacture of 46
  matching 309
  moisture contents of 322
  storage of 142, 321
  types of 47
  varieties 48
Volutes and spirals 373

WALL UNITS 430, 440
Wardrobes 440
Warp, correcting 500
Warping 40, 119, 148, 149, 153, 155
Water stones 109
Wax polish 505
Webbings, upholstery 475
Wedge jointing, veneers 303
Wet and dry papers 86
Winding-sticks 92
Wood, advantages of solid 57
  bending 322
  -boring insects 28
  buttons 199
  buying 39
  calculations 44
  choosing 40
  classification 1
  coloration 21
  defects 22
  diseases and pests 26
  drying times 12
  durability 21
  felling 5
  finishes, compatibility of 511
  finishing 505, 509
  fire resistance of 22
  grain, texture and figure 18

growth and structure 2
jointing 150
laminates 66
laminations 337
marking and measuring 44
moisture contents 9, 12
  measurement of 9, 13
  meter for 15
moulds and fungi 30
movement 18, 32
odour 21
pests 28
preparation of 146
properties 32
saw-milling 5, 7
seasoning 9
shrinkage 16, 244
species 1
stacking 10
staining 510
stains in 30
thicknessing 148
trade terms 41
truing 149
waste factors 7
Woodboring bits, types of 111
  sharpening 113
Woods, list of 32
Wood-scribe 45
Work-benches 145
Working-drawings 348, 361, 363
Workshop automation 140
  drawing 363
  equipment 352, 363
  furnishings/layout 141
  geometry 363
  heating 142
  layout/furnishings 141
  lighting 141
  planning 141
  regulations 507
  safety precautions 511
Woodworker's vice/vise 87
Woodworm 29

YORKITE CROSSBAND VENEER 307